HANDBOOK OF RESEARCH ON ECONOMIC LIFE

Handbook of Research on Gender and Economic Life

Edited by

Deborah M. Figart

The Richard Stockton College of New Jersey, USA

and

Tonia L. Warnecke

Rollins College, USA

Edward Elgar

Cheltenham, UK • Northampton, MA, USA

Published by
Edward Elgar Publishing Limited
The Lypiatts
15 Lansdown Road
Cheltenham
Glos GL50 2JA
UK

Edward Elgar Publishing, Inc.
William Pratt House
9 Dewey Court
Northampton
Massachusetts 01060
USA

A catalogue record for this book
is available from the British Library

Library of Congress Control Number: 2013932067

This book is available electronically in the ElgarOnline.com
Economics Subject Collection, E-ISBN 978 0 85793 095 8

ISBN 978 0 85793 094 1 (cased)

Typeset by Servis Filmsetting Ltd, Stockport, Cheshire
Printed and bound in Great Britain by T.J. International Ltd, Padstow

Contents

PART VII CONTEMPORARY GLOBAL ISSUES

Figures

Tables

Contributors

Randy Albelda is Professor of Economics and Senior Research Fellow at the Center for Social Policy at University of Massachusetts Boston, USA. Her focus is a broad range of economic policies affecting low-income families. Her coauthored books include *Glass Ceilings and Bottomless Pits: Women's Work, Women's Poverty, Unlevel Playing Fields: Understanding Wage Inequality* and *Discrimination*, and *The War on the Poor: A Defense Manual*. She is an Associate Editor of the award-winning journal, *Feminist Economics*.

Nina Banks is Associate Professor of Economics at Bucknell University, USA. She received her PhD in economics from the University of Massachusetts Amherst. She is preparing an edited volume of the speeches and writings of Sadie Alexander, the US's first black woman economist, which focuses on economic and political justice. Professor Banks' research also analyzes the effects of racial and gendered ideologies on African American migrants in Pittsburgh during the World War I Great Migration era. She is published in a number of journals, including the *Review of Black Political Economics*, *Feminist Economics*, and the *Review of Social Economy*.

Drucilla K. Barker is Professor in the Department of Anthropology and Director of Women's & Gender Studies at the University of South Carolina, USA. Her research interests are gender and globalization, feminist political economy, and feminist methodology. Her work ranges from explorations of the gendered nature of economic efficiency to poststructuralist and interdisciplinary explorations of social science methodologies. She is a founding member of the International Association for Feminist Economics and was the founding director of the Gender and Women's Studies Program at Hollins University. Her books include *Liberating Economics, Toward a Feminist Philosophy of Economics*, and *Feminist Economics and the World Bank*.

Suzanne Bergeron is Professor of Social Sciences and Women's Studies and Director of Women's and Gender Studies at the University of Michigan-Dearborn, USA, where she teaches courses on development economics, feminist theory, and gender and development. Her work on the implications of recent economic innovations for gender and development policy has been published in the *International Feminist Journal of Politics*, *Globalizations*, the edited volume *Development, Sexual Rights and Global Governance*, and elsewhere. Her authored book is *Fragments of Development: Nation, Gender, and the Space of Modernity* (University of Michigan Press, 2005).

Heather Boushey is Senior Economist at the Center for American Progress. She co-edited *The Shriver Report: A Woman's Nation Changes Everything* (Simon & Schuster ebook, 2009). Her research has been published in academic journals and has been covered widely in the media, including regular appearances on the PBS Newshour and in *The New York Times*, where she was called one of the 'most vibrant voices in the field' Boushey received her PhD in economics from the New School for Social Research and her BA from Hampshire College.

Elissa Braunstein is Associate Professor in the Department of Economics at Colorado State University in Fort Collins, USA, and an Associate Editor for the journal *Feminist Economics*. She works primarily on issues related to gender and macroeconomics, with particular emphasis on international and development dynamics. In addition to gender and central bank policy, Professor Braunstein's recent work considers how to account for patriarchal institutions in econometric growth models as well as how to incorporate care in structuralist macroeconomic models.

S. Charusheela is Associate Professor of Interdisciplinary Arts and Sciences at the University of Washington, Bothell, USA. Her work straddles the intersection of post-colonial theory, Marxism, and feminism. She currently serves as Editor of *Rethinking Marxism*. Recent publications include 'Gender and the stability of consumption: a feminist contribution to Post Keynesian economics' (*Cambridge Journal of Economics*, 2010) and 'Response: history, historiography, and subjectivity' (*Rethinking Marxism*, 2011).

Zohreh Emami is Professor of Economics and former Associate Dean and Vice President for Academic Affairs at Alverno College, USA. She teaches courses in international and development economics, globalization and democracy, women and the economy, women and leadership, and the economic environment. She consults with colleges and universities on teaching, learning, assessment, and curriculum design and writes on economics, education, and democracy. Her book with Paulette Olson entitled *Engendering Economics: Conversations with Women Economists in the United States* was published in April 2002.

Deborah M. Figart is Professor of Education and Economics at The Richard Stockton College of New Jersey, USA. She is one of the 50 founding members of the International Association for Feminist Economics (IAFFE) and served as President of the Association for Social Economics in 2006–07. She is an internationally known scholar in the field of labor and employment issues, writing on subjects such as pay equity and wage discrimination, labor–management relations, working time, emotional labor at work, minimum and living wage issues, job evaluation, and career ladders. She is currently co-editor of the *Review of Social Economy* and has served on the editorial board of numerous professional journals.

Amie Gaye is an expert in international development statistics who has worked for the past six years as a Policy Specialist for the UNDP Human Development Report (HDRO), where she contributed to the conception of the Report's recently introduced Gender Inequality Index. Before joining HDRO, Gaye worked at the UNDP Office in Namibia as a Technical Advisor for three years, supporting the National Poverty Reduction and Equity Programme. She also worked at the Gambia Bureau of Statistics for 20 years, holding various positions including as head of its Gender Statistics Unit. She holds an undergraduate degree in statistics from the University of Ghana and a Master's degree in Population Research from the University of Exeter, UK.

Julie Ham is a doctoral student in criminology at Monash University, Australia, and an associate of the Global Alliance Against Traffic in Women (GAATW). Her research explores how the criminalization and regulation of sex work and migration influences migrant sex workers' security, mobility, and agency. She has published on anti-trafficking, participatory action research, and activist efforts by trafficking survivors, sex workers, and domestic workers. Her work includes community-based research with sex workers, immigrant communities, women substance users, low-income urban communities, and anti-violence organizations.

Cilja Harders has been director of the Center for North African and Middle Eastern Studies at the Otto-Suhr Institute for Political Sciences at Freie Universität Berlin, Germany, since 2007. She received her PhD in political sciences from the University of Hamburg, Germany. She has extensive research experience in the Middle East (Egypt, Jordan, Syria, Lebanon, the Gulf, and Morocco). Her research focuses on Middle Eastern politics and politics 'from below', foreign policy and Arab–European relations, and gender and violence. She coedited *Beyond Regionalism? Regional Cooperation, Regionalism and Regionalisation in the Middle East* (Ashgate, 2008).

Ariane Hegewisch is a Study Director at the Institute for Women's Policy Research, a thinktank based in Washington, DC, USA. Her research concerns workplace discrimination, work–life reconciliation and job quality. Prior to coming to the United States in 2001, she researched and taught comparative European human resource management at Cranfield School of Management, UK. After receiving a BSc in economics from the London School of Economics and an MPhil in development studies from the IDS, Sussex, she began her career in local government in the UK as a policy advisor on local economic development.

Elizabeth Hirsh is Associate Professor of Sociology and Canada Research Chair in Social Inequality and Law at the University of British Columbia, Canada. Her research and teaching are in the areas of gender and race inequality, organizations, and the law. Much of her work focuses on employment discrimination and the impact of anti-discrimination laws and workplace diversity policies on gender, race, and ethnic inequality at work. Her recent scholarship appears in the *Law and Society Review*, *Research on the Sociology of Work*, and the *American Sociological Review*.

Hazel Hollingdale is a PhD student in sociology at the University of British Columbia, Canada. Her primary research interests are in gender, work, and the effects of organizational structures on social processes and inequality. She is currently completing a study on the organizational response to occupational health and safety issues in high-risk, male-dominated fields.

Barbara E. Hopkins is Associate Professor of Economics at Wright State University in Dayton, Ohio, USA. She teaches courses on comparative economics, capitalism, gender, and the global economy. Her research focuses on the interaction between the economic system and the gender system, consumption choices, and pluralism in economics. She has published in *Feminist Economics*, *Feminist Studies*, the *Review of Radical Political Economics*, and in several edited volumes.

Marlene Kim is Professor of Economics at the University of Massachusetts-Boston, USA. She specializes in race and gender discrimination in employment and the working poor. She has published *Race and Economic Opportunity in the Twenty-First Century* (Routledge, 2007) as well as numerous scholarly articles on these topics. She is the recipient of IAFFE's first Rhonda Williams Prize for her work on race and gender discrimination and serves as Associate Editor of *Feminist Economics* and on the editorial boards of *Industrial Relations*, the *Review of Radical Political Economics* and *Pan Economics*. She holds a PhD in economics from the University of California, Berkeley.

Elizabeth M. King is Director of Education of the World Bank. In this position, she is the World Bank's senior spokesperson for global policy and strategic education issues in developing countries. Prior to her current position, she headed the Bank's research group that focuses on human development. She has published on topics such as household investments in human capital; the linkages between education, poverty, and economic development; gender issues in development, especially women's education; education finance, and the impact of decentralization reforms. She has a PhD in economics from Yale University and a BA from the University of the Philippines.

Jeni Klugman is the Director, Gender and Development, World Bank. She was the former director and lead author of the three global Human Development Reports published by the United Nations Development Programme: on human mobility (2009), pathways to human development (2010) and equity and sustainability (2011). Klugman has published a number of books, papers, and reports on topics ranging from poverty reduction strategies and labor markets to conflict, health reform, education, and decentralization. She holds a PhD in economics from the Australian National University. She also has graduate degrees in development economics, as well as in law, from Oxford University where she was a Rhodes Scholar.

Milorad Kovacevic is Chief Statistician at the Human Development Report Office of UNDP. Before joining UNDP, he was working as a methodologist at Statistics Canada, the national statistical office of Canada, for more than 17 years, of which for the last 11 years he was chief of research in data analysis methods unit at the methodology branch. He also worked for the Federal Statistical Office of Yugoslavia and was teaching statistics at the University of Belgrade, Serbia, and the University of Iowa, Iowa City, United States. He has published in the area of analysis of complex survey data, inference on finite populations, and income inequality and polarization. He received a PhD in statistics from the University of Belgrade.

Karl Krupp is the Program Director for Public Health Research Institute of India and a Research Associate at Florida International University in Miami. He has an MSc in public health from London School of Hygiene and Tropical Medicine. Over the last decade, he has carried out mixed methods research on a variety of issues related to women's health including HIV prevention, reproductive health, cancer prevention, and maternal health. His current research interests include the genetic causes of chronic disease, healthcare access for women, and research ethics.

Dominique Lallement has over 40 years of experience in international development, mostly with the World Bank. Trained as an economist at Princeton University, she is now engaged as an international development consultant, focusing on gender equality in infrastructure investments and services, trade and labor markets, and agriculture and rural development. She has worked extensively in Sub-Saharan Africa and Latin America, in the Middle East and North Africa, and in South and East Asia. She serves on the Board of three NGOs, focused respectively on scholarships for women from developing countries, energy grants to Africa, and cultural heritage, and is a volunteer mentor to youth entering the job market.

Hannah Liepmann is a PhD student in economics at Humboldt-University, Berlin, Germany. Her research interests include empirical labor economics and gender economics. She has a BSc in economics from European-University Viadrina in Germany. In 2010, she interned for six months with the Institute for Women's Policy Research in Washington, DC.

Purnima Madhivanan is an Associate Professor in Epidemiology at Robert Stempel College of Public Health and Social Work at Florida International University in Miami, USA. She is a physician by training with an MPH and PhD in epidemiology from the University of California, Berkeley. Her research focuses on women's health issues across the life span, particularly among disadvantaged populations. Her current projects include interventions integrating antenatal care and HIV testing among rural populations in India; and studies identifying barriers and facilitators to increased uptake of primary and secondary prevention of cervical cancer in the US and India.

Nisrine Mansour is a social researcher and documentary filmmaker holding a PhD in social policy from the London School of Economics and an MA in documentary filmmaking from the London College of Communication, UK. She is a former research fellow at the University of Oxford's Refugee Studies Centre and has taught on the MSc in Social Policy and Development at the London School of Economics. She has several publications on the intersections between gender, family law, religion, civil society, forced migration, and statelessness in Lebanon and the Middle East and is currently working on multimedia research projects on related topics.

Elaine McCrate teaches Economics and Women's and Gender Studies at the University of Vermont, USA. Her current research examines contemporary changes in the social coordination of time, especially between the workplace and the family.

Lynn McIntyre is currently Professor and Canadian Institutes for Health Research (CIHR) Chair in Gender and Health in the Department of Community Health Sciences, Faculty of Medicine, University of Calgary, Alberta, Canada. Dr McIntyre holds both a medical degree and Master's degree in community health and epidemiology from the University of Toronto. She is also a Fellow of the Royal College of Physicians of Canada in Public Health and Preventive Medicine. She has studied food insecurity for 20 years using a variety of methods and with diverse disadvantaged populations both in Canada and globally.

Nidhiya Menon is Associate Professor of Economics at Brandeis University, USA. Her areas of research and teaching are empirical development economics, labor, and demography. She received a BA from Mount Holyoke College in 1994 and a PhD in economics from Brown University in 2001.

Julie A. Nelson is a Professor of Economics at the University of Massachusetts Boston, USA. She is the author of *Economics for Humans* (2006) and *Feminism, Objectivity, and Economics* (1996); coeditor of *Beyond Economic Man* (1993) and *Feminist Economics Today* (2003); and the author of many articles in journals including *Econometrica*,

American Economic Review, *Journal of Economic Perspectives*, *Signs: Journal of Women in Culture and Society*, and *Hypatia: Journal of Feminist Philosophy*.

Vy T. Nguyen is an Education Economist at the World Bank's Human Development Network, Education Unit. Her current work focuses on issues of inequalities in education. In her role as an economist, she provided assistance to the development of the World Bank Group Education Strategy 2020 and conducted research in a number of topics including education, women's fertility and labor force participation, and financial market development. She received a PhD in economics from The American University, Washington, DC, with a dissertation focused on financial market liberalization policies and development.

Amy North works in the field of gender, education, and international development. She has worked in a range of NGOs and research organizations in Latin America, Africa, and the UK and is currently based at the Institute of Education, University of London, UK. Her particular research interests include global policy on gender and education and the role of NGOs and international agencies; and women's literacy and adult education, particularly in the context of migration.

Patricia E. (Ellie) Perkins is a Professor in the Faculty of Environmental Studies, York University, Canada, where she teaches and advises students in the areas of ecological economics, community economic development, and critical interdisciplinary research design. Her research focuses on feminist ecological economics, climate justice, participatory community, and watershed-based environmental education. She currently directs an international research project on climate justice and equity in watershed management with partners in Mozambique, South Africa, and Kenya, and works with the GreenXChange Project on green community development in northwest Toronto. She holds a PhD in economics from the University of Toronto.

V. Spike Peterson is a Professor in the School of Government and Public Policy at the University of Arizona, USA, with courtesy appointments in the Department of Gender and Women's Studies, Institute for LGBT Studies and International Studies. Her 2003 book, *A Critical Rewriting of Global Political Economy: Reproductive, Productive and Virtual Economies*, introduced an alternative analytic for examining intersections of ethnicity/race, class, gender, and national hierarchies in the context of neoliberal globalization. Her current research focuses on informalization, intersectionality, and global insecurities.

Anandita Philipose is a development professional who has been working with the United Nations in the areas of gender, health, education, and food insecurity for several years. She has worked on these issues in a variety of different contexts in Africa, Asia, Europe, and North America. This builds on her work grounded in her Master's degree program in Public Administration from Cornell University, New York, USA. She has previously published articles on gender, food insecurity, and mother and child health, and contributed to numerous articles on development issues through her work with the UN.

Janneke Plantenga is Professor of Economics at University of Utrecht, The Netherlands. She is a member and coordinator of the European Expert Group on Gender, Social Inclusion and Employment. Her research interest focuses on labour market flexibilization, the reconciliation of work and family, and European social policy. She has written widely on redistribution of unpaid work, changing working-time patterns, childcare issues, and modernizing social security. She is the Dutch expert and coordinator of the the European Network of Experts on Gender Equality (ENEGE).

Marilyn Power is Professor of Economics at Sarah Lawrence College, USA. She is coauthor, with Deborah M. Figart and Ellen Mutari, of *Living Wages, Equal Wages: Gender and Labor Market Policies in the United States* (Routledge, 2002). She has also served on the elected Board of Directors of the International Association for Feminist Economics.

Chantal Remery is Assistant Professor at the Utrecht School of Economics, The Netherlands, and is a coordinator of the European Network of Experts on Gender Equality (ENEGE). She has worked on other European projects with a gender focus including WELLKNOW and NESY and has written on reconciliation, flexible working time and employers' policy. She is coauthor, with Janneke Plantenga, of *The Provision of Childcare Services: A Comparative Review of 30 European Countries* (European Commission, 2009).

Yana van der Meulen Rodgers is Associate Professor of Women's and Gender Studies at Rutgers University, USA. She teaches and conducts research on gender and economic development and economics of the family. She received her BA from Cornell University in 1987 and her PhD in economics from Harvard University in 1993. In 2011, she was elected President-Elect of the International Association for Feminist Economics.

Krista Rondeau is a registered dietitian and holds a Master's degree in health promotion studies from the University of Alberta, Canada. For her thesis, she conducted qualitative research on how farmwomen in Canada conceptualized food safety within the context of their daily food provisioning practices. She is currently a Senior Research Associate with the Department of Community Health Sciences at the University of Calgary and works on both domestic and international-focused household food insecurity and food-provisioning research projects.

Mishka Saffar is a development expert who has worked for the United Nations and the European Commission. Following her Master's program in Politics of Development at Stockholm University, Sweden, she has specialized in the areas of food security, agricultural development, humanitarian assistance, and sustainable management of natural resources, in Uganda, India, Europe, and Brazil. Through her work with the UN and the European Commission, she has contributed to policy-making and program design, as well as to several reports and articles on development issues. Currently based in Brazil, she works as a freelancer, with a focus on food security, alternate livelihoods, and water resources management.

Stephanie Seguino is Professor of Economics at the University of Vermont, USA. Prior to obtaining a PhD from The American University, she served as an economist in Haiti for several years in the 'Baby Doc' era. Her current research explores the relationship between inequality, growth, and development. A major focus of that work explores the effect of gender equality on macroeconomic outcomes. She is Research Associate at the School of Oriental and African Studies (SOAS), University of London, Research Scholar at the Political Economy Research Institute, instructor in the African Program for Rethinking Development Economics (APORDE), and Associate Editor of *Feminist Economics* and the *Journal of Human Development and Capabilities*.

Irene van Staveren is Professor of Human Resources and Local Development at the International Institute of Social Studies, Erasmus University, The Netherlands. She has published widely in development economics, ethics, feminist economics, and heterodox economics. Her published book is *The Values of Economics: An Aristotelian Perspective* (Routledge, 2001).

Natasha Stecy-Hildebrandt is a PhD student in sociology at the University of British Columbia, Canada. Her broad research interests lie in gender, work, family, and inequality. She is currently completing a study of parental leave-taking among fathers in Canada.

Sarah Twigg is a consultant in the World Bank's Gender and Development Unit. Prior to joining the World Bank, she worked as a researcher for two global Human Development Reports (2010 and 2011) published by the United Nations Development Programme, and as a gender and climate finance consultant for UN Women. She also has experience practicing as a commercial lawyer in New Zealand and New York. She holds a Master's degree in international politics and business from New York University and Bachelor's degrees in law and political science from the University of Otago, New Zealand.

Elaine Unterhalter is a Professor of Education and International Development at the Institute of Education, University of London, UK. She has more than 25 years experience working on themes concerned with gender, race, and class inequalities and their bearing on education. Her specialist interests are in the capability approach and human development and education in Africa, particularly South Africa. Her current concerns are with education, poverty, and global social justice. Her book *Gender, Schooling and Global Social Justice* won first prize in the Society of Education Studies book awards in 2008. She is currently working with a number of UN agencies on aspects of gender and the Millennium Development Goals.

Tonia L. Warnecke is Assistant Professor of International Business at Rollins College, USA. She has a PhD in economics from the University of Notre Dame, USA. She is internationally known for her research on the gender dimensions of development, particularly with regard to informal labor, social welfare, and international finance. In 2009, she was awarded the Young Scholars award by the European Society for the History of Economic Thought and in 2012 she received a Best Paper Award for her research on female entrepreneurship in China and India. She currently serves on the board of the Association for Institutional Thought, the executive council of the Association for Social Economics, and the board of two professional journals.

Rita Watterson spent several years traveling and working throughout Asia and Latin America following her undergraduate studies at McGill University, Canada, and it was during these experiences that she was introduced to global health issues. Upon returning to Canada, she completed a Master of Public Health degree at Simon Fraser University. In 2010, she began a medical degree at the University of Calgary in order to pursue front-line global health work and population-level research.

Doris Weichselbaumer is Associate Professor at the Department of Economics as well as at the Department for Gender and Women's Studies at the University of Linz, Austria. Her research interests include feminist economics and labor economics as well as gender and postcolonial studies.

Brigitte Young has retired from a professorship at the Institute of Political Science, University of Muenster, Germany. She has taught at the Free University Berlin, and was Research Associate at Georgetown University, Science-Po (CERI) in Paris and Lille, and Warwick University. She is presently Guest Professor at the Central European University in Budapest and the German delegate and Working Group leader for New Global Finance and Financial Stability (EU-COST project). Her research areas include global financial markets and crises with an emphasis on the eurozone and the role of Germany, and theories of international political economy. She has published widely in English and German (with translations in other languages).

Eduardo Zambrano is Associate Professor of Economics at Cal Poly in San Luis Obispo, California, USA. His research spans the fields of general equilibrium theory, game theory, decision theory, political economy, and welfare economics. Professor Zambrano worked in 2002 as a consultant to Venezuela's Congressional Budget Office and in 2003 as a Senior Researcher at Venezuela's Central Bank. He has also worked as a consultant to the Human Development Report Office of the United Nations Development Programme in matters regarding the measurement of human development, the measurement of gender inequality, and the measurement of the impact of environmental sustainability on human development.

Foreword

This excellent handbook goes far beyond mere disaggregation of economic agents by sex to challenge the mainstream definition of economics as the optimum allocation of scarce resources, and to focus instead on economics as a process of provisioning for well-being, shaped by social norms, including gender norms. It clarifies that gender identities are social constructions that are influenced by, and in turn influence, economic life.

The volume includes contributions from leading feminist economists and scholars from related disciplines, covering both theory and policy, which stem from a commitment to use research to improve economic well-being, especially for the most disadvantaged. The book is relevant to both industrialized and industrializing countries and is written in an accessible style that reflects a multidimensional understanding of economic life. As well as labor market and human development issues, the handbook includes analysis of global and national institutions, macroeconomic and financial policies, and global issues such as migration, environment, and conflicts.

This book will be an invaluable resource for courses at the undergraduate and postgraduate levels that aim to introduce students to a feminist approach to economics, rather than simply adding 'women' or 'gender' to conventional therorizing. It demonstrates how this kind of feminist economics is not just about discrimination, narrowly understood, but about the gendered character of all aspects of economies and economic policies.

No matter what your specific interest, there is something in the handbook that will illuminate the topic. It should inspire a new generation of researchers to use the tools of feminist social science to investigate the contours and contradictions of economic life in a rapidly changing world in which provisioning for the well-being of the many is challenged by maximizing the profits and wealth of the few.

Diane Elson
Emeritus Professor, University of Essex, UK

Introduction
Deborah M. Figart and Tonia L. Warnecke

Economic life involves more than buying and selling things. The economic lives of women and men around the world are diverse – in the kinds of activities they engage in, the motivations that prioritize their choices, and the institutional and cultural contexts that can both narrow or enrich their options. In fact, our economic lives, and therefore our economies, are something that we continuously create and recreate through our daily activities.

We purposefully chose 'Gender and Economic Life' for the title and theme of this research handbook to reflect the interdisciplinary nature and global scope of the topic. We conceptualize economic life as a process of provisioning for well-being. Many of the activities of our daily lives, both paid and unpaid, are part of the process of provisioning for ourselves and those close to us. As such, understanding the ways in which gender relates to economic life requires much more than an understanding of economic theory. The economy does not exist in a vacuum; the economy is embedded in society, so all factors shaping societal behavior shape the economy as well. To understand economic life, then, we must explore the sociocultural norms that shape agency, the political and institutional forces that shape individual opportunity, and the multifaceted linkages (and disconnects) between policy intent and what actually happens 'on the ground'.

Feminist scholarship has long noted that gender is a human construction, one that is created and recreated through our daily lives and activities. Candace West and Don Zimmerman (1987) refer to this process as 'doing gender'. The fact that gender is a human construction is often invisible to us as we unconsciously pursue our daily lives (Lorber, 1994, p. 13). Yet the identity of being a man or being a woman takes on different meanings in different historical periods and cultural contexts due to the agency of human actors. Feminists, therefore, are keenly aware that our economic life is one arena in which we produce and reproduce gender identities; at the same time, our gender identities shape the economy that we create (Figart et al., 2002). Who can own or inherit property, who is defined as a 'breadwinner' deserving a family wage, the relative social value ascribed to paid and unpaid labor, and the degree of flexibility in labor markets are all examples of aspects of economic life that have been influenced by and in turn have reproduced prevailing gender norms.

To foster this exploration, we are pleased to present original, cutting-edge work from a variety of academics, practitioners and activists around the globe. The book is divided into seven parts. Part I, Analytical Tools, presents a variety of lenses through which feminist analysis of economic life occurs. Feminist scholars are often asked what feminist analysis is and whether it is simply a matter of investigating women's lives as compared to men's. Gender as an organizing principle of economic life is more complex. We want to give readers an understanding of possible entry points for gender-based analysis and some key facets of such analysis. Thus, the six chapters in Part I comprise an investigation of economics as social provisioning and how this differs from the mainstream definition of economics as the process of allocating scarce resources; the ways that feminist scholarship has evolved over time and the cutting edge of analytical focal points in this field; the cross-cutting influences of gender, race, and class; the complications of defining (and thus attaining) well-being; the integral role that caring plays in economic life; and how our conceptualizations of economic life influence the teaching and learning process.

Part II is titled Institutional Contexts for Provisioning. Our lives are constantly influenced by the institutions that surround us, and though formal institutions and rules are certainly significant, it is equally important to consider informal institutions. Informal institutions such as social norms and legislative norms operate outside of official channels, but play a major role in structuring 'the rules of the game' for economic life processes. In this part, four chapters illustrate the gendered impacts of both formal and informal institutions, detailing the varieties of capitalisms as they shape provisioning; the role of international development institutions; infrastructure and institutional development; and the ways that institutions can constrain women's empowerment.

This leads us to Part III, Informal and Formal Work. The existence and quality of paid employment opportunities play a significant role in shaping our lives. While most policy-making is based on a narrow conceptualization of work that includes only waged production in the formal sector of the economy, women in most countries around the world are more likely to work in the informal sector. But – as the five chapters in this part show – employment inequalities take many forms, from occupational segregation and the glass ceiling to discrimination in hiring, promotions, and firing based on sex, race and ethnicity, and sexual orientation.

Part IV, Employment Policies, focuses on methods (successful or not) to address these gendered employment outcomes. Because employment policy generally targets the formal sector, and the majority of employment in the global North occurs within this sector, chapters in this part focus on the developed world. Four chapters discuss policies impacting low-wage mothers, work-schedule flexibility, work–family reconciliation, and work-family conflict.

We then shift focus to the macro economy, finance, and credit. In comparison with paid labor, the gender dimension of the macro economy has been less studied, but is particularly important to analyze given the recent global economic downturn and emphasis worldwide on restructuring macroeconomic policies to support recovery. The first chapter in Part V provides an excellent overview of the linkage of gender to the macro economy, both in the short run and the long run, and the current state of research in this area. The next three chapters delve more deeply into central bank policy, credit and self-employment, debt, and the housing/financial crisis.

Part VI takes us on a tour around the world, investigating key issues of human development, education, and health as we do so. We learn about ways to measure human development (and limitations therein) before analyzing various facets of human development. Two chapters center on education, focusing on girls' schooling, the evolving way education has been integrated into the global development agenda, and the multiple ways educational inequality arises. The next two chapters provide a current, comprehensive overview of the health of the world's women as well as an investigation into gendered hazards and health effects for ultra-poor women. Our discussion of human development would be incomplete without the last chapter in this part, which delves into the crucial issue of food security.

Part VII concludes the book with an exploration of the gender dimension of contemporary 'hot topics' commonly seen in the news and addressed by popular culture. Examples from these four chapters include migration (documented and undocumented), environmental degradation and sustainability, peace, war, violence, and trafficking.

What unifies the diverse topics, perspectives, and methodologies of the 33 contributions to this volume is a commitment to using scholarship to advance economic well-being, especially for those who often struggle at the margins of our economy. Each author brings a unique perspective that contributes to our understanding. Weaving together the fabric of these different threads, the volume advances feminist scholarship on economic life.

REFERENCES

Figart, Deborah M., Ellen Mutari and Marilyn Power (2002), *Living Wages, Equal Wages, Gender and Labor Market Policies in the United States*, London: Routledge.
Lorber, Judith (1994), *Paradoxes of Gender*, New Haven, CT: Yale University Press.
West, Candace and Don Zimmerman (1987), 'Doing gender', *Gender & Society*, 1(2), 125–51.

PART I

ANALYTICAL TOOLS

1. A social provisioning approach to gender and economic life
Marilyn Power

I   INTRODUCTION

What is economic life? How have scholars defined the parameters of their study of the provisioning process – that is, the production and reproduction of human material life? Economic thinkers have offered a range of answers to this question. Classical economist Adam Smith focused his analysis in *The Wealth of Nations* around general well-being (or 'general opulence' as he termed it), defined as the production of the 'necessaries and conveniences of life' produced by labor (Smith, 1776 [2003], p. 1). While most of his analysis focused on the role of markets in producing these necessaries and conveniences, production outside of markets and exchange relations could easily fit within his definition. In *Capital*, Karl Marx (1867 [1967]), building upon Smith's analytic base, pointed out that market production of exchange values may deliver, rather than general opulence, inequality, miserable working conditions, and economic crisis.[1] Once again, focus was primarily on market production, as Marx argued that commodity production and exchange was the heart of a capitalist economic system. Still, within his analysis – while adhering to his period's cultural assumptions about 'natural' differences between women and men – he addressed the role of women's nonmarket production in the well-being of working-class families, which was jeopardized by capitalism's relentless demand for labor (ibid., p. 395fn).

Institutional economist Thorstein Veblen, in *The Theory of the Leisure Class*, examined the cultural institutions that organized economic life and that mediated the conflict between human impulses toward constructive action and toward competitive display and domination. He viewed gendered divisions of labor through this lens, arguing that women's cultural roles and subordinate position had their origins in competitive male displays of 'conspicuous consumption', rather than the necessities of nonmarket production (Veblen 1899 [1967], pp. 81–5).

Contemporary neoclassical economics, arising in the late nineteenth century, focused entirely on economic exchange within markets. Such mainstream scholars left aside questions of the provisioning *process* (meaning the process of producing use and/or exchange values), whether within or outside markets. Further, they took cultural institutions, distributions of income and wealth, and gender roles as given, outside the realm of economic analysis, restrictions that continue largely unchanged into the present. In this methodology, as typified in a best-selling mainstream textbook, *Essentials of Economics*, economic life is reduced to the choice within markets using scarce resources (Krugman et al., 2007, p. 6).

These differing methodologies provided very different lenses on economic life, leading to diverging recommendations for economic policy. They coexisted more or less uneasily during the early twentieth century, culminating in a period that historians of economic thought often identify as the period of 'interwar pluralism' (Morgan and Rutherford, 1998). However, in the period after World War II, the neoclassical paradigm became increasingly dominant, and the political economic and institutional schools of thought were allowed increasingly less space in the curriculum of economics departments, particularly in the major research institutions; were less welcome in the most prestigious academic journals; and represented fewer economists invited to advise the government.

This dominant approach left many aspects of economic life out of the discussion. With the rise of the women's movement in the late 1960s, persistent questions about (i) occupational segregation, discrimination, and wage inequality in the labor force and (ii) the complex array of provisioning activities outside the paid economy (predominantly engaged in by women) led to dissatisfaction with the mainstream model, and a search for an economic methodology that would better illuminate the dynamics of gender and economic life. This chapter first gives an account of the rise of heterodox and feminist economics (Section II) and then describes the emergence of a methodology I term 'social provisioning' (Section III). I divide the methodology into five components, and illustrate each with examples that show the rich and varied uses of the concept of social provisioning by feminist economists (Section IV). Section V concludes.

II   THE RISE OF HETERODOX AND FEMINIST ECONOMICS

By the end of the 1960s the dominance of the neoclassical (often referred to as 'mainstream') model was quite established. But during this tumultuous decade of increased political activism over civil rights, the Vietnam War, and at the end of the decade, a revived women's movement, a growing discontent with the narrowness of the dominant model led to a broadening of the economic questions asked, moving beyond the scope of the neoclassical framework and leading to renewed interest in classical and institutional economics among activists and academics concerned with issues of inequality, underdevelopment, and economic justice. For these groups, an understanding of economic life centered on differences in power and the related inequality in outcomes, with a growing focus on broader issues of well-being. Their analyses, therefore, needed to go beyond narrow questions of choice within market constraints to investigations of historically based and culturally specific institutions, relations of economic and political power, and the dynamics of production and distribution both within and outside of formal markets.

The re-emergence of a feminist movement in the US and Europe in the late 1960s brought with it pressing economic questions about the role and condition of women within the economy. Research revealed pervasive economic disadvantages for women and also marked differences in economic position and prospects for women across lines of race, ethnicity, class, and country. Attempts to explain these results within existing economic paradigms were limited by models that often marginalized women's experience, assumed away discrimination or differentials of power, or assumed that any observed differences were the outcome of 'essential' differences between men and women, and therefore were natural, inevitable, and even desirable. While this resistance was particularly true of neoclassical economics, political and institutional economists were also often reluctant to open their fields to these new feminist questions and analyses.

The establishment in 1992 of the International Association for Feminist Economics (IAFFE) reflected the sense of frustration and marginalization felt by feminist economists who believed that the constraints of existing schools of thought were an obstacle to answering the questions they found most pressing. With the introduction of the journal *Feminist Economics* in 1995, feminist economists had a forum for theoretical and empirical analysis that could both allow their voices to be heard and further the development of a methodology that would allow the full breadth of women's economic lives to become visible.

In the wonderfully fruitful period since the inception of IAFFE, feminists have been able to persist in their tradition of collaboration across paradigms, embracing a wide range of methodologies, listening with respect to each other's arguments, and offering constructive criticisms. To Diana Strassmann's important question of who gets to speak and who is expected to listen (1993), feminist economists so far have been able to answer with striking openness. At the same time, within this diversity of approaches, a study of the growing body of feminist economic literature suggests certain basic principles as points of analytic departure for feminist economic research.

Feminist economics emerged from dissatisfaction with the mainstream model for all the elements of economic life left out and rendered invisible, particularly traditionally female responsibilities for housework, childcare, and broader care of the family and community. Feminist economists come from a range of backgrounds in economics, from neoclassical to institutionalist to Marxist. But impelled by these broader questions, their analyses have begun to coalesce around a methodology that incorporates aspects of providing a living outside the market, and motives that go beyond self-interest, such as caring and responsibility to community and family. Feminists raise questions not only of efficiency, but also of the quality of life, and economic justice.

These concerns lead feminist economists to a broader and richer understanding of 'economic life'. All of us are engaged in economic activity any time we interact with other people and the natural environment in the process of providing a living. How this process is organized is a rich, complex, and dynamic story that is historically specific and integrally related to cultural, political, and social institutions, as well as the economic organization of the society. Factors such as property rights, the class structure, and gender rules – including, but not limited to the gender division of labor and the racial and ethnic divisions of the society – all affect our interdependent social processes of providing a living for ourselves and our families. We inherit these dynamics from the past, but we also can affect and change them in the present. Economic life is not something that just happens to us; it is the outcome of human agency, both our own and that of others who impact us.

III   A SOCIAL PROVISIONING APPROACH TO ECONOMIC LIFE

Feminist economists began using the terms 'provisioning' or 'social provisioning', which have also been used in institutional and heterodox economic analyses, to describe the processes involved in providing a living, both within the paid labor force and through unwaged labor, as well as through the public sector (Jennings, 1993; Nelson,

1993; Dugger, 1996; Benería, 2003; Lee, 2009; Jo, 2011). While the terms have often been used interchangeably, I have suggested (Power, 2004) that 'social provisioning' draws attention more effectively to the interdependent and multilayered process of providing a living. Without further elaboration, provisioning can become a study solely of individual acts and choices; it does not automatically highlight the interdependence or social embeddedness of economic processes. Social provisioning emphasizes the analysis of economic activities as interdependent social processes. To define economics as the study of social provisioning is to emphasize that at its root, economic activity involves the ways people organize themselves collectively to provide a living and sustain households.

Social provisioning draws attention away from images of pecuniary pursuits and individual competition, and toward notions of sustenance, cooperation, and support. Rather than naturalized or taken as given, capitalist institutions and dynamics become subjects to be examined and critiqued. Social provisioning need not be done through markets; it need not be done for selfish or self-interested motives, although neither of these is inconsistent with social provisioning. Thus, the concept allows for a broader understanding of economic activity that includes women's unpaid and nonmarket activities and for understandings of motivation that do not fall under narrow or tautological notions of self-interest. The term also emphasizes process as well as outcomes. The methods by which we provide for ourselves, both paid and unpaid, are included in the analysis. And social provisioning emphasizes the importance of social norms (Himmelweit, 2002) in affecting both the process and the outcome of economic processes.

Starting economic analysis from this standpoint illuminates the ways a society organizes itself to produce and reproduce material life. This organization is a set of social activities, rather than individual choices, and its outcome is social production and reproduction rather than individual happiness (although, of course, individual choices do occur and individual happiness is directly relevant – the point is that this is not utility maximization). Social provisioning is a classical, not a neoclassical, concept, a descriptive category rather than a motivation. At any historical moment within a given economic system, a specific aspect of provisioning can be carried out in myriad ways. The dynamics of economic relations (themselves embedded within power relations) interact with societal institutions and social divisions such as class, race, and gender to construct specific outcomes. In this sense, social provisioning is closely related to feminist historians' notion of social reproduction (Glenn, 1992), because culture, ideology, and social institutions help determine the specific organization of provisioning at a given moment. In turn, the organization of social provisioning interacts with and changes the social environment, for example, by rendering some groups poor or economically dependent.

This definition points to several important characteristics of social provisioning. First, because it is a process, it is in a state of continuous change. Second, it is situated in a social, cultural, and political context, and as such, it is complex, messy, and nondeterministic. Third, and related to the preceding two characteristics, it will be affected by the class, racial-ethnic, and gender dynamics of the society, and will affect these dynamics in turn. Finally, the organization of social provisioning is not a 'natural' outcome of market and emotional forces. Rather its organization reflects relations of power and can become an object of sharp political struggle.

IV FIVE COMPONENTS OF THE SOCIAL PROVISIONING APPROACH

In my review of feminist economic analyses, I have identified five common characteristics of what I have been terming a social provisioning methodology. This field is of course evolving, and differences in approach and method continue to enrich the dialogue. Still, there appears to be an implicit consensus among many feminist economists around the following five methodological starting points.

First, caring labor and domestic labor are vital parts of any economic system and should be incorporated into the analysis from the beginning, not shoehorned in as an afterthought. One implication of this view is that interdependent and interconnected human actors are at the center of the analysis, rather than the isolated individual (Ferber and Nelson, 1993; Folbre, 1994; Himmelweit, 1995; Akram-Lodhi, 1996; Gideon, 1999; Benería, 2003; Addabbo et al., 2010).

The journal *Feminist Economics*, recognizing the importance of understanding the role of unpaid work in economic life, particularly for women, published two volumes on the subject of 'Unpaid Work, Time Use, Poverty, and Public Policy' (July 2010 and October 2011). The articles in these volumes range across developed and developing countries across the globe, and demonstrate through time-use studies the importance of including unpaid domestic and caring labor in analyses of economic life, detailing results such as the increased 'work intensity' as women struggle to combine paid and unpaid work in the same moments in Thailand (Floro and Pichetpongsa, 2010); the 'time poverty' experienced by women who must combine long hours of paid and unpaid labor in an attempt to provide for their families in Guinea (Bardasi and Wodon, 2010); and the corrosive 'time bind' experienced by low-income single mothers in the United States caught between the difficulties of caring for their families with inadequate resources and the demands of welfare policy that prioritizes paid work (Albelda, 2011).

Separately, a group of Canadian researchers carried out a study in communities of low-income households to discover 'how women undertake the various dimensions of provisioning work in family, market, and public arenas for their households and communities' (Collins et al., 2009, p. 24). This extension of the investigation of provisioning work into the community adds a very useful dimension to the concept, emphasizing that the interdependence involved in the process of providing a living extends well beyond the household. Stephanie Collins et al. found that the women in their study, for example, provided informal oversight for unsupervised children; kept each other informed about the availability of resources such as 'where to get day-old bakery products or how to obtain a season pass for children to the community swimming pool'; and participated more formally in community-support programs such as the council of a community center (pp. 27–8). Cutbacks in government funding for social service organizations have resulted in a transfer of provisioning from the public to the private sector, and low-income women scramble to take on the burden. Collins et al., echoing studies by Diane Elson (2009) and Susan Himmelweit (2002) among others, emphasize that this transfer had negative effects on the well-being of the women and their families, creating increased vulnerability and deprivation rendered largely invisible by the absence of an accounting for nonwage labor.

Second, human well-being should be a central measure of economic success. Properly

evaluating economic well-being requires attention not only to aggregate or average distributions of income and wealth, but also to individual entitlements and what economics
Nobel laureate Amartya Sen has identified as the heterogeneity of human needs (Sen,
1999; see also Floro 1995; Aslaksen et al., 1999). An emphasis on well-being is present in
much of the literature in feminist economics, whether implicitly or explicitly. The Maria
Floro and Anant Pichetpongsa (2010) article cited above, for example, is concerned
particularly with the effects of the work intensity they observed on the well-being and
quality of life of the women home-based workers they studied.

Much of this literature begins with Sen's capabilities approach, which understands
well-being as the ability to lead a life one values (Sen, 1999). Feminist economists have
emphasized that the definition should include care for others (Folbre, 2008), and,
building on Martha Nussbaum's work, feelings of dignity and emotional well-being
(Nussbaum, 2003). Floro and Pichetpongsa (2010) emphasize that well-being is affected
by the material factors that organize a person's life; since 'engagement in work . . . constitutes an essential element of life . . . the manner in which a person spends time and
performs these activities may be important, along with income and consumption data, in
determining the quality of their life' (p. 6).

Deborah Figart, in her keynote address as President of the Association for Social
Economics, notes that our living standard includes 'tangible as well as intangible, privately owned commodities and public goods and services' (Figart, 2007, p. 396). Because
of this, a social provisioning approach emphasizes public processes, not solely individual
choices, as necessary to well-being. However, not all public policy improves quality of
life. As Figart explains,

> If social provisioning entails the ways people organize themselves collectively to get a living,
> we need to examine how we, as a society, are currently organized to accomplish this task and
> the implicit assumptions about capabilities and functionings that underlie this set of social
> practices . . . I am not simply asserting an ethical judgment that society *should* take a role in
> defining living standards; I am saying that it already does. The problem is that the way that
> we go about it now presents major obstacles to the achievement of human flourishing. (2007,
> p. 397; original italics)

Third, human agency is important. Processes as well as outcomes should be examined in evaluating an economic event. This emphasis on agency means that questions
of power, and unequal access to power, are part of the analysis from the beginning
(Albelda, 2002; Hill, 2003; Peter, 2003; Berik et al., 2009). Emphasizing human agency
also helps us to conceptualize development as a multidimensional, relational, and collective process (Benería, 2003, p. 167). Benería stresses that development should lead 'to
shifts in the balance of power toward those who hold very little of it. Development is
much more than increases in GDP and the growth of markets; it's about the fulfillment
of human potential, in all its dimensions – for each and everyone. It's about economic as
well as political democracy' (pp. 167–8).

When processes are recognized as important, case studies become an even more valuable tool for analysis (Berik et al., 2009, fn 20, p. 27). Writing in the *Feminist Economics*
special issue on Inequality, Development, and Growth, Jeanne Koopman examined
the largely negative effects of development policies aimed at 'modernization' (and particularly structural adjustment policies that emphasized production for export) on the

well-being of women agriculturalists in the Senegal River Valley. Successful agricultural policy, she demonstrated, must pay attention to gender (as well as caste and class) divisions of labor, women's traditional land rights, and the realistic possibilities for unsubsidized agricultural exports from developing countries to compete with the heavily subsidized products of the developed world. Most importantly, development policies are unlikely to improve women's position unless the processes implemented include participation by women stakeholders from the onset. As Koopman concludes:

> [N]o matter how good outsiders' ideas for improving women's farming seem, all efforts to promote women's access to improved technology and/or land must be planned and implemented with the active and continual participation of the rural women whose lives and livelihoods will be affected. Only women themselves can fully understand the complexities of local culture and politics that affect the pros and cons of a particular policy change or technology in their villages. (2009, pp. 273–4)

Fourth, ethical judgments are a valid, inescapable, and in fact desirable part of an economic analysis (Benería, 2003; Nussbaum, 2003; Robeyns, 2003), though it is important to clearly state one's assumptions/beliefs so that the reader understands where those ethical judgments are coming from. In feminist economic writing, the emphasis on analyzing inequality, power differentials, and well-being begins with a deeply held belief in the social responsibility for well-being. Each issue of the journal *Feminist Economics* itself begins with the statement that its goal is 'not just to develop more illuminating theories, but to improve the conditions of living for all children, women, and men'. These ethical concerns bring with them responsibilities. Figart asserts, for example, that a social provisioning approach leads to the conclusion that 'there should be social responsibility for living standards' (2007, p. 391). Contributing to the debates about global climate policy, feminist economists have employed an approach based on provisioning to argue that ethical and just policies must prioritize the most vulnerable populations, both within and across nations (Power, 2009; Nelson, 2011).

Fifth, feminist scholars tend to incorporate considerations of class, race-ethnicity, sexual preference and other factors into their research, recognizing the limits of theorizing 'women' as a homogeneous category (Power and Rosenberg, 1995; Badgett and Hyman, 1998; Figart et al., 2002). For example, the July 2002 issue of *Feminist Economics*, dedicated to issues of 'gender, color, caste, and class,' represents 'steps toward an intersectional analysis' (Brewer et al., 2002, p. 7) in which the interactions of race, gender, and other historically specific social categories can be better understood. A study on the effects of the 'Great Recession' of 2007–08, reported by the Institute for Women's Policy Research, illustrates the importance of recognizing difference in vulnerability to hardship by gender, class, race and ethnicity, finding that women, and particularly women of color, had fewer resources than men to cushion periods of unemployment (Hayes and Hartmann, 2011, p. viii).

Also important has been the recognition of differing standpoints in illuminating women's varying experiences across cultures. The expanding literature by feminists from countries of the South has been crucial to this process. For another example, feminist economists in Europe have focused in recent years on the phenomenon of the 'migrant in the family' (Bettio et al., 2006; Lyberaki, 2011), the growing reliance on immigrant women from Southeast Asia and Eastern Europe as a low wage workforce providing caring and domestic labor that enables their female employers to seek paid labor. The authors arrive at different conclusions, with Francesca Bettio et al. pointing out that the availability of cheap, relatively skilled labor generates institutional arrangements that rely upon and perpetuate low-wage caring and domestic labor – such as a limited supply of specialized public services (2006, p. 282). By contrast, Antigone Lyberaki posits more of a win–win dynamic, as the Greek female employers in her study were enabled to seek employment outside their patriarchal families, and the immigrant women they hired were able to earn much-needed income for the families they left behind (p. 122).

While these five components of the social provisioning approach fit together into a coherent whole, they do not constitute a 'check list' that feminist economic analyses must incorporate into their papers. Different approaches and differing circumstances mean that in any given study the use of some components may be more prominently displayed, and at times social provisioning may be recognized as an implicit frame for the research question, without being explicitly recognized. Still, the outcome is an analysis that illuminates a more complex, holistic, and ethically based view of economic life. For example, a study of women's empowerment in a desperately poor rural area of Bangladesh incorporated many aspects of the social provisioning approach, without explicitly using the term. An experiment had been conducted by a UK development project, which provided extremely poor village women with money to purchase (usually) cattle, hoping that this material resource would empower women and thereby raise their (and their families') economic condition. Investigating the results of this project, researcher Lucy Scott asked questions about the results in terms of empowering the women, but she deviated from the frequent measure of empowerment as a set of (mostly economic) outcomes. Instead, since gender poverty is an outcome of social and economic relations, particularly women's subordinate position to men (Scott, 2012, p. 4), Scott emphasized that empowerment must be seen as a *process*, 'or change from a position of disempowerment, during which people are able to exercise greater choice' (p. 5). Addressing the gender division of labor, Scott noted that providing women with more economic resources without giving them more autonomy in choices about how to live their lives can simply leave them with more work and more responsibilities instead of an improved standard of living.

In order to understand how the acquisition of cattle affected the empowerment of the women in the study, the author conducted semi-structured interviews of each woman twice, at the beginning and at the end of the study period, looking for effects on the women's experience along four dimensions: economic, sociocultural, interpersonal, and psychological. Although Scott makes no reference in her study to Sen's work on well-being, her focus in these four categories seems to be on the women's capabilities, their ability to make choices that allowed them to lead lives they valued. She noted that major strategic life choices occur infrequently, so may not be observed in a study, but that a woman's empowerment in small things (like the ability to pay school fees with her own money or pick out her own sari) may lead cumulatively to a position of improved self-esteem and greater respect within the family, outcomes that were most evident in a decrease in domestic violence and a greater confidence among the women to speak out and assert their presence within the village (ibid. p. 18). It is clear from Scott's discussion that this greater confidence among the women is seen as progress in and of itself, not solely for its effects on the economic condition of the women and their children.

In all, although she did not explicitly reference the social provisioning approach, Scott's paper illustrates many aspects of the methodology. She examined the effects on the division of labor within the home as well as on income; she defined empowerment as a process of developing greater autonomy and personal security, reflecting both the emphasis on process and the importance of well-being; and she ended her analysis with a clear ethics-based call:

> The ability to make strategic life choices is closely related to perceptions of the choices available and to the costs associated with making, or not making, them ... Increasing people's knowledge of their rights and laws through social development interventions is one way of doing this. Raising awareness has to be accompanied by other interventions which reduce the economic and social risks associated with individuals making certain strategic choices. (Ibid., p. 17)

V　CONCLUSION

What difference does it make to use a social provisioning approach in an evaluation of the economy and economic life and livelihood? Starting places matter. In teaching, the concepts and arguments introduced at the beginning of the course become repeating themes that inform the material for the entire semester. In economic analysis, where the analysis begins limits what will be examined and what will be ignored. Feminists have done considerable work in demonstrating the role that gender has played in affecting outcomes in concrete, specific historical instances. In the process, feminist research has illuminated the greater complexity of human social, economic, and political organization, combining a search for universal themes with attention to the diversity and historical specificity of human outcomes. At its best, this attention to detail and willingness to avoid neat outcomes has resulted in a richer and deeper understanding of social organization and the roles that gender relations (in conjunction with other relations such as class and race-ethnicity) play.

Social provisioning broadens the scope of economic analysis away from simply choice in the marketplace, to the rich, complex, and interdependent processes involved in providing a living. It recognizes caring for family and community, and the long hard hours spent, most especially by women, in provisioning outside the exchange economy. By asking how well we are providing for ourselves, a social provisioning approach draws attention to questions of well-being, and in the process, to the importance of voice, dignity, and the meaningfulness of economic life. It illuminates the fundamental bases for human material existence in the combining of labor with nature – and the necessity of cooperation. At the same time, it acknowledges differences, the economic, social, and cultural practices that divide and create invidious distinctions. As such, the analysis developed will be complex, messy, and nondeterministic; but also rich, multilayered, and deeply humane.

I believe that social provisioning is a fruitful beginning for an economic analysis that has at its core a concern with human well-being, with the empowerment of subordinated groups, and in Lourdes Benería's words, with 'the fulfillment of human potential in all its dimensions–for each and everyone' (2003, pp. 167–8). Starting points matter because of where they take you and, as such, must be chosen with great care.

NOTE

1. 'Exchange value' refers to the price at which a commodity trades. Exchange value is influenced by market conditions affecting supply and demand. It can be contrasted with 'use value', the intrinsic value of any produced good or service. For example, in the classic diamond-water paradox, water has a much higher use value than diamonds while their relative exchange values are reversed.

REFERENCES

Addabbo, Tindara, Diego Lanzi and Antonella Picchio (2010), 'Gender budgets: a capability approach', *Journal of Human Development and Capabilities*, **11**(4), 479–501.

Akram-Lodhi, A. Haroon (1996), '"You are not excused from cooking": peasants and the gender division of labor in Pakistan', *Feminist Economics*, **2**(2), 87–106.

Albelda, Randy (2002), 'Fallacies of welfare-to-work policies', in Randy Albelda and Ann Withorn (eds), *Lost Ground: Welfare Reform, Poverty, and Beyond*, Boston, MA: South End Press, pp. 79–94.

Albelda, Randy (2011), 'Time binds: US antipoverty policies, poverty, and the well-being of single mothers', *Feminist Economics*, **17**(4), 189–214.

Aslaksen, Iulie, Ane Flaatten and Charlotte Koren (1999), 'Explorations on economics and quality of life', *Feminist Economics*, **5**(2), 79–82.

Badgett, M.V. Lee and Prue Hyman (1998), 'Toward lesbian, gay, and bisexual perspectives in economics: why and how they may make a difference', *Feminist Economics*, **4**(2), 49–54.

Bardasi, Elena and Quentin Wodon (2010), 'Working long hours and having no choice: time poverty in Guinea', *Feminist Economics*, **16**(3), 45–78.

Benería, Lourdes (2003), *Gender, Development, and Globalization: Economics as if People Mattered*, London: Routledge.

Berik, Gunseli, Yana van der Meulen Rodgers and Stephanie Seguino (2009), 'Feminist economics of inequality, development, and growth', *Feminist Economics*, **15**(3), 1–33.

Bettio, Francesca, Annamaria Simonazzi and Paola Villa (2006), 'Change in care regimes and female migration: the care drain in the Mediterranean', *Journal of European Social Policy*, **16**(3), 271–85.

Brewer, Rose, Cecilia Conrad and Mary C. King (2002), 'The complexities and potential of theorizing gender, caste, race, and class', *Feminist Economics*, **8**(2), 3–17.

Collins, Stephanie Baker, Sheila Neysmith, Elaine Porter and Marge Reitsma-Street (2009), 'Women's provisioning work: counting the cost for women living on low income', *Community, Work & Family*, **12**(1), 21–37.

Dugger, William M. (1996), 'Redefining economics: from market allocation to social provisioning', in Charles J. Whalen (ed.), *Political Economy for the 21st Century*, Armonk, NY: M.E. Sharpe, pp. 31–43.

Elson, Diane (2009), 'Gender equality and economic growth in the World Bank *World Development Report 2006*', *Feminist Economics*, **15**(3), 35–59.

Ferber, Marianne A. and Julie A. Nelson (eds) (1993), *Beyond Economic Man: Feminist Theory and Economics*, Chicago, IL: Chicago University Press.

Figart, Deborah (2007), 'Social responsibility for living standards: presidential address, Association for Social Economics, 2007', *Review of Social Economy*, **65**(4), 391–405.

Figart, Deborah M., Ellen Mutari and Marilyn Power (2002), *Living Wages, Equal Wages: Gender and Labor Market Policies in the United States*, London: Routledge.

Floro, Maria Sagrari (1995), 'Women's well-being, poverty, and work intensity', *Feminist Economics*, **1**(3), 1–25.

Floro, Maria S. and Anant Pichetpoongsa (2010), 'Gender, work intensity, and well-being of Thai home-based workers', *Feminist Economics*, **16**(3), 5–44.

Folbre, Nancy (1994), *Who Pays for the Kids? Gender and the Structures of Constraint*, London: Routledge.

Folbre, Nancy (2008), *Valuing Children: Rethinking the Economics of the Family*, Cambridge, MA: Harvard University Press.

Gideon, Jasmine (1999), 'Looking at economies as gendered structures: an application to Central America', *Feminist Economics*, **5**(1), 1–28.

Glenn, Evelyn Nakano (1992), 'From servitude to service work: historical continuities in the racial division of paid reproductive labor', *Signs: Journal of Women in Culture and Society*, **18**(1), 1–43.

Hayes, Jess and Heidi Hartmann (2011), 'Women and men living on the edge: economic insecurity after the Great Recession', testimony, IWPR #C387, Institute for Women's Policy Research, Washington, DC.

Hill, Marianne (2003), 'Development as empowerment', *Feminist Economics*, **9**(2/3), 117–36.

Himmelweit, Susan (1995), 'The discovery of unpaid work', *Feminist Economics*, **1**(2), 1–20.
Himmelweit, Susan (2002), 'Making visible the hidden economy: the case for gender-impact analysis of economic policy', *Feminist Economics*, **8**(1), 49–70.
Jennings, Ann L. (1993), 'Public or private? Institutional economics and feminism', in Ferber and Nelson (eds), pp. 111–29.
Jo, Tae-Hee (2011), 'Social provisioning process and socio-economic modeling', *American Journal of Economics and Sociology*, **70**(5), 1094–116.
Koopman, Jeanne E. (2009), 'Globalization, gender, and poverty in the Senegal River Valley', *Feminist Economics*, **15**(3), 253–85.
Krugman, Paul, Robin Wells and Martha L. Olney (2007), *Essentials of Economics*, New York: Worth Publishers.
Lee, Frederic (2009), *A History of Heterodox Economics*, London: Routledge.
Lyberaki, Antigone (2011), 'Migrant women, care work, and women's employment in Greece', *Feminist Economics*, **17**(3), 105–31.
Marx, Karl (1867 [1967]), *Capital*, Vol. 1, New York: International Publishers.
Morgan, Mary S. and Malcolm Rutherford (1998), 'American economics: the character of the transformation', *History of Political Economy*, **30**(Supplement), 1–26.
Nelson, Julie A. (1993), 'The study of choice or the study of provisioning? Gender and the definition of economics', in Ferber and Nelson (eds), pp. 23–36.
Nelson, Julie A. (2011), 'Ethics and the economist: what climate change demands of us', Global Development and Environment Institute Working Paper no. 11–02, Tufts University, Medford, MA.
Nussbaum, Martha (2003), 'Capabilities as fundamental entitlements: Sen and social justice', *Feminist Economics*, **9**(2/3), 33–60.
Peter, Fabienne (2003), 'Gender and the foundations of social choice', *Feminist Economics*, **9**(2/3), 13–32.
Power, Marilyn (2004), 'Social provisioning as a starting point for feminist economics', *Feminist Economics*, **10**(3), 3–19.
Power, Marilyn (2009), 'Global climate policy and climate justice: a feminist social provisioning approach', *Challenge*, **52**(1), 47–66.
Power, Marilyn and Sam Rosenberg (1995), 'Race, class, and occupational mobility: black and white women in service work in the United States', *Feminist Economics*, **1**(3), 40–59.
Robeyns, Ingrid (2003), 'Sen's capability approach and gender inequality: selecting relevant categories', *Feminist Economics*, **9**(2/3), 61–92.
Scott, Lucy (2012), 'Contested relationships: women's economic and social empowerment, insights from the transfer of material assets in Bangladesh', UNU World Institute for Development Economics Research Working Paper No. 2012/2, available at: http://www.wider.unu.edu/publications/working-papers/2012/en_GB/wp2012–002/ (accessed February 25, 2012).
Sen, Amartya (1999), *Development as Freedom*, New York: Anchor Books.
Smith, Adam (1776 [2003]), *An Inquiry into the Nature and Causes of the Wealth of Nations*, New York: Bantam Dell.
Strassmann, Diana (1993), 'The stories of economics and the power of the storyteller', *History of Political Economy*, **25**(1), 147–65.
Veblen, Thorstein (1899 [1967]), *The Theory of the Leisure Class*, New York: Penguin Books.

2. Feminist economics as a theory and method
Drucilla K. Barker

I INTRODUCTION

Several years ago while teaching at a liberal arts college, I had a conversation with a colleague at a similar institution regarding the long-run economic viability of institutions such as ours. I mentioned I was a 'feminist' economist, to which he politely replied that was just a good economist. My use of the modifier feminist seemed to him utterly unnecessary. So why is it necessary? This is really a variant of an old question first put in this form by Simone de Beauvoir; she asked in the introduction to the *Second Sex* why it was necessary that she be described as a female philosopher (de Beauvoir, 1949 [1974]). Her answer was that women are defined with reference to men, but men are not defined in terms of reference to women. Men are human beings. Of course so are women, yet somehow they remain different.

The same is true for feminist economics. It is defined in reference to economics unmodified, whether it is neoclassical, Marxist, or institutionalist. Economics is the study of human beings and economic processes; feminist economics, because it puts women at the center, is somehow different. I agree that it is both different and necessary because – even with decades and decades of scholarship, teaching, and activism – questions about women's roles in economic life endure. More importantly, despite the advances that elite women have made in economics, politics, and society in general (although there is still a long way to go before gender equality is reached, even for this group), women still bear a disproportionate bulk of the burdens of poverty, social and economic exclusion, and the ecological damage caused by climate change. Feminist economics is absolutely necessary to change this.

The many different chapters in this volume attest to the myriad and varied roles women play in economic life in both the private and the public sectors. This chapter does not attempt to provide a definitive answer to the question of what feminist economics is; rather, it examines the underlying epistemological foundations and methodologies that characterize feminist economics. It begins with a brief exploration of feminist economics and its epistemological and methodological differences and similarities to economics unmodified (Section II). I then examine some of the epistemological and methodological debates within feminist economics itself (Section III). Section IV offers a brief speculation of the philosophical future of feminist economics. Section V concludes.

II FEMINIST ECONOMICS: DIFFERENCES AND SIMILARITIES TO MAINSTREAM ECONOMICS

Feminist economics is a pluralistic and sometimes interdisciplinary knowledge project that works toward a transformation of economics. This transformation entails critically examining the dimensions of gender, race, ethnicity, caste, and class embedded and naturalized in economics unmodified. Although much of what I have to say will also apply to the institutionalist and Marxist approaches to women's economic issues, I will couch this section in terms of what is commonly referred to as neoclassical or mainstream economics. For most economists and lay people, neoclassical economics *is* economics.[1]

In this version of economics, the economy is seen as an entity comprised of rational economic agents. These individuals maximize their utility subject to the constraints placed on them, prices, incomes, and in more complex models, time. Formal mathematical models trace the consequences of the decisions made by consumers and firms. These consequences are determined at the margin by comparing the marginal, or incremental, benefits and costs. Equilibrium prices and quantities for commodities and for factors of production are determined by the intersections of their respective supply and demand functions and any imbalance between demand and supply exerts pressures on prices to adjust to new market-clearing levels. In the absence of market imperfections, the price system will result in an economically efficient allocation of resources.

The epistemological aspects of the neoclassical approach are characterized by a commitment to the notion that adherence to a rigidly prescribed 'scientific' methodology based on the concepts of self-interested individualism, contractual exchange, and constrained optimization results in unbiased economic science. Mathematical modeling is at the center of the project because that is where the claim to science lies. As Gerard Debreu put it in his 1990 Presidential address to the American Economic Association meeting, 'A global view of an economy that wants to take into account the large number of its commodities, the equally large number of its prices, the multitude of its agents and their interactions requires a mathematical model' (1991, p. 3).

Feminist economists have been critical of the assumption of self-interested individualism and the lack of any interactions, except those organized according to the principles of self-interested contractual exchange, because these assumptions excluded considerations of the dependent children, the elderly, and the infirm (see Strassmann, 1993; Folbre, 1995; Folbre and Nelson, 2000). Using gender as an analytical category, feminist economists show that unquestioned and unexamined masculinist values are deeply embedded in both theoretical and empirical economic scholarship. Absent feminist analyses, economics rationalizes and naturalizes existing social hierarchies based on gender, race, ethnicity, and sexuality. Although this is especially true of issues germane to women's lives such as labor market segregation and the wage gap, the feminization of poverty, and the provision of domestic labor, it is no less true of issues such as international trade and macroeconomics. All economic phenomena are likely to have asymmetric impacts on women and men since they occupy different social locations.

Much of feminist economics can be categorized as feminist empiricism, a type of feminist science practice that has its origins in the work of feminist scholars in biology and related life sciences.[2] Scholars recognized that standard answers to many questions involving sex and gender reflected a distinct androcentric and/or sexist bias (Harding, 1986). For proponents of this approach, the problem is not science, but rather that researchers are simply not doing good science. In this case, mainstream economists are not doing good economics. Androcentric biases and blind adherence to the ideologies of free markets can be eliminated if the economics community would seriously examine their implicit assumptions and values. This would lead to better economic practice in the sense of being less biased and more objective. Feminist economists and the inclusion of women and other underrepresented groups are necessary to this endeavor because they are the ones most likely to notice the gendered asymmetric effects of economic theories and policies that are hidden by conventional theorizing.

A popular radio show in the US, *MarketPlace*, provides an excellent example of the problems using purely abstract models peopled by rational economic agents rather than people differentiated by various categories of social difference. In an episode, one of the Freakonomics bloggers, Stephen Dubner (2012), made a compelling case for sending plastic flowers rather than real flowers for Mothers Day.[3] The host of the show, Kai Ryssdal, demonstrated his feminist sensibilities immediately by revealing, in a sort of 'man to man' way, that he left this particular task to his wife. But, never mind. The point is that Dubner made an excellent case, based on neoclassical microeconomic principles, that sending real flowers was simply not a 'green' thing to do after the costs and benefits of transportation and storage were taken into account. I agree completely.

As Dubner pointed out, nearly all cut flowers are imported from the equatorial parts of the world and the carbon footprint associated with this particular type of international trade is enormous. What he left out, though, was any consideration of the workers who planted, weeded, and cut the flowers. They are mainly young women and due to the use of pesticides and fungicides the work is terribly dangerous to their long-term health. In Dubner's cost–benefit analysis these costs to the workers were simply not important. I would argue that it was precisely because they are women in the global South that they remained invisible. This is just one example of why we still need 'economics modified' – feminist economics.

Feminism provides the conceptual framework that allows feminist economists to reveal the androcentric, classist, racist, and heterosexist values that have shaped economics (Barker, 2005a). It also allows us to put the work that women do at the center of the analysis rather than at the margin. Feminist economics is about people and so gender, race, ethnicity, caste, sexuality, and class matter. Domestic labor is recognized as real work that is essential to the reproduction of the labor force. Its value can be accounted for and when it is, estimates show it is equivalent to approximately 33 percent of GDP (Cloud and Garrett, 1996). Moreover, women bear a disproportionate share of the burden of domestic labor. Rachel Krantz-Kent (2009) found that in the 2003–07 time period women spent an average of 10.8 hours more per week doing unpaid household work than did men. Feminist economics also interrogates, among other things, questions about the social devaluation of work associated with women, the feminization of the labor force both nationally and internationally, the race and gender wage gap, and the importance of caring labor (Barker and Feiner, 2004).

As I have argued earlier, feminist economists are faced with the same dilemmas that other feminist researchers in other social sciences face: the instability of women as a category; the intersectionality of gender, race, class, nationality, and sexuality; and the relationship between the researcher and the people or phenomena being studied (Barker, 2005a). However, its objects of study – such as the division of labor by sex, race, ethnicity, class, and nation; the value of unpaid household labor; the supply of caring labor; and women's roles and status in labor markets – mean that feminist economists face these dilemmas in ways that are particular to their discipline. It is about women, but it is not only about women. It studies 'women's work', but destabilizes that designation. It presumes to speak for the well-being of poor women and their families, but does so from positions of relative power and privilege. It inherits the scientific prestige of economics and, to a certain extent, questions the methodologies that accord it its status as a science.[4]

This last issue is perhaps the most pressing. Feminist economists are trying to both transform the discipline and work within it. We work within a discipline that calls itself 'the queen of the social sciences', and its scientific status is derived from its 'rigorous', read mathematical, modeling and by a strict allegiance to the separation of positive (what is) and normative economics (what ought to be). Although this distinction has been thoroughly debunked in both the philosophy of science and feminist economics literature, it remains a truism in most introductory economics textbooks (Sen, 1973; Ferber and Nelson, 1993; Putnam, 2002). Textbook authors justify this by saying that economics relies on models and all models must simplify (Walsh, 1987). However, as Vivian Walsh points out, these authors never discuss the implicit values that determine what is put in the model and what is left out. Feminist economists have explicit values: gender equity, racial equality, environmental sustainability and so forth. We recognize that economics is not about elegant models and theories, but rather it is about the lives of actual living people and their descendants. The dilemma for many feminists is how to explicitly reveal these values while working within the discipline. To borrow a phrase from anthropology, we are insider/outsiders to the profession.

Feminist economists want a seat at the table; that is to say, we want to influence public policy at both the local and global levels. To do so we must speak not only the language of feminism but also the language of economics. It is this latter requirement that creates the tension because it is a language that is distinctly unfriendly to feminist concerns (Barker, 2005b). Still, tremendous strides have been made. The journal *Feminist Economics* continues to thrive; the work on engendering macroeconomic models continues (despite a lack of an institutional home), and the International Association for Feminist Economics (IAFFE) remains a healthy organization with an annual conference each 'summer' (located both within and outside North America) and a continued presence at the Allied Social Science Association/American Economic Association annual meetings. One distinctive feature about both the journal and the conferences is the heavy reliance on modeling (the theoretical side) and on quantitative measurement (the empiricist side).

Formal modeling, reliance on stylized facts and mathematical models and quantitative empirical work all contribute to the reputation of economics as a science. Understanding the economy as an isolated phenomenon, which can be understood separately from culture, power, and ideology, is a commitment to a particular epistemological view. That is to say, it is a way of knowing that assumes that phenomena can be best understood by breaking them down into their component parts. Given the complexity of economic phenomena, an economic model is a mathematical map that isolates the relevant variables and deduces the causal relationships between them. Econometrics provides the tools necessary to empirically verify hypothesized causal relationships.

For examples I will use the abstracts from three articles in a recent special issue of *Feminist Economics* dealing with unpaid work, time use, poverty, and public policy to illustrate the use of formal modeling by and of empirical studies in feminist economics. The abstracts are useful because they illustrate how the authors are speaking both the language of mainstream economics and the language of feminism.

The first by Elissa Braunstein, Irene van Staveren and Daniele Tavani is titled, 'Embedding care and unpaid work in macroeconomic modeling: a structuralist approach,' and the abstract is quoted in full below:

This study embeds paid and unpaid care work in a structuralist macroeconomic model. Care work is formally modeled as a gendered input into the market production process via its impact on the current and future labor force, with altruistic motivations determining both how much support people give one another and the economic effectiveness of that support. This study uses the model to distinguish between two types of economies – a 'selfish' versus an 'altruistic' economy – and seeks to understand how different macroeconomic conditions and events play out in the two cases. Whether and how women and men share the financial and time costs of care condition the results of the comparison with more equal sharing of care responsibilities making the 'altruistic' case more likely. (Braunstein et al., 2011, p. 5)

I chose this abstract for three reasons: first, because the authors are highly respected feminist economists and it is an innovative and important article; second, because it shows how to speak the dual languages of feminism and economics; and third, because it is an excellent example of theoretical work in feminist economics. It explicitly values gender equity, it uses gender as a category of analysis and it offers concrete public policy solution. Its innovative use of a structuralist model allows the authors to explicitly consider how the 'social structures of production matter for economic outcomes' (p. 6).

In this case, it allows them to show that gender equity, in the sense of a more equal sharing of 'reproductive responsibilities' makes an 'altruistic' outcome more likely. The altruistic case results in better economic outcomes because productivity at work 'depends on the extent to which one is supported and replenished at home' (p. 10). Thus, the feminist insight, from a wide variety of academic disciplines, that both care work and an equitable sharing of reproductive labor are important to the social good is demonstrated using language that is acceptable to the mainstream.

The second article is by Chang Hongqin, Fiona MacPhail and Xiao-yuan Dong and is titled, 'The feminization of labor and the time-use gender gap in rural China'. I choose it for the same reasons as above, but this one illustrates the empirical dimensions of feminist economics:

This contribution investigates the impact of economic development on the feminization of labor in rural China between 1991 and 2006. Using data from the China Health and Nutrition Survey (CHNS; 1991–2006), this study estimates time use in three sectors (farm, off-farm and domestic) and analyzes the contribution of four features of economic development to changes in time use. Women's share of paid and unpaid work has increased in both the farm and off-farm sectors and migration is a critical determinant. Economic development is associated with a rise in absolute work time, although not an increase in the time-use gender gap. Measuring the feminization of labor with time use rather than labor force participation data may be relevant to feminist analyses in other regions and countries, since it enables a more nuanced evaluation of the impacts of economic development on changes in the well-being of women. (Hongqin et al., 2011, p. 93)

The authors make a compelling case for investigating the effects of the feminization of labor in rural China and couch their arguments in terms of women's well-being and overall economic well-being. The feminization of labor is an established feature of economic development and is generally measured by the increase in women's labor force participation, but it has contradictory effects. In increasing women's access to wages the feminization of labor potentially increases their well-being; however, to the extent that it increases their total work time it decreases their well-being.

Hongqin et al. use accepted econometric and statistical methods to estimate changes in total work hours and show that women 'still provide more hours of total paid and unpaid work than men . . . the data also show that women continue to provide more unpaid hours per day than men do in the domestic sector' (p. 107). This indicates that women continue to bear a disproportionate burden of unpaid household labor. However, the authors also show that economic development is associated with a shift in time-allocation patterns that may have a positive effect on women's well-being. So, while the authors do not solve the contradictions, their analysis illuminates the features of economic development that increase women's well-being.

These two articles are both excellent contributions to the literature and to economic knowledge that can benefit women and their families. They are also typical of the two types of articles that characterize contemporary feminist economics, at least as represented by *Feminist Economics*, the official journal of the organization. Their ability to write in both the language of feminism and the language of economics will contribute to the establishment of feminist economics as a legitimate field of economic inquiry, and I have no doubt will aid many fledging feminist economists on their journeys toward job offers, tenure, and promotion.

Feminist economists working in this tradition have made considerable strides in changing some of the androcentric assumptions and adding important but previously overlooked economic variables. The radical edge of this work, however, is blunted in the sense that it reinscribes the mainstream prescription of what economics is and what economics is not. It is about theory, understood as mathematical modeling, and it is about empirical testing, understood as measurement and establishing causal relationships.

A second important line of feminist economic inquiry further broadens the field by incorporating history, institutions, and other actual rather than only stylized facts. It uses descriptive statistics and qualitative arguments to show what mainstream economics leaves out about the lives of women.[5] It is interdisciplinary in that it draws from other social sciences such as anthropology, gender studies, sociology, and history as well as advocacy groups. It is also heterodox in that it draws on the insights of both institutionalism and neoclassical economics. I would argue, however, that it is primarily disciplinary in terms of the phenomena it examines: the influences of race, class, and gender on labor force participation, occupational segregation and the gender wage gap, domestic labor and social reproduction, public policies, and economic globalization.

The abstract for 'Welfare-to-work, farewell to families? US welfare reform and work/family debates' by Randy Albelda provides an excellent example of the language and methodology of this approach:

There are large research, policy and economic gaps between the ways US researchers and policy makers address the work/family bind amongst middleclass professionals and poor lone mothers. This is clearly seen in US welfare reform, an important piece of work/family legislation in the 1990s. The new rules make the work/family binds worse for low-income, poor mothers and do not alleviate poverty. With its clear expectation that poor mothers be employed, the legislation opens up new avenues to revamp low-wage work for breadwinners and to socialize the costs of caring for family. Closing the literature gap may help to close the policy gap, which, in turn, would promote more income equality. (Albelda, 2001, p. 119).

Through a careful analysis of the history of social insurance and social assistance programs dating from 1935, Albelda shows that they have all been shaped by the notion that men are the breadwinners and women are the caretakers. However, the underlying presumptions behind social protection programs no longer hold. Women have increased their labor force participation; there has been a decline in married couple families, and a growth in single-mother families. Moreover, the number of jobs that would allow one breadwinner to support a family has declined. During the late 1980s and early 1990s, these demographic changes, plus an increase in African American women's use of government assistance led to a political consensus that poor mothers must become more reliant on their own wages. Anti-poverty programs were replaced by work-support programs, and poor women were required to find paid employment if they wished to keep childcare assistance and health insurance while they transitioned to paid work.

Among the many problems with this policy change is that poor women do not have enough time or other resources to adequately care for their children, perform other necessary household tasks, participate in paid employment, and navigate the bureaucracy of government support programs. The predictable result is that children get less parental care. All other government assistance programs share this notion of 'free time' and thus 'intensify the time poverty that single mothers already face'. This article provides important and useful insights into the ways that the rhetoric around self-sufficiency and family values leads to policies that are ill-suited not only to poor women turning to government assistance for their survival, but also to the needs of the working poor in general. It is an example of using empirical facts to construct a feminist argument around an important policy debate that is central to the well-being of many women today.

III   EPISTEMOLOGY, INTERDISCIPLINARITY, AND FEMINIST ECONOMICS

Methodologies in feminist economics that use accepted economic concepts and categories to frame feminist arguments for women's economic and social equality are well positioned to propose concrete public policy solutions that work toward these goals. There is much to be gained by remaining within this disciplinary framework in that it provides a common language that legitimates and valorizes feminist approaches. However, I would argue for an approach that is interdisciplinary in both its methods and in its subject matter. Why?

First, an interdisciplinary approach would be contextual and intersectional. It could conceptualize economics not as an isolated aspect of the social world, but rather as an integral part of culture, politics, and competing and contradictory ideologies. It could incorporate insights from other disciplines and fields such as cultural studies, queer studies, and social theory. Most importantly, it would invite an analysis of the relationship between power, knowledge, and privilege.

As I have argued earlier, feminist economists have had only limited success in challenging the hegemony and prestige of neoclassical economics (Barker, 2005a). We are not alone here. Marxists, institutionalists, Post Keynesians, and other heterodox schools have likewise had little success in this endeavor. And it could be the case that no amount of 'better' science and analysis will ever replace the scientism that characterizes neoclassical economics. Because neoclassical economics does one thing very, very well: it articulates the ideology of contemporary capitalism in a manner that makes it seem natural, inevitable, and beneficent. Neoclassical economics does not 'speak truth to power', but on the contrary, accommodates and naturalizes it. Answering this challenge entails an examination of power, knowledge, and privilege, including the power and privilege that attaches to feminist economics. The modernist position within which the intellectual – embedded though she may be within social institutions of power and control – could still step outside of power and find a neutral vantage point from which to take an ethical, oppositional stand will no longer suffice (Sandoval, 2000).

The empiricist epistemology shared by the vast majority of feminist economists presupposes a separation between the real and the metaphorical in which the former refers to material objects in the world and the latter to discursively constructed systems of meaning and value. As I have previously argued, many, if not most, feminist economists would argue that it is only the real that is relevant to the feminist economics project (Barker, 2005a). Lourdes Benería, a prominent feminist economist, articulates this position clearly. She argues that postmodern work emphasizing identity, difference, and agency have enriched our understanding of identity politics, postcolonial realities, and the intersections of gender and race. This scholarship has, however, 'run parallel' to changes on the material side of life, particularly the resurgence of neoliberalism (Benería, 2003, p. 25). The problem, according to her, is that postmodern work tends to deemphasize the economic and generate an imbalance between the need to understand economic reality and 'the more predominant focus on 'words,' including issues such as difference, subjectivity and representation' (p. 25). It is not that work on these issues is wrong, but rather that it needs to be linked to an understanding of the socioeconomic aspects of life. This is the task for feminist economics.

Benería is not alone in making this argument. Consider the comments of Julie Nelson, another prominent feminist economist. In an essay that discusses the range of work in feminist economics, she notes the lack of deconstructionist or poststructuralist scholarship relative to the humanities (Nelson, 2000; see also Nelson, 1995). This is not a problem in her opinion. Indeed, she argues that poststructuralist thought creates barriers for scholars not educated in 'obscurant literatures/techniques', and 'promulgate[s] a bloodless and lifeless view of the world and fail[s] to take into account lived experience' (2000, p. 1180).

The importance of the contributions of Benería, Nelson, and other members of the feminist economics community to understanding the material dimensions of women's lives is uncontested. It is not my intention to disparage them here. Rather, my intention is to argue that analyses of identity and representation, knowledge and power, and authenticity and culture are crucial to understanding economic and political structures. It is to argue for a rethinking of the empiricist position and a valorizing of postmodern, poststructuralist, and postcolonial theoretical commitments (Peterson, 2003). Although there are differences among these three theoretical commitments, for the purpose of this chapter I will use the term 'post-positivist' to refer to them as a group that shares particular significant ontological and epistemological assumptions.

A post-positivist approach to feminist economics and feminist political economy would, at a minimum, entail a commitment to the notion that the material and symbolic are not radically separate. The feminist economist Gillian Hewitson (1999) puts it most clearly. She argues for a rejection of an empiricist view of language in favor of one that sees language as a system of relationships within which meaning is produced. Metaphors are not just descriptive, they are productive and a referential view of language masks these productive effects. For economics, including feminist economics, this means that underlying processes of the economy are constituted through economic discourse. While this is certainly a minority view among feminist economists, I will argue that it is an important perspective to bring to the table.

The concept of discourse refers not only to language, but also to social institutions and practices. Since power constitutes and legitimates itself through a variety of institutions and discursive practices, it is important to understand that knowledge production is 'power laden and power producing' (Peterson, 2003, p. 24). Considering the relationship between knowledge and power is a way to emancipate knowledge production from the subjugation of science and to create alternative knowledges that are capable of opposition to and struggle against the coercion of a unified, formal, and scientific discourse (Foucault, 1980). Again, this is not to argue against science, empirical investigations, systematic inquiry, or comparative studies. As a practical matter in today's political and cultural climate we need to emphasize the importance of good science, especially good economic science. Nonetheless, I want to argue for recognition of the contingent and local nature of the claims of economics and to explicitly acknowledge the situated position of feminist economists who are simultaneously both inside and outside of economic discourse (Barker, 2005b).

IV POST-POSITIVIST APPROACHES TO FEMINIST ECONOMICS

There are a handful of scholars trained in feminist economics who engage in interdisciplinary work with other scholars in cultural studies, feminist and queer studies, and social theory. The work that has emerged from these conversations opens up feminist economics to a more radical transformation of what we think of as the 'economy', and raises questions that were heretofore obscure. Take one familiar issue, for example: caring labor. As I have argued previously, the distinction in feminist economics between caring labor and other forms of domestic labor, articulated in terms of feelings of genuine nurturance and affection, is problematic for several reasons (Barker and Feiner, 2009). It masks the ways in which domestic labor is racialized and feminized and it restricts the concept of care metaphorically to the domestic sphere, which makes it a private rather than a collective issue and reinforces heteronormative scripts about appropriate family forms.

Suzanne Bergeron (2009) has noted the implicit heteronormative assumptions in feminist economics and demonstrated how common it is within feminist economic scholarship to assume that households, the site of where most domestic labor is done, comprise two heterosexual adults who conform to 'dominant gender scripts' (p. 55). Similarly, Colin Danby has argued that heteronormativity and race have long been linked in US history. Normal, healthy, and private realms were 'contrasted to pathological personal, familial and kin practices that do not merit the social or juridical support that 'normal' private life receives. Efforts by abjected groups to cross over this division and achieve respectability simply mark its existence and importance' (Danby, 2007, p. 41). The importance of these insights from queer theory to the discussions of domestic labor is that they aid in explaining two important, but overlooked questions in the literature. The first is why some groups are entitled to be cared for and cared about while others are not afforded this privilege (Barker, 2012). Perhaps more important is the question asked by the post-positivist feminist sociologist Encarnación Gutiérrez Rodríguez: 'why is domestic work linked to the dehumanization of those who work to ensure that others have agreeable surroundings for living and recreating life?' (2007, p. 72).

Understanding this question entails interrogating the role that feminism plays in maintaining race, class, and caste privilege. Women in the global South, like many black and Latina women in the global North, have demonstrated a deep ambivalence toward white, western feminism. Theorists and activists such as Audre Lourde (1984) and bell hooks (1984) argue that feminists need to deal with differences among women, differences that arise from differing oppressions, especially racial oppression. Others argue that for the majority of the world's poor women, the class oppression created by globalization and the international division of labor is far more devastating than gender oppression (Mies, 1986). Similarly, the academic construction of 'Third World Women' has been shown to be a problematic construct of liberal feminism (Mohanty, 1988; Narayan, 1997; Barker, 1998; Zein-Elabdin and Charusheela, 2004). Taking these considerations seriously means that feminist scholars need to examine the implicit values and ideological claims that are embedded in their analyses and interrogate the roles they play in maintaining and reproducing the unequal social hierarchies.

Let me illustrate this last point by examining a familiar issue: the relationship between women's education, women's empowerment, and economic growth. The importance of education for girls, women, and other disenfranchised populations is taken as axiomatic. For example, goal three of the Millennium Development Goals, Promote Gender Equality and Empower Women, has as its first target the elimination of gender disparity in primary and secondary education (United Nations Development Programme, n.d.). Similarly, a World Bank publication on the education of girls in the twenty-first century states that 'educating girls is one of the most cost-effective ways of spurring development. [It] creates powerful poverty-reducing synergies and yields enormous intergenerational gains' (Phumaphi and Leipziger, 2008, p. xvii). The report goes on to say that 'greater investment in girls' education is vital for increasing female participation and productivity in the labor market' (p. xviii).

Now let me be very, very clear: I am most definitely not arguing against the importance of education for girls and women. I do think, however, that the way in which it is framed by the United Nations, the World Bank, and various NGOs can be problematic in the sense that it reproduces the very power structures and inequalities that feminists challenge. This argument is aptly developed in an article by S. Charusheela (2009) in which she analyzes a conversation between the philosopher Martha Nussbaum and the Africanist feminist philosopher Nikiru Nzegwu. Nussbaum uses the capabilities approach developed by economist Amartya Sen to develop a universalist ethics. Literacy is one of Nussbaum's essential capabilities and she argues that women's education ought to be a central task for feminists today. For Nussbaum, not only is literacy important in its own right, it is essential for women's economic empowerment. Charusheela argues, however, that Nussbaum's argument rests on implicit assumptions about the structure of institutions that organize the production of knowledge and culture. What Nussbaum overlooks is that it is these same institutions and the types of education they provide that 'exclude subaltern groups and privilege educated elites' (p. 1140).

Drawing on Nzegwu's work, Charusheela goes on to argue that not only did illiterate Igbo women play strong political and social roles in Igbo society and claim a long tradition of organized political protest to maintain their status, but that it was the '*literate* privileged women from the emerging upper classes who showed a lack of political consciousness through an internalization of Western patriarchal norms in the colonial period' (Charusheela, 2009, p.1142, original italics). Not all education is the same in either its content or its methods. I would argue that just as trade schools and technical colleges in the global North filter individuals into different segments of the labor market (or into the permanent ranks of the unemployed), education and literacy campaigns in the global South fulfill the same function. In this case education produces workers for the factories and sweatshops necessary for global capitalism on the bottom and a small handful of the elite to fulfill the technocratic professions on the top. Thus while education is empowering, literacy and the lack thereof also justify unequal political, social, and economic conditions.

One of the important contributions of postcolonial scholarship in general has been to show the ways that the colonizers of the 'new world' used education to inculcate western patriarchal values into a class of indigenous elites. It was through education that colonized populations internalized the values and belief systems of the colonizers. What multiple and contradictory functions do the educational policies advocated by the World Bank and other similar institutions play in the global political economy of today? The Bank does acknowledge that 'schooling as an institution may marginalize and diminish the power of local indigenous knowledge', but its answer is to give children the space to 'reclaim their power and right to be heard as experts about their own gendered and sexual lives' (Mannathoko, 2008, p. 134; see also Bergeron, 2006). To do so, however, they must speak within the discursive framework of the educated elites if their voices are to be heard and intelligible. The problem does not have an easy solution because while education is necessary for the emancipation of women today, it is also a process through which the values associated with global capitalism are internalized. This is another example of how a critical and interdisciplinary approach can contribute to feminist economics.

Finally, interdisciplinary, post-positivist approaches to feminist economics allow feminist economists to connect to what J.K. Gibson-Graham (2008) has termed an 'ontological project'. That is, the way we think about, talk about and represent economic phenomena discursively constitute the phenomena we study. It allows us the potential to bring new and alternative economies into being and to imagine a way out of dualisms such as private/public, family/market, and nation-state/global governance.

V   CONCLUSION

This is not to say that everyone has to do everything. If we are reading this book, it is because we are scholars or academics or activists who are committed to our work. That commitment engenders the really good, progressive work. What I am arguing for is a pluralistic approach to feminist economic methodology that takes seriously critical evaluations of the dialectic between power and knowledge and between the material and the symbolic.

This does not mean that feminist economists should give up either the tools or prestige of economics. To resist power and work for social change, we need to speak the language of power, in this case the language of high-status economics. It is, however, important to recognize that this is only one language, one system of knowledge production. Its elite status and hegemonic influence stems not from its superior fidelity to the real, but rather from its connection to power (Barker, 2005b). This likewise entails replacing the notion of science as representation with the notion of science as a set of practices (Harding, 2003, 2008; Peter, 2003). Thus, the methodological pluralism I am advocating is a radical one. It is one in which the goals of feminist economics – to improve the lives of women and create a more just and equitable society – are facilitated by a variety of seemingly incommensurate interventions, tactics, and discourses.

NOTES

1. See Barker (1999) for an examination of some of the foundational critiques by both institutional and Marxist critics.
2. There is an extensive literature on this in the feminist epistemology literature. See Barker (2004) for a summary.
3. Personally I prefer silk or cloth flowers.
4. This, in turn, has the potential to demonstrate the disparity between the social, cultural and political authority enjoyed by mainstream economics and its manifest failings as a science.
5. There are many excellent examples of this approach in feminist economics, and there are several anthologies that provide a good guide here. See, for example, Ferber and Nelson (1993), Kuiper and Sap (1995), Mutari and Figart (2003), Barker and Kuiper (2009), and Benería et al. (2011).

REFERENCES

Albelda, Randy (2001), 'Welfare-to-work, farewell to families? US welfare reform and work/family debates', *Feminist Economics*, **7**(1), 119–35.
Barker, Drucilla K. (1998), 'Dualisms, discourse and development', *Hypatia*, **13**(3), 83–94.
Barker, Drucilla K. (1999), 'Neoclassical economics: critique', in Phil O'Hara (ed.), *Encyclopedia of Political Economy*, Vol. 2, London: Routledge, pp. 793–7.
Barker, Drucilla K. (2004), 'From feminist empiricism to feminist poststructuralism: philosophical questions in feminist economics', in John Davis, Alain Marciano and Jochen Runde (eds), *Elgar Companion to Economics and Philosophy*, Cheltenham, UK and Northampton, MA, USA: Edward Elgar, pp. 213–29.
Barker, Drucilla K. (2005a), 'Beyond women and economics: rereading "women's work"', *Signs: Journal of Women in Culture and Society*, **30**(4), 2189–209.
Barker, Drucilla K. (2005b), 'A seat at the table: feminist economists negotiate development', in Drucila K. Barker and Edith Kuiper (eds), *Feminist Economics and the World Bank*, London: Routledge, pp. 209–17.
Barker, Drucilla K. (2012), 'Querying caring labor', *Rethinking Marxism*, **24**(4), 574–91.
Barker, Drucilla K. and Susan F. Feiner (2004), *Liberating Economics: Feminist Perspectives on Families, Work, and Globalization*, Ann Arbor, MI: University of Michigan Press.
Barker, Drucilla K. and Susan F. Feiner (2009), 'Affect, race and class: an interpretive reading of caring labor', *Frontiers: A Journal of Women Studies*, **30**(1), 41–54.
Barker, Drucilla K. and Edith Kuiper (eds). (2009), *Feminist Economics: Critical Concepts*, 4 vols, London and New York: Routledge.
Benería, Lourdes (2003), *Gender, Development and Globalization: Economics as if All People Mattered*, New York: Routledge.

Benería, Lourdes, Ann Mari May and Diana L. Strassmann (eds) (2011), *Feminist Economics*, Cheltenham, UK and Northampton, MA, USA: Edward Elgar.

Bergeron, Suzanne (2006), 'Colonizing knowledge: economics and interdisciplinarity in engendering development', in Edith Kuiper and Drucilla K. Barker (eds), *Feminist Economics and the World Bank: History, Theory and Policy*, London and New York: Routledge, pp. 127–41.

Bergeron, Suzanne (2009), 'An interpretive analytics to move caring labor off the straight path', *Frontiers: A Journal of Women Studies*, **30**(1), 55–64.

Braunstein, Elissa, Irene van Staveren and Daniele Tavani (2011), 'Embedding care and unpaid work in macroeconomic modeling: a structuralist approach', *Feminist Economics*, **17**(4), 1–27.

Charusheela, S. (2009), 'Social analysis and the capabilities approach: a limit to Martha Nussbaum's universalist ethics', *Cambridge Journal of Economics*, **33**(6), 1135–52.

Cloud, Kathleen and Nancy Garrett (1996), 'Inclusion of women's household human capital production in analyses of structural transformation', *Feminist Economics*, **2**(3), 93–120.

Danby, Colin (2007), 'Political economy and the closet: heteronormativity in feminist economics', *Feminist Economics*, **13**(2), 29–53.

de Beauvoir, Simone (1949 [1974]), *The Second Sex*, New York: Vintage Books.

Debreu, Gerard (1991), 'The mathematization of economics', *American Economic Review*, **81**(1), 1–7.

Dubner, Stephen J: (2012), 'Don't buy your mom fresh flowers', Interviewed by Kai Rysdall, available at: http://www.marketplace.org/topics/life/freakonomics-radio/dont-buy-your-mom-fresh-flowers (accessed September 7, 2012).

Ferber, Marianne A. and Julie A. Nelson (eds) (1993), *Beyond Economic Man: Feminist Theory and Economics*, Chicago, IL: University of Chicago Press.

Folbre, Nancy (1995), '"Holding hands at midnight": the paradox of caring labor', *Feminist Economics*, **1**(1), 73–92.

Folbre, Nancy and Julie A. Nelson (2000), 'For love or money – or both?', *Journal of Economic Perspectives*, **14**(4), 123–40.

Foucault, Michel (1980), *Power/Knowledge: Selected Interviews and other Writings, 1972–77*, edited by Colin Gordon, New York: Pantheon Press.

Gibson-Graham, J.K. (2008), 'Diverse economies: performative practices for "other worlds"', *Progress in Human Geography*, **32**(5), 613–32.

Harding, Sandra G. (1986), *The Science Question in Feminism*, Ithaca, NY: Cornell University Press.

Harding, Sandra G. (2003), 'After objectivism vs. relativism', in Drucilla K. Barker and Edith Kuiper (eds), *Toward a Feminist Philosophy of Economics*, London: Routledge, pp. 122–33.

Harding, Sandra G. (2008), *Sciences from Below: Feminisms, Postcolonialities and Modernities*, Durham, NC: Duke University Press.

Hewitson, Gillian J. (1999), *Feminist Economics: Interrogating the Masculinity of Rational Economic Man*, Cheltenham, UK and Northampton, MA, USA: Edward Elgar.

Hongqin, Chang, Fiona MacPhail and Xiao-yuan Dong (2011), 'The feminization of labor and the time-use gender gap in rural China', *Feminist Economics*, **17**(4), 93–124.

hooks, bell (1984), *Feminist Theory from Margin to Center*, Boston, MA: South End Press.

Krantz-Kent, Rachel (2009), 'Measuring time spent in unpaid household work: results from the American Time Use Survey', *Monthly Labor Review*, **132**(7), 46–59.

Kuiper, Edith and Jolande Sap (eds) (1995), *Out of the Margin: Feminist Perspectives on Economics*, London: Routledge.

Lourde, Audre (1984), *Sister Outsider: Essays and Speeches*, Trumansburg, NY: Crossing Press.

Mannathoko, C. (2008), 'Promoting education quality through gender-friendly schools', in Mercy Tembon and Lucia Forte (eds), *Girl's Education in the 21st Century: Gender, Equality and Economic Growth*, Washington, DC: International Bank for Reconstruction and Development/World Bank, pp. 127–42.

Mies, Maria (1986), *Patriarchy and Accumulation on a World Scale: Women in the International Division of Labour*, London: Zed Books.

Mohanty, Chandra Talpade (1988), 'Under western eyes: feminist scholarship and colonial discourses', *Feminist Review*, **30**(1), 61–88.

Mutari, Ellen and Deborah M. Figart (eds) (2003), *Women and the Economy: A Reader*, Armonk, NY: M.E. Sharpe.

Narayan, Uma (1997), *Dislocating Cultures: Identities, Traditions and Third-World Feminism*, New York: Routledge.

Nelson, Julie A. (1995), *Feminism, Objectivity and Economics*, London: Routledge.

Nelson, Julie A. (2000), 'Feminist economics at the millennium: a personal perspective', *Signs: Journal of Women in Culture and Society*, **25**(4), 1177–81.

Peter, Fabienne (2003), 'Foregrounding practices: feminist philosophy of economics beyond rhetoric and realism', in Drucilla K. Barker and Edith Kuiper (eds), *Toward a Feminist Philosophy of Economics*, London: Routledge, pp. 105–21.

Peterson, V. Spike (2003), *A Critical Rewriting of Global Political Economy: Integrating Reproductive, Productive and Virtual Economies*, London: Routledge.

Phumaphi, Joy and Danny Leipziger (2008), 'Forward', in Mercy Tembon and Lucia Fort (eds), *Girl's Education in the 21st Century: Gender, Equality and Economic Growth*, Washington, DC: International Bank for Reconstruction and Development/World Bank, pp. xvii–xxii.

Putnam, Hilary (2002), *The Collapse of the Fact/Value Dichotomy and Other Essays*, Cambridge, MA: Harvard University Press.

Rodríguez, Encarnación Gutiérrez (2007), 'The "hidden side" of the new economy: on transnational migration, domestic work and unprecedented intimacies', *Frontiers: A Journal of Women Studies*, **28**(3), 6–83.

Sandoval, Chela (2000), *Methodology of the Oppressed*, Minneapolis, MN: University of Minnesota Press.

Sen, Amartya (1973), *On Economic Inequality*, Oxford: Clarendon Press.

Strassmann, Diana L. (1993), 'Not a free market: the rhetoric of disciplinary authority in economics', in Ferber and Nelson (eds), pp. 54–68.

United Nations Development Programme (n.d.), *We Can End Poverty 2015*, available at: http://www.undp.org/content/undp/en/home/mdgoverview.html (accessed September 7, 2012).

Walsh, Vivian (1987), 'Models and theory', in John Eatwell, Murray Milgate and Peter Newman (eds), *The New Palgrave: A Dictionary of Economics*, Vol. 3, 1st edn, New York: Stockton Press, pp. 482–3.

Zein-Elabdin, Eiman O. and S. Charusheela (2004), 'Introduction: economics and postcolonial thought', in Zein-Elabdin and Charusheela (eds), *Postcolonialism Meets Economics*, London: Routledge, pp. 1–18.

3. Intersectionality
S. Charusheela

I INTRODUCTION TO MULTIPLE OPPRESSIONS

This chapter explores the value of intersectionality as a research framework. Initially developed within the context of US black/women of color feminism, the concept has traveled, and now takes its place as a cross-cutting analytic frame within and outside feminist scholarship. The term is usually credited to the critical legal scholar Kimberlé Crenshaw (1989). While we conventionally date its emergence to the late 1980s and 1990s, scholars such as Crenshaw and Patricia Hill Collins (2000) use the term in ways that mark their debt to, and indicate their situation within, the terrain of US black feminist thought. As such, intersectionality is best seen as a term that gestures to a broad body of thought already developed and circulating within and among minority/US women of color feminist scholars and activists.

In 'Jane Crow and the law: sex discrimination and Title VII', Pauli Murray and Mary Eastwood write (1965):

> If 'sex' had not been added to the equal employment opportunity provisions of the Civil Rights Act of 1964, Negro women would have shared with white women the common fate of discrimination since it is exceedingly difficult to determine if a Negro woman is being discriminated against because of race or sex. Without the addition of 'sex,' Title VII would have protected only half of the potential Negro workforce. (p. 243)

Murray, a 1950s and 1960s US civil rights activist and member of the President's Commission on the Status of Women, insisted that the National Association for the Advancement of Colored People (NAACP) address issues of 'sex' (or what we may today call 'gender'). Her work was crucial for placing some aspects of the concepts we group under intersectionality on the table. The question she raises about the impossibility of addressing race discrimination without addressing sex discrimination (and vice versa) when it comes to minority women is the one taken up by intersectionality.

This was pushed further by Crenshaw in 'Demarginalizing the intersectionality of race and sex: a black feminist critique of antidiscrimination doctrine, feminist theory, and antiracist politics', the 1989 piece to which we conventionally attribute the coining of the term. Crenshaw argues that specific aspects of minority women's lives are not captured by the sum of the two axes of race and gender. The inseparable simultaneity or *intersection* of the two oppressions generates a specific life experience that neither axis alone, nor even the two axes additively combined, can capture. As a result, we cannot assume that the discrimination faced by minority women can be addressed through a simple summation of laws to address racial discrimination, and laws to address gender discrimination – what she calls 'single axis' theories of discrimination. One implication is that we need laws designed to address the unique experience of minority women.

Even at this initial exploration of the concept, we can see the value of intersectionality for a wide range of scholars interested in questions of social inequality. The editors of the special issue of *Feminist Economics* on gender, color, caste, and class, Rose Brewer, Cecilia Conrad and Mary King, note that economic 'studies of the determinants of earnings tend to focus either on racial differences or on gender differences, but rarely on both' (2002, p. 7). The special issue provides a wide range of examples of intersectional research on questions of discrimination and inequality.

This chapter addresses several aspects of intersectionality in order to frame scholarship on gender and economic life.[1] First, I examine how intersectionality draws attention to structural inequality (Section II). Next I highlight the role of interdisciplinarity and reflexivity in intersectional research (Section III), and provide some examples of the ways the concept of intersectionality has traveled outside its context of origin (Section IV). Section V discusses four areas of tension in the deployment of the concept. Section VI concludes.

II   INTERSECTIONALITY AS STRUCTURE[2]

If the identity category 'minority woman' cannot be seen as the simple addition of the categories of 'minority' and 'woman', it requires a framework adequate to its particularity. It is thus unavoidable that intersectionality is bound up with disputes about identity. Intersectionality derives from a tradition that sees identity categories as socially constituted, rather than a property of the individual or social group. At stake in intersectional research, then, is the analytical status of the categories of race, class, gender, or any other categories of domination that may intersect to constitute a social identity.

Intersectional analyses by Crenshaw and Collins note their debt to black feminist thought – for example, the Combahee River Collective Statement.[3] While its tone and sensibility is different from Pauli Murray's work, it reflects the same broader appreciation of life at the intersections of oppression (Combahee River Collective, 1977): 'We are actively committed to struggling against racial, sexual, heterosexual, and class oppression, and see as our particular task the development of integrated analysis and practice based upon the fact that the major systems of oppression are interlocking'. As in Crenshaw's analysis, the statement highlights the synthesis of multiple oppressions, locating the action of intersection within a structure where each axis of oppression draws on and reinforces the other within an overall structure of domination. The Collective continues:

> We believe that sexual politics under patriarchy is as pervasive in Black women's lives as are the politics of class and race . . . We know that there is such a thing as racial-sexual oppression which is neither solely racial nor solely sexual, e.g., the history of rape of Black women by white men as a weapon of political repression. (Ibid.)

For the Collective, liberation requires the destruction of a structure that bell hooks (1981) famously came to call 'white supremacist capitalist patriarchy'.

This issue of structural power and its social effects has important implications for research. One implication is that we cannot analyze the effects of axes of power if we examine them in isolation; no single axis of domination operates or sustains itself independent of the other. This insight has been central for scholarship on the social construction of race, class, and gender. For example, US women of color scholars such as Evelyn Nakano Glenn (1981, 1991) and Bonnie Thornton Dill (1988) examine caring/reproductive labor for different groups of women. The historical institutionalization of this intersection between paid and unpaid labor in US minimum wage policies is tracked by Deborah Figart, Ellen Mutari and Marilyn Power (2002).

A second implication is that we cannot take the nature of the categories as self-evident. Since intersectionality takes place at the intersection of axes of domination within a structure, the ways in which the axes work and the meanings attached to each of the identity axes vary depending on the historical and geographic context. This is given analytical vocabulary through, for example, Michael Omi and Howard Winant's (1994) use of 'racial formation' (rather than simply the category 'race'). A related implication is that intersectionality is not a framework one uses only when looking at minority women, or social groups defined through more than one social category of identification, exclusion, or domination. If, for example, axes of class and race are crucial for constituting the axes of gender and vice versa, then one can no longer study the lives of white men, white women, or black men outside intersectionality. While not enough work has been done within political economy on this front, examples in the US context can be found in historical scholarship by Karen Brodkin (1998), David Roediger (1999), and Pem Buck (2001); this work sheds light on the ways the racial order both changes in response to, and in turn changes, the logic of economic orders.

III   INTERSECTIONALITY AND RESEARCH METHODS

The concept of intersectionality emerged from broad traditions attuned to the influence of power. This included an apprehension of the ways structural power has become ingrained in institutions to the point of normalization. Thus, scholars developing these analytical frameworks recognized how power has shaped our interpretations of the social world. To address this, women of color began to excavate the meaning of their own experience, and in the process provided two further key contributions: interdisciplinarity and reflexivity.

Intersectional research is of necessity interdisciplinary. If the social construction of domination and subordination takes place within intersecting structures of power, making sense of them requires us to see how multiple axes and locations of power interact with each other. We cannot separate our study of economic life, political structures, cultural meaning, and historical constitution if we hope to apprehend how power has become built into the structures of daily life. As Brewer et al. (2002, p. 8) note, economic analysis tends to 'separate labor market from other economic interactions', but this is not the only issue: many academic disciplines neglect useful theories from other disciplines. Scholars taking up intersectionality explore the role of cultural stereotypes in shaping law and public policy, the role of law and public policy in shaping material life, and of material life in shaping cultural meaning. They examine how institutions normally examined by different branches of academia interact to constitute the terrain through which structural power operates.

In addition to being interdisciplinary, intersectional research tends to be reflexive, that is, attentive to the politics of knowledge creation. Reflexivity is necessary in approaching the 'materials' we use for our research, and ensuring that the voices and experiences of marginalized groups and the texture of life at the intersection of oppressions is adequately accounted for. Since this attentiveness must come against the grain of dominant narratives, and requires unlearning received common sense about people's lives, it also requires attentiveness to the researcher's own location within structures of power. This location shapes both the process of undertaking research and of interpreting materials. Thus, reflexivity in this framework has two aspects, that of marginalized voice and that of researcher location.

The first aspect is, in large part, a legacy of black feminist/US women of color feminist thinkers. The impetus for new ways of analyzing the social world came from efforts to make sense of their experience through categories provided by single-axis theories, which they found inadequate. Their turn to experience called for new scholarship. The Combahee River Collective (1977) noticed a correlation between 'smart' and 'ugly' in people's perceptions, realizing that 'the sanctions in the Black and white communities against Black women thinkers are comparatively much higher than for white women, particularly ones from the educated middle and upper classes'. Here, experience both provides the raw material for analysis and becomes the ground on which to develop an analysis of social structure, showing how a race-gendered system constitutes an opposition between thought (masculine) and beauty (feminine) within the social order.[4]

The second aspect is equally important, as it asks researchers to account for their own frames of reference. This is crucial, since our frames of reference are not innocent but reflect the hold of oppressive structures on our understanding of the world. For example, in my own research (Charusheela, 2003), I show how our understanding of work experience shifts depending on how we distinguish between different ways of utilizing bargaining frameworks in feminist research. From one frame of reference, work is always liberating and should be seen as empowering women and increasing their bargaining position. From another, work can fail to liberate and may instead be a marker of personal or familial need, indicating an absence of rather than an increase in bargaining power. The perspective deployed depends on whether one understands difference as deviance, as diversity, or as forged by and reflective of structural power.

IV   TRAVELING INTERSECTIONALITY

Black feminist scholars developed their ideas within the context of rich conversations and exchanges with other minority feminist scholars, both within and outside the US.[5] Thus, many of the ideas raised here are not unique to them, and in developing their ideas they remained attentive to the relationship between their struggles and the struggles of minority women in various countries.[6] Given the tendency to think of the minority feminist scholar as local/localized rather than engaging with a global audience, the capacity of this concept to travel deserves its own section.

Kanchana Ruwanpura (2008) uses intersectionality to critique existing economics frameworks for labor market discrimination. Drawing on Crenshaw and others, she analyzes two legal cases in the UK with a 'multiple-discrimination framework to acknowledge the complexities and nuances of labor market reality' (p. 77). In the special *Feminist Economics* issue on gender, color, caste, and class, Ashwini Deshpande (2002) examines the overlap between caste and gender in constraining Dalit women's lives. This may seem like a simple transposition of race onto a different context, but Brewer et al. write in their introduction to the special issue (2002, p. 4), 'Is race caste? Technically, the answer is no, but the caste system is based on descent, and the major caste structure in India correlates with skin color. The Dalits, or untouchables, face tremendous social barriers that are closely akin to racial apartheid (Human Rights Watch, 2001)'.[7] Deshpande's work also calls attention to the need for a careful investigation of the meanings of the categories used in intersectional analysis, lest the analogy between caste and race end up obscuring more than it reveals as the conceptual frame of intersectionality travels across borders. Charu Gupta's (2010) historical scholarship on Dalit masculinities considers the construction of social identity in colonial North India, producing the genealogical background necessary for illuminating the origins and meanings of the categories deployed in Deshpande's work.

The scholarship in the recent *Symposia on the Contributions of Patricia Hill Collins* (2012) also showcases the traveling of intersectionality. In her discussion of intersectionality and global gender inequality, Christine Bose (2012) highlights multiple avenues through which the framework has traveled. For example, she discusses the 2009 issue of the *International Feminist Journal of Politics* on institutionalizing intersectionality in the European Union (ibid.). She writes that 'feminists in European Union (EU) countries, where gender mainstreaming is common and where crossnational equality policies are being developed, view intersectionality as directly useful for such policies and considerably better than approaches that tend to foster a sense of competing oppressions' (p. 68; see also Kantola and Nousiainen, 2009). Bose's comments provide a context within which we can situate Ruwanpura's work extending concepts of intersectionality to the UK (see also Yuval-Davis, 2006).

Bose goes on to note that as intersectionality travels, new groups of scholars intervene in its elaboration. Drawing on the work of Hae Yeon Choo and Myra Marx Ferree (2010), Bose explains that she uses a complex systems approach to examine gender inequalities across many nations.[8] She finds 'this transnational angle on intersectionality a useful alternative to the broad brush that paints national-level gender inequalities as fundamentally all the same, differentiated only between the global North and South, or all unique' (Bose, 2012, p. 70).

Of special value is attention to the process of traveling itself, as in Hae Yeon Choo's (2012) discussion of her work in translating *Black Feminist Thought* into Korean:

> My diasporic position as an outsider within has been salient in a different way in South Korea, where I wanted to bring Collins's work on intersectionality into the sociological dialogue. As I prepared to leave South Korea to pursue graduate study in the United States, a progressive feminist professor of mine revealed her sense of disappointment. 'Why the U.S.?' she asked. 'Don't you think you need to do nationalist (*minjok*) sociology?' Her comment was based on a critical stance – not uncommon among Korean progressives – of resistance to the hegemonic production of knowledge on a global scale; in her view, I was becoming part of this hegemonic production by joining an academic institution in the metropole. More bluntly, my decision was seen as selling out at a personal level, and even worse, selling out the nation in pursuit of Western/colonial academic consumption. Although I empathize with the need for critical revision of knowledge production, I am doubtful about the adequacy of the nationalist scholarship for such endeavors, as the South Korean nation-state is increasingly confronting the question of migrants' rights and belonging in the absence of shared nationhood. (p. 42)

This attentiveness to her own positioning, and exploration of the structures of power within which acts of translation and travel take place, is a different example of intersectionality's reflexiveness (discussed in the previous section).

Intersectionality has also traveled beyond its original terrain to integrate new axes of oppression. This difference in types of oppression is not in itself new. Even in its origins, we see deeper attention to, for example, issues of sexuality in the Combahee River Collective and Collins's work than in the development of the concept within critical legal theory. More recently, Yvette Taylor, Sally Hines and Mark Casey (2011) provide examples of efforts to address sexuality in an intersectional frame that navigates, rather than essentializes, sexual identity as it crosses borders. Disability studies provides another example of how intersectionality travels across categories; this is not surprising given the increasing focus on questions of access to healthcare, education, and workplaces placed on the agenda by disability rights activists.

Bente Meyer (2002) examines how intersectionality travels to a European context as she links disability with other axes of power. Like the contributors to the Taylor et al. (2011) volume on sexuality and intersectionality, she brings together two frames of analysis often thought to be hostile to each other: poststructuralist feminist thought and intersectionality. Taking up Judith Butler's (1990) interventions on the construction of gender, Meyer writes: 'If the body is a troubled site for the construction and experience of identity, as several conference speakers claimed, then it is essential that feminist and gender research take an interest in how gender identity intersects with other body categories, for instance race, homosexuality and disability' (2002, p. 168).

As intersectionality travels, and the structural axes it accounts for shift, its analytical contours must also shift. If Ruwanpura's work extends Crenshaw to show how economic theories of labor market discrimination are inadequate for multiple oppressions, disability activists similarly show us how extant mainstream economic approaches to inequality are inadequate. Neoclassical perspectives on labor markets have tended to take wage- or asset-ownership-based resource access as the primary legitimate mode for claiming a share of national output. If feminist scholarship on women's unpaid labor challenges this, so does the disability rights movement, albeit from a different angle. This suggests that scholars undertaking intersectional research may be able to provide more robust analyses of the structures of exclusion if they begin with alternate heterodox frameworks such as institutionalist, capabilities, provisioning, or Marxist approaches to political economy that are more attuned to the interplay between household, market, and state in constituting the nexus of resource access and distribution.

V TENSION POINTS

This section discusses four key areas of debate surrounding the deployment of intersectionality. I begin with the problem of categories. Next is standpoint or experience. A further problem the intersectional scholar needs to pay attention to is the structural context for research. Finally, one category in particular, the nation-state, has raised questions for intersectional analysis.

Intersectionality and the Problem of Categories

Since identity categories are socially constituted, the question of genealogy – how the meanings of categories have been generated – becomes unavoidable. Many of the categories of social difference have their roots in the biopolitical apparatuses of state power. Thus, in a Foucauldian sense, scholarship that seeks to 'reveal' the nature of experience within a particular identity category stands in danger of reifying the category itself. But failure to account for this experience, however reified and state-constituted, can in turn create a failure to adequately account for and address inequality.

Navigating this terrain requires simultaneously tracking the historical construction of categories and formulating research that takes them as given for tracing their effects on specific groups. An example of this tension can be seen in Cecilia Conrad's (2004) discussion of Karen Graubart's (2004) historical analysis of race categories. Examining the historical archive of census records, Graubart shows how racial categories in colonial Peru were constituted in and through state apparatuses for tracking people. Conrad, in turn, contends that however constructed the racial categories, and regardless of the role of the census in constituting and consolidating them, scholars today cannot simply abandon census-based categories; we need the data in order to show the material effects of such categorization. This is not unlike the ways in which feminist scholars both use the simple 'sex' binaries that provide us with data categorization for tracking inequality in pay and opportunities, and show the shifting meanings and social constructedness of gender as a way to describe how the inequality gets socially constructed and reproduced in institutions. We need to both provisionally suggest that some unified element or aspect of social life legitimately allows us to aggregate data by sex, and also show that there is actually no single, essential universal quality of femininity underlying this aggregation.

Being able to do both these things – historicize the categories and recognize their instability and discursive constitution as well as track their effects via data that is constructed by taking the stability of categories at face value – requires scholars working with intersectional frames to use different types of approaches for conceptualizing categories. Leslie McCall (2005) presents three different approaches – anticategorical, intracategorical, and intercategorical – which correspond roughly to different ends of the research continuum in terms of whether we treat the categories as unstable or stable. Quantitative research, which constructs data by taking the categories as stable in order to enable aggregation, is essential to tracking the effects of difference on groups and highlights the value of intercategorical approaches (see Kim, Chapter 14, this volume). Qualitative methods provide insight into the complex nature of experience in intersectional identity categories and the processes through which group experience is constituted, showcasing the value of intracategorical approaches. And discursive methods help us tease apart the assumptions through which difference gets stabilized, normalized, and constituted, highlighting the value of anticategorical approaches. Scholarship drawing on combinations of these methods can illuminate the structural origins of social difference.

Standpoint Theory and the Problem of Experience

Intersectional research has also drawn on the voices and experiences of marginalized women. Following poststructuralist analysis, feminist scholarship suggests that experience, even the experience of marginalized subjects, cannot be taken at face value as a ground for critical knowledge.[9] The argument is that experience is accessed and communicated through language, and language and discourse are already constituted through the categories of the social structure. Hence, our understanding of our experience is not free of influence from the social structure, and so cannot be used at face value to ground alternative epistemologies that escape the norming role of power contained in discourse. More generally, identity is an unstable category formed and stabilized through the very social structure we seek to critique. When poststructural research explodes identity, it threatens to remove the grounds for using identity-based experience to create dissident knowledge.

Not surprisingly, the initial presentation of this problem was experienced as a hostile turn toward 'theory' that would silence minority women's voices. As Collins (1998) notes, the unraveling of the identity category posed problems for black feminist thought: 'What good is a theory that aims to dismantle the authority that Black women in the United States have managed to gain via group solidarity and shared traditions? . . . who benefits from a methodology that . . . dismantles notions of subjectivity, tradition, and authority just when Black women are gaining recognition for these attributes?' (pp. 144–5).

It is in this context that one can see Collins's reworking of standpoint theory to enable the possibility of a political subjectivity that can be taken as a ground for theoretical intervention, similar to Chandra Mohanty's 1991 argument that 'Third World' can be seen not as a shared 'identity' but as a shared subjectivity emerging from a shared structural location. Collins (1998) provides an epistemic repositioning of the knowledge produced by or from the perspective of the 'Outsider Within', akin to postcolonial scholars' noting of double consciousness or migrant liminality as a space from which knowledge about the structures of discursive containment can be produced.[10]

Now, more than two decades after these theoretical struggles, feminists are better able to navigate the terrain of discourse and construction, and no longer make the mistake of presuming that the 'fact' of discursive construction evacuates the ground of analysis.[11] Indeed, it is no longer possible to provide easy divisions that mark scholars off as postmodern or modern in their approach to issues of discourse, identity, and experience. Collins herself is someone whose work falls between any strict division between analysts interested in the discursive constitution of categories and meanings, and those interested in experience. Perhaps it is not entirely surprising that Brewer et al. (2002) highlight Anne McClintock's (1995) *Imperial Leather*, a classic of poststructuralist feminist scholarship, as a key resource for thinking about how the categories of race, class, and gender are constructed.

As the best intersectional scholarship shows, intersectional analysis cannot afford to ignore poststructural analyses of discourse. For example, Leslie Salzinger (1997) examines how gendering is generated in and through the practices and discourses of the factory floor in maquiladoras, rather than presuming pre-existing and given gendered meanings of labor within a gender division of labor. In discussing how Martha Nussbaum interprets African women's voices, my own scholarship scrutinizes the discourse of universalism (Charusheela, 2009). Drucilla Barker (2005) rereads conceptual frames used to think about women's work to resituate the question of gendered labor. Suzanne Bergeron (2009) discusses the ways normalized conceptions of the household undergird economic policies, including many policies we tend to imagine as pro-women in the context of development.

Intersectionality and the Question of Structure

Even within the US context, the structure and meaning of racial difference varies dramatically between slavery, antebellum, and post-civil rights eras, even if we limit our attention to simply black–white racial formations. If we add a multi-racial landscape, the problem gets even more complicated, since the ways race and gender get imagined and consolidated vary across groups. For example, Amy Kaminsky (1994) shows how the concept of Hispanic has shifted in the US depending on foreign policy, and how this differs from the concept of Hispanic in Latin American countries at different historical junctures. Here, gender conceptions and norms 'stabilize' unstable and shifting racial categories, even as racial imaginations stabilize shifting conceptions of gender. Similarly, Bandana Purkayastha (2012) suggests that post 9/11, intersectional theorists may need to rethink questions of transnationalism and religion, especially the tendency to think of religious difference as operating via a different logic than racial difference.

Intersectionality, Rights, and the Nation-state

Among the categories that present a particular difficulty in intersectional analysis is that of the nation-state. This is not accidental. The state is one key audience for our scholarship, as intersectional analysts seek to intervene in law and social policy to generate inclusion. However, the nation-state, both as idea and institution, is also a key generator of social difference – both within the state itself and between states. Thus, in our efforts to address the state, we risk reifying the categories it has generated to manage and organize populations. We also risk limiting our vision of where and how change happens as we naturalize the state itself.[12]

The naturalization of the nation-state poses a particular problem for politics imagined through civil rights activism – an activism for inclusion into the civic national body that was central to the US movements out of which the conceptual terrain of intersectionality emerged.[13] When the aim is not a firmer attachment to nation-state but rather sovereignty and decolonization, there are problems with an approach that seeks to address the question of difference through a politics of equal rights and inclusion into the national body. For example, Marie Anna Jaimes Guerrero (1997) shows how the concept of dual citizenship (that structures indigenous women's rights through both US and tribal laws) results in a net diminution of rights and a reduction of tribal sovereignty.

From a different angle, the transnational politics of migration and citizenship – which have led to the increasing presence of migrants, immigrants, refugees, and stateless people – throw the politics of belonging into question. Jacqueline Stevens (1999) shows how the nation-state is defined through heteronormativity, given the central role of birth (parentage and location) in allocating citizenship and the rights attendant to that across the globe. Eithne Luibhéid (2002) shows how heteronormativity and homophobia shape border policing and immigration. In the context of immigration politics, Monisha Das Gupta (2006) takes up the politics of South Asian immigrants in the US, noting how they piece together varied possibilities for gaining political space. Nira Yuval-Davis (1997) provides an intersectional analysis that integrates the question of the relation between gender and nation into contemporary feminist frameworks for social analysis.

The politics of state belonging, immigration, and migration are, of course, tightly tied to issues of political economy, since the state acts both as arbiter of rights and as the key agent for redress of inequality through social policy. The nation-state, both in its exclusions and in its structural constitution, thus becomes an additional aspect of the structures of difference that intersectional scholars must account for in their work. Bergeron (2001) examines the ways in which 'globalocentric' representations of the 'economic' in political economy discourses render invisible any alternative, gendered terrains of global networks and activity from below. Barker and Susan Feiner (2010) link questions of consumption to the gendering of labor under globalization. Colin Danby (2012) shows how assumptions about normative households and social reproduction are built into the very numbers used to track national output and population. All of this scholarship shows the difficulty of articulating a simple policy of 'inclusion' into structures of economy and nation-state to resolve the problem of difference, exploitation, and oppression.

The question of the nation-state brings together two traditions of thought normally seen as being at sharp odds with each other: queer theoretic investigations of biopolitical regulation following Foucault on the one hand, and intersectional analyses rooted in the history of US women of color feminism and identity politics on the other. But if we recognize intersectionality as structure, and equally recognize that the nation-state is a key structure engaged in constituting group membership and allocating rights through such membership, it becomes increasingly important that the two broad traditions noted above find their point of contact. Currently, this point of contact seems to be emerging in the terrain of transnational feminism – perhaps not surprising given that the question of the nation-state, both in its consolidation and its margins and dissolutions, looms large in this field.

The question of biopolitics in relation to traveling intersectionality and transnational feminism is not solely a question of research accuracy. At stake here is the question of advocacy; advocacy requires an imagination of how a group envisages a future. What future beyond inclusion into the nation-state and body politic do we imagine? We must imagine a possibility of the political beyond the institutional structures of the nation-state.

VI CONCLUSION

In the early period of the development of intersectionality, caught within feminist debates about identity, experience, and social construction, feminist scholars often turned to the 'truth' of identity and experience as a way to defend female-centered understandings of the world against the perceived onslaught of postmodernism and the turn to discourse. More recently, intersectionality has traveled across multiple locales, and has emerged as a powerful frame for feminist scholarship. But its very success poses a danger, since the institutionalizing of the frame can freeze categories of analysis as researchers simply apply the frame, converting intersectionality into a mere buzzword (Davis, 2008). Scholars deploying intersectional frameworks need to take care, lest they inadvertently essentialize identity and experience, in the process reifying the very structures they seek to undo.

On the flip side, the move away from intersectionality toward a terrain of pure constructedness may leave us without a mooring for social and political intervention. This has problematic implications: it obscures the origin of the intersectionality concept in anti-racist politics; it rephrases the critique of exclusion as a general problem of identification; and it empties intersectional analysis 'of its political dimension, which means that, finally, it can be turned against black feminists and queers (and other marginalised subjects) who insist on a politics of location' (Erel et al., 2011, p. 66).

Where does this leave us? Feminist scholarship has come a long way since the early debates that saw poststructuralist/textual/deconstructionist and experiential/feminist-empiricist approaches as irredeemably opposed. Intersectionality's ability to draw attention to overlooked aspects of experience, and foreground the effects of social difference through the overlap of categories makes it a powerful and valuable analytic for feminist scholars. Yes, intersectional analysis carries with it the danger of freezing categories or presuming a universal set of meanings for identity. But as long as researchers remain attentive to context and are thoughtful about how they use the frame, this danger can be mitigated. At its best, such scholarship brings together the quantitative, qualitative, historical, genealogical, and discursive to provide a rich mapping of the structures that shape and constrain our lives and imaginations.

NOTES

1. For additional introductions to intersectionality, see McCall (2005) and Hancock (2007).
2. This section draws its title from a rearrangement of 'structural intersectionality', a section header in Crenshaw (1996).
3. A detailed discussion of this tradition is beyond the purview of this chapter. Patricia Hill Collins (2000) and Joy James and T. Denean Sharpley-Whiting (2000) provide excellent introductions to this tradition.
4. The broader terrain within which the turn to experience gets linked to epistemology comes from Nancy Hartsock's (1983) adaptation of Lucaks' 'standpoint of the proletariat' to develop the concept of the feminist standpoint.
5. See, for example, the collection *This Bridge Called My Back* (Moraga and Anzaldua (1981 [2002]), which both showcases and is generative of the cross-community conversations that formed US women of color feminism.
6. Recognizing the collaborative space within which the framework emerged should not be taken as a reduction or dismissal of the central role played by black feminist scholars in developing this set of ideas. The question of intellectual origins is fraught, since minority scholars often find that their contributions are not acknowledged, and recognition of the shared or co-generative nature of their frameworks is often presented in ways that diminish the worth and weight of their intellectual contributions. But these were scholars and activists who were not only linking analysis to their own experience; they were also thinking about and generating these analyses in the context of intellectual networks that spanned multiple terrains, reaching out both to transnational thinkers as part of postcolonial movements, and to US scholars and activists from other minority communities and movements. It would be a serious mistake to presume that this scholarship can, or even should, be taken to reflect the thinking of a community in isolation working through primarily parochial concerns. Indeed, it is precisely because this is not the product of an isolated community (located is not the same as localized) that these frameworks manage to travel across so many socio-spatial formations, providing the basis for the translocational value of this work.
7. See also Center for Human Rights and Global Justice, NYU School of Law, and Human Rights Watch (2007).
8. Choo and Ferree (2010) highlight group-, process-, and system-centered approaches to intersectional research, depending on whether the researcher focuses on the voices of group members, the institutional processes that generate differential experience, or the systemic articulation of the intersecting categories.
9. See, for example, Joan Scott (1991). This is the counterpart of the argument that identities are socially constituted by the structures of oppression, and the act of consolidating identity reifies the structures of oppression and exclusion, a point taken up more extensively by Nitasha Kaul (2007).

10. See Sandra Harding (2004) for further discussion of the ways in which feminist scholars have reworked standpoint theory to navigate the terrain between epistemic authority and discursive knowledge constitution.
11. See Kathy E. Ferguson (1993) for an extended discussion of the differences, but also necessary symbiotic and dialectical relationships, between the two broad strands of feminist analysis that imagined and represented themselves in opposition to each other through the late 1980s and early 1990s: feminist empiricism/realism/materialism on the one hand, and feminist genealogy/poststructuralism/postmodernism on the other.
12. This is a problem that faces all scholars, but scholars working in the terrain of economics and public policy are especially susceptible to this difficulty. In these fields, relevance is often measured in terms of ability to shape public policy – which means treating the state, lawmaker, or policymaker as key audience, and thus entering into the imagination of the modern nation-state and adopting its categories in our search for persuasiveness and relevance (see Scott, 1998).
13. The actual politics of civil rights in the US was, of course, much more complicated than simple inclusion into the national body, and entailed a middle ground – or rather, a negotiation – between inclusion and rejection/separation (see Crenshaw, 2000). But as rights concepts travel in terms of a law-based movement for human rights, the question of civil rights as rights in the terrain of nation-state and civil society – rather than as a term used to denote a specific social movement at a particular moment in the US – has to be addressed. A non-US discussion of the limits of rights-based approaches for addressing multiple oppressions, and problems with the universalizing modes of 'traveling' of such frames, can be found in Nivedita Menon (2000).

REFERENCES

Barker, Drucilla (2005), 'Beyond women and economics: rereading "women's work"', *Signs: Journal of Women in Culture and Society,* **30**(4), 2189–209.

Barker, Drucilla K. and Susan F. Feiner (2010), 'As the world turns: globalization, consumption, and the feminization of work', *Rethinking Marxism*, **22**(2), 246–52.

Bergeron, Suzanne (2001), 'Political economy discourses of globalization and feminist politics', *Signs: Journal of Women in Culture and Society*, **26**(4), 983–1006.

Bergeron, Suzanne (2009), 'Querying feminine economics' straight path to development: household models reconsidered', in Amy Lind (ed.), *Development, Sexual Rights and Global Governance*, New York: Routledge, pp. 54–64.

Bose, Christine (2012), 'Intersectionality and global gender inequality', *Gender & Society*, **26**(1), 67–72.

Brewer, Rose M., Cecilia A. Conrad and Mary C. King (2002), 'The complexities and potential of theorizing gender, caste, race, and class', *Feminist Economics*, **8**(2), 3–18.

Brodkin, Karen (1998), *How Jews Became White Folks: And What That Says About Race in America,* Rutgers, NJ: Rutgers University Press.

Buck, Pem Davidson (2001), *Worked to the Bone: Race, Class, Power, and Privilege in Kentucky*, New York: Monthly Review Press.

Butler, Judith (1990), *Gender Trouble: Feminism and the Subversion of Identity*, London: Routledge.

Center for Human Rights and Global Justice, NYU School of Law, and Human Rights Watch (2007), 'Hidden Apartheid: Caste Discrimination Against India's "Untouchables", A Shadow Report to the UN Committee on the elimination of Racial discrimination', available at: http://www.hrw.org/sites/default/files/reports/india0207webwcover_0.pdf (accessed November 17, 2012).

Charusheela, S. (2003), 'Empowering work? Bargaining models reconsidered', in Drucilla Barker and Edith Kuiper (eds), *Toward a Feminist Philosophy of Economics*, London: Routledge, pp. 287–303.

Charusheela, S. (2009), 'Social analysis and the capabilities approach: a limit to Martha Nussbaum's universalist ethics', *Cambridge Journal of Economics*, **33**(6), 1113–18.

Choo, Hae Yeon (2012), 'The transnational journey of intersectionality', *Gender & Society*, **26**(1), 40–45.

Choo, Hae Yeon and Myra Marx Ferree (2010), 'Practicing intersectionality in sociological research: a critical analysis of inclusions, interactions, and institutions in the study of inequalities', *Sociological Theory*, **28**(2), 129–49.

Collins, Patricia Hill (1998), *Fighting Words: Black Women and the Search for Justice,* Minneapolis, MN: University of Minnesota Press.

Collins, Patricia Hill (2000), *Black Feminist Thought*, New York: Routledge.

Combahee River Collective (1977), 'The Combahee River Collective Statement', available at: http://circuitous.org/scraps/combahee.html (accessed September 24, 2012).

Conrad, Cecelia (2004), 'Econometrics and postcolonial theory: a comment on the fluidity of race', in Eiman Zein-Elabdin and S. Charusheela (eds), *Postcolonialism Meets Economics*, London: Routledge, pp. 271–4.

Crenshaw, Kimberlé (1989), 'Demarginalizing the intersectionality of race and sex: a black feminist critique of antidiscrimination doctrine, feminist theory, and antiracist politics', *University of Chicago Legal Forum*, 1989, 139–67.

Crenshaw, Kimberlé (1996), 'Mapping the margins: intersectionality, identity politics, and violence against women of color', in Kimberlé Crenshaw, Neil Gotanda, Gary Peller and Kendall Thomas (eds), *Critical Race Theory: The Key Writings That Formed the Movement*, New York: New Press, pp. 357–83.

Crenshaw, Kimberlé (2000), 'Were the critics right about rights? Reassessing the American debate about rights in the post-reform era', in Mahmood Mamdani (ed.), *Beyond Rights Talk and Culture Talk: Comparative Essays on the Politics of Rights and Culture*, New York: St. Martin's Press, pp. 61–74.

Danby, Colin (2012), 'Postwar norm', *Rethinking Marxism*, **24**(4), 499–515.

Das Gupta, Monisha (2006), *Unruly Immigrants: Rights, Activism, and Transnational South Asian Politics in the United States,* Durham, NC: Duke University Press.

Davis, Kathy (2008), 'Intersectionality as buzzword: a sociology of science perspective on what makes a feminist theory successful', *Feminist Theory*, **9**(1), 67–85.

Deshpande, Ashwini (2002), 'Assets versus autonomy? The changing face of the gender–caste overlap in India', *Feminist Economics*, **8**(2), 19–35.

Dill, Bonnie Thornton (1988), 'Our mothers' grief: racial ethnic women and the maintenance of families', *Journal of Family History*, **13**(4), 415–31.

Erel, Umut, Jin Haritaworn, Encarnación Gutiérrez Rodríguez and Christian Klesse (2011), 'On the depoliticisation of intersectionality talk: conceptualising multiple oppressions in critical sexuality studies', in Taylor et al. (eds), pp. 56–77.

Ferguson, Kathy E. (1993), *The Man Question: Visions of Subjectivity in Feminist Theory*, Berkeley, CA: University of California Press.

Figart, Deborah M., Ellen Mutari and Marilyn Power (2002), *Living Wages, Equal Wages: Gender and Labor Market Policies in the United States*, London: Routledge.

Glenn, Evelyn Nakano (1981), 'Occupational ghettoization: Japanese American women and domestic service, 1905–1970', *Ethnicity*, **7**(4), 352–86.

Glenn, Evelyn Nakano (1991), 'Racial ethnic women's labor: the intersection of race, gender, and class oppression', in Rae L. Blumberg (ed.), *Gender, Family and Economy: The Triple Overlap*, Newbury Park, CA: Sage, pp. 173–200.

Graubart, Karen (2004), 'Hybrid thinking: bringing postcolonial theory to colonial Latin American economic history', in Eiman Zein-Elabdin and S. Charusheela (eds), *Postcolonialism Meets Economics*, London: Routledge, pp. 215–34.

Gupta, Charu (2010), 'Feminine, criminal or manly? Imaging Dalit masculinities in colonial North India', *Indian Economic Social History Review*, **47**(3), 309–42.

Hancock, Ange-Marie (2007), 'When multiplication doesn't equal quick addition: examining intersectionality as a research paradigm', *Perspectives on Politics*, **5**(1), 63–79.

Harding, Sandra (ed.) (2004), *The Feminist Standpoint Theory Reader*, New York: Routledge.

Hartsock, Nancy (1983), 'The feminist standpoint: developing the ground for a specifically feminist historical materialism', in Sandra Harding and Merrill B. Hintikka (eds), *Discovering Reality: Feminist Perspectives on Epistemology, Metaphysics, Methodology, and Philosophy of Science* (Synthese Library, Vol. 161), Dordrecht: D. Reidel, pp. 283–310.

hooks, bell (1981), *Ain't I a Woman? Black Women and Feminism*, Cambridge, MA: South End Press.

Human Rights Watch (2001), 'Caste: Asia's Hidden Apartheid', available at: http://www.hrw.org/legacy/campaigns/caste/presskit.htm (accessed November 17, 2012).

Jaimes Guerrero, Marie Anna (1997), 'Civil rights versus sovereignty: Native American women in life and land struggles', in Chandra Talpade Mohanty and M. Jacqui Alexander (eds), *Feminist Genealogies Colonial Legacies, Democratic Futures*, New York: Routledge, pp. 101–21.

James, Joy and T. Denean Sharpley-Whiting (eds) (2000), *The Black Feminist Reader*, Malden, MA: Blackwell.

Kaminsky, Amy (1994), 'Gender, race, raza', *Feminist Studies*, **20**(1), 7–31.

Kantola, Johanna and Kevät Nousiainen (2009), 'Institutionalizing intersectionality in Europe: introducing the theme', *International Feminist Journal of Politics*, **11**(4), 459–77.

Kaul, Nitasha (2007), *Imagining Economics Otherwise: Encounters with Identity/Difference*, London: Routledge.

Luibhéid, Eithne (2002), *Entry Denied: Controlling Sexuality at the Border*, Minneapolis, MN: University of Minnesota Press.

McCall, Leslie (2005), 'The complexity of intersectionality', *Signs: Journal of Women in Culture and Society*, **30**(3), 1771–800.

McClintock, Anne (1995), *Imperial Leather: Race, Gender and Sexuality in the Colonial Contest*, New York: Routledge.

Menon, Nivedita (2000), 'State, community and the debate on the uniform civil code in India', in Mahmood Mamdani (ed.), *Beyond Rights Talk and Culture Talk: Comparative Essays on the Politics of Rights and Culture*, New York: St. Martin's Press, pp. 75–95.

Meyer, Bente (2002), 'Extraordinary stories: disability, queerness and feminism', *NORA: Nordic Journal of Feminist and Gender Research,* **10**(3), 168–73.

Mohanty, Chandra T. (1991), 'Cartographies of struggle: third world women and the politics of feminism', in Chandra Mohanty, Ann Russo and Lourdes Torres (eds), *Third World Women and the Politics of Feminism*, Bloomington, IN: Indiana University Press, pp. 1–47.

Moraga, Cherrie and Gloria Anzaldua (1981 [2002]), *This Bridge Called My Back: Writings by Radical Women of Color*, 3rd edn, Berkeley, CA: Third Women Press.

Murray, Pauli and Mary Eastwood (1965), 'Jane Crow and the law: sex discrimination and Title VII', *The George Washington Law Review*, **34**(2), 232–56.

Omi, Michael and Howard Winant (1994), *Racial Formation in the United States: From the 1960s to the 1990s*, 2nd edn, New York: Routledge.

Purkayastha, Bandana (2012), 'Intersectionality in a transnational world', *Gender & Society*, **26**(1), 55–66.

Roediger, David (1999), *The Wages of Whiteness: Race and the Making of the American Working Class*, rev. edn, New York: Verso.

Ruwanpura, Kanchana N. (2008), 'Multiple identities, multiple discrimination: a critical review', *Feminist Economics*, **14**(3), 77–105.

Salzinger, Leslie (1997), 'From high heels to swathed bodies: gendered meanings under production in Mexico's export processing industry', *Feminist Studies*, **23**(3), 549–74.

Scott, James C. (1998), *Seeing Like a State: How Certain Schemes to Improve the Human Condition Have Failed*, New Haven, CT: Yale University Press.

Scott, Joan Wallach (1991), 'The evidence of experience', *Critical Inquiry*, **17**(4), 773–97.

Stevens, Jacqueline (1999), *Reproducing the State*, Princeton, NJ: Princeton University Press.

Symposia on the Contributions of Patricia Hill Collins (2012), *Gender & Society*, **26**(1).

Taylor, Yvette, Sally Hines and Mark E. Casey (eds) (2011), *Theorizing Intersectionality and Sexuality*, New York: Palgrave Macmillan.

Yuval-Davis, Nira (1997), *Gender and Nation*, London: Sage.

Yuval-Davis, Nira (2006), 'Intersectionality and feminist politics', *European Journal of Women's Studies*, **13**(3), 193–209.

4. Gender, well-being and civil society
Nisrine Mansour

I INTRODUCTION

How to optimize women's well-being? This question has occupied the imagination of feminist researchers and activists since the start of the feminist movement more than a century ago. Feminist influences on development studies, economics, and political science developed the concept of women's well-being as a way to reach the broader goal of gender equality and engage more effectively in collective action through civil society channels. Of course, answering this question depends on how we understand women's identity and agency, and how we formulate well-being, gender equality, and civil society.

Some of the most important contributions formulate women's well-being in terms of economic achievement. Economic well-being is defined according to objective structural indicators such as gross domestic product (GDP) and income levels, as well as poverty, literacy, and life expectancy indicators (Diener et al., 2009). This perspective intends to highlight the economic discrimination that many women around the globe face, particularly regarding labor market indicators. In the Middle East, for instance, the gender gap in employment is wider than in any other region; 67.7 percent of Middle Eastern men are employed, compared to only 20.5 percent of women (ILO, 2011, Table A5).

However, the economic perspective of well-being often assumes a causal link between women's economic empowerment and well-being. This causal link is sometimes disproved in cases when gender inequality persists despite improvement in economic situation. One example is the relatively small gender employment gap in East Asia where 64.1 percent of women (and 75.7 percent of men) are employed (ibid., Table A5). This high female employment rate has not translated into greater gender equality at the level of family relations, as women in China and Korea for instance suffer from discrimination such as gender-based abortions and forced marriages. While economic achievement contributes to greater material means that could lead to greater economic power for women, it remains one single factor among other social and political influences (Jordan, 2008).

Another popular perspective considers well-being in relation to psychological perceptions of happiness. In the last four decades, measuring well-being focused on subjective indicators such as the personal experience of pleasure and pain, and the 'eudemonic' side of well-being such as our psychological need for autonomy, control, and connectedness (Dolan et al., 2011). The psychological indicators of well-being reveal the importance of perceptions and psycho-social factors that affect women's agency and their ability to break away from gender discrimination (Rao et al., 2003). While psychological analyses highlight the psychological effects of gender discrimination, they tend to neglect the broader sociopolitical factors influencing the construction of a 'womanhood identity'. Borrowing from Simone de Beauvoir's (1993) famous quote 'one is not born a woman, but becomes one', women's identity is shaped in the social spheres, and the family in particular is recognized to be a crucial social institution where the politics of gender are reproduced (Okin, 1991). The development of women's identity in the family connects to the various areas of gender equality. Perhaps unsurprisingly, gender dynamics within families have also proven to be too controversial, as they have failed to generate widespread political support and substantive collective action in comparison to other gender issues (Taylor et al., 1999). Hence, the analysis of well-being and gender equality needs to incorporate the sociopolitical dimension of gender equality in the family and its implications for shaping women's identity and feminist civil society action.

In this chapter, I analyze the sociopolitical factors that contribute to the shaping of women's identity and agency, drawing on examples of women's condition in Arab countries, starting with the rise of the feminist movement in the early twentieth century until the recent (2010) revolutions of the Arab Spring. I draw on disciplinary intersections of legal, gender, social and political analyses with special focus on women's well-being in the family. The chapter starts by tracing the evolving concepts of gender equality and well-being within the feminist movement (Section II). I then present various schools of feminist thought that have contributed to analyses of gender equality and well-being. In Section III, I explore the concept of civil society as an activist space, discussing civil society actors and institutions along with the way it contributes to furthering women's rights and well-being. Section IV explores a dynamic approach to understanding feminist collective action and women's well-being. Section V concludes by suggesting a sociopolitical framework of analysis that incorporates gender equality in the family as part of the overall well-being of women. I argue that women's position in the family constitutes the primary source of inequity that affects their well-being in various aspects of socioeconomic and public life.

II   APPROACHES TO WOMEN'S WELL-BEING AND GENDER EQUALITY

Debates around equality have long circled around questions regarding what type of equality we seek, and for whom should equality be achieved and preserved. With regard to gender, these debates can be traced in four historically evolving and competing feminist perspectives: statutory, structural, cultural, and poststructural.

Gender Inequality as Liberal Statutory Discrimination

In the western world, the battle for women's rights began around the end of the nineteenth and the early twentieth centuries, an era witnessing significant changes in the way nations and populations negotiated their citizenship entitlements. European empires were competing against each other over colonies, and various nationalist movements were demanding a more solid framework of citizenship. While there was a strict gender divide between the public and private spaces, with the public domain considered the territory of men and the private (household) domain considered women's 'natural place', changes in labor force composition threatened this arrangement. In the public space, working-class women were a driving labor force in the factories developed by the industrial revolution two centuries earlier, working under harsh employment terms. Middle- and upper-class women were active in the political, philanthropic, and even military scenes without formal recognition of their efforts.

Against this backdrop, women activists in various western countries demanded further recognition in the public space, turning to political rights. From the late 1800s, the Suffragettes in Great Britain and the United States launched campaigns to demand the right to vote. By focusing on the vote (also termed the franchise), early feminists in this 'first wave' understood gender equality in *statutory* terms and asked for entitlements in the political sphere drawing upon the tenets of classical liberalism. However, since these early activists did not belong to the working class, they did not pay much attention to women's economic entitlements and their employment conditions. The agenda of first-wave feminists was also adopted by the first wave of Arab feminists in countries such as Lebanon, Syria, and Egypt, where from the 1930s onward, feminist groups called for participation in political and public life, demanding voting rights, the abolition of the veil, and the adoption of western modernist attire (Thompson, 2000).

Similarly, first-wave feminists did not dedicate much attention to women's position in the family. Since the private sphere of the household is, for liberals, the beacon of individual freedoms, it used to be largely unregulated.[1] However, while this appeared to protect the household as a 'free' private space, it favored men's position as the head of the household. It did not question the compromised position of women in the family, and disguised it under a 'false gender neutrality' (Okin, 1998, p. 120).

Because first-wave feminists viewed the domestic role of woman as part of her 'natural' occupation, they sought only to reform the legal structure (for example, Wollstonecraft, in Tong, 1998) and lobby for access to 'public' issues of voting, education, and health (Okin, 1998). 'Second-wave' liberal feminists, such as Betty Friedan (1963 [2001]), showed dissatisfaction with their domesticity as a 'feminine mystique' and turned to joining men in the public sphere, instead of probing into the conditions of their domestic plight (Whelehan, 2007).

In a leftist critique of liberal feminism, Iris Young (1998) noted the problems created by the privileging of the public sphere, arguing that both public and private issues need to be debated and addressed. Pioneering work by feminists such as Carole Pateman (1988) denounced marriage contracts as a major area of discrimination; gender bias in the family tied women through marriage into a 'sexual contract'. Until the second half of the twentieth century, many western countries had marriage legislation that did not recognize married women as individuals. Rather, women were considered as an extension of their male spouse, disowned from any right to own property or conduct separate business. At this stage, gender inequality in the private sphere was mainly considered as a legal or statutory issue that could be remedied with changing legislation.

In the second half of the twentieth century, legal or statutory gender equality was considered a universal issue that applied to non-western contexts. The newly established institutions of the United Nations formulated international legislation that recognized women's rights in all domains: the public as well as the private spheres. These rights are stipulated in the 1948 Universal Declaration of Human Rights (UDHR), the 1966 International Covenant on Civil and Political Rights (ICCPR), the 1966 International Covenant on Economic, Social and Cultural Rights (ICESCR), and the 1979 Convention on the Elimination of all forms of Discrimination Against Women (CEDAW).[2]

While these legal entitlements represent a major achievement, they are far from being applied at a universal level. Many countries (including Arab states) signed these treaties, but held reservations on some clauses, specifically ones relating to women's well-being in the family (Welchman, 2007). One main limitation of statutory approaches such as these is that they equate legal entitlements with *effective* access to gender equality (Tong, 1998). Another limitation is the conceptualization of legal provisions as a comprehensive, definitive, and largely fixed body of legislation dissociated from sociopolitical influence (Esposito and Burgat, 2003; Amirmokri, 2004; Rehman, 2007). Hence, legalistic approaches depoliticize gender equality and ignore structural, cultural, and institutional factors that hinder the achievement of women's well-being.

Gender Inequality as Structural Injustice

In the 1970s, socialist feminists provided the most pertinent contribution to the economic concept of women's well-being. For a long time, the household was considered an economic black box where resource distribution was assumed to be equitable. However, this was not the case. Pointing to women's uneven economic power within the household and society, socialist feminists argued that women were held in uneven personal relationships through their purse strings. Women remained unpaid for their contribution to domestic work, so the control of income by male members of the family facilitated the oppression of women in the household (Whelehan, 2007). This shift added a materialist dimension to gender equality. Thus, socialist feminists lobbied for structural changes to economic relations within the structure of the family, as well as outside it (see, for example, Eisenstein, 1978). Several Arab women's groups adopted a structural approach to gender equality, lobbying to increase women's access to education and employment (Moghadam, 2007).

Women's well-being gained further prominence through research concerned with women's economic inequality in developing country contexts. Martha Nussbaum's use of the capabilities approach, developed with Amartya Sen is an example of this perspective (see Nussbaum and Sen, 1993; Nussbaum and Glover, 1995). The capabilities approach acknowledges that individual freedoms are curtailed by structural constraints and is concerned with providing the basis for individuals' abilities to flourish in various areas of life. In order to remedy any gap in meeting capabilities, it is necessary to reform the distribution of resources within the household.

The structural approach, advocated by both socialist and development feminists, assumed that by reforming male-dominated structures in the public and private spheres (such as installing quotas for women representatives, or issuing more equitable provisions in the workplace), women would automatically make use of them. Hence, the main limitation of this approach is that it portrays women as being endowed with unconstrained choices and autonomy that would allow them to exploit any opportunities they are presented with (Charusheela, 2009), regardless of any pressure from the largely male-dominated society.

Anne Phillips (2001) found that analyzing gender equality in terms of choice is inadequate because it understands it as sufficiency rather than substantive equality. A sufficiency approach to women's living conditions is concerned with a relative assessment of their situation and ensuring a relative and selective improvement similar to the concept of subjective well-being (Casal, 2007). Hence sufficiency might improve some aspects of women's lives to a certain degree, such as a relative increase in their income in comparison to men or securing some improvements in divorce provisions rather than a reform of the family law, but does not seek to achieve full legal or material equality. In contrast, substantive equality refers to equality in outcomes that go beyond formal or legal gains, and ensure actual material outcomes to women's daily lives, for example reforming family law legislation toward full equality and ensuring that the judges in courts are applying these reforms effectively.

The structural approach held another limitation, mainly by considering the state as a single homogeneous entity. Hence, 'the state' was responsible for the various exclusionary economic mechanisms that marginalize women and keep them within the grip of uneven household relations. However, it is increasingly recognized that the state is composed of fragmented and often competing structures and actors (see Hopkins, Chapter 7, this volume). This limitation applies especially to non-western contexts where customary or religious entities and frameworks overlap and compete with governmental ones. For example, when Arab feminist groups blame 'the state' for sustaining discrimination in family law, they falsely assume that state bodies and the religious institution are separate entities. In fact, in these contexts, the religious institution spreads over both state and civil society spaces (Mansour, 2011). It is a state entity recognized in many constitutions as a legislative authority in family law jurisprudence (Rabo, 2011). It also simultaneously occupies civil society spaces through the community religious groups and practices affiliated to the state bodies. One example is the Higher Muslim Council in Lebanon, which is registered as a charity, but headed by the *Mufti* (a governmental official that heads the Lebanese Sunni religious courts).

Gender inequality as cultural subordination

In an attempt to recognize the social influences on women's well-being (beyond statutory and economic frameworks), feminists focused on analyzing patriarchal culture as the driving force behind gender discrimination. Patriarchy was defined as an institutional structure of fixed, traditional, male-biased cultural norms maintained through customary and religious influences that perpetuate gender inequality in various areas including family law (Walby, 1989).[3]

In western contexts, women's inequality in the family was exposed by radical feminists, who followed Carol Hanisch's (1969) iconic statement 'the personal is political'. This statement recognized the crucial impact of gender discrimination in family relations as part of the broader feminist struggle to achieve women's well-being.[4] As such, this approach was an invitation to consider the pervasiveness of uneven sexual power between men and women (MacKinnon, 2005). Cultural feminists believed that deeply entrenched patriarchal (that is, male-biased) practices oppressed women in all areas of life, starting with forced sexual practices (in their extreme form, rape). At the time, this view constituted a revolutionary approach that held support groups for victims of domestic violence and ran shelters for battered women. In western contexts, a radical strand of cultural feminism, namely lesbian feminists, denounced the pervasive patriarchal order and the heterosexual marriage institution, and called for a segregationist approach based on 'women for women' support. This school saw equality as independence/disengagement/distinction. The concept of violence against women was elaborated as part of this broad cultural approach to expose sexual aggression by pinning it down to cultural norms and practices. However, this approach was critiqued for sustaining essentialist cultural distinctions between men and women.

Development feminists also investigated the ways that cultural practices confined women in the family. They rejected traditional and 'backward' local customs that disadvantaged women and sought to apply a universal understanding of equality. Advocating a modernist secular-religious divide, they adapted various ideas from liberal, radical, and socialist feminism. They incorporated western liberal approaches to formal equality through advocating legislation change. Similarly, they considered economic discrimination as a hindrance to equality within the family. They also adopted radical views flagging the role that men have in oppressing women in the family and adopted these western-centric approaches in the global discourse on Violence Against Women (VAW).

Within Arab contexts, the discourse of VAW appealed to feminist groups because it was formulated in terms of cultural backwardness, ignoring the influence of religious institutions on formulating and perpetuating gender discrimination within religious legal family law texts and practice. For example, several women's groups formed common platforms that provided support for abused women through hotlines and counseling services, as well as establishing the Permanent Arab Court to Resist Violence Against Women in 1996. In this formulation, men and the family institution were flagged as propagators of outdated and oppressive patriarchal norms, without much discussion of the religious influence (Mansour, 2011).

In an alternative take on cultural influence, religious feminists denounced local cultural norms as a major hindrance for achieving women's equality within religious frameworks. They considered religion as an exceptional moral order that had the capacity to provide answers to transcend gender inequality. Equality was understood as equity and fairness that surpasses manmade conceptions of justice (King, 1994; Badran, 2009). The assumption is that when men and women follow religious doctrine closely, they do not leave room for inequality. From this perspective, inequality occurs only when men and women misinterpret religious doctrine and fail to apply it.[5]

In Islamic contexts, recent feminist scholarship finds that multiple interpretations of Islamic Sharia can provide opportunities for a progressive reading and application of women's rights in the family (Mir-Hosseini, 2003, 2006; Mayer, 2007). The 1980s saw a surge in Islamic feminist groups in Egypt among other countries. These groups claimed that Islamic law is misunderstood, misinterpreted, and co-opted by regressive cultural patriarchal forces. They called for reverting to the 'authentic' teachings of Islam that in theory have the potential to bring equity to women (Badran, 2009). Claiming a schism between 'high' equitable religious teachings, and 'low' discriminatory religious practices, however, is a flawed argument; it sustains the artificial difference between the two religious orders, thus ignoring the amalgamation of the two through institutional and social discursive practices.

In these cultural perspectives, women are also perceived as inherently different from men. Womanhood as an identity was essentialist and fixed. However, they conceptualized it in terms of positive emotions of motherhood and care as well as an innate concern for nature and peace (see Gilligan, 1982; Mies and Shiva, 1993). In these views, women held generative and nurturing qualities. A celebration of women's maternal identity also extended to drawing a link with the natural powers of mother earth (Tong, 1998).

As men were believed to lack these nurturing qualities, women were deemed to operate in the special moral framework of emotions that is outside of rigid rational masculinist logic (Elshtain, 1995). The perceived abundance of the maternal logic was an antidote to the male oppressive rational logic. From this view, the gender roles involved in personal relations were complementary. It also implied that women had a common core identity of 'womanhood' translated within a sense of 'sisterhood'. The assumption that women's identity was homogeneous, however, was problematic (Naghibi, 2007). Examples of this approach proliferate within Arab women's groups. For instance, Lebanese women's groups based in liberal and leftist ideologies often insist on attributing positive and essentialist qualities to womanhood, framed within notions of self-sacrifice and obedience (Mansour, 2011).

Although emphasizing culture helped to shed light on more obstacles to enhancing women's well-being, this approach holds two main limitations. In the case of development feminists, they advocated secular and universal norms of gender equality. Hence, they assumed that secular frameworks do not discriminate against women. This assumption is false because many secular frameworks have been influenced by religious norms, such as the case of most European civil marriage legislation in the mid-twentieth century (Sharma and Young, 1999). The second limitation relates to religious feminists. Their approach is to consider religious doctrine as an elevated and pure ideal; they thus create a false distinction between the concept and the practice of religion. However, if we consider that any legislation, whether based on secular or on religious doctrine, is effectively articulated and enforced by an authority (be it judges, the police, or spouses themselves), it is always subject to interpretation (Caputo and Derrida, 1997). Thus, it is not possible to reach a pure essence of religion.

This section has discussed three approaches to gender equality. Statutory approaches focus on changing legislation to enhance women's well-being. Gender equality is considered as a right, yet no provisions are in place to enhance effective practice. Structural approaches expand gender equality toward economic and social justice. They focus on the financial empowerment of women by encouraging increased work opportunities and labor rights as well as enhanced education. Although structural approaches expect women to earn more and thus enhance their position in the household, they do not explain why some women fail to do so despite the improvement in their earning power. Cultural approaches attribute such failure to patriarchy, a system of male-dominated norms that is deeply entrenched in society. Despite their differences, these three approaches are similar in the way they explain women's identity and solidarity. They assume that women's sense of self and conceptualization of equality are fixed and are shared among women across the globe, albeit to varying degrees. The next section discusses these limitations in relation to the role of civil society in fostering gender equality and well-being.

III   CIVIL SOCIETY AND FEMINIST ADVOCACY

I now turn to the historical development of civil society and the extent to which it accommodates gender equality. I discuss the rise of the concept of civil society and the gender bias it contains. Then I turn to a broader understanding of feminist collective action[6] as a way to accommodate the variation in women's interests, issues and needs.

Civil Society: The Rise of a Male-biased Space for Action?

The early notions of a western concept of civil society grew from liberal/enlightenment scholarly thought that was concerned with citizens' relationship to the state. Civil society was considered a social and political space where citizens gather to exchange ideas about world affairs and join in common activities aimed at improving their society. Conceptualizing civil society as a free and democratic space, the liberal approach built on Adam Ferguson's view that civil society is an alternative space between the 'savagery' of communal space and the control of the state (Oz-Salzberger, 1995). This understanding became popular in the recent revival of the role of civil society and especially non-governmental organizations in the 1990s as part of the neoliberal agenda (Lewis, 2006).

An alternative radical view of civil society emerged in the 1920s from the work of the Italian political activist and thinker Antonio Gramsci (1971), who was imprisoned under Mussolini's fascist regime. In Gramsci's view, civil society is not necessarily an open and democratic space. Rather it is an arena where groups of different ideologies, both progressive and restrictive, clash with others. Hence, according to this view civil society has a dark side; it can accommodate pervasive ideas such as discrimination, racism, and gender bias.

In fact, throughout their historical development, civil society spaces were male dominated both in terms of numbers and male-centered issues, while women were underrepresented (Howell and Mulligan, 2004). Due to this schism, feminist activists advocated a sense of sisterhood among all women in western and non-western contexts based on the idea that women hold similar attributes and go through similar experiences (Naghibi, 2007). In this view, women are assumed to have common grievances and interests and by proxy would have a unity and willingness to work on common goals (Elshtain, 1995). Activists gathered and formed platforms for feminist collective action within or in parallel to mainstream civil society spaces. This pattern is noticeable within various Arab women's groups. For instance, two of the most prominent leftist feminist groups in Lebanon initially organized as the women's branches of the male-dominated political groups Lebanese Communist Party and the Communist Labor Organization (Mansour, 2011), in order to provide 'female-oriented' charitable activities such as literacy classes and employment skills workshops to disadvantaged women.

Feminist collective action merged various feminist approaches discussed in the previous section with liberal and radical notions of civil society by relying on sisterhood solidarity. Many feminist liberal groups lobbied for legal or statutory reforms such as holding allocated seats for women in electoral systems. Radical feminist groups organized into 'women for women' support groups against rape and domestic violence. Sisterhood solidarity extended globally and permeated various contexts. Women's groups organized by and for women became the typical form of association around women's issues (Mohanty, 2003).

Sisterhood and the Clash of Multiple Women's Interests

However, the concept of sisterhood solidarity has been questioned as conflict within the feminist movement started appearing in the 1970s. Feminists in the margin contested the western, white, and mainstream approach of dominant feminist groups. Third world and multicultural feminists in both western and developing countries objected in international forums that their issues were marginalized by the mainstream global feminist agenda (Basu, 2003). In these forums, western women's issues were considered global while those of third world women were considered local (McCann and Kim, 2003). As a result and in response to this division, third world feminists gathered as separate interest groups within or in parallel to international women-focused forums (Basu, 2003). These developments created a divide between global North and global South feminist civil society.

As women were increasingly recognized to have diverse needs and issues around the world, it became necessary to reject a plain sisterhood solidarity and move to understanding women as a social group rather than an aggregate (Young, 1998). In this sense, women do not necessarily share the same ideals or issues. Rather, they relate to other women – at least partly – based on a particular sense of history and understanding of social relations, personal possibilities, and other experiences. Hence, feminist civil society groups can be varied in their goals and activists can leave or enter several groups and adhere to various ideas at once. Like other disadvantaged groups, what brings various women together is a sense of oppression. Iris Young (1998) drew conditions for oppression as follows: (i) exploitation in work activity; (ii) marginalization from participation in the social scene, powerlessness, and submission to others' authority; (iii) cultural imperialism, when the group is stereotyped while at the same time is prevented from voicing its experience; and finally (iv) subjugation to random violence or harassment.

However, other perspectives emphasized that the meaning of oppression can vary across individuals and groups. For example, standpoint feminism recognized that women experience discrimination in various ways according to their lived experiences and the specific power dynamics that they engage in. Hence it focused on the importance of considering knowledge about gender relations as being socially embedded within social power dynamics, arguing that disadvantaged groups are capable of articulating the discrimination they face according to various social vantage points of women's experiences (Harding, 2004). However, while standpoint feminists recognized variation in women's experiences, they had a fixed understanding of power that accentuated the gap between center (the west) and margin (the developing world). They did not elaborate on the variations within the power relations that shape women's experiences in every context.

These gaps were addressed by the poststructural perspectives that focused on opening up the analysis of women's well-being. Poststructural feminism is part of third-wave feminism and moves away from analyzing womanhood as a fixed identity toward focusing on power dynamics and knowledge as forces that shape women into 'subjects' whose perceptions of self and experiences change across time and context.[7] With their focus on tracing the history of gendered knowledge and power relations, they reformulated patriarchy as part of a dynamic process of oppression that shifts according to contextual time-bound norms and values (Butler, 2003).

IV MULTIDIRECTIONAL WOMEN'S GROUPS AGENCY AND GENDER EQUALITY OUTCOMES

Foucault's concept of power is useful to understand the ways in which women's groups articulate knowledge on gender equality and women's well-being. Power is a net-like phenomenon that circulates through social relations and is exercised between individuals, groups, and institutional actors. It is generated by rules and norms and 'surmounts the rules of right which organise and delimit it and extends itself beyond them, invests itself in institutions, becomes embodied in techniques, and equips itself with instruments and eventually even violent means of material intervention' (Foucault, 1980, p. 96). Power is an enactment rather than a status, and an exercise of discursive influence that could go in either positive or negative directions, depending on one's position on the normative divide.

As various actors push their agendas, the policy process becomes a set of 'interactions of individuals, interest groups, social movements, and institutions through which problematic situations are converted to policy problems, agendas are set, decisions are made, and actions are taken' (Rein and Schön, 1993, p. 145). Action and power are thus reconciled as 'all relations bring together unequal actors by the very fact that any relation, directly or indirectly, relates actors who are directing this intervention with one who is on the receiving end of it. All relations include power relations. There is no purely horizontal social relation' (Touraine, 1998, p. 49).

Saba Mahmood (2005) elaborates on the notion of women's agency. She contends that formulations of agency in feminist accounts were useful in contesting earlier views of women as passive or repressed actors. However, Mahmood argues that women's agency – and by proxy women's groups – is not necessarily of a 'progressive nature' and does not lead to resistance and subversion of gender-biased norms.[8] Rather it is context specific, and responds to specific historical and cultural dynamics that 'enable specific modes of being, responsibility, and effectivity' (ibid., p. 14).

In the same vein, Wendy Brown turned the attention to the dynamics within civil society. As women's groups' agency is shaped by many institutional and discursive influences, it is not immune of discriminatory ideology and practices. Thus the progressive nature of civil society and women's groups' agency needs to be questioned as

> [I]t could harbour the same injustices or power relations than hegemonic institutions, it is important to question other claims of political solutions when they codify and entrench existing social relations, when do they mask them, and when do they directly contest or transform them. (Brown, 1995, p. 9)

Building on this view, civil society action is a process of social construction that can take multiple directions, and does not necessarily follow a linear progressive path. To illustrate the point, I draw on an example from my research on gender equality in family law in post-conflict Lebanon (Mansour, 2011). In the early 1990s, women's groups contributed to establishing the National Commission for Lebanese Women's Rights, with the aim of pressing the Lebanese government to ratify the CEDAW agreement. The government ended up ratifying the convention in 1996 and placed reservations on Article 16 in relation to gender equality in family law. These reservations were meant to preserve the religious power-sharing legislative system that has been in place since Ottoman and French colonial times and that only allows religious marriages to be conducted in various religious Christian and Muslim courts. Women's groups followed up on the issue throughout annual follow-up monitoring reports requested by the CEDAW committee.

In the earliest three reports, women's groups' construction of women's subjectivity changed as the process went along.[9] In the first report, women's groups called for establishing a compulsory civil family law and banishing the current religious legislation. In this sense, they constructed women as secular subjects who were oppressed by religion. In the second report, they called for an optional civil family law, hence dividing women into two secular and religious categories. In this way, they considered religious women as rational subjects who subscribe to the values of religious law and hence were not affected by the inherent discrimination in family law. In the third report, women's groups made a U-turn and dropped calls for a secular family law. Instead, they called for reforms within religious family law jurisdiction and the court system.

By doing so, they recognized that women could in fact identify themselves as religious beings and adhere to the dominant social and legal religious frameworks. Yet they denied women the possibility of identifying with a secular legal and social framework. Hence, they placed all women within a religious category and ignored the fact that during their lifetime, women's own perception of themselves can be fragmented, multiple, and conflicting, in the sense that they can identify themselves as religious and secular at different points in time and circumstances. For example, women with family law problems reported that contracting a religious marriage was part of the common practice of the time, and they were not aware of the inherent discrimination in legislation. Rather, at the time of marriage, their subjectivity was constructed within a desirability of being a married woman. Hence, their married status mattered more than the form within which they contracted their marriage.

This example supports the view of Rosemary Pringle and Sophie Watson (1998) who argue that women's interests are not fixed. Women's interests are produced by historically specific discourses, that is, norms and values that are created by and disseminated in society through individuals, groups (political, civil society, community), and institutions (such as the educational system, the family, and the legal system). Interests are defined as 'precarious historical products which are always subjected to processes of dissolution and redefinition' (ibid., p.216). These discourses evolve through time and reshape individuals and groups' perspectives. While groups contribute in shaping these discourses, they also get influenced by them and develop new discourses on gender equality. This view implies that 'every social practice . . . involves a continuous process of constructing new differences' (ibid., p.216). These discourses can take various directions, developing into a range of restrictive or progressive directions depending on the changing power relations between various social and political actors as a result of the broader influences of sociopolitical factors within the specific context.[10]

Such a poststructuralist perspective sheds some light on the complex dynamics of women's solidarity and alliance around gender equality. It also implies two things. First, since feminist interests are numerous and at times conflicting, the issues selected for civil society action are manifold. Second, the feminist agenda is not necessarily progressive, but can take different directions. The style of civil society action is also discursively shaped. Women's groups, like other civil society actors, select their advocacy platforms within the constraints imposed by other influential social and political actors (such as the religious institution or the state) and within the historical setting (such as the colonial or political history). Finally, since women do not necessarily hold common platforms, it is hard to decide which groups legitimately represent women's interests. One example is Lebanese women's groups' conflict over the International March for Women (IMW) in 2000 (Mansour, 2011).

IMW is an international event where various women's groups draft a common agenda of the most crucial gender advocacy issues in their countries. The Lebanese organizers of the IMW disagreed over including an optional secular family law as part of the reform demands. Leftist women's groups insisted on including it among the priorities, while other liberal and religious women's groups rejected this proposal. Their stand was supported by two conservative women members of parliament who called for boycotting the march if family law reforms were to be included and effectively did so, creating a schism within the Lebanese feminist movement. This incident resonates with the claims of poststructural feminists who argue for analyzing feminist collective action as a multitude of collective interests that are shaped within the broader sociopolitical historical frameworks of governance.

By focusing on the dynamics of women's interactions in social spaces, it is possible to untangle the process of shaping individual and collective agency, and the ways women experience and practice different types of agency. Hence, the analysis of collective action becomes more complex than the standard notions of submission and resistance, allowing us to question the plain roles usually attributed to women's groups as actors of feminist resistance (Braig and Wölte, 2002; Mateo Diaz, 2005). Their ideals and practices need to be analyzed in relation to the contradictions inherent in the civil society spaces (Fisher, 1997; Chatterjee, 2004). This will contribute to a shift in the analysis, focusing on the ways in which family law frameworks construct women's agency and equip them with variable degrees of influence over their personal relations and ultimately their well-being.

V CONCLUSION

This chapter argued that, in order to optimize well-being in the family, we need to move beyond fixed approaches despite their historical contribution to feminist thought. Fixed approaches – whether statutory, structural, or cultural – fail to capture the complex and dynamic factors surrounding our understanding of well-being and gender equality. There is a need to move beyond economic and psychological parameters, also taking into account the broader social and political factors that hinder women's greater well-being; this can shed more light on the complex processes of shaping women's identity and collective action.

In particular, focusing on the institutional, historical, legal, and sociopolitical influences on gender equality in the family shows how women's groups developed within a male–dominated social space of civil society. When sociopolitical factors are considered, we realize that women's groups do not necessarily have an emancipatory purpose. Rather, they can host the broader discriminatory discourses relating to women's well-being and gender equality.

Adapting Michel Foucault's concept of power enables a greater understanding of the complex role of women's groups in influencing the policy process. Liberal conceptions of these groups posit them as guardians of freedom, democratic values, and gender equity, a critic of the state, and a catalyst for change (Aubrey, 1997; Molyneux, 2000; Naples and Desai, 2002; O'Neill and Gidengil, 2006). However, the way that women-based civil society affects well-being and equality is far more convoluted than the often-claimed linear emancipatory impact. Women's groups need to be recognized as major players in the policy process, and specifically in relation to their crucial role as experts in the field of gender analysis and gender equality and well-being (King, 1999; Petersen et al., 1999).

The past four decades have seen women's groups become more influential, pushing for policy reform at the international level through UN mechanisms and at national levels through state reforms. But since women's groups hold various ideological differences on what constitutes gender equality, they have competed over legitimacy and representation of women's issues, acting as buffers that control what issues are to be upheld or sidelined. This conflict often translated into a shy commitment to gender equality in family law, despite it being the most influential component in furthering women's well-being.

NOTES

1. First-wave feminists adopted a liberal approach to women's rights. Liberalism, developed by Enlightenment thinkers such as John Locke, theorizes governance around the ideas of individual freedoms and liberty and consensual rule by populations. The pioneer of liberal feminism is the British philosopher Mary Wollstonecraft, who wrote *A Vindication of the Rights of Woman* in 1792, critiquing the exclusion of women from the public sphere and calling for the inclusion of women in governance and the political structure through voting rights. One main critique of liberal thought and liberal feminism is its placement of the family sphere at the core of individual freedoms, meaning that the family was deemed outside the bounds of state control. This approach meant that gendered relations – and in particular discrimination against women – within the family remained unexplored.
2. The rights approach was critiqued for being based on universalist grounds (Spivak and Harasym, 1990). The term 'universalist' refers to a popular research perspective claiming individuals' entitlements and rights to be uniform and applicable across various cultural and political contexts. This view is in fact western-centric, based on a framework of human rights that developed from within the western tradition of democracy and governance and which is recognized and promoted by UN institutions. The universalist approach is contrasted to a communitarian approach that recognizes different rights for different groups and individuals within and across various societies.
3. Patriarchy was later critiqued for providing a fixed and essentialist view of gendered norms and values.
4. Liberal feminists tried to distance themselves from radical feminists, and blamed them for an overemphasis on victim feminism, hostility to men, and focus on sexual violence.
5. This latter view relies on a relativist stand that contests the moral–legal and political framework of secular equality. It relates to other cultural relativist feminists who argue for different frameworks.
6. Feminist collective action is included within the broad citizens' space of civil society, usually organized as loose structures of voluntary women's groups or women's movements (Molyneux and Razavi, 2002), or with a more bureaucratic structure as nongovernmental organizations.
7. Third wave feminism started in the 1980s until the present day. It destabilized the first and second waves' focus on the issues of white women in the industrialized world. By relying on development, postcolonial and poststructural theories it acknowledged the differences of women's experiences across ethnicity and geography, and included feminist strands such as development, cultural, standpoint, and poststructural feminism. Unlike other third wave strands, poststructural feminism highlighted the power differences *within* the conditions of women in developing countries and thus destabilized the fixed gendered categories of race, ethnicity, culture, and religion.
8. Mahmood questions the notion of 'desire for freedom' as western-centric focused on individual autonomy. She (2005, p.14) suggests that the 'desire for freedom . . . is not an innate desire that motivates all beings at all times, but is also profoundly mediated by cultural and historical conditions'. In other words, motivations for people's actions – in this case women's groups – can emerge from other considerations than subordination or subversion.
9. Following poststructural understandings of subjectivity (Foucault and Rabinow, 1997), I use the term

'subjectivity' to refer to the ways individuals understand themselves ontologically and ethically as constituted from within positions of power within which they are located. The subject 'is constructed through
acts of differentiation that distinguish the subject from its constitutive outside, a domain of abjected alter-
ity conventionally associated with the feminine, but clearly not exclusively' (Butler, 1992, p. 12).

10. 'Situated knowledge' recognizes the variety of women's experiences.

REFERENCES

Amirmokri, Vida (2004), L'islam *et Les Droits de L'homme: L'islamisme, Le Droit International et Le
Modernisme Islamique*, Québec: Presses de l'Université Laval.
Aubrey, Lisa M. (1997), *The Politics of Development Co-Operation: NGOs, Gender and Partnership in Kenya*,
London: Routledge.
Badran, Margot (2009), *Feminism in Islam: Secular and Religious Convergences*, Oxford: Oneworld.
Basu, Amrita (2003), 'Globalization of the local/localization of the global: mapping transnational women's
movements', in McCann and Kim (eds), pp. 68–79.
Braig, Marianne and Sonje Wölte (2002), *Common Ground or Mutual Exclusion? Women's Movements and
International Relations*, London: Zed Books.
Brown, Wendy (1995), *States of Injury: Power and Freedom in Late Modernity*, Princeton, NJ: Princeton
University Press.
Butler, Judith (1992), 'Contingent foundations: feminism and the question of "postmodernism"', in Scott and
Butler (eds), pp. 3–21.
Butler, Judith (2003), 'Performative acts and gender constitution: an essay in phenomenology and feminist
theory', in McCann and Kim (eds), pp. 415–27.
Caputo, John D. with Jacques Derrida (1997), *Deconstruction in a Nutshell: A Conversation with Jacques
Derrida*, New York: Fordham University Press.
Casal, Paula (2007), 'Why sufficiency is not enough', *Ethics*, **117**(2), 296–326.
Charusheela, S. (2009), 'Social analysis and the capabilities approach: a limit to Martha Nussbaum's universal-
ist ethics', *Cambridge Journal of Economics*, **33**(6), 1135–52.
Chatterjee, Partha (2004), *The Politics of the Governed: Reflections on Popular Politics in Most of the World*,
New York: Columbia University Press.
de Beauvoir, Simone (tr. H.M. Parshley) (1993), *The Second Sex*, New York: Alfred A. Knopf.
Diener, Ed, Richard Lucas, Ulrich Schimmack and John Helliwell (eds) (2009), *Well-Being for Public Policy*,
Oxford: Oxford University Press.
Dolan, Paul, Richard Layard and Robert Metcalfe (2011), 'Measuring subjective wellbeing for public policy:
recommendations on measures', London Special Paper No. 23, Centre for Economic Performance, March.
Eisenstein, Zillah R. (ed.) (1978), *Capitalist Patriarchy and the Case for Socialist Feminism*, New York:
Monthly Review Press.
Elshtain, Jean Bethke (1995), 'Feminism, family, and community', in Penny A. Weiss and Marilyn Friedman
(eds), *Feminism and Community*, Philadelphia, PA: Temple University Press, pp. 259–72.
Esposito, John L. and François Burgat (2003), *Modernizing Islam: Religion in the Public Sphere in the Middle
East and Europe*, New Brunswick, NJ: Rutgers University Press.
Fisher, William F. (1997), 'Doing good? The politics and antipolitics of NGO practices', *Annual Review of
Anthropology*, **26**, 439–64.
Foucault, Michel (1980), 'Two lectures', in Michel Foucault (ed. Colin Gordon), *Power/Knowledge: Selected
Interviews and Other Writings, 1972/1977*, New York: Pantheon Books, pp. 78–108.
Foucault, Michel and Paul Rabinow (1997), *Ethics: Subjectivity and Truth*, New York: The New Press.
Friedan, Betty (1963 [2001]), *The Feminine Mystique*, New York: W.W. Norton.
Gilligan, Carol (1982), *In a Different Voice: Psychological Theory and Women's Development*, Cambridge, MA:
Harvard University Press.
Gramsci, Antonio (1971), *Selections from the Prison Notebooks*, New York: International Publishers.
Hanisch, Carol (1969), 'The personal is political', paper presented to the Women's Caucus of the Southern
Conference Educational Fund (SCEF), February, available at: http://www.carolhanisch.org/CHwritings/
PersonalisPol.pdf (accessed July 29, 2012).
Harding, Sandra (2004), *The Feminist Standpoint Theory Reader*, London: Routledge.
Howell, Jude and Diane Mulligan (eds) (2004), *Gender and Civil Society: Transcending Boundaries*, London:
Routledge.
International Labour Organization (ILO) (2011), *Global Employment Trends 2011: The Challenge of a Jobs
Recovery*, Geneva: ILO.

Jordan, Bill (2008), *Welfare and Well-being: Social Value in Public Policy*, Bristol, UK: Policy Press.
King, Desmond S. (1999), *In the Name of Liberalism: Illiberal Social Policy in the USA and Britain*, Oxford: Oxford University Press.
King, Ursula (1994), *Feminist Theology from the Third World: A Reader*, London: SPCK/Orbis.
Lewis, David (2006), *The Management of Non-Governmental Development Organizations*, London: Routledge.
MacKinnon, Catherine A. (2005), *Women's Lives, Men's Laws*, Cambridge, MA: Belknap Press of Harvard University Press.
Mahmood, Saba (2005), *Politics of Piety: The Islamic Revival and the Feminist Subject*, Princeton, NJ: Princeton University Press.
Mansour, Nisrine (2011), 'Governing the personal: family law and women's subjectivity and agency in post-conflict Lebanon', PhD thesis, London School of Economics, London.
Mateo Diaz, Mercedes (2005), *Representing Women? Female Legislators in Western European Parliaments*, Colchester: ECPR Press (European Consortium for Political Research).
Mayer, Ann Elizabeth (2007), *Islam and Human Rights: Tradition and Politics*, Boulder, CO: Westview Press.
McCann, Carole and Seung-kyung Kim (eds) (2003), *Feminist Theory Reader: Local and Global Perspectives*, London: Routledge.
Mies, Maria and Vandana Shiva (1993), *Ecofeminism*, Halifax: Fernwood Publications.
Mir-Hosseini, Ziba (2003), 'The construction of gender in Islamic legal thought and strategies for reform', *Hawwa: Journal of Women in the Middle East and the Islamic World*, **1**(1), 1–28.
Mir-Hosseini, Ziba (2006), 'Muslim women's quest for equality: between Islamic law and feminism', *Critical Inquiry*, **32**(4), 629–45.
Moghadam, Valentine M. (ed.) (2007), *From Patriarchy to Empowerment: Women's Participation, Movements, and Rights in the Middle East, North Africa, and South Asia*, New York: Syracuse University Press.
Mohanty, Chandra Talpade (2003), *Feminism without Borders: Decolonizing Theory, Practicing Solidarity*, Durham, NC: Duke University Press.
Molyneux, Maxine (2000), *Women's Movements in International Perspective: Latin America and Beyond*, Basingstoke, UK: Macmillan.
Molyneux, Maxine and Shahra Razavi (eds) (2002), *Gender Justice, Development, and Rights*, Oxford: Oxford University Press.
Naghibi, Nima (2007), *Rethinking Global Sisterhood: Western Feminism and Iran*, Minneapolis, MN: University of Minnesota Press.
Naples, Nancy A. and Manisha Desai (2002), *Women's Activism and Globalization: Linking Local Struggles and Global Politics*, London: Routledge.
Nussbaum, Martha C. and Jonathan Glover (eds) (1995), *Women, Culture, and Development: A Study of Human Capabilities*, Oxford: Clarendon Press.
Nussbaum, Martha C. and Amartya Sen (eds) (1993), *The Quality of Life*, Oxford: Clarendon Press.
O'Neill, Brenda and Elisabeth Gidengil (2006), *Gender and Social Capital*, London: Routledge.
Okin Susan Muller (1991), *Justice, Gender, and the Family*, New York: Basic Books.
Okin, Susan Muller (1998), 'Gender, the public and the private', in Anne Phillips (ed.), *Feminism and Politics*, New York: Oxford University Press, pp. 116–32.
Oz-Salzberger, Fania (1995), 'Introduction', in Oz-Salzberger (ed.), *An Essay on the History of Civil Society*, Cambridge: Cambridge University Press.
Pateman, Carole (1988), *The Sexual Contract*, Cambridge: Polity Press.
Petersen, Alan, Ian Barns, Janice Dudley and Patricia Harris (1999), *Poststructuralism, Citizenship, and Social Policy*, New York: Routledge.
Phillips, Anne (2001), 'Feminism and liberalism revisited: has Martha Nussbaum got it right?', *Constellations*, **8**(2), 249–66.
Pringle, Rosemary and Sophie Watson (1998), 'Women's interests and the poststructuralist state', in Anne Phillips (ed.), *Feminism and Politics*, New York: Oxford University Press, pp. 203–20.
Rabo, Annika (2011), 'Syrian transnational families and family law', in Anne Hellum, Shaheen Sardar Ali and Anne Griffiths (eds), *From Transnational Relations to Transnational Laws: Northern European Laws at the Crossroads*, Farnham, UK: Ashgate, pp. 29–50.
Rao, Kiran, Mridula Apte and D.K. Subbakrishna (2003), 'Coping and subjective wellbeing in women with multiple roles', *International Journal of Social Psychiatry*, **49**(3), 175–84.
Rehman, Javaid (2007), 'The Sharia, Islamic family laws and international human rights law: examining the theory and practice of polygamy and talaq', *International Journal of Law, Policy and the Family*, **21**(1), 108–27.
Rein, Martin and Donald Schön (1993), 'Reframing policy discourse', in Frank Fischer and John Forester (eds), *The Argumentative Turn in Policy Analysis and Planning*, Durham, NC: Duke University Press, pp. 145–66.
Scott, Joan W. and Judith P. Butler (eds) (1992), *Feminists Theorize the Political*, London: Routledge.

Sharma, Arvind and Katherine K. Young (eds) (1999), *Feminism and World Religions*, Albany, NY: State University of New York Press.

Spivak, Gayatri Chakravorty (author) and Sarah Harasym (ed.) (1990), *The Post-Colonial Critic: Interviews, Strategies, Dialogues*, London: Routledge.

Taylor, Betty W., Sharon Rush and Robert John Munro (1999), *Feminist Jurisprudence, Women and the Law: Critical Essays, Research Agenda, and Bibliography*, Littleton, CO: F.B. Rothman.

Thompson, Elizabeth (2000), *Colonial Citizens: Republican Rights, Paternal Privilege, and Gender in French Syria and Lebanon*, New York, Columbia University Press.

Tong, Rosemarie (1998), *Feminist Thought: A More Comprehensive Introduction*, Boulder, CO: Westview Press.

Touraine, Alain (1988), *Return of the Actor: Social Theory in Postindustrial Society*, Minneapolis, MN: University of Minnesota Press.

Walby, Sylvia (1989), 'Theorising patriarchy', *Sociology*, **23**(2), 213–34.

Welchman, Lynn (2007), *Women and Muslim Family Laws in Arab States: A Comparative Overview of Textual Development and Advocacy*, Amsterdam: Amsterdam University Press.

Whelehan, Imelda (2007), *Modern Feminist Thought*, Edinburgh: Edinburgh University Press.

Young, Iris Marion (1998), 'Polity and group difference: a critique of the ideal of universal citizenship', in Anne Phillips (ed.), *Feminism and Politics*, New York: Oxford University Press, pp. 401–26.

5. Gender and caring
Julie A. Nelson

I INTRODUCTION

'Care' can, in one sense, refer to activities such as childcare or nursing. Such activities further the development of another, usually in a face-to-face and personal way. Care recipients are typically people who could not flourish without it, such as the very young or ill. Another meaning of 'care' is that it is a motivation based on concern for someone or something outside of oneself. There is a general sense that 'care activities' are of highest quality when accompanied by, and motivated by, authentic emotional commitments, or 'caring feelings'.[1]

How does caring figure into economic life? From the viewpoint of orthodox neoclassical economics, it does not figure in at all. From this viewpoint, economics is centrally defined around the topics of (i) markets in which the goods and services are exchanged for money and (ii) the choice behavior of the rational, autonomous, self-interested agents thought to populate these markets. 'Economic man' then, is imagined as a creature who neither needs care nor has any responsibility or motivation to provide it. The model of the economy that, in theory, is created by these creatures is often taken as an accurate portrayal of real-world capitalism and a simple description of a heartlessness that is presumed to be of its essence. As a result, over the centuries, many supporters for a more caring economy have called for the dismantling of individualist capitalism in favor of a more solidaristic state socialism and/or local, nonprofit familial and community systems of cooperation and sharing.

A gender perspective brings fresh insights to this well-trampled territory, for two reasons. First, the vast amount of labor that women around the world have historically devoted to unpaid household caring labor is in sharp contrast to views that look only to the market or state for the means of human sustenance and flourishing. Some of this work has been transferred to childcare centers, hospitals, schools, and so on and become paid. Even then, the work tends to be primarily done by women, and has been presumed to be motivated by something other than complete self-interest. Feminist sociologists and economists have, in recent decades, extensively explored the phenomenon of 'caring labor' both unpaid and paid, while philosophers have debated the motivations implied by an 'ethic of care'. Some of this now vast literature on care as a phenomenon that is distinctively different from (what is presumed to be) normal market behavior and motivations will be reviewed in Section II.

A second and more radical implication of a gender perspective has, however, so far been less extensively investigated. What *is* normal market behavior? While researchers of caring labor and care ethics have performed an extremely valuable service in bringing to light types of work and motivations that were previously unrecognized, the discussion too often accepts what I believe is an excessive emphasis on gender difference. Care is thought to be primarily the domain of women, families, close personal relations, emotionality, organic connections, and/or informal and nonprofit local (and perhaps state) institutions, while – right in line with orthodox neoclassical teaching – men, markets, global economic connections, and money are assumed to be inherently mechanical and care-free. Section III deals with the gender dualisms that have created biases in the very core of our beliefs about economics and economies, and reviews the small but growing literature on care as a phenomenon *within* markets – assuming care-free markets (and care-free men) have, in fact, created dangerous self-fulfilling prophecies. Section IV concludes.

II   CARING LABOR AS A DISTINCT PHENOMENON

A great deal of academic literature in economics and sociology has now developed around the concept of 'caring labor' as a form of labor that is distinctive from other sorts of labor. To the extent that the issue of motivation comes up, this social science literature also overlaps with the philosophical and psychological literatures on the 'ethic of care'. Literatures have grown up around unpaid caring labor, the nexus between unpaid caring labor and paid labor, and paid caring labor.

Unpaid Caring Labor

During the 1970s, a number of feminist scholars and activists around the world began to argue that the economic contribution of women's traditional unpaid work in the home should be recognized. One manifestation of this was a 'wages for housework' discussion (see, for example, Graber and Miller, 2002). Another was the argument, most notably made by Marilyn Waring (1988), that the economic value of women's unpaid work should be included in the calculation of measures of national output, such as gross domestic product. This has remained a topic of discussion among some feminist economists, with discussions revolving around whether the work should be valued on a replacement cost basis (for example, the cost per hour of a nanny, driver, cook, and so on) or opportunity cost basis (that is, the lost income of the woman herself), and what the effect of including unpaid labor would be on our understanding of national economies and on policies (Ironmonger, 1996; Wagman and Folbre, 1996). Time-use surveys, recently instituted in a number of countries, have made the empirical study of unpaid caring labor more viable (Budlender, 2010). Other feminists (Bergmann, 1986) have rejected the call for studying or recognizing the value of housework, arguing that this movement only serves to reinforce women's ties to the home, and draw attention away from women's lack of access to real money and power.

It was also recognized, early on, that not all activities traditionally accomplished by homemakers are of the same nature. Some activities of 'caring for a family' are done on behalf of people who could, in fact, take care of themselves. The assignment of, for example, washing the clothes of a husband or teenager to the wife/mother of a family generally has more to do with tradition (and oppression) than ability or need. So a distinction was made between caring for those who are not vulnerable in some way and those who are. Most of the care literature has focused on care for people who are in some way dependent. Another axis of distinction came about from noticing that some activities such as cleaning, laundry, and food preparation can be relatively easily contracted out to people who do the work 'for the money'. The nature of the good or service may change in some ways with this shift, but such tasks seem less intrinsically personal than the hands-on and often deeply relational work involved in childcare or care of sick or elderly family members. The literature on unpaid care, as it has developed, has tended to move away from housework in general to focus on personalized care for the vulnerable, within the context of (hopefully) loving relationships (Himmelweit, 1995; Gardiner, 1997; England and Folbre, 1999).

How much care can be contracted out? As a later section will discuss, it is possible for authentic caring relationships to develop between paid caregivers – such as nannies, early childhood educators, nurses, social workers, foster parents, paid companions for the elderly, therapists, physicians, and so on – and the vulnerable people they serve. Yet, is there some distinct kernel of traditionally familial caring labor that is nontransferable? Such questions arise, as a matter of policy, in questions of how many hours in day care might be too much for a child, whether special day-care centers for sick children are a good idea, whether kibbutzim-style (socialized) child-raising should be developed or avoided, or whether social service agencies should focus on helping children within troubled families or removing them to foster care. Caring labor and caring relationships are, at some level, intimately associated. Most individuals and families appear to value at least some amount of personally given intra-family care, even when they also rely to a large extent on extra-family sources.

Empirical work on unpaid household caring labor has confirmed that, while men participate, it is still disproportionately done by women, both nationally and globally (Budlender, 2008). Discussions of the meaning to be given to this empirical fact have created splits within feminist circles, with cultural or relational feminists tending to argue that women are by nature more caring and nurturing, while liberal feminists tend to emphasize similarities between men and women. Certain radical and postmodern feminists may refuse to recognize gender binaries at all. In my own work, I have sought to find a middle ground in which insights of various groups are appreciated, but the level of analysis is moved from a question of inherent sameness/difference to questions about social beliefs and social and economic structures.

I believe we do better to think of caring as a *human* capacity that can be *developed* rather than an inherent female talent. Participation in caring activities can develop a person's caring attitudes and caring skills. To the extent this is so, one must be very careful about drawing conclusions based on patterns of caring labor that have themselves been pre-shaped by stereotyping and inequalities of power.

Work–Family Issues

When people with caregiving responsibilities also engage in paid work, conflicts can arise between the demands of care and the demands of employers. Large literatures in human resource management and sociology, and smaller literatures in economics and law, have grown up around this issue of work – family conflict.[2] One visible result of these conflicts is what has been called the 'motherhood penalty' – the tendency of women with children to earn less than other women, controlling for education, hours, skills, and so on.

To a large extent, these problems arise because paid jobs are often structured around the image of the ideal worker – someone with no caring responsibilities, who can work late, change hours or travel at a moment's notice, and never asks for time off for a sick child or an elderly parent's doctor's appointment (Williams, 2001). Historically, of course, men were expected to approximate this ideal, with women performing all of the caring labor invisibly and without recognition of their work's importance in supporting paid employment. A (white) middle-class married woman was expected to engage in market work only to the extent that it did not interfere with her household responsibilities. The problems of women in poorer and/or single-parent families, who are expected to somehow both work and simultaneously care, often receive less attention.

One sort of response to this conflict maintains the gendered identification of care with women, and proposes special treatment such as 'mommy track' career ladders, maternity leaves to ease women's participation in both paid work and family, and/or the encouragement of female entrepreneurship (to the extent that this may provide more flexibility in hours and locations of work). To the extent that policies such as maternity leaves make women more expensive to employ than men, however, they may encourage even more discrimination against women in the paid workforce. To the extent that workplace policies are only available to women, they also do not support – and may even discourage – the engagement of men in caring activities. Female entrepreneurship – now encouraged by many microcredit schemes worldwide – may be a solution to some women's problems, but may also trap women in small-scale, low-paying types of work.

Another line of response looks to somewhat more gender-neutral policies such as parental leaves, or sick leaves or personal days that can be used by either men or women employees to care for family members. In the absence of strong encouragement of men to take advantage of such programs, however, social pressures continue to assure that it is largely (though not entirely) women who use them. Sweden has taken more forceful steps, by instituting a 'use it or lose it' policy in its parental leaves, in which only the father is allowed to use some weeks of the guaranteed paid parental leave that is offered. The degree to which caring is supported by state institutions varies widely across countries (Bettio and Plantenga, 2004).

A continuing problem, however, is that even when policies are available, employees may be afraid to use them for fear of being seen as less than serious about their job. This will not change until the image of the 'ideal worker' stops being a widespread social norm. Shouldn't the image of the care-free person, unattached and lacking in responsibilities, be a target of social censure, instead of an ideal? Isn't there something rather sad about people who are never needed enough by the people who they should be closest to, that they never have to say 'no' to their employer?

Paid Caring Labor

Some of the mostly highly sex-segregated occupations in modern market economics clearly fall into the category of caring labor. In the United States, for example, 92 percent of nurses, 95 percent of childcare workers, and 82 percent of elementary school teachers were women in 2009 (US Bureau of Labor Statistics, 2010). A somewhat broader definition of caring labor includes more face-to-face services. Paula England, Michelle Budig and Nancy Folbre (2002), for example, include in their empirical study any occupation that helps to develop a person's capabilities, including physical and mental health and cognitive skills, in ways that may be more short term or intermittent. Under this definition, all of healthcare (including the work of doctors and technicians), all of education (including at the university level), and social services are also considered to be forms of care. The conceptual and empirical study of paid work with dependency, emotional and/ or other-regarding components has recently become a frequent endeavor of feminist economists and sociologists (for example, Himmelweit, 1999; Folbre and Nelson, 2000, 2006; Macdonald and Merrill, 2002; England and Folbre, 2003; Swartz, 2004).

Besides tending to be dominated by women, another empirical regularity that has been observed is the 'care penalty' – the tendency for occupations that involve face-to-face healing and nurturing services to pay less than other occupations, controlling for factors such as educational requirements, and even controlling for the sex of the job holder (England et al., 2002). The existence of this penalty tends both to disadvantage the people who go into these fields, and to create problems in the quality and size of the care labor force. Many explanations have been put forth for why this care penalty exists. As reviewed by sociologist Paula England (2005), a number of scholars, for example, have hypothesized that there is a systematic devaluation of work associated with females.

Another concept that I believe might help explain why the persistence of this devaluation has taken hold is what some economists call 'hysteresis', or the tendency of historical events to affect current economic patterns. Nursing and the teaching of small children, for example, were historically accomplished within families for free (that is, without monetary payment), and then when they moved outside the household first tended to be done by nuns or young unmarried women. While trade unionists and others often argued for 'family wages' for men, the argument for good wages for women was weakened by the fact that women doing caring work had often taken vows of poverty or had no dependants to support. Once established, however, patterns of relative wages tend to persist over time (Albelda et al., 2001). This could be one reason why wages have not caught up with the reality that caregiving work is now often done by people who are primary – or at least major – earners for their families. The vulnerability of care recipients adds a further complication to using union tactics to raise wages: economist Nancy Folbre created the phrase 'prisoner of love' to describe the paid caregiver who is unwilling to withhold care – for example, to go out on strike – as a tactic for increasing wages or improving working conditions (2001, p. 38).

Another problem is the failure to recognize the real human skills involved in care work (Meagher, 2002). In the US, for example, someone paid to care for children is paid about the same as someone paid to 'care for' parked cars (US Bureau of Labor Statistics, 2009). Even though the skills involved for good care should be vastly higher for the former occupation, there remains a popular perception that childcare is something that any warm (female) body can do. The relational skills involved in nursing are similarly often either neglected or romanticized (Folbre and Nelson, 2006; Adams and Nelson, 2009).

Some standard economics concepts can also be applied to this issue. For example, a number of scholars have discussed the public good nature of care: that is, many of the benefits of good care – such as healthy and educated fellow-citizens – cannot be restricted only to the people who contribute resources towards it. This weakens people's willingness to pay for care (England, 2005). Another explanation for low wages comes from arguments about productivity. A number of sectors of the economy have experienced increases in productivity and (at least until recent decades) concomitant increases in wages due to economies of scale and the introduction of new technologies. The personal nature of caring work, on the other hand, means that it is afflicted by the 'cost disease of the service sector' that prevents such cost savings (England et al., 2002; Himmelweit, 2007).

Another explanation for low wages for care that comes out of conventional economics is the idea that care pays a compensating wage differential – that is, that because people like the work, they are willing to accept a lower wage and 'take part of their pay in hugs'. Such an argument, however, is problematic for two reasons. First, it vastly oversimplifies the issue of motivation. Much caring labor is very unlikely to be undertaken for reasons of personal gratification (for example, diaper changing), but rather is motivated by a sense of duty or responsibility that is completely ignored in the model of self-interested economic man (Nelson, 2009). Second, it relies on fallacious economic reasoning that confuses individual choice with market wage determination. While *individuals* might choose to take a lower-paying job if they receive nonpecuniary benefits from it, the level of wages for an *occupation* also depends crucially on the level of demand for specific workers (Nelson, 1999). Surgeons or engineers, for example, can both enjoy their work *and* receive high pay, because both private and public actors devote considerable resources to advanced medical care and skillful technological development. This sort of high demand for quality – backed up by money to spend – does not yet characterize most markets for caring labor.

Yet another explanation for low wages receives support not only from some conventional (nonfeminist) economists, but also – unfortunately, from my point of view – from some scholars and activists who consider themselves feminist. This is the belief that money motivations corrupt caring, and that therefore authentic caring labor needs to be protected in some way from markets and money. There is, indeed, psychological literature on how extrinsic motivators, such as monetary gain, can crowd out intrinsic motivations such as caring feelings, if the structure of the relationship of the employer and employee is perceived of as controlling. But what these arguments neglect is that the same literature finds that receipt of monetary rewards can crowd in (that is, increase) intrinsic motivations if the relationship is perceived of as acknowledging the recipient's own humanity, agency, skills, and motivations. The danger of a protection argument is that it can protect caregivers from good wages! (See Nelson, 1999; Folbre and Nelson, 2000; Nelson and England, 2002; Nelson, 2006b.) More implications of such dualistic thinking about care and markets will be explored below.

The issue of the care penalty is, however, not the only interesting issue in the economics of paid care. It seems, for example, in the United States now that the main pressing issue facing Registered Nurses (that is, nurses with at least two to four years of specialized education) is not so much about pay, as about working conditions. The numbers of patients per hospital nurse has risen, while the job has become 'Taylorized' through the increasing use of technology and the assignment of tasks to lower-paid aides and assistants. This has reached a point where many nurses no longer feel able to provide the sort of person-to-person care that they believe patients need, and that they went into nursing to provide (Buresh and Gordon, 2000).

Another aspect of paid caring labor that has received considerable attention among some social scientists is what has been called the 'global care chain' (Hochschild, 2000). When women in rich countries are under pressure to be ideal workers, one possible response is for them to hire women from poor countries as nannies and housecleaners. This system only works, of course, to the extent that the wages of the hired domestic workers are low relative to wages for rich-country natives. Many writers in this literature not only decry the inequality that this system exploits, but also emphasize and even dramatize the fact that some nannies have to leave their own children back home (Hochschild, 2002). Portraying this as traumatic for all concerned, the global care chain is considered to be the result of a 'vast and tragic global politics' (Ehrenreich and Hochschild, 2002, p. 12). While I would not want to downplay the hardships of poverty and economically motivated migration, I find much of this literature to be a bit over-wrought, with its narrow focus and unrelenting negative portrayal of migrant care work.

It is not clear that leaving one's children behind in order to take care of someone else's children should be so much more appalling than leaving one's children behind in order to cut up chickens – or do any of the other (usually more unpleasant than childcare) jobs often taken up by immigrants. Yet the larger issues about migration of *all* workers do not seem to be as much discussed. There also seems to me to be a flavor of moral condemnation surrounding discussions of both the migrant care workers who leave their children and of those who hire them, which may more reflect the writers' biases and feelings of guilt than the actual feelings, motivations, and contexts of the women involved. Certainly, there is much to be done in making the world more just toward women (and men), both within countries and across, but it is not clear to me that the hand-wringing tone and rather simplistic economics of care chain analysis moves this project ahead.

Care Ethics

While economists and sociologists have been intent on studying the tasks and economic relations involved in care work, psychologists, educators, and moral philosophers have focused on the motivations for it, and in particular, on what has come to be called the ethic of care. The idea of a care orientation toward ethics originated in the work of psychologist Carol Gilligan (1982, p. 56), who noticed that a number of subjects in her study of moral development seemed to speak in 'a different voice' than that recognized in prevailing 'ethic of justice' theories. A care orientation, Gilligan suggested, prioritizes empathy, the preservation of particular authentic relationships, and responsiveness to needs, in contrast to the rationality, universal principles, and the adjudication of rights among individuals prominent in the ethic of justice. The notion of care ethics was further developed by a large number of gender scholars in philosophy, political philosophy, and other fields (Noddings, 1984; Tronto, 1994; Held, 1995; Sevenhuijsen, 1998), and continues as a vibrant field today (for example, Lynch et al., 2009).

Care ethics is sometimes even referred to as 'the feminine' or 'the feminist' approach to ethics. Later research, however, indicated that both care and justice orientations are called upon by both women and men, in a variety of mixtures and degrees, and in various cultures and contexts (Jaffee and Hyde, 2000). The question of what is – and is not – feminist about care ethics is also a topic of lively debate (Borgerson, 2007; Tong and Williams, 2009). To the extent that care ethics is associated only with women, it tends to reinforce the idea of women as being more naturally suited for caring work – and thereby lets men off the hook. To the extent that it is often applied primarily to private, familial, and face-to-face interactions, it fails to challenge classic liberal (and economic man) understandings of larger social, political, economic realms. Thinking, instead, of caring as a *human* capacity that can be developed in broader realms, however, can lead to some perhaps startling – and perhaps deeply liberating – fresh views of our economic life.

III 'CARING LABOR' AS AN ECONOMY-WIDE NECESSITY

It is tempting to study care work, in the sense of face-to-face intimate care for individuals, in isolation, and emphasize its *differences* from other kinds of work – such as in carpentry, marketing, information technology, or business management. What I would like to suggest, instead, is that in our contemporary global and densely interconnected world, in which the actions of each of us impact others, *all* work involves, in an even larger sense of 'care', caring responsibilities. All work, to be done properly and in the service of not only ourselves but also the common good, requires a sensitivity to interdependence and the expression of our compassion. That we do not recognize this, and in fact often may do our other sorts of work in ways that are directly *harmful* rather than caring, is not due to some fundamental differences in the natures of the economic, familial, and public spheres. Rather, it is due to our currently abominably low ethical standards for economic behavior. Where did these standards come from?

Orthodox economics preaches that markets and business firms are spheres in which people are rational, self-interested, and autonomous. Rational consumers buy the goods that maximize their utility, rational workers try to get the highest wage for the lowest effort, and rational firms single-mindedly maximize profits. Yet not even orthodox economists believe that people are so thoroughly monomaniacal: the man assumed to be self-interested in his market dealings is assumed, by notable conservative University of Chicago School economists, to turn into an 'altruist' in the home (Nelson 1996, ch. 5). More progressive economists see that there is a role for caring in issues related to economics, but assign concern for well-being or the environment to the government. The marketplace, it seems, is the one area of social behavior in which no one expects caring to occur.

Where did this idea come from? In previous work, I have traced its roots to an exaggeration of eighteenth century philosopher Adam Smith's notion of the economy as a machine (Nelson, 2006b); to embellishments of John Stuart Mill's early nineteenth century suggestion that, to be a science, economics must assume self-interest and rationality (Nelson 2011a, 2011b); to Victorian notions of the hard-driving industrial breadwinner versus the 'angel in the house' (Nelson, 1999); and to developments throughout the history of science and economics that have prioritized masculine-stereotyped traits and concerns over feminine-associated ones, due to a misunderstanding about the nature of objectivity (Nelson, 1996). These divisions are illustrated in Table 5.1.

Rather than identify these dualisms as reflecting something at the core of masculine and feminine natures, I see them as being at the very heart of virulent sexism. At one level, sexism stereotypes men and women, discouraging men from developing their caring and interdependent sides, and discouraging women from developing their individuality and reason. At another level, these dualisms are also hierarchical: in modern western societies, high status and real political and economic power are given to masculine concerns,

Table 5.1   Conventional economic analysis

Economics	*Not* economics
Market	Home
Mind	Body
Reason	Emotion
Autonomy	Interdependence
Self-interest	Care and compassion
Knowledge	Virtue
Masculine	*Feminine*

while feminine ones are considered soft, of secondary concern, and often assumed to be invisibly self-maintaining – a convenient belief for denying care activities a healthy share of resources.

As a result of such dualistic habits of thought, thinking about care in market and economic relations is not only neglected, it is actively discouraged. Thinkers on the political right, who believe in so-called free markets, say that care is *unnecessary* in economic dealings since the market will solve all problems. Thinkers on the political left, who deplore global capitalism, say that care is *impossible* in economic dealings since the driving force of commerce is greed. Both sides appeal to what they believe are 'the facts' of economics and law to support their points.

But what if they are wrong? There is, in fact, plenteous evidence that the idea that economies are *intrinsically* uncaring is wildly off the mark. The biased nature of this belief can be examined at three organizational levels: the level of human individuals, the level of businesses, and the level of markets.

Workers and Managers Are Social Beings

Starting with the simplest organizational unit – the human individual – there is, in fact, considerable empirical evidence that people do not leave their feelings, values, ethics, sociality, and search for meaning behind when they enter commercial life. The vast literature on the psychology of employee motivation, for example, shows that people are complex social animals, even when at work (Herzberg, 1987; Fehr and Falk, 2002). Research on motivation finds that people are generally motivated by a mix of intrinsic rewards (such as enjoyment or a feeling of contributing to something worthwhile) and extrinsic rewards (such as money or status) (Ryan and Deci, 2000). Phenomena of care, including caring about one's coworkers or customers, caring about the quality of the product or service one provides, or caring about the impact of one's business on the world, are endemic to well-run businesses – as well as often missing in poorly run ones (Kusnet, 2008). Caring, as well as other kinds of 'emotional labor', are demanded by many kinds of jobs, not just those held by women (Steinberg and Figart, 1999). Of course, other human motivations besides caring – including a desire for dominance, for example – show up in the workplace as well. But the point here is that the unemotional, a-social employee who gets only disutility from expending effort at work, and utility from pay, is a fiction invented by economists.

While business leaders are assumed to care only about profits, this is not necessarily the case. For example, David Packard (of Hewlett-Packard) once said, 'Profit
. . . is not the proper end and aim of management – it is what makes all of the proper
ends and aims possible', with the proper aim being to 'make a contribution to society'
(Collins and Porras, 1994, p.56). Surveys of business leaders suggest that shareholders
are often only one of many constituencies considered in decision-making (along with
workers, communities, suppliers, creditors, and so on).[3] Some executives, of course,
have bought into pure bottom-line, money-oriented, short-term thinking – but is this a
necessity determined by the nature of commerce, or a self-fulfilling prophecy brought
about by the widespread influence of orthodox economic theory? I argue that it is the
latter.

Businesses Are Social Entities

Now, even if one grants that an *individual* businessperson can care about the social
good, it may be argued that the *structure* of businesses will either extinguish that impulse
(perhaps by causing that person to be fired for poor profit-making performance) or
make it ineffective (through procedural or groupthink factors) – because, of course,
firms *must* maximize profits.

University of Chicago School of Economics professor Milton Friedman famously
said that the only duty of corporate officials is to 'make as much money as possible'
for their shareholders (Friedman, 1970). But this is just so much conservative ideology.
Many people falsely believe that profit maximization is mandated by law. But an actual
examination of the relevant legal codes and case law shows that this is not so. In fact,
rather than Friedman's view reflecting a given reality, the popularity of Chicago School
thinking is perversely shaping reality, by shaping our beliefs about what firms are and
can do (Nelson, 2006b, 2011b; Bratton, 2011).

If firms are not single-minded profit-maximizing machines, what are they? Firms are
complexly structured social organizations. A firm is not made up of one individual, with
one goal. Rather, it is made up of executives, managers, and workers engaged in a joint
activity, embedded in relationships with suppliers, customers, shareholders, creditors,
communities, governments, the natural environment, and so on. The fields of business
management, organizational behavior, and economic sociology would have far less work
to do, of course, if businesses were as simple as conventional economics assumes them
to be.

There are many reasons to believe, right now, that many businesses are ethically
broken, and that substantial changes are needed in firm structure, governance, and regulation to get businesses back on track. But the reason firms are ethically broken is not
because they automatically profit maximize. They do not. Instead, the belief in economic
man and narrow goals has itself served, over time, to corrupt earlier notions of business responsibility, in a sort of self-fulfilling prophecy. The first thing that needs to be
changed is the *belief* that businesses can or should be care-free zones.

My argument here is not that businesses should care for workers, communities,
customers, or the environment in exactly the same way that, for example, a mother
cares for a young child. But there are varieties of care – varieties of attentiveness, responsibility, responsiveness, and concern for the most vulnerable – that are

appropriate for businesses, and a small but growing literature has begun to explore these (Wicks et al., 1994; Solomon, 1997; Eisler, 2008; Engster, 2011; Koehn, 2011; Nelson, 2011d; Palmer and Stoll, 2011; Puka, 2011). Since care on a corporate level requires more than just good intentions on the part of some individuals, investigation is also needed into how internal structures such as lines of communication and responsibility, as well as external pressures such as laws and regulation, can best be structured to support ethical decision-making and care in the business world (Paine, 2002; Stout, 2011).

Of course, it may be granted that individual *people* and individual *firms* may be essentially human and social, but then argued that *the market* is the ultimate impersonal, uncaring mechanism.

Markets Are Social Institutions

Don't the forces of market competition demand that firms squeeze out every last penny of profit, or they will go out of business? Doesn't market competition, in itself, reinforce dog-eat-dog competition, values of greed and self-interest, and a race to the bottom on social and environmental protections? There are two flaws in this argument.

First, markets are not, in fact, nearly as competitive as portrayed in the abstract, mechanical model of orthodox economics. Walmart, ExxonMobil, IBM, Verizon, Microsoft, and the like are hardly the sort of anonymous, powerless companies that populate the neoclassical theory of perfect competition. Since many businesses are not on a razor's edge of competition, their decisions can be made with some discretion. This opens the possibility of realizing that business practices are complex and laden with ethical possibilities and ramifications.

Second, the idea that markets are somehow mechanical also assumes that the market somehow exists itself, separable from society and government, and separable from more cooperative social values such as trust and cooperation. Considered from a different point of view, market interactions can be seen to be *entirely dependent* on values of trust and cooperation, systems of social mores, and government laws and regulations. In order for a trade to take place, for example, the trading partners have to trust each other – that is, trust that the items being exchanged have the value that is claimed for them. This requires ethical norms of honesty, backed up by social institutions such as business reputations, ratings bureaus, government regulations concerning disclosure or product quality, and the courts. Market exchange also requires a physical environment that is not unduly polluted or depleted, again requiring coordinated social and political action. Insufficient care for children, for the poor, for people's health, for the environment – all create long-term deficits that impede, not aid, healthy commercial functioning (Nelson, 2006b, 2011c, 2011d).

The more honest and considerate trading partners are – the more they see their exchange as a cooperative endeavor to benefit both parties and society, rather than a selfish grab – the more smoothly markets can run. Take away a concern for appropriate care, and the result is a train wreck – as we have learned from the 2008 (and ongoing) financial crisis. Everyone from mortgage brokers to lending institutions to rating agencies followed the neoclassical advice to relentlessly pursue self-interest, and the result was not market bliss, but market disaster.

Economies Are Part of Society

Since people do not leave their caring capacities at the door, firms rely on cooperative relations, and markets require environments of trust, phenomena of care are *not* irrelevant to the economic life, in its broadest sense. A small but dynamic literature is now growing up around the social dimensions of economies (Nelson and England, 2002; Williams and Zelizer, 2005; Nelson, 2006a, 2006b, 2011a, 2011d; Healy and Fourcade, 2007; Zelizer, 2011).

To be very clear, I am not taking a 'Pollyanna' stance toward corporations and markets. I do not deny that a great number of horrendously uncaring things have been done in the name of profits. What *does* need to be discredited is the false belief that there is something intrinsic in the economic or legal structure of commerce that forces firms, inexorably, as if run on rails, to neglect values of care and concern in order to strive for every last dollar of profits. This widespread belief detracts from human and ecological welfare, for two reasons. First, it lets shareholders, directors, and managers of corporations morally off the hook for the social and environmental consequences of business decisions. Second, it puts the entire burden for caring behavior onto nonbusiness entities, such as government, nonprofits, and families. But such organizations may be (and too often are) overwhelmed, lack resources, or – romanticized images aside – themselves problematic (for example, corrupt, mismanaged, or abusive). If we are seriously interested in making economies that serve human life and life on the planet, we cannot afford to buy into stale, dualistic, and sexism-biased beliefs about the existence of an inherently care-free economic realm.

IV   CONCLUSION

Despite the huge role played by caring activities and caring motivations in provisioning for the survival and flourishing of life, the phenomenon of care has been neglected by conventional economic analysis. Women's traditional work caring for the most vulnerable in society has traditionally been considered 'not economic'. Moreover, a masculinist-biased view of economics has caused aspects of relationality and care present in business and marketplace relationships to be denied and suppressed. Economic life is not what Milton Friedman or any other expert economist tells you it is: economic life is what you live every day, and care is a good part of what allows you to live it.

NOTES

1. The distinctions between care as an activity and care as a motivation have been discussed by, among others, Kari Waerness (1984), Joan Tronto (1987), Susan Himmelweit (1996), and Nancy Folbre and Thomas Weisskopf (1998).
2. Unpaid work within the household is of course also 'work', but I follow the tradition in the literature here of using 'work' in this context to refer to paid employment.
3. Jay W. Lorsch and Elizabeth Maciver, *Pawns or Potentates* (1989) as cited in D. Gordon Smith (1998, p.291). See also the discussion in Sen (1983).

REFERENCES

Adams, Valerie and Julie A. Nelson (2009), 'The economics of nursing: articulating care', *Feminist Economics*, **15**(4), 3–29.

Albelda, Randy, Robert W. Drago and Steven Shulman (2001), *Unlevel Playing Fields: Understanding Wage Inequality and Discrimination*, Bosto, MA: Dollars & Sense.

Bergmann, Barbara (1986), *The Economic Emergence of Women*, New York: Basic Books.

Bettio, Francesca and Janneke Plantenga (2004), 'Comparing care regimes in Europe', *Feminist Economics*, **10**(1), 85–113.

Borgerson, Janet L. (2007), 'On the harmony of feminist ethics and business ethics', *Business and Society Review*, **112**(4), 477–509.

Bratton, William W. (2011), 'At the conjunction of love and money: comment on Julie A. Nelson, does profit-seeking rule out love? Evidence (or not) from economics and law', *Washington University Journal of Law and Policy*, **35**, 109–15.

Budlender, Debbie (2008), 'The statistical evidence on care and non-care work across six countries', Gender and Development Programme Paper 4, United Nations Research Institute for Social Development, Geneva.

Budlender, Debbie (ed.) (2010), *Time Use Studies and Unpaid Care Work*, London: Routledge.

Buresh, Bernice and Suzanne Gordon (2000), *From Silence to Voice: What Nurses Know and Must Communicate to the Public*, Ottawa: Canadian Nurses Association.

Collins, James C. and Jerry I. Porras (1994), *Built to Last*, New York: Harper Business.

Ehrenreich, Barbara and Arlie Russell Hochschild (eds) (2002), *Global Woman: Nannies, Maids and Sex Workers in the New Economy*, New York: Metropolitan Books.

Eisler, Riane (2008), *The Real Wealth of Nations: Creating a Caring Economics*, San Francisco, CA: Berrett-Koehler.

England, Paula (2005), 'Emerging theories of care work', *Annual Review of Sociology*, **31**, 381–99.

England, Paula and Nancy Folbre (1999), 'The cost of caring', *Annals of the American Academy of Political and Social Science*, **561**, 39–51.

England, Paula and Nancy Folbre (2003), 'Contracting for care', in Marianne A. Ferber and Julie A. Nelson (eds), *Feminist Economics Today*, Chicago, IL: University of Chicago Press, pp. 61–79.

England, Paula, Michelle Budig and Nancy Folbre (2002), 'Wages of virtue: the relative pay of care work', *Social Problems*, **49**(4), 455–73.

Engster, Daniel (2011), 'Care ethics and stakeholder theory', in Maurice Hamington and Maureen Sander-Staudt (eds), *Applying Care Ethics to Business*, Dordrecht: Springer, pp. 93–110.

Fehr, Ernst and Armin Falk (2002), 'Psychological foundations of incentives', *European Economic Review*, **46**(4–5), 687–724.

Folbre, Nancy (2001), *The Invisible Heart: Economics and Family Values*, New York: New Press.

Folbre, Nancy and Julie A. Nelson (2000), 'For love or money – or both?', *Journal of Economic Perspectives*, **14**(4), 123–40.

Folbre, Nancy and Julie A. Nelson (2006), 'Why a well-paid nurse is a better nurse', *Nursing Economics*, **24**(3), 127–30.

Folbre, Nancy and Thomas Weisskopf (1998), 'Did father know best? Families, markets, and the supply of caring labor', in Avner Ben-Ner and Louis G. Putterman (eds), *Economics, Values, and Organization*, Cambridge: Cambridge University Press, pp. 171–205.

Friedman, Milton (1970), 'The social responsibility of business is to increase its profits', *New York Times*, September 13.

Gardiner, Jean (1997), *Gender, Care, and Economics*, New York: Macmillan.

Gilligan, Carol (1982), *In a Different Voice: Psychological Theory and Women's Development*, Cambridge, MA: Harvard University Press.

Graber, Lena and John Miller (2002), 'Wages for housework: the movement and the numbers', *Dollars & Sense*, September–October, 45–46.

Healy, Kieran and Marion Fourcade (2007), 'Moral views of market society', *Annual Review of Sociology*, **33**, 285–311.

Held, Virginia (ed.) (1995), *Justice and Care: Essential Readings in Feminist Ethics*, Boulder, CO: Westview.

Herzberg, Frederick (1987), 'One more time: how do you motivate employees?', *Harvard Business Review*, September–October, 109–20.

Himmelweit, Susan (1995), 'The discovery of "unpaid work": the social consequences of the expansion of "work"', *Feminist Economics*, **1**(2), 1–19.

Himmelweit, Susan (1996), 'Conceptualising caring', paper presented at the International Association for Feminist Economics Conference, Washington, DC, July.

Himmelweit, Susan (1999), 'Caring labor', *Annals of the American Academy of Political and Social Science*, **561**(January), 27–38.

Himmelweit, Susan (2007), 'The prospects for caring: economic theory and policy analysis', *Cambridge Journal of Economics*, **31**(4), 581–599.

Hochschild, Arlie (2000), 'The nanny chain', *The American Prospect*, **11**(4), January 3, 32–6.

Hochschild, Arlie Russell (2002), 'Love and gold', in Barbara Ehrenreich and Arlie Russell Hochschild (eds), *Global Woman: Nannies, Maids and Sex Workers in the New Economy*, New York: Henry Holt & Company, pp. 15–30.

Ironmonger, Duncan (1996), 'Counting outputs, capital inputs and caring labor: estimating gross household product', *Feminist Economics*, **2**(3), 37–64.

Jaffee, Sara and Janet Shibley Hyde (2000), 'Gender differences in moral orientation: a meta-analysis', *Psychological Bulletin*, **126**(5), 703–26.

Koehn, Daryl (2011), 'Care ethics and unintended consequences', in Maurice Hamington and Maureen Sander-Staudt (eds), *Applying Care Ethics to Business*, Dordrecht: Springer, pp. 141–53.

Kusnet, David (2008), *Love the Work, Hate the Job: Why America's Best Workers Are More Unhappy than Ever*, Hoboken, NJ: John Wiley & Sons.

Lynch, Kathleen, John Baker and Maureen Lyons (2009), *Affective Equality: Love, Care and Injustice*, New York: Palgrave Macmillan.

Macdonald, Cameron Lynne and David A. Merrill (2002), '"It shouldn't have to be a trade": recognition and redistribution in care work advocacy', *Hypatia*, **17**(2), 67–83.

Meagher, Gabrielle (2002), 'Making care visible: performance measurement in welfare services', UnitingCare Burnside Discussion Paper No. 2, Sydney.

Nelson, Julie A. (1996), *Feminism, Objectivity and Economics*, London: Routledge.

Nelson, Julie A. (1999), 'Of markets or martyrs: is it OK to pay well for care?', *Feminist Economics*, **5**(3), 43–60.

Nelson, Julie A. (2006a), 'Can we talk? Feminist economists in dialogue with social theorists', *Signs: Journal of Women in Culture and Society*, **31**(4), 1052–74.

Nelson, Julie A. (2006b), *Economics for Humans*, Chicago, IL: University of Chicago Press.

Nelson, Julie A. (2009), 'A response to Bruni and Sugden', *Economics and Philosophy*, **25**(2), 187–93.

Nelson, Julie A. (2011a), 'Care ethics and markets: a view from feminist economics', in Maurice Hamington and Maureen Sander-Staudt (eds), *Applying Care Ethics to Business*, Dordrecht: Springer, pp. 35–53.

Nelson, Julie A. (2011b), 'Does profit-seeking rule out love? Evidence (or not) from economics and law', *Washington University Journal of Law and Policy*, **35**, 69–107.

Nelson, Julie A. (2011c), 'For love or money: current issues in the economics of care', *Journal of Gender Studies (Ochanomizu University)*, **14**(March), 1–19.

Nelson, Julie A. (2011d), 'The relational economy', in Laszlo Zsolnai (ed.), *Ethical Principles and Economic Transformation: A Buddhist Approach*, Dordrecht: Springer, pp. 21–33.

Nelson, Julie A. and Paula England (2002), 'Feminist philosophies of love and work', *Hypatia*, **17**(2), 1–18.

Noddings, Nel (1984), *Caring: A Feminine Approach to Ethics and Moral Education*, Berkeley, CA: University of California Press.

Paine, Lynn Sharp (2002), *Value Shift*, New York: McGraw-Hill.

Palmer, Daniel E. and Mary Lyn Stoll (2011), 'Moving toward a more caring stakeholder theory: global business ethics in dialogue with the feminist ethics of care', in Maurice Hamington and Maureen Sander-Staudt (eds), *Applying Care Ethics to Business*, Dordrecht: Springer, pp. 111–25.

Puka, Bill (2011), 'Taking care of business: caring in competitive corporate structures', in Maurice Hamington and Maureen Sander-Staudt (eds), *Applying Care Ethics to Business*, Dordrecht: Springer, pp. 175–99.

Ryan, Richard M. and Edward L. Deci (2000), 'Intrinsic and extrinsic motivations: classic definitions and new directions', *Contemporary Educational Psychology*, **25**, 54–67.

Sen, Amartya (1983), 'The profit motive', *Lloyds Bank Review*, (147), 1–20.

Sevenhuijsen, Selma (1998), *Citizenship and the Ethics of Care*, New York and London: Routledge.

Smith, D. Gordon (1998), 'The shareholder primacy norm', *Journal of Corporate Law*, **23**, 277–323.

Solomon, Robert C. (1997), 'Competition, care, and compassion: toward a nonchauvinist view of the corporation', in Andrea Larson and R. Edward Freeman (eds), *Women's Studies and Business Ethics: Toward a New Conversation*, New York: Oxford University Press, pp. 144–73.

Steinberg, Ronnie J. and Deborah M. Figart (1999), 'Emotional demands at work: a job content analysis', *Annals of the American Academy of Political and Social Science*, **561**, 177–91.

Stout, Lynn A. (2011), *Cultivating Conscience: How Good Laws Make Good People*, Princeton, NJ: Princeton University Press.

Swartz, Teresa Toguchi (2004), 'Mothering for the state', *Gender & Society*, **18**(5), 567–87.

Tong, Rosemarie and Nancy Williams (2009), 'Feminist ethics', in Edward N. Zalta (ed.), *Stanford Encyclopedia of Philosophy*, available at: http://plato.stanford.edu/archives/fall2009/entries/feminism-ethics/ (accessed September 29, 2012).

Tronto, Joan (1987), 'Beyond gender difference to a theory of care', *Signs: Journal of Women in Culture and Society*, **12**(4), 644–63.

Tronto, Joan (1994), *Moral Boundaries: A Political Argument for an Ethic of Care*, New York: Routledge.

US Bureau of Labor Statistics (2009), 'Occupational employment and wages, May 2009', Washington, DC: US Department of Labor: Tables 39–9011 and 53–6021.

US Bureau of Labor Statistics (2010), 'Women in the labor force: a databook (2010 edition)', Washington, DC: US Department of Labor: Table 11.

Waerness, Kari (1984), 'Caring as women's work in the welfare state', in Harriet Holter (ed.), *Patriarchy in a Welfare Society*, Oslo: Universitetsforlaget, pp. 67–87.

Wagman, Barnet and Nancy Folbre (1996), 'Household services and economic growth in the U.S., 1870–1930', *Feminist Economics*, **2**(1), 43–66.

Waring, Marilyn (1988), *If Women Counted: A New Feminist Economics*, San Francisco, CA: Harper & Row.

Wicks, Andrew C., Daniel R. Gilbert Jr. and R. Edward Freeman (1994), 'A feminist reinterpretation of the stakeholder concept', *Business Ethics Quarterly*, **4**(4), 475–97.

Williams, Joan C. (2001), *Unbending Gender: Why Family and Work Conflict and What to Do About It*, New York: Oxford University Press.

Williams, Joan C. and Viviana A. Zelizer (2005), 'To commodify or not to commodify: that is not the question', in Martha M. Ertman and Joan C. Williams (eds), *Rethinking Commodification: Cases and Readings in Law and Culture*, New York: New York University Press, pp. 362–82.

Zelizer, Viviana A. (2011), *Economic Lives: How Culture Shapes the Economy*, Princeton, NJ: Princeton University Press.

6. Teaching and learning for economic life
Zohreh Emami

I INTRODUCTION TO LEARNING AND ECONOMIC DEVELOPMENT

Feminist social economists have long recognized the interconnection between the teaching of the discipline and the goals of reformulating assumptions and transforming knowledge necessary for achieving ethical and fair development and progress in economic life. Seeing knowledge, including its categories of race and gender, as socially constructed, for feminist economists the practices of teaching and the knowledge content of the discipline are integrally related. As teacher-scholars participating in the production, dissemination, and institutionalization of knowledge, we have acknowledged the contradictions involved in coupling emancipatory feminist research with traditional hierarchical teaching practices. For feminists these practices reinforce inequalities based on biased and disempowering values, assumptions, categories, and institutional arrangements and are therefore anathema to the underlying values of fairness, equality, and dignity (see Ferber and Nelson, 1993; Bartlett, 1997; Aerni et al., 1999; Peterson and Lewis, 1999; Strassmann, 1999; Aerni and McGoldrick, 2002; Mutari and Figart, 2003; Barker and Feiner, 2004).

The assumption that social economic development and progress are more than the growth of gross domestic product or rise of personal incomes or industrialization or technological advance is the foundation of my thinking in this chapter. Supporting Nobel laureate in economics Amartya Sen, I see development as a process of expanding the reach of substantive freedoms that people enjoy in the context of social and economic arrangements and institutions including families, communities, for-profit, not-for-profit and nonprofit organizations, and governments. The focus of development here is the expansion of 'capabilities' individuals have in order to lead the kinds of lives they value. This approach therefore shifts attention from an exclusive focus on income poverty (without denying its importance in understanding deprivation) toward capability deprivation, thus providing a broader and more inclusive informational base for understanding deprivation and development in human lives and how systemic inequalities are sustained and can be addressed (see Sen, 1999).

Social economic development thus is a dynamic relationship between the extent to which institutional contexts enhance capabilities and the impact of individual capabilities on changing institutional policies and practices. The two-way relationship between the impact of social institutional cultures and practices on individual freedoms on the one hand, and the potential of individuals to create more appropriate and effective social arrangements on the other, makes the issue of participation and voice central to the reach and impact of development. Development then depends on individuals' ability to participate in economic, social, political, community, cultural, and educational conversations and activities in current institutional contexts and to help initiate change and create future ones. Participatory freedom in turn depends in part on how learning and by implication teaching in service of these goals are understood and practiced.

Two approaches to teaching and learning are contrasted in this chapter. In terms of their impact on sustaining inequalities, bell hooks compares these two approaches as 'the difference between education as the practice of freedom and education that merely strives to reinforce domination' (hooks, 1994, p. 4). The conventional approach (in the United States) sees learning as the acquisition of knowledge and information and teaching as the delivery of these. Teaching as delivery is built, if only implicitly, on a strict distinction between research/scholarship versus teaching, content versus pedagogy, and thus theory versus practice. With its focus on the teacher as the source of knowledge, this approach treats the individual learner as a passive recipient of received knowledge. In economics, this approach entails presenting economics as a 'way of knowing', often a-historically, and as if there are no controversies or debates regarding its ethical commitments, relevance, and usefulness to economic lives (Aerni et al., 1999; Nelson, 2006).[1]

For the alternative approach, learning is a dynamic developmental process of integration of knowledge and the necessary abilities to participate actively in composing a life and building communities one has reason to value. In this second approach, teaching involves rejecting as false the dichotomy between theory and practice, knowing and action, and curriculum and pedagogy. Moreover, this approach recognizes multiple modes of knowing and intelligence, the social character of learning, and the significance of collaboration in the acquisition, diffusion and application of knowledge about the real world. Feminists have long acknowledged the necessity of sharing ideas, engaging in conversations that cross boundaries, and creating spaces where assumptions are questioned and challenged for creating social economic progress. It is in the spirit of multidisciplinary collaboration that I will explore the intersection of feminist scholarship and research in neuroscience, cognitive science, and organizational behavior. I believe that scientific research on individual and social learning provides strong support for feminist economists' call for an inclusive economics that recognizes the impact of race and gender as social economic constructs with significant implications for economic life and individuals' capability to function and lead the life they have reason to value.

Below I draw on neuroscience, especially the work of John Bransford, Ann Brown and Rodney Cocking for the National Research Council (Bransford et al., 2000), which synthesizes the outpouring of research in recent decades in neuroscience and cognitive science on how people learn and the implications of this research for teaching (Section II–IV). I then explore research by organizational behavior theorists Anne Baker, Patricia Jensen and David Kolb on conversational learning and its implications for teaching (Section V). The objective is to bring women's lived experiences from the periphery to the center of disciplines, recognize the problematic character of the claims to universality of white, western, masculine knowledge and rationality, and reject the privileging of abstract rationality over other forms of knowing (Nelson, 1993; Grapard, 1995; Barker and Kuiper, 2003). Section VI concludes.

II LEARNING ABOUT LEARNING FROM NEUROSCIENCE

Neuroscientists have explored the relationship between learning and changes in the physical structure and functional organization of the brain. They have shown that the human brain has a relatively small proportion of its synaptic wiring at birth and that it adds two-thirds of its synapses after birth. More specifically, the brain goes through two stages of addition of synaptic connections. First, during the early period of development after birth, synapses are overproduced and then selectively lost. The second stage, however, takes place throughout the life span, is in fact more important later in life, and is primarily driven by experience. It is at this second stage of brain development where the significance of learning is strongly evident at the cellular level. More specifically, research evidence from multiple animal studies demonstrates that learning through direct experiential contact (for example, hands-on exposure to a variety of problem-solving tasks and opportunities for exploration) as well as interaction in social groups lead to the creation of 20–25 percent more new synapses, fewer errors when starting an activity, and faster learning from mistakes. In short, neuroscientists have shown that the brain is a dynamic organ that is shaped, organized, and reorganized to a great extent by learning not just at the early stages of life but throughout life (Bransford et al., 2000; Willis, 2006; Doidge, 2007).

There are two broad implications that can be drawn from the research in neuroscience. First, the common wisdom that the brain anatomy is fixed, 'hardwired', and permanent, and that after childhood the brain changes only by going through the long process of decline has been debunked. It is this static understanding of the brain that is at the root of often sexist and racist explanations for what people can and cannot learn and beliefs that certain people have fundamental limitations in certain areas – for example, that women are not good in learning math and science. In fact, neuroscience has shown that the brain is changeable and malleable, that it has plasticity, and that the structure and the function of the brain changes through thought, learning, and activity. Second, given the dynamic potential of the brain and the place of learning and experience in reaching this potential, and since educational institutions at every level today fail most notably in helping disadvantaged populations reach their potential, understanding the nature of how people learn can have significant policy implications and equalizing effects on societies' responses to systemic inequalities.

III LEARNING ABOUT LEARNING FROM COGNITIVE SCIENCE

For our purposes, systematic studies of the human mind by cognitive scientists are especially relevant. Cognitive science emerged in the late 1950s attempting to avoid the crude Behaviorism (with a big B) of the early twentieth century with its emphasis on the relationship between stimuli and response. Recognizing the complexity of the human mind, cognitive scientists approach learning from a multidisciplinary perspective integrating learning from several branches of psychology, anthropology, philosophy, linguistics, computer science, and neuroscience. Using experimental tools and qualitative research methodologies, cognitive scientists have reached three major and interrelated conclusions regarding how people learn (Bransford et al., 2000; Schwartz and Begley, 2002).

First is the importance of *prior learning*. Cognitive scientists have argued that even from infancy, humans bring a point of view to learning and that therefore humans construct new understanding and knowledge based on what they already know and believe. The personal meanings created through prior learning experiences are more likely to be stored in long-term memory and affect individuals' ability to retrieve information later. Second, in order to understand the extent and impact of learning, it is especially important to understand the kind of learning experiences that lead to the ability to extend and *transfer* what has been learned in one context to other contexts. Transfer is more likely to occur through practice, repetition, and continued engagement with the material. Third, people learn better when they are self-reflective and have *awareness* of themselves as learners. It is in this context that the role of such things as emotions, physical need, space, and self-made choice make a difference in how people learn (Bransford et al., 2000; Schwartz and Begley, 2002; Willis, 2006). It is through the interplay between prior learning, possibilities for transfer of learning, and awareness of self that cognitive scientists have demonstrated the significance of social and cultural contexts for learning, thus confirming the significance of the social construction of categories of identity that have been a significant foundation of feminist thought.

IV   TEACHING LESSONS FROM COGNITIVE SCIENCES

In this section, I explore the implications of the significance of prior learning, transfer, and self-awareness for teaching in general and teaching economics in particular. The impact of prior learning on how people learn can surface in at least three different ways (Bransford et al., 2000) that have a number of implications for teaching about economic life. First, learners might have knowledge relevant to a particular learning context that might not be activated in a learning environment unless intentionally elicited. Tapping into and building on their existing knowledge can assist learners in developing a voice as well as a more coherent and thorough understanding of disciplinary content by helping them make connections that might otherwise seem unrelated (ibid.; Mentkowski, 2000; Willis, 2006; Wlodkowski, 2008).

In the economics profession, those who have been critical of the assumptions, analytical focus, policy prescriptions, and in general ethical vision of mainstream economics are the ones who have explored learning experiences that engage the students actively in understanding the economy by building on their prior learning. For example, for a symposium on teaching heterodox economics in the *Forum for Social Economics* in 2009, Daniel Leclerc, Ed Ford and E.J. Ford discuss a constructivist and cooperative learning approach through in-class learning experiments focused on poverty and inequality that builds on the student's own economic experience (Leclerc et al., 2009).

On the other hand, there are times when one's existing knowledge is in fact misleading and/or mistaken, thus making it difficult to learn new and different information and knowledge. In these circumstances, new ideas often seem incomprehensible to learners. But even here, making the learners' thinking visible can help find and reconceptualize misleading prior knowledge (Alverno College Faculty, 2005; see also Bransford et al.,

2000). Teaching for comprehension, analysis, and comparison of multiplicity of economic data often is a valuable strategy in breaking down inaccurate preconceptions. In circumstances in which students bring misleading or mistaken prior understanding, it is often helpful to take students outside their comfort zones through creating safe opportunities for articulation of existing knowledge, careful dialogues aimed at exploration of the assumptions and 'facts' underlying this knowledge, and directed student research and presentations of relevant data. In the example above, Leclerc et al. ask students to

> provide estimates of expenses associated with different qualitatively described living standards. They estimated the living expenses of a modest middle income family, one living at the poverty line and a family living the 'American Dream.' The students' expense estimates were then compared with actual US income distribution data. The resulting comparisons revealed that the amount of income required to support these living standards is only available to a much smaller proportion of the population than the students might have predicted. (p. 202)

The ultimate goal of students exploring varied sources and information that reveal the misconceptions they come with is that they would develop the capability to resist parochialism and learn to take multiple perspectives. Listening to the voices of those near and far and recognizing the inescapable plurality of realities and priorities is a way of scrutinizing not just what they value but what they might have 'reason' to value (Sen, 2009; Simkins and Maier, 2009).

Of particular relevance to feminists has been the significance of the prior knowledge that learners bring to formal learning contexts as a result of such factors as their race, gender, class, sexual orientation, and ethnic and cultural affiliations. Formal learning experiences can either reinforce or conflict with this kind of shared prior learning. Feminist arguments regarding the consequences of ignoring the relevance of these factors (Badgett, 1995; Bartlett, 1997; Feiner and Roberts, 1999; Hirschfield et al., 1999) are supported by research in cognitive science and learning theory (Dweck, 2006; Barnett and Rivers, 2011). More specifically, evidence has shown that evaluations of learners' success or failure and strength versus deficit are affected by lack of recognition of the significance of prior learning connected to these factors (Ginsberg and Wlodkowski, 2009). For example, feminist economists have long emphasized the ways in which mainstream economics devalues women's economic experiences in the workplace and in the family (see Badgett, 1995; Folbre, 1995; Folbre and Nelson, 2003; Strober, 2003; Adams and Nelson, 2009). The prior learning women bring to learning economics contains much knowledge that is deemed irrelevant and unconnected to what is conventionally considered the economy. Ignoring the social context of the students' prior learning hinders their further learning and is ineffective teaching.

Students of economics are often unaware of the criteria they already have for an effectively working economy. Acknowledging their prior learning by helping them explicitly articulate their own vision and criteria for the economy gives learners the opportunity to take stock of what they value, enter economic conversations from where they are, and understand economic perspectives and the foundations of their own often implicit values. Here also feminist economists have guided the way by often beginning their economic analysis with an explicit definition of the role and purpose of economics and clear elucidations of the criteria for a well-working economy. Feminist economists have defined economics as the study of provisioning, thus expanding our understanding of the economy by including the essential role of households, families, and communities in economic life (see, for example, Nelson, 1993, 2006; Barker and Feiner, 2004). Based on this definition, these economists have utilized five criteria to evaluate economic performance – fairness, improved quality of life over time, economic security, extent of waste of human and nonhuman resources, and opportunities for meaningful work (ibid.). Surprisingly, in my experience as an educator in economics, drawing from their own experiences, new students of economics often come up with a very similar list of criteria for good economic performance. Starting with the relevant knowledge they already have increases their curiosity and grounds them more effectively by helping them make connections, which they might not otherwise make automatically, between their study of and participation in economic life. An exercise engaging students in creating a vision for the economy can be done in conjunction with them creating a narrative for their own life exploring their own history, the sources of their values, and any transformations they might have gone through. Engaging learners in exploring their own histories is a step in the process of helping them become conscious of the forces that have shaped their thinking and ultimately is an opportunity to celebrate and scrutinize their inherited traditions, customs, and identities (Amott and Matthaei, 1991). Exploring their multiple identities (and conflicting loyalties and commitments these entail) makes it possible for learners to more effectively scrutinize external authority as well as their own values and to establish what David Hodge, Marcia Baxter Margola and Carolyn Haynes have called 'self-authorship', which they define as the internal authority to define their own identities and the kind of lives they aspire to construct (Hodge et al., 2009).

In terms of the significance of the ability to transfer what is learned in one context to varied contexts outside the formal learning environment, the circumstances of needed transfer of appropriate economic understanding are many, given the permeation of economic issues in so many facets of the life of families, organizations, and communities. Teaching for student transfer of economic knowledge from the classroom to debates about economics of families, local, national, and global communities therefore requires students' understanding of the theoretical perspectives underlying these debates (their analytical framework as well as their assumptions and foundational values), exploration of the relevant evidence and facts about the issues, practice in and evaluation of the varied arguments, as well as varied opportunities for students' individual voices in presentation, conversations and debate (Emami, 2005; Emami and Davis, 2009; Mallin, 2009; Schneider, 2009; Warnecke, 2009; Wheat, 2009; Wunder et al., 2009).

For effective learning to occur, cognitive scientists have not only emphasized the need for recognition and acknowledgment of prior learning and focus on transference of knowledge from the classroom to varied contexts outside the classroom; they have also stressed the significance of *reflexivity* and *self-awareness* on the part of the learner (Alverno College Faculty, 2000; Bransford et al., 2000; Willis, 2006). The ability to observe and analyze oneself as a learner is not necessarily innate, but it can be taught and learned. However, perceptive and persistent observation, accurate and at times brutally honest analysis and interpretation of patterns of emotions, thought and behavior, and exercise of imagination and planning for future learning are in fact often quite challenging. By the same token, it is often easier to teach for knowledge and the analytic and valuing abilities needed in understanding and problem-solving real-world issues than it is to help learners develop an understanding of themselves as learners. Developing a meta-cognitive understanding of where one started as a learner, how one's learning has evolved, and what dimensions of learning come naturally and which areas need work requires a level of reasoned self-scrutiny comparable to what is needed for understanding the world around us. Teaching and learning reflexivity and self-awareness depend on the context of the learning and the learner and require practice, time, and ongoing and varied conversations to make observations about the quality and application of knowledge, interpret the areas and patterns of misunderstanding, and plan for practical learning strategies to focus on.

Finally, it is important to emphasize here the relationship between teaching, learning, and assessment. Teaching is not only the design and facilitation of learning experiences that actively engage students by acknowledging who they are and fostering their sense of self, but it also involves the assessment of and providing feedback on their learning. Assessment of student learning is a multidimensional process, integral to learning, that involves observing an individual learner in action and judging her performance on the basis of explicit criteria with resulting feedback to the student (Alverno College Faculty, 1994; Gibbs, 1995; Carpenter and Bach, 2010). It is through the sharing of explicit criteria which integrate knowledge and abilities necessary for satisfactory performance that students are brought in on the expected standards of performance and develop an awareness of themselves as learners. Explicit criteria help students develop the language and the ability to observe themselves in action and to evaluate what they can and cannot do.

Assessment of student learning is not equivalent to measurement. It is rather a dynamic qualitative judgment of student performance 'through multiple, cumulative, and time-extended observations' (Rogers, 1994, p. 151; Sternberg et al., 2011). The validity of an assessment instrument is the degree to which it integrates learning goals that have relevance to who the learner is and what the learner needs to know and be able to do in the context of the world today as an individual, a professional, and a citizen. As opposed to testing, which happens after the student has finished with the required learning, assessment itself is a learning experience, a time when students have the opportunity to do something with what they know – reflect on a specific issue, collaborate with others to define and propose possible solutions to a problem, listen and think on their feet in a debate, or write a persuasive editorial to a specific audience.

Testing students' understanding of content knowledge through various methods is, of course, useful in providing the teacher information about whether the students are doing the necessary preparations, have memorized and internalized key definitions, and know and can use specific techniques and frameworks. When it comes to evaluation of learning itself, however, it is opportunities for the integration and application of knowledge, and the subsequent descriptive, prescriptive, and summative feedback that facilitates the transfer of learning outside the classroom. In other words, learning is more than knowing, it is being able to act on knowledge so that one can analyze, evaluate, scrutinize, make decisions, engage in civil discourse, and so on.

Assessments of student learning also provide the data and feedback loop which teachers need to evaluate the effectiveness of their teaching in helping students acquire and use economic knowledge in varied contexts. They can provide information on such issues as the effectiveness of specific assessment instruments in fulfilling their intended goals, students' intellectual development and preparedness, the appropriateness of the expectations, and students' understanding of the integrated criteria. Assessments can also be a significant source of feedback to faculty regarding the extent of our success in creating inclusive learning by building on the diversity of students' experiences in terms of such things as gender, ethnicity, sexual orientation, class, and nationality.

V   LEARNING IN CONVERSATION

One of the most significant contributions of feminists across the disciplines has been their powerful criticism of dualistic habits of thought – reason/emotion, fact/value, objective/subjective, universal/particular, science/humanism, distance/immersion (Nelson, 1993; Jennings, 1999; Lewis, 1999) – and the connection of these dualisms to justification and maintenance of social economic distinctions and inequalities. More specifically, feminists have shown that binary thinking produces understandings of sameness and difference that render the 'other' invisible or invariably inferior. It is my contention that the literature on conversational learning strongly confirms these feminist insights by emphasizing the need to move beyond dualistic thinking and by providing holistic and dynamic understandings of how learning can happen in conversation.

The roots of the literature on conversation as learning go back to the work of philosophers and educational reformers John Dewey (1938) and Paulo Freire (1992), among others. In this section, I will draw on learning and organizational behavior scholars Ann Baker, Patricia Jensen and David Kolb's analysis of learning through conversation, which is grounded in this literature. Baker et al. describe conversational learning as 'a learning process whereby learners construct meaning and transform experiences into knowledge through conversations' (2002, p. 51). For them, conversation leads to learning through five processes involving the interplay of opposites and contradictions that are resolved by rejecting dualistic either/or conclusions in favor of balanced both/and resolutions.

The first process is that of *knowing*, which consists of the tension between two inseparable yet distinct dimensions: apprehension or concrete knowing and comprehension or abstract knowing. Baker et al. consider concrete knowing/apprehension as 'an immediate, feeling-oriented, tacit, subjective process largely based on older regions of the human brain that serve as physiological and emotional gatekeepers that monitor the emotional dimensions of learning' (p. 55). Abstract knowing/comprehension is 'a linguistic, conceptual, interpretative process based in the relatively newer left cerebral cortex of the brain' (p. 55). Learning is the result of a complex interrelationship between these coequal processes of knowing in conversation, and as such, is more than simply an exchange of concepts; it is a sensual experience that involves the engagement of all the senses. As Baker et al. note, 'Conversation is typically thought of as speaking and listening, but . . . conversational experiences that take place in varied contexts enhance or restrict different senses and hence affect what is heard and perceived in the conversation' (p. 56).

Feminist economists have rejected exclusive reliance on abstract knowing as top down and removed from the social context of construction and exchange of knowledge. They have instead pointed to the need for a balance between intuitive and tacit knowledge on the one hand and abstract knowledge on the other. The recognition of the significance of tacit knowledge provides the needed bottom-up dimension that takes into account the actual reality of individual lives and communities. This more balanced approach uses all the relevant sources of information and knowledge rather than relying exclusively on abstract a priori analysis. Recognizing the need for a balance between tacit and abstract knowledge, KimMarie McGoldrick and Janice Peterson (2009) have developed class projects in public scholarship that involve students in collaborative processes of inquiry within their communities. These major course projects are designed around the creation of relationships and conversations between the student researchers and varied communities that debunk the privileging and primacy of abstract knowledge by intentionally acknowledging the community as a significant source of knowledge and reaffirming integration of tacit and abstract knowing in knowledge generation.

The second process of learning through conversation is that of *praxis* involving the dynamic interplay of two distinguishable yet interconnected dimensions of learning, namely, intention/reflection on the one hand and extension/action on the other. As Baker et al. (2002) put it: 'Learning is like breathing; it follows a rhythm of taking in and putting out, of incorporating ideas and experiences to find meaning and expressing that meaning in thought, speech and action' (p. 57). As humans we do not learn if our learning is only focused on either reflection or action alone. The banking concept of education, where the educator makes deposits in the empty head of the learner (who is simply the recipient of the deposit and not engaged in any form of intentional action), is neither conversation nor learning. Effective learning in conversation happens when a conversational space is created 'where the praxis between reflection and action is fully recognized' (p. 58). The assessment process, described above, is an example of the relationship between reflection and action in learning. Engagement in an authentic assessment creates the opportunity for the student to demonstrate the integration of knowledge and abilities and learn by doing/action. It also creates a safe conversational space between the teacher and the student for sharing of feedback as well as student self-reflection and self-assessment where both the cognitive and the emotional dimensions of learning are recognized and valued and the learner hears and is heard. In fact, the early Latin etymology of the verb 'to assess' is 'to sit down beside as an assistant judge', implying a conversation that happens as the judge 'sits down besides' and 'assists', in our case, the student to learn.

The third conversational dynamic is *temporal* and is represented in the connection with and tension between the discursive versus the recursive processes of learning. This interrelationship involves two temporal dimensions, namely, linear time that guides the discursive process and cyclical time that provides the rhythm of the recursive process. The discursive process is linear in that it moves from assumptions and prejudgments which frame the conversation and proceeds to naming where the implications of those assumptions are elucidated. In the recursive process, the conversation returns to the original ideas and experiences to question and further explore the framed assumptions and subsequent conclusions, and to sort through what to keep in and what to leave out. It is the simultaneous engagement of the discursive and the recursive processes that embed learning in a complex network of previous and future conversations and in many ways determine the depth and quality of learning generated.

Effective teaching therefore involves persistence in helping students understand that to the extent that conversations remain primarily within the linear discursive process, and thus simply move from assumptions and prejudgments framing the conversations to the elucidation of the implications of these, one could reasonably expect the recurrence of biased and faulty generalizations. Effective learning requires consistent balance in the engagement of both the discursive and the recursive processes where the framed assumptions and the subsequent conclusions are questioned and the stage is set for effective learning. I have found that the engagement of the discursive process requires conversational spaces where multiple perspectives are brought forth with the intention of conducting inquiry about their assumptions, values, problem definition, and so on versus advocacy and control on my part. The recursive process involves revisiting the assumptions and values through exploration of their limitations, who and what they leave out, and who and what are devalued. The recursive dimension of conversation usually involves more probing on my part to help students explore what is not being said, and often sending students out on fact-finding missions.

Fourth is the process of interaction between individuality and relationality. This is an intersubjective process of the individual maintaining a sense of self in the midst of relationships, connections, and influences of others. Feminist economists have rejected the atomistic individual conception of mainstream economic theory in favor of a balanced approach to economic conversations that provide the space for individuals to retain a sense of self in the midst of a wide array of social economic relationships (England, 1993; Nelson, 1993, 2006; Folbre, 1995; Grapard, 1995; Adams and Nelson, 2009). Rejecting the Robinson Crusoe view of the individual as ethically and empirically flawed, social economists have argued that it is only through a socially embedded conception of the individual that economic conversations create learning environments that benefit from the diversity of human experiences (Davis, 2003).

Conversational learning is a matter of the tension and balance between the possibility of individual autonomy, uniqueness, and independence on the one hand, and relatedness, reciprocity, connection, and empathy on the other. Unbalanced conversations which, for example, overemphasize individuality often only pay lip service to the significance of individuals by in fact restricting individuals' ability to retain a sense of self through the full range of their experiences and by imposing a narrow, one-size-fits-all understanding of individual motivation and behavior (Davis, 2003; see also Peterson and McGoldrick, 2009). On the other hand, conversations that assume and pre-assign specific identities to individuals deny the possibility of multiple identities, and can therefore also be restrictive. Effective learning requires that conversations balance the requirements for individuality and relationality.

In my experience as an educator, students who have gone through transformative learning experiences are those who have been allowed the opportunity to compose an identity through being heard, interacting with, listening to, and hearing others. Projects in which students interview members of their families or communities to explore personal and economic histories, for instance, can be opportunities for them to engage with the processes of individuality and relationality in conversation. These conversations, if planned through the development of questions integrating feminist insights, often help students recognize and honor caring, supportive relationships they might not have acknowledged, while also confronting idealized notions of security that suggest safety in group memberships (such as families or nations), thus seeing how for example sexist roles are often upheld in traditions through viewing domination as natural.

The fifth and final significant process for conversational learning is that of the interrelationship between status and solidarity. Baker et al. see status as 'one's positioning or ranking in the group' and solidarity as 'the extent to which one is linked interpersonally with others in a network of relationships' (p. 62). It is the interplay between this ranking and the subsequent interpersonal linking that carries on and sustains a conversation. Conversation and learning are sustained depending on the balance between status/ ranking and solidarity/linking. Status and expertise are often instrumental in initiating, leading, and learning in conversations. Without solidarity, however, through which participants link to and build on each other, conversations often lose connection and relevance by lacking multiple perspectives and diverse expertise.

The relationship between status/authority/expertise and solidarity is particularly interesting, especially when it comes to teaching women students. Imagining the world as it should be and taking action to make it happen requires leadership in initiating conversations and collaborations. Leadership in the exercise of moral imagination and for action requires learning a healthy balance between claiming and asserting the authority and status that comes with the acquisition of expertise on the one hand, and the necessary tentativeness and humility that comes with awareness and appreciation of and solidarity with others.

Baker et al. argue that when any one of the dimensions in the interplay of the above five processes dominates, conversational learning is impeded:

> Speaking without listening or listening without speaking is futile. Similarly … reflection without action turns into 'idle chatter' and activism by itself becomes action for action's sake. Discourse without recourse is brute force. … Extreme individualism – 'I touch no one and no one touches me' – can result in alienation, while total relatedness can lead to conversations that go nowhere. Totalitarian hierarchy crushes voice, while total egalitarianism might sacrifice individual uniqueness and distinctiveness. (p. 64)

VI   CONCLUSIONS

This chapter shares the view of those who define the economy broadly as the domain of social and economic arrangements, including families, market and community-based organizations, and government and nongovernmental institutions, and economics as the study of provisioning. Moreover, it considers social economic progress as the dynamic interaction between the extent to which institutional arrangements enhance individuals' capabilities to lead lives they value in varied institutional settings, on the one hand, and the ability of individuals to participate in changing current arrangements and create new ones, on the other.

Building on feminist commitments to the value of interdisciplinary collaboration, this chapter has drawn upon neuroscience's demonstration of the plasticity of the human brain and people's potential for learning throughout life to emphasize the place of teaching and learning for society's response to systemic inequalities. It has explored the intersection of feminist social economics and cognitive science's conclusions regarding the importance of prior learning, opportunities for the transfer of learning to varied contexts outside the classroom, and self-awareness for learning that lasts. It has also drawn connections between the work of experiential learning scholars in organizational behavior on the dynamics of learning in conversation and feminist insights regarding the role of static dualistic thinking in the maintenance of systems of inequality and domination.

More specifically, it has drawn on the five dynamic processes involved in conversational learning – apprehension/comprehension, reflection/action, discursive/recursive, individuality/relationality, status/solidarity – to support feminist understandings of the interaction of abstract and concrete knowing, the necessity of engaged and active learning, the need for questioning of assumptions, the relationship between autonomy and relatedness, and the balance between authority and solidarity for women's leadership.

Two general arguments have permeated this chapter. First, the scholarship of teaching benefits from and needs to intentionally build on the science of learning. As educators, developing an understanding of the nature of learning, how people learn, and what enhances and hinders learning is an important aspect of our responsibility. Second, effective teaching involves the integration of the science of learning within the context of our disciplines to ask what learners have to know and be able to do as a result of learning our discipline. As economists with the responsibility for explaining the economy, we need to show how people really learn in order for our discipline to make a contribution to the world.

Finally, it is my contention that economic conversations are powerful instruments for understanding the economic environment, constructing economic life, and creating economic progress and development. The capability that people have for participating in and influencing these conversations, therefore, provides a broader informational base for understanding economic lives and dealing with deprivation of human lives and systemic inequalities, including those that are gender based. Economists have an enormous influence in these conversations not only in terms of their scholarship, but also as teachers with responsibility for communicating economic content as well as facilitating the development of abilities required to access and enter economic conversation, debates, facts, and evidence. Conversations on and about how people teach and learn are, thus, an integral part of the extent to which systemic inequalities are practiced and maintained and the possibility of envisioning and creating economic lives of dignity.

NOTE

1. David Colander (2006) has been one of the rare exceptions among economists in his interest and scholarship on the teaching of the discipline. Colander is critical of teaching the 'economic way of thinking' that assumes people are perfectly rational and selfish. He urges economists to challenge students to re-examine their views and argues in favor of the 'common sense wisdom' approach to teaching economics. In contrast to feminist economists, however, he makes a strict distinction between content and pedagogy, claims to only deal with 'what' we teach and not 'how' we teach. He assumes that the processes of teaching are only a matter of the utilization of techniques and independent of its content and that therefore, it is possible to talk about one without the other.

REFERENCES

Adams, Valerie and Julie A. Nelson (2009), 'The economics of nursing: articulating care', *Feminist Economics*, **15**(4), 3–29.
Aerni, April Laskey and KimMarie McGoldrick (2002), *Valuing Us All: Feminist Pedagogy and Economics*, Ann Arbor, MI: Michigan University Press.
Aerni, April Laskey, Robin L. Bartlett, Margaret Lewis, KimMarie McGoldrick and Jean Shackelford (1999), 'Toward a feminist pedagogy in economics', *Feminist Economics*, **5**(1), 29–44.

Alverno College Faculty (1994), *Assessment as Learning*, Milwaukee, WI: Alverno Productions.

Alverno College Faculty (2000), *Self Assessment at Alverno College*, Milwaukee, WI: Alverno Productions.

Alverno College Faculty (2005), *Ability-Based Learning Outcomes*, Milwaukee, WI: Alverno Productions.

Amott, Teresa L. and Julie A. Matthaei (1991), *Race, Gender, and Work*, Boston, MA: South End Press.

Badgett, Lee M.V. (1995), 'Gender, sexuality, and sexual orientation: all in the feminist family', *Feminist Economics*, **1**(1), 121–41.

Baker, Anne C., Patricia Jensen and David Kolb (2002), *Conversational Learning: An Experiential Approach to Knowledge Creation*, Westport, CT and London: Quorum Books.

Barker, Drucilla K. and Susan Feiner (2004), *Liberating Economics: Feminist Perspectives on Families, Work, and Globalization*, Ann Arbor, MI: University of Michigan Press.

Barker, Drucilla K. and Edith Kuiper (eds) (2003), *Towards a Feminist Philosophy of Economics*, London and New York: Routledge.

Barnett, Rosaline and Caryl Rivers (2011), *The Truth About Girls and Boys: Challenging Toxic Stereotypes About Our Children*, New York: Columbia University Press.

Bartlett, Robin (ed.) (1997), *Introducing Race and Gender into Economics*, London and New York: Routledge.

Bransford, John D., Ann L. Brown and Rodney R. Cocking (2000), *How People Learn: Brain, Mind, Experience, and School*, Washington, DC: National Academy Press.

Carpenter, Andrew N. and Craig Bach (2010), 'Learning assessment: hyperbolic doubts versus deflated critiques', *Analytical Teaching and Philosophical Praxis*, **30**(1), 1–11.

Colander, David (2006), *The Stories Economists Tell: Essays on the Art of Teaching Economics*, New York: McGraw-Hill.

Davis, John B. (2003), *The Theory of the Individual in Economics: Identity and Value*, London and New York: Routledge.

Dewey, John (1938), *Experience and Economics*, New York: Macmillan.

Doidge, Norman (2007), *The Brain that Changes Itself*, London: Penguin.

Dweck, Carol (2006), *Mindset: The New Psychology of Success*, New York: Random House.

Emami, Zohreh (2005), 'Making economics matter to students', in Tim Riordan and James Roth (eds), *Disciplines as Frameworks for Student Learning: Teaching the Practice of the Disciplines*, Sterling, VA: Stylus, pp. 59–74.

Emami, Zohreh and John Davis (2009), 'Democracy, education and economics', *International Journal of Pluralism and Economics Education*, **1**(1/2), 37–46.

England, Paula (1993), 'The separative self: androcentric bias in neoclassical assumptions', in Ferber and Nelson (eds), pp. 37–54.

Feiner, Susan F. and Bruce B. Roberts (1999), 'Hidden by the invisible hand: neoclassical economic theory and the textbook treatment of race and gender', in April Laskey Aerni and KimMarie McGoldrick (eds), *Valuing Us All: Feminist Pedagogy and Economics*, Ann Arbor, MI: University of Michigan Press, pp. 43–66.

Ferber, Marianne A. and Julie A. Nelson (eds) (1993), *Beyond Economic Man: Feminist Theory and Economics*, Chicago, IL and London: University of Chicago Press.

Folbre, Nancy (1995), 'Holding hands at midnight: the paradox of caring labor', *Feminist Economics*, **1**(1), 73–93.

Folbre, Nancy and Julie A. Nelson (2003), 'For love or money – or both?', in Mutari and Figart (eds), pp. 108–23.

Freire, Paulo (1992), *Pedagogy of the Oppressed*, New York: Continuum.

Gibbs, Graham (1995), *Improving Student Learning through Assessment and Evaluation*, Oxford: Oxford Brookes University.

Ginsberg, Margery B. and Raymond J. Wlodkowski (2009), *Diversity and Motivation: Culturally Responsive Teaching in College*, San Francisco, CA: Jossey-Bass.

Grapard, Ulla (1995), 'Robinson Crusoe: the quintessential economic man', *Feminist Economics*, **1**(1), 33–53.

Hirschfeld, Mary, Robert L. Moore and Eleanor Brown (1999), 'Exploring the gender gap on the GRE subject test', in April Laskey Aerni and KimMarie McGoldrick (eds), *Valuing Us All: Feminist Pedagogy and Economics*, Ann Arbor, MI: University of Michigan Press, pp. 137–52.

Hodge, David C., Marcia B. Baxter and Carolyn A. Haynes (2009), 'Engaged learning: enabling self-authorship and effective practice', *Liberal Education*, **95**(4), 16–23.

hooks, bell (1994), *Teaching to Transgress: Education as the Practice of Freedom*, New York and London: Routledge.

Jennings, Ann (1999), 'Dualisms', in Peterson and Lewis (eds), pp. 142–53.

Leclerc, Daniel C., Ed Ford and E.J. Ford (2009), 'A constructivist learning approach to income inequality, poverty and the "American Dream"', *Forum for Social Economics*, **38**(2–3), 201–8.

Lewis, Margaret (1999), 'History of economic thought', in Peterson and Lewis (eds), pp. 433–42.

Mallin, Sean (2009), 'Teaching alternative approaches to the firm', *International Journal of Pluralism and Economics Education*, **1**(1/2), 87–93.

McGoldrick, KimMarie and Janice Peterson (2009), 'Public scholarship and economics: engaging students in the democratic process', *Forum for Social Economics*, **38**(2–3), 220–47.

Mentkowski, Marcia (2000), *Learning That Lasts*, San Francisco, CA: Jossey-Bass.

Mutari, Ellen and Deborah M. Figart (eds) (2003), *Women and the Economy: A Reader*, Armonk, NY: M.E. Sharpe.

Nelson, Julie A. (1993), 'The study of choice or the study of provisioning', in Ferber and Nelson (eds), pp. 23–37.

Nelson, Julie (2006), *Economics for Humans*, Chicago, IL and London: University of Chicago Press.

Peterson, Janice and Margaret Lewis (eds) (1999), *The Elgar Companion to Feminist Economics*, Cheltenham, UK and Northampton, MA, USA: Edward Elgar.

Peterson, Janice and KimMarie McGoldrick (2009), 'Pluralism and economic education: a learning theory approach', *International Review of Economics Education*, **8**(2), 73–90.

Rogers, Glenn (1994), *Assessment Update*, San Francisco, CA: Jossey-Bass, January–February.

Schneider, Geoff (2009), 'Teaching heterodox economics: introduction to the special issue', *Forum for Social Economics*, **38**(2–3), 91–6.

Schwartz, Jeffrey M. and Sharon Begley (2002), *The Mind and the Brain*, New York: Harper Perennial.

Sen, Amartya (1999), *Development as Freedom*, New York: Random House.

Sen, Amartya (2009), *The Idea of Justice*, Cambridge, MA: Harvard University Press.

Simkins, Scott and Mark Maier (2009), 'Using pedagogical change to improve student learning in the economics major', in David Colander and KimMarie McGoldrick (eds), *Educating Economists: The Teagle Discussion on Re-evaluating the Undergraduate Economics Major*, Cheltenham, UK and Northampton, MA, USA: Edward Elgar, pp. 83–91.

Sternberg, Robert R., Jeremy Penn and Christie Hawkins (2011), *Assessing College Student Learning: Evaluating Alternative Models, Using Multiple Methods*, Washington, DC: AAC&U.

Strassmann, Diana (1999), 'Feminist economics', in Peterson and Lewis (eds), pp. 360–71.

Strober, Myra H. (2003), 'Rethinking economics through a feminist lens', in Mutari and Figart (eds), pp. 5–13.

Warnecke, Tonia (2009), 'Teaching globalization from a feminist pluralist perspective', *International Journal of Pluralism and Economics Education*, **1**(1–2), 93–108.

Wheat, David I. (2009), 'Empowering students to compare ways economists think: the case of the housing bubble', *International Journal of Pluralism and Economics Education*, **1**(1/2), 65–87.

Willis, Judy (2006), *Researched-Based Strategies to Ignite Student Learning*, Alexandria, VA: ASCD.

Wlodkowski, Raymond J. (2008), *Enhancing Adult Motivation to Learn*, San Francisco, CA: Jossey-Bass.

Wunder, Timothy A., Thomas Kemp and Scott England (2009), 'Fact-based economic education', *Journal of Economic Issues*, **43**(2), 467–75.

PART II

INSTITUTIONAL CONTEXTS FOR PROVISIONING

7.   Gender and provisioning under different capitalisms
Barbara E. Hopkins

I   INTRODUCTION

At the heart of economic life is the process of providing for oneself and one's family – provisioning. This process varies depending on the location in society and the structure of the economic system. Most of us live under some form of capitalism. Although capitalism is defined by markets, families and the state also play important roles in the provisioning process. This chapter explains how different forms of capitalism shape provisioning and how the experience of these different forms of capitalism is different for women and men. Parallel to different forms of capitalism, different gender regimes – the variety of ways to differentiate rules for men and women – also shape the way men and women experience different capitalisms.

The two most popular models for categorizing capitalisms are the varieties of capitalism (VOC) approach and the three worlds of welfare capitalism approach. These models are both based primarily on men's experience of labor markets, mediated by state regulation and social policies. Feminist scholars have criticized this literature and offered modifications. For women, and especially mothers, the role of the family and the state in provisioning is more obvious than for men. Thus, feminist analyses of welfare states emphasize the role of the state in altering women's dependence on family to provide for themselves and their children.

In this chapter, I argue that understanding how gender influences provisioning in different capitalisms requires a focus on two previously neglected aspects of economic systems. First, since families are important centers of women's economic lives, models of capitalism need to incorporate families as important economic structures that limit choices. Thus, different family regimes are as important to understanding capitalisms as different corporate governance structures are in the VOC approach. The different family regimes are affected by state policy as laid out in the feminist literature of welfare states and also by cultural factors. Second, gender conflict is as important a process for capitalist economies as class conflict. Struggles over distribution of work and goods shape economic structures and outcomes. I begin with an explanation of the process of provisioning under capitalist systems (Section II), then discuss various alternative models and critiques (Section III), and family regimes as important structures of capitalism and gender conflict as an important process (Section IV). Section V concludes.

II   PROVISIONING UNDER CAPITALISMS: THE MARKET, THE FAMILY, AND THE STATE

Capitalism is an economic system based on the private ownership of property and market exchange. The property that is privately owned generally refers to productive assets: tools and machinery that can be used to produce other goods. The owners of these assets can provide for themselves and their families by using them to produce for their own consumption, using them to produce goods for sale either through their own labor or hired labor, or renting them out to others. However, property rights are not as simple as stating that a private individual owns a piece of property. Rules vary from one capitalist society to the next. Furthermore, private property and markets are not the only institutions that play important roles in the process of provisioning in capitalist economies. Families play a significant role in providing for members of capitalist societies; ownership by a family complicates the concept of property rights. The state also plays an important role, both by providing for its citizens and by shaping the rules under which markets and families distribute and produce goods and services.

In a traditional analysis of capitalism, property defines class and class shapes inequality. This distinction between those who own property and those who do not has been the primary basis for the stratification into classes. Those who do not own enough productive assets to generate an adequate income are forced to sell their labor to those who do. Those who own, and thus control property have more options and more bargaining power to ensure that they receive a larger share of the goods produced or the income generated than the workers who are dependent on labor markets for their livelihoods.

But property ownership remains a source of inequality along gender lines. Historically, a common solution to inadequate ownership of property for women was marriage, but this often facilitated access to (not ownership of) property. Women often lack legal rights to shared property because it is nominally owned by husbands. Contributions by wives to the family home either directly, for the purchase price or upkeep, or indirectly, through household production, may not be recognized by property law. For example, Irish law did not recognize the right of wives to any say in the control of the marital home until the Family Home Protection Act of 1976. Furthermore, this law only granted wives the right to limit their husband's rights to the property, but did not confer ownership rights to wives (Yeates, 1999). Additionally, inheritance laws often disadvantaged daughters (Beckert, 2010). Even when inheritance laws allowed discretion, property law disadvantaged women because after marriage a woman's husband became the legal owner of her property.

In Great Britain and the United States, both early adopters of capitalism, married women had no legal right to property until later in the nineteenth century (Braunstein and Folbre, 2001). Women's property rights have improved in industrialized countries. However, equality has not been achieved. Norway ranks highest on the International Property Rights Index Gender Equality Ranking, but still merits only 10.2 out of 12 and the US only 9.3. For developing countries the situation is much worse. Bangladesh ranks at the bottom with a score of 2.3 (Horst, 2007). Clearly, the specifics of property rights matter. Differential access to property creates and maintains inequality between men and women, because women cannot control their own livelihoods.

Property rights are just one aspect of the institutional structure of capitalism. The institutional structure is the set of rules, norms, assets, and preferences that constrain the choices of those in the economic system. These constraints could be formally codified in law, or they could be norms of behavior informally enforced through social sanctions, or they could represent limited access to certain assets that are themselves shaped by norms and laws. As with property rights, markets are mediated by different sets of rules that affect how goods are produced and distributed. Capitalist economies differ depending on the institutional structure that exists within the broad framework of an economic system based on property rights and markets.

The concept of the institutional structure is not like the concept of regulation. Although regulations are part of the institutional structure, the rhetoric about regulations often frames the debate around whether there should be more regulations or less. This type of debate cannot apply to the institutional structure. While there are different institutional structures, and different institutional structures can advantage or disadvantage different groups within a society and be more or less efficient, there is not more or less structure. There is no 'natural' state for the institutional structure.

Different institutional structures within capitalism affect the process of provisioning through market exchange. Prices for goods that people produce and the wages they receive for their work are affected by the institutional structure. The institutional structure can also affect whether others wish to buy one's goods, services, or labor. As such, they affect the distribution of income and wealth and the ability for different segments of a population to provide for themselves and their families. Furthermore, institutions can affect the stability of the prices for goods and wages. So incomes can fluctuate a little or a lot. This further affects the ability to provision over time.

Families are as much a part of the institutional structure of capitalism as are markets. Families share production and pool income to address some of the risks of market fluctuations. However, families rarely distribute the work or the income equally (see for example, Strober and Chan, 1998; Bonke and Browning, 2009; Meulders and O'Dorchai, 2010). Nevertheless, almost all of us are born dependent on our families for subsistence. Those few who are not are dependent on the state, which in turn looks for families to whom responsibility can be assigned. Even for those old enough to sell their labor, almost 40 percent of women and over 20 percent of men aged 15–64 years in OECD countries in 2010 were not in the labor force.[1] Among those working, 26 percent of women and 10 percent of men were working part-time. Combining these figures into a crude measure of female reliance on nonmarket relationships for provisioning, over half of women in the OECD are relying on some source other than selling their labor in markets for support.[2] Many of them are relying on family for their subsistence. As Table 7.1 demonstrates, there is a great deal of international variation within the OECD: Sweden is at the low end with 37 percent and Italy and the Netherlands are at the high end with 64 and 71 percent, respectively.

While a full-time job is almost a requirement for the market to provide for subsistence, it is often not enough. Women generally earn lower wages and face a greater risk of poverty (Fagan et al., 2006). A study in the UK found that 15 percent of lone parents who worked full-time were at risk of poverty, while the risk for a couple if one works full-time and one part-time was only 6 percent (Lister, 2005). A more recent study by Eurostat (2010) also demonstrates that single-parent households are at much greater risk of poverty than households with two adults and one or more children. In Germany, the Netherlands, Sweden, and Finland, single-parent households face a risk of poverty three or more times that of households with two adults and children. In Belgium, Ireland, the UK, France, Austria, and Portugal, the poverty risk for single-parent households is two or more times. Even in households that are not responsible for children, individuals face a greater risk of poverty alone than households with two or more adults.

Table 7.1   Measure of female reliance on nonmarket relationships for provisioning, in percent, 2010

Country	Percent	Country	Percent
Turkey	76.4	Greece	50.2
Netherlands	71.1	France	48.3
Mexico	65.5	North America	48.1
Italy	64.5	Poland	48.0
Ireland	60.8	Spain	47.4
Chile	60.2	Hungary	45.8
Switzerland	58.2	Norway	45.7
Luxembourg	57.8	Canada	44.9
Belgium	57.6	Denmark	42.9
United Kingdom	56.4	Czech Republic	42.0
Australia	56.1	United States	41.7
Europe	56.1	Slovak Republic	41.6
Germany	55.4	Slovenia	39.4
OECD average	*54.4*	Finland	38.5
Japan	54.0	Sweden	36.8
Austria	52.8	Iceland	36.6
Israel	51.3	Portugal	35.9
New Zealand	50.9	Estonia	34.9
Korea	50.6	Russian Federation	34.7

Note: Part-time work is defined as less than 30 hours per week.

Source: Author's calculation based on data from OECD Labor Force Statistics dataset and Incidence of Full-time Part-time Dataset.

The age at which young people are able to achieve self-sufficiency and start their own household is increasing in industrialized countries. Especially in Continental Europe, young adults are more likely to be living with their parents because there has been a decline in the income adequacy of households headed by young adults (Bell et al., 2007). The upward trend flattened out between 2005 and 2010, but still represents a significant share of young people. Among the EU15[3] in 2010, 49.9 percent of men and 38 percent of women between the ages of 18–34 years were living with their parents. Again, this reflects a great deal of international variation. In Sweden, 27.5 percent of young men and 21 percent of young women were living with their parents, while in Italy 66.1 percent of young men and 54.8 percent of young women were living with their parents.[4] The US falls below the EU average with 30 percent of 18–34-year-olds living with a parent. The gender gap is large with 33 percent of young men and only 27 percent of young women living with a parent.[5] Clearly, income pooling, not just within generations, but also across generations, is an important provisioning strategy. However, provisioning involves more than using income. In households with only one wage-earner, other family members contribute labor to the production of services and sometimes goods in the household. In households at risk of poverty, it is often women who are responsible for managing the provisioning process with meager budgets (Lister, 2005; see also Albelda, Chapter 16, this volume).

The state also plays an important role in provisioning in the modern capitalist economy. Not only do states play a role in setting the rules under which families and markets operate, they also participate in directly providing for people's needs. Some form of unemployment insurance, state participation in pension schemes, disability insurance, and state involvement in either health insurance or direct involvement in providing healthcare all represent state participation in providing for the members of the society. The greater independence from family for both women and young adults in Sweden alluded to above is largely the result of state support. State funding for maternity leave benefits along with state support for childcare facilitate a more equitable balance between work and family life (Government Offices of Sweden, 2012a,b). Similarly, housing benefits along with various child supports help young families achieve economic security (Newman and Aptekar, 2007; Government Offices of Sweden, 2012b).

Ultimately, human beings in capitalist economies are dependent on all three sources of provision: market, family, and state. Periodically, social movements develop that attempt to increase independence from one of these sources. For example, in the United States, the Grey Flannel movement and the Beat movement represent a rebellion by men against dependency on the market for subsistence (Ehrenreich, 1983). Similarly, the liberal feminist movement can be interpreted as a movement against economic dependency on family. The conservative calls for 'personal responsibility' represent a backlash against dependency on the state. However, unlike the previous examples, calls for independence from the state are usually not made by those who are most dependent on it.

The variety in the institutional structure that shapes how the market, the family, and the state are able to contribute to the process of provisioning represents the differences in capitalisms. The best way to understand how these different rules arise is through Nancy Folbre's analysis of the structures of constraint. She defines the structures of constraint 'as sets of asset distributions, rules, norms, and preferences that empower given social groups' (Folbre, 1994, p. 51). As illustrated in the examples above, different institutional structures in different capitalist countries have served to create different opportunities for employment for men, women, and young adults in those countries. Relative wages, unemployment, the cost of necessities, access to childcare or healthcare, and many other factors that affect the ability of people to provide subsistence are shaped by the institutional structure. It is important to distinguish this framework from the new institutionalist approach of scholars such as Douglass North (1990), who argue that societies are searching for the most *efficient* set of institutions. Folbre's analysis leads to a set of institutions that result from a negotiated process between different groups who may not share the same interests in a particular structure.

III POPULAR UNDERSTANDINGS OF CAPITALISMS AND THEIR FEMINIST CRITICS

Two basic frameworks that have been applied to categorize and analyze the variations in capitalist economies have sparked debate among feminist scholars. The 'varieties of capitalism' approach is focused on different production regimes (Hall and Soskice, 2001). Gøsta Esping-Andersen's (1990) three worlds of welfare capitalism approach is focused on alternative systems of social protection. Bernhard Ebbinghaus and Philip Manow

(2001) attempt to bring the two concepts together. However, if we begin, as I did above, with the idea that economic systems represent different mechanisms for provisioning rather than the idea that economic systems represent different mechanisms for formal production, as the varieties of capitalism approach does, or the idea that the economic system is a mechanism for governmental intervention in the system of production and distribution, as the welfare capitalism framework does, the obvious gap in the existing theoretical analyses is the failure to incorporate families as part of the economic system. This is a well-established problem with research on economic systems (see Hopkins and Duggan, 2011) and with economics in general (Folbre, 1996). Esping-Andersen is a sociologist and he later attempted to incorporate family into his project (Esping-Andersen, 1999). Nevertheless, feminists still find fault with the way that each of these frameworks fails to describe women's experience in their respective spheres. These criticisms tend to fall into two categories: those that simply challenge whether women's experiences would lead to similar evaluations of the different types and those that challenge the basic understanding of capitalisms.

To begin, the varieties of capitalism (VOC) approach distinguishes between liberal market economies (LMEs) and coordinated market economies (CMEs). This approach emphasizes the idea of complementarity of institutions that lead to different kinds of comparative advantages in production for different models. This can be distinguished from the various literatures that focus on one institution, such as the level of unionization, and estimate some kind of correlation with economic growth or some other macroeconomic variable. CMEs have better job security combined with better coordination among businesses and between businesses and workers. This allows for a comparative advantage for goods that require more complex business processes. LMEs, by contrast, have a comparative advantage in the production of simple mass-produced goods (Whitley, 1999; Soskice, 2005).

The VOC literature tends to favor CMEs, arguing that the inequality generated by LMEs is not a requirement for efficient production (Hall and Soskice, 2001). The most common criticism of the VOC literature is that other dimensions besides coordination are important and that there are many more varieties than two (see Amable, 2003). For example, Esping-Andersen's (1999) categorization relies on the form of social protection rather than the degree of nonmarket structural coordination between enterprises. Bruno Amable (2003) defines different types of capitalisms based on institutional differences in the financial sector, employment relationships, and the education sector. He divides the CMEs into a social-democratic model, exemplified by the Scandinavian economies minus Norway; a European Integration model, consisting of France, Germany, and the Netherlands; an Alpine version, including Switzerland and Austria; a Mediterranean variant, including Spain, Italy, Greece, and Portugal; and a Mesocorporatist model, including South Korea and Japan. Like Amable, most alternative categorizations largely distinguish between different CMEs, leaving the market variant intact. Richard Whitley's (1999) business systems model, for example, distinguishes between Germany and Northern Italy. However, most of these alternatives still represent different categorizations of production systems.

Within the VOC framework, there have been efforts to incorporate gender (Estévez-Abe, 2009). Primarily, this literature asks whether women benefit from the kinds of labor market and worker institutions that benefit men in CMEs. Indeed it argues that these institutions can actually increase inequality between men and women by reinforcing patriarchal norms. For example, Margarita Estévez-Abe (2009) argues that the institutions of CMEs can increase occupational segregation, undermining gender inequality. Similar arguments have been made without referencing the VOC approach (Rubery et al., 1999).

Asking the question, 'Are women better off under the same system that benefits men?' also raises questions about whether women of different classes benefit from the same institutional arrangements. Research by Marie Evertsson et al. (2009) found that women with low education, and thus lower economic opportunities, benefit from state provision of childcare (as in the Swedish model) more than labor market policies for women's equality. For women at the higher end of the labor market, the provision of relatively inexpensive childcare and domestic services in liberal market economies facilitates shorter unpaid working hours for those who can afford it (ibid.), though the UK is an exception (Esping-Andersen, 1999).

However, a greater concern is whether the descriptions of different typologies in the VOC approach are adequate to capture the differences in women's experience in different economic systems. One key point made by feminists is that women have a different relationship with formal markets than men do. While a typical pattern for men is continuous full-time participation in the labor force from the completion of schooling until retirement, women take time out of the labor force to care for children and often work part-time. Nevertheless, the OECD reports wage statistics based on full-time work, unemployment compensation based on continuous full-time work, and pension replacement rates based on the average man.[6] Given that women's working lives differ from men's, how much they differ is shaped by the various different institutions of capitalisms. The relative costs of taking time away from paid employment to care for children in terms of skill formation and future employability, pension loss, and tax implications will vary depending on differences in policies and institutional structure that are abstractions in the VOC typology and most other typologies focused on formal employment. Jill Rubery (1992, 2009) provides numerous examples of how our understanding of labor markets thus needs to be broadened.

Another limitation of the VOC approach is that it is poorly equipped to deal with family policy as part of the economic system and families as significant providers of goods and services (Folbre, 2009). The complementarity of the VOC approach is focused on institutions affecting formal production taking place in businesses. It ignores the role of the state in processes of reproduction. It considers how the state influences differences in labor force participation, but ignores the role of policy to influence differences in unpaid work. The VOC approach also differs from Folbre's (1994) analysis in its emphasis on the political power of business, ignoring other interest groups in the formation of state policy. Folbre's more nuanced analysis recognizes a variety of overlapping interest groups that include not only business and workers, as implied by the Marxist framework of class struggle, but also groups formed based on gender identity or racial and ethnic identities. Individual political–economic actors will belong to several groups and may have conflicting interests.

The second theoretical analysis of capitalism is provided by Esping-Andersen (1990). Esping-Andersen's typology represents a slightly more complex one, though his focus is more on social policy rather than production as in the VOC literature. For example, he is not particularly concerned with enterprise governance structures or the independence of the central bank, but rather with the state's intervention in the market in order to enhance welfare. Esping-Anderson's original formulation defines three different welfare capitalisms – liberal welfare states; social-democratic welfare states; and conservative welfare states – which are classified by the basis on which an individual is entitled to provisions from the state. In *liberal welfare states*, which also correspond to liberal market economies, means testing is the primary mechanism for determining eligibility. Individuals are entitled to provisions if they lack the means to provide for themselves and their dependents. In *conservative welfare states*, comprising Amable's (2003) European integration, Alpine, and Mediterranean groupings, entitlements are based on employment history. In *social-democratic welfare states*, such as the Nordic countries, entitlements are based on citizenship. Esping-Andersen (1990) also distinguishes the social-democratic approach by arguing that they socialize the caring costs of families. However, Folbre (1994) points out that old-age pensions and family allowances were implemented in Nordic and Northern European countries at roughly the same time, but that the specific policies chosen in the Nordic countries offered women more options and were less punitive toward families with working mothers.

The original focus was to investigate how the different types of welfare state regimes succeed in de-commodifying labor and in altering stratification in the society. The de-commodification of labor means decreasing the dependence that workers have on the market for their livelihood. Stratification refers to the way in which the social structure divides people up into classes with different life chances. Since individuals must rely on the market, family, or the state, Esping-Andersen is most interested in the ways that state policy can reduce people's reliance on the market or equalize people's life chances.

His original schema does not adequately incorporate the role of families in provisioning and is concerned only with stratification along class lines, ignoring stratification based on gender, race or ethnicity, discussed below. Thus, his analysis finds that the social-democratic societies, with citizen-based entitlements, achieve the highest level of de-commodification. The three types can be ranked in terms of increasing stratification from the social democratic, to the conservative, to the liberal. Social-democratic societies reduce stratification because there is an emphasis on equality across skill types, and entitlements such as healthcare are provided to all citizens. Conservative welfare states create stratification between insiders, who have jobs and thus access to entitlements and insurance against job loss, and outsiders, who are not employed, including unpaid wives and mothers and young potential workers. Liberal welfare states create stratification through market-determined inequalities and punitive social safety nets.

Feminists have challenged whether Esping-Andersen's categorization based on the foundations for entitlement captures women's experience. Given the significant role that family plays in women's experience of provisioning, family structure is a key variable. In particular, ideological expectations of family structure are part of the foundation of welfare state policies. For example, Diane Sainsbury (1994, 1996) develops alternative characterizations of welfare state policies based on the alternative foundations of a male-breadwinner model and a model of individual entitlement. The male-breadwinner model assumes that husbands and fathers are the breadwinners while wives and mothers are financially dependent and available to provide care and other services in the household. The model of individual entitlement treats husbands and wives separately; in Sainsbury's formulation, the models for entitlement (the right to provisions from the state) empha-size the differences between a woman's access to entitlement through a male head of household rather than by her own right. One interesting dimension that illustrates this distinction is that of taxation. Under the male-breadwinner ideology, married couples are taxed jointly. In the individual model, husbands and wives are taxed separately. Under progressive joint or split taxation, highly paid married men are taxed relatively less because they are seen as supporting others. Married women, on the other hand, are taxed relatively more because their lower income is taxed at their husband's marginal rate, often creating a disincentive for women to work (see Smith, 2003; Warnecke, 2008; de Villota, 2011). However, as Portugal illustrates split taxation methods can be designed to advantage dual-earner families over single-earner families and favor women's labor force participation (Marques and Pereira, 1999).

Feminists have also challenged Esping-Andersen's evaluation of his types. Esping-Andersen (1990) treats the conservative welfare regime as superior to the liberal welfare state because in liberal welfare states dual labor markets generate a large share of 'bad' jobs and the losers in the liberal economies face social humiliation and meager benefits offered by the means-tested entitlements. In contrast, conservative welfare regimes offer strong job security combined with social protections to workers that partially liber-ate them from dependence on markets. However, feminists have argued that welfare state policies in conservative welfare states, instead of being liberating, were reinforcing patriarchal relationships by reinforcing female dependence on men (Meyer, 1994).

The concepts of de-commodification and of class stratification do not capture gender inequality as well as they capture class inequalities. Specifically, the concept of de-commodification reflects men's experience more than women's (Bussemaker and van Kersbergen, 1994; Daly, 1994; Sainsbury, 1999). Women do not have the same access to labor markets as men. Lack of adequate childcare limits mothers from entering the labor market (Evertsson et al., 2009). Responsibility for housework limits women's ability to be available for work. A lack of part-time employment can limit women's opportunity to combine household responsibilities with work (Yeandle, 1999). Furthermore, part-time work often does not generate the same entitlements as full-time work. Mary Daly points out that rather than de-commodifying women, welfare states were just as likely to com-modify women, because the expansion of some welfare states created opportunities for women in paid employment (Daly, 1994). However, this varied depending on the form and in particular, the degree of direct provision of services.

Feminists have reframed Esping-Andersen's notion of de-commodification to look instead at de-familialization (Daly, 1994). Thus, welfare regimes could be evaluated not just on how they support independence from the market, but how they support women's independence from men. For example, policies that provide child benefits, but pay them to the male head of household, reinforce dependency on men. Policies that support women's employment, especially mothers' employment, increase a woman's ability to provide for an acceptable standard of living for her and her child without her husband. This not only reduces poverty for lone mothers and their children, but also increases the ability for women to negotiate for a better deal within shared households: a better divi-sion of labor, a better distribution of goods, and more decision-making power.

Esping-Andersen's analysis also fails to consider labor market stratification based on gender. Policies aimed at promoting full employment have often been based on the idea of a male-breadwinner model, thus leaving out women (Rubery, 1997; Bruegel et al., 1998). Most of these differences are better covered under the production regime orientation of the VOC literature, but welfare state benefits also have an impact. Means testing for unemployment insurance in the UK that is based on heterosexual couples that pool income effectively excludes women from unemployment insurance because their husbands earn too much, and also creates a disincentive for low-skill wives of unemployed men to work for pay (Rubery, 1997). Different patterns of labor market activity create inequalities, not just in terms of pay, but also in terms of pension benefits over a lifetime (Scheiwe, 1994). Alternatively, generous support for maternity leave, such as that offered in Sweden, creates discrimination against women in labor markets and in part contributes to occupational segregation (Stark, 2008). Different strategies for dealing with pay inequities affect women differently from men (Rubery, 1992; O'Connor, 1999).

Esping-Andersen's (1999) response has been to incorporate families into his analysis. This does not change his analysis significantly. He argues that conservative welfare states are familialist, although to varying degrees, while social-democratic states are attempting de-familialization. Sainsbury (1999) argues that the social-democratic state policy toward family varies. Sweden encourages an individual, earner–carer model, while Norway reinforces separate roles for men and women. This Norwegian approach reinforces women's role as carer and men's role as earner, through labor market policies that favor men and entitlements differentiated by different roles. These two welfare states reflect differences in feminist theories of equality. In Sweden, a 'gender-neutral' approach to equality was taken, while in Norway, a 'separate but equal' approach that grants women special entitlements based on their role as mothers was the approach (Stark, 2008). Esping-Andersen's (1999) newer approach emphasizes that family structure is changing, even in welfare states that discourage women's employment. Women's labor force participation is increasing everywhere and welfare state reform needs to take account of it. As such he is less interested in feminist critiques than in focusing on inequalities in labor markets.

IV   RETHINKING CAPITALIST STRUCTURES AND PROCESSES: FAMILY AND GENDER CONFLICT

Both of the popular frameworks discussed – VOC and welfare state regimes – limit our understanding of capitalisms. First, both are focused on the state. The VOC approach and most economic typologies focus on formal production, emphasizing the market and state regulation of the market. The welfare capitalisms representation focuses on the state's role in provisioning and (in Esping-Andersen's revision) on state regulation of families. The structures of capitalism are broader than the state. Understanding the institutions of capitalism requires an understanding of families. The feminist literature building on and critiquing Esping-Andersen incorporates families, but is still focused primarily on state entitlements and regulation of families.

Second, both VOC and welfare capitalisms treat class conflict as the only basis for political struggles over the distribution of work, resources, and goods. VOC is focused on the level of coordination between firms and workers which reduces conflict and increases productivity and innovation. The focus of the welfare state capitalisms approach defines different forms of stratification, but all are based on one's place in labor hierarchies and class distinctions. As Folbre (1994) points out, our analysis of groupings that represent cooperative actors in an economic system should also include other divisions for social conflict, such as race or gender. This chapter lays out the implications of gender conflict.

First, let us consider families and the various institutions that influence them besides state regulation (which was described above). While the role of the state in providing for people's needs and in setting the rules of the game is important for understanding economic systems, especially the relative importance of families in the provision process and the relative distribution of work and goods within families, the state does not unilaterally control these processes. (Not all institutions of capitalisms are controlled by the state.) Although the gendered division of labor in households may be influenced by such policies as parental leave that fathers must take, it is also influenced by cultural norms that in turn influence employers' attitudes. Cultural norms are expectations of behavior that if violated result in some form of social sanctions. These represent informal rules in the system that will vary from one country to another. The social consequences of violating these norms shape the choices women and men make. For example, attitudes about women's, and especially mothers', employment affect the opportunities for women to work and the willingness of employers to invest in training for women workers, and, in turn, women's dependence on families (Crompton and Harris, 1997). Similarly, if mothers are expected to take leave but fathers are not, employers may be more likely to penalize fathers who take leave than mothers, even when the preferences of the individual family would lead to a more egalitarian distribution of unpaid work.

A variety of institutions shape these norms and expectations. In Sweden, for example, the Lutheran church was instrumental in promoting universal literacy, and thus the education of girls long before the development of feminist movements (Gazdar, 2008). Business culture also shapes family norms. The extension of benefits to domestic partners in the United States provides an example of how change can be enacted outside of government policy, and also how government policy can be affected by other nongovernmental institutions. Domestic partnership was a policy innovation in the sphere of labor markets, not a policy shift made by the state (Knauer, 1998). While political leaders resist innovations in policy to address cohabiting couples, especially same sex couples that offend the sensibilities of the religious right in the United States, businesses have discovered that providing health insurance and other benefits to 'domestic partners' allows them to attract good employees.

Different norms for the distribution of paid work and care can be categorized into different family regimes. Structural approaches to categorizing family regimes parallel welfare state categorizations and emphasize government policies such as tax policies, social security systems, and state spending on childcare (see, for example, Lewis, 1992). Thus, as described in the previous section, government policies can advantage or penalize male-breadwinner families and policies can enable dual-earner families to support children or not. Cultural approaches emphasize social attitudes, values, and norms. Birgit Pfau-Effinger (2004) has classified the cultural norms for family structure, focusing on participation in employment by each parent and the source of care for children. The male-breadwinner/female-home-carer model depicts what has generally been recognized as the traditional family, in which fathers work in formal employment and mothers stay at home and care for children.

However, the male-breadwinner model does not always represent an accurate reflection of the average family, even historically. For example, in the US, where the male-breadwinner/housewife model dominated ideology before second-wave feminism, it did not reflect reality for many families (Coontz, 1992). Furthermore, the male-breadwinner model does not represent a universal tradition. An egalitarian form of the family economic gender model was the norm in Finland during the 1950s (Pfau-Effinger, 2004). The family economic gender model refers to a family business such as a store or a farm in which all family members, including children, work. Work and care for children is combined with work on goods or services for sale in the market. This model can be relatively egalitarian, as in the Finnish case, or it can be patriarchal, as in the household arrangements described by Elissa Braunstein and Folbre (2001).

The cultural norms for family structure have been evolving in capitalist economies. In Finland, the norms have shifted from the family economic gender model to the dual-breadwinner/state-carer model. In this model both parents work and the welfare state takes over some of the responsibility of caring for children through provision of high-quality childcare. In the Netherlands, cultural change has led to an evolution from the male-breadwinner/female-carer model to the dual-breadwinner/dual-carer model. Again, both parents work, but domestic work is equally shared. This is facilitated by some combination of purchase of domestic services and a work structure that allows for domestic responsibility. In former West Germany, the shift has been from the male-breadwinner/female-home-carer to the male-breadwinner/female-part-time-carer model (Pfau-Effinger, 2004). The male-breadwinner/female-part-time-carer model refers to a family in which fathers still hold the primary responsibility for earning income in the market, but mothers work part-time and take primary responsibility for caring for children.

A synthesis of the cultural typology of family regimes with the structural typology permits an analysis of how policies and culture interact (Haas, 2005). The synthesis consists of the traditional breadwinner model; a modified breadwinner model, which is comparable to the male-breadwinner/female part-time-carer model; the egalitarian employment model, in which both parents work, but women are still held primarily responsible for household work and care work; the universal-carer model, which is a theoretical model in which both parents share responsibility for care equally; and the role-reversal model, in which women work longer hours in paid employment and men take responsibility for childcare. Only the egalitarian employment model reflects the de-familialization concept that feminists have used to modify Esping-Andersen's evaluation of different models of welfare states. In breadwinner models women are dependent on men. In the role-reversal model men are dependent on women. And in the universal-carer model, both parents are dependent on each other.

In actual societies culture can complement or contradict policy. Different state policies are likely to be contradictory, and the actual practice of families may differ from culture or the intent of policymakers. For example, the universal-carer model (which is analogous to Pfau-Effinger's (2004) dual-breadwinner/dual-carer model) is an ideal in some countries, but is not the dominant form of family anywhere. The role-reversal model is not the ideal, either culturally or among policymakers anywhere, but is clearly practiced by some families.

This contradiction between ideal and actual family regimes is exemplified by Barbara Haas's (2005) study including Austria and the Netherlands. Austria is a country that is culturally a modified breadwinner model, but policies are ambiguous, providing benefits for both traditional breadwinner families and egalitarian employment families. In practice, the lack of part-time work available in the labor market prevents many families from adopting the culturally preferred family regime. In the Netherlands, the culture supports a universal-carer model (Pfau-Effinger, 2004; Haas, 2005). However, in practice unpaid work is not equally divided (ibid.). Mothers retain primary responsibility for their children and are less likely to allow working time to interfere with care responsibilities than men (Roeters et al., 2012). Only 16 percent of fathers participate in childcare and housekeeping 'often'; those 16 percent represent the top three of five categories of caring fathers in the Netherlands study (Duindam and Spruijt, 1997). In the top category, the average time spent by fathers is more than mothers, but in the category second in the degree of paternal involvement, mothers spent twice the time of fathers (ibid.).

Both the egalitarian employment model and the universal-carer model require that many different institutions come together to facilitate women working in paid employment and, in the case of the universal-carer model, men participating in care work. For example, the egalitarian employment model requires some mechanism for working mothers to arrange care. In the Swedish model, or state-carer model, the state takes responsibility for childcare. In liberal market economies the viability of a low-wage domestic sector allows for childcare that is affordable, at least to those at higher income levels. This solution of purchasing care in the market is increasingly facilitated in Europe through the accession to the European Union of poorer Eastern European states and the subsequent migration of care workers who are necessary for the economy but excluded from full membership in the society (Tronto, 2011). Nevertheless, the lack of workable childcare presents a serious barrier to the egalitarian employment model in Southern Europe (see, for example, Warnecke, 2008). Ultimately, policies that facilitate the egalitarian employment model are crucial for combating child poverty, since employment is an important provisioning strategy for lone mothers.

The universal-carer model requires that men contribute more time to household work and caring for children. This requires much more control over work hours for both parents than most workers have. However, the debate over liberalization of European labor markets continues and is likely to intensify with the current downturn. The pressure to increase employment could lead to increasing bargaining power for employers, allowing them greater leverage over working hours as in liberal market economies, or it could lead to solutions that shorten work hours for everyone as in the Netherlands (see, for example, Pascal and Lewis, 2004; Pontusson, 2005). Even if the work structure permitted it, men will not increase care work unless they want to. Government policies can do very little to increase incentives for them to do this. They may not want to increase care work because it could decrease their income, which at lower incomes may undermine family provisioning, or they may not want to give up the power that comes with the existing division of labor (MacLennan and Purdy, 1999). Governments can promote modified breadwinner models by fostering part-time work through changes in labor market regulations and they can promote egalitarian employment models through individual taxation, hiring regulations, and equal pay provisions, along with subsidies for childcare. However, the only policy adopted that affects childcare is limited to the first years of a child's life: mandatory daddy leaves. Indeed, the new European policies of individualization, intended to reduce dependence on family, have created a crisis of care where not enough care work is being undertaken (Pascall and Lewis, 2004). It should be noted that additional institutions would be required to facilitate universal care in the context of divorced or separated parents.

In practice, sharing of caring responsibilities by enlisting fathers has not been fully successful anywhere. In dual-earner families in the United States, where the model might be described as dual-earner/paid-caregiver for those families that can afford it, fathers have increased the time spent engaging in direct interaction with their children to about 44 percent of the time mothers spend and the time they are accessible to their children to about 66 percent of the time mothers spend (Lamb, 2000). This is up from studies a decade earlier, but it hardly constitutes equality. Furthermore, this does not clearly reflect responsibility. Time spent by fathers does not seem to be affected by the mothers' employment. The shares are higher for dual-earner families not because fathers were spending more time, but because mothers were spending less (ibid.). Across countries there has been a trend toward less time spent on housework by women and more time spent by men, but the gender gap remains large. The gender gap is the lowest in the social-democratic countries and the highest in conservative welfare states, though the absolute time spent in housework does not correspond to welfare regimes (Sayer, 2010).

The second consideration to expand our understanding of capitalisms is to recognize the role that gender plays in distributional conflict. Neoclassical economists ignore conflict and understand the economic actors in capitalist systems as individual agents making decisions to buy, sell, produce, and work for pay based on the incentives created by market prices and individual preferences. The Marxian understanding of economic actors also includes individuals organized into groups, specifically classes that either own the tools for production or have to sell their labor to survive. These classes collectively have different interests and benefit from different institutions. Thus, their interests are in conflict. Folbre's (1994) feminist model of economic systems includes men and women as groups of individuals whose interests differ, and thus benefit differently from different sets of rules and economic institutions. Folbre also includes other standard groupings such as racial categories, age, and sexual identity, for example. These categories clearly overlap creating various different groups of women and men that have different economic interests. Furthermore, collective interests also incorporate strategic interests to maintain or develop a relative power advantage. Thus, men as a group may be interested in policies that undermine overall efficiency and well-being but enhance patriarchal power.

One outcome of conflict is likely to be contradictory and unstable state policies (ibid.). Since policies are the result of political compromises between different interests, the compromise in one policy debate is likely to conflict with the compromise in another. Indeed, such contradictory policy may be the compromise. Furthermore, the precise compromise is likely to shift as the relative bargaining power of different groups changes. The policy move toward individualization in Europe provides an example. Mary Daly (2011) argues that recent policy shifts reflect contradictory movement both toward and against familialization despite the rhetoric in support of individualization. For example, tax policy is becoming individualized, but also reflects a different kind of familialization. The trend is to calculate taxes based on individual income. At the same time, there is an expansion of pension credits for time spent caring for children. This implies a different kind of familialization, in which mothers are dependent on family, but retired women are not. However, conflict affects many of the structures of economic systems, not just the state policies. Cultural norms, preferences, and the distribution of assets are all influenced by gender conflict. Thus, many of the structures of economic systems will be contradictory and unstable, in the sense that any particular configuration reflects a delicate balance between competing interests that may change.

The cultural norms will also be the outcome of conflict between different groups. It is important to remember that norms evolve over time. As more and more wives and mothers choose to work, norms change. As feminist movements demand better labor market opportunities, norms change. However, understanding cultural norms as the outcome of gender-based distributional conflict allows us to see that progress toward greater gender equality is not guaranteed. One institution that affects cultural norms is the media. Attitudes about the proper role for women are shaped by the media. For example, in Italy, feminist opposition to former Italian Prime Minister Silvio Berlusconi was not simply about his role as prime minister, but also the representation of women on his private television stations.[7] Feminist movements also experience opposition. After decades of success that has surpassed most other countries but has not led to equality in pay or unpaid working time, Swedish feminists are facing new opposition by those who think gender equality has gone too far (Sümer, 2009).

The preferences of an economic system are also the result of a negotiated process involving conflict. However, preferences are separate from 'rules'; preferences do not simply mean different policy choices as described in the comparative welfare states literature. Preferences mean that different people will make different choices when faced with the same alternatives. Even private choices can be the result of negotiation. Many choices involve synergies, in which benefits exist when many people make the same choice. Work hours illustrate this point. Different individuals will inevitably have different innate preferences. Nevertheless, societies develop 'normal working hours', and workers with different preferences may have a hard time finding jobs that allow for different work hours. As different societies negotiate these norms, we would expect different outcomes. For example, although American observers assert that Swedes work shorter hours in response to tax incentives (Burtless, 1987), an equally plausible explanation is that shorter work hours reflect a preference for a different work–life balance that can also be revealed in tax policy. As another example, women tend to have different preferences than men on work–life balance. Yet, almost everywhere, the structure of work follows a male pattern (Nagy, 2008). These differences in preferences disadvantage women in most economies, but less so in Sweden. Thus, the outcome in Sweden appears to reflect the relative strength of the feminist movement in its ability to shift national preferences closer to feminist ideals.

Finally, distributional conflict also affects the assets available to different groups in society. In the case of class, it is the unequal distribution of productive assets that defines the Marxist conception of capitalism. Viewing this unequal distribution as both the result and the source of conflict means that the rules and processes that lead to that distribution are the result of a contested political process in which different groups have different interests. The ruling class has an inherent interest in maintaining a set of rules that distribute to them more assets. In the case of gender distribution, assets should be considered more broadly than just physical productive assets. Assets represent not only the resources and wealth of an economy, but also technology, skills, and knowledge more generally. Many assets are not equally distributed across genders. Conflict arises when men have an interest in blocking women from access to and control over assets.

Access to resources, skills, technology, and credit shape the opportunities one faces to start a business as a means to provide for oneself and one's family. Access to skills and knowledge, as well as the distribution of resources and technology within an organization, affect the opportunities for workers to be judged as productive and, thus, financially rewarded. Differential control over shared assets in the family affects intrahousehold bargaining power and women's dependence on the family, as well as the ability for widows to manage their affairs. The distribution of assets is shaped by cultural norms and by the formal rules of both the government and private organizations. For example, entrance requirements for universities and financial support for students affect access to knowledge and skill development. In some countries, these are controlled exclusively by the state, while in others these factors are also influenced by private institutions. Even knowledge at the most basic level, knowing the income of your household, is an important factor in women's ability to provide for their families. In southern Italy, for instance, many housewives do not know how much money their husbands earn, shaping their ability to make 'rational' decisions (Addis, 2010). Furthermore, many of the issues I have raised above reflect unequal distribution in assets. The VOC literature describes how different varieties of capitalism value different kinds of skill formation and that this affects the opportunities for women (Estévez-Abe, 2009; Rubery, 2009). Property rights clearly represent rules that shape the distribution of assets (Yeates, 1999; Braunstein and Folbre, 2001; Beckert, 2010). The cultural norms and formal rules are the outcome of conflict between different interest groups.

V   CONCLUSION

While conventional descriptions of capitalism are focused on the market, I have demonstrated that understanding women's experience of capitalisms requires a shift in focus to families. Feminists researching welfare states have refocused attention to families and the state policies that regulate them. However, it is also important to consider other influences on family structure including cultural traditions, churches, and business practices. Ultimately, the choices available to women and the possibilities for different combinations of family, state, and market in their strategies for providing for themselves and their children will depend on family regimes and the policies of the state that shape family regimes.

Capitalisms differ in the opportunities they create for women to earn a living in markets and to raise their children and the degree to which they foster dependence on men for financial support or as partners for household management and parenting. Women's and men's experience of capitalism is shaped by different cultural expectations for women's proper role in economic life as a breadwinner and as a caregiver; various policies developed by businesses including the benefits they provide, such as maternity leave or who counts as family for leave or healthcare benefits; and various regulation by states mandating benefits, or providing subsidies for childcare at home by parents or provided as a service by the private sector for a fee or by government, or taxing different family forms differently. A categorization of capitalisms that incorporates traditional variables of production and business systems with family regimes and government policies has not yet been developed.

I also argued that understanding capitalisms requires an analysis of conflict between groups defined by gender. However, this should not be taken to mean that one can reduce social groupings to just men and women. Men and women also belong to other groups and are divided by race, ethnicity, class, age, marital status, and many other aspects of identity that can create differing economic interests. The concept of group conflict, as a key process of capitalism, means that policy outcomes, expectations, socially determined preferences, and distribution can be contradictory and unstable as social groups negotiate compromises that differ not just between capitalisms, but within capitalisms and across time. One cannot expect that societies will make uninterrupted progress toward gender equality or even that women will all agree on what policies constitute relatively more gender equality. To date, gender equality in all capitalisms is partial. As women retreat from care work to enter paid labor, men have not made up for the loss. Thus, women are divided as to whether the egalitarian employment model is better than a modified breadwinner model with protections for economic security such as pension credits for care work. Policy and norms will continue to vary and will change to reflect shifting compromises between interest groups.

NOTES

1. Data from OECD StatExtracts (http://stats.oecd.org/Index.aspx), 'LFS by sex and age – indicator, labor force participation rate, women, total ages' and 'Incidence of FTPT employment – common definition, women, total ages, total employment'.
2. This measure adds the percentage of women not in the labor force to the percentage of women in the labor force who are working less than 30 hours. It is not a perfect measure of dependency. It may overstate reliance on nonmarket relationships; a 61-year-old retiree relying on a pension obtained through the market (but not in the labor force) and a college student borrowing from credit markets to fund living expenses (but only working part-time) would be included in this measure, even though both individuals rely on markets for subsistence. However, in practice, both of these individuals would most likely also be relying on state support, either through state-supported pension schemes or state support for higher education, directly to colleges and universities, grants made directly to students, or indirectly through loan guarantees. The measure is also likely to be understated because many women who work full-time may earn substantially less than their husbands and, thus, rely on intrahousehold redistributions for their standard of living.
3. The EU-15 refers to the member countries of the EU prior to May of 2004. This omits the post-socialist members of the European Union and Cyprus and Malta.
4. Data are available from Eurostat at: http://appsso.eurostat.ec.europa.eu/nui/show.do?dataset=ilc_ lvps08&lang=en (accessed June 5, 2012).
5. Data were calculated from CPS data available at the Census Bureau: www.census.gov/hhes/families/files/ cps2010/tabA2-all.xls (accessed June 4, 2012). Based on tables for additional years available at: http:// www.census.gov/hhes/families/data/cps.html, there is a slow but unsteady trend upward in the share of young adults living with their parents rising from 27 percent in 2001 to 31 percent in 2011.
6. Women's noncontinuous labor force participation generally leads to lower pensions, but these vary a great deal because policies for dealing with full-time caregivers vary.
7. This insight is thanks to Elisabetta Addis who was active in organizing demonstrations on February 13, 2011 as part of *Se Non Ora, Quando*. A video of the rally with English subtitles can be found at http://www. archive.org/details/SeNonOraQuandoEnglishSubtitles.

REFERENCES

Addis, Elisabetta (2010), 'Gender, money, and capabilities', in Tindara Addabbo, Cristina Borderias, Marie-pierre Arrizabalaga and Alastair Owens (eds), *Gender Inequalities, Households and the Production of Well-being in Modern Europe*, Farnham, UK: Ashgate, pp. 235–52.
Amable, Bruno (2003), *The Diversity of Modern Capitalism*, Oxford: Oxford University Press.
Beckert, Jens (2010), 'Are we still modern? Inheritance law and the broken promise of the enlightenment', MPIfG Working Papers 10/7, Max-Planck-Institut für Gesellschaftsforschung, Köln.
Bell, Lisa, Gary Burtless, Janet Gornick and Timothy M. Smeeding (2007), 'Failure to launch: cross-national trends in the transition to economic independence', in Sheldon Danzinger and Cecilia Elena Rouse (eds), New York: Russell Sage Foundation, pp. 27–55.
Bonke, Jens and Martin Browning (2009), 'The distribution of well-being and income within the household', *Review of Economics of the Household*, **7**(1), 31–42.
Braunstein, Elissa and Nancy Folbre (2001), 'To honor and obey: efficiency, inequality, and patriarchal property rights', *Feminist Economics*, **7**(1), 25–44.
Bruegel, Irene, Deborah M. Figart and Ellen Mutari (1998), 'Whose full employment? A feminist perspective on full employment and work redistribution', in Jane Wheelock and John Vail (eds), *Work and Idleness: The Political Economy of Full Employment*, Dordrecht: Kluwer Academic Publishers, pp. 69–83.
Burtless, Gary (1987), 'Taxes, transfers, and Swedish labor supply', in Barry P. Bosworth and Alice Rivlin (eds), *The Swedish Economy*, Washington, DC: The Brookings Institution, pp. 185–242.
Bussemaker, Jet and Kees van Kersbergen (1994), 'Gender and welfare states: some theoretical reflections', in Diane Sainsbury (ed.), *Gendering Welfare States*, London: Sage, pp. 1–7.
Coontz, Stephanie (1992), *The Way We Never Were: American Families and the Nostalgia Trap*, New York: Basic Books.
Crompton, Rosemary and Fiona Harris (1997), 'Women's employment and gender attitudes: a comparative analysis of Britain, Norway and the Czech Republic', *Acta Sociologica*, **40**(2), 183–202.
Daly, Mary (1994), 'Comparing welfare states: towards a gender friendly approach', in Diane Sainsbury (ed.), *Gendering Welfare States*, London: Sage, pp. 101–17.
Daly, Mary (2011), 'What adult worker model? A critical look at recent social policy reform in Europe from a gender and family perspective', *Social Politics: International Studies in Gender, State and Society*, **18**(1), 1–23.
de Villota, Paloma (2011), 'A gender perspective approach regarding the impact of income tax on wage-earning women in Spain', in Kim Brooks, Åsa Gunnarson, Lisa Philipps, and Maria Wersig (eds), *Challenging Gender Inequality in Tax Policy Making: Comparative Perspective*, Oxford: Hart, pp. 109–34.
Duindam, Vincent and Ed Spruijt (1997), 'Caring fathers in the Netherlands', *Sex Roles*, **36**(3/4), 149–70.
Ebbinghaus, Bernhard and Philip Manow (2001), *Comparing Welfare Capitalism: Social Policy and Political Economy in Europe, Japan, and the USA*, London and New York: Routledge.
Ehrenreich, Barbara (1983), *The Hearts of Men: American Dreams and the Flight from Commitment*, Garden City, NY: Anchor Press/Doubleday.
Esping-Andersen, Gøsta (1990), *The Three Worlds of Welfare Capitalism*, Princeton, NJ: Princeton University Press.
Esping-Andersen, Gøsta (1999), *Social Foundations of Post-industrial Economies*, Oxford: Oxford University Press.
Estévez-Abe, Margarita (2009), 'Gender, inequality, and capitalism: the "varieties of capitalism" and women', *Social Politics: International Studies in Gender, State and Society*, **16**(2), 182–91.
Eurostat (2010), 'In-work poverty in the EU', Eurostat Methodologies and Working Papers, KS-RA-10-015-EN-N, Publications Office of the European Union, Luxembourg.
Evertsson, Marie, Paula England, Irma Mooi-Reci, Joan Hermsen, Jeanne De Bruijn and David Cotter (2009), 'Is gender inequality greater at lower or higher educational levels? Common patterns in the Netherlands, Sweden, and the United States', *Social Politics: International Studies in Gender, State and Society*, **16**(2), 210–41.
Fagan, Colette, Peter Urwin and Kathryn Melling (2006), *Gender Inequalities in the Risks of Poverty and Social Exclusion for Disadvantaged Groups in Thirty European Countries*, Luxembourg: European Commission.
Folbre, Nancy (1994), *Who Pays for the Kids? Gender and the Structure of Constraint*, New York: Routledge.
Folbre, Nancy (1996), *The Economics of the Family*, Aldershot, UK and Brookfield, VT, USA: Edward Elgar.
Folbre, Nancy (2009), 'Varieties of patriarchial capitalism', *Social Politics: International Studies in Gender, State and Society*, **16**(2), 204–9.
Gazdar, Haris (2008), 'The transition to mass literacy', in Naila Kabeer, Agneta Stark and Edda Magnus (eds), *Global Perspectives on Gender Equality: Reversing the Gaze*, London: Routledge, pp. 19–39.

Government Offices of Sweden (2012a), 'Childcare voucher system and universal pre-school for three-year-olds', available at: http://www.regeringen.se/sb/d/7172/a/172234 (accessed May 30, 2012).

Government Offices of Sweden (2012b), 'Parental insurance and allowances to parents in Sweden', available at: http://www.regeringen.se/sb/d/15473/a/183497 (accessed May 30, 2012).

Haas, Barbara (2005), 'The work–care balance: is it possible to identify typologies for cross-national comparisons?', *Current Sociology*, **53**(3), 487–508.

Hall, Peter A. and David W. Soskice (2001), *Varieties of Capitalism: The Institutional Foundations of Comparative Advantage*, Oxford: Oxford University Press.

Hopkins, Barbara E. and Lynn S. Duggan (2011), 'A feminist comparative economic systems', *Feminist Economics*, **17**(3), 35–69.

Horst, Alexandra C. (2007), 'International Property Rights Index 2007 Report', International Property Rights Index, Washington, DC, available at: http://web.undp.org/legalempowerment/pdf/PRA_Interior_LowRes.pdf (accessed June 21, 2012).

Knauer, Nancy J. (1998), 'Domestic partnership and same-sex relationships: a marketplace innovation and a less than perfect institutional choice', *Temple Political and Civil Rights Law Review*, **7**(2), 337–61.

Lamb, Michael E. (2000), 'The history of research on father involvement: an overview', *Marriage and Family Review*, **29**(2/3), 23–42.

Lewis, Jane (1992), 'Gender and the development of welfare regimes', *Journal of European Social Policy*, **2**(3), 159–73.

Lister, Ruth (2005), 'Women's and children's poverty: making the links', Women's Budget Group, London.

MacLennan, Barbara and David Purdy (1999), 'Engendering the redistribution of work', in Olwen Hufton and Yota Kravaritou (eds), *Gender and the Use of Time: Gender et emploi du temps*, The Hague: Kluwer, pp. 505–19.

Marques, Ana Cristina Lino and Pedro Telhado Pereira (1999), 'Taxes and women in the labour force in a Southern European country: the case of Portugal', *Labour*, **13**(4), 797–819.

Meulders, Danièle and Síle O'Dorchai (2010), 'Revisiting poverty measures towards individualisation,' DULBEA Working Paper 10–03.RS, Département d'économie appliquée Université Libre de Bruxelles, Brussels.

Meyer, Traute (1994), 'The German and British welfare states as employers: patriarchial or emancipatory?', in Diane Sainsbury (ed.), *Gendering Welfare States*, London: Sage, pp. 62–81.

Nagy, Beata (2008), 'Challenging the male norm of employment: evidence from Sweden, Norway, and Hungary', in Naila Kabeer, Agneta Stark and Edda Magnus (eds), *Global Perspectives on Gender Equality: Reversing the Gaze*, London: Routledge, pp. 87–110.

Newman, Katherine and Sofya Aptekar (2007), 'Sticking around: delayed departure from the parental nest in Western Europe', in Sheldon Danzinger and Cecilia Elena Rouse (eds), New York: Russell Sage Foundation, pp. 207–30.

North, Douglass (1990), *Institutions, Institutional Change and Economic Performance*, Cambridge: Cambridge University Press.

O'Connor, Julia S. (1999), 'Employment equality strategies in liberal welfare states', in Diane Sainsbury (ed.), *Gender and Welfare State Regimes*, Oxford: Oxford University Press, pp. 47–74.

Pascall, Gillian and Jane Lewis (2004), 'Emerging gender regimes and policies for gender equality in a wider Europe', *Journal of Social Policy*, **33**(3), 373–94.

Pfau-Effinger, Birgit (2004), *Development of Culture, Welfare States and Women's Employment in Europe*, Burlington, VT: Ashgate.

Pontusson, Jonas (2005), *Inequality and Prosperity: Social Europe vs. Liberal America*, Ithaca, NY: Cornell University Press.

Roeters, Anne, Tanja Van der Lippe and Ester S. Kluwer (2012), 'Parental work demands and the frequency of child-related routine and interactive activities', *Journal of Marriage and Family*, **71**(5), 1193–204.

Rubery, Jill (1992), 'Pay, gender and the social dimension to Europe', *British Journal of Industrial Relations*, **30**(4), 605–21.

Rubery, Jill (1997), 'What do women want from full employment?', in John Philpott (ed.), *Working for Full Employment*, London: Routledge, pp. 63–80.

Rubery, Jill (2009), 'How gendering the varieties of capitalism requires a wider lens', *Social Politics: International Studies in Gender, State and Society*, **16**(2), 192–203.

Rubery, Jill, Mark Smith and Colette Fagan (1999), *Women's Employment in Europe: Trends and Prospects*, London: Routledge.

Sainsbury, Diane (1994), 'Women's and men's social rights: gendering dimensions of welfare states', in Diane Sainsbury (ed.), *Gendering Welfare States*, London: Sage, pp. 150–69.

Sainsbury, Diane (1996), *Gender, Equality and Welfare States*, Cambridge: Cambridge University Press.

Sainsbury, Diane (1999), 'Gender and social-democratic welfare states', in Diane Sainsbury (ed.), *Gender and Welfare State Regimes*, Oxford: Oxford University Press, pp. 75–115.

Sayer, Liana C. (2010), 'Trends in housework', in Judith Teas and Sonja Drobnič (eds), *Dividing the Domestic: Men, Women and Household Work in Cross-national Perspective*, Stanford, CA: Stanford University Press, pp. 19–38.

Scheiwe, Kirsten (1994), 'German pension insurance, gendered times and stratification', in Diane Sainsbury (ed.), *Gendering Welfare States*, London: Sage, pp. 132–49.

Smith, Nina (2003), 'The effects of taxation on married women's labour supply across four countries', *Oxford Economic Papers*, **55**(3), 417–39.

Soskice, David (2005), 'Varieties of capitalism and cross-national gender differences', *Social Politics: International Studies in Gender, State and Society*, **12**(2), 170–79.

Stark, Agneta (2008), 'Don't disturb the men: a viable gender-equality strategy?', in Naila Kabeer, Agneta Stark and Edda Magnus (eds), *Global Perspectives on Gender Equality: Reversing the Gaze*, London: Routledge, pp. 229–43.

Strober, Myra H. and Agnes Miling Kaneko Chan (1998), 'Husbands, wives, and housework: graduates of Stanford and Tokyo universities', *Feminist Economics*, **4**(3), 97–127.

Sümer, Sevil (2009), *European Gender Regimes and Policies: Comparative Perspectives*, Burlington, VT: Ashgate.

Tronto, Joan (2011), 'Privatizing neo-colonialism: migrant domestic care workers, partial citizenship, and responsibility', in Hanne Marlene Dahl, Marja Kevänen and Anne Kovalainen (eds), *Europeanization, Care, and Gender: Global Complexities*, London: Palgrave, pp. 165–81.

Warnecke, Tonia L. (2008), 'Women as wives, mothers or workers: how welfare eligibility requirements influence women's labor force participation – a case study of Spain', *Journal of Economic Issues*, **42**(4), 981–1004.

Whitley, Richard (1999), *Divergent Capitalisms: The Social Structuring and Change of Business Systems*, Oxford: Oxford University. Press.

Yeandle, Sue (1999), 'Women, men, and non-standard employment: breadwinning and caregiving in Germany, Italy, and the UK', in Rosemary Crompton (ed.), Oxford: Oxford University Press, pp. 80–104.

Yeates, Nicola (1999), 'Gender, familism and housing: matrimonial property rights in Ireland', *Women's Studies International Forum*, **22**(6), 607–18.

8. International development institutions, gender and economic life
Suzanne Bergeron

I INTRODUCTION

International development institutions (IDIs) have had a significant and wide-ranging impact on gender and economic life for the past half century. While the stated goal of development has been to improve the economic fortunes of all members of society, the economic and societal transformations associated with it have had mixed results on gender hierarchies and relations. While some initiatives have promoted gender equity, many others have contributed to the immiseration of women, indigenous populations, sexual minorities, and other subordinate groups, even as development itself has undergone numerous shifts in direction.

Agencies such as the World Bank, the United Nations (UN), and the United States Agency for International Development (USAID), among others, have long implemented agricultural and industrialization policies that structure access to resources such as land, credit, and paid employment in ways that assume a heteronormative male worker/female caregiver household, often limiting women's access to paid labor and other earning opportunities and exacerbating a variety of gender inequalities in the process. While the male worker assumption lost some ground in the 1970s with the promotion of export production in feminine-coded clothing and electronics manufacturing, women's insertion into these jobs had uneven effects in terms of improving women's lives (see Kabeer, 1994; Fernández-Kelly and Wolf, 2001). In the 1980s and early 1990s, the neoliberal turn of many IDIs toward structural adjustment resulted in fiscal, monetary, and exchange rate policies that heightened economic insecurity and increased work burdens for poor women. In contrast, in the recent shift away from strict neoliberalism, there has been greater attention to tackling gender issues within the human rights, anti-poverty, and growth mission of the IDIs.

Feminist researchers, practitioners, and activists have maintained pressure on the IDIs through all of these phases of development, and after some initial resistance, the institutions have become more attuned to gender issues. With its involvement in the decade on women starting with the 1975 Mexico City conference, the UN was an early pioneer in mainstreaming gender concerns across its many agencies. USAID established an office of Women in Development in the 1970s due to feminist initiatives in US foreign policy (Jaquette and Staudt, 2006). The World Bank's initial resistance was slowly whittled away throughout the 1970s and 1980s, and more recently this institution has come around to arguing that gender inequality deserves a central emphasis in its anti-poverty policy (Murphy, 1995; World Bank, 2012). The Organisation for Economic Co-operation and Development (OECD) identifies gender inequality as a core problem to be tackled in its anti-poverty guidelines. The UN Millennium Development Goals (MDGs), which aim to achieve key development outcomes in the 1990–2015 period, include the goals of promoting gender equality and empowering women. After decades in which women were underrepresented in professional and managerial positions at the IDIs, equal opportunity and inclusion is now high on the agenda (World Bank Group, 2010). In 2011 the International Monetary Fund (IMF) appointed its first female director, Christine Lagarde, who is also a well-known advocate for women's rights. The World Bank's choice of gender equality as the theme of its 2012 *World Development Report* is only the most recent evidence of how high gender has risen on the development agenda.

However, this heightened attention does not necessarily mean that gender equity issues have been adequately addressed within the IDIs. Scholarly considerations of development's transformed policy terrain demonstrate a number of unresolved tensions around this project, including a conflict between women in development (WID) versus gender and development (GAD) approaches, framings of gender in the instrumental terms of 'smart economics' versus those that focus on equity issues and enhancing human capabilities, emphases on enhancing women's paid labor force participation versus supporting women's role in social reproduction, difficulties of translating feminist insights into practice at these bureaucratic and technocratic institutions, and the IDIs' lack of accountability to the women in the global South they claim to be serving. This chapter pulls together feminist scholarship on gender and the IDIs to show how these tensions structure debates about the role of IDIs in creating more equitable economic outcomes for women in the global South.

The outline of the chapter is as follows. Section II summarizes the initial feminist challenges to the IFIs' male-biased policy frameworks that led to the implementation of WID policy initiatives in the 1970s. In Section III, I discuss the conceptual shift in development policy from the liberal WID approach of integrating women into existing institutions to the GAD focus on transforming institutional dimensions of power. Section IV examines the negative effects on women's lives associated with the sidelining of gender equity issues at the IDIs during the 1980s and early 1990s market-liberalization, 'Washington Consensus' years. In Section V, I highlight the role of feminist scholarship and women's movements in the push away from the Washington Consensus and toward a focus on social and equity concerns at the IDIs. This section also summarizes recent innovations in development policy that have increased support for previously neglected work in social reproduction, and highlighted the role of masculinities in development. The concluding section summarizes the progress and pitfalls associated with efforts to mainstream gender into the IDIs over the past few decades.

II   INTEGRATING WOMEN INTO DEVELOPMENT

Historically, the IDIs have been male-dominated in both institutional culture and numbers. While the creation of women's bureaus such as the International Research and Training Institute for the Advancement of Women at the UN and the World Bank's Women's Office provided more opportunities for women to rise to leadership positions in the 1970s, only since the late 1980s have more than a token number of women served managerial and professional ranks (Murphy, 1997; World Bank, 2010).[1] Given the narrow range of perspectives, experiences and voices, policy at the IDIs from the

1950s through the late 1970s reflected a male bias in development (Elson, 1991). What little attention was paid to women in development was confined to what Caroline Moser has dubbed a 'welfare approach' that emphasized making women better mothers and wives (Moser, 1989). These assistance projects focused on areas such as training women in nutrition, cooking, and sewing. The welfare approach did not serve to challenge gender inequalities, for it reflected a norm of the male breadwinner/female caregiver that, depending on the context, reinforced or helped to produce a gendered productive/reproductive sexual division of labor based on a western middle-class ideal (Wood, 2003). Contributing to these flawed notions is that development policies were based on a unitary economic model of the household and its assumptions about the efficiency of the gender division of labor, as well as a notion of the household as a site of harmony rather than conflict in which the (typically) male head makes decisions for the well-being of all.

It was not until the 1970s, with the implementation of the first Women in Development (WID) initiatives, that the IDIs began to pay explicit attention to questions of gender equity in economic development. While pressure from activists, feminist researchers and women's advocates inside the IDIs was instrumental here, the emergence of WID should also be viewed in the context of a broader paradigm shift in development from growth and modernization to a greater focus on poverty and inequality, which created more space for feminist concerns to get a hearing. For instance, the United Nations Development Programme (UNDP), which was early in taking women and economic development issues seriously, first broached the idea of integrating women into development at a 1972 conference aimed at addressing widening socioeconomic disparities in development more generally (Tinker, 2006).

WID initiatives were sparked by a growing body of research that demonstrated the adverse impact of development on women. Particularly influential was the pioneering work of Ester Boserup, whose *Women's Role in Economic Development* showed that development policy was hardly gender neutral in its effects (Boserup, 1970). Boserup's research on agricultural assistance in Africa demonstrated the failures of policies that did not acknowledge or support women's productive labor. In their attempts to modernize agriculture, the IDIs invisibilized women's contributions to farming by relying upon western notions of masculine and feminine tasks in which men were associated with the modern market sector and women with the subsistence sector (ibid.). With these assumptions guiding policy, men now had a monopoly on technology, seeds, fertilizer, credit, and land rights, while women lost access to resources, income, and power. These outcomes were not only inequitable but inefficient by underutilizing women as an economic resource. With little support for women's farming, many projects failed on their own terms. For instance, in some cases, the failure to recognize women's work led to flawed policies that offered support to male farmers for crops that only women grew (Staudt, 1978), while in other cases inattention to intrahousehold complexities led to failed food security policies by wrongly assuming that women would pitch in with growing crops owned and controlled by their husbands (Dey, 1981).

Such concerns were taken up successfully by WID advocates working within the IDIs. WID was able to gain traction in these institutions for the following reasons. First, by connecting equity with efficiency-based arguments, WID advocates were able to justify investments in women in terms that other Bank and USAID staffers could support – as contributing to the bottom line of productivity and growth (Kardam, 1991). Bringing together gender equity and productivist efficiency concerns was a powerful political strategy for keeping development planners' focus on gender issues (Razavi and Miller, 1995). Further, WID's liberal feminist solution of integrating women into economic arenas in which they had been left out suggested that exclusion from the marketplace – rather than gendered power dynamics – was the cause of women's subordination. While WID's feminist demands for women's equality were certainly threatening to many working within the IDIs, the idea that the fix lay in the creation of well-functioning and inclusive markets, rather than the need to transform gender relations, was more palatable to the key players in those institutions (Tinker, 1990). And finally, because Boserup made the argument that women and men in Africa had been relatively equal prior to male-biased development interventions, gender equity could not be rejected as a culturally inappropriate 'western' import (Jaquette, 1990).

In addition to the effectiveness of advocates working on the inside, the role of women's movements and organizations put political pressure on the IDIs to transform development from the outside. The United Nations Commission for Women played a crucial role in transforming the policy landscape by launching the UN Decade for Women in 1975, which brought together numerous organizations for transnational dialogue at the World Conference on Women in Mexico City, Mexico, and then Nairobi, Kenya, 10 years later. This also contributed to the momentum of WID. Another influential organization during this period was the women's caucus of the Society for International Development, which mobilized to integrate gender issues into the World Bank and USAID (Tinker, 1990). As a result of these initiatives, by the middle of the 1970s, all of the major development institutions had a WID office.

This is not to suggest that the implementation of WID resulted in a dramatic shift within the institutional bureaucracies of the major donor agencies. At the World Bank, for example, there was only one officer assigned to WID, and the small amount of funding given to women's projects has led analysts to charge the Bank with paying no more than lip service to women's issues (Kardam, 1991). While the UN and other organizations were slightly more attentive to WID concerns, as a group, development institutions did not make gender equity a priority in terms of funding. Still, WID made some gains with regard to women's economic well-being, including targeted programs to train development practitioners to challenge their male biases, programs to provide support to woman farmers, and income generation projects of all kinds, including those aimed at women-headed households that had previously been ignored in heteronormative development frameworks (Jaquette and Staudt, 2006). WID also provided an initial challenge to market-centered definitions of work by collecting data on previously ignored productive activities such as women's unpaid labor on family farms (Razavi and Miller, 1995).

III   CONCEPTUAL SHIFTS IN POLICY: FROM 'WOMEN' TO 'GENDER'

While the WID approach offered a progressive shift in development away from seeing women only as mothers, its near-exclusive focus on integrating women into the market failed to adequately address women's unpaid care work or the linkages between the productive and reproductive spheres. WID also offered little analysis regarding the relational aspects of women's subordination. There was a tendency to treat women as a homogeneous group rather than identifying class, race, sexuality, and other differences among women. Further, WID policies of integrating women into the development process were not making much headway in improving women's lives, and many started to believe that what needed changing was development itself. The instrumental cast of WID that views gender equity as a means to an end, not as a goal unto itself, was failing to address the systematic nature of gender injustice (Baden and Goetz, 1998). These and other critiques of WID began emerging from a variety of feminist quarters by the early 1980s, leading to the emergence of a new approach that focused more squarely on gender power relations that were keeping women from benefiting from development.

This emerging gender and development (GAD) approach drew upon a social construction of gender model that could acknowledge how gender experiences varied by race, class, nationality, location, and so forth rather than viewing women as a homogeneous group (Moser, 1989). Further, while WID's focus on minimizing discrimination against women was laudable, it offered little challenge to the current capitalism-centered development paradigm. GAD theorists began to link the social construction of gender to the power relations embedded in many development initiatives, asking how patriarchy, capitalism and modernization come together to systematically assign women inferior roles. They also began to move beyond questions of how women could be integrated into the economy to broader questions of how women could be empowered through organizing and activism (Sen and Grown, 1987).

As GAD gained traction within academic and activist circles, its concepts and language began to filter into the IDIs as well. But the relevance of gender relations analysis was a contested issue in policy circles, and the central focus of GAD was often lost in these institutional contexts. The more politicized meaning of GAD, in terms of addressing structural inequalities based on gender power dynamics, is not as easily adopted into development strategies and programs coming out of the IDIs. Many projects aimed at women, despite being touted as emanating from a GAD perspective, still reflect the WID approach.

As one example, the term 'gender' is typically viewed as a stand-in for 'women'. This has been the case in gender-focused anti-poverty approaches investigating the causes of women's poverty in ways that do not examine gender power dynamics at the intimate, institutional, or transnational level. For instance, most programs aimed at reducing women's poverty retain their market-oriented focus on integrating women into the labor market, even though these low-wage, often undervalued feminine-coded jobs often fail to lift them out of poverty. Further anti-poverty policies place an emphasis on the rise of women-headed households as the problem, even though the data do not bear out the assumption that women in single-headed households are necessarily worse off than other women (Chant, 2003).

In other contexts gender was used as a way to take the focus away from women and on the troublingly feminist implications of challenging inequities (Razavi and Miller, 1995). As Eudine Barriteau argued at the NGO Forum at the World Conference on Women in Beijing, the shift in discourse from women to gender in Jamaica had led to a focus away from women to men at risk, and to denying the very existence of women-specific inequities (see Baden and Goetz, 1998). In addition, a common institutional reading of how to do gender in development has been to generate gender-disaggregated data. While these data are useful, they also limit attention to questions about gender and social relations by reducing women's needs to a set of gaps that need to be filled, rather than a more transformative project focused on changing power relations (ibid.).

An additional critique of GAD discourse is that it often frames gender oppression only in terms of local patriarchy that ignores colonial legacies, and often represents women of the global South in colonial terms as helpless victims of gender power dynamics who need to be saved by western women. This also serves to redirect attention from global economic exploitation as a potentially greater cause of women's subordination than the cultural construction of gender in their own societies (Mohanty, 1991). Finally, while a social construction of gender approach could yield sophisticated and intersectional understandings of women's and men's lives, in practice GAD often traded in reified gender characteristics and attitudes. Representing women and men as if they embody a set of given characteristics is troubling not just because it obscures differences among each group, but also because it suggests generalized gender differences in behavior that can be relied on in creating policy, such as the idea that all women are carers (Jackson, 2002).

However, it would be unfair to say that the conceptual shift left no impression on the IDIs. The transition from WID to GAD did open up space for change in development thinking and policy at the IDIs in a few key ways. First, it created an impetus for examining the gendered implications of all development policies that allowed gender to be mainstreamed rather than isolated in a women's programs office. Further, this led to widespread gender training within the IDIs that put the impact of development policies on gender relations on the radar of many practitioners. This allowed for more attention to gender inequities in the direction of policy, as well as leverage for activists both inside and outside of these institutions to call for attention to gender.

IV   THE WASHINGTON CONSENSUS, GENDER AND NEOLIBERAL RESTRUCTURING

At the time that this shift from WID to GAD was occurring at the IDIs, however, there was a broader conceptual shift in development that derailed much of the attention to gender equity in these institutions. This was an emerging 'Washington Consensus' of market efficiency, financial balance, and growth as the focus of key players in development in Washington, DC, such as the World Bank, USAID, and the IMF, replacing an earlier emphasis on inequality and basic needs (Williamson, 1989). Central to this policy shift was the implementation of structural adjustment policies (SAPs) undertaken at the behest of the IDIs by borrowing countries. SAPs often included dramatic reform requirements as conditionality for receiving loans, and these interventions were aimed at addressing symptoms related to debt crisis in countries of the global South, such as high inflation, fiscal deficit, and external imbalance. These symptoms were more often than not the result of structural economic dislocations due to significant changes in the global economy in the previous decade, including rising global prices for key commodities and the pushing of loans on these countries by a corporate banking system that found itself awash in petrodollars to lend in the 1970s (Pastor, 1987).

The World Bank and the IMF – the latter reinventing itself during this period from an agency that monitored exchange rates into a development and international finance institution – undertook hundreds of SAPs in the developing countries from the late 1970s and early 1990s. Other IDIs such as USAID and the Asian Development Bank oriented their lending toward adjustment programs as well. It should be noted that the Washington Consensus approach to development that focused on liberalization, privatization, and market efficiency was not limited to the IMF and the World Bank, or to structural adjustment conditionalities. It also took hold of the broader imagination of development during this period, as the Keynesian economic model upon which state-led development interventions were based was being challenged in many quarters, including the influential sites of US and UK government. But the SAPs, which had an enormous impact on people's lives in the global South and are most emblematic of this period of development policy-making, will be the focus of this section of the chapter.

Under the structural adjustment requirements placed on countries that required loans and refinancing, several policies were typically pursued. IDIs called for the removal of price supports on basic foods, subsidies for housing and education, minimum wage laws, and safety nets for the poor. Countries were forced to focus on export promotion in an attempt to draw in foreign exchange, in many cases resulting in less food available for domestic consumption and increased economic insecurity in an unstable global market. Export-oriented industry was encouraged through the establishment of free trade zones in which minimum wage laws, workplace safety, and other protections were loosened or nonexistent. To create a positive environment for foreign investment, the Bank and the IMF called for environmental regulations to be scrapped. Imported food, clothing, and other necessities became far more expensive as currencies were devalued to make exports from the home country more attractive. As the Bank and Fund's standard formula for fixing the developing economies called for a tight monetary policy, credit was difficult to obtain and high interest rates crippled farmers and small business owners. Under conditionality mandates, governments sold off state-owned enterprises such as utilities to private firms, making these basic goods more expensive. While the goal of SAPs was to move each country toward fiscal, monetary, current account, and capital account balance, in many cases these policies failed on their own terms. Further, SAPs fell hard on the poor and vulnerable (Cornia et al., 1987).

As a significant body of research has documented, SAPs had a generally negative economic impact on women, who bore the brunt of adjustment in terms of losing access to social supports from the state and being laid off from state-funded jobs in the social service, health, and education fields.[2] Women faced pressure to work more hours in formal and informal sectors due to rising prices for basic goods and heightened economic insecurity (Elson, 1991). Multinational firms drawn to developing countries by export promotion incentives made hiring and production decisions that typically impeded rather than furthering gender equity goals. As economic conditions became worse at home, women became part of a wave of immigrant labor moving north to escape the poverty fueled by structural adjustment. Sometimes this migration was explicitly encouraged by developing country governments. For example, the government of the Philippines encouraged women to migrate and send home remittances, which provided much-needed foreign exchange (Parrenas, 2001). Many women across the global South did not accept these difficult economic conditions, and throughout the 1980s and 1990s women's organizations mounted significant protests against structural adjustment (Keck and Sikkink, 1998).

Despite these negative effects on women and the activist outcry against SAPs, the IDIs paid minimal attention to women and gender in the framing, implementation, or assessment of these policies. Women's concerns were rendered invisible by the abstractions of the neoclassical economic theoretical models that undergirded SAPs, as well as the technocratic, undemocratic nature of how they were imposed upon the nations of the global South. As Isabella Bakker dryly notes, structural adjustment represented a gender paradox in policy-making in which gender became unimportant at precisely the moment when it was most salient (Bakker, 1994). Of particular concern to many feminists working in development was the neglect of the reproductive sector, which, while crucial to economic well-being, was often ignored by economic models. For instance, one pernicious and false assumption made in adjustment programs in the 1980s and 1990s was that the supply of reproductive labor was perfectly elastic and would be forthcoming to pick up services such as childcare and eldercare that were once provided by the state (Elson, 1991). Because the sphere of social reproduction was not included in national accounts and macroeconomic policy, SAPs easily relied upon the unaccounted-for household sector to absorb the costs of adjustment. This contributed to a crisis of social reproduction in the developing countries and spurred feminist economists' demands to include unpaid reproductive labor in national accounts (Benería and Feldman, 1992). As one UNICEF report critical of structural adjustment stated, the 'crisis of social disinvestments is financed from a social fund provided by the superhuman efforts of poor women' (Cornia et al., 1987, p. 38).

But the crisis of social reproduction was not the only gendered effect of market-oriented restructuring and structural adjustment. The export orientation required within many SAPs led to significant changes in gender relations and economic life. While the move toward export promotion by developing country governments cannot be laid entirely at the feet of the IDIs, it was certainly a cornerstone of conditionalities for receiving aid and assistance during the 1980s and 1990s. The effects of export-oriented development and trade liberalization included gender shifts and inequalities in employment, wages, access to consumer goods, and labor distribution within households. Women have been drawn into garment, textile, and electronics jobs in those countries that have specialized in those exports (Standing, 1999), but in other places have lost employment when liberalized trade led to import displacement of these goods. Access to income from these industrial jobs can improve women's economic fortunes and give them leverage to challenge gender inequities, and the equity benefits of factory work are often touted by IDIs such as the World Bank and USAID. However, as many of these plants are exploiting gender inequities for gain (Enloe, 2000), the IDIs often overstate the equity effects. Positions in these industries are typically characterized by significant vertical and horizontal segregation, with women confined to undervalued female-dominated jobs that are characterized by low wages and vulnerability in working conditions when compared to male-identified ones, which are more likely to be higher-paid positions and supervisory roles.

Thirty years of feminist scholarship on the subject suggests that whether access to paid work intensifies gender oppression, challenges it, and/or transforms it must be examined on a case-by-case basis. For instance, in a case study of Mexico, it was shown that while women face long hours, terrible working conditions, and are offered little in terms of job security in positions that do little to challenge gender stereotypes, access to income gave them leverage to break free of sometimes stifling patriarchal expectations in their homes and communities (Fernández-Kelly and Wolf, 2001). In a case study of Bangladesh, in contrast, women's access wages in export industries were not shown to increase their leverage at home or their overall empowerment within society (Ahmed, 2004). Attention to how jobs and opportunities are stratified not only by gender by also by class, race, ethnicity, and sexuality is key to understanding the impact of export industrialization on gender and economic life.

Moving to the agriculture sector, in some cases export-promotion strategies resulted in a feminization of labor, and thus increased access to labor market income for women. Employment opportunities opened up for women in large commercial farms and processing aspects of agro-export production, particularly in cut flowers and packing produce (Barrientos and Dolan, 2001). These jobs, however, are more precarious than men's positions in these industries, as men are more likely to occupy managerial or permanent roles (ILO, 2003). In cases where women lost control over income-generating opportunities, particularly as smallholder agricultural sectors moved away from locally consumed crops toward export-oriented goods controlled by men, women's fortunes declined. Statistically speaking, women do not typically make decisions or control the income from commercialized export crop production, and women's contribution to export production on family farms often comes at the expense of their other economic activities. So as households moved away from domestic production to export-oriented crops, another effect has been that the extra demand on women's labor time in social reproductive tasks is often taken up by girls at the expense of their education, particularly in the context of the implementation of user fees for education as a cost recovery fiscal measure under structural adjustment, which contributed to the opportunity cost of educating girls (Katz, 1995; Van Staveren et al., 2007).

V   GENDER AND DEVELOPMENT IN THE POST-WASHINGTON CONSENSUS YEARS

By the mid-1990s, mounting criticism of the neoliberal market-based approach to development in general, and structural adjustment in particular, was emerging from numerous quarters. Anti-poverty, anti-globalization, indigenous rights, women's, and environmental organizations pressured national governments and IDIs such as the World Bank and the IMF to address the inequalities, social dislocations, and environmental effects of liberalization and usurious debt repayment on poor countries. Women's organizations were particularly active in these efforts. For example, the negative impact of structural adjustment on women was a focus of the NGO sessions at the 1995 World Conference on Women in Beijing, China, where Women's Eyes on the World Bank was formed to pull that organization in a direction of being more accountable and responsive to women's needs (Kerr, 1999).

As discussed above, the growing body of scholarship documenting the negative impacts of neoliberal reform and structural adjustment on gender equity was making these impacts harder for the IDIs to ignore. Armed with this research, advocates both outside and inside the IDIs were gaining traction in their push for change. The growing influence of the human development approach at the UN, which published its first *Human Development Report* in 1990, also contributed to the breakdown of the Washington Consensus model, creating more space for gender-sensitive policy. Human development emerged as a critical response to the social costs of the market-centric approach of the 1980s, and traced its conceptual roots to economist Amartya Sen's capabilities theory, which focused on the expansion of human choices rather than per capita GDP as the goal of development (Sen, 1988).

Finally, within the context of this push toward a social turn in development and away from a strict focus on liberalization, new innovations in mainstream economics played a decisive role. As former World Bank chief economist Joseph Stiglitz states, a paradigm shift in mainstream economics toward a greater consideration of institutions, culture, distributional factors, and market failures in determining economic outcomes – through the development of new institutionalist and information-theoretic approaches – was crucial in challenging the old state/market dichotomies that had anchored development policy during the 1980s (Stiglitz, 1998). Because it is believed to be the most rigorous of the social sciences, traditional economic theory is highly influential in development in general and the World Bank in particular, and those approaches that do not incorporate it are more likely to encounter resistance. Thus the paradigm shift in economics made attention to social and institutional factors, especially those related to gender inequalities, more legitimate in the policy circles of the major IDIs (Bergeron, 2003).

The influence of all of these factors – pressure from social movements, academic research on the inequalities and dislocations associated with adjustment, the emergence of the alternative human development approach, and the paradigm shift in mainstream economics – worked together to transform development thinking in general and gender policy specifically in the post-Washington Consensus years. For instance, in the early 1990s, the World Bank instituted an operational policy on gender, resulting in a third of its projects including gender-related components, with the notable exception of adjustment lending (Murphy, 1995). Another marker of this shift at the World Bank was the publication of its first flagship research report on gender, *Engendering Development* (World Bank, 2001).

The report's emphasis on the social and cultural factors that influence women's capabilities and agency, along with its focus on social development concerns such as education and healthcare, represents a real improvement over the Bank's earlier market efficiency, growth-fetishized approach. Conceptually, it drew upon innovations in economics to make its case for gender-sensitive policy more acceptable to a range of audiences inside and outside of the Bank. For instance, intrahousehold bargaining approaches were used to bring attention to the need to frame policies in ways that are attentive to power dynamics and work distribution in households (Bergeron, 2006). By addressing women's disproportionate burdens in care work, the report also signaled that the Bank had finally acknowledged a major feminist critique of earlier restructuring policy: the invisibility of social reproduction (Bedford, 2009).[3]

At the UN, there has also been a shift to more emphasis on gender equity as a goal of development, both through the impact of the World Conferences on Women, as well as the shift toward the human development paradigm in the 1990s. An early pioneer in gender mainstreaming in development projects, the UN linked gender equity to health, education, labor market, growth, and efficiency outcomes. In 1995, it began publishing two important indices of gender inequality, the Gender Empowerment Measure (GEM) to capture achievements and opportunities to improve women's capabilities in decision-making such as parliamentary representation, labor force participation and managerial positions, and the Gender-Related Development Index (GDI), which uses gender-disaggregated data on life expectancy, educational attainment, and per capita GDP as the basis of its measure (see Gaye et al., Chapter 24, this volume). Attention to these indices has pushed policy-making in the direction of focus on the relationships between institutional discrimination, education level, women's and girls' health, gender violence, political representation, and labor market participation as markers of women's access to economic opportunities that would expand their capabilities.

This focus on human development and a human rights approach has created space for feminist economists and policy advocates to explore the complexities of gender equality. For instance, feminist work has traced the relationships between gender violence and property ownership (Panda and Agarwal, 2005), and integrated gender equity into macroeconomic policies on human rights grounds (Balakrishnan and Elson, 2008). It has spawned policy interventions that include changing land titles, providing women with microcredit in order to jump-start income-generating activities, getting women more involved in politics, and challenging barriers that keep women from pursuing market labor.

The IDIs have also broadened their toolkits to address women's poverty and disempowerment, and are now utilizing approaches such as gender budgeting and microcredit lending despite initial resistance to these 'unorthodox' tools and methods. Gender budgeting emerged from feminist economists' concerns regarding the differential impact of structural adjustment on women and men, and calls for government planning that identifies gender biases and gaps in government policies and budgets (Budlender et al., 2002). UN Women has taken the lead in supporting these gender budgeting initiatives, with programs at the national or local level in 45 countries spanning the regions of Africa, the Middle East, Eastern Europe, Asia, and Latin America. These have been drawn upon to support policies addressing women's unpaid social reproductive work, education for girls, and gender-based violence (UN Women, 2012).

In tandem with this work on gender budgets has been a move to engender national income accounts and other statistics in order to provide gender-disaggregated data on which to make policy. While much of this work has been initiated independently by governments, the IDIs have also played a role. For example in 1993 the UN, building upon the pioneering work on gender biases in national accounts by Marilyn Waring (1989), revised the system of national accounts to take into account women's unpaid productive activities and is assisting developing economies in preparing these satellite accounts. This represents a remarkable shift after decades of resistance to the idea of counting women's unpaid labor as work in official statistics (Banerjee, 2002), and provides an improved statistical measure upon which to base gender-sensitive policy-making. Countries such as the United Kingdom, Finland, and Australia have produced fully fledged satellite accounts while the developing economies have engaged in more limited approaches because of lack of data (Esquivel, 2011). Some limited policy implementation based on these satellite accounts has included investment in infrastructure and subsidies to support care work (Bryson, 2008). Feminist economists have been instrumental in pushing for increased integration of these accounts into gender-sensitive policy (Esquivel et al., 2008; Budlender, 2010).

The idea of microcredit as an anti-poverty strategy, and one aimed particularly at women, had been around for almost 20 years before the IDIs took it up in the 1990s. 1995 was declared the year of microcredit by the UN and the World Bank began supporting microfinance projects in 1996, later extending its program to target the poorest of the poor in developing countries. Microcredit involves lending small sums of money to the poor to invest in improvements in their business or farm, or to spur entrepreneurship and new ventures. Given the poverty of the borrowers, even a small sum of money, often less than $100, can make a difference, particularly as they have no access to more traditional forms of borrowing. The vast majority of IDI microfinance programs are pitched toward women as a way to assist them in escaping poverty, as women are often the poorest of the poor, and gender discrimination interferes with other means of obtaining credit.

In addition to anti-poverty goals, there are also gender empowerment factors that have been associated with microcredit. Women's access to finance is assumed to increase their economic agency in their households and communities, including greater bargaining power within the family leading to more control over resources and a fairer division of tasks (see Menon and van der Meulen Rodgers, Chapter 22, this volume). Lending to women has been touted as smart economics because women are assumed to be more likely to invest in productive activities and their children's well-being than men (Khandker, 1999). This is a major turnaround from the previous policy regime of extending credit to men only.

While there is much to celebrate in this shift toward targeting women as clients of development, framing gender-aware policy, focusing on women's human rights and capabilities, and expanding the toolkit to better meet women's needs, a number of scholars have pointed out that the shift is not as dramatic a change as it appears at first glance. Gender is still considered secondary to the supposed fundamentals of growth and market efficiency, against which social goals such as gender equity must accommodate themselves (Elson and Çagatay, 2000). Central to much feminist critique is the fact that the IDIs seem incapable of addressing the fact that paid work, or integration into the market through microcredit, is not necessarily empowering to women (see Charusheela, 2003). About microcredit specifically there has been much debate, for IDIs often tout it as a 'magic bullet' for women's empowerment, but the actual results are mixed and not particularly inspiring. The anti-poverty impact is not very great for the poorest of the poor, and loans are more often than not used to cover basic needs rather than jump-start new ventures. Further, in terms of women's empowerment the outcomes are also mixed, as women do not always have control over the loans, and even in cases they do, a small bank loan cannot substitute for the more transformative interventions needed to empower women (Kabeer, 2005; Barker and Feiner, 2006).

There has also been significant concern about the instrumental emphasis of policy discourse that links investing in women with 'smart economics,' in which gender equity is framed as being worth pursuing only if it contributes to goals of growth and efficiency (Balakrishnan and Elson, 2008; Zuckerman, 2009). By framing gender equity as a project of granting rights in order to liberate previously untapped resources of women's labor, the World Bank's recent social turn seems less of a move away from neoliberalism than a reformed version of the neoliberal project of marketization and efficiency enhancement (Bergeron, 2011). And while this shift has utilized the discourse of GAD, most of its projects have adhered more closely to the WID approach, which is focused on integrating women into markets and the global cash nexus as the road to empowerment, rather than transforming gender relations.

But there have been some areas in which GAD has taken hold of the development imagination, notably in the shift toward male inclusion in the past 15 years, placing attention to how masculinities work to structure power and privilege as well as the role that men can play in reducing gender inequalities. Development interventions to address gender struggles related to masculine role expectations, as well as those focused on transforming men's role in the relational aspect of gender inequality, have been central to this shift. Rethinking gender policy to take masculinities into account, particularly within the context of the UN, has drawn upon contemporary feminist masculinities scholarship (for example, Grieg et al., 2000). While the preponderance of masculinities work in development is focused on sexual health and violence, some recent interventions have focused explicitly on gender and economic life.

One key concern has been men's exclusion from the economic gains of development. There are now higher ratios for girls' enrollment in secondary school in approximately half of the developing countries, and 49 out of 92 reporting countries show higher female enrollment in tertiary education (Jacobson, 2006). Further, while female participation rates remain lower than men's, the changing structure of work has led to a decline in male participation rates in a high percentage of developing countries, with long-term unemployment in Latin America and Africa falling hardest on men (ibid.). As Ian Bannon and Maria Correia (2006) of the World Bank argue, dislocations related to economic restructuring make it difficult for men to fulfill their breadwinner role, leading them toward violence, alcoholism, substance abuse, and unsafe sex as ways to affirm their manhood. This underwrites codes of masculinity that allow men to shirk their responsibilities and women to be overburdened, which leads to further social breakdown. Policies aimed at addressing these issues have focused on promoting responsible fatherhood to challenging violent attitudes among men.

Development has also become concerned with the relational aspect of gender in development policy, particularly in addressing the unequal burden of housework in families. As Kate Bedford's case study of World Bank gender policy in Ecuador and Argentina shows, the goal of sharing partnerships in which women and men jointly make equitable decisions about household work and resource distribution has been a key part of gender equity strategy in those countries. Encouraging women to work outside the home, augmented by gender training for men in more equitable versions of masculinity, was pursued by Bank staffers as a way of getting men to share household labor (Bedford, 2009). Since this line of research utilizes the conceptual framework of intrahousehold bargaining models, however, the emergent policy solutions rest on the assumption that women's increased income will improve their bargaining power at home. This is problematic for reasons discussed above.

While the goals are laudable, there are some troubling aspects of the discourse of masculinities in economic development worth mentioning. First, it reinforces stereotypes of men in developing economies as inherently profligate and blameworthy, as well as failing to take into account differences among men. As Andrea Cornwall notes, while many men have access to positions of power, we cannot assume that all men have this power or even wish to take it up (Cornwall, 2000). Further, with regard to sharing couplehood approaches, the heteronormative, nuclear family assumption leaves out female-headed households, non-heterosexual households, households that do not conform to dominant gender roles, and all manner of alternative arrangements. Sharing couplehood also offers a neoliberal, privatized solution to the crisis of social reproduction by keeping care work in the realm of the household (Bergeron, 2011). Further, the focus on the need to promote sharing partnerships because of a crisis of hyper-masculinity is a top-down strategy that also reinforces the colonial assumption of non-western men as backward (Bedford, 2009). More critical and effective initiatives utilize ground-up approaches rooted in local norms and strategies for resistance, recognize differences among men, acknowledge the fact that many men do not benefit from hegemonic masculinity, and engage men as allies and advocates in challenging restrictive gender roles (Esplen, 2006).

The question of care work, and how to address the crisis of social reproduction in development, is currently a matter of significant debate in the field. While attention to formerly ignored unpaid care labor has certainly been welcomed by those working in the field, there are concerns about the policy options pursued by the IDIs to support care. The sharing partnership solution outlined above has its shortcomings, as do other key approaches to supporting care work in current social policy circles. For example, there have been a number of World Bank and UN funded programs that offer cash transfers to mothers in exchange for enrolling their children in educational and health programs as a way of supporting social reproduction. But these programs rely upon an essentialist notion that women are more caring, and tend to confirm rather than challenge women's role as unpaid care providers. It also keeps care in the private sector instead of putting some of the responsibility on the public sector (Molyneux, 2006). Some recent policy interventions have tried to sidestep such maternalist and heteronormative assumptions by providing the cash transfer to a non-gender-specified parent or guardian, open to men and women in many different kinds of household care arrangements. One example of this is the Child Support Grant in South Africa, offered to the child's primary caretaker (not necessarily the mother) and not contingent on the child attending school, participation in nutrition and health classes, or the caretaker's performance of community work, all of which were troubling features of childcare benefits instituted by IDIs in developing countries (Razavi, 2007).

VI   CONCLUSION

Based on the current rhetoric of the IDIs, it appears that gender equity is now a central concern of development policy. The MDGs, which structure the focus of much development policy at the UN, include the goal of gender empowerment, and campaigning to get women into elective office, training women as managers, and integrating them into paid employment are pursued as a way of achieving this goal. In an unprecedented move, the World Bank made gender issues the core theme of its annual *World Development Report* (World Bank, 2012). But the extent to which this expanded discourse reflects a real transformation of policy-making at the IDIs remains an open question. While gender has been mainstreamed into many key initiatives, there is little monitoring or assessment of gender impacts, and therefore not much accountability for gender outcomes (UN, 2009).

Further, the spending on gender remains low. For instance, only 1.6 percent of the

World Bank's budget was invested in gender and social inclusion in 2010 (World Bank, 2010). Other estimates of total development assistance, taking into account all of the IDIs as well as private aid sources, show a more promising trend with approximately 25 percent of aid estimated to focus on some aspect of gender equity (OECD, 2008), but the vast majority of those funds have gone to health and education, with few resources channeled to improve women's economic situation. While there has been increased attention to human rights, rather than instrumental approaches, in development discourse, with the World Bank adopting human rights language regarding gender equity on par with the UN (World Bank, 2012), equality for women is still generally presented in terms of achieving efficiencies and other instrumental payoffs, and otherwise tethered to the conceptual constraints of neoclassical economics (Griffin, 2010). Policy discourse continues to conflate paid labor with empowerment for women in official statistics and elsewhere, thus ignoring the fact that for many, insertion into the sometimes precarious and low-wage labor force, or similarly precarious self-employment through microcredit lending, is hardly empowering. Further, the barriers to gender equity are often framed as backward cultural beliefs that place barriers on women's empowerment, which fails to capture the complex realities of local histories, global transformations, and women's and men's lives, and thus fails to locate solutions to poverty and inequality (Zein-Elabdin and Charusheela, 2003).

It is difficult to make any sort of sweeping claims regarding the impact of these policies on women's lives on a global scale because of many factors, including the lack of consistent series in data collection, the difficulties of parsing out the effects of aid from other influences on gender equity, and the limited work that has been done in identifying and assessing targeted gender mainstreaming activities (UN, 2009). As this chapter has emphasized throughout, the results of IDI policy on economic life have been mixed, and vary based on national, regional, and local context as well as the differing social locations that women occupy with regard to class, race, sexuality, ethnicity, and so forth. But drawing upon some of the IDIs' own statistics, it seems that the progress is not as great as one would expect from reading official documents.

Improvements have mostly come in areas such as health (particularly maternal mortality declines) and female to male education ratios, which are certainly factors related to women's economic well-being that should not be discounted. But for improvement in indicators related specifically to economics, the pace of change has been slow, and women continue to experience high rates of poverty, burdens of unpaid work, and lack of access to and control over economic resources (UN, 2009). For example, with all of the effort placed on integrating women into paid labor in World Bank gender policy, there has only been a 2 percent increase in women's labor force participation worldwide from 1980 to 2009 (World Bank, 2012, p. 200). Examining a consistent series of data on Latin America carefully prepared by a team of feminist development practitioners at FLACSO shows that the wage gap in this region closed during the 1995–2003 period by 4 percentage points, or ½ percent per year (FLACSO, 2005), despite a considerable push for change in this area through UN and World Bank gender policy. A careful longitudinal and comparative study of gender wage gaps in selected occupations in developed and developing countries found that from the 1980s to 2000 there was no decline in the wage gap in lower-income countries (Oostendorp, cited in UN, 2009, p. 31). As Cornwall et al. (2004) write:

> Gender is now well established in development . . . But the extent of change in women's lives does not match this discursive landslide. For many gender and development advocates, it appears that the more women and poverty are equated in development discourse, the more many women experience entrenched poverty; the more gender is mainstreamed, the less we find effective gender equality policies within key policy spaces and documents. (p. 1)

This suggests that rather than seeing the IDIs' recent turn toward gender as a victory for feminist economic goals, it should be viewed as a particular sort of opening for pushing forward those goals. The recent centrality of gender as a rhetorical feature of international development can be used strategically, as it provides fresh opportunities to call for accountability of the IDIs with regard to gender policy. Being attentive to the constraints and the shifting gender discourse of these institutions, and not buying into their rhetoric, allows feminist advocates to be more effective change agents with regard to gender and economic life.

NOTES

1. By 1995, all of the major IDIs made a commitment to gender equity in hiring through the Organizational and Institutional Gender Information Network (ORIGIN). From 1995 to the present, the number of women in managerial positions rose from 13 to 32 percent at the World Bank, from 8 to 20 percent at the IMF, and from 11 to 26 percent at the United Nations (World Bank, 2010; Applebaum and Stoleberg, 2011).
2. See, for instance, Commonwealth Secretariat (1989), Palmer (1991), Benería and Feldman (1992), Bakker (1994), Sparr (1994), and Çagatay et al. (1995).
3. For an account of *Engendering Development* from a feminist economics perspective, see Kuiper and Barker (2006).

REFERENCES

Ahmed, Fauzia (2004), 'The rise of the Bangladeshi garment industry: globalization, women workers and voice', *NWSA Journal*, **16**(2), 34–45.
Applebaum, Binyamin and Sheryl Gay Stoleberg (2011), 'At I.M.F., men on prowl and women on guard', *New York Times*, May 19.
Baden, Sally and Anne Marie Goetz (1998), 'Who needs [sex] when you can have [gender]?', in Cecile Jackson and Ruth Pearson (eds), *Feminist Visions of Development: Gender, Analysis and Policy*, London: Routledge, pp. 19–38.
Bakker, Isabella (1994), *The Strategic Silence: Gender and Economic Policy*, London: Zed Books.
Balakrishnan, Radhika and Diane Elson (2008), 'Auditing economic policy in light of obligations on economic and social rights', *Essex Human Rights Review*, **5**(1), 32–54.
Banerjee, Nirmala (2002), *Gender Sensitive Statistical Measures for the Informal Sector*, New York: UNIFEM.
Bannon, Ian and Maria Correia (2006), 'Introduction', in Ian Bannon and Maria Correia (eds), *The Other Half of Gender: Men's Issues in Development*, Washington, DC: World Bank, pp. xvii –xxiv.
Barker, Drucilla K. and Susan Feiner (2006), 'Microcredit and women's poverty', *Dollars and Sense*, 268, available at:http://dollarsandsense.org/archives/2006/1106feinerbarker.html (accessed, September 9, 2012).
Barrientos, Stephanie and Catherine Dolan (2001), 'Gender and ethical trade: a mapping of the issues in African horticulture', Natural Resources Institute Report 2624, Natural Resources Institute, available at:www.nri.org/NRET/genderet.pdf (accessed August 16, 2012).
Bedford, Kate (2009), *Developing Partnerships: Gender, Sexuality and the Reformed World Bank*, Minneapolis, MN: University of Minnesota Press.
Benería, Lourdes and Shelly Feldman (1992), *Unequal Burden: Economic Crises, Persistent Poverty and Women's Work*, Boulder, CO: Westview.

Bergeron, Suzanne (2003), 'The post-Washington consensus and economic representations of women in development at the World Bank', *International Feminist Journal of Politics*, **5**(2), 397–419.

Bergeron, Suzanne (2006), 'Colonizing knowledge: interdisciplinarity in *Engendering Development*', in Kuiper and Barker (eds), pp. 127–41.

Bergeron, Suzanne (2011), 'Economics, performativity and social reproduction in global development', *Globalizations*, **8**(2), 151–61.

Boserup, Ester (1970), *Women's Role in Economic Development*, London: Allen & Unwin.

Bryson, Valerie (2008), 'Time-use studies: a potentially feminist tool', *International Feminist Journal of Politics*, **10**(2), 135–53.

Budlender, Debbie (ed.) (2010), *Time Use Studies and Unpaid Care Work*, New York: Routledge.

Budlender, Debbie, Diane Elson, Gillian Hewitt and T. Mukhopadhyay (2002), *Gender Budgets Make Cents*, London: Commonwealth Secretariat.

Çagatay, Nilufer, Diane Elson and Caren Grown (1995), 'Introduction: gender, adjustment and macro-economic models', *World Development*, **23**(8), 1827–36.

Chant, Sylvia (2003), 'New contributions to the analysis of poverty', CEPAL Women and Development Unit, United Nations, New York.

Charusheela, S. (2003), 'Empowering work? Bargaining models reconsidered', in Drucilla Barker and Edith Kuiper (eds), *Toward a Feminist Philosophy of Economics*, London: Routledge, pp. 287–303.

Commonwealth Secretariat (1989), *Engendering Adjustment for the 1990s*, London: Commonwealth Secretariat.

Cornia, Giovanni, Richard Jolly and Frances Stewart (1987), *Adjustment with a Human Face*, Oxford: Clarendon Press.

Cornwall, Andrea (2000), 'Missing men: reflections on men, masculinities and gender in GAD', *IDS Bulletin*, **31**(2), 1–16

Cornwall, Andrea, Elizabeth Harrison and Ann Whitehead (2004), 'Repositioning feminisms in gender and development', *IDS Bulletin*, **35**(4), 1–10.

Dey, Jennie (1981), 'Gambian women: unequal partners in rice development projects?', *Journal of Development Studies*, **17**(3), 109–22.

Elson, Diane (1991), *Male Bias in the Development Process*, Manchester: Manchester University Press.

Elson, Diane and Nilufer Çagatay (2000), 'The social content of macroeconomic policies', *World Development*, **28**(7), 1347–64.

Enloe, Cynthia (2000), *Bananas, Bases and Beaches: Making Feminist Sense of Global Politics*, Berkeley, CA: University of California Press.

Esplen, Emily (2006), *Engaging Men in Gender Equality: Positive Strategies and Approaches*, Brighton, UK: Institute for Development Studies.

Esquivel, Valeria (2011), 'Sixteen years after Beijing: what are the new policy agendas for time-use collection', *Feminist Economics*, **17**(4), 215–38.

Esquivel, Valeria, Debbie Budlender, Nancy Fobre and Indira Hirvway (2008), 'Explorations: time use surveys in the south, *Feminist Economics*, **14**(3), 107–52.

Fernández-Kelly, Maria Patricia and Diane Wolf (2001), 'A dialogue on globalization', *Signs: Journal of Women in Culture and Society*, **26**(4), 1243–9.

FLACSO (Facultad Latinoamericana de Ciencias Sociales) (2005), *1995–2003: Have Women Progressed? Latin American Index of Fulfilled Commitment*, Santiago, Chile: FLACSO.

Grieg, Alan, Michael Kimmel and James Lang (2000), *Men, Masculinities and Development: Broadening Our Work towards Gender Equality*, New York: United Nations.

Griffin, Penny (2010), *Gendering the World Bank*, London: Palgrave Macmillan.

ILO (2003), *Time for Equality at Work*, Geneva: International Labour Office.

Jackson, Cecile (2002), 'Disciplining gender?', *World Development*, **30**(3), 497–509.

Jacobson, Joyce (2006), 'Men's issues in development,' in Ian Bannon and Maria Correia (eds), *The Other Half of Gender: Men's Issues in Development*, Washington, DC: World Bank, pp. 1–28.

Jaquette, Jane (1990), 'Gender and justice in economic development', in Tinker (ed.), pp. 54–69.

Jaquette, Jane and Katherine Staudt (2006), 'Women, gender and development', in Gale Summerfield and Jane Jaquette (eds), *Women and Gender Equity in Development Theory and Practice*, Durham, NC: Duke University Press, pp. 17–52.

Kabeer, Naila (1994), *Reversed Realities*, London: Verso.

Kabeer, Naila (2005), 'Is microfinance a "magic bullet" for women's empowerment? Findings from South Asia', *Economic and Political Weekly*, **40**(44/45), 4709–18.

Kardam, Nukut (1991), *Bringing Women In: Women's Issues in International Development Programs*, Boulder, CO: Lynne Rienner.

Katz, Elizabeth (1995), 'Gender and trade within the household: observations from rural Guatemala', *World Development*, **23**(2), 327–42.

Keck, Margaret and Kathryn Sikkink (1998), *Activists Without Borders*, Ithaca, NY: Cornell University Press.

Kerr, Joanna (1999), 'Responding to globalization: can feminists transform development?', in Marianne Porter and Ellen Judd (eds), *Feminists Doing Development: A Practical Critique*, London: Zed Books, pp. 190–205.

Khandker, Shahidur (1999), *Fighting Poverty with Microcredit*, Washington, DC: World Bank.

Kuiper, Edith and Drucilla K. Barker (eds) (2006), *Feminist Economics and the World Bank: History, Theory and Policy*, New York: Routledge.

Mohanty, Chandra Talpade (1991), 'Cartographies of struggle: third world women and the politics of feminism', in Chandra Mohanty (ed.), *Third World Women and the Politics of Feminism*, Bloomington, IN: Indiana University Press, pp. 51–80.

Molyneux, Maxine (2006), 'Mothers at the service of the new poverty agenda: Progresa/Oportunidades, Mexico's conditional transfer programme', *Social Policy & Administration*, **40**(4), 425–49.

Moser, Caroline (1989), 'Gender planning in the third world: meeting practical and strategic gender needs', *World Development*, **17**(11), 1799–825.

Murphy, Josette (1995), *Gender Issues in World Bank Lending: A World Bank Operations Evaluation Study*, Washington, DC: World Bank.

Murphy, Josette (1997), *Mainstreaming Gender in World Bank Lending: An Update*, Washington, DC: World Bank.

OECD (2008), *Gender and Sustainable Development: Maximizing the Economic, Social and Environmental Role of Women*, Paris: OECD.

Palmer, Ingrid (1991), *Gender and Population in the Adjustment of African Economies: Planning for Change*, Geneva: International Labour Organization.

Panda, Pradeep and Bina Agarwal (2005), 'Marital violence, human development and women's property status', *World Development*, **33**(5), 823–50.

Parrenas, Rhacel (2001), *Servants of Globalization*, Stanford, CA: Stanford University Press.

Pastor, Manuel (1987), *The International Monetary Fund and Latin America*, Boulder, CO: Westview Press.

Razavi, Shahra (2007), 'The political and social economy of care in a development context', Gender and Development Program Paper 3, United Nations Research Unit for social Development, Geneva.

Razavi, Shahra and Carol Miller (1995), 'From WID to GAD: conceptual shifts in the women and development discourse', United Nations Development Program Occasional Paper 1, United Nation Research Unit for Social Development, Geneva.

Sen, Amartya (1988), *The Standard of Living*, Cambridge: Cambridge University Press.

Sen, Gita and Caren Grown (1987), *Development Crises and Alternative Visions: Third World Women's Perspectives*, New Delhi: DAWN.

Sparr, Pamela (ed.) (1994), *Mortgaging Women's Lives: Feminist Critique of Structural Adjustment*, London: Zed Books.

Standing, Guy (1999), 'Globalization through flexible labor: a theme revisited', *World Development*, **27**(3), 583–602.

Staudt, Kathleen (1978), 'Agricultural productivity gaps: a case study of male preference in government policy implementation', *Development and Change*, **9**(3), 439–57.

Stiglitz, Joseph (1998), 'Towards a new paradigm for development: strategies, policies, and processes', Prebisch Lecture, UNCTAD, Geneva.

Tinker, Irene (ed.) (1990), *Persistent Inequalities: Women and World Development*, New York: Oxford University Press.

Tinker, Irene (2006), 'Empowerment just happened: the unexpected expansion of women's organizations', in Gale Summerfield and Jane Jaquette (eds), *Women and Gender Equity in Development Theory and Practice*, Durham, NC: Duke University Press, pp. 268–302.

UN Women (2012), *Gender Responsive Budgeting*, available at: http://www.unifem.org/gender_issues/women_poverty_economics/gender_budgets.php (accessed August 16, 2012).

United Nations (2009), *World Survey on the Role of Women in Development*, available at: http://www.un.org/ga/search/view_doc.asp?symbol=A/64/93 (accessed August 16, 2012).

Van Staveren, Irene, Diane Elson, Caren Grown and Nilufer Çagatay (eds) (2007), *Feminist Economics of Trade*, London: Routledge.

Waring, Marilyn (1989), *If Women Counted*, London: Macmillan.

Williamson, John (ed.) (1989), *Latin American Readjustment: How Much Has Happened*, Washington, DC: Institute for International Economics.

Wood, Cynthia (2003), 'Economic marginalia: postcolonial readings of unpaid domestic labor and development', in Drucilla K. Barker and Edith Kuiper (eds), *Toward a Feminist Philosophy of Economics*, New York: Routledge, pp. 304–20.

World Bank (2001), *Engendering Development through Gender Equality in Rights, Resources, and Voice*, Washington, DC: World Bank/Oxford University Press.

World Bank (2010), *Annual Report of the World Bank*, Washington, DC: World Bank.
World Bank (2012), *World Development Report*, Washington, DC: World Bank/Oxford University Press.
World Bank Group (2012), *Commemorating the 15th Anniversary of ORIGIN: From Gender to Diversity and Inclusion*, Washington, DC: World Bank.
Zein-Elabdin, Eiman and S. Charusheela (2003), *Postcolonialism Meets Economics*, London: Routledge.
Zuckerman, Elaine (2009), *Problems in the World Bank's Gender Action Plan and Gender Policy*, Washington, DC: Gender Action.

9. Infrastructure and gender equity
Dominique Lallement*

I INTRODUCTION

To many, the subject of gender and infrastructure is still an enigma even though policy-makers and development workers have increasingly been thinking about and working toward gender equality in all economic and social spheres.[1] Targeted analyses exist, of course, describing the gender dimension of infrastructure sectors such as energy, water and sanitation, transport, and information technologies. This literature highlights the human costs of the lack of infrastructure services, or the ways such services can improve women's access to new economic opportunities. In several countries, research projects have facilitated significant insights regarding the integration of gender equality in sectoral policies and projects. However, the linkage between gender equality and infrastructure as a whole has not yet been extensively researched or documented, neither methodologically nor empirically, with the result that limited macro data and empirical evidence are available to guide policies and practices.

The World Bank (2006) broke new ground when it included infrastructure in its gender action plan for 2007–10. The action plan recognizes infrastructure as essential for increasing women's access to the four key markets: land, finance, product, and labor. Given the plan's emphasis on the United Nations' third Millennium Development Goal (MDG3) – Promote Gender Equality and Empower Women (United Nations, 2012) – the contribution of infrastructure is focused on potential savings of women's time when access to infrastructure services increases, time that they can then reallocate to market/economic activities, knowledge and skill acquisition, and to some extent leisure. In the annual World Development Report focused on gender equality (World Bank, 2012), the references to infrastructure are broader.[2] Besides the linkages among infrastructure, time savings, and the reallocation of time to market activities or leisure, the report draws on sectoral analyses to highlight the need for infrastructure to achieve more of the MDGs. For example, it recognizes that rural roads and transport services are indispensable to improve access to health services and reduce maternal mortality.

This chapter is written primarily from a perspective of developing economies, where blatant gender disparities in access to and benefits from infrastructure development have significant implications for women and men, for the growth of these economies and for the reduction of household poverty. I address two pivotal questions: (i) does infrastructure development influence the outcome on gender equality, that is, does it enable women and men to have equal voice, rights, freedom, living conditions, and opportunities and (ii) does infrastructure development generate opportunities for gender equity, that is, does it generate a process for correcting gender disparities in endowments, incomes, welfare, and agency?

I begin by showing why the linkages between gender equality and infrastructure are so important in the development paradigm, from both economic (Section II) and social

(Section III) development perspectives. Then I review some operational tools for practitioners to identify and analyze gender and infrastructure issues, design operational solutions, and measure results and impacts (Section IV). I conclude with priority actions for policy-makers and areas for further research (Section V). Practical examples are used throughout the chapter, including experiences shared during training workshops I conducted on mainstreaming gender equality into infrastructure policies, programs, and projects for several development organizations. Whenever relevant, references and lessons from industrialized countries have also been included.[3] Ultimately, I highlight the paramount importance of pursuing gender equality in infrastructure policies and projects to capitalize on the talents of women and men, accelerate economic growth across generations, and ensure that economic growth will benefit equitably and meet the needs of both women and men.

II INFRASTRUCTURE AND ECONOMIC GROWTH

Infrastructure is a very broad term, and in this chapter infrastructure refers to both the physical structures and services derived from the physical structures needed for an economy and a society to function and develop. In the electricity sector, for example, power plants, transmission lines, substations, and distribution networks are the physical infrastructure needed to produce, transport, and distribute electricity. However, electricity is both an intermediate good and a service for final industrial, commercial, and domestic consumption. From an economic and social welfare perspective, water is a resource, but it requires infrastructure (pumping and purification stations, water mains, canals and drains, and distribution pipes) to become a usable commodity/good. I refer mainly to energy, information and communication technologies (ICTs), transport, water, and sanitation, but also mention infrastructure such as irrigation, markets, housing, schools, and health facilities.[4]

Development economists such as Albert Hirschman describe infrastructure as 'social overhead capital' (World Bank, 1994, p. 2) that supports services to productive and social activities. In that sense, infrastructure complements direct productive capital, contributes to enhancing productivity, and assists in the realization of the potential ability of human capital (Kim, 2006). Infrastructure is therefore most important for women and men to reach their full potential.

As both a societal and a development goal, gender equality is achieved when men and women have equal rights, freedom, conditions, and access to endowments and social and economic opportunities for realizing their capabilities and for contributing to and benefiting from economic, social, cultural, and political development. Gender equality thus means that women's and men's rights, responsibilities, and opportunities do not depend on whether they are born male or female; society values women and men equally for their similarities and differences and for the diverse roles they play. Furthermore, gender equality concerns both women and men. A related concept is gender equity, the process of being fair to women and men. To ensure equity, measures must often be taken to compensate (or reduce disparity) for historical and social disadvantages that prevent women and men from otherwise operating on an equitable basis. Equity leads to equality, and empowerment aims at creating both equality and equity between individuals and social groups.

From an economic perspective, there are at least four compelling reasons for exploring the linkages between gender equality and infrastructure, and these are based on the contribution of infrastructure to economic development. First, infrastructure is critical for economic growth, as it affects production and consumption. It also increases the productivity of natural resource endowments, capital, and labor, attracts large flows of government spending, and creates positive and negative externalities, particularly but not exclusively relating to environmental sustainability and climate change. Viewing these reasons through the gender lens leads scholars and policy-makers to ask if men and women benefit equally from infrastructure. Specifically, those concerned with gender equity pose questions regarding to what extent infrastructure's impacts on productivity increases and poverty reductions affect women, and whether government spending to finance infrastructure benefits both men and women equally. Unfortunately, these questions have not been equally researched and documented.

The correlation between infrastructure and economic growth is well documented even though there is a wide range of estimates of the growth impact of infrastructure investments (Munnell, 1992; Pedroni and Canning, 2004). The World Bank (1994) stated that over the long term, 'a 1 percent increase in the stock of infrastructure is associated with a 1 percent increase in gross domestic product (GDP) in all countries' (p. 2). The densification of efficient transport networks (Boarnet and Haughwout, 2000), energy systems, and more recently telecommunications networks has been amply demonstrated in the growth of industrialized, emerging, and developing economies, from Europe, Japan, Korea, and the United States to Brazil, China, Mexico, Mauritius, Morocco, Turkey, South Africa, and many other countries. In Latin America, 25 percent of the variation in economic growth between 1981 and 2000 was explained by differences in the quantity and quality of infrastructure stocks (Vinod, 2007).

The economic development literature and empirical evidence both document that infrastructure investments must keep up with growth and adapt to changing patterns of demand (World Bank, 1994, p. 2); for example, China has had to add about 100,000 megawatts (MW) of electric power annually since 2005 to keep up with 10 percent average annual growth rates of the economy (US EIA, 2012). It is also clear that infrastructure needs evolve over time. Who would have predicted 40 years ago the dependency of women's small business creation on the penetration of mobile telephones? However, there is virtually no macroeconomic research available on the distribution of benefits from infrastructure-led growth on women and men, and whether such growth has enabled greater gender equality. Macroeconomic research appears to assume that infrastructure development and economic growth are gender neutral. Agenor and Canuto (2012) have just published one of the first papers attempting to develop and test a methodology to analyze the linkages between gender in/equality, infrastructure development, and growth. They conclude that gender inequality in access to education, health, and formal sector employment (common in developing economies) is partially due to lack of infrastructure and this remains a major constraint to growth.

The literature on infrastructure development and productivity is extensive, generally finding a positive correlation between infrastructure development and productivity growth, both at the macroeconomic and microeconomic levels (for example, in terms of land and product value or firm-level output). Some research (such as Haughwout, 2000), however, cautions that infrastructure can also lead to productivity decline, for example, when investments in one area influence factor prices and consumer preferences in another. This is particularly the case for the development of urban infrastructure that leads to a densification of economic activities, affects the distribution of jobs, and may lead to lower productivity in adjacent or other areas (Munnell, 1990).

Whether women and men benefit equally from infrastructure-led productivity increases is a critical question to address. In Bangladesh, for instance, public sector investments in rural electrification have led to private sector investments in modern textile factories; this has considerably increased rural labor productivity and benefited poor women who find employment in the factories (World Bank, 2010a). By contrast, in Peru, the labor productivity of rural areas relatively close to Lima, the capital city, has declined considerably despite good agricultural potential, as men have migrated to urban jobs (Lallement, interview, 2012). Women are left behind to face lower productivity agriculture and lower incomes due to the shortage of male labor. Similar situations are common in several countries of South and Central America (Segura Consulting, 2011).

Infrastructure attracts large amounts of government spending and international financing that potentially generates massive employment, regardless of the countries' levels of economic development. World Bank data (2011) show that public capital formation from infrastructure can absorb from 4 to 20 percent of GDP in transition and developing economies, and a bit less in OECD countries. For countries with significant natural resource endowment such as hydrocarbon-rich countries in the Middle East, Africa, or Latin America, rates of public spending on infrastructure increase as countries' revenues increase from exports of oil or gas. In a new report by the World Bank (Ianchovichina et al., 2012), the authors estimate that the needs for infrastructure investments in the Middle East and North Africa region could represent 7 percent of GDP. The long-term job creation could be extremely high. A related report estimates that 'the employment response induced by infrastructure investment resulting in a 1 percentage point additional growth is expected to be 9 million additional jobs in the course of ten years, [representing the equivalent of] approximately 30 percent of the jobs created in the region during the 2000s' (Freund and Ianchovichina, 2012, p. 3). Estimates made for Sub-Saharan Africa infrastructure needs are much greater: 15 percent of the regional GDP (Foster and Briceño-Garmendia, 2010), from which a million jobs could be created. A key question, however, is whether women and men will benefit equally from these jobs, directly or indirectly. Unfortunately, this gender question has not been adequately addressed.

Assumptions about potential job creation from infrastructure investments have been underlying all public works programs for decades. During long periods of drought in the 1970s, food for work programs in India were a way of providing minimum employment to both women and men. Most recently, similar assumptions were made to determine the share of 'financial rescue packages' allocated to infrastructure in the US and other countries. In 2009, the International Labour Office carried out a survey of 54 countries on their response with stimulus packages to the global economic recession: 87 percent allocated additional fiscal spending on infrastructure, and one third of these included specific employment components, often with targets for disadvantaged groups, but no indication of the results on male and female employment (ILO, 2010).[5]

Recognizing the correlation among infrastructure growth, economic development, and employment, financial assistance programs of institutions like the World Bank, the Regional Development Banks for Africa (AfDB), Asia (ADB), and Latin America (IDB), and the European Commission continue to be dominated by the infrastructure sectors, with transport and energy sectors occupying the prime positions in terms of both lending and technical assistance (TA) support. For example, in 2009, infrastructure lending reached 59.9 percent of the total loan portfolio with transport[6] and energy constituting the bulk of activities; over the 1990–2009 period, these same sectors occupied almost one-third of the ADB grant portfolio (ADB, 2010).

In recent years, some progress has been made in mainstreaming gender in the infrastructure portfolios financed by international financial institutions. The ADB may be at the forefront, having set up a systematic process to review *ex ante* all activities through the gender lens, and to design a gender-action plan for each activity where gender opportunities exist. The World Bank incorporated actions to reduce gender disparity in 36 percent of infrastructure projects in 2009 (World Bank, 2010a), and the AFDB is also striving to make its infrastructure operations more gender responsive.

In the wake of the recent global economic downturn, it is also worth considering the gender sensitivity of stimulus packages. In Asia, for example, most stimulus packages were directed at infrastructure, while some were more gender sensitive than others, both in terms of employment creation and the selection of infrastructure (United Nations Development Fund for Women [UNIFEM], 2009). UNIFEM suggested that investing in social infrastructure such as health centers, schools, and community centers could benefit women directly even if the actual construction jobs went to men. However, it is also possible to support activities where both men and women can access employment:

> Enacted in 2005, [India's National Rural Employment Guarantee Act] NREGA is a demand-driven scheme which guarantees employment in rural areas for 100 days in a year. Priority is given to labor-intensive projects, and laborers are paid the prevailing rate of minimum wages in the state. The NREGA mandates that at least one third of the workers should be women, and that crèche facilities should be provided to support women with children. The crèche facilities also relieve girls from the burden of having to take care of younger siblings while their mothers are at work. As of 2008, the share of women beneficiaries was 40 percent at the national level (Ibid., 2009, pp. 24–5; see also Jaffer, 2009)

In postconflict countries, quantitative targets for women's participation in infrastructure reconstruction programs were used as a way to create employment and income sources and to stimulate growth. In Liberia, although women were at an initial disadvantage for lack of formal diplomas and skills, the 30 percent employment quota in urban and rural infrastructure reconstruction programs provided sufficient seed income for them to start developing new economic activities in agriculture and trade (Lallement, 2007).

Since traditionally infrastructure is considered a 'male business', reducing gender disparities in the infrastructure job market can be challenging. Even when women have obtained infrastructure-related jobs, gender bias often prevents their career progression. For example, a study of the career progress of 440 male and 440 female construction workers in India attempted to find out why women in the construction sector were not able to acquire skills for higher-paid masonry work. The study found that there was a shared belief that women construction workers are unfit to be trained informally like men in the construction sector even though they have the necessary skills, capability, and desire to become masons (Barnabas et al., 2009).

Still, changes are happening slowly but surely. In Haiti, a training program was designed to train women as heavy machinery operators for the road construction industry (Global Communities, 2011, p. 1). Mining companies in countries such as Chile, Ghana, and Papua New Guinea that have hired female heavy machinery operators (trucks, excavators) have found that women maintain their machinery better and the rate of wreckage is less; heavy mining equipment operated by women is therefore more efficient and incurs lower operating costs than equipment operated by men (Eftimie et al., 2009, p. 10).

With proper political and societal support, there are no limitations as to the sectors or positions in which women can be employed in infrastructure, from locomotive conductor in Burkina Faso to CEOs of large infrastructure companies (for example, Sophie Boissard, one of the Executive Managers of the French Railways since 2009, or Anne Lauvergeon, CEO of French Nuclear Power Company AREVA from 2001 to 2011). Depending on the cultural context, companies may even perceive female construction supervisors as having a strategic advantage, as was the case for the renovation of the postnatal department of a hospital in Bethlehem (ANERA, 2012).

In Brazil, in view of the increasing number of female-headed households (from 26 percent in 1998 to 35 percent in 2005), the 39 percent wage disparity between women and men, and the higher rate of unemployment and job precariousness among women, the government designed the 'Next Step Program' as part of its growth program. Established in 2008–09 (Santos et al., 2011, p. 3), the Next Step Program aimed to train women technicians for infrastructure jobs, to encourage infrastructure enterprises to hire women, and to reduce the stereotypes and income disparities between women and men. As a result, more than 130,000 women became engaged in the construction industry; in two large power companies women respectively represented 15 and 20 percent of their technical staff; and higher-paying jobs occupied by women ranged from welders to carpentry supervisors, drill operators, dynamite operators, and many others (de Mello, 2009).

While it is important to assess the linkages between infrastructure and gender equality and the way they affect economic growth, income generation, and financing mobilization, it is also essential to assess externalities. Among positive or negative externalities generated by infrastructure, environmental sustainability, and climate change are the ones receiving the most attention today, as in the recent Rio+20 (Vaughan, 2012). Environmental impact assessments for large infrastructure projects (highways, dams, power plants, and irrigation) have challenged technology choices and uniquely highlighted differentiated social impacts on women and men, in particular with respect to resettlement and health issues. As a result, there is an abundant literature on the subject (UNDP, 2009; Kapoor et al., 2011a and 2011b; Skinner, 2011). In the case of climate-related extreme events, there is mounting evidence that women are at greater risk than men: more women than men perish in floods, women bear the brunt of water and fuel scarcity from droughts, and the poor, mostly women, live in flood-prone urban centers (World Bank, 2011). However, in post-disaster situations men find themselves with new roles as caretakers, for which some are ill-prepared.

Infrastructure plays a key role in shaping approaches to disaster prevention, climate change mitigation and adaptation: flood control dikes in low lands; irrigation systems to offset the impacts of droughts; adequate water and sanitation systems to maintain supplies and avoid contamination; adoption of low carbon emission technologies; and planning of evacuation roads. In terms of gender, frequently made recommendations include recruiting women and men to design appropriate solutions and capitalizing on women's traditional knowledge and social skills. A recent study in Bangladesh revealed that women are emerging as change agents, as gender responsive disaster management and climate adaptation activities are saving lives. In disaster forecasting, women now make the announcements over microphones and radio in rural areas; women indicated that they would be more mindful if the announcement came from women. Large numbers of young women are also trained as volunteers to take women and children to shelters and provide the needed support while they are in the shelter. As a result, more women are going to shelters and the number of victims in disasters has reduced drastically. In 1991, over 140,000 people perished in a cyclone; this number was reduced to around 3,000 in 2007 in a cyclone of the same intensity. The ratio of male–female deaths was also reduced from 1:14 in 1991 to 1:5 in 2007 (Ahmad, 2012).

III   INFRASTRUCTURE AND SOCIAL DEVELOPMENT

From a social development perspective, various studies have documented major differences between men and women with respect to development, maintenance, access to, and use of infrastructure. First, women and men have different needs and priorities for the type and location of physical infrastructure and infrastructure services. Second, they have unequal opportunities to participate in decision-making on the choice of infrastructure services, both within households and communities, and unequal opportunities to participate in the design and implementation of infrastructure programs and in the delivery of services. Finally, women and men face significant disparities in access to and impact from infrastructure services. Gender disparities in infrastructure needs, priorities, and potential benefits can be analyzed using a simple framework comprised of four main elements that are also linked to the main components of gender equality, as shown in Figure 9.1: human capital, social capital, risks, and economic empowerment. As in the macroeconomic or growth perspective, these four elements raise questions for scholars and policy-makers about the measures governments take to ensure that infrastructure needs are met for both women and men.

The economic empowerment of both women and men from access to infrastructure has three main dimensions: time savings, productivity increases, and income gains. Asymmetries in the allocation and valuation of women's and men's time have been extensively documented (Ilahi, 2000). Empirical data indicate that men's time allocation focuses on market income, while women's is divided between their multiple societal roles as primary contributors to the household economy (child and elderly care, water and fuel supply, agriculture, food processing and other household productive tasks) and to the market economy (urban services and industries, agriculture, or other rural industries and services). Even though time is an economic good, and despite the prominent work of Gary Becker and others, the household economy remains unaccounted for in national accounts. Time allocated to the household economy – mostly women's time and labor – is not given any financial value. And yet, the development of the market economy depends on the availability of women's and men's time to engage in it. Many studies (for example, Blackden and Wodon, 2006; Parikh, 2007) have also documented

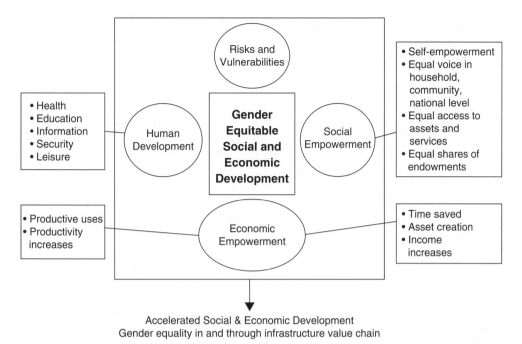

Figure 9.1   Framework for analyzing gender and infrastructure

the disparities between men's and women's workday, the latter averaging 4 to 6 hours more, in particular among the poorest income groups. In Nepal, women were found to work 50–80 percent more than men (Ilahi, 2000). Disparities also exist between regions, depending on social norms, and between rural and urban areas.

Infrastructure services facilitate time savings and reduce the opportunity costs of women's time spent delivering infrastructure services (carrying water and transporting firewood and agricultural commodities on foot) or spent on domestic and care work. Electrification in rural South Africa, for instance, has increased women's labor force participation by about 9 percent (World Bank, 2012, p. 30). Time saved can be invested in productive activities (market work for wages or home-based businesses) to increase incomes; acquiring information, education and skills (which can also be facilitated by infrastructure services) to access more profitable segments of the labor or product markets; and leisure or rest (which can positively affect women's health and productivity). Women's decisions on time allocation are also influenced by how well labor and goods markets function. In many parts of the world, with the increasing feminization of the rural economy due to HIV/AIDS or men's migration to urban areas or abroad for higher income-earning opportunities, the opportunity cost of women's time is increasing. Investing in infrastructure to increase the productivity of women's time can generate high economic and social returns, and be an opportunity to promote gender equality. In Mexico, for instance, the benefits per rural household from investments in a rural water supply project were estimated at 3,358 pesos (2004) in time saved and reinvested in income-earning activities (IDB, 2005).

In developing economies, women may provide up to two-thirds of the cultivation, harvesting, packaging, and marketing labor force, particularly for subsistence agriculture and high-value export crops (vegetables, cotton, groundnuts). However, women are 'left behind' in terms of land ownership, and access to credit and other financial services (due to lack of collateral). This limits their ability to invest in infrastructure and factors of production to increase their productivity, and create their own agricultural or infrastructure businesses. Projects that specifically address these issues generate substantial productivity and income improvements as well as further growth and employment benefits through enterprise creation. In Gambia, the involvement of women in an integrated watershed development project financed by the AFDB and the International Fund for Agricultural Development provided land security to more than 72,000 women (52 percent of project beneficiaries), and improved access to productive land with water control. As a result, land under rice cultivation increased, women gained skills in water infrastructure management and maintenance, productivity for all cereal crops increased from 10 to 30 percent, and food security increased by about 12 percent (Chileshe, 2011). In Zambia, through partnerships between communities and the water company supported by the German International Cooperation Agency – GIZ, selling safe and affordable quality water has become an important small business for women who earn a 40 percent commission on water sales (Simasiku, 2011). Investment in infrastructure can also be instrumental in building social cohesion through the direct employment impact and be a step towards private sector job creation (World Bank, 2012, p. 19).

The availability of infrastructure contributes to poverty reduction as well. Remoteness and isolation, along with lack of infrastructure services such as potable water and sanitation, are considered critical components of poverty. While poverty strikes both women and men, women constitute 70 percent of the world's poor (UN-Women, 2012). Improved infrastructure, particularly transport (Barwell, 1996), but also energy and ICT leads to new activities and opportunities, and results in increased access to product and labor markets and socioeconomic services that in turn contribute to reducing poverty and improving welfare. Although women are at a particular disadvantage when accessing infrastructure, infrastructure development policies and the design of investments can be adjusted to address such disparities.

For example, the rural electrification program in Lao PDR was specifically designed to address the needs of the poorest women. The program quadrupled access to network electricity from 16 percent in 1995 to 95 percent in 2010, reaching more than 750,000 households, of which about 10,400 households were disadvantaged (Tang, 2011). In 2004, however, a study revealed that 20 to 40 percent of households in connected villages still lacked access, mostly poor female-headed households that made up 80 percent of poor households (EdL, 2005; Tang 2011). These households could not afford the $100 cost of connections and indoor wiring. Electricité du Laos (EdL), the power company, adopted a two-year pilot program, Power to the Poor, that included an interest-free credit of $80 for the initial connection and indoor wiring to be repaid through $2.50 monthly installments over three years as part of the electricity bill. The repayment scheme was designed to be cash-neutral as compared to the previous level of energy expenditures (candles, kerosene, car batteries). In the 20 pilot villages, connection rates increased from 81 percent in 2009 to 97 percent in 2011; female-headed households' connection rate increased from 63 to 90 percent, and recurrent expenses decreased from

$3 to $1 on average. The pilot program was subsequently expanded nationally, leading to an overall rural electrification rate of 96 percent. With 95 percent of female-headed households connected, the program almost reached gender parity (ibid.).

In addition to reducing poverty, it is now recognized that infrastructure services contribute to meeting broader human development objectives such as health and education and others captured in the MDGs (Willoughby, 2004). Asymmetry in women's and men's access to social infrastructure assets and services is one of the main impediments to improving women's health, education, productivity, and ability to fulfill more productively economic opportunities and social responsibilities. Women and girls carry the greater load-carrying burden of firewood and water, together with the risks on their health and security. Boys, however, are often left out of health education programs of sanitation projects (Sibijsma, 2009). Exposure to pollution caused by the lack of access to improved energy services (cleaner fuels or improved stoves) continues to be a leading cause of premature death and high morbidity among women and young children. Infant boys and girls are equally affected, but girls are the ones suffering most as they grow up and share cooking tasks with their mothers at a young age. Women and girls are therefore the ones who benefit most from projects which address cooking fuels, indoor air pollution (Denton, 2002), and water and sanitation projects, even though families are not always aware of the correlation between reduced air pollution and the reduction in respiratory diseases. Women and girls also benefit most from rural transport projects that include improvements of rural footpaths used to fetch wood and water.

Improved roads and transport services, improved water and sanitation, increased access to affordable, sustainable, and efficient energy, and the expansion of all telecommunication services have been found to improve access to health services, to education, and information. When reflecting on how to achieve the MDG on reducing maternal mortality, for example, faster progress would be obtained if the physical infrastructure and infrastructure services were available: clean water, proper lighting for safe birth delivery, and adequate road transport to clinics (Babinard and Roberts, 2006). Similarly, studies undertaken to assess constraints to girls' access to schools found that lack of dedicated sanitation facilities for girls was among the main reasons for keeping girls at home, especially after puberty.

Promoting gender equity in infrastructure policies and projects also hinges on complex social variables. According to the World Bank (2011), social empowerment and agency are critical when assessing 'an individual's or a group's ability to make effective choices and transform those choices into effective outcomes' (p. 150). Agency is 'the process through which women and men use their endowments and take advantage of economic opportunities to achieve desired outcomes; [it] is key to understanding how gender outcomes emerge and why they are equal or unequal' (p. 150). But experience shows that compared to men, women are more often left out of planning processes for infrastructure, with the result that their needs are not met. In some other cases, the infrastructure remains unused. A Nigerian highway was planned and paved without taking into account that women needed an access path for their daily marketing activities (MDB, 2011). In Paraguay, new and more modern village water points remained unused for many years until consultations with women led to understanding that their location did not meet the needs of the women (Sotomayor, 2007).

Infrastructure development is also associated with significant and well-documented gender asymmetries in exposure to risks and vulnerabilities (FAO/IFAD/World Bank, 2008). Identifying them is essential in order to integrate mitigation measures into policies and project designs. For example, in the case of resettlement due to road construction, women, children, and the elderly are most negatively affected by the loss of land and of natural resource-based sources of livelihood. Payment of resettlement compensation to those with legal title is intrinsically gender biased because land and property are usually registered to men's names. Changes in resource-use patterns increase women's workload, for example, to collect firewood and water, and relocation to distant lands results in greater loss of incomes for women than men, largely because women derive incomes from the informal sector (World Bank, 2010b) and men from wage employment.

When displaced, widows and deserted women are particularly vulnerable. Displacement and resettlement often lead to the breakdown of community networks, further destroying an important source of help for women in hard times. Men are also vulnerable to infrastructure development risks, especially in transport. As men use more motorized transport than women, they are more accident prone on newly paved roads. HIV/AIDS is one of the greatest risks associated with the development of inter-city and rural transport infrastructure because of increased mobility and the influx of male temporary labor force in many large construction sites that attracts the development of prostitution. Contractors' obligation to provide HIV/AIDS information and free condom distribution to their labor force has been a successful mitigation measure used in many countries.[7]

In terms of intergenerational equity, Richard Agénor and Otavio Canuto (2012) are among the first to have methodically concluded that the lack of infrastructure feeds into the poverty cycle of future generations, for example by limiting access to health and education services. They showed that women deprived of access to infrastructure (such as reasonable access to potable water and roads) in childhood and adolescence had lower wages into adulthood. As a result, these women were not able to adequately invest in their own education and health, or their children's education and health (ibid.). Thus the adult gender gap in employment and wages may partially result from differentiated access to infrastructure in childhood and adolescence.

IV   ADDRESSING GENDER EQUALITY

It is easier to integrate gender equality in infrastructure policies, programs, and projects in countries that already have a legal framework on gender equality. Such a framework can span the country's constitution and laws on human rights or labor as well as such practices as national gender budgeting. Assessing the overall framework for gender equality is usually a prerequisite for establishing the basic principles for integrating gender in various infrastructure sector policies. However, it is the choice and design of investments that are likely to yield the greatest impact on gender equality.

The key objective is therefore to undertake a gender-sensitive needs assessment and to get a sense for the potential participation of both women and men in the design and future implementation of the investments. In such assessments, the main questions aim to document the gender-disaggregated socioeconomic profile of the area where the infrastructure is to be developed. Understanding the ethnic or racial composition of the population as well as the specific gender issues relevant to each group will provide the foundation knowledge to anchor the operational design of the proposed investments. Such assessments need to include a fair amount of detail, documenting, for example, the gender distribution of female- and male-headed households, the gender control of assets (land, tools, equipment) and whether men and women have equal access to credit. Similarly, questions need to be asked about the gender and age distribution of productive and welfare tasks in the community and at the household level; the main productive activities in which women and men are engaged, as household members, labor or entrepreneurs; time poverty for women and men; respective infrastructure needs of the main target groups; and whether there are any differences between women's and men's priorities (including those in different ethnic groups).

The lack of organized gender-specific groups is an issue that often emerges at the stage of investment identification or planning and limits the capacity to give women and men equal voice. The challenge in such cases is one of sequencing interventions. Can the preparation of an investment project be initiated or should some 'social engineering' effort first be undertaken to develop the community structures that will empower women and men in all groups to have equal voice in selecting infrastructure priorities and designing project interventions? In Paraguay, a rural water program had to be put on hold until they organized women's groups and were able to consult with them on the location and daily schedule for the use of water points (Sotomayor, 2007).

In designing infrastructure investments, the key elements are to include gender and the welfare and economic objectives relevant to poverty reduction. One must include design features that will address the objectives; develop arrangements to optimize the opportunities for both women and men to participate in project implementation; analyze the benefits and risks through a gender lens; and identify the project performance and outcome indicators. There are a number of specific design questions that need to be asked and answered. For instance, it is important to assess which design feature is needed to address women's and men's time scarcity, enabling them to increase their productivity, alleviate the burden of household tasks and increase their economic/income earning opportunities. Is a priority improving footpaths for women or paving an access road, improving household fuel availability and use or electrification? One must also ascertain whether the infrastructure project will generate equal labor and business opportunities for both women and men during implementation. Another issue is whether there are specific risks from the project's infrastructure investments, and how these are distributed and alleviated by gender. For example, if the project is in an area at climate risk, how will the infrastructure be secured or how will the selection of the specific infrastructure investment help mitigate the climate risk for both women and men? All of these questions raise an overarching concern about the ability to gather, document and assess gender-disaggregated data on infrastructure development and impact.

Execution and supervision is the real opportunity to 'make things happen'. The development of infrastructure involves many parties, both from the public and the private sector. Procurement documents and contracts provide opportunities to integrate gender equality obligations. Even when project objectives and design do not have a specific gender focus, it is never too late during project execution and supervision to introduce a gender element if the project team is convinced that this would enhance project effectiveness. Women, including poor women, can participate very effectively in the management of infrastructure services. This is the case when women participate in water user associations, in road maintenance committees, or on the boards of rural power utilities or irrigation schemes. Such participation is often an opportunity for improving their self-esteem and developing their decision-making capabilities.

A good example can be found in the Peru Rural Road Projects, which rehabilitated nearly 15,000 kilometers of rural roads and 7,000 kilometers of nonmotorized tracks used mostly by women and children. Multiple consultations with women, and their representation on various rural road committees, helped define the nonmotorized tracks to be rehabilitated. To accomplish this, 20 percent of the members of the road committees had to be women, which required training implementation agencies and men to accept women coworkers. Over time, however, women's representation on road committees increased to 24 percent of the total, more than what was required (Caballero and Peltier, 2008). An impact evaluation reported increased availability of transport services, decreased travel times, and new engagement of women in civic activities such as voting. Over two-thirds of women interviewed said they felt safer, and traveled more frequently and for longer distances; a smaller number said they obtained access to temporary employment. Importantly, the program trained women and set quotas for women to become micro-entrepreneurs to manage the routine maintenance of sections of rehabilitated roads. The implementation of such initiatives requires sensitivity to and understanding of the local culture, economic activities, and social realities, and more importantly, it requires trust that it can work. Including gender-sensitive experts in project teams is a good strategy to integrate gender equality in infrastructure projects, not only for project design but for project supervision as well.

Monitoring gender results and evaluating impacts on women and men from infrastructure investments is possibly the most effective tool for obtaining positive gender outcomes. It is important that development partners have processes and procedures in place to assess the impact of their infrastructure portfolio on gender equality; during the investment design phase, monitoring indicators and the means to document them should be identified, and at project completion the gender results should be assessed. When routine measures do not exist or are not gender disaggregated, it is important to assist implementation agencies in building systems that do so, with simple tools.

Several useful tools are available. Gender audits can assess the gender maturity of sets of organizations involved in infrastructure, from public works ministries to private enterprises. For example, these audits help benchmark the gender composition of staff, the degree of gender knowledge, and the preparedness of these organizations to give equal opportunities to women and men – both in their business practices and in serving their clients. Gender budgeting (Sulmont, 2004; Raes, 2006) can identify gender gaps in access to infrastructure services, analyze infrastructure budget allocations, and monitor whether women and men benefit equally from infrastructure investments and services. Both gender audits and gender budgets help to increase gender accountability and transparency. Household and sector surveys, normally carried out by statistical services, are essential to identify gendered consumption and expenditure patterns for infrastructure services, and to establish baseline indicators. Project gender action plans are practical tools encompassing the whole project cycle from the identification of women's and men's infrastructure needs, to project design elements, budgets, implementation and operational processes, and results and impact monitoring from a gender perspective. The Asian Development Bank has been at the forefront of using such gender action plans

(ADB, 2012). Finally, sectoral toolkits can provide detailed samples of questionnaires and methodologies to integrate gender equality into policies and programs (UNDP and Energia, 2004; Care International, 2009).

V CONCLUSION: THE WAY FORWARD

The central policy arguments for providing infrastructure that will take gender equality into account are that it will promote economic efficiency and growth, contribute to poverty alleviation, especially for women, and eventually create a win–win situation whereby both women and men will see improved welfare and wealth in the current and future generations. Is there a case for targeting women in infrastructure policies and projects? The human rights argument is to prevent them from being left behind from the benefits of growth and to enable them to escape poverty. The socioeconomic argument is that as women are more empowered economically, they become the intermediaries passing on infrastructure benefits to other members of the household, including children. Adopting a strategy to target women in infrastructure investments therefore also potentially addresses concerns of intergenerational equity.

What policy-makers and infrastructure planners should have is a thorough understanding of the inefficiencies and inequities in their current infrastructure service provision, the obstacles they are posing to the development of other sectors, and how these differentially affect women and men. Suggestions of how this can be done include sensitivity training for officials; technical education for infrastructure jobs; training for enterprise managers on the creation of safe workplaces for women and men, in particular on construction sites; appointment of women to senior infrastructure positions; gender-sensitive budgeting in infrastructure ministries/departments; accounting for gender results in the public and the private sector; and equal opportunity in procurement.

A variety of approaches can work. In the World Bank-financed rural roads and infrastructure projects in Bangladesh, women participated in all project elements, including decision-making on where women's markets and women's sanitation facilities should be situated. Affirmative action enabled women to obtain employment in construction and maintenance, as well as create and manage their own labor contracting companies (Quader, 2011). In Uganda, contractors were encouraged to use task rates instead of daily rates, adopt flexible working times, and provide separate sanitation facilities (Tanzarn, 2003). In Liaoning, China, an urban transport survey with focus groups on women raised concerns about safety issues related to the lack of street lighting and lack of off-peak bus services, which had created a barrier to employment possibilities (Chen and Mehndiratta, 2007).

Notwithstanding this progress, it is indispensable that more research be done to measure the benefits and costs of gender in/equality and infrastructure, both at the macro level and at the investment level. The results of such research are needed to inform policy-makers and to improve the selection and design of infrastructure investments. Mainstreaming the gender dimension in infrastructure is an opportunity to implement gender equality and to recognize the dynamic role that women can play in their countries' economic life. At the same time, it is an opportunity to provide women with greater control over socioeconomic resources to benefit both present and future generations.

NOTES

*   This chapter has benefited from suggestions and inputs from Rekha Dayal and Nilufar Ahmad, gender specialists and international development consultants.
1. Gender equality is a key objective of the eight Millennium Development Goals (MDGs) adopted by the UN and all development partners in 2000 with the objective of reducing world poverty by half by 2015. Progress is measured through 21 targets and 60 monitoring indicators. These can be found at http://mdgs. un.org.
2. The World Development Reports published by the World Bank capture the most up-to-date research results, including policy and project experience from the majority of development partners.
3. Since the chapter is focused on the socioeconomic aspects of gender equality and equity, it does not address other aspects including legal issues and human rights.
4. 'Soft infrastructure' is also relevant; it includes the institutions or complementary services that are necessary to ensure access to infrastructure services such as credit, but does not address in detail the services needed to generate the intended value added from infrastructure, such as education and healthcare systems.
5. In the note, the ILO reports the following on the employment impact of infrastructure spending: 'A theoretical model-based assessment of the impact of infrastructure spending on employment concluded that US$1 billion on large projects generates around 28,000 jobs, both directly and indirectly in equal proportions. Infrastructure spending in developing countries has a substantially high employment impact. US$1 billion in Latin America generates 200,000 direct jobs. A similar amount on labor-intensive rural projects can create up to 500,000 jobs' (ILO, 2010, pp. 1–2). The article does not mention whether the model generates sex-disaggregated data.
6. The transport sector comprises the roads and highways subsector and the rail subsector. Other subsectors such as ports and communications had been included in ADB's funding portfolio in the past. However, with the increased private sector participation in these subsectors, ADB has refocused its involvement to exclude them from its 2011 Country Strategy Programs.
7. The World Bank's Procurement Policy for Transport requires contractors to offer training on HIV/AIDS, free voluntary diagnosis, free condom distribution, and free treatment to employees and family if needed.

REFERENCES

Agénor, Richard and Otavio Canuto (2012), 'Access to Infrastructure and Women's Time Allocation: Evidence and a Framework for Policy Analysis', Working Paper/P45, Fondation pour les Études et Recherches sur le Développement International-FERDI, Clermont-Ferrand, France.
Ahmad, Nilufar (2012), 'Gender and climate change in Bangladesh: the role of institutions in reducing gender gaps in adaptation program', Social Development Network Working Paper No. 126, World Bank,Washington, DC, available at: http://www-wds.worldbank.org/external/default/WDSContentServer/WDSP/IB/2012/04/04/000333038_20120404010647/Rendered/PDF/678200NWP0P1250C0in0Bangladesh0web2.pdf (accessed October 21, 2012).
ANERA (2012), 'Right engineer for this [Bethlehem, Palestine] hospital upgrade', available at: http://www.anera.org/newsResources/RightEngineerforHospitalUpgrade.php (accessed October 21, 2012).
Asian Development Bank (ADB) (2012), 'Project gender action plans', available at: http://www.adb.org/themes/gender/project-action-plans (accessed October 21, 2012).
Asian Development Bank (ADB) (2010), 'Annual Report on 2009 Portfolio Performance', Reference Number RPE:OTH 2010–2, Asian Development Bank, Manila, August.
Babinard, Julie and Peter Roberts (2006), 'Maternal and child mortality development goals: what can the transport sector do?', Transport Paper No. 12, World Bank, Washington, DC.
Barnabas, Annette, Joseph Anbarasu and Clifford Paul (2009), 'A study on the empowerment of women construction workers as masons in Tamil Nadu, India', *Journal of International Women Studies*, **11**(2), 121–41.
Barwell, Ian (1996), 'Rural transport in developing countries', in *Engendering Development*, Policy Research Report, Washington, DC: World Bank.
Blackden, Mark C. and Quentin Wodon (eds) (2006), 'Gender, time use, and poverty in Sub-Saharan Africa', Working Paper No. 73, World Bank, Washington, DC.
Boarnet, Marlon and Andrew Haughwout (2000), 'Do highways matter? Evidence and implications of highways' influence on metropolitan development', Working Paper, The Brookings Institution, Washington, DC.

Caballero, Luz and Nicolas Peltier (2008), 'Gender equity in the Peru rural roads program', Project Brief, MDB-Mainstreaming Gender Equality in Infrastructure Projects: Asia and Pacific Regional Meeting, World Bank, Manila.

Care International (2009), *Climate Vulnerability and Capacity Analysis*, available at: http://www.careclimate-change.org/cvca/CARE_CVCAHandbook.pdf.

Chen, Wenling and Shomik Mehndiratta (2007), 'Lighting up her way home: integrating gender issues in urban transport project design through public participation. A case study from Liaoning, China', Transport Forum 2011, World Bank, Washington, DC.

Chileshe, Paxena (2011), 'Participatory integrated watershed management project, the Gambia, AfDB/IFAD', presentation at the Gender and Infrastructure Workshop, Addis Ababa, Ethiopia, March 22–24.

de Mello, Janine (2009), 'Presentation at the regional workshop on gender and development', Casa Civil da Presidência da República, Lima, unpublished paper.

Denton, Fatma (2002), *Gender – the Missing Link to Energy for Sustainable Development*, Johannesburg: Enda Tiers Monde.

Eftimie, Adriana, Katherine Heller and John Strongman (2009), 'Gender dimensions of extractive industries: mining for equity', Extractive Industries and Development Series No. 8, August, World Bank, Washington, DC.

Électricité du Laos (EdL) (2005), 'Social impacts and management survey 2004', February, cited in *Implementation Completion Report, Laos People's Democratic Republic Southern Provinces Rural Electrification Project*, Report No. 32004, June, available at: http://www.sunlabob.com/data/documents/energy_issues/WB-05_06-Rural_electrification_project.pdf (accessed October 21, 2012).

Food and Agricultural Organizaton (FAO/IFAD/World Bank) (2008), *Gender and Agricultural Sourcebook*, Module 9: Rural Infrastructure, Washington, DC: FAO, available at: ftp://ftp.fao.org/docrep/fao/011/aj288e/aj288e.pdf (accessed October 13, 2012).

Foster, Vivien and Cecilia Briceño-Garmendia (2010), *Africa's Infrastructure, A Time for Transformation*, Washington, DC: Agence Française de Développement and the World Bank.

Freund, Caroline and Elena Ianchovichina (2012), 'Infrastructure and employment creation in the Middle East and North Africa', MENA Knowledge and Learning, Quick Notes No. 54, World Bank, Washington, DC, January.

Global Communities (CHF) Haiti (2011), 'Empowering women through heavy machinery training', available at: http://www.chfinternational.org/node/34828 (accessed October 21, 2012).

Haughwout, Andrew F. (2000), 'State infrastructure, the distribution of jobs, and productivity', Federal Reserve Bank of New York, available at: http://www.newyorkfed.org/research/economists/haughwout/paper2.pdf (accessed October 22, 2012).

Ianchovichina, Elena, Antonio Estache, Renaud Foucart, Grégoire Garsous and Tito Yepes (2012), 'Employment creation in the Middle East and North Africa', Policy Research Working Paper No. 6164, World Bank, Washington, DC.

Ilahi, Nadeem (2000), 'The intra-household allocation of time and tasks: what we have learned from the empirical literature', Working Paper Series No. 13, Development Research Network/Poverty Reduction and Economic Management Network, World Bank, Washington, DC.

Inter-American Development Bank (IDB) (2005), 'Proposal for a loan for a program for the sustainability of water supply and sanitation in rural communities II', IDB, Washington, DC.

International Labour Office (ILO) (2010), 'Investments in infrastructure – an effective tool to create decent jobs', Global Jobs Pact Policy Brief No. 1, Geneva.

Jaffer, P.C. (2009), 'The process of NREGA, a case study of Gulbarga District (Karnataka)', available at: http://pcjaffer.blogspot.com/2009/07/process-of-nrega-case-study-of-gulbarga.html (accessed October 21, 2012).

Kapoor, Aditi, Anupma Rai and Paromita Chowdhury (2011a), 'Why women matter: the gender dimension of climate change adaptation policies', Alternative Futures, New Delhi, available at: http://www.seachangecop.org/seachange/files/documents/2011_10_AlternativeFutures_-_Policy_Brief_Why_Women_Matter.pdf (accessed October 21, 2012).

Kapoor, Aditi, Anupma Rai and Paromita Chowdhury (2011b), *Engendering the Climate for Change: Policies and Practices for Gender-Just Adaptation*, New Delhi: Alternative Futures and Heinrich Böll Foundation (HBF).

Kim, Byoungki (2006), 'Infrastructure development for the economic development in developing countries: lessons from Korea and Japan', Graduate School of International Cooperation Studies, GCICS Working Paper Series No. 11, Kobe University, Japan.

Lallement, Dominique (2007), 'Liberia: women's economic empowerment through infrastructure projects', Consultant's Report to the Gender and Development Department, World Bank, Washington, DC.

Lallement, Dominique (2012), Interview with Maximo Rivero, International Food Policy Research Institute (IFPRI), Washington, DC, February 27.

Multilateral Development Banks (MDB) (2011), 'Regional workshops to mainstream gender equality in infrastructure policies and projects', Africa Regional Workshop, Addis Ababa, Ethiopia, March 22–24, available at: http://www.afdb.org/fileadmin/uploads/afdb/Documents/Generic-Documents/final%20program%20 English_01.pdf (accessed October 22, 2012).

Munnell, Alicia H. (1990), 'Why has productivity declined? Productivity and public investment', *New England Economic Review*, (January–February), 13–22.

Munnell, Alicia H. (1992), 'Infrastructure investment and economic growth', *Journal of Economic Perspectives*, **6**(4), 189–98.

Parikh, Jyoti (2007), 'Gender and climate change: framework for analysis, policy and action', IRADE and UNDP, New Delhi.

Pedroni, Peter and David Canning (2004), 'The effect of infrastructure on long run economic growth', Working Paper 2004–04, Department of Economics, Williams College.

Quader, M.A. (2011), 'Enhancing women's economic opportunities in transport investment in Bangladesh: rural roads', presentation at MDB Gender and Infrastructure Workshop, Addis Ababa, Ethiopia, March 22–24, available at: http://siteresources.worldbank.org/EXTGENDER/Resources/workshop-032211-Day-1-Qader.pdf (accessed October 21, 2012).

Raes, Florence (2006), 'What can we expect from gender sensitive budgets? Strategies in Brazil and Chile in a comparative perspective', Network Women in Development Europe – WIDE, available at: www.gender-budgets.org/index.php (accessed October 21, 2012).

Santos, Pacheco Leonor Maria, Romulo Paes-Sousa, Edina Miazagi, Tiago Falcão Silva and Ana Maria Medeiros da Fonseca (2011), 'The Brazilian experience with conditional cash transfers: a successful way to reduce inequity and to improve health', draft background paper, World Conference on the Determinants of Health, Rio de Janeiro, Brazil, October 19–21.

Segura Consulting LLC (2011), 'Doing agribusiness in Latin America and the Caribbean', Nicaragua Final Report to USAID, July, Guatemala Final Report to USAID.

Sibijsma, Christine (2009), 'Thematic note 4: rural water supply and sanitation', in *Gender and Agricultural Sourcebook*, Washington, DC: World Bank, pp. 399–406, available at: ftp://ftp.fao.org/docrep/fao/011/ aj288e/aj288e05.pdf.

Simasiku, Precious (2011), 'Learning from the water kiosks in Zambia', presentation at Gender and Infrastructure Workshop, Addis Ababa, Ethiopia, March 22–24, available at: http://siteresources.world-bank.org/INTGENDER/Resources/336003–1289616249857/PreciousSimasiku_ZambiaWater_kiosks. pdf (accessed October 21, 2012).

Skinner, Emmeline (2011), *Gender and Climate Change: Overview Report*, Brighton, UK: Bridge/Institute of Development Studies, available at: http://www.seachangecop.org/files/documents/2011_10_BRIDGE_ Gender_and_climate_change.pdf (accessed October 10, 2012).

Sotomayor, Maria Angélica (2007), 'Presentation at a World Bank sustainable development network-SDN training', World Bank, Washington, DC, February.

Sulmont, Denis (2004), 'Pérou: Gestion d'un District Urbain: L'expérience de Villa El Salvador', Alterinfos América Latina, April, available at: http://www.alterinfos.org/spip.php?article1045 (accessed October 15, 2012).

Tang, Jie (2011), 'Shining the light on the poor and and women: rural electrification in Lao PDR', presentation at IDB Sponsored Workshop on Social and Gender Dimension in Rural Energy Projects, La Paz, Bolivia, November 8–9, available at: http://events.iadb.org/calendar/eventDetail.aspx?lang=En&id=3265 (accessed October 15, 2012).

Tanzarn, Nite (2003), 'Integrating gender in World Bank financed transport programs: case study Uganda', World Bank, Washington, DC, June.

United Nations (2012), *The Millennium Development Goals Report 2012*, July, New York: UN.

United Nations Development Fund for Women (UNIFEM) (2009), 'Making Economic Stimulus Packages Work for Women and Gender Equality', UNIFEM Working Paper draft, New York, June 19, available at: http://www.unifem.org/attachments/events/UNIFEM_Working_Paper_Making_Economic_Stimulus_ Packages_Work_for_Women.pdf (accessed October 9, 2012).

United Nations Development Program (UNDP) (2009), *Gender and Climate Change Resource Guide*, New York: UNDP.

United Nations Development Program (UNDP) and Energia (2004), *Gender and Energy for Sustainable Development: A Toolkit and Resource Guide*, New York: UNDP.

UN-Women (2012), 'Women, poverty & economics', available at: http://www.unifem.org/gender_issues/ women_poverty_economics/ (accessed September 20, 2012).

US Energy Information Administration (ETA) (2012), China Country Report, September 4, available at: http://www.eia.gov/countries/analysisbriefs/China/china.pdf (accessed October 12, 2012).

Vaughan, Kit (2012), 'Rio+20: equity and resilience for a sustainable future', PECCN, Global Climate Change Advocacy Coordinator, CARE International (2010), available at: http://www.careclimatechange.org/files/ CARE_docs/2012_PECCN_PAGES_April.pdf (accessed October 2, 2012).

Vinod, Thomas (2007), 'The difference inclusive growth makes', Latin American Emerging Market Forum, discussion draft, Washington, DC.

Willoughby, Christopher (2004), 'Infrastructure and the Millennium Development Goals', commissioned by DFID for the second, Berlin workshop of the DAC POVNET Task Force on Infrastructure for Poverty Reduction, Berlin, October 27–29.

World Bank (1994), *Infrastructure and Economic Development*, World Development Report, Washington, DC: World Bank.

World Bank (2006), *Gender Equality as Smart Economics: A World Bank Gender Action Plan Fiscal Years 2007–2010*, August, Washington, DC: World Bank.

World Bank (2010a), *Making Infrastructure Work for Women and Men: A Review of World Bank Infrastructure Projects (1995–2009)*, Social Development Department, Sustainable Development Network, December, Washington, DC: World Bank.

World Bank (2010b), *Mainstreaming Gender in Road Transport: Operational Guidance for World Bank Staff*, Transport Papers – TP 28, March, Washington, DC: World Bank.

World Bank (2011), *Gender Equality and Development*, World Development Report 2012, Washington, DC: World Bank.

World Bank (2012), *Jobs*, World Development Report 2013, Washington, DC: World Bank.

10. How gendered institutions constrain women's empowerment

*Irene van Staveren**

I INTRODUCTION

Since the 1980s, gender policies at the international level have emphasized women's participation in the economy. In particular, international gender policies tend to concentrate on the promotion of women's access to resources, such as jobs, education, land, other assets, and credit. Recent literature acknowledges that women's empowerment involves more than access to resources but also implies agency and an enabling institutional context, which together help women to achieve better well-being (Kabeer, 2001; Narayan, 2005a; Alsop et al., 2006; Ibrahim and Alkire, 2007). In light of the recent literature on women's empowerment, this chapter undertakes an innovative exploratory analysis of the role of resources relative to women's agency, captured by gendered institutions that limit this agency. Nonmarket institutions that constrain women's economic position as well as economic development in general are measured, like all other variables, at the macro level.

Whereas most scholarship on women's empowerment is at the micro level, the empirical analysis here is cross-country. The advantage of a cross-country empirical analysis is that it allows for much more variation in institutions, and, hence, it helps to understand more fully how these affect women's agency and access to resources. (At the micro level, for example, a negative effect of gender norms on women's bargaining power has been demonstrated, even to the extent that it overrides a positive effect of resources.) In support of a macro-level analysis of empowerment, a useful database has become available with indicators for gendered institutions for most countries of the world (OECD, 2006). Obviously, data on institutions that are qualitative have their limitations for quantitative analysis and require a careful assessment in terms of measurement and multicollinearity. These limitations will be discussed.

Section II will briefly discuss the literature on empowerment. Sections III and IV will introduce exploratory models and the data as well as the empirical analysis. Finally, Section V examines policy implications. I conclude that we need to transform formal and informal gendered institutions throughout society.

II WOMEN'S EMPOWERMENT

Recently, the empowerment literature has been enriched by conceptual and empirical work around issues of measurement, comparison, subjective/objective dimensions, and the recognition of different domains of empowerment (Narayan, 2005a; Walby, 2005; Alsop et al., 2006; Ibrahim and Alkire, 2007). One of the definitions of empowerment emerging from this literature has been formulated by Deepa Nayaran (2005b, p. 5): 'Empowerment is the expansion of assets and capabilities of poor people to participate in, negotiate with, influence, control, and hold accountable institutions that affect their lives.' Although there are some differences, the literature tends to agree that women's empowerment is a process involving *agency* (referred to in the definition above with words such as 'negotiate', 'influence', and 'control'), access to *resources* (or assets), and *institutions*, which together affect how women are able to improve their well-being absolutely, and more importantly, relative to men. Moreover, research suggests that the three constitutive elements of empowerment – agency, resources, and institutions – tend to be closely related, so that the absence of one element cannot, or can only partially, be compensated by the presence of another. Indeed, as the capability approach has pointed out, agency without resources is rather meaningless when being able to make one's own choices and having the self-confidence to do so are not matched by any real opportunities to choose from (Alkire, 2002; Robeyns, 2003). The other way around is equally compelling in cases where women may have access to resources but feel constrained by internalized oppression from actually making use of the available resources (Sen, 1990; Nagar and Raju, 2003).

The role of resources for women's empowerment is well understood. Already in 1986, Pampel and Tanaka demonstrated a U-shaped relationship between economic development and the female labor force participation rate, in which the latter might be considered, though with qualifications, as a proxy for empowerment. More recent empirical studies have shown that access to land (Agarwal, 1994; Deere and Doss, 2006; Allendorf, 2007), access to credit (Kabeer, 2001) and access to education (Jejeebhoy, 1995) are all important for women's empowerment, and, as other studies show, also for economic development (Klasen, 2002; Lagerlöf, 2003). However, human capital investment is arguably most effective in a context of medium or high economic development, which is not always the case in agricultural economies relying on low technology. In such cases, education, in particular for women, may not be translated effectively through labor market participation into higher incomes and GDP growth (Barro, 2000).[1] In general, however, the literature indicates that education, at least primary education, tends to have a positive effect on development, and for women through more routes than for men including lower fertility, which may contribute to women's empowerment.

The role of agency on women's empowerment, however, has only recently come to the attention of researchers. Agency has been defined 'as an actor's or group's ability to make purposeful choices' (Alsop et al., 2006, p. 11), recognizing that psychological as well as social factors are crucial for this. The authors explain that 'actors need a raised level of consciousness if they are to translate their assets into choices – that is, to become "agents"' (p. 11). Drawing on this insight, Solava Ibrahim and Sabina Alkire (2007, p. 8) define agency, embedded in the social realm, as 'the ability to act on behalf of what you value and have reason to value'. Both understandings of agency combine psychological factors with social factors of having control over assets and facing real options. This understanding of agency as embedded in the social realm points at a relationship of agency with the third element for empowerment, namely institutions.

Women face a variety of intangible constraints to plan their lives, to choose their goals, and to make their own choices, inside and outside households, often more so than men. Such constraints, understood as *gendered institutions* (Goetz, 1997), limit their opportunities both in terms of access to resources as well as their agency (Narayan, 2005b). Both formal and informal institutions reflect power relations, since institutions tend to be supported and defended by those who derive advantages from them; for gendered institutions, these power relations are embedded in formal and informal expressions of patriarchy (Folbre, 1994; Goetz, 1997).

Formal gendered institutions then can be interpreted as codified gendered social norms such as inheritance laws, property rights, or the fiscal system, with different effects for women and men. On the other hand, informal gendered institutions can be understood as the set of noncodified social norms and cultural practices that impact differently on men and women. The influence of informal gendered institutions leads to stereotypes of masculine and feminine agency, as Bina Agarwal (1997, p. 1) has explained, by 'ascribing to women and men different abilities, attitudes, desires, personality traits, behaviour patterns, and so on'. This not only results in adaptive preferences (Sen, 1990) that are an internalization of gender inequalities, but experimental research has indicated that gender stereotypes also lead to different self-evaluations, lowering women's self-esteem, motivation, and confidence (Biernat et al., 1998; Shih et al., 2006).

Most studies that pay attention to the impact of gendered institutions on women's empowerment have been carried out at the micro level. While these studies in general find a positive impact of access to resources on women's empowerment, empirical studies using detailed survey data and case study data indicate that this is not always the case due to the influence of gendered norms, networks, beliefs, and practices (Blumberg, 1991; Mayoux, 2001; Odebode and van Staveren, 2007). For example, a detailed household bargaining study on China has recently found that the standard hypothesis on the role of resources in empowerment, 'that an increase in women's relative household income contribution will enable them greater household decision-making control, is not supported by any regression results' (MacPhail and Dong, 2007, p. 114). Or, to give another example, Sharada Srinivasan and Arjun Bedi (2008) have found for Tamil Nadu that higher levels of education for women do not reduce the incidence of daughter elimination. So, the higher women's educational levels, the more often women undertake sex-selective abortions, and the stronger the inequality in the state's sex ratio. These findings therefore suggest that it is relevant for the understanding of women's empowerment to focus not only on access to resources but also on the intangible constraints that prevent women from benefiting from them.

One way to analyze the impact of institutions on agency is a cross-country analysis in which differences in countries' gendered institutions are included in the analysis of women's empowerment. There are only very few studies available that have analyzed gendered institutions in relation to women's well-being at the macro level. They have found that labor market segmentation, discrimination, high female unemployment rates, and the gender wage gap all limit the benefits that women may derive from their education and labor force participation (Jayaweera, 1997; Elson, 1999; Seguino, 2000; Casale, 2004; Busse and Spielmann, 2006). Moreover, a macro-level study by Klasen and Wink (2003) on China, Taiwan, South Korea, India, Pakistan, Bangladesh, Sri Lanka, Turkey, Syria, Afghanistan, Iran, Egypt, Algeria, and Tunisia confirms the micro analyses of a positive relationship between women's education and daughter elimination referred to above. What is much less clear from the literature is which types of gendered institutions are responsible for the negative, or at least not positive, effects of women's increased access to resources on their empowerment. This requires a cross-country analysis in which a range of formal and informal gendered institutions is included in order to explore the relative impacts of resources and institutions on women's empowerment.

III   WOMEN'S EMPOWERMENT: A CROSS-COUNTRY STUDY

The Empowerment Model

Given the limitations of working with a cross-country dataset with rather crude estimates of variables and no observations over time, which does not allow for panel estimations, I will employ a simplified model. In this model, variables express gender gaps rather than absolute values, because the concepts of gender and empowerment are relative and not absolute. Women's achievements are measured as gender gaps in health, education, and decision-making power. Resources are defined in terms of women's relative access to education (gender gaps in combined primary and secondary school enrollment rates) and to jobs (female share of the nonagricultural labor force). Gender gaps are mostly measured as ratios of female scores over male scores, for example in education. In a few cases, they are taken as percentages of female out of the total. Variable construction will be explained below.[2] The two categories of institutions, formal and informal, each consist of three variables that are taken from the OECD–GID (Gender, Institutions and Development) database (see explanation below). The empowerment model is presented in Figure 10.1: formal and informal institutions influence women's access to resources, whereas these institutions and women's access to resources together influence women's achievements.

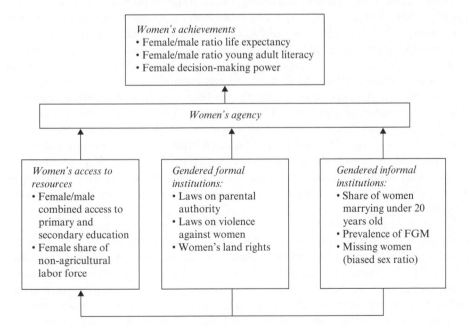

Figure 10.1   Women's empowerment model

This role of gendered institutions reflects the views in the empowerment literature that gendered institutions not only affect women's and men's access to resources but also that they impact directly on women's achievements, through affecting their agency. Obviously, the direction of causality is not straightforward and various endogeneity effects may occur. For example, in looking at the access to resources box in Figure 10.1, a higher ratio of female education is likely to increase the female nonagricultural labor force participation rate, whereas higher women's empowerment may increase the average age at marriage. Hence, the regression results should be taken with caution, because coefficients and their estimated level of significance and/or R square may be biased upwards due to the implicit accumulation of feedback effects. But, as indicated earlier, the dataset has no observations over time. The estimations presented here only serve an exploratory purpose. The results may therefore best be interpreted as descriptive. Further research is clearly needed and will hopefully be able to reduce endogeneity effects (for a further discussion of measuring and modeling empowerment, see Khwaja, 2005). Hence, gendered institutions are not only likely to constrain women's access to resources, as others have argued with bivariate regression analysis of the same dataset (Morrisson and Jütting, 2005), but they are also likely to affect women's agency, directly affecting women's empowerment, irrespective of women's access to resources.

Variables and Data

Data are from the World Bank's *World Development Indicators* (2008) and the OECD–GID database. These are the only two datasets with a substantial number of developing countries included for which gender disaggregated data are available. For achievements, the three variables selected are: female/male ratio in life expectancy, female/male ratio in young adult literacy (15–24 years), and female decision-making power in politics and the economy. The life expectancy variable reflects women's relative health status, taken as the ratio of female over male life expectancy. The young adult literacy variable, as a ratio, was chosen because it reflects how current levels of illiteracy may be affected by resources and institutions. Moreover, literacy was preferred over school enrollment because literacy is an expected outcome of school enrollment, so it is more suitable as an achievement measure of well-being. The third achievement variable that was selected is a composite index of female decision-making power, which is available in the dataset as an unweighted average of three indicators that all refer to senior positions: the share of female parliamentarians in the political arena, the share of women among administrators and managers in the administrative arena, and the share of women among professionals and technical specialists, which are top occupations in the standard classifications of occupations.

The two resource variables are key variables in the empowerment literature: access to education and paid employment. They are measured as the gender gap (a ratio) in the combined primary and secondary school enrollment rate and the female share (a percentage) of the nonagricultural labor force. The first one broadly reflects women's relative educational levels compared to men, excluding tertiary education since in many developing countries there is only a small minority of both men and women enrolled at that level. The second resource variable, the female share of the nonagricultural labor force, reflects women's relative access to paid labor. Women's share of the agricultural labor force was excluded because in many developing countries, this includes a large proportion of unpaid family workers who do not derive an independent income from their work.

The variables on gendered institutions lie between zero and one: the more asymmetric the institutions are, disadvantaging women, the closer the values are to one. The variables for gendered institutions for this chapter were chosen from the 13 gendered institutions in the GID database. I have selected these using the following two criteria.[3] First, variables that are very country or religion specific were dropped, such as polygamy and the obligation to wear a veil in public. Second, there is a risk of multicollinearity when including all available variables in the regression equation. I selected correlations of less than 0.50, with one exception: the Pearson zero-order correlations between the four property rights variables are quite high: inheritance laws, land rights, credit rights, and other property rights.[4] From these four variables, I therefore selected only one, namely the variable for land rights. The reason is that these are key for women in developing countries, probably more urgent than other property rights.

Six gendered institutional variables are useful for the empirical analysis, representing three formal and three informal institutions. The three formal gendered institutions (FGIs) included are:

- parental authority: measures whether women have the same right to be a legal guardian of a child during marriage, and whether women have custody rights over a child after divorce;
- land rights: measures women's right and de facto access to agricultural land; and
- laws against violence against women: measures the existence of women's legal protection against violent attacks such as rape, assault, and sexual harassment.

The three informal gendered institutions (IFGIs) included are:

- female genital mutilation (FGM): measures the share of women who have been subjected to any type of female genital cutting;
- early marriage: measures the percentage of girls between the ages of 15 and 19 who are married, divorced, or widowed, providing an indication of forced or arranged marriages; and
- missing women: son preference reflects the economic valuation of women; the variable missing women measures gender bias in mortality due to sex selective abortions or insufficient care given to baby girls.

The GID institutional database has in most cases transformed qualitative information into quantitative data, which necessarily involves some degree of subjectivity. On the other hand, much of the information refers to laws, which are either in place or not, while a few other variables are already quantitative, such as the extent of early marriage.[5] A second limitation of the GID database is that it uses a single observation about gendered institutions for a variety of years because of lack of availability of all information for every single year. This, however, should not be a very serious problem because gendered institutions tend to change slowly over time, as is the case with institutions in general (Hodgson, 2006). The GID database contains the kind of institutional data that others also have used in analyzing women's empowerment, for example: Karen Oppenheim Mason (2005), using data on freedom of movement and wife beating for five Asian countries; and Jayaweera (1997) and Christiaan Grootaert (2005), using the UNDP Gender Development Index (GDI) and Gender Empowerment Measure (GEM) for the analysis of women's empowerment in developing countries and in transition economies. The empirical analyses in the models shown below include between 53 and 153 countries, depending on data availability for the variables used in the various models.

IV   EMPIRICAL ANALYSIS[6]

Resource Models

The first step in the empirical analysis, as portrayed in Figure 10.1, is the testing of the resource models for education and employment. The two models have independent variables for resources (RES_i), with i referring to women's relative access to education and their share in the nonagricultural labour force. The dependent variables are a constant, C, the six gendered institutions, referred to as GI_j, with ε as the error term:

$$RES_i = C + \beta_1 GI_j + \varepsilon.$$

The differential impact of formal and informal gendered institutions can be analyzed by aggregating the institutional variables into two composite indexes, one for formal and one for informal gendered institutions, FGI and IFGI, respectively.

The results of the regressions with the resource models, using aggregate variables for the gendered institutions, are shown in Table 10.1. The regressions show that both variables have the expected negative sign and are statistically significant. Hence, both types of gendered institutions seem to be influential, with parameter values between 0.30 and 0.41. In order to test for any statistical problems, a residual analysis was done. The plots of standardized residuals and standardized predicted values do not show any non-normal pattern, nor any serious sign of heteroskedasticity. This suggests that the models are indeed linear, that there are no clear outliers that could have biased the regression results, and that the variation is rather constant around the regression line.

Table 10.2 presents the exploratory regression results for the two disaggregated resource models. The results for the education model show that five out of six coefficients have the expected negative sign and that three coefficients are statistically significant: land rights (–0.13), early marriage (–0.27), and female genital mutilation (–0.10). Hence, the lower women's access to land ownership and the higher the prevalence of early marriage and female genital mutilation, the lower is women's access to education. Whereas marriage between 15 and 19 years is a clear direct constraint on women's school enrollment, lack of land ownership and experience of female genital mutilation are expressions of a patriarchal norm that regards women as men's property, handed over from fathers' to husbands' control, which therefore does not stimulate women's individual accumulation of knowledge and skills.

For the second empirical model, with the female share of the nonagricultural labor force as the dependent variable, results again show three of the six institutional variables

Table 10.1   Resource models with aggregate institutions

Independent variables	Female/male education	Female nonagricultural labor share
Formal gendered institutions	–0.30***	–0.41***
	(–3.63)	(–5.44)
Informal gendered institutions	–0.38***	–0.32***
	(–4.50)	(–4.17)
Constant[a]	***	***
	(64.09)	(32.10)
Adjusted R^2	0.36***	0.42***
	(40.88)	(55.04)
N	142	153

Note:
Standardized coefficients (beta) with *t*-statistics in brackets. Level of significance for *t*-statistics for independent variables and for *F*-statistic for adjusted R^2: = $p < 0.1$; ** = $p < 0.05$; *** = $p < 0.01$.
[a] For the constant, the SPSS software provides significance tests, not a coefficient. The size does not matter for the analysis.

Source: GID.

Table 10.2   Resource models with disaggregate institutions

Independent variables	Female/male education	Female nonagricultural labor share
Parental authority	0.00	–0.09***
	(0.04)	(0.03)
Land rights	–0.13***	0.01
	(0.04)	(0.03)
Violence against women	–0.03	–0.07
	(0.06)	(0.05)
Early marriage	–0.27**	–0.34***
	(0.11)	(0.09)
Female genital mutilation	–0.10*	0.05
	(0.05)	(0.04)
Missing women	–0.02	–0.19***
	(0.07)	(0.06)
Constant	1.06***	0.49***
	(0.03)	(0.02)
R^2	0.50***	0.58***
	(*F*-statistic 15.058)	(*F*-statistic 21.269)
N	96	99

Note: Coefficients with standard errors in brackets. Level of significance: * = $p < 0.1$; ** = $p < 0.05$; *** = $p < 0.01$.

Source: GID online: http://stats.oecd.org/WBOS/default.aspx?DatasetCode=GID&lang=en. (accessed November 17, 2008).

being statistically significant, but only one is the same as in the education model. Of the three nonsignificant variables two have an unexpected sign, which is difficult to interpret, but parameter values are low. The three variables that are statistically significant all have expected negative signs: parental authority (−0.09), early marriage (−0.34), and missing women (−0.19). In other words, the more parental authority is granted to the father and the higher the extent of early marriage and missing women, the lower is women's access to the nonagricultural labor force. These negative relationships can be explained by underlying patriarchal norms that limit women's freedom to earn an independent income outside a family farm and apart from domestic responsibilities.

Although both models have women's access to resources as dependent variables, they clearly have different results. This is because access to education and access to nonagricultural employment measure two different types of resources, which do not necessarily go together. In some countries, women have higher levels of education than men (Argentina and Lesotho, for example), while having relatively low levels of labor force participation, whereas in other countries women's education is very low while they participate in the nonagricultural labor force at a rate that does not differ very much from men, as is the case in various African and South Asian countries. Education provides women with knowledge and information to make their own choices, while paid employment provides them with the actual means to make choices that would require resources and may go against the will of a male partner in the household. Therefore, they do not measure the same thing. As a result, we would not expect a high correlation coefficient between these two dependent variables. This was confirmed in a test with cross-correlations between the female/male education ratio and the female share of the nonagricultural labor force, which resulted in $r = 0.45$.

The exploratory resource models have two implications. First, they show that the more asymmetric gender norms and practices are, the less is women's access to resources. This confirms the bivariate results obtained by the initiators of the GID database, Christian Morrisson and Johannes Jütting (2005). Second, the models suggest that informal gendered institutions are more often a constraint for women's access to resources than formal gendered institutions: in each of the two models, two informal against one formal institutional variable were statistically significant. This suggests that social norms put a stronger constraint on women's access to resources than laws and regulations.

Achievement Models

The models for women's achievements can be specified as follows, in line with the model in Figure 10.1:

$$ACH_1 = C + \beta_2 GI_j + \beta_3 GDP\ln + \beta_4 GDP\ln SQ + \beta_5 RES_i + \varepsilon.$$

Achievements (ACH_1) are measured with three variables: the female/male ratio in life expectancy and the female/male ratio in the young adult literacy rate, as well as the average share of women as parliamentarians, administrative persons and managers, and professionals and technicians. Gross domestic product is included in logarithmic form as *GDP* (ln) and *GDP* (ln) squared, as control variables for level of development. It is

Table 10.3   Empowerment model with aggregate institutions

Independent variables	Female/male life expectancy	Female/male youth literacy	Female decision-making power
Formal gendered institutions	–0.27***	–0.25***	–0.50***
	(–3.09)	(–3.19)	(–6.31)
Informal gendered institutions	–0.25***	–0.60***	–0.17**
	(–2.78)	(–7.60)	(–2.12)
Constant[a]	***	***	***
	(216.28)	(52.21)	(24.18)
Adjusted R^2	0.20***	0.57***	0.37***
	(20.39)	(64.02)	(45.07)
N	153	96	149

Note:
Standardized coefficients (beta) with *t*-statistics in brackets.
Level of significance for *t*-statistics for independent variables and for *F*-statistic for adjusted R^2; * = $p < 0.1$; ** = $p < 0.05$; *** = $p < 0.01$.
[a] For the constant, the SPSS software provides significance tests, not a coefficient. The size does not matter for the analysis.

Source: GID and World Development Indicators 2006.

also included as a squared variable in order to account for possible nonlinearity, since the dataset includes both developing and developed countries. The achievement model for literacy has a new variable, namely primary school enrollment, with a time lag, so it refers to the year 1991. This variable replaces the current education variable which would lead to high autocorrelation. It is expected to have a high coefficient, because there is a likely strong relationship between school enrollment in the past and youth literacy today. The two resource variables (RES_i) are the ratio of female over male education and the share of women in the nonagricultural labor force, as before, and also the six gendered institutions are the same as before.

The results for the aggregate achievement models are shown in Table 10.3, and for the disaggregate achievement models results are shown in Table 10.4. It is important to note here that lack of data for some variables has seriously reduced the number of countries included, in particular for model 2 on youth literacy. Thus the results of the second model are not strictly comparable with the other two models.

The results presented in Table 10.3 indicate again that both formal and informal gendered institutions impact negatively upon women's empowerment. In all three aggregate achievement models, both types of institutions appear to be statistically significant, with similar parameter sizes. The results indicate quite varied relationships for women's empowerment. The achievement model for the gender gap in health, measured as the male/female ratio in life expectancy, shows that the level of GDP per capita has a relatively strong positive impact (0.09). The squared income variable is also significant, but negative (–0.01), implying a nonlinear effect of income. This may suggest that men are catching up with women's life expectancy rate when countries get richer, with women following less healthy lifestyles, including smoking and becoming overweight, in richer countries (for a study on the US, see Ezzati et al., 2008). Of the two resource variables,

Table 10.4   Achievement models: women's achievements in health, education, and decision-making

Independent variables	Female/male life expectancy	Female/male youth literacy	Female decision-making power
GDP (ln)	0.09**	0.15	0.21*
	(0.04)	(0.10)	(0.10)
GDP (ln) squared	–0.01**	–0.01*	–0.01*
	(0.00)	(0.01)	(0.00)
Parental authority	–0.02**	–0.02	–0.03
	(0.01)	(0.02)	(0.03)
Land rights	–0.04***	–0.00	–0.00
	(0.01)	(0.03)	(0.03)
Violence against women	0.02	0.03	–0.05
	(0.01)	(0.04)	(0.04)
Early marriage	0.04	–0.29***	0.09
	(0.04)	(0.08)	(0.10)
Female genital mutilation	0.00	–0.01	0.01
	(0.01)	(0.04)	(0.04)
Missing women	–0.03	0.01	–0.06
	(0.02)	(0.04)	(0.05)
Female % non-agricultural labor	0.04	–	0.23**
	(0.03)		(0.09)
Female/male education	–0.06**	–	0.12
	(0.03)		(0.07)
Female/male primary school '91	–	0.79***	–
		(0.07)	
Constant	0.70***	–0.33	–0.95**
	(0.16)	(0.41)	(0.46)
R^2	0.55***	0.94***	0.63***
	(F-stat. 9.600)	(F-stat. 70.403)	(F-stat. 13.154)
N	90	53	90

Note: In the second model, the female/male ratio of primary education enrollment in 1991 replaces the current education enrollment variable, which would otherwise be very similar to the dependent variable and hence would cause strong auto-correlation. Coefficients with standard errors in brackets. Level of significance: * = $p < 0.1$; ** = $p < 0.05$; *** = $p < 0.01$.

Sources: World Development Indicators, World Bank, 2008: http://data.worldbank.org/products/data-books/WDI-2008 and GID online: http://stats.oecd.org/WBOS/default.aspx?DatasetCode=GID&lang=en. (accessed November 17, 2008). Empowerment data on achievements for 2003–05 and 1991 for FMprim91.

only one is statistically significant, women's access to education (−0.06), but it has a negative sign, which is difficult to interpret. Two formal gendered institutions do have a statistically significant negative impact on women's relative health: parental authority (−0.02) and land rights (−0.04). This suggests that gender-biased laws and regulations have a stronger impact on women's relative health achievements than gender norms and beliefs.

The achievement model for the gender gap in youth literacy shows that GDP is not statistically significant, whereas GDP squared is only barely so, and negative. Income, hence, does not seem to be a strong determinant of women's relative educational achievements. As expected, the gender gap in the lagged primary school enrollment rate is positive and statistically significant (0.79) (see Table 10.4). This may suggest that the international efforts to achieve the third goal of the Millennium Development Goals, which is on gender equality in education, may not depend so much on economic development in general but on spending on girls' education. In addition, the informal institution of early marriage appears to be influential (−0.29), and statistically significant, which has a clear link to girls' access to education.

The final achievement model in Table 10.4, the model for women's decision-making power in the last column, shows again a different picture. Here, the level of economic development has a relatively strong statistically significant impact, again suggesting nonlinearity (0.21 for GDP and −0.01 for GDP squared). Women's relative access to jobs has a relatively strong positive and statistically significant impact on women's decision-making power (0.23). This may be explained probably not only by the income effect but also by the social participation effect – that is, a strengthening of women's agency – of nonagricultural jobs for women. This effect is important for taking up leadership positions in politics, administration, and management. Finally, when looking at the results for gendered institutions, we see that none of the coefficients is statistically significant. Hence, it is not so much unequal laws or biased social norms that constrain women's leadership roles, but rather low labor force participation and low level of economic development which form hurdles for women to break through the glass ceiling in the economy and politics.

V   CONCLUSIONS AND POLICY IMPLICATIONS

The overall picture from the extended women's empowerment model and exploratory empirical results is fourfold. First, the level of development has an important impact on women's achievements in health and political and economic decision-making power, but not on literacy. Also, income seems to have a nonlinear effect on women's achievements. Second, in each of the three achievement models, one of the two resource variables is statistically significant (even though the negative sign could not be explained in the health achievement model). Third, depending on the type of achievement, different gendered institutions play a role, or none at all. For health, formal institutions appear to be significant constraints, for education it was an informal institution that appears to limit women's achievements, whereas for political and economic influence, none of the gendered institutions seems to matter. The results suggest that gender policies would be more effective when contextualized to a country's binding constraints in terms of specific laws, regulations, social norms, and cultural practices that may negatively affect particular dimensions of women's empowerment. Thus, legal changes may need to be prioritized to improve women's relative health, whereas the traditional practice of early marriage would be a more likely candidate to address for achieving MDG3. Fourth, the results point out that women's access to resources is important but not sufficient for women's empowerment. Formal and informal gendered institutions both put a constraint on women's agency, which prevents them from turning their resources effectively into well-being achievements.

Of course, these are only exploratory results that require further exploration beyond the descriptive analysis provided here. They suggest, however, that gender policies may become more effective when they are contextualized, and not only help women to increase their access to resources, but also address the constraints to their agency from laws, regulations, norms, and practices that underlie particular gendered institutions.

Indeed, two types of policies are relevant: (i) legal changes toward equal treatment of women and men, and the enforcement of such laws, focusing on changing formal gendered institutions; (ii) awareness campaigns and civil society pressure toward abandoning traditional norms and cultural patterns, focusing on informal gendered institutions. I will briefly discuss examples of policies in both areas, drawing from the development literature.

Women tend to be the major food growers in the developing world. They work on family land, communal land, and land owned by male relatives (only a very small percentage of women owns the land that she works). This lack of land titles has several consequences for women's role as food producers, limiting their empowerment and leading to inefficiencies. First, without a land title, she cannot obtain credit for improving land productivity, because she cannot use the land she works as collateral. This, for example, will not allow poor women to join irrigation projects or to purchase draught animals or fertilizer. Hence, there will be underinvestment in the land that women grow, and women will find it difficult to meet the needs for sufficient food in their households, or will spend inefficient amounts of labor time (Agarwal, 1994).

Second, without a legitimate hold on the land, she has little decision-making power over the use of the land (Doss, 1999). This may lead to the use of (parts of) the land for cash crops by her husband or other male relatives, or the sale of the land to satisfy cash needs of male owners. This puts pressure on women's role, as part of the gender division of labor in rural households, as food provider: a woman would need to purchase food if she can no longer grow it, and therefore needs to find wage work, which is scarce and often very hard work, without a formal contract.

Third, the lack of legitimacy of her land claim also leads to limited control over her own labor time for production on the land: other household members tend to claim women's labor time for cash crop production on their own lands, without compensation. Research has pointed out, however, that with a shift of resources such as labor and fertilizer from male to female plots, total household production would increase (Udry et al., 1995). Moreover, when men claim women's labor to work on their own land without compensation, this can result in an aggregate undersupply of cash crops, because of the low work input or effort that women will provide without any sharing in the cash crop earnings (Warner and Campbell, 2000).

In addition, women's land rights contribute to women's bargaining power in other realms of life, simply because their value to the household goes up. This contributes directly to their empowerment. The research referred to above has pointed at women's land rights leading to lower fertility, lower unpaid workload, better health status, and more education for their daughters.

A second policy affecting women's empowerment involves the power of civil society action where the enforcement of law is lacking, as in the successful action of groups in various African countries to ban harmful practices. An illustrative example comes from Ethiopia, where I studied women's empowerment and bargaining in households (Mabsout and van Staveren, 2010). In Ethiopia, for example, female genital mutilation (FGM) is prohibited, polygamy has been abolished and the legal minimum marriage age for girls has been increased from 15 to 18 years (Vaughan and Tronvoll, 2003; Bevan and Pankhurst, 2007). Informal norms, however, remain strong, so that the practices are still widespread. Seventy-four percent of the women are circumcised according to household survey data from the Demographic and Health Survey 2005, and polygamy still occurs (Bevan and Pankhurst, 2007), while traditional practices and customs dominate marriage practices, such as kidnapping and girl child brides, in spite of the legal reforms (Fafchamps and Quisumbing, 2002).

The federal government has limited capacity to enforce the laws (WHO, 1999), whereas various Ethiopian states have been granted full sovereignty, which allows them to practice earlier laws that discriminate against women (World Bank, 1998). Philippa Bevan and Alula Pankhurst (2007) add a similar argument on the widespread practice of female circumcision: 'female circumcision is widely supported by males and females throughout rural Ethiopia; uncircumcised girls/women (depending on cultural context) bring shame on their families, cannot get married, and cannot be buried in churchyards' (p. 12). Indeed, the household survey data for 2005 show that 31 percent of women support the continuation of female circumcision.

In several African countries, including Ethiopia, civil society campaigns have emerged and appear to be quite effective in changing the harmful cultural practice of FGM, precisely because they are not state-led and initiated neither by donor countries nor by foreign NGOs. Hence, they are not perceived as top-down intrusions on local culture. They are very local based, often emerging from a small group of women who stand up against these practices and do not want their daughters to be mutilated with a razor blade at a young age by older village women who reinforce this practice by referring to norms of chastity and women's subordination to men and the family lineage. One example is the Senegalese NGO Tostan, which has organized discussions in many villages across the country about FGM, in which the villagers themselves discuss the topic. Such discussions often reveal negative side-effects and encourage people to speak about these. One father told about the death of his daughter, probably from tetanus, after circumcision. Also, the campaigns turn enlightened religious leaders into their allies by requesting them to confirm and tell the people that FGM is not supported in the holy books, whether it is Islam or Christianity. Many of the campaigns result in declarations denouncing FGM practices signed by complete villages.

In Ethiopia, the strategy has combined a state-led with a civil society approach, in which village discussions were supported with training and workshops on a wider set of issues related to women's health, morality, gender relations, and religious norms and values. The project evaluation in 2005 indicated clear advancements in reducing FGM, but it also signaled that the government's involvement was not sustainable due to upcoming elections and changes in government (Feldman-Jacobs and Ryniak, 2006). This lesson reinforces the need to have civil society as the driving force for abandoning particular harmful practices against women, and hence, changing informal gendered institutions from the bottom up.

NOTES

*   This chapter is based on Irene van Staveren. 'An exploratory cross-country analysis of gendered insti-
     tutions', *Journal of International Development*, **25**(1), 2013, pp. 108–21. It has benefited from discussion
     with Arjun Bedi and Francesca Bettio.
1.   There is additional empirical research about the relationship between gender inequality or female labor
     participation and economic growth not cited here. Others have provided overviews of women's position
     across countries, such as UNIFEM, UNDP, and the World Economic Forum, but have not included
     empirical analyses with possible underlying variables, also omitted.
2.   The list of all variables is available from the author.
3.   It should be noted that for some variables, for developed countries there is (almost) no variation. But
     excluding the developed countries from the analysis would result in a dramatic reduction in the number
     of cases, with subsequent negative impact on the econometric results. For property rights and parental
     authority the values are zero for all but one OECD country. Only for violence is there considerable vari-
     ation for OECD countries, with a mean of 0.31 and a standard deviation of 0.16. Early marriage also has
     some variation for OECD countries.
4.   A table of these correlations is available from the author.
5.   For more detailed information about the opportunities and constraints of the database, see Christiaan
     Morrisson and Johannes Jütting (2005).
6.   All models were run using linear regression analysis with SPSS version 16. The countries included are all
     countries for which data were available, the majority being developing countries in Africa, Asia, and Latin
     America, including China and India and excluding small island economies. There are no weights for popu-
     lation size, following the standard in cross-country analyses with social data.

REFERENCES

Agarwal, Bina (1994), *A Field of One's Own. Gender and Land Rights in South Asia*, Cambridge: Cambridge
     University Press.
Agarwal, Bina (1997), '"Bargaining" and gender relations: within and beyond the household', *Feminist
     Economics*, **3**(1), 1–51.
Alkire, Sabina (2002), *Valuing Freedoms. Sen's Capability Approach and Poverty Reduction*, Oxford: Oxford
     University Press.
Allendorf, Keera (2007), 'Do women's land rights promote empowerment and child health in Nepal?', *World
     Development*, **35**(11), 1975–88.
Alsop, Ruth, Metter Frost Bertelsen and Jeremy Holland (2006), *Empowerment in Practice: From Analysis to
     Implementation*, Washington, DC: World Bank.
Barro, Robert J. (2000), 'Inequality and growth in a panel of countries', *Journal of Economic Growth*, **5**(1),
     5–32.
Bevan, Philippa and Alula Pankhurst (2007), 'Power structures and agency in rural Ethiopia: development lessons
     from four community case studies', paper prepared for the Empowerment Team in the World Bank, June 14.
Biernat, Monica, Christian S. Crandall, Lissa V. Young, Diane Kobrynowicz and Stanley M. Halpin (1998),
     'All that you can be: stereotyping of self and others in a military context', *Journal of Personality and Social
     Psychology*, **75**(2), 301–17.
Blumberg, Rae Lesser (ed.) (1991), *Gender, Family, Economy. The Triple Overlap*, Newbury Park, CA: Sage.
Busse, Matthias and Christian Spielmann (2006), 'Gender inequality and trade', *Review of International
     Economics*, **14**(3), 362–79.
Casale, Daniela (2004), 'What has the feminization of the labour market, "bought" women in South Africa?
     Trends in labour force participation, employment and earnings, 1995–2001', *Journal of Interdisciplinary
     Economics*, **15**(3–4), 251–75.
Deere, Carmen Diana and Cheryl Doss (2006), 'The gender-asset gap: what do we know and why does it
     matter', *Feminist Economics*, **12**(1–2), 1–50.
Doss, Cheryl R. (1999), 'Twenty-Five Years of Research on Women Farmers in Africa: Lessons and
     Implications for Agricultural Research Institutions, with an Annotated Bibliography', CIMMYT Economics
     Program Paper No. 99–02, CIMMYT, Mexico D.F.
Elson, Diane (1999), 'Labour markets as gendered institutions: equality, efficiency and empowerment issues',
     World Development, **27**(3), 611–27.
Ezzati, Majid, Ari Friedman, Sandeep Kulkarni and Christopher Murray (2008), 'The reversal of fortunes:

trends in county mortality and cross-county mortality disparities in the United States', *PLOS Medicine*, **5**(4), 557–68.

Fafchamps, Marcel and Agnes Quisumbing (2002), 'Control and ownership of assets within rural Ethiopian households', *Journal of Development Studies*, **38**(6), 47–82.

Feldman-Jacobs, Charlotte and Sarah Ryniak (2006), 'Abandoning female genital mutilation/cutting: an in-depth look at promising practices', Population Reference Bureau, USAID, Washington, DC.

Folbre, Nancy (1994), *Who Pays for the Kids? Gender and the Structures of Constraint*, London: Routledge.

Goetz, Anne-Marie (ed.) (1997), *Getting Institutions Right for Women in Development*, London: Zed Books.

Grootaert, Christiaan (2005), 'Assessing empowerment at the national level in Eastern Europe and Central Asia', in Narayan (ed.) (2005a), pp. 309–40.

Hodgson, Geoffrey (2006), 'What are institutions?', *Journal of Economic Issues*, **60**(1), 1–25.

Ibrahim, Solava and Sabina Alkire (2007), 'Agency and empowerment: a proposal for internationally comparable indicators', OPHI Working Paper Series, Oxford Poverty and Human Development Institute, Oxford.

Jayaweera, Swarna (1997), 'Women, education and empowerment in Asia', *Gender and Education*, **9**(4), 411–24.

Jejeebhoy, Shireen (1995), *Women's Education, Autonomy, and Reproductive Behavior: Experience from Developing Countries*, New York: Oxford University Press.

Kabeer, Naila (2001), 'Conflicts over credit: re-evaluating the empowerment potential of loans to women in rural Bangladesh', *World Development*, **29**(1), 63–84.

Khwaja, Asim Ijaz (2005), 'Measuring empowerment at the community level: an economist's perspective', in Narayan (ed.) (2005a), pp. 267–84.

Klasen, Stephan (2002), 'Low schooling for girls, slower growth for all? Cross-country evidence on the effect of gender inequality in education on economic development', *World Bank Economic Review*, **16**(3), 345–73.

Klasen, Stephan and Claudia Wink (2003), '"Missing women": revisiting the debate', *Feminist Economics*, **9**(2–3), 263–300.

Lagerlöf, Nils-Petter (2003), 'Gender equality and long-run growth', *Journal of Economic Growth*, **8**(4), 403–26.

Mabsout, Ramzi and Irene van Staveren (2010), 'Disentangling bargaining power from individual and household level to institutions: evidence on women's position in Ethiopia', *World Development*, **38**(5), 783–96.

MacPhail, Fiona and Xiao-yuan Dong (2007), 'Women's market work and household status in rural China: evidence from Jiangsu and Shandong in the late 1990s', *Feminist Economics*, **13**(3/4), 93–124.

Mayoux, Linda (2001), 'Tackling the down side: social capital, women's empowerment and micro-finance in Cameroon', *Development and Change*, **32**(3), 435–64.

Morrisson, Christian and Johannes Jütting (2005), 'Women's discrimination in developing countries: a new data set for better policies', *World Development*, **33**(7), 1065–81.

Nagar, Richa and Saraswati Raju (2003), 'Women, NGOs and the contradictions of empowerment and disempowerment: a conversation', *Antipode*, **35**(1), 1–13.

Narayan, Deepa (2005a), *Measuring Empowerment. Cross-Disciplinary Perspectives*, Washington, DC: World Bank.

Narayan, Deepa (2005b), 'Conceptual framework and methodological challenges', in Narayan (ed.) (2005a), pp. 3–38.

Odebode, Sunbo and Irene van Staveren (2007), 'Gender norms as asymmetric institutions: a case study of Yoruba women in Nigeria', *Journal of Economic Issues*, **61**(4), 903–25.

Oppenheim Mason, Karen (2005), 'Measuring women's empowerment: learning from cross-national research', in Narayan (ed.) (2005a), pp. 89–102.

Organisation for Economic Co-operation and Development (OECD) (2006), Gender Institutions Database, available at: http://stats.oecd.org/WBOS/default.aspx?DatasetCode=GID&lang=en (accessed November 17, 2008).

Pampel, Fred and Kazuko Tanaka (1986), 'Economic development and female labor force participation: a reconsideration', *Social Forces*, **64**(3), 599–619.

Robeyns, Ingrid (2003), 'Sen's capability approach and gender inequality: selecting relevant capabilities', *Feminist Economics*, **9**(2/3), 61–92.

Seguino, Stephanie (2000), 'Gender inequality and economic growth: a cross-country analysis', *World Development*, **28**(7), 1211–30.

Sen, Amartya (1990), 'Gender and cooperative conflicts', in Irene Tinker (ed.), *Persistent Inequalities: Women and World Development*, Oxford: Oxford University Press, pp. 123–49.

Shih, Margaret, Todd Pittinsky and Amy Trahan (2006), 'Domain-specific effects of stereotypes on performance', *Self and Identity*, **5**(1), 1–14.

Srinivasan, Sharada and Arjun Bedi (2008), 'Daughter elimination in Tamil Nadu, India: a tale of two ratios', *Journal of Development Studies*, **44**(7), 961–90.

Udry, Christopher, John Hoddinott, Harold Alderman and Lawrence Haddad (1995), 'Gender differentials in farm productivity: implications for household productivity and agricultural policy', *Food Policy*, **20**(5), 407–23.

Vaughan, Sarah and Kjetil Tronvoll (2003), 'The culture of power in contemporary Ethiopian political life', SIDA Studies no. 10, SIDA, Stockholm.

Walby, Sylvia (2005), 'Measuring the progress of women in a global era', *International Social Sciences Journal*, **57**(184), 371–87.

Warner, James and D.A. Campbell (2000), 'Supply response in an agrarian economy with non-symmetric gender relations', *World Development*, **28**(7), 1327–40.

World Bank (1998), *Implementing the Ethiopian National Policy for Women: Institutional and Regulatory Issues*, in cooperation with the Women's Affairs Office, Federal Democratic Republic of Ethiopia, Washington, DC: World Bank.

World Bank (2008), *World Development Indicators*, available at: http://data.worldbank.org/products/data-books/WDI-2008 (accessed November 17, 2008).

World Health Organization (WHO) (1999), 'Female genital mutilation programmes to date: what works and what doesn't', Report by Department of Women's Health, Health Systems and Community Health, WHO, Geneva.

PART III

INFORMAL AND FORMAL WORK

11. Informal work
V. Spike Peterson

I   INTRODUCTION: WHO AND WHAT COUNTS IN ANALYSES OF ECONOMIC LIFE?

Most adults in the world work, but most of their work does not 'count'. Dominant approaches to the study of economics tend to focus on formal (official, recorded, taxed, regulated) activities that generate forms of monetary and presumably market-based compensation. This focused attention excludes the socially necessary but unpaid domestic labor that ensures household survival and has traditionally been assigned to women. Indeed, 'women's work' is the enduring stereotype of the most familiar of these domestic reproductive activities: cooking, cleaning and caretaking.[1] At the same time, a narrow focus on formal, market-based production marginalizes myriad forms of 'work' that constitute the primary source of income in the global South, shape the resource-pooling strategies of households worldwide, and are an increasingly significant aspect of economic life in the global North.[2]

Informal activities, informality and informalization share a reference to laboring activity – that is, *work* – that falls outside of formal (regulated, taxed) economic arrangements. Manuel Castells and Alejandro Portes offered an early and widely cited definition that characterized as informal 'all income-earning activities that are not regulated by the state in social environments where similar activities are regulated' (1989, p. 12). Barbara Harriss-White's recent, succinct definition states that 'informal activity is work outside the regulative ambit of the state' (2010, p. 170). For most of the twentieth century, this activity did not appear to count for much; economists viewed informality as marginal to formal market transactions and expected it to wane as states underwent modernizing processes and industrialized economic production.

Most observers agree, however, that the scale and significance of informality have – in part due to neoliberal policies since approximately the 1970s – expanded worldwide, and especially so in the context of late twentieth and twenty-first-century financial crises.[3] The basic insight here is that the extent of informal work is shaped by both the absence of formalized (industrialized, regulated) market arrangements and/or the erosion of formal employment where it previously existed. More specifically, recent studies indicate that informal activities constitute more than one-half of all economic output of most developing countries and their extent is increasing in advanced industrialized economies (Chant and Pedwell, 2008; ILO, 2008; Barta, 2009; Harriss-White, 2010; Peterson, 2010a; Godfrey, 2011). Difficulties of documentation and measurement render estimates of informality unreliable, but they are generally assumed to understate rather than overstate the extent of informal work (Joshi et al., 2011, p. S144). Even when unpaid domestic labor is excluded, Arne Kalleberg concludes that 'most workers in the world find themselves in the informal economy' (2009, p. 6, citing Webster et al., 2008). And concluding a recent and exceptionally comprehensive survey of the literature, Paul Godfrey states that 'informal economic arrangements represent a dominant form of exchange for many of the world's peoples and, depending on how one defines informality, may be the dominant model of economic organization' (2011, p. 270).

Hence, while informal work is conventionally marginalized in economic studies, it is much more important – socioculturally, economically, and politically – than is generally acknowledged. Most obvious through even conventional lenses is the dramatic expansion of informal work already noted. What is less visible but growing in significance are disturbing linkages between precarious – uncertain, unreliable, risky – forms of work and widely experienced conditions of *insecurity*. The latter include, but are not limited to, conditions of direct and indirect (structural) violence that are conventionally understood in political, military and geopolitical terms (for example, Kalleberg, 2009; Peterson, 2010a).

Informal work has additional significance for feminist and other critical approaches to the study of economic life. First, the *systemic* aspect of informalization is key to theorizing 'gendered economics': informality cuts across and links the conditions and activities of unpaid domestic (caring) labor (assigned primarily to women and neglected in most economic theory) with the conditions and monetized valorization of formal market activities (focused on in economic theory and increasingly 'feminized').[4] Second, how symbolic devalorization of feminized work and workers is 'translated' into material devalorization is especially visible through a lens on informalization. Power operates in informalization through intersections of feminized, racialized work, histories of exploitative colonization, geopolitical hierarchies, and global migration flows. While informal work may appeal to and be rewarding for some individuals, the vast majority of informal labor is precarious and poorly paid. In effect it constitutes devalorized (feminized) work, and structural hierarchies of gender, ethnicity/race, class, and nation shape which devalorized (feminized) workers are most likely to be doing it: poor people, ethnic minorities, women, youth, migrants, the urban underclass, the global South. The point here is that theorizing informal work invites, indeed requires, analyses that can address how 'differences' are cross-cutting (intersecting), and intersectional analyses are a particular strength of feminist scholarship.

To illuminate the expansive terrain of 'informal work' presumed in this chapter, I first turn to the complexities of definition and offer an inclusive conceptualization (Section II). Section III reviews how informal activities have historically been characterized and theorized through various lenses. This is followed in Section IV by summary comparisons of prevailing – and sometimes overlapping – approaches to the topic: mainstream/orthodox, critical/structuralist and feminist/intersectional. A short conclusion reviews how and why informalization matters: economically, politically, and analytically (Section V).

II   DILEMMAS OF DEFINITION

Recognizing that the significance and expansion of informality warrants greater attention does not easily translate into specifying what counts as, or how we might generate adequate accounts of, informal work. Virtually every article on the topic begins by acknowledging the controversies that attend defining, documenting, measuring, and interpreting informal activities. At issue for economists are no less than fundamental premises: what activities 'count' in terms of 'work', 'productivity', 'growth', 'value' and discipline-defining boundaries (Gaughan and Ferman, 1987; Mingione, 1991).[5] For feminists, the issues involve whether and how 'women's work' counts, how it relates to productivity and contributes to growth, how it is valued, and how gender is addressed (or not) in economic theories and the policies and politics they generate (for example, Barker, 2005; Hoskyns and Rai, 2007; Peterson, 2012).

Definitional issues are compounded by the sheer heterogeneity and ubiquity of informal activities. They range from food provisioning, care of dependents, and domestic labor to street vending, entertainment services, home-based production, and seasonal harvesting, to trade in drugs, body parts, small arms, and nuclear materials. They variously occur in rural and urban locales, in developing, transitional, and industrialized countries, and in household, corporate, and government spheres. Similarly, motivations for participating in informal work range from 'family' values to pursuit of profits and 'national security'. And the effects of informalization are felt across sites and scales, as shifts in divisions of labor alter subjective identities, social imaginaries, institutional arrangements, and power relations.

Defining informality is also difficult due to continuously shifting relationships among workers, entrepreneurs, regulatory practices, market arrangements, governmental policies, and transnational dynamics. Most obviously, the scale and *forms* of informality differ between more industrialized states with a history of institutionalized regulatory regimes and welfare provisioning, in contrast to poorer and less industrialized states where informal work prevails. At the same time, these and other differences variously (re)shape the informal–formal relationship *within* nations. If we include unpaid domestic labor, many individuals are simultaneously engaged in informal and formal work; others intermittently move between formal and informal work; and all variously respond to local conditions that are continually interacting with larger, even global, forces. Both small and large enterprises may turn to informal workers to supplement productivity or increase growth. Whereas earlier analyses tended to assume an adversarial relationship between informal actors and regulatory regimes, recent studies confirm that informality can be 'useful' for states and the latter may implicitly and even explicitly support informal arrangements (Centeno and Portes, 2006; Andreas and Greenhill, 2010; Harriss-White, 2010). In short, 'formality breeds informality' (Fernandez-Kelly, 2006, p. 3) and states, as well as corporations, variously decry and also accommodate, support, and benefit from informality.

It is worth noting that how the formal–informal boundary is drawn, and hence what is included and what is excluded, depends on which questions are focal and whose concerns are being privileged. With this in mind, it is less surprising that dominant accounts exclude domestic, unpaid labor in the household, and most treat 'illegal' (criminal) activities as a distinctive area of inquiry. Cumulative evidence indicates, however, that no categorical distinction between formal and informal can be sustained; changing conditions complicate definitive boundaries; and informality is best understood as a matter of degree. For the purposes of this chapter, then, an inclusive, relational orientation encourages the examination of linkages. In the proposed framing, formal and informal activities are understood as interactive and overlapping, along a *continuum* that permits a variety of distinctions without presuming discrete categories.

At the least formal end are activities involving socially necessary labor and voluntary work (childcare, housework, neighborhood projects). These are rarely considered illicit; cash compensation is typically not expected; intervention by the state is usually considered inappropriate; and regulation is not presumed. These merge with a vast array of activities involving 'nonstandard' work (microenterprise, street vending, petty trade, sex work, drug dealing). In these activities, some form of enterprise and payment is presumed. Activities may be licit *or* illicit, but legal regulation is either difficult to enforce or intentionally evaded. At the most formal end of this continuum are activities that are the focus of conventional economic accounts (waged labor, industrialized production, corporate business). Here, not only paid compensation but legality, labor regulation, and regulatory institutions are presupposed.

On the one hand, this inclusive and expansive conceptualization is atypical. First, it encompasses unpaid domestic labor, which is rarely counted by mainstream economists but is indispensable for gendering the study of economic life. Second, it includes illicit and criminal activities, which are apparently so outside the frame of regular economic analysis that they are treated in a separate body of research (Portes and Haller, 2005) or explicitly excluded (Godfrey, 2011, p. 235).[6] On the other hand, a continuum framing better fits current research trends. In brief, as 'economic' activities worldwide are transformed by deteriorating conditions of work and changing regulatory frameworks, any pretense of discrete categories and unproblematic boundaries is increasingly problematic (Fernandez-Kelly, 2006).

III   PAST AND PRESENT OF INFORMALITY[7]

For most of the twentieth century, dominant theories of economic life paid little heed to informality. After World War II, attention was focused on industrializing processes and the reconstruction of war-torn countries. In effect, economic theories were 'silent on informality in order to enhance formality' (Ferman et al., 1987, p. 10). Those who were interested in third world development tended to make several assumptions about informal activities: that they were remnants of 'traditional', kin-based societies, appeared to be minimal in advanced economies, and would soon disappear in developing countries as their markets and governments modernized. A model of dual (traditional and modern) sectors initially seemed adequate for explaining the remnant – as economic 'backwardness' typical of pre-industrial conditions – and positing its eventual absorption into formal markets as industrialization proceeded (Tabak, 2000, p. 2).

Field research by development economists in the early 1970s revealed that the traditional sector not only continued with modernization but was often quite robust, including profitable self-employment and other creative income-generating activities (ILO, 1972; Hart, 1973). These persistent findings prompted a shift in terminology – 'traditional' was upgraded to 'informal' – and theories of informality were revised.

In the 1980s, studies of informalization extended into new areas, investigating survival strategies of the urban poor, especially in the United States, and the parallel or underground economy in socialist planned economies (Ferman et al., 1987; Portes and Borocz, 1988; Sampson, 1988). Feminists investigated informal activities in relation to social reproduction and increasingly demonstrated that women's work *mattered* for generating 'better economic theory' and designing more effective development policies (see Boserup, 1970; Tinker et al., 1976; Benería, 1982; Jaquette, 1982; Mies, 1982, 1986 [1998]; Leacock and Safa, 1986; Elson, 1991). As research findings accumulated, the model of separate (dual) spheres lost ground to acknowledging linkages between formal and informal activities (Pahl, 1985; Mingione, 1991), with some analysts arguing that the formal economy *depended* on an extensive and foundational informal economy.

Neoliberal policies promoted in recent decades have systemically restructured economic arrangements, with pervasive though varying effects on informal–formal conditions of work.[8] Flexibilized work conditions favor some, and certainly a small elite has prospered from deregulation. For the majority, historical, sociocultural and geopolitical differences shape the positive and negative effects of restructuring. In general, restructuring increases the unpaid work of women, worsens men's un- and underemployment, undercuts the power of organized labor and systemically erodes the availability of secure, formal work. In particular, decentralization of production, flexibilization of labor, and expansion of outsourcing and subcontracting spur informal activities worldwide.

Flexibilization refers to shifts in production processes away from large, integrated factory work sites, unionized workers, and mass production of standardized consumer goods to spatially dispersed (global) production networks, increasingly casualized and informalized workers, and small batch, 'just in time' procurement and production. In important respects, flexibilization – and its associated practices of informalization – constitutes a global *feminization* of employment, understood simultaneously as an embodied transformation of work practices (more women engaged in formal and informal income generation), a conceptual characterization of devalued labor conditions (more precarious and poorly paid jobs), and a reconfiguration of worker identities (more feminized management styles and more female breadwinners).[9] Flexibilization thus fuels informalization, and both involve feminization (Peterson, 2003).

In the global South, informal activities expanded as structural adjustment policies (SAPs) increased unemployment and compromised smaller enterprises oriented to local and national (rather than export) markets (Bakker, 1994; Sparr, 1994; Sassen, 2000). During the 1990s, the informal sector became a focus of those studying transitional economies where the 'secondary' economy quickly appeared to dominate market transactions (Einhorn and Yeo, 1995; Feige and Ott, 1999). And processes of informalization became increasingly visible where they were least anticipated: in the advanced, prosperous economies of the global North (Portes et al., 1989; Standing, 1999; Tabak and Crichlow, 2000).

Also unanticipated was the growing significance of illicit informal activities in zones of conflict. At issue here is how economic informalization is structurally linked to *political* informalization (weak or eroded state capacity). The latter is a conventional concern of international relations analysts, especially those focused on the topics of in/security, conflict, and war (Peterson, 2010a).[10] Yet economists and security scholars tend to compartmentalize – and I argue compromise – their analyses by: (i) assuming formal and informal activities are non-overlapping categories, (ii) separating illicit activities from other manifestations of informalization, and (iii) excluding all work of social reproduction.

Social reproduction refers to activities in support of ensuring the daily and generational continuity of individuals, collectivities, and social institutions. Access to market, community, and government resources variously shapes conditions of social reproduction, but most of the work involved is unpaid, assigned to women, and situated in households. Feminists argue that economic theory is impoverished by its failure to account for this socially necessary labor and its structural importance. In addition to ensuring social reproduction, this 'hidden' work produces intangible social assets and significantly shapes the quality and quantity of labor, goods, services, and financial assets available within and beyond the household (for example, through production, consumption, savings, and intergenerational transmission of assets). Because unpaid domestic labor underpins and articulates with paid work (informal and formal), 'counting' the former is necessary for generating adequate accounts of the latter. This is especially pertinent as we pursue systemic analyses and consider appropriate policies in response to recurring crises.

In summary, critics argue that decades of neoliberal policies have reduced most states' capacity for and/or commitment to public welfare provisioning, while these same policies have eroded the power of labor, exacerbated un – and underemployment (especially of men), and deepened inequalities within and between nations. Deteriorating economic conditions increase the vulnerability of the global majority, who face limited options. Most seek work however and wherever they can, yet economic restructuring has reduced the availability of 'decent work' (formal, secure, safe), which tends to reduce the monetized component of household resource pooling. Insofar as flexibilization avoids taxation, it worsens the decline in resources devoted to public welfare provisioning, just when the 'need' for such support is growing. Loss of income and/or state-centric support increases pressure on nonmonetized (unpaid) work – done primarily by women – to ensure household survival.

These entwined developments reveal tensions between state capacities, patterns of capital accumulation, and the viability of households as basic socioeconomic units.[11] Feminists refer to a *crisis of social reproduction* as pressure increases – primarily on women as caregivers and household sustainers – to 'make up the difference' between an amplification of care needs (emotional and physical) and a reduction of monetized income and public welfare (Bakker and Gill, 2003; Hoskyns and Rai, 2007; Bakker and Silvey, 2008). Economic downturns compound these dynamics and suggest the urgency of generating more systemic analyses of household–market–state–linkages (Elson, 1998; Peterson, 2010a, 2010b).

IV   THEORIZING INFORMALITY IN ECONOMIC LIFE

Analyses of informality differ along a number of dimensions, including underlying assumptions, selection of research data, methodological preferences, and geopolitical perspective. The dominant approach is that of mainstream or orthodox economists, who subscribe to neoclassical assumptions and advocate free markets. For the most part, these economists adopt a favorable view of informal activities and enterprises (excluding those that are criminal) (Maloney, 2004; Bosch and Maloney, 2008). Informal activities are often seen as a breeding ground for small-scale enterprises (ibid.); as stimulating the formal economy by injecting otherwise unavailable revenues (Bajada and Schneider, 2005, p. 2); or as flexible responses to inefficient or excessive regulation (De Soto, 1989, 2000).

Positive interpretations are not surprising when we consider the prevailing focus: on small-scale *enterprises*, family-owned businesses, and self-employment. These versions of informal work contribute to conventional growth objectives and entail esteemed (masculinized) qualities: a strong work ethic, spirit of independence, entrepreneurial creativity, and willingness to take risks. Hence, policy recommendations feature reducing governmental intervention in market and labor activities, so that creativity and competition can flourish. This perspective underlies policies promoted in recent decades by the World Bank and the International Monetary Fund. (Recurring financial crises prompt calls for reform and more transparency, but fundamental assumptions do not appear to be disturbed).

The major contrasting approach is typically labeled 'critical' or 'structuralist', and variously informed by Marxist political economy and/or world systems theories. This approach focuses less on enterprises than on the *structural vulnerability* of informal (and formal) workers, understood as an effect of capitalism's exploitative dynamics. The more historical orientation favored here reveals how capitalist accumulation is both constant and cyclical (Tabak, 2000). It is *constant* in the sense of continually seeking profits gained through formal mechanisms of production and exchange. But profits also depend, and continuously, on accumulation secured through an array of nonformal – unregulated, artisanal, subsistence, and domestic/household – economic activities. The crucial insight here is that the latter (informal) activities sustain accumulation by absorbing costs of social reproduction, subsidizing formal wages through provision of cheap goods and services, and exerting downward pressure on wages. At the same time, informality is *cyclical*: when economic downturns recur (linked to cycles of expansion and contraction), profit margins are squeezed and capital responds by cutting costs (reducing labor inputs, implementing technologies) to reconstitute profits. In recent decades, flexibilization, casualization, outsourcing, and subcontracting have constituted such cost-cutting measures.

Compared to the mainstream, structural approaches are more historical, more reflexive (critical), and less exclusively focused on the global North. Their policy recommendations range from mitigating the excesses of the dominant system to proposing more radical transformations of how we organize economic life. While they move theorizing beyond the limits of the orthodoxy, they typically marginalize social reproduction and rarely engage the critiques raised by feminist and postcolonial (critical race) scholars (such as Gibson-Graham, 1996; Hewitson, 1999; Barker and Kuiper, 2003; Charusheela, 2003; Peterson, 2003, 2005; Kaul, 2008; Griffin, 2009).

Feminist studies of informality variously build upon and move beyond mainstream and structuralist approaches. They typically start from the vantage point of women and women's work in relation to informalization, social reproduction, and larger socioeconomic issues. The questions they focus on include how gendered divisions of labor shape and are shaped by informalization; the relationship of social reproduction and household provisioning to informal and formal economies; and how globalization and informalization are shaping inequalities and conditions of feminized labor. Feminists approach these questions from differing epistemological and political orientations, disciplinary perspectives, and spatial and temporal locations within the globalizing dynamics of capitalism.

Most feminist scholarship begins by investigating gender as an empirical category – the embodied variable of sex difference – in order to illuminate male – female differentiations in agency, action, and effect. As an empirical variable, gender can be incorporated in the models and quantitative, calculable methods accorded credibility in the discipline, and this now extensive empirical research is indispensable for feminist theorizing. Without dismissing gender as a variable, feminists also investigate gender as an *analytical* category, that is, a governing code that normalizes gender hierarchy by privileging masculinized over feminized qualities. Key here is that 'gender' pervades discourse and collective meaning systems, and the coding it entails orders (governs) our ideational and material practices–not the least with respect to who/what is valued. This more constructivist or poststructuralist orientation illuminates how identities and ideologies, which are pervasively gendered, are operating in the political economy of work, informalization, and globalization. It thus affords deeper interrogations of masculinism in definitions of work and how to count it, the meaning and desirability of development, men's absence in social reproduction, and (western-centric) narratives of victimization that deny women's agency.

These variations in vantage points shape how informal work is studied. When we investigate gender as an empirical variable, the following *descriptive* picture emerges.[12] Gendered divisions of labor worldwide reflect both traditional patterns and shifting arrangements. Informal work is the primary source of earnings for women in the global South (i.e., the economically most vulnerable populations worldwide), and in advanced economies, women more often than men are engaged in informal work (a situation exacerbated by the 2008 financial crisis). The global gender gap in earnings is larger in the informal than the formal economy; where we observe decreases in this gap, studies indicate that this is more the effect of a downward trend in men's earnings than an upward trend in women's. The structural subordination and disadvantages of the informal sector (relative to the formal and global economy) are compounded when gender differences are taken into account: women tend to have less education, lower skill levels, less access to credit, technologies, and elite contacts, etc. And compared with men, women are more likely to be positioned as own account traders or producers, piece-rate and other home-based workers, and domestic workers; hence, in the most insecure and poorly compensated informal activities.

When we investigate gender as an analytical category – a symbolic code carrying hierarchical valorization – a more *explanatory* picture emerges. We are better able to interpret how and why women and men are differently situated and differently valued. This picture reveals how expectations, subjectivities, conceptual frameworks, and institutionalized practices are both produced by and tend to reproduce gendered inequalities (that are racialized as well). To begin with, personal investments in conforming to normative masculinity and femininity figure importantly, though often unconsciously, with respect to interests in, access to, and development of aptitudes, skills, and capabilities that are economically valued. The resilience of (racialized) gender stereotyping continually shapes women's (and men's) expectations and experiences while also perpetuating various gendered dichotomies that underpin conceptualizations of work and economics. Sex-segregated labor markets persist worldwide, and women cluster where feminized skills (personal service, caring labor) are preferred but poorly paid (Heinz, 2006). Subcontractors prefer feminized workers they assume will be less demanding, docile but reliable, available for part-time and temporary work, and too structurally vulnerable to contest low wages. Women working informally at home can earn often desperately needed income while simultaneously providing socially necessary domestic labor and care of dependents – all without disturbing gender normative appearances (Snyder, 2005).

In brief, feminist approaches move beyond dominant economic theories and critical structural analyses, and deploy a variety of historical, quantitative, qualitative, and constructivist methods. They illuminate how *gender* shapes divisions of identity, labor, resources, authority and status, and how masculinism devalues socially necessary labor and feminized identities, skills and work in formal and informal activities. The diversity among feminist researchers produces a wide array of recommendations. Many advocate better access to formal employment and the benefits it may entail. Some support the ILO's 'decent work' initiatives (opportunities, rights, protection, and voice) that begin to take informal work seriously (see Torres, 2001; Chen, 2005), although within a capitalist framework and with little attention to racialized, gendered differences. In the face of multiple crises – of poverty, care, social reproduction, environmental degradation, and so on – many feminists endorse short-term reforms as crucial for ameliorating the already stark and deteriorating conditions of the global majority.

Feminist scholars and activists thus produce richer and more nuanced accounts of informal as well as formal work. This important scholarship significantly advances our understanding of gender and economic life, and warrants much closer attention from mainstream and structuralist scholars. At the same time, feminists share with other approaches several problematic tendencies. With the exception of human trafficking (primarily in relation to sex work), there is little attention to illicit or criminal informal activities. North – South inequalities are often challenged in the context of development studies and ethnic/racial hierarchies feature in many case studies, but *racism* as a systemic feature of capitalist practices is rarely interrogated. Few of these strategies fundamentally disturb capitalist premises; and typical employment strategies often ignore the work women are already doing within households. And finally, feminists join others in too often presuming the family is heteronormative and avoiding the politics of sexuality, which too often leaves the politics of hetero-patriarchy in place (see critiques by Bedford, 2009; Griffin, 2009; Lind, 2010; Bergeron, 2011).

V CONCLUDING THOUGHTS ABOUT THE INFORMAL ECONOMY AND WOMEN'S LIVES

Studies of informality hold great promise, not least because they reveal structural linkages among household, market, and government arrangements. More specifically, characteristics of informalization cut across and 'bridge' unpaid domestic labor, which ensures the social reproduction of households, and compensated formal labor, which predominates in market-based economic theory. At the same time, the 'political' (public) power of states is inextricable from (private) economic forces that are increasingly empowered by neoliberal principles that have systemic implications for 'work' inside and outside of households. Hence, our theoretical framing needs to view social reproduction, informality, formal market activities, and governance not in isolation but in relation, as overlapping and interdependent fields of activity. In combination, these practices shape how economic resources – and *relations of power correlated with resources* – are distributed worldwide.

In sum, informalization matters *economically* because of its extent and value, its effects on working conditions, tax revenues, wages and profits, and its tendency to exacerbate inequalities within and between nation-states. Informal work articulates with 'regular' market activities to constitute patterns of monetized income that shape (gendered) household strategies of resource pooling and social reproduction. Informalization matters *politically* because it compromises effective governance: tax evasion reduces public resources, unreliable accounts of work and production generate misguided policies, unregulated work practices pose safety, health, and environmental risks, and criminal activities thwart collective interests in law and order. And it matters *analytically* in terms of economic theory and foundational assumptions. Contrary to expectations, informalization is neither marginal nor waning, and it illuminates conditions of work that defy the either–or logic of conventional categorizations. In particular, it *blurs* (gender coded) binary distinctions that are cornerstones of social science inquiry: public–private, paid–unpaid, productive–reproductive, licit–illicit, modern–traditional. For example, the (unpaid, reproductive) work of household members often enables or increases the income generated in (paid, productive) activities such as street vending, family businesses, subcontracted piecework, and formal employment. In effect, informalization forces us to think across conventional boundaries, to focus not on social reproduction *or* informal *or* formal activities but their interconnections and systemic effects.

NOTES

1. Feminists have long understood and argued for the centrality of caring and domestic labor and promoted its inclusion in economic theorizing (see, for example, Dalla Costa, 1973; Ferber and Birnbaum, 1980; Picchio, 1992; Folbre, 1986, 1994, 2001; Himmelweit, 1995; Gardiner, 1997; Nelson, 2006).
2. I prefer 'global South' and 'global North' to signify social locations of subordination and privilege, respectively, though the Eurocentric, geopolitical characterizations of advanced and developing economies appear when contextually appropriate.
3. Informality features in a burst of journal special issues. Through 2000 alone these include *World Development*, 1978; *Social Justice*, 1988; *Yale Law Journal*, 1994; *International Journal of Urban and Regional Research*, 1994; *Journal of International Affairs*, 2000; *International Journal of Sociology and Social Policy*, 2000.
4. I understand 'feminization' as effectuating the *de*valuation of ideas, identities, bodies, practices, and skills associated with the feminine/femininity (not all women or only women). This devalorization is both ideational *and* material, as exemplified in the typically lower status of and compensation for labor characterized as 'women's work', whether or not it is done by women. Devalorized femininity is the corollary of privileging or overvaluing that which is associated with – especially, hegemonic – masculinity (not all men or only men). This 'linkage' and its costs to women and feminized others is often noted and variously documented in feminist scholarship. For theoretical elaboration of this claim and its wider application, see Peterson (2007, 2009b) and Barker and Feiner (2010).
5. Harrod (1987) articulates an early critique of the 'informal economy' as a conceptual category. The *Journal of International Affairs* (2000) discusses definition and measurement issues. Schneider and Enste (2002) offer an extensive account that includes international estimates. Bhattacharyya (2004) and Portés and Haller (2005) provide overviews.
6. Informality in conflict zones is of growing interest to international relations security scholars, who tend to focus on underground and transnational criminal activities without analyzing these in relation to more systemic aspects of informalization.
7. Material in this section draws variously on Peterson (2010a and 2012), which provide more developed argumentation and extensive citations.

8. An extensive literature supports the general claims that follow (for example: Cornia, 2004; Wade, 2004; Milanovic, 2005 on worsening inequalities; Sassen, 1998; Hoogvelt, 2001; Rai, 2002; Peterson, 2003; Scholte, 2005; Rupert and Solomon, 2006; Ong, 2006; Klein, 2007; Peck, 2010; Peterson and Runyan, 2010; Marchand and Runyan, 2011 for critical overviews).
9. On the feminization of economic restructuring, see Standing (1999); Benería (2003); Peterson (2003); Hoskyns and Rai (2007); Berik et al. (2009).
10. While international relations security scholars increasingly acknowledge the salience of economic *in*securities, they rarely acknowledge how these processes are gendered. On gendering informality in war economies, see Peterson, (2008, 2009a, 2013); on feminist critiques of entwined economic and geopolitical insecurities, see Eisenstein (1998, 2007); Enloe (2007); Peterson and Runyan (2010); Peterson (2010b); Marchand and Runyan (2011).
11. I refer to 'households' (rather than families) as basic economic units to emphasize the pooling of material and non-material resources from multiple activities to ensure well-being and reproduction of the collective unit (which may or may not be kinship based) over time. The global care economy and global householding are linked phenomena. Douglass (2006, p. 423) deploys the term 'householding' to underscore how 'creating and sustaining a household is a continuous process of social reproduction that covers all life-cycle stages and extends beyond the family'. *Global* householding references the many ways in which these processes increasingly occur across national boundaries, for example, through transborder marriages, overseas education, labor migration, and war displacements (see Douglass, 2006; Peterson, 2010c; Safri and Graham, 2010).
12. While recognizing the problematic nature of data on informality, generalizations presented in this section are widely accepted.

REFERENCES

Andreas, Peter and Kelly M. Greenhill (eds) (2010), *Sex, Drugs, and Body Counts: The Politics of Numbers in Global Crime and Conflict*, Ithaca, NY: Cornell University Press.

Bajada, Christopher and Friedrich Schneider (eds) (2005), *Size, Causes and Consequences of the Underground Economy: An International Perspective*, Aldershot: Ashgate.

Bakker, Isabella (ed.) (1994), *The Strategic Silence: Gender and Economic Policy*, London: Zed Books.

Bakker, Isabella and Stephen Gill (eds) (2003), *Power, Production and Social Reproduction: Human In/security in the Global Political Economy*, Basingstoke: Palgrave Macmillan.

Bakker, Isabella and Rachel Silvey (eds) (2008), *Beyond States and Markets: The Challenges of Social Reproduction*, London: Routledge.

Barker, Drucilla K. (2005), 'Beyond women and economics: rereading "women's work"', *Signs*, **30**(4), 2189–209.

Barker, Drucilla and Susan F. Feiner (2010), 'As the world turns: globalization, consumption and the feminization of work', *Rethinking Marxism*, **22**(2), 246–52.

Barker, Drucilla K. and Edith Kuiper (eds) (2003), *Toward a Feminist Philosophy of Economics*, London and New York: Routledge.

Barta, Patrick (2009), 'The rise of the underground', *Wall Street Journal*, March 14: Global Economics, W1.

Bedford, Kate (2009), *Developing Partnerships: Gender, Sexuality and the Reformed World Bank*, Minneapolis, MN: University of Minnesota Press.

Benería, Lourdes (ed.) (1982), *Women and Development: The Sexual Division of Labor in Rural Societies*, New York: Praeger.

Benería, Lourdes (2003), *Gender, Development and Globalization: Economics as if All People Mattered*, New York: Routledge.

Bergeron, Suzanne (2011), 'Governing gender in neoliberal restructuring: economics, performativity, and social reproduction', in Marchand and Runyan (eds), pp. 66–77.

Berik, Günseli, Yana van der Meulen Rodgers and Stephanie Seguino (2009), 'Feminist economics of inequality, development, and growth', *Feminist Economics*, **15**(3), 1–33.

Bhattacharyya, D.K. (2004), 'On the use of the hidden economy estimates', *Public Choice*, **118**(1/2), 169–81.

Bosch, Mariano and William Maloney (2008), 'Cyclical movements in unemployment and informality in developing countries', Policy Research Working Paper 4648, World Bank, Washington DC.

Boserup, Esther (1970), *Women's Role in Economic Development*, New York: St. Martin's Press.

Castells, Manuel and Alejandro Portes (1989), 'World underneath: the origins, dynamics, and effects of the informal economy', in Portes et al. (eds), pp. 11–37.

Centeno, Miguel Angel and, Alejandro Portes (2006), 'The informal economy in the shadow of the state', in

Patricia Fernández-Kelly and Jon Shefner (eds), *Out of the Shadows*, University Park, PA: Pennsylvania State University Press, pp. 23–48.

Chant, Sylvia and Carolyn Pedwell (2008), *Women, Gender and the Informal Economy: An Assessment of ILO Research and Suggested Ways Forward*, Geneva: ILO.

Charusheela, S. (2003), 'Empowering work? Bargaining models reconsidered', in Barker and Kuiper (eds), pp. 287–303.

Chen, Martha (2005), 'Rethinking the informal economy: from enterprise characteristics to employment relations', in Neema Kudva and Lourdes Benería (eds), *Rethinking Informalization*, Cornell Open Access, available at: http://ecommons.library.cornell.edu/handle/1813/3716 (accessed November 2007).

Cornia, Giovanni Andrea (ed.) (2004), *Inequality, Growth, and Poverty in an Era of Liberalization and Globalization*, Oxford: Oxford University Press.

Dalla Costa, Mariarosa R. (1973), *The Power of Women and the Subversion of the Community*, Bristol: Falling Wall Press.

De Soto, Hernando (1989), *The Other Path: The Invisible Revolution in the Third World*, New York: Harper & Row.

De Soto, Hernando (2000), *The Mystery of Capital: Why Capitalism Triumphs in the West and Fails Everywhere Else*, New York: Basic Books.

Douglass, Mike (2006), 'Global householding in Pacific Asia', *International Development Planning Review*, **28**(4), 421–45.

Einhorn, Barbara and Eileen Janes Yeo (eds) (1995), *Women and Market Societies: Crisis and Opportunity*, Aldershot, UK and Brookfield, VT, USA: Edward Elgar.

Eisenstein, Zillah R. (1998), *Global Obscenities: Patriarchy, Capitalism, and the Lure of Cyberfantasy*, New York: New York University Press.

Eisenstein, Zillah R. (2007), *Sexual Decoys: Gender, Race and War in Imperial Democracy*, London: Zed Books.

Elson, Diane (ed.) (1991), *Male Bias in the Development Process*, Manchester: Manchester University Press.

Elson, Diane (1998), 'The economic, the political and the domestic: businesses, states and households in the organization of production', *New Political Economy*, **3**(2), 189–208.

Enloe, Cynthia (2007), *Globalization and Militarism: Feminists Make the Link*, Lanham, MD: Rowman & Littlefield.

Feige, Edgar L. and Katarina Ott (eds) (1999), *Underground Economies in Transition*, Brookfield, VT: Ashgate.

Ferber, Marianne A. and Bonnie G. Birnbaum (1980), 'Housework: priceless or valueless?', *Review of Income and Wealth*, **26**(4), 387–400.

Ferman, Louis A., Stuart Henry and Michele Hoyman (eds) (1987), *The Informal Economy*, The Annals of the American Academy of Political and Social Science, London: Sage.

Fernández-Kelly, Patricia (2006), 'Introduction', in Fernández-Kelly and Jon Shefner (eds), *Out of the Shadows: Political Action and the Informal Economy in Latin America*, College Park, PA: Pennsylvania State University Press, pp. 1–22.

Folbre, Nancy (1986), 'Hearts and spades: paradigms of household economics', *World Development*, **14**(2), 245–55.

Folbre, Nancy (1994), *Who Pays for the Kids?*, London: Routledge.

Folbre, Nancy (2001), *The Invisible Heart: Economics and Family Values*, New York: New Press.

Gardiner, Jean (1997), *Gender, Care and Economics*, London: Macmillan.

Gaughan, Joseph P. and Louis A. Ferman (1987), 'Toward an understanding of the informal economy', in Ferman et al., (eds), Vol. 493 (September), pp. 15–25.

Gibson-Graham, J.K. (1996), *The End of Capitalism (As We Knew It): A Feminist Critique of Political Economy*, Cambridge, MA: Blackwell.

Godfrey, Paul C. (2011), 'Toward a theory of the informal economy', *The Academy of Management Annals*, **5**(1), 231–77.

Griffin, Penny (2009), *Gendering the World Bank: Neoliberalism and the Gendered Foundations of the World Bank*, Basingstroke: Palgrave Macmillan.

Harriss-White, Barbara (2010), 'Work and wellbeing in informal economies: the regulative roles of institutions of identity and the state', *World Development*, **38**(2), 170–83.

Harrod, Jeffrey (1987), *Power, Production, and the Unprotected Worker*, New York: Columbia University Press.

Hart, Keith (1973), 'Informal income opportunities and urban employment in Ghana', *Journal of Modern African Studies*, **11**(1), 61–89.

Heinz, James (2006), 'Globalisation, economic policy and employment: poverty and gender implications',: International Labour Office, Geneva available at: www.ilo.org/public/english/employment/strat/download/esp2006-3 (accessed June 2008).

Hewitson, Gillian J. (1999), *Feminist Economics: Interrogating the Masculinity of Rational Economic Man*, Cheltenham, UK and Northanpton, MA, USA: Edward Elgar.

Himmelweit, Susan (1995), 'The discovery of "unpaid work"', *Feminist Economics*, **1**(2), 1–19.

Hoogvelt, Ankie (2001), *Globalization and the Postcolonial World: The New Political Economy of Development*, 2nd edn, Baltimore, MD: Johns Hopkins University Press.

Hoskyns, Catherine and Shirin M. Rai (2007), 'Recasting the global political economy: counting women's unpaid work', *New Political Economy*, **12**(3), 297–317.

International Journal of Sociology and Social Policy (2000), Special Issue: Informal Sector, **20**(9/10).

International Journal of Urban and Regional Research (1994), Special Issue: Informal Economy and Family Strategies, **18** (March).

International Labour Organization (ILO) (1972), *Employment, Incomes and Equality: a Strategy for Increasing Productive Employment in Kenya*, Geneva: ILO.

International Labour Organization (ILO) (2008), *World of Work 2008*, Geneva: International Labour Organization.

Jaquette, Jane S. (1982), 'Review essay. Women and modernization theory: a decade of feminist criticism', *World Politics*, **34**(January), 267–84.

Joshi, Kaushal, Glenita Amoranto and Rana Hasan (2011), 'Informal sector enterprises: some measurement issues', *Review of Income and Wealth Series*, **57**(May), S143–65.

Journal of International Affairs (2000), Special Issue: The Shadow Economy, **53**(2).

Kalleberg, Arne L. (2009), 'Precarious work, insecure workers: employment relations in transition', *American Sociological Review*, **74**(1), 1–21.

Kaul, Nitasha (2008), *Imagining Economics Otherwise: Encounters with Identity/Difference*, London: Routledge.

Klein, Naomi (2007), *The Shock Doctrine: The Rise of Disaster Capitalism*, New York: Metropolitan.

Leacock, Eleanor and Helen I. Safa (eds) (1986), *Women's Work: Development and the Division of Labor by Gender*, South Hadley, MA: Bergin & Garvey.

Lind, Amy (ed.) (2010), *Development, Sexual Rights, and Global Governance*, London: Routledge.

Maloney, W. (2004), 'Informality revisited', *World Development*, **32**(7), 1159–78.

Marchand, Marianne H. and Anne Sisson Runyan (eds) (2011), *Gender and Global Restructuring: Sightings, Sites and Resistances*, 2nd ed., London: Routledge.

Mies, Maria (1982), *Lacemakers of Narsapur: Indian Housewives Produce for the World Market*, London: Zed Books.

Mies, Maria (1986 [1998]), *Patriarchy and Accumulation on a World Scale: Women and the International Division of Labour*, New edn with preface, London: Zed Books.

Milanovic, Branko (2005), *Worlds Apart: Measuring International and Global Inequality*, Princeton, NJ: Princeton University Press.

Mingione, Enzo (1991), *Fragmented Societies*, Trans. Paul Goodrick, Oxford: Basic Blackwell.

Nelson, Julie A. (2006), *Economics for Humans*, Chicago, IL: University of Chicago Press.

Ong, Aihwa (2006), *Neoliberalism as Exception*, Durham, NC: Duke University Press.

Pahl, R.E. (1985), 'The restructuring of capital, the local political economy and household work strategies', in Scott Lash and John Urry (eds), *Social Relations and Spatial Structures*, Basingstoke: Macmillan, pp. 242–64.

Peck, Jamie (2010), *Constructions of Neoliberal Reason*, Oxford: Oxford University Press.

Peterson, V. Spike (2003), *A Critical Rewriting of Global Political Economy: Integrating Reproductive, Productive, and Virtual Economies*, London: Routledge.

Peterson, V. Spike (2005), 'How (the meaning of) gender matters in political economy', *New Political Economy*, **10**(4), 499–521.

Peterson, V. Spike (2007), 'Thinking through intersectionality and war', *Race, Gender & Class*, **14**(3–4), 10–27.

Peterson, V. Spike (2008), '"New wars" and gendered economies', *Feminist Review*, **88**(1), 7–20.

Peterson, V. Spike (2009a), 'Gendering informal economies in Iraq', in Nadje Al-Ali and Nicola Pratt (eds), *Women and War in the Middle East: Transnational Perspectives*, London: Zed Books, pp. 35–64.

Peterson, V. Spike (2009b), 'Interactive and intersectional analytics of globalization', *Frontiers*, **30**(1), 31–40.

Peterson, V. Spike (2010a), 'Informalization, inequalities and global insecurities', *International Studies Review*, **12**(2), 244–70.

Peterson, V. Spike (2010b), 'A long view of globalization and crisis', *Globalizations*, **7**(1), 179–93.

Peterson, V. Spike (2010c), 'Global householding amid global crises', *Politics and Gender*, **6**(2), 271–81.

Peterson, V. Spike (2012), 'Rethinking theory: inequalities, informalization and feminist quandaries,' *International Feminist Journal of Politics*, 14(1), 1–31.

Peterson, V. Spike (2013), 'Insecurities, informalization and gendering "new wars"', in Christina Ewig, Myra Marx Ferree and Aili Mari Tripp (eds), *Gender, Violence and Human Security: New Perspectives*, New York: New York University Press (in press).

Peterson, V. Spike and Anne Sisson Runyan (2010), *Global Gender Issues in the New Millennium*, 3rd edn, Boulder, CO: Westview Press.

Picchio, Antonella (1992), *Social Reproduction*, Cambridge: Cambridge University Press.

Portes, Alejandro and Jozsef Borocz (1988), 'The informal economy under capitalism and state socialism: a preliminary comparison', *Social Justice*, **15**(3–4), 17–28.

Portes, Alejandro and William Haller (2005), 'The informal economy', in Neil Smelser and Richard Swedberg (eds), *The Handbook of Economic Sociology*, Princeton, NJ and Oxford: Princeton University Press, pp. 403–25.

Portes, Alejandro, Manuel Castells and Lauren A. Benton (eds) (1989), *The Informal Economy: Studies in Advanced and Less Developed Countries*, Baltimore, MD: Johns Hopkins University Press.

Rai, Shirin M. (2002), *Gender and the Political Economy of Development*, Cambridge: Polity.

Rupert, Mark and M. Scott Solomon (2006), *Globalization and International Political Economy: The Politics of Alternative Futures*, Lanham, MD: Rowman & Littlefield.

Safri, Maliha and Julie Graham (2010), 'The global household: toward a feminist postcapitalist international political economy', *Signs*, **36**(1), 99–125.

Sampson, Steven (1988), '"May you live only by your salary!" The unplanned economy in Eastern Europe', *Social Justice*, **15**(3–4), 135–59.

Sassen, Saskia (1998), *Globalization and its Discontents*, New York: New Press.

Sassen, Saskia (2000), 'Women's burden: counter-geographies of globalization and the feminization of survival', *Journal of International Affairs*, **53**(2), 503–24.

Schneider, Friedrich and Dominick H. Enste (2002), *The Shadow Economy: An International Survey*, Cambridge: Cambridge University Press.

Scholte, Jan Aart (2005), *Globalization: A Critical Introduction*, 2nd edn., Basingstoke: Palgrave Macmillan.

Snyder, Karrie Ann (2005), 'Gender segregation in the hidden labor force: looking at the relationship between the formal and informal economies', *Advances in Gender Research: Gender Realities*, **9**[annual], 1–27.

Social Justice (1988), Special Issue: Dynamics of the Informal Economy, **15**(3–4).

Sparr, Pamela (ed.) (1994), *Mortgaging Women's Lives: Feminist Critiques of Structural Adjustment*, London: Zed Books.

Standing, Guy (1999), 'Global feminization through flexible labor: a theme revisited', *World Development*, **27**(3), 583–602.

Tabak, Faruk (2000), 'Introduction: informalization and the long term', in Tabak and Crichlow (eds), pp. 1–19.

Tabak, Faruk and Michaeline A. Crichlow (eds) (2000), *Informalization: Process and Structure*, Baltimore, MD and London: Johns Hopkins University Press.

Tinker, Irene, Michele Bramsen and Mayra Buvinić (eds) (1976), *Women and World Development*, Washington, DC: Overseas Development Council.

Torres, Raymond (2001), *Towards a Socially Sustainable World Economy: An Analysis of the Social Pillars of Globalization*, Geneva: ILO.

Wade, Robert H. (2004), 'Is globalization reducing poverty and inequality?', *World Development*, **32**(4), 567–89.

Webster, Edward, Rob Lambert and Andries Bezuidenhout (2008), *Grounding Globalization: Labour in the Age of Insecurity*, Oxford: Blackwell.

World Development (1978), Special Issue on Urban Informal Sector **6**(9–10 September–October), 1031–98.

Yale Law Journal (1994), Symposium: The Informal Economy, **103**(8).

12. Gender inequality in the workplace
Elizabeth Hirsh, Hazel Hollingdale and
Natasha Stecy-Hildebrandt

I INTRODUCTION

Despite legal and organizational efforts to alleviate gender inequality at work, gender differences in career opportunities and the allocation of workplace rewards persist. Women are segregated into lower-paying occupations, passed over for promotions, and paid less than equally qualified men. The persistence of gender inequality in the workplace is rooted in a 'gender subtext' – a set of often concealed, gendered power-based processes and organizational arrangements that differentially confer value on men and women (Benschop and Doorewaard, 1998). In this chapter, we argue that this gender subtext informs cultural understandings of who is deemed competent and worthy in workplace settings and is embedded in the very organizational structures that govern workplace decisions and the allocation of rewards, including pay, status, and opportunities for career advancement. In Sections II and III we review research that documents the cultural and structural nature of gender inequality, respectively. In Section IV we suggest several policy remedies designed to dislodge the cultural valuation system that disadvantages women and alter organizational structures to ensure gender-neutral evaluation and reward decisions. Section V concludes.

In reviewing the sources of gender inequality at work, we take a decidedly sociological approach. While neoclassical economic perspectives on gender inequality see differences in employment outcomes for men and women stemming from differences in individuals' human capital (that is, education, training, experience, and productivity) or preferences (such as commitment to employment, interests, or competing family obligations) (see Becker, 1985), sociologists see gender inequality as rooted in broader social processes of categorization, ranking, and power (Tilly, 1998; Reskin and Bielby, 2005). As sociologists note, it is natural to categorize individuals on the basis of personal characteristics such as gender, but categorization often gives way to status distinctions and ranking, which facilitate inequality in the distribution of resources across social groups. As in the case of gender, those in the higher-ranking social group (that is, men) seek to maintain their privilege over those in subordinate group(s) (that is, women) by enacting cultural systems and implementing institutional structures that either explicitly or implicitly preference the dominant group. As we detail below, many cultural values and institutional structures operating in today's workplace are seemingly neutral on face value but have unequal effects by gender.

Understanding the sources of gender inequality at work and their remedies is important for women's overall well-being. Discrimination affects employee morale, turnover, productivity, and performance, not to mention physical and mental health. Unlike traditional or mainstream economists, we argue that gender inequality at work has cultural and structural sources and therefore requires varied solutions, in the economy and within organizations.

II   CULTURAL SOURCES OF GENDER INEQUALITY

Culture can be thought of as a 'mindset [that] explains and controls behavior and beliefs', and at the same time, a process of social interaction that 'both constitutes and is constituted by the individuals who engage in it' (Green, 2005, pp. 630, 631). In other words, social actors have choices in how they behave, interact, and construct their identities, yet are constrained by and contribute to the values and beliefs operating around them. In the workplace, culture sets expectations about how to behave, dress, and converse, about how attributes – such as competence – are assigned, and importantly, which behaviors are deemed appropriate, and therefore expected, of men and women.

According to Cecilia Ridgeway and Shelley Correll (2004b), cultural beliefs and expectations about men's and women's appropriate behaviors are not neutral. They confer advantage to men and women differentially. In fact, these feminist scholars argue that what maintains the gender system, a system for establishing and maintaining differences between men and women, are the 'widely held cultural beliefs that define the distinguishing characteristics of men and women and how they are expected to behave' (ibid., p. 511). More than stereotypes, these cultural or 'gender beliefs' are abstract, hegemonic, and universal understandings of who men and women are and what they do, guiding the behavior of actors in social relational contexts. In these contexts, gender beliefs ultimately bias the behavior and evaluations of self and others in ways that are consistent with the gender system. Because differences in status are attached to these gender beliefs, their enactment results in different and unequal workplace outcomes – in terms of recruitment, hiring, promotion, and rewards – for women, relative to men. In this section, we discuss several cultural and gendered beliefs that put women at a disadvantage in the workplace.

The Ideal Worker Norm

One cultural norm that appears to be neutral in its distribution of status but has gendered effects is that of the ideal worker (Acker, 1990; Williams, 2001). Though not strictly a gender belief, the ideal worker norm is based on assumptions and expectations that have a clear gender subtext. According to the ideal worker norm, the best and most competent workers are those that demonstrate full devotion to their paid employment (ibid.), evidenced by putting in long hours (Simpson, 1998; Rutherford, 2001), organizing and accommodating outside responsibilities – such as caregiving – around paid work, and a willingness to relocate or travel upon request (Kelly et al., 2010). This norm is gendered insofar as women, and particularly mothers, cannot conform to its expectations in the same way that men and fathers can, given that women continue to be responsible for the majority of childcare and household labor, and tend to be socialized accordingly (see Rutherford, 2001; Hochschild, 2003; Coltrane, 2004; Davis and Greenstein, 2009). The ideal worker, and the abstract jobs filled by this worker, are constructed around men's bodies (Acker, 1990), yet women are evaluated against this norm.

Maternal and Motherhood Bias

One characteristic that is especially vulnerable to negative evaluation on the basis of the ideal worker norm is motherhood. Joan Williams and Nancy Segal coined the term 'maternal wall' (2003) to refer to the discrimination mothers face at work before they even reach sight of the glass ceiling.[1] Using data from the National Longitudinal Survey of Youth, Jane Waldfogel (1998, p. 512) reported a parenthood gap of 20 percentage points for women: at age 30, mothers earned 70 percent of men's pay, while nonmothers earned 90 percent of men's pay. This parenthood wage gap is due in part to how mothers are perceived in the workplace based on our cultural beliefs of motherhood. For example, Ridgeway and Correll argue that motherhood is a status characteristic, a categorical distinction for which 'widely-held cultural beliefs associate greater status worthiness and competence with one category of the distinction (for example nonmothers) than another (for example mothers or primary child caretakers . . .)' (2004a, p. 684). Because gendered cultural systems confer lower status and competence on caregiving as compared to other roles, motherhood is often associated with biased evaluations of women's competence on the job. The normative obligations of mothers are thought to be inconsistent with the obligations of a committed, ideal worker since mothers are culturally defined as intensively devoted to children (Hays, 1996), nurturing, and communal, rather than instrumentally agentic, a quality more readily associated with paid work (Ridgeway and Correll, 2004a). When evaluators hold such beliefs, motherhood status can trigger biased evaluations of mothers' competence, which in turn undermine mothers' perceived suitability for positions of authority, as authority and leadership are culturally associated with masculinity (Collinson and Hearn, 1994). Nurturance is not seen as critical to success in senior positions. As an undervalued status characteristic, motherhood also results in a double standard wherein mothers' ability may be perceived as lower, but the standards they must meet to prove their ability are higher, relative to men and women without children (Fuegen et al., 2004).

One recent study on the motherhood disadvantage examined the tension between cultural understandings of motherhood and the ideal worker norm (Correll et al., 2007). The investigators asked undergraduate students to evaluate fictitious resumes of mothers, nonmothers, fathers, and nonfathers in a laboratory setting and also sent resumes to actual employers. They found that, holding qualifications and background experiences constant, student evaluators gave lower competence and commitment ratings to mothers, as compared to nonmothers, and the nonmothers fared better with respect to hiring, promotion, and salary decisions. When the fictitious resumes were sent to actual employers, mothers were called back half as often as nonmothers. At the same time, student evaluators offered fathers higher starting salaries, relative to childless men, attesting to raters' perceptions of fathers as highly committed to paid work and the compatibility of fatherhood and the ideal worker norm.

Caregiving Responsibilities

While perceptions and biases associated with motherhood as a status characteristic clearly disadvantage women in the workplace, the assumed or actual caregiving responsibilities that women and mothers shoulder can also lead to workplace disadvantages relative to men and fathers. For instance, using a sample of gender discrimination cases brought before the Ohio Civil Rights Commission, Donna Bobbitt-Zeher (2011) found that descriptive stereotypes of women's assumed characteristics made up the majority of discriminatory practices in these cases. Female workers were seen as 'women first [and] workers second', suggesting that assumptions about women's roles and responsibilities outside of the workplace affected employers' assessments of their reliability and commitment.

Similarly, as Paula England (2005) explains, one of the major determinants of the gender gap in pay is women's responsibility for childrearing, which affects employment continuity, part-time employment, and exclusivity of career focus. As many women take some time away from work after the birth or adoption of a child and to care for young children, career interruptions can result in less experience, fewer skills, and less seniority, relative to women without children. This is evidenced in Michelle Budig and Paula England's (2001) classic study of motherhood wage penalties. They report that mothers experience, on average, a 7 percent wage penalty per child. However, after controlling for years of job experience lost due to caregiving, mothers still experience a 5 percent penalty per child. The fact that pay penalties remain even after controlling for mothers' work suggests that motherhood wage penalties are not reducible to lost job experience alone (see also Wakabayashi and Donato, 2005). Employers hold cultural assumptions about mothers that affect their remuneration at work.

To help women maintain their labor force attachment and reduce the risk of dropping out of the workforce, many advocate for organizations to offer work–family policies, including leave policies (see Boushey, Chapter 19, this volume; Plantenga and Remery, Chapter 18, this volume). However, leave policies also carry risks. For example, researchers using Swedish data found that mothers who took parental leaves of 15 months or longer were significantly less likely to experience an upward occupational move, as measured by the standard international occupational prestige scale (SIOPS), upon return to their job and within a 10 year period following their return, net of individual human capital characteristics, such as education, as well as sector, number of children, and even of differences in selectivity between mothers who select short versus long leaves (Evertsson and Duvander, 2010).

While many studies have documented the negative effects of motherhood and caregiving on workplace advancement and wages, research has pointed to the positive effects of fatherhood. For example, in their study using longitudinal data, Melissa Hodges and Michelle Budig (2010) found that earnings bonuses for fathers remained, even after controlling for human capital characteristics, labor supply, family structure, and wives' employment status. Men identified by culturally favored markers of hegemonic masculinity – those who are white, married, in traditional households, college graduates, professional or managerial, and who work in employment demanding head work rather than physical strength – received the largest earning bonuses. This may be related to the historical and cultural linking of fatherhood with breadwinning, although fathers are also held to lower performance and time commitment standards than the hypothetical ideal worker (see Fuegen et al., 2004).

Devaluation of Women's Work

Women may also experience negative career outcomes because of the specific kind of paid work that they do and cultural valuations systems that under-reward women's work. For instance, work that involves caring for or nurturing others (rather than production or sales) is paid less than comparable work that does not involve care. Using panel data from the National Longitudinal Survey of Youth, England, Budig, and Nancy Folbre (England et al., 2002) found a 5–6 percent wage penalty for those in occupations requiring care work (relative to the wages that might be expected for individuals with similar qualifications in jobs with similar requirements but not involving care work) even after controlling for individual human capital variables, such as experience and education, occupation and industry characteristics, and stable characteristics of individuals. This care pay gap held for both men and women, yet to the extent that care-related jobs are overwhelmingly held by women, they suffer disproportionately from this pay penalty.

Women also experience a wage penalty for working in female-dominated sectors, even in occupations that do not involve care. Rebecca Glauber (2012) investigated the motherhood wage penalty within female-dominated (70 percent or more of workers are female), male-dominated (women constitute 30 percent or fewer of workers), and integrated workplaces (between 30 and 70 percent of workers are female). Mothers working in female-dominated workplaces, relative to women working in other jobs, experience a 7 percent wage penalty for one or two children and a 15 percent penalty for three or more children, after controlling for labor market experience. Women who work in male-dominated or integrated jobs do not experience a wage penalty for one or two children, but they pay a 10 percent or more wage penalty for three or more children. The reason for this wage penalty in female-dominated workplaces is not related to compensating differentials; in other words, mothers are not compensated for their lost wages with greater job satisfaction or access to workplace flexibility measures, health insurance, or other benefits. In fact, Glauber found that access to flexibility, health insurance, and paid leave (maternity leave, sick and vacation time) were positively correlated with wages (see also McCrate, Chapter 17, this volume).

The fact that women experience negative career consequences from caregiving, doing care-typed work, and working in female-dominated sectors attests to an underlying cultural framework that not only devalues the work that women do but also devalues female-typed work. In light of this, one possible solution would be for women to strive for male-typed work to upset cultural norms linking women to care and female-typed work. However, research indicates that when women are employed in male-typed jobs – such as leadership/managerial positions – and demonstrate success in these positions, they are often disliked by raters, which in turn has deleterious consequences for evaluations and reward allocation (Heilman et al., 2004).

Corporate Culture

For male-dominated and male-typed work, the argument may be that women lack the necessary 'fit' with corporate culture. For example, Karen Lyness and Madeline Heilman (2006) found that a perceived lack of fit between stereotypical attributes of women and requirements of managerial line jobs (which control essential organizational activities), as compared to managerial staff jobs (which provide support and expertise to line managers) was related to lower performance ratings for women in line jobs, relative to women in staff jobs or men in either staff or line jobs. These findings support lack-of-fit arguments that more negative evaluations of women occur when there is a perceived gap between job requirements and women's culturally assigned attributes.

However, relying on cultural fit in hiring decisions does not necessarily disadvantage women candidates. For example, research has revealed that homophily (the preference for similar others) based on shared cultural characteristics and experiences, such as tastes, life histories, hobbies, interests, values, and demeanor not only plays an explicit role in hiring in elite professions, such as law and investment banking, but also can work to women's advantage if they share a similar cultural background with their interviewers. In fact, whether candidates demonstrated organizational 'fit' – or similarity to firms' current employees on measure such as leisure pursuits, educational background, and demeanor – was deemed to be more important than skills relevant to job competence, particularly at the interview stage (Rivera, 2008).[2] Ascriptive homophily – based on similarity in gender and race – was actually less impactful on evaluations than cultural and experiential homophily. Importantly, a focus on organizational fit was not detrimental to women's hiring, as 60 percent of interviewers named a cross-sex candidate when asked to describe the 'best candidate' they had interviewed recently. Thus, in contexts where corporate fit includes personal characteristics that go beyond hegemonic, ideal worker norms, women can benefit.

III   STRUCTURAL SOURCES OF GENDER INEQUALITY

Although it is widely recognized that the workplace is a site of gender inequality, often the structure of organizations is overlooked as a cause of women's disadvantage. The structure of an organization refers to the procedures and activities that enable individuals to meet the goals of the organization (Pugh, 2007). Organizational structure, which is often, but not always, manifested in written policies and regulations, includes activities such as the allocation of responsibilities, decision-making processes, evaluation and wage-setting procedures, and hiring and promotion practices. In this section, we discuss how the very structure of an organization can affect how employees are rewarded and can contribute to gender inequality in explicit and subtle ways.

A pioneer in the feminist analysis of gender and organizations is sociologist Joan Acker. Acker (1990) has argued that most onlookers begin with the erroneous assumption that organizations are gender neutral. Although many organizations are male dominated, the gendered nature of organizations is more deeply engrained than simply the gender composition of a workforce. Just as gendered notions of the ideal worker influence assessments of who is recognized as competent, dedicated, and deserving of workplace rewards, norms favoring a 'masculine ethic' of rationality, stoicism, and the exclusivity of career focus are embedded in organizational structures (Kanter, 1993). What is more, because structures – such as hiring and promotion practices, evaluation systems, and labor contracts – are shrouded in an air of objectivity, they are often seen as gender neutral, making it difficult to uncover the gendered assumptions that underpin them. By examining the gendered foundations of organizational structures, we can understand how key organizational functions generate gender inequality.

Recruitment and Hiring Practices

Recruitment and hiring practices operate as the proverbial 'gatekeeper' of workplace opportunity and rewards. The major factors that determine who gets hired is how employers choose to recruit and screen applicants. Employers can use formalized recruitment and hiring procedures, such as advertising widely for jobs, using employment agencies, and screening workers based on specific qualifications and skills. Or employers can use informal procedures, such as word-of-mouth recruitment and hiring based on social networks and affiliations.

While formal recruitment and hiring procedures tend to generate a more diverse applicant pool, recruitment and hiring via informal networks is convenient, cheap, and less risky, and thus an attractive option for many employers. However, to the extent that social networks are homophilous (see Fernandez and Sosa, 2005), recruitment through informal networks can lead to gender-segregated applicant pools and hiring. For instance, Barbara Reskin and Debra Branch McBrier (2000) examined how the hiring practices of a representative sample of work organizations in the US affected the gender composition of management. They found that, even when accounting for the gender composition of labor supply, when companies recruited from informal networks, women were less likely to be in management. The use of formalized, open recruitment methods, such as advertising or using employment agencies, however, were associated with more women holding management jobs. Reskin and McBrier argued that structural inertia, sex-based ascription, and power dynamics all affect the hiring practices, as employers rely (whether consciously or not) on gender-based stereotypes and in-group preference to make hiring decisions in the absence of formal, objective criteria and procedures (see also Reskin, 2000).

Sex Composition and Segregation

The sex composition of the workforce and within occupations is an important component of organizational structure. Sex composition refers to the representation of men and women in the labor force, workplace, or jobs while occupational sex segregation refers to the concentration of men and women in specific occupations. Rather than a division of labor based on innate abilities, sex segregation relies on 'exaggerated' notions of biological traits and can lead to assumptions about men's and women's personality, preferences, and behavior (Reskin and Bielby, 2005). Occupational segregation can be horizontal or vertical. Horizontal segregation refers to segregation *across* occupations, such as women being concentrated in service work and men concentrated in blue-collar professions (Charles, 2003). Vertical segregation refers to the hierarchy that exists *within* a given occupation or organization, which results in men holding the highest status positions within a given occupation or organization (ibid.). Occupational segregation is a major determinant of the gender earnings gap, even when controlling for possible confounding individual and macro-level variables (see Petersen and Morgan, 1995; Cotter et al., 1997). Indeed, David Cotter and et al. (1997) suggest, echoed by many feminist economists, that the gender gap in earnings could be substantially reduced if occupational sex segregation was eradicated.

High levels of occupational sex segregation also reinforce stereotypes regarding the gender appropriateness of certain jobs and sectors, which not only leads to the devaluation of women's work, as discussed above, but also to stereotyping and bias in hiring and promotion practices (Cohen and Huffman, 2003). When hiring and promotion decisions are based on notions of the gender appropriateness of jobs, women may be steered toward positions that are deemed most appropriate for them. Moreover, to the extent that the existing sex composition of a workforce and occupations is a reflection of prior management decisions, if sex has been explicitly or implicitly used as an indicator of competence in the past, positions may be 'reserved' for either men or women based on the preconceptions of sex-based competencies (Cohen et al., 1998). While broader cultural beliefs about gender certainly influence such steering, the sheer number of women in specific jobs and sectors reinforce conceptions of gender-appropriate work.

Although sex composition of the workforce can be a source of gender stereotyping, it can also help women gain access to organizational positions. In an effort to understand how cultural beliefs can be effectively debunked, Lisa Cohen, Joseph Broschak and Heather Haveman (1998) collected and analyzed data on managerial employees, and set out to test whether women were more likely to be hired into such positions when gender-based preconceptions had already been challenged by women making inroads into managerial positions. They found that firms with higher proportions of female managers had a greater probability of hiring and promoting other women into that level. However, the relationship disappeared when the *majority* of higher-level positions were held by women. In other words, a minority of women in positions serves as a catalyst for more equal representation but when substantial representation is achieved, the push for additional representation ceases. Thus, composition reveals a troubling paradox: while the presence of women can lead to gender stereotyping and steering, particularly in female-typed work, in order to get more women into desirable positions, there must already be some women present.

Hierarchy and Promotion Ladders

It is often assumed that promotions and hiring practices are carried out through merit-based principles, with those who are most deserving, based on their competency and superior performance, being hired and promoted into the most desirable and suitable positions. However, nonmeritocratic practices, such as reliance on personal networks and preferences, often lurk beneath seemingly objective promotion structures, resulting in unequal outcomes.

Joe Magee and Adam Galinsky (2008) argue that those in positions of power within organizations act in ways that perpetuate the very structure of the organization: they expect, recognize, and reward behavior that aligns with and reflects the existing structure. This means that individuals who reflect that organization's status quo in terms of gender (and also race and ethnicity) are often preferred in the allocation of workplace opportunities and rewards compared to subordinate group members. For instance, researchers have documented that white men are more likely to receive callbacks after interviews, receive opportunities to work on high-profile cases, and are given responsibility for more complex, firm-specific tasks, as compared to women and people of color (Bielby and Baron, 1986; Hinds et al., 2000; Bertand and Mullainathan, 2004). If the evaluation of employees' competence and capability is founded on the ideal worker norm – as is argued above – then it is the ideal (male) worker who will most readily be recognized as deserving of mobility opportunities, and, in turn, will uphold the system. Indeed, women are given fewer opportunities than men to perform more complex work, and are not recognized as being as competent in male-dominated sectors, which effectively results in the sorting of women into lower-ranking positions of organizations (Bielby and Baron, 1986; England, 1992; Petersen and Morgan, 1995).

One mechanism that relegates women to lower-ranking and lower- paying positions has been dubbed the 'sticky-floor' effect, or the tendency for women to be trapped in the lower rungs of the organizational hierarchy. Using personnel records on over 22,000 employees from a large Canadian firm, Margaret Yap and Alison Konrad (2009) found that women were less likely than their male counterparts to be promoted, and the disadvantage was most severe for those in lower-status positions, providing support for the sticky-floor hypothesis. Although some argue that these discrepancies can be accounted for by sex-based choice, with the assumption that women often choose family responsibilities over work advancement (Baker, 2003), these choices are often shaped by extraneous cultural and structural influences, as discussed above (see also Van Vianen and Fischer, 2002). In addition, feminized jobs, which are often low paid, are not only undervalued, but once in them, women face increased barriers to pursuing better-paid jobs, as they do not often provide opportunities for career development or advancement (Rainbird, 2007).

A second mechanism – the glass-ceiling effect – refers to organizational structural barriers that inhibit women from advancing to higher rungs of the workplace hierarchy, irrespective of their qualifications (Powell and Butterfield, 1994). Although women have increasingly gained access to management positions, they often become stuck in middle management, and have not gained equivalent representation in senior management positions (Powell, 1999; Van Vianen and Fischer, 2002). Glass-ceiling effects are not explained by job-relevant characteristics of the employee alone, but rather are differences that remain even when controlling for education, experience, motivation, and abilities (Cotter et al., 2001).[3] The barriers to women's advancement stem from both conscious and unconscious discriminatory practices, including prescriptive stereotypes regarding expectations of conformity to gender-appropriate roles (Kaufmann et al., 1996; Eagly and Karau, 2002). Such gender biases can be cumulative, worsening as women advance through their careers (Jackson and O'Callaghan, 2009). Organizational supports, such as acknowledgment of problems, mentoring programs, increased representation of women in senior positions, emphasis on employee development and promotion, and formalized hiring and promotion practices have been found to help crack the glass ceiling (Scanlon, 1997; Reskin, 2000; Chesterman et al., 2003; Goodman et al., 2003).

The promotion and hierarchical structure of organizations can also contribute to unequal career outcomes for men and women by serving a motivational function (Tannenbaum et al., 1974). Rosabeth Moss Kanter (1993) hypothesized that the unequal opportunity structure in sex-segregated sectors discourages women from having lofty career aspirations, because the structural limitations in organizations make it so that they hold little hope of realizing those goals. In keeping with Kanter's theory, Naomi Cassirer and Reskin (2000) empirically identified location in the organizational hierarchy as a causal factor in women's career aspirations. Using data from the 1991 General Social Survey, they found men attached more importance to promotion than women, but this was largely due to the fact that men were more often in organizational positions that gave better chances for promotion. When controlling for experience and organizational location, sex was not found to be associated with attitudes or aspirations toward promotion, suggesting that structural limitations shape upward mobility for women. The motivational function of hierarchy is largely not recognized as a structural constraint, and instead is internalized as personal choice, leading individuals to be unaware of how structural forces influence their career trajectories (see Correll, 2004).

Performance and Evaluation Systems

Most organizations use some form of performance and evaluation system as a way of assessing employees' competencies and skills, which helps determine promotion decisions. Although there are many different modes and systems of assessment, all have the general aim of providing a systematic way of evaluating an individual's skills or competencies against established criteria (Manasa and Reddy, 2009). Although many assessments appear to be objective, due to standardized practices, there is evidence that they often reinforce existing biases, and can result in discriminatory practices.

Standardized evaluation systems are predicated and informed by cultural values and assumptions, which, if ignored, lead to inequitable appraisals when evaluating workers who differ from the 'ideal worker' norm. One notable example is the Hay Guide Chart-Profile methodology, which is a standardized job evaluation system, originally established in the 1940s and widely used for setting pay rates. Ronnie Steinberg (1992) argues that the underlying assumptions of the Hay system are rooted in the gendered norms and values from the era in which it was created. This assessment tool, she argues, creates a devaluation of women's roles, and leads to inequitable outcomes for women at work (see also Kim, 1989; Figart, 2000). The Hay system overvalues management duties, which are common of male-dominated jobs, and devalues nonmanagement duties, which are typical of female-dominated jobs. Thus, simply by relying on this outdated job evaluation structure, organizations systematically devalue work done by women and overvalue the work of men. This provides a clear example of how the use of a seemingly standardized evaluation system perpetuates gender inequalities to this day.

Even merit-based reward systems do not guarantee against gender bias. Using human resources data from a large service organization, Castilla (2008) demonstrated that even when women and men scored equally on merit-based evaluations, women and minorities received less compensation when compared to white men. Here, although merit-based evaluations were used to evaluate employee performance, employers were found to discount these ratings on the basis of gender, race, and nationality, resulting in discriminatory outcomes. Similarly, in a study of gender differences in promotions of Finnish metalworkers, Tuomas Pekkarinen and Juhana Vartiainen (2006) found that men were more likely to be promoted than women, despite being assessed as equally competent using merit-based measures. Women had to overperform at the same duties as men, and be more productive than men in order to be promoted, indicating that a different 'promotion threshold' existed for men than for women. This suggests that the establishment of formalized and more objective evaluation systems is a necessary but not sufficient mode of remedying gender inequalities.

IV REMEDIES AND POLICY RECOMMENDATIONS

Strategies to remedy gender discrimination must address both cultural and structural sources of inequality. Altering cultural beliefs about the ideal worker or gendered expectations regarding care work will be ineffective if these new norms are not written into and reinforced by workplace policies and procedures. Likewise, altering policies may result in change on the books but not in practice if the ideal worker norm and gendered expectations of behavior are not dislodged. We discuss several remedies for gender inequality – both in theory and in practice – with an eye toward integrating workplace culture and structures.

At the cultural level, much of the inequality faced by women and mothers results from their evaluation against an ideal worker norm (Acker, 1990). It is important to emphasize the socially constructed nature of these norms and expectations, and in doing so, their mutability. To the extent that the ideal worker norm is a social construction, it is possible that transformations in cultural understandings of whom and what constitutes the 'ideal worker' can occur, moving from a 'breadwinner with backstage support' model to a norm of 'work–life balance' for all workers.

For instance, in a comparative study of German and Finnish bank managers, researchers found that in both Germany (a context with a gender order emphasizing a male-breadwinner model) and Finland (a context emphasizing an egalitarian, dual-earner model), the ideal worker norm shifted from a male model of full-time, lifelong employment, 24-hour a day socializing with clients, and expertise in corporate banking *before* organizational reforms during the 1980s and 1990s to a gender-ambiguous model in the case of Germany and a feminized model in the case of Finland (Tienari et al., 2002). In Germany, ideals changed to full-time, entry-level employment, relaxed socializing requirements, and an emphasis on expertise in team management, sales, and retail. In Finland, new feminized ideal-work attributes were emphasized: sales skills in retail banking, team leadership, and trouble-shooting; full-time, career-stage employment with the possibility of family-related career breaks; and a reduced emphasis on after-work social events.

There is also evidence that transformation of the ideal worker norm can occur through attempts to change workplace culture by altering the very organization of work and the workday. A study of the workplace culture of Best Buy corporate head-quarters demonstrates how the 'Results-only Work Environment' (ROWE) initiative challenged the ideal worker norm and the devaluation of unpaid work, particularly when initiatives were targeted at and supported by men as well as women (Kelly et al., 2010). ROWE – implemented at the team level through a series of workshops and orientations – is described as an 'adaptive culture change strategy' (p. 284) that is not targeted specifically at mothers or parents.[4] Under this framework, expectations of face-time hours worked, as a measure of productivity, are replaced with a focus on outcomes and results. A key focus of the initiative was to critically examine old norms about productivity and commitment, signaled through visible busyness, long hours, and imme-diate responsiveness to unplanned work, which tend to advantage men and childless women, and instead, give workers new ways of responding to workplace expectations and effectively organize their time.

In theory, this initiative and others like it provide an opportunity to construct a new ideal of effective organization of work and life for all workers. But, in practice, many gendered cultural norms remained intact. Most notably, ROWE was treated by many as a women's-only initiative, and on countless occasions, men attempted to actively dis-tance themselves from it, most visibly when senior managers actively resisted efforts for ROWE-driven changes in their departments.

This resistance on the part of men points to two major challenges of enacting cultural change in organizational contexts. The first lies in attempts to exact social change in a context such as a work organization, without seeing the same changes made at the broader cultural level. Insofar as gendered norms remain in society at large, it is dif-ficult to upset the ideal worker norm in individual workplaces. Efforts must be made at the societal level to promote norms of work–life balance for both women and men and increase awareness of the ways in which gendered norms regarding work and family are activated and can be deactivated. As recently as 2010, the US Census Bureau defined fathers caring for their children while mothers worked for pay as a 'childcare arrange-ment' while mothers caring for their children while fathers worked for pay were simply parenting (Laughlin, 2010). Such antiquated cultural (and institutional) definitions that assume that caregiving responsibilities are the purview of mothers and effectively desig-nate fathers as second-order parents need to be altered before workplaces can displace ideal worker norms. This is not to suggest that a simple modification of definitions at the US Census Bureau will bring about cultural change, but it would certainly be a step in the right direction for altering gendered norms about work and family obligations.

The second challenge of enacting cultural change in organizations lies in the actual division of care work and the empirical fact that mothers continue to shoulder the lion's share of care and domestic work. One way of easing the burden for women is through the adoption of work–family policies, such as paid maternity leave, flextime (see Boushey, Chapter 19, this volume; Plantenga and Remery, Chapter 18, this volume), and reduced work weeks. However, as noted above, the extended use of leave policies can carry risks associated with career disruption and, because they are often framed as 'accommoda-tions' or 'perks' (Lewis, 2010), such policies can marginalize caregivers if they are seen as being given special treatment. In addition, work–family policies are more readily avail-able to those in higher-status, better-paying jobs, and thus are not an option for many workers (see McCrate, Chaper 17, this volume). The limited provision of work–family policies and their framing in the language of accommodation can actually reinforce the separation of paid and unpaid labor, which further marginalizes those in the former sphere, while privileging those doing paid employment (Williams, 2001; Lewis, 2010).

Instead, some commentators have argued that individual men and fathers need to take on more domestic duties, in order to help redress gender inequities within the workplace and facilitate work–life balance. Michael Selmi (2007), for instance, argues that many of the arguments against men engaging in childcare prove to be based upon erroneous assumptions, such as the notion that fathers face greater economic losses, relative to mothers, when they set aside work to engage in care. The adoption and implementation of state-sponsored paid parental leaves – for both parents – and publicly subsidized childcare are just two measures that could ease women's real and perceived responsibility for caregiving, undo gender norms regarding care work, and mitigate the workplace penalties that women typically experience. For parental leave provisions, offering fathers a period of nontransferable paid leave on a 'use-it-or-lose-it' basis is especially important for encouraging fathers to take leave. And using paid leave can provide an important opportunity for fathers to participate in caregiving at the beginning of a child's life, when caregiving/breadwinning patterns tend to be established in families. Such programs would not only ease women's actual caregiving burden and offset the negative consequences women experience at work but also begin to alter gendered cultural norms regarding caregiving and domestic responsibilities.

In addition to promoting work–life balance through cultural change and extended policy provisions, organizations need to restructure recruitment, hiring, and promotion practices to ensure that decisions are based on objective criteria rather than ideal worker norms or subjective – and often homophilous – preferences of managers. As Reskin and McBrier (2000) note, recruitment and hiring is a 'critical stage' and the most effective site for change because recruitment and hiring practices ultimately shape the gender composition of the workforce which, in turn, influences future opportunities for women. Using open recruitment methods, such as public job postings or employment agencies rather than relying on informal networks or personal referrals, will diversify the applicant pool. The voluntary use of affirmative action policies, with goals and timetables to increase the representation of women in key occupations, would also generate more gender diversity in the applicant pool. At the evaluation stage, replacing subjective criteria, such as vague notions of being a 'team player', 'fitting in', or 'competence' with clearly operationalized, objective criteria, such as test performance or interview rankings would help to eradicate subjectivity and bias in evaluation and hiring (Heilman, 2001). The use of strict seniority systems would ensure that women move beyond glass ceilings and encourage women's mobility aspirations. Finally, replacing antiquated job evaluation systems that under-reward skills typically associated with women's work with gender-neutral systems that assign wages based on job value would minimize wage differentials between predominantly female and predominantly male jobs that are comparable in skills, responsibility, and working conditions (see Figart and Lapidus, 1996) and chip away at the cultural devaluation of women's work.

Such changes in workplace structure and culture must involve both top-down commitment and bottom-up involvement. Organizational leadership must be committed to altering long-standing sources of gender inequality and must be willing to involve rank-and-file workers in their efforts. Otherwise changes will be ceremonial and perfunctory, both in form and function. Susan Sturm's (2001) case study of the efforts of a large US accounting/consulting firm, Deloitte & Touche, to enhance gender equality is illustrative. Prior to the gender equity initiative, women were underrepresented in high-level occupations and had high turnover rates as compared to men. The gender equity program, which was very effective, included participatory task forces that engaged employees in possible solutions. These task forces were responsible for assessing causes of gender gaps in promotions and turnover, making recommendations to change the underlying problems and implementing a retention program for female employees. Any changes made were to be transparent, measurable, and sustainable, ensuring clear, ongoing, and effective solutions. Importantly, the impetus for these actions did not stem from a threat of legal action, but recognition from the CEO of the company that a gender gap existed and was an ongoing problem. The experience of Deloitte & Touche highlights the importance of a multifaceted approach to gender equity and attests to the importance of commitment from organizational leadership as well as involvement from employees.

It is important to note that while many of the policy recommendations we have suggested would be enhanced by federal legislation and state support (that is, broader affirmative action requirements, paid parental leave, subsidized childcare, and comparable worth), all of the policies mentioned above can be voluntarily adopted at the organizational level by individual firms. Because state and federal law is slow to change, policy implementation can occur most readily at the organizational level. This is not to excuse state, local, and federal governments from legislating against gender discrimination and in favor of work–life balance, but while waiting, firms can and should go it alone.

V   CONCLUSION

In this chapter, we have argued that gender inequality at work stems from a gender subtext rooted in the ideal worker norm; this subtext informs cultural understandings of who is deemed worthy of workplace rewards and biases personnel and evaluation structures that are seemingly neutral on face value. Accordingly, policies designed to remedy gender inequality at work must promote new norms of work–life balance for both women and men and systematize personnel practices and evaluation procedures to ensure that workplace decisions are gender neutral. Finally, to be most effective, workplace policy changes must be accompanied by broader social change as well as commitment from organizational leadership. To the extent that gender inequality at work directly affects women's economic security, family relations, health, and political power, giving women equal access to jobs, wages, and career advancement will result in more-equitable arrangements for women at work, home, and in the public sphere.

NOTES

1. The glass ceiling commonly refers to the 'invisible' (not stated or overt) barriers that prevent women from reaching top positions.
2. However, the interviewers did make the point that the interview stage would only be reached if candidates met a certain, predetermined baseline level of job-relevant skills, such as appropriate prior work experience.
3. Interestingly, men in female-dominated professions do not face similar barriers to advancement, and in fact have been found to ride the 'glass escalator'. This term refers to hidden structural advantages that allow men to be assessed as more competent in these professions, and advance more overall than their female counterparts (see Williams, 1992).
4. Ultimately, mothers came to champion the initiative more so than other groups of workers, including men who, not surprisingly, saw less of a need for it.

REFERENCES

Acker, Joan (1990), 'Hierarchies, jobs, bodies: a theory of gendered organizations', *Gender & Society*, **4**(2), 139–58.

Baker, Joe G. (2003), 'Glass ceilings or sticky floors? A model of high-income law graduates', *Journal of Labor Research*, **24**(4), 695–711.

Becker, Gary (1985), 'Human capital, effort and the sexual division of labour', *Journal of Labour Economics*, **3**(1), 33–58.

Benschop, Yvonne and Hans Doorewaard (1998), 'Covered by equality: the gender subtext of organizations', *Organizational Studies*, **19**(5), 787–805.

Bertrand, Marianne and Sendhil Mullainathan (2004), 'Are Emily and Greg more employable than Lakisha and Jamal? A field experiment on labor market discrimination', *American Economic Review*, **94**(4), 991–1013.

Bielby, William T. and James N. Baron (1986), 'Men and women at work: sex segregation and statistical discrimination', *American Journal of Sociology*, **91**(4), 759–99.

Bobbitt-Zeher, Donna (2011), 'Gender discrimination at work: connecting gender stereotypes, institutional policies, and gender composition of workplace', *Gender & Society*, **25**(6), 764–86.

Budig, Michelle J. and Paula England (2001), 'The wage penalty for motherhood', *American Sociological Review*, **66**(2), 204–25.

Cassirer, Naomi and Barbara R. Reskin (2000), 'High hopes: organizational position, employment experiences, and women's and men's promotion aspirations', *Work and Occupations*, **27**(4), 438–63.

Castilla, Emilio J. (2008), 'Gender, race and meritocracy in organizational careers', *American Journal of Sociology*, **113**(6), 1479–526.

Charles, Maria (2003), 'Deciphering sex segregation: vertical and horizontal inequalities in ten national labor markers', *Acta Sociologica*, **46**(4), 267–87.

Chesterman, Colleen, Anne Ross-Smith and Margaret Peters (2003), 'Changing the landscape? Women in academic leadership in Australia', *McGill Journal of Education*, **38**(3), 421–35.

Cohen, Lisa E., Joseph P. Broschak and Heather A. Haveman (1998), 'And then there were more? The effect of organizational sex composition on the hiring and promotion of managers', *American Sociological Review*, **63**(5), 711–27.

Cohen, Philip N. and Matt L. Huffman (2003), 'Occupational segregation and the devaluation of women's work across labor markets', *Social Forces*, **81**(3), 881–908.

Collinson, David and Jeff Hearn (1994), 'Naming men as men: implications for work, organization and management', *Gender, Work & Organization*, **1**(1), 2–22.

Coltrane, Scott (2004), 'Research on household labor: modeling and measuring the social embeddedness of routine family work', *Journal of Marriage and Family*, **62**(4), 1208–33.

Correll, Shelley J. (2004), 'Constraints into preferences: gender, status, and career aspirations', *American Sociological Review*, **69**(1), 93–113.

Correll, Shelley J., Stephen Bernard and In Paik (2007), 'Getting a job: is there a motherhood penalty?', *American Journal of Sociology*, **112**(5), 1297–339.

Cotter, David A., JoAnn Defoire, Joan M. Hermsen, Brenda Marsteller Kowalewski and Reeve Vanneman (1997), 'All women benefit: the macro-level effect of occupational integration on gender earnings equality', *American Sociological Review*, **62**(5), 714–34.

Cotter, David A., Joan M. Hermsen, Seth Ovadia and Reeve Vanneman (2001), 'The glass ceiling effect', *Social Forces*, **80**(2), 655–82.

Davis, Shannon N. and Theodore N. Greenstein (2009), 'Gender ideology: components, predictors, and consequences', *Annual Review of Sociology*, **35**, 87–105.

Eagly, Alice H. and Steven J. Karau (2002), 'Role congruity theory of prejudice toward female leaders', *Psychological Review*, **109**(3), 573–98.

England, Paula (1992), *Comparable Worth: Theories and Evidence*, New York: Aldine de Gruyter.

England, Paula (2005), 'Gender inequality in labor markets: the role of motherhood and segregation', *Social Politics*, **12**(2), 264–88.

England, Paula, Michelle Budig and Nancy Folbre (2002), 'Wages of virtue: the relative pay of care work', *Social Problems*, **49**(4), 455–73.

Evertsson, Marie and Ann-Zofie Duvander (2010), 'Parental leave – possibility or trap? Does family leave length effect Swedish women's labour market opportunities', *European Sociological Review*, **27**(4), 435–50.

Fernandez, Roberto M. and M. Lourdes Sosa (2005), 'Gendering the job and recruitment at a call center', *American Journal of Sociology*, **111**(3), 859–904.

Figart, Deborah M. (2000), 'Equal pay for equal work: job evaluation in an evolving social norm', *Journal of Economic Issues*, **34**(1), 1–19.

Figart, Deborah M. and June Lapidus (1996), 'The impact of comparable worth on earnings inequality', *Work and Occupations*, **23**(3), 297–318.

Fuegen, Kathleen, Monica Biernat, Elizabeth Haines and Kay Deaux (2004), 'Mothers and fathers in the workplace: how gender and parental status influence judgments of job-related competence', *Journal of Social Issues*, **60**(4), 737–54.

Glauber, Rebecca (2012), 'Women's work and working conditions: are mothers compensated for lost wages?', *Work and Occupations*, **39**(2), 115–38.

Goodman, Jodi S., Dail L. Fields and Terry C. Blum (2003), 'Cracks in the glass ceiling: in what kind of organizations do women make it to the top?', *Group Organization Management*, **28**(4), 475–501.

Green, Tristin K. (2005), 'Work culture and discrimination', *California Law Review*, **93**(3), 623–84.

Hays, Sharon (1996), *The Cultural Contradictions of Motherhood*, New Haven, CT: Yale University Press.

Heilman, Madeline E. (2001), 'Description and prescription: how gender stereotypes prevent women's ascent up the organizational ladder', *Journal of Social Issues*, **57**(4), 657–74.

Heilman, Madeline E., Aaron S. Wallen, Daniella Fuchs and Melinda M. Tamkins (2004), 'Penalties for success: reactions to women who succeed in male gender-typed tasks', *Journal of Applied Psychology*, **89**(3), 416–27.

Hinds, Pamela J., Kathleen M. Carley, David Krackhardt and Doug Wholey (2000), 'Choosing work group members: balancing similarity, competence, and familiarity', *Organizational Behavior and Human Decision Processes*, **81**(2), 226–51.

Hochschild, Arlie R. (with Anne Machung) (2003), *The Second Shift*, New York: Penguin Books.

Hodges, Melissa J. and Michelle J. Budig (2010), 'Who gets the Daddy bonus? Organizational hegemonic masculinity and the impact of fatherhood on earnings', *Gender & Society*, **24**(6), 717–45.

Jackson, Jerlando F.L. and Elizabeth M. O'Callaghan (2009), 'What do we know about glass ceiling effects? A taxonomy and critical review to inform higher education research', *Research in Higher Education*, **50**(5), 460–82.

Kanter, Rosabeth Moss (1993), *Women and Men of the Corporation*, rev. edn, New York: Basic Books.

Kaufmann, Geir, Scott G. Isaksen and Ken Lauer (1996), 'Testing the "glass ceiling" effect on gender differences in upper level management: the case of innovator orientation', *European Journal of Work and Organizational Psychology*, **5**(1), 29–41.

Kelly, Erin L., Samantha K. Ammons, Kelly Chermack and Phyllis Moen (2010), 'Gendered challenge, gendered response: confronting the ideal worker norm in a white-collar organization', *Gender & Society*, **24**(3), 281–303.

Kim, Marlene (1989), 'Gender bias in compensation structures: a case study of its historical basis and persistence', *Journal of Social Issues*, **45**(4), 39–49.

Laughlin, Linda (2010), 'Who's minding the kids? Child care arrangements: Spring 2005/Summer 2006', Current Population Reports, US Census Bureau, Washington, DC.

Lewis, Suzan (2010), 'Restructuring workplace cultures: the ultimate work–family challenge?', *Gender in Management: An International Journal*, **25**(5), 355–65.

Lyness, Karen S. and Madeline E. Heilman (2006), 'When fit is fundamental: performance evaluations and promotions of upper-level female and male managers', *Journal of Applied Psychology*, **91**(4), 777–85.

Magee, Joe C. and Adam D. Galinsky (2008), 'Social hierarchy: the self-reinforcing nature of power and status', *The Academy of Management Annals*, **2**(1), 351–98.

Manasa, K.V.L. and Nivedita Reddy (2009), 'Role of training in improving performance', *The IUP Journal of Soft Skills*, **3**(3 & 4), 72–80.

Pekkarinen, Tuomas and Juhana Vartiainen (2006), 'Gender differences in promotion on a job ladder: evidence from Finnish metalworkers', *Industrial and Labor Relations Review*, **59**(2), 285–301.

Petersen, Trond and Laurie A. Morgan (1995), 'Separate and unequal: occupation' – establishment sex segregation and the gender wage gap', *American Journal of Sociology*, **101**(2), 329–65.

Powell, Gary N. (1999), 'Reflections on the glass ceiling: recent trend and future prospects', in Powell (ed.), *Handbook of Gender and Work*, Thousand Oaks, CA: Sage, pp. 325–46.

Powell, Gary N. and D. Anthony Butterfield (1994), 'Investigating the "glass ceiling" phenomenon: an empirical study of actual promotions to top management', *Academy of Management Journal*, **37**(1), 68–86.

Pugh, Derek S. (2007), *Organization Theory: Selected Classic Readings*, 5th edn, London: Penguin Books.

Rainbird, Helen (2007), 'Can training remove the glue from the "sticky floor" of low-paid work for women?', *Equal Opportunities International*, **26**(6), 555–72.

Reskin, Barbara F. (2000), 'Proximate causes of employment discrimination', *Contemporary Sociology*, **29**(2), 319–28.

Reskin, Barbara F. and Denise D. Bielby (2005), 'A sociological perspective on gender and career outcomes', *Journal of Economic Perspectives*, **19**(1), 71–86.

Reskin, Barbara F. and Debra Branch McBrier (2000), 'Why not ascription? Organizations' employment of male and female managers', *American Sociological Review*, **65**(2), 210–33.

Ridgeway, Cecilia and Shelley Correll (2004a), 'Motherhood as a status characteristic', *Journal of Social Issues*, **60**(4), 683–700.

Ridgeway, Cecilia and Shelley Correll (2004b), 'Unpacking the gender system: a theoretical perspective on gender beliefs and social relations', *Gender & Society*, **18**(4), 510–31.

Rivera, Lauren (2008), 'Cultural reproduction in the labor market: homophily in job interviews', Working Paper, Department of Sociology, Harvard University, Cambridge, MA.

Rutherford, Sarah (2001), '"Are you going home already?" The long hours culture, women managers and patriarchal closure', *Time & Society*, **10**(2–3), 259–76.

Scanlon, Karen C. (1997), 'Mentoring women administrators: breaking through the glass ceiling', *Initiatives*, **58**(2), 39–59.

Selmi, Michael (2007), 'The work–family conflict: an essay on employers, men and responsibility', *University of St. Thomas Law Journal*, **4**(3), 573–98.

Simpson, Ruth (1998), 'Presenteeism, power and organizational change: long hours as a career barrier and the impact on the working lives of women managers', *British Journal of Management*, **9**(1), 37–50.

Steinberg, Ronnie J. (1992), 'Gendered instructions, cultural lag and gender bias in the Hay system of job evaluation', *Work and Occupations*, **19**(4), 387–423.

Sturm, Susan (2001), 'Second generation employment discrimination: a structural approach', *Columbia Law Review*, **101**(3), 458–568.

Tannenbaum, Arnold S., Bogdan Kavčič, Menachem Rosner, Mino Vianello and Georg Wieser (1974), *Hierarchy in Organizations: An International Comparison*, San Francisco, CA: Jossey Bass.

Tienari, Janne, Sigrid Quack and Hildegard Theobald (2002), 'Organizational reforms, "ideal workers" and gender orders: a cross-societal comparison', *Organizational Studies*, **23**(2), 249–79.

Tilly, Charles (1998), *Durable Inequality*, Bervicley, CA: University of California Press.

Van Vianen, Annelies E.M. and Agneta H. Fischer (2002), 'Illuminating the glass ceiling: the role of organizational culture preferences', *Journal of Occupational and Organizational Psychology*, **75**(3), 315–37.

Wakabayashi, Chizuko and Katharine M. Donato (2005), 'The consequences of care giving: effects on women's employment and earnings', *Population Research and Policy Review*, **24**(5), 467–88.

Waldfogal, Jane (1998), 'The family gap for young women in the United States and Britain: can maternity leave make a difference', *Journal of Labor Economics*, **16**(3), 505–45.

Williams, Christine L. (1992), 'The glass escalator: hidden advantages for men in the "female" professions', *Social Problems*, **39**(3), 253–67.

Williams, Joan C. (2001), *Unbending Gender: Why Family and Work Conflict and What to Do about It*, New York: Oxford University Press.

Williams, Joan C. and Nancy Segal (2003), 'Beyond the maternal wall: relief for family caregivers who are discriminated against on the job', *Harvard Women's Law Journal*, **26**(77), 77–162.

Yap, Margaret and Alison M. Konrad (2009), 'Gender and racial differentials in promotions: is there a sticky floor, a mid-level bottleneck, or a glass ceiling?', *Industrial Relations*, **64**(4), 593–619.

13. Occupational segregation and the gender wage gap in the US
Ariane Hegewisch and Hannah Liepmann*

I INTRODUCTION

Women are now roughly half of the workforce, but that parity in the overall labor force has not translated into a balanced distribution of men and women across jobs and occupations. Occupational segregation, with men working in jobs that are predominantly male and women working in jobs that are predominantly female, remains a strong feature of the labor market in the US and other industrialized countries. In the 1970s and 1980s, occupational segregation fell rapidly, as women moved into fields and jobs such as law, accounting, pharmacy, bus driving, and postal mail carriers, which previously had been virtually closed to them. Yet other occupations such as nursing (female) or engineering (male) saw hardly any change in their stark gender distribution. Moreover, since the late 1990s, there has been no further progress toward integration of occupations and indeed, if anything, the trend seems to be toward further segregation. This holds for all age groups, including younger women. In the US in 2010, among full-time workers, over four out of five women (41.1 percent) and close to five out of 10 men (49.3 percent) worked in an occupation where at least 75 percent of other workers were also of that gender (Hegewisch et al., 2011).[1]

Women's lives and livelihoods are affected greatly by occupational segregation. First, such stark gender segregation might be an indication of barriers in the labor market that discourage the underrepresented gender from following their talents and inclinations (see Hirsh et al., Chapter 12, this volume). This would result in an inefficient allocation of people between jobs. Second, female-dominated occupations on average pay lower wages and salaries than male-dominated or more-integrated occupations, and thus occupational segregation is one factor in the gender-based wage gap. This has particularly pernicious consequences for women (and their families) who toil at the bottom end of the labor market (see Albelda, Chapter 16, this volume). For researchers and policy-makers concerned with women's economic self-sufficiency and security, occupational segregation is a primary reason for women's lower earnings, and hence a contributing factor to women's lower ownership of financial assets, reduced ability to save for retirement or emergencies, and higher poverty rates among women during their working lives and in retirement.

In this chapter, we will provide an overview of trends in gender segregation and its link to the gender wage gap, highlighting the stagnation in trends toward occupational integration (Section II). In Section III we will then review competing explanations for these trends and the debates on why or whether there seems to have been so little progress. While the link between women's share of an occupation and lower earnings is undisputed, the explanations for occupational segregation are contested. Some economists focus on supply-side factors and human capital, suggesting that women choose certain occupations because these fit in better with their family responsibilities and are paid lower wages because their productivity is lower as a result of more disrupted working lives. Others focus on demand-side factors and discrimination. Section IV concludes.

II   OCCUPATIONAL SEGREGATION IN THE LABOR MARKET

During the last few decades, the face of the American workforce has changed dramatically as more and more women entered and remained in the labor force and also moved into occupations that were previously barred to them or where they were only a small share of the total. Occupational integration progressed significantly during the 1970s and 1980s, supported by the passage of Title IX of the Educational Amendments of 1972 that required colleges, universities, and vocational institutions to open their doors to women and minority students. Active enforcement of anti-discrimination laws and of affirmative action obligations of federal contractors complemented these efforts by challenging discrimination in hiring and pay (see, for example, Bergmann, 1986; US Department of Labor, Women's Bureau, 1998). Other factors contributing to reduced occupational segregation were the rapid growth of occupations, particularly in business and financial services, which were less segregated (Reskin and Roos, 1990; Blau et al., 1998; Cotter et al., 2004). Yet as several commentators and scholars have noted, progress toward further integration slowed considerably during the 1990s (ibid.; England, 2005; Tomaskovic-Devey et al., 2006) and stalled if not reversed during the last decade (Hegewisch et al., 2010; Blau et al., 2012).

One way of showing the quantitative change in occupation segregation is the Index of Dissimilarity, a methodology originally developed by Otis Duncan and Beverly Duncan (1955) to analyze residential segregation by race. Applied to occupational segregation, the index estimates how many women and men would have to change occupations for the gender distribution in each occupation to mirror the gender distribution of the workforce as a whole. The index spans from 1.00 (total segregation) to 0.00 (total integration) and is weighted so that changes in larger occupations affect the index more than changes in smaller occupations. Figure 13.1 tracks the change in occupational segregation from 1972 to 2011 for all US workers, and separately for college-educated workers (with at least four years of college) and workers with lower levels of education. Occupational segregation for all workers declined consistently for the first 25 years, from the early 1970s until the mid-1990s. The index reached its lowest point in 2002 with a value of 0.5011, meaning that 50 percent of men and women would have to move occupations for workers' distribution across jobs to reach the same general distribution of women and men in the labor market. The value for the index stagnated, and even slightly increased for the rest of the decade, suggesting that there was no further integration of the workforce. During 2010 and 2011, the index has fallen marginally.

Change in the Index of Dissimilarity can come from two sources: (i) actual change within different occupations, called the 'composition effect', for example, due to an increase in the proportion of women among accountants or pharmacists; and (ii) differential employment growth between occupations, called the 'mix effect', for example, due

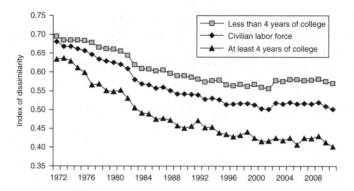

Note: Occupations are consistently classified according to 1990 Census occupational classifications. The analysis is restricted to the civilian labor force, and to workers aged 25 to 64.

Source: Authors' compilations based on the Current Population Survey, March/Annual Social and Economic Supplement (ASEC), as provided by King et al. (2010).

Figure 13.1   Index of Dissimilarity, 1972–2011

to accounting (with a relatively even gender distribution) adding jobs, or construction (with a very uneven gender distribution in most occupations) losing jobs, without either occupation actually changing its gender composition. Ariane Hegewisch et al. (2010, p. 16, based on Blau and Hendricks, 1979), estimated the impact of the mix and composition effects on the index for each decade. The composition effect was negative in each of the decades (that is, occupations actually became more integrated), but the size of the negative impact fell sharply each decade and was almost zero between 2000 and 2009. The mix effect was positive in all decades apart from the 1990s, suggesting that for most of the time growth was stronger in less integrated than more integrated occupations.[2]

Figure 13.1 also shows that college-degree level occupations on the whole have been more likely to be gender integrated than occupations requiring less education. Yet within this broad generalization, different occupations have changed at different rates (see Hegewisch et al., 2010). Forty years ago, fewer than one in 20 lawyers, dentists, engineers, electricians, or carpenters were women, and fewer than one in eight pharmacists or postal mail carriers. By 2010, one in two pharmacists and at least three in 10 dentists and lawyers were women, but occupations such as civil engineers, electricians, or carpenters were still as firmly male dominated in 2010 as they were in the early 1970s. Other occupations, such as nurses, pre-school and kindergarten teachers, and dental assistants, are almost as exclusively female now as they were four decades ago. Four of the 10 most common occupations for women (including nurses, secretaries, other administrative support workers, and teachers) are nontraditional occupations for men, and five of the 10 most common occupations for men (truck drivers, sales representatives in wholesale and manufacturing, laborers, construction workers, and computer programmers) are nontraditional jobs for women (Hegewisch et al., 2011). The occupation of computer programmers illustrates that progress toward a more even gender balance is not irreversible. In the 1980s, when computer programming first became an important field, women's share steadily increased, reaching about a

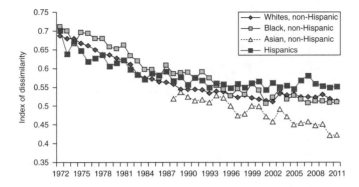

Notes: Occupations are consistently classified according to 1990 Census occupational classifications. The analysis is restricted to the civilian labor force, and to workers aged 25 to 64. Whites, blacks and Asian groups are non-Hispanic. 'Asians' include 'Asian only' as well as 'Hawaiian/Pacific Islander' (data available only from 1988 onward).

Source: See Figure 13.1.

Figure 13.2 Comparison between men and women within race/ethnicity group, 1972–2011

third of the workforce, only to steadily decline again during the 1990s and 2000s, with women's share falling to just one in five computer programmers by 2009 (Hegewisch et al., 2010).

Figure 13.2 shows change in the Index of Dissimilarity over time for each major race/ethnic group, comparing women to men of the same background. Once different levels of education are taken into account, change over time in occupational segregation for men and women within each major race/ethnic group is fairly similar to the trend for all men and women. Asian women and men are most likely to have at least a four-year college degree, and are most likely to work in the same occupations compared to other race/ethnic groups. Hispanic women and men, on the other hand, as a group are least likely to have college-level education (National Center for Education Statistics, 2011) and are also least likely to work in the same occupations.

Paula England (2005, p. 267) noted that 'the concentration in gendered jobs does not vary much by race,' especially once different levels of education are taken into account (although Price (2002) finds that in the construction trades race and ethnicity are clearer predictors of women's jobs, and earnings, than gender). Yet even if gender segregation overall is more pronounced than race or ethnic segregation, occupations do differ by race/ethnic background. The Index of Dissimilarity between black and white women, for example, suggests that still almost three of 10 women would have to change occupations for black and white women to be equally likely to work in all occupations. As between men and women, segregation among women is less for college educated than for women with lower educational qualifications.[3]

Perhaps surprisingly, younger women have not made much more headway in terms of occupational integration than older women. During the 1980s and 1990s, women in the youngest age group, 25–34 years, the most recent entrants to the labor market, were considerably more likely than older women to work in more-integrated occupations, but

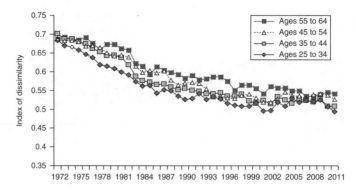

Note: Occupations are consistently classified according to 1990 Census occupational classifications. The analysis is restricted to the civilian labor force, and to workers aged 25 to 64.

Source: See Figure 13.1.

Figure 13.3   Index of Dissimilarity, 1972–2011, by age groups (in a given year)

by the 2000s, trends shifted. From 2002 to 2009, there was a disappointing move away from integration for this group (see Figure 13.3).

One of the challenges of comparing occupational segregation over time is the periodic readjustment of the definitions of occupations to capture the rise of new occupations, such as call-center operators, for example, and the decline of older ones, such as elevator operators. The above data take the 1990 definition of occupations as their reference point, using a dataset specifically developed to allow longitudinal analysis of approximately 390 occupations (Ruggles et al., 2010).[4] Francine Blau, Peter Brummund and Albert Liu (2012) instead use the 2000 occupational reclassification as their reference point for an examination of change in occupational integration between 1970 and 2009. They argue that the 2000 reclassification, particularly where it took the form of splitting one occupation into two or more new occupations, with the new occupations having different gender balances than the old occupation, potentially overstated integration by up to 5 percentage points. They develop a crosswalk between the old and new classifications for comparing trends over time. Overall, their results are broadly similar to the ones shown above, but find a continued if small decline in occupational gender segregation between 2000 and 2009, by 1.1 percentage points.[5]

Donald Tomaskovic-Devey et al. (2006) use a different estimate of change in the occupational distribution by race and gender. They base their study on the EEO-1 reports that private sector employers must submit annually to the US Equal Employment Opportunity Commission (EEOC), with information about the distribution by gender and race/ethnicity of the workforce across nine broad job groups. The EEO-1 categories are less detailed than the occupational data in other studies, but they make it possible to study change within organizations over time. Between 1966 and 2003, the authors document a pronounced decline in gender segregation, but find that 'after an initial burst of desegregation along race/ethnic lines, workplace segregation stalled at essentially 1980 levels for black-white and Hispanic-white segregation' (Tomaskovic-Devey et al., 2006, p. 573).

Francesca Bettio and Alina Verashchagina (2009) review trends in occupational segregation from 1992 to 2007 in the European Union, and also find little progress toward integration during the time period. The European Union uses a different index for occupational segregation in official labor market analysis, the IP index (Karmel and MacLachlan, 1988), although trends over time closely mirror trends in the Index of Dissimilarity for Europe (see Bettio and Verashchagina, 2009, for a more detailed discussion). Overall European trends, however, mask distinct regional patterns. Several European countries saw an increase in segregation from the late 1990s; all of these countries had also seen a strong increase in women's labor force participation during the same period and had comparatively low levels of segregation previously (Bulgaria, Ireland, Italy, Latvia, Romania, and Spain). Other countries, most of them with already high levels of female labor force participation, saw a significant decrease in segregation (Austria, the Czech Republic, the Nordic countries, and the UK); previously segregation was reported to be comparatively high in the Nordic countries, and comparatively low in southern Mediterranean countries.

The Index of Occupational Dissimilarity and the IP index provide a broad picture of what people do and how this has changed over time. It suggests that we are still far from gender integration at work. If anything, the indices are likely to overstate the actual level of integration because sample size and changing occupational definitions over time reduce the number of occupations that can be separately analyzed, and aggregation of smaller occupations into one broader occupational category may overstate the actual level of integration. Take, for example, the occupation 'physicians and surgeons'. In 2010, approximately three of 10 physicians and surgeons in the United States were female; the category of physicians and surgeons, however, is an aggregation of many different medical specialties. In some of these specialties, women were only a small minority; in others, they made up over two-thirds of the workforce (Goldin and Katz, 2011). In their pathbreaking book, *Job Queues, Gender Queues*, Barbara Reskin and Patricia Roos (1990) similarly find that the apparent move toward greater gender balance in many occupations masks re-segregation into subgroups within an occupation. For example, the occupation of real estate agents saw a significant increase of women during the 1970s and 1980s; but women's inroads were limited to residential real estate agents, while (higher-earning) commercial real estate agents remained very much a male-dominated occupation.

Research about occupational segregation within establishments, occupations, or industries (rather than nationwide) provides rich input for the story. Sociologists of organizations William Bielby and James Baron (1986) studied the gender distribution across occupations within different establishments in California in the 1960s and early 1970s. They found that within establishments, occupations were further subdivided, with men and women being given different job titles, status, and earnings but only marginally different job content so that occupational subdivisions were created along gender lines: 'Men and women may share occupational designations in a few types of work; but even then they almost always work in different organizations or hold different job titles within an establishment' (p. 777). For example, the occupational classification of 'packer' is an occupation with a comparatively even gender balance (55 percent female). Yet among the 2,000 workers whose work was classified as packers, the vast majority did not work with workers of the other gender; establishments had either a solely male or a solely female workforce, and in the few instances where both male and female packers worked in the same establishment, they had different job titles segregated along gender lines. In the total sample, only 8 percent of all women workers shared the same job title with a male worker.

A related study by Erica Groshen (1991) analyzed establishment-level wage data in five industries in the 1970s and 1980s and found it rare for men and women to work in the same occupation. Interestingly, where they did, wage differences were insignificant between men and women (leading her to argue that a strategy primarily focused on equal pay for equal work is unlikely to make a significant dent in the gender wage gap);[6] more typically, female workers in an occupation worked in different (lower-paying) establishments from male workers in the same occupation. Researchers have also found that a major share of the wage gap among lawyers is due to women being more likely than men to work in smaller firms and establishments than men (Wood et al., 1993). Bielby and Baron explain this process of establishment segregation by employers' 'mental discrimination function' (1986, p. 781); employers cluster jobs into those requiring stereotypically male (upper body strength, numerical skills, spatial ability) and female (finger dexterity, verbal skills, clerical perception, adaptability) skills and in the process small technical differences in job requirements become amplified into large gender differences in hiring and promotions. Such stereotypical hiring and promotion decisions, they stress, are not simply due to employer prejudice or socialization but may also reflect rational concerns with preventing adverse male reaction when female workers are hired to work side by side with men.

Reskin and Roos (1990) enhance economist Lester Thurow's concept of job queues to understand why and how occupations change their gender balance. Thurow suggests that employers have preferences for certain types of workers (for example, male, white) and workers have preferences for certain jobs (for example, higher earnings, autonomy, prestige); when filling jobs, employers will fill jobs with the most preferred workers they can attract: 'As a result, the best jobs go to the most preferred workers, and less attractive jobs go to workers lower down the queue; bottom-ranked workers may go jobless, and the worst jobs may go unfilled' (1972, p. 73). They further this line of argument to explain under what circumstances women (less preferred workers) may move into previously male occupations: when demand for an occupation expands beyond the available pool of suitably qualified 'preferred' workers or when higher-ranked occupations expand, reducing the pool of preferred (male) workers, employers are forced to move 'down' their worker ranking. Then, the researchers' empirical applications draw on detailed occupational case studies to show that typically, gender integration during the 1970s and 1980s was accompanied by a downgrading of the occupation and its earnings potential (although they stress that women's earnings in these occupations were still higher than in traditionally female sex-typed occupations). For example, women moved into typesetting and printing when technological changes reduced skill requirements and the prestige of the occupation. Women were able to move into residential real estate during a period when the housing market was volatile and the earnings potential from commissions was falling. Women were hired when men were less willing to work in the 'integrating' occupations. The continued supply of men willing to work in blue-collar craft and manufacturing occupations, on the other hand, explains why, with few exceptions, women's share of construction occupations and truck driving has remained marginal.

III LINKING OCCUPATIONAL SEGREGATION AND THE GENDER WAGE GAP: EVIDENCE AND EXPLANATIONS

Research suggests a clear link between gender segregation and the gender wage gap. In fact, just two factors, occupation and industry, together account for over 40 percent of the gender wage gap (Blau and Kahn, 2007). And job segregation within firms explains about 35 to 40 percent of the gender wage gap (Treiman and Hartmann, 1981). Further, a significant portion is also explained by the fact that the highest-paying firms are most likely to hire men, so that even in the same occupation, women – particularly black and Hispanic women – are less likely to work in the best-paid jobs (see also Groshen, 1991).

A number of studies find that the higher the proportion of women in an occupation, the lower the pay (Jacobs and Steinberg, 1990; England, 1992; Sorensen, 1994; England et al., 2000).[7] Hegewisch et al. (2010) estimate that workers in female-dominated highly skilled occupations have median earnings of only 67 percent of workers in male-dominated highly skilled occupations. Figures 13.4 and 13.5 provide an updated analysis by estimating trends separately for men and women. The results confirm that both men and women are paid substantially less when working in a highly skilled female occupation. Women gain somewhat, but not as much, from working in male-dominated medium-or low-skilled occupations. Men, on the other hand, experience more of a wage penalty than women from working in female-dominated low-skilled jobs.[8] What Figures 13.4 and 13.5 also demonstrate, however, is that, whatever the skill level or share of women in an occupation, men have higher earnings than women.

Yet while it is clear that occupational gender segregation contributes to the gender wage gap, there is less agreement on the causal links between occupational segregation

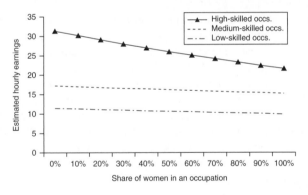

Note: The analysis is restricted to full-time, year-round workers of the civilian labor force, aged 25 to 64.

Source: Illustration of authors' regression analysis. The model is specified as: 'ln(hourly earnings) = constant + b1*Percent female + b2*Medium-skilled + b3*Medium-skilled*Perc. female + b4*High-skilled + b5*High-skilled*Perc. female + error term'. Hourly earnings are for each worker imputed as total wage and salary earnings divided by the number of weeks worked multiplied with the hours usually worked per week. Data are from the 2011 Current Population Survey, March/Annual Social and Economic Supplement (ASEC). Skill levels are defined according to US Department of Labor, Bureau of Labor Statistics (2008) as described in Hegewisch et al. (2010).

Figure 13.4   *Correlation between the occupational gender composition and the estimated hourly earnings of women, 2010*

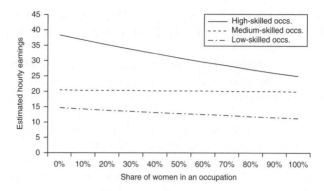

Note: The analysis is restricted to full-time, year-round workers of the civilian labor force, aged 25 to 64.

Source: See Figure 13.4.

Figure 13.5   *Correlation between the occupational gender composition and the estimated*
        hourly earnings of men, 2010

and earnings, or indeed on the reasons for occupational segregation being such a stub-
born feature of paid work. Central to the debate is whether women work in female-
dominated occupations primarily by choice or primarily because of lack of choice, that
is, because of discrimination; and whether lower wages are due to actual differences
in male and female productivity and preferences for certain work characteristics, or
instead are due to a social undervaluation of women's work and discrimination. In sum,
the debate concerns the primacy of supply-side versus demand-side factors in explaining both occupational patterns and wage differences. Supply-side economists focus on
women's lower productivity or human capital as a result of the unequal gender division
of domestic and caring work; demand-side explanations focus on employers' discrimination in hiring and remuneration. Additionally, the contested terrain concerns the efficacy
of labor markets, that is, whether over time, absent of discrimination, wage rates will
reflect men's and women's productivity or whether labor markets differ from markets
for other goods and services when it comes to typically male and female work, reflecting the social undervaluation of work that was traditionally done by women even when
women are no longer the majority of workers in such occupations.

Supply-side Explanations

Initial proponents of supply-side explanations are human capital theorists Jacob Mincer
and Solomon Polachek (1974). They propose that because of the sexual division of
labor in marriage, women are more likely to disrupt their working lives when they have
children and hence are less likely to invest in training and education than men, thus
acquiring less human capital than men. By the same token, their choice of careers and
occupations will be influenced by the extent of penalties for having interrupted working
lives. At the same time, given that married women are likely to spend less time in paid
work over their lifetime than men, employers have fewer incentives to train women on
the job (see also Polachek, 2007). That is, women have incentives to seek lower-skilled

jobs, and they are in lower-waged jobs as a reflection of their lower investment in human capital. Gary Becker (1985) also argues that the division of labor within marriage gives women reduced incentives to invest in their human capital. Yet, additionally, he argues that women's wages will also be lower because the strains and efforts of raising children are likely to reduce their productivity at work, inducing them to look for jobs which require less effort and focus, and hence pay lower wages. Polachek (1981) expands this argument further to suggest that because of their expectations of a more interrupted working life, women will choose occupations that do not require a frequent updating of skills.[9]

This line of reasoning was strongly criticized, particularly by feminist sociologist Paula England. England (1982, 1984) analyzed the penalties for career interruptions in male-and female-dominated jobs, but, unlike suggested by the theory, does not find there to be less penalty in female dominated careers. England et al. (1988) suggest that the theory would predict that, other factors being equal, starting wages in male-dominated jobs should be lower than in female-dominated jobs, given that male occupations are predicted to more strongly depend on on-the-job training to increase workers' productivity over their working lives, and again does not find this to be the case. Tony Tam (1997) finds significant differences in vocational training required for male compared to female occupations in support of a human capital explanation of lower wages in female-dominated occupations. But England et al. (2000) suggest that such differences disappear once educational attainment is included as a variable as well as vocational training.

Margarita Estevez-Abe (2006) has extended this focus on incentives to invest in training and education to explaining cross-national differences in occupational segregation. Occupational segregation is a common feature of all industrialized economies, yet there are significant differences in the degree of segregation. She argues that lack of investment in education *per se* can no longer be an explanatory factor given that in many countries, including the United States, women have equalized if not outpaced men in terms of educational credentials. Thus what matters are not just educational credentials, but how these are delivered, or rather the extent of employers' involvement in their delivery. Where skills are firm or industry specific and strongly involve employers' investment in the delivery of such training, as in apprenticeships in the trades or in manufacturing, 'the micro-logic of employers' risk calculation', in the context of women's more interrupted working lives, will lead employers to discriminate against women 'purely on the basis of economic cost calculations' (ibid., 2006, p. 154). These effects are more pronounced in countries with strong employment protection, encouraging men (with more continuous careers) to invest in firm-specific human capital, but providing incentives to women, who are likely to have more disrupted careers, to invest in general rather than specific skills. Estevez-Abe finds a strong correlation with women's underrepresentation in skill-intensive manufacturing jobs and the delivery and certification of vocational training, but also finds that such a framework is less helpful for understanding women's overrepresentation in the service sector.

A related explanation for women's lower wages is that of 'compensating differentials': women are willing to accept lower wages because they seek jobs which make it easier to reconcile work and family. Jennifer Glass (1990) tests that assumption and finds that although there are significant differences in the fringe benefits that come with male-and female-dominated occupations, the effects are opposite to the predicted direction: on the whole, women and men in female-dominated occupations have less flexibility and fewer work–family friendly working conditions than workers in male-dominated occupations. Likewise, Lonnie Golden (2001) finds that men are more likely to have access to flexible working schedules than women, and Elaine McCrate that working mothers in particular are unable to control their working times. As McCrate (2002, p. 1, original italics) summarizes her findings: 'contrary to the expectations of many economists, workers who do enjoy flexible hours earn *more*, not less, than those with rigid work schedules' (see also McCrate, Chapter 17, this volume). Sociologists Jerry Jacobs and Ronnie Steinberg (1990) test the related argument that men are paid higher wages because they are willing to take less attractive and more physically dangerous jobs. They examine the relationship between earnings and 15 different job characteristics including adverse ones such as working in hot, cold, or noisy conditions, cleaning other people's dirt, engaging in strenuous physical activity, and risking injury, and find that contrary to the predictions of 'compensating differentials' proponents, on the whole such conditions are associated with lower rather than higher earnings, for both men and women.

Most recently, Claudia Goldin and Lawrence Katz (2011) have argued that flexibility in working hours, both in the numbers of hours worked and in scheduling, is a key explanatory factor for changes in the gender composition of jobs and the gender wage gap in different highly skilled professions. They combine Mincer and Polachek's human capital explanation with Sherwin Rosen's (1986) model of compensating differentials. They argue that over time the costs of working fewer hours or of career interruptions have fallen in some professions more than others, and that this at least partly explains a comparative rise of women working in these professions, as well as possibly changes in earnings in these occupations.

Veterinary sciences, for example, which is now majority female has seen a change in the structure of service delivery. Independent practices requiring 24/7 services have become less predominant; independent practitioners are more likely to be able to work with veterinary clinics which can provide overnight/24-hour services where needed, but also provide more opportunities for work sharing. The ownership structure has changed with it, requiring fewer capital investments for individual practitioners. All these factors, they argue, have made the industry more attractive to women with caregiving responsibilities. By contrast, such changes have not occurred in dentistry, where small or single-owner practices remain common, requiring larger capital investments as well as longer working hours and less scope for career interruptions, and where women's share has remained much lower.

In their model, the gender wage gap, and earnings overall, in these occupations may have fallen because these external changes to the industry have made it cheaper to provide flexibility (they stress that in their view this was primarily a change independent of women's move into these professions). In the past, women or men who were able to work long hours would have been able to command higher premiums. The greater ease in providing cover has reduced such premiums and has provided incentives for men to move into other medical professions where such premiums are still greater. Interestingly, Goldin and Katz also find that with the greater availability of reduced hours work, the average length of maternity leaves has fallen dramatically and the wage penalty for taking leaves or working reduced hours has almost disappeared.

Demand-side Explanations

Demand-side explanations are focused on discrimination in limiting the range of occupations in which women may work. Gary Becker (1957), in a new theory of discrimination, suggests that some employers, and customers, may have a 'taste for discrimination', and pay for such preferences by having to pay higher wages to the, say, male workers they prefer because they artificially restrict labor supply to such jobs. Becker adds that in perfectly competitive product markets, employers without such discriminatory tastes will have a competitive advantage by being able to get equally qualified female, or black, workers at cheaper rates; thus, in the long run, the discriminating employers would become uncompetitive and forced out of business because of their higher labor costs. In the context of less than perfect competition, however, discrimination might continue. Scholars have found support for the first part of the argument: that in less than fully competitive product markets employers who employed higher shares of women tended to be more profitable, and empirical tests of the second part show that deregulation of the banking industry resulted in a decrease of the gender wage gap as well as an increase of women's share in managerial and professional positions in banking (Hellerstein et al., 1997; Black and Strahan, 2001). Another study likewise found that as a result of the deregulation of long-distance bus travel in the US, women's earnings rose and men's fell, but only in the industry segment which had previously been regulated; in the previously deregulated segment of the market the gender wage gap stayed unchanged (Schwartz-Miller and Talley, 2000).

Barbara Bergmann (1971, 1974) developed the concept of occupational crowding as an explanation for race and sex differentials in earnings. Bergmann developed an index of occupational crowding which compares the supply of suitably qualified workers (those having finished high school) of different races to their share of different occupations to highlight underrepresentation. She argued that because of discrimination, the highest productivity jobs are restricted to white males; black workers and women workers of all races are restricted to work in a narrower range of lower-productivity occupations, leading to lower earnings both because wages reflect the lower productivity of work, and because there is oversupply of workers in the narrow range of occupations open to them. Once formal discrimination became illegal with the passage of the Equal Pay Act, Title VII of the Civil Rights and Title IX, the strength of enforcement of anti-discrimination provisions becomes a key factor (Bergmann, 1986).

Karen Gibson, William Darity and Samuel Myers (1998) use Bergmann's index of occupational crowding to examine race and gender segregation in two US counties in 1990, and include occupations requiring college-level education. Among jobs requiring higher levels of education, both black men and black women have made some inroads into public sector jobs but are underrepresented in such jobs in the private sector. Access to higher-level skilled craft and manufacturing jobs is restricted for both black men and black women, and they are also proportionately underrepresented in better-paid clerical and administrative jobs. When manufacturing declined, the growth of business and financial services opened up lower-paid clerical jobs to black women; strong gender typing of those jobs, however, prevented black men from moving into such jobs, a contributing factor to high rates of male unemployment.

In sum, both demand- and supply-side explanations are supported by empirical evidence. Research also suggests that changes both in women's labor market behavior and in the discriminatory barriers women face contributed to the decline in occupational segregation in the 1980s. Reuben Gronau (1988) aptly names this the 'chicken versus egg' problem, suggesting that employers partly restrict women's employment opportunities because of women's greater family responsibilities, but some women may underinvest in their careers and prioritize family over work because their career options are more restricted than men's. It is not clear what started this, but both factors play a role and interact, perhaps causing feedback effects that reinforce one another. Pinning causation down empirically, however, has been more of a challenge. As Francine Blau and Lawrence Kahn (2000) suggest: 'While it is likely that both changes in women's behavior and changes in the amount of discrimination they faced played a role in women's occupational shifts, we are not aware of any research unraveling this complex causation' (p. 91).

The Undervaluation of Women's Work

Both demand- and supply-side explanations acknowledge that the gender division of labor and resulting labor market decisions by women, men, and employers may reflect social values, but these values are taken as a given, as external to their model. Sociologists and feminist economists have put greater emphasis on socialization as an explanatory factor both for supply- and demand-side decisions (see Blau et al., 2009). Sociological perspectives have added insights on how social values translate into practices that reduce women's opportunities and structure men and women's preferences and expectations in relation to work (see, for example, Reskin and Bielby, 2005).

More important perhaps is the emphasis on social values as an explanation for the lower earnings of work that is predominantly done by women (Treiman and Hartmann, 1981). This view challenges the emphasis on human capital and skill acquisition in explaining wage differences between male- and female-dominated occupations. Instead, lower earnings in female-dominated jobs are seen to reflect a social undervaluation of work traditionally done by women in the home, such as childcare or other caring work. This approach was formalized into the 'equal pay for work of equal value' or 'comparable worth' perspective to pay inequity, showing that there was systematic gender bias in the way organizations set pay rates. For example, organizations' job evaluation/grading schemes may provide extra pay points for the job of (predominantly male) waste collectors for having to work in dirty conditions and lift heavy objects; but they would not provide similar points to the job of (predominantly female) care or nursing assistants for having to remove soiled bedding or for lifting patients. Such an approach was actively promoted by trade unions and activists concerned with pay equity during the 1980s and resulted in the adjustment of pay rates, particularly in the public sector. In many industrialized countries, although not the United States, equal pay legislation was specifically adjusted to encompass an equal value perspective (see Acker, 1989; Evans and Nelson, 1989; Sorensen, 1994; Figart and Kahn, 1997).

Paula England et al. (2007) have tried to empirically test how far the undervaluation of women's work is dependent on women doing the work, or persists when the gender balance changes in an occupation; and whether over time the causal mechanism runs from low wages to jobs being female dominated (the 'queuing or attractiveness thesis') or the other way around, from female dominated to low wages (the devaluation thesis). The authors find no empirical support for the queuing thesis; that is, a fall in wages of an occupation does not lead to increased feminization, at least during the time period they observe. They find only weak evidence for the devaluation thesis; that is, when more women join an occupation wages marginally fall for all workers, including men. They conclude that the social undervaluation of women's work initially played a significant role in wage levels, but that institutional inertia or the 'stickiness' of labor markets and wage setting leads to relative stability over time in the way occupations are valued.

Social Values

These supply- and demand-side explanations were developed primarily in the 1960s and early 1970s when differences in male and female labor force participation rates, particularly for mothers, were pronounced and discrimination in access to jobs and educational opportunities were still both legal and widespread. Arguably, they reflected an expectation that occupational segregation and earnings differences would continue to get smaller over time. As we discussed earlier, however, improvement in occupational integration and a reduction in the gender-based wage gap slowed markedly in the 1990s. Forward progress has stagnated since the beginning of the last decade, just when women overtook men in educational achievements and when women's labor force participation rates were closer to men's than ever before.

Researchers have moved to assess social values as one explanatory factor. One new study, for example, finds that change toward more gender egalitarian social attitudes toward women's caregiving roles, and women's and men's work, stalled at the same time as labor force participation and occupational integration plateaued (Cotter et al., 2011). England (2010) has put forward an intergenerational theory for explaining differences in the rate of integration of different occupations. She argues that women take their mothers as a reference point; in the context of upward mobility and the fact that women's jobs pay less than men's, daughters of mothers who work in typical female occupations requiring a graduate degree, such as teachers, have to move into nontraditional professions to do better than their mothers. Daughters of mothers who worked in lower-skilled, typically female occupations, such as cashiers or administrative assistants, can improve their social position relative to their mothers by pursuing careers that require higher levels of education but are female dominated, such as teachers, secretaries, and psychologists. In addition, in the professions, women have financial incentives for putting up with discrimination and hostile behavior from employers and male coworkers, but at lower levels of the skills spectrum, women can move up without having to put up with male resistance. This argument has led to a lively debate (see Bergmann, 2011; Prokos, 2011, and also England, 2011, for a reply). Her critics argue that England relies too strongly on women's choices and underplays discrimination, particularly for working-class women, so her view of (lack of) change is too monolithic and pessimistic. The debate between supply- and demand-side explanations continues. As Anastasia Prokos (2011) concludes, 'Perhaps England's biggest challenge to the feminist movement is her evidence that we have not succeeded in challenging the fundamentally devalued status of women's activities' (p. 79).

IV   CONCLUSION AND POLICY IMPLICATIONS

Almost 30 years ago, Barbara Reskin wrote in testimony before the US Congress: 'As more women participate in the labor force and as they stay there longer, the number of women affected by the negative consequences of segregation increases accordingly. Foremost among these consequences is the depressing effect on women's wages' (Reskin et al., 1984, p. 4). In the intervening years, women's working lives have changed dramatically and they have made progress by breaking into many areas of work. Yet occupational segregation has remained amazingly stable, and continues to present a significant challenge to both feminist theorists and activists concerned with achieving gender equality. Working in female-dominated occupations carries a significant wage penalty for both men and women, and has a long-term impact on women's capacity to provide for themselves and their families during their working life and in old age. Lower earnings mean less money to build up retirement savings, pay for housing or education and provide supports for one's children.

As we have seen, it is not easy to isolate a single explanatory factor for occupational segregation, and hence to point to a single policy solution. Many factors contribute to the differences in men's and women's occupations: traditional social attitudes to appropriate male and female work, discrimination in recruitment and promotion, the steering of women to lower-paid areas within occupations, lack of proactive career counseling, and working hours which make some jobs more difficult to combine with caregiving obligations than others. And, of course, just as important as opening up higher-paid stereotypically male occupations to women is the re-evaluation and better remuneration of much of the work that is stereotypically female. Yet perhaps the biggest challenge is not identifying policies to address occupational segregation. As can be seen from the research reviewed in this chapter, the damaging impact of occupational segregation both for families and the economy has been on the agenda of feminist economists and sociologists for many decades, as have been policy proposals to address it, ranging from gender-aware educational methods and proactive enforcement of recruitment and retention to comparable worth policies. What seems to be lacking is the political will and sense of urgency to implement such policies.

NOTES

*   This chapter draws heavily on an earlier paper by Hegewisch et al. (2010).
1.   The definition of traditional/nontraditional occupations is based on the 1998 Carl D. Perkins Vocational and Technical Education Act, which defines an occupation as nontraditional for one sex if at least 75 percent of the workers in the occupation are of the other sex.
2.   The estimate for the last decade does not fully capture the impact of the Great Recession but given the disproportionate job loss in male-dominated industries such as construction and manufacturing, it is likely to result in a negative impact of the 'mix' effect.
3.   Our findings for the 2011 Index of Dissimilarity for women are: White versus Black = 0.2755; White versus Asian = 0.2958; and White versus Hispanic = 0.2986. Women with less than four years of college: White versus black = 0.2825; White versus Asian = 0.3465; White versus Hispanic = 0.3875 (authors' calculations).
4.   See http://cps.ipums.org/cps-action/variables/OCC1990#description_tab for technical details on the variable Occ1990 (accessed July 2012).
5.   The two calculations use different datasets; the data shown in Figures 13.1–5 is based on the Current

Population Survey, and uses continuous annual data from 1972 to 2011; Blau et al. (2012) use data from the decennial census for 1970, 1980, 1990, and 2000, and the American Community Survey for 2005 to 2009; hence the results are not strictly comparable.

6. Groshen chose industries and occupations that at the time of her study had a low incidence of merit or performance-related pay, a factor that might have contributed to relative equality in earnings. Research suggests that merit-and performance-related pay are a source of potential bias and wage inequality within the same job and establishment.

7. Barón and Cobb-Clark's (2010) study of Australia suggests that this relationship between female-dominated occupations and women's earnings is not universal.

8. A discussion of how high, medium, and low are defined and how this relationship was estimated can be found in Hegewisch et al. (2010).

9. Readers interested in additional pioneering articles on supply-side explanations will find several reproduced in Ferber (1998, Vol. I, Part IIb).

REFERENCES

Acker, Joan (1989), *Doing Comparable Worth: Gender, Class, and Pay Equity*, Philadelphia, PA: Temple University Press.

Barón, Juan D. and Deborah A. Cobb-Clark (2010), 'Occupational segregation and the gender wage gap in private – and public-sector employment: a distributional analysis', *Economic Record*, **86**(273), 227–46.

Becker, Gary S. (1957), *The Economics of Discrimination*, Chicago, IL: University of Chicago Press.

Becker, Gary S. (1985), 'Human capital, effort, and the sexual division of labor', *Journal of Labor Economics*, **3**(1), S33–S58.

Bergmann, Barbara R. (1971), 'The effect on white incomes of discrimination in employment', *Journal of Political Economy*, **79**(2), 294–13.

Bergmann, Barbara R. (1974), 'Occupational segregation, wages and profits when employers discriminate by race or sex', *Eastern Economic Journal*, **1**(2), 103–10.

Bergmann, Barbara R. (1986), *The Economic Emergence of Women*, New York: Basic Books.

Bergmann, Barbara R. (2011), 'Sex segregation in the blue-collar occupations: women's choices or unremedied discrimination? Comment on England', *Gender & Society*, **25**(1), 88–93.

Bettio, Francesca and Alina Verashchagina (2009), *Gender Segregation in the Labour Market, Root Causes, Implications and Policy Responses in the EU*, Luxemburg: Publications Office of the European Union.

Bielby, William T. and James N. Baron (1986), 'Men and women at work: sex segregation and statistical discrimination', *American Journal of Sociology*, **91**(4), 759–99.

Black, Sandra E. and Philip E. Strahan (2001), 'The division of spoils: rent sharing and discrimination in a regulated industry', *American Economic Review*, **91**(4), 814–31.

Blau, Francine D. and Wallace E. Hendricks (1979) 'Occupational segregation by sex: trends and prospects', *Journal of Human Resources*, **14**(2), 197–210.

Blau, Francine D. and Lawrence M. Kahn (2000), 'Gender differences in pay', *Journal of Economic Perspectives*, **14**(4), 75–99.

Blau, Francine D. and Lawrence M. Kahn (2007), 'The gender pay gap', *The Economists' Voice* **4**(4), article 5, 1–6.

Blau, Francine D., Peter Brummund and Albert Yung-Hsu Liu (2012), 'Trends in occupational segregation by gender 1970–2009: adjusting for the impact of changes in the occupational coding system', IZA Discussion Paper No. 6490, Bonn.

Blau, Francine D., Marianne A. Ferber and Anne E. Winkler (2009), *The Economics of Women, Men, and Work*, 6th edn, Englewood Cliffs, NJ: Prentice-Hall.

Blau, Francine D., Patricia Simpson and Deborah Anderson (1998), 'Continuing progress? Trends in occupational segregation in the United States over the 1970s and 1980s', *Feminist Economics*, **4**(3), 29–71.

Cotter, David A., Joan M. Hermsen and Reeve Vanneman (2004), *Gender Inequality at Work*, New York, NY: Russell Sage Foundation and Population Reference Bureau.

Cotter, David A., Joan M. Hermsen and Reeve Vanneman (2011), 'The end of the gender revolution? Gender role attitudes from 1977 to 2008', *American Journal of Sociology*, **117**(1), 259–89.

Duncan, Otis D. and Beverly Duncan (1955), 'A methodological analysis of segregation indexes', *American Sociological Review*, **20**(2), 210–17.

England, Paula (1982), 'The failure of human capital theory to explain occupational sex segregation', *Journal of Human Resources*, **17**(3), 358–70.

England, Paula (1984), 'Wage appreciation and depreciation: a test of neoclassical economic explanations of occupational sex segregation', *Social Forces*, **62**(3), 726–49.

England, Paula (1992), *Comparable Worth: Theories and Evidence*, New York: Aldine de Gruyter.
England, Paula (2005), 'Gender inequality in labor markets: the role of motherhood and segregation', *Social Politics*, **12**(2), 264–88.
England, Paula (2010), 'The gender revolution: uneven and stalled', *Gender & Society*, **24**(2), 149–60.
England, Paula (2011), 'Reassessing the uneven gender revolution and its slowdown', *Gender & Society*, **25**(1), 113–23.
England, Paula, Paul Allison and Yuxiao Wu (2007), 'Does bad pay cause occupations to feminize, does feminization reduce pay, and how can we tell with longitudinal data?', *Social Science Research*, **36**(3), 1237–56.
England, Paula, Joan M. Hermsen and David A. Cotter (2000), 'The devaluation of women's work: a comment on Tam', *American Journal of Sociology*, **105**(6), 1741–51.
England, Paula, George Farkas, Barbara Kilbourne and Thomas Dou (1988), 'Explaining occupational sex segregation and wages: findings from a model with fixed effects', *American Sociological Review*, **53**(4), 544–58.
Estevez-Abe, Margarita (2006),'Gendering the varieties of capitalism: a study of occupational segregation by sex in advanced industrial societies', *World Politics*, **59**(1), 142–75.
Evans, Sara M. and Barbara J. Nelson (1989), *Wage Justice: Comparable Worth and the Paradox of Technocratic Reform*, Chicago, IL: University of Chicago Press.
Ferber, Marianne A. (1998), *Women in the Labor Market*, Vols I and II, Cheltenham, UK and Lyme, NH, USA: Edward Elgar, The International Library of Critical Writings in Economics.
Figart, Deborah M. and Peggy Kahn (1997), *Contesting the Market: Pay Equity and the Politics of Economic Restructuring*, Detroit, MI: Wayne State University Press.
Gibson, Karen J., William A. Darity and Samuel L. Myers (1998), 'Revisiting occupational crowding in the United States: a preliminary study', *Feminist Economics*, **4**(3), 73–95.
Glass, Jennifer (1990), 'The impact of occupational segregation on working conditions', *Social Forces*, **68**(3), 779–96.
Golden, Lonnie (2001), 'Flexible work schedules: which workers get them?', *American Behavioral Scientist*, **44**(7), 1157–78.
Goldin, Claudia and Lawrence F. Katz (2011), 'The cost of workplace flexibility for high-powered professionals', *Annals of the American Academy of Political and Social Science*, **638**(1), 45–67.
Gronau, Reuben (1988), 'Sex-related wage differentials and women's interrupted labor careers – the chicken or the egg', *Journal of Labor Economics*, **6**(3), 277–301.
Groshen, Erica L. (1991), 'The structure of the female/male wage differential: is it who you are, what you do, or where you work?', *Journal of Human Resources*, **26**(3), 457–72.
Hegewisch, Ariane, Claudia Williams and Amber Henderson (2011), 'The gender wage gap by occupation', IWPR Fact Sheet, Washington, DC, available at: http://www.iwpr.org/initiatives/pay-equity-and-discrimination/#publications (accessed March 15, 2012).
Hegewisch, Ariane, Hannah Liepmann, Jeffrey Hayes and Heidi Hartmann (2010), 'Separate and not equal? Gender segregation in the labor market and the gender wage gap', Institute for Women's Policy Research Briefing Paper, Washington, DC, available at: http://www.iwpr.org/publications/pubs/separate-and-not-equal-gender-segregation-in-the-labor-market-and-the-gender-wage-gap/ (accessed March 15, 2012).
Hellerstein, Judith K, David Neumark and Kenneth Troske (1997), 'Market forces and sex discrimination', Working Paper 6321, National Bureau of Economic Research, Cambridge, MA.
Jacobs, Jerry and Ronnie J. Steinberg (1990), 'Compensating differentials and the male–female wage gap: evidence from the New York State comparable worth study', *Social Forces*, **69**(2), 439–68.
Karmel, Tom and Maureen MacLachlan (1988), 'Occupational sex segregation: increasing or decreasing?', *Economic Record*, **64**(186), 187–95
King, Miriam, Steven Ruggles, J. Trent Alexander, Sarah Flood, Katie Genadek, Matthew B. Schroeder, Brandon Trampe and Rebecca Vick (2010), 'Integrated Public Microdata Series, Current Population Survey: Version 3.0' (Machine-readable database), University of Minnesota, Minneapolis, MN.
McCrate, Elaine (2002), 'Working mothers in a double bind: working moms, minorities have the most rigid schedules, and are paid less for the sacrifice', Economic Policy Institute Briefing Paper, Washington, DC, available at: http://www.epi.org/page/-/old/briefingpapers/124/124.pdf (accessed July 7, 2012).
Mincer, Jacob and Solomon Polachek (1974), 'Family investments in human capital: earnings of women', *Journal of Political Economy*, **82**(2), S76–S108.
National Center for Education Statistics (2011), 'Table 8. Percentage of persons age 25 and over and 25 to 29, by race/ethnicity, years of school completed, and sex: selected years, 1910 through 2010', *Digest of Education Statistics 2010*, available at: http://nces.ed.gov/pubs2011/2011015.pdf (accessed July 7, 2012).
Polachek, Solomon W. (1981), 'Occupational self-selection: a human capital approach to sex differences in occupational structure', *Review of Economics and Statistics*, **63**(1), 60–69.
Polachek, Solomon W. (2007), 'Earnings over the lifecycle: the Mincer earnings function and its applications', IZA Discussion Paper, DP No. 3181, Bonn.

Price, Vivian (2002), 'Race, affirmative action, and women's employment in US highway construction', *Feminist Economics*, **8**(2), 87–113.

Prokos, Anastasia (2011), 'An unfinished revolution: England symposium introduction', *Gender & Society*, **25**(1), 75–80.

Reskin, Barbara F. and Denise D. Bielby (2005), 'A sociological perspective on gender and career outcomes', *Journal of Economic Perspectives*, **19**(1), 71–86.

Reskin, Barbara F. and Particia A. Roos (1990), *Job Queues, Gender Queues: Explaining Women's Inroads into Male Occupations*, Philadelphia, PA: Temple University Press.

Reskin, Barbara F., Ronnie J. Steinberg, Lois Haignere, Congressional Caucus for Women's Issues, and Women's Research and Education Institute (1984), *Gender at Work: Perspectives in Occupational Segregation and Comparable Worth*, Women's Research and Education Institute of the Congressional Caucus for Women's Issues, Washington, DC.

Rosen, Sherwin (1986), 'The theory of equalizing differences', in Orley Ashenfelter and Richard Layard (eds), *Handbook of Labor Economics*, Vol. 1, Amsterdam: North-Holland, pp. 641–92.

Ruggles, Steven, J. Trent Alexander, Katie Genadek, Ronald Goeken, Matthew B. Schroeder and Matthew Sobek (2010), 'Integrated Public Use Microdata Series: Version 5.0' (Machine – readable database), University of Minnesota, Minneapolis, MN.

Schwartz-Miller, Ann and Wayne K. Talley (2000), 'Motor bus deregulation and the wage gap: a test of the Becker hypothesis', *Eastern Economic Journal*, **26**(2), 145–56.

Sorensen, Elaine (1994), *Comparable Worth: Is It a Worthy Policy?*, Princeton, NJ: Princeton University Press.

Tam, Tony (1997), 'Sex segregation and occupational gender inequality in the United States: devaluation or specialized training?', *American Journal of Sociology*, **102**(6), 1652–92.

Thurow, Lester C. (1972), 'Education and economic equality', *The Public Interest*, **28**(Summer), 66–81.

Tomaskovic-Devey, Donald, Catherine Zimmer, Kevin Stainback, Corre Robinson, Tiffany Taylor and Tricia McTague (2006), 'Documenting desegregation: segregation in American workplaces by race, ethnicity, and sex 1966–2000', *American Sociological Review*, **71**(4), 565–88.

Treiman, Donald J. and Heidi Hartmann (1981), *Women, Work, and Wages: Equal Pay for Jobs of Equal Value*, Washington, DC: National Academy Press.

US Department of Labor, Bureau of Labor Statistics (2008), 'Table 1.11. Education and training measurements by detailed occupation, 2008', available at: http://www.bls.gov/emp/ep_table_111.htm (accessed June 11, 2010).

US Department of Labor, Women's Bureau (1998), *Equal Pay: A Thirty Five Year Perspective*, Washington, DC: US Department of Labor.

Wood, Robert G., Mary E. Corcoran and Paul N. Courant (1993), 'Pay differences among the highly paid: the male–female earnings gap in lawyers' salaries', *Journal of Labor Economics*, **11**(3), 417–71.

14. Race and ethnicity in the workplace
Marlene Kim

I INTRODUCTION

Race and ethnicity significantly affect the employment opportunities and earnings of workers, hence their livelihoods and economic well-being. Racial and ethnic minorities are more likely to have lower incomes and higher poverty rates than white Americans. These disparities are largely due to earnings differentials and labor market segregation; research on racial differences in earnings and employment suggest that discrimination is a factor in these outcomes. The result is reduced economic well-being that affects minority populations in many aspects of their lives, including their ability to pay their bills, meet their rent or mortgage obligations, and receive medical treatment.

Because of the nexus of race and gender, women of color are especially at risk of lower standards of living and economic well-being; women of color work in the lowest-paid jobs and have lower earnings than both minority men and white women. In this chapter, I examine the economic status of racial and ethnic minorities, and especially women of color in the US, regarding their earnings, income, and jobs (Sections II and III). I describe the various explanations for lower economic outcomes, including how employment discrimination can lead to lower pay, income and economic well-being (Sections IV and V). I then explore the ways researchers have examined this issue as well as the results they have found (Section VI). Section VII concludes.

II RACIAL AND ETHNIC DIFFERENCES IN ECONOMIC OUTCOMES

Race and ethnicity affect the livelihoods of workers in many different ways. Perhaps the clearest way to observe this is by examining racial differences in family income. Median family income of blacks and Hispanics is only 59 and 60 percent that of white families, whereas Asian Americans earn more than white families.[1] Because of their lower family incomes, the US Census Bureau reports that poverty rates for blacks and Hispanics are much higher – three times the rate of white families.[2]

Why do these racial differences exist? There are numerous reasons. First, many racial and ethnic minorities have a more difficult time obtaining jobs. In the United States, unemployment among blacks and Hispanics, is typically 200 and 130 percent the level of whites, respectively. For example, the US Bureau of Labor Statistics reported that unemployment in 2011 for black men was 15.2 percent and for Hispanic men, 9.5 percent, compared to 7.1 percent for white men.[3] Unemployment also varies by gender. Hispanic and Asian women have higher rates (at 10.2 and 6.8 percent, respectively), but white and black women have lower rates (6.5 and 11.9 percent, respectively) than men of their same

Table 14.1   Occupations by gender and race

	All	White	Black	Asian	Hispanic (of any race)
Men					
Management, business and financial operations	16.5	17.4	9.7	16.9	7.7
Professional and related	17.9	17.6	13.8	32.3	7.9
Service	14.7	13.8	22.3	14.2	21.9
Sales and related	10.4	10.7	8.2	10.4	7.8
Office and administrative support	6.3	6.0	9.9	6.7	6.8
Farming, fishing, forestry	1.1	1.1	0.5	0.2	2.8
Construction and extraction	9.4	10.3	5.9	2.8	17.1
Installation, maintenance, and repair	6.3	6.6	5.3	3.5	6.2
Production	7.8	7.8	8.1	7.8	9.8
Transportation and material moving	9.5	9.0	16.5	5.3	12.0
Women					
Management, business and financial operations	14.2	14.7	11.2	15.4	8.9
Professional and related	27.0	27.6	22.9	29.0	16.3
Service	21.1	19.9	28.0	21.8	31.2
Sales and related	11.6	11.6	11.5	11.4	12.2
Office and administrative support	19.9	20.2	19.3	14.9	19.6
Farming, fishing, forestry	0.3	0.4	0.1	0.2	1.1
Construction and extraction	0.2	0.3	0.1	0.1	0.4
Installation, maintenance, and repair	0.3	0.3	0.2	0.3	0.3
Production	3.5	3.2	4.1	6.0	7.1
Transportation and material moving	1.9	1.8	2.6	0.9	3.0

Source: US Bureau of Labor Statistics, *Employment and Earnings*, Table 10, at: www.bls.gov/opub/ee/2012/cps/annavg10_2011.pdf.

race. Among women, all women of color – black, Hispanic, and Asian – have higher unemployment rates than white women.

Unemployment has severe effects on workers, leading to depression, reduced self-esteem, and higher stress levels, which affect one's health, including increased mortality (see Ruhm, 1991; Jacobson et al., 1993; Stevens 1997; Chan and Stevens, 2001; von Wachter et al., 2007; Sullivan and von Wachter, 2009). The aftermath of the recent Great Recession led to many of the unemployed relying on charity after they lost their homes (Goodman and Healy, 2009; Healy, 2009; Abel, 2010; Brown, 2010).

Second, even when racial and ethnic minorities obtain jobs, these are often the lowest paying. As Table 14.1 shows, black and Hispanic men are underrepresented in high-paid management and professional occupations and overrepresented in lower-paid transportation and material-moving jobs. Hispanic men are also more likely to work in the lower-paid occupations of farming, fishing, forestry, construction and extraction, and production. Thus black and Hispanic men are relegated to traditional male occupations requiring physical labor but that are also racialized: they hold the traditionally male jobs that are low paid.

Like their male counterparts, black and Hispanic women are similarly relegated to

Table 14.2   Industry distribution by race and gender

	Women	Black	Asian	Hispanic
Total	46.9	10.8	4.9	14.5
Agriculture	24.7	2.3	1.0	23.2
Mining	12.1	4.5	1.6	16.0
Construction	9.2	5.5	1.5	24.4
Manufacturing, durable	24.8	7.2	6.5	12.7
Manufacturing, nondurable	35.2	11.1	5.2	18.9
Wholesale trade	28.5	7.5	4.6	15.6
Retail trade	48.6	10.8	4.5	14.6
Transportation and utilities	22.6	15.6	3.9	15.1
Information	40.2	10.8	5.6	9.5
Finance and insurance	57.6	9.3	6.2	9.7
Real estate and rental and leasing	47.6	9.6	4.0	12.8
Professional and technical services	42.5	5.9	8.3	6.9
Management, administrative and waste services	38.6	12.8	2.9	26.3
Educational services	68.4	10.7	3.7	9.6
Healthcare and social assistance	78.5	16.0	5.5	11.1
Arts, entertainment, recreation	45.3	8.6	5.1	11.1
Accommodation and food services	51.9	12.0	6.8	22.1
Repair and maintenance	10.7	6.4	4.0	20.3
Personal and laundry services	74.6	11.1	12.7	14.4
Membership organizations and associations	54.6	10.1	3.0	7.6
Private household services	89.3	8.4	3.7	35.2
Public administration	44.7	15.3	3.2	10.1

Source: US Bureau of Labor Statistics, *Employment and Earnings*, Table 18, at: www.bls.gov/opub/ee/2012/cps/annavg18_2011.pdf.

lower-paid jobs along racial patterns. They are less likely to work in higher-paying management and professional jobs compared to white workers, and instead hold jobs in lower-paid service occupations and occupations that require physical labor. As Table 14.1 shows, compared to white women, black and Hispanic women are more likely to hold production, transportation and material-moving jobs, which tend to be lower paid. But their jobs are also delineated by gender: women are overrepresented in typically female jobs such as office and administrative support and sales and related occupations (see Hegewisch and Liepmann, Chapter 13, this volume). In addition, women of all races are more likely to hold these jobs compared to their same-race male counterparts. Jobs by industry are similarly defined by race and gender (see Table 14.2).

These patterns in employment result in lower earnings by gender and by race (see Table 14.3). Within every racial group, women earn less than same-race men: 23 percent less for Asian women, 18 percent for white women, and 9 percent for black and Hispanic women. Gender wage disparities are thus prevalent and pervasive among all races. Race also lowers earnings. Among men, the earnings for blacks and Hispanics are less than that of whites: black men earn 77 percent of white male earnings, and Hispanic men, 67 percent. The confluence of lower earnings by race and by gender results in women of

Table 14.3   *Weekly earnings of full-time wage and salary workers by race and gender (2011 annual averages)*

	White		Black		Asian		Hispanic	
	Women	Men	Women	Men	Women	Men	Women	Men
Median weekly earnings ($)	703	856	595	653	751	970	518	571
Wages of women								
Compared to same race men (%)	82		91		77		91	
Compared to white men (%)	82		70	76	88	113	61	67

Source: US Bureau of Labor Statistics, at: www.bls.gov/opub/ee/2012/cps/annavg37_2011.pdf.

color earning the least. As Table 14.3 shows, black women earn 69 percent, Hispanic women 68 percent, and Asian women 88 percent of white male earnings.

These lower earnings lead to high poverty rates. Poverty is much greater for female-headed families (compared to married couple families or other families not headed by a woman), and families headed by black or Hispanic women have the highest rates. Forty-one percent of black female-headed families and 44.5 percent of Hispanic female-headed families are poor. In comparison, 24.8 percent of white female-headed families are poor, and 7.4 percent of all (not just female-headed) families are poor.[4]

III   HETEROGENEITY AMONG RACIAL-ETHNIC MINORITIES: HISPANICS AND ASIANS

Hispanics and Asians have certain characteristics that need further explanation. First, fewer are native born. Thirty-seven percent of Hispanics and two-thirds of Asian Americans are born abroad, compared to 4 percent of whites and 8 percent of blacks. Consequently, a significant proportion – one-third – does not speak English well. In comparison, fewer than 3 percent of black and white workers speak English less than well.[5] The ability to speak English may be affecting their ability to perform in higher-paid jobs that could lead to higher earnings and income levels. Indeed, research indicates that being foreign born, English ability, and the number of years living in the US affect the earnings of both Hispanics and Asians (Reimers, 1985; Trejo, 1997, 2003; O'Neill and O'Neill, 2005; Kim, 2007; Kim and Mar, 2007; Lopez, 2012). Among Hispanics, although the first generation earns less than white workers, later generations earn the same or almost the same, especially among some ancestries (Trejo, 1997, 2003; Antecol and Bedard, 2002).

Finally, because so many are foreign born, the country of origin plays a significant role in their economic outcomes. Among Hispanics, those from Spain fare the best, with the highest education levels, incomes, and earnings, and the lowest levels of unemployment and poverty. Hispanics from South America also fare relatively well using these measures, followed by Hispanics from Cuba. In contrast, those from Mexico, Puerto Rico, the Dominican Republic, and Central America have lower than average earnings and income and higher poverty rates. These and other salient differentials are portrayed in Table 14.4.

Table 14.4 *Characteristics of Hispanics*

	All	Mexican	Puerto Rican	Cuban	Dominican	Central American	South American	Spanish	Other
Demographic Characteristics									
Educational attainment									
Less than high school	38.4	44.3	26.3	23.7	35.4	47.2	16.4	11.6	23.5
High school degree	26.2	25.9	29.2	27.7	25.5	23.7	26.1	22.9	29.7
Some college	22.4	20.6	28.5	24.0	23.8	18.0	27.3	34.6	30.4
College degree	8.9	6.6	10.8	15.3	10.8	7.9	19.5	18.0	10.8
Graduate degree	4.1	2.6	5.2	9.2	4.4	3.1	10.7	13.0	5.6
Percent foreign born	37.5	36.2	1.1	58.7	57.0	64.9	66.5	13.6	13.3
Speaks English less than very well	36.1	36.9	18.8	41.0	45.4	53.6	41.1	7.6	13.8
Labor Force Characteristics									
Unemployment rate	10.9	10.7	13.8	10.7	12.9	10.4	8.8	9.7	10.8
Occupation									
Management	18.8	15.9	26.9	31.5	18.2	12.7	28.6	40.3	26.1
Service	25.8	26.0	22.6	18.1	31.3	31.8	24.7	16.0	23.0
Sales and office	22.3	21.2	29.1	27.2	25.5	17.6	23.8	27.2	27.4
Natural resources, construction, maint.	16.2	18.8	7.7	10.2	7.2	19.4	10.0	8.0	11.0
Production, transp., material moving	16.9	18.2	13.7	13.0	17.6	18.4	12.9	7.8	12.4
Industry									
Ag., forestry, fishing, hunting, mining	3.3	4.7	0.4	0.6	0.2	0.1	0.5	1.5	1.7
Construction	11.1	12.4	4.5	7.5	4.3	15.5	8.2	6.2	8.1
Manufacturing	10.9	11.9	9.0	8.1	9.3	10.6	9.0	7.2	7.8
Wholesale trade	3.2	3.2	2.8	3.8	3.1	3.1	3.3	2.9	2.7
Retail trade	11.3	11.1	13.0	12.0	14.2	10.0	11.3	11.4	12.8
Transp., warehousing, utilities	4.8	4.3	6.0	6.8	6.8	4.4	5.4	4.6	5.1

Information	1.6	1.4	2.3	2.4	1.8	1.2	2.3	2.9	2.2
Finance/insur., real estate, rental/leasing	5.0	4.1	7.6	8.0	6.3	4.5	6.9	7.9	6.2
Prof., scientific, mgt., admin. and waste mgt	10.5	9.9	9.8	11.7	9.7	12.7	12.1	11.5	9.9
Educ. services, health care, social assist.	16.2	14.5	24.2	20.9	23.0	12.0	18.4	23.2	21.1
Arts, entertain., recreat., accom., food serv.	13.0	13.7	10.0	8.6	10.9	14.3	12.5	9.7	11.6
Other services (excl. public admin.)	5.8	5.4	4.4	5.5	7.6	8.4	7.6	4.3	5.0
Public administration	3.4	3.3	6.0	3.9	2.7	1.6	2.6	6.8	5.8
Income									
Median household income	40,914	40,040	37,654	42,154	34,560	42,331	51,448	54,406	41,517
Mean earnings	54,362	51,046	56,854	67,725	49,181	53,704	68,133	74,275	57,985
Median family income	42,151	40,451	42,240	50,308	35,821	41,491	54,674	65,216	48,135
Per capita income	15,356	13,688	17,265	23,025	15,002	15,397	22,186	28,034	17,288
Median income female householder	24,775	23,880	22,162	31,033	22,488	26,798	33,124	33,673	26,216
Poverty rates									
Poverty rate, all	20.9	22.7	22.8	12.5	25.5	19.2	10.9	8.8	16.3
Poverty rate, families with children	26.5	28.2	29.4	15.4	31.0	24.0	14.2	13.2	22.3
Female householder	38.8	41.3	42.7	25.2	40.7	34.5	23.1	21.6	33.8
Female householder with children	46.2	48.5	49.0	32.7	47.5	41.9	30.1	28.9	41.0

Note: Populations are those over age 16 unless otherwise specified. Unemployment rates are for the civilian population. Hispanics can be of any race.

Source: US Census Bureau, American Community Survey, 2008–10, 3-year estimates.

Because of their unusual economic outcomes, it is important to examine Asian Americans in more detail. Asians have higher earnings than white Americans; consequently they have higher family incomes (see Table 14.3). Due to their economic success, many consider Asians to be model minorities – successful despite their race – and thus all minorities can follow their lead and obtain high education levels and affluence. The implication of this argument is that race does not matter and can be overcome by hard work and high skill levels. But these overall patterns among Asians are deceiving. First, family income is greater in Asian families because these households have more family members and more workers per family. When examining income per capita, Asians have lower incomes than do whites, earning $30,000 per capita compared to $32,000 (Kim and Mar, 2007).[6]

Second, not all measures indicate economic success. Asians have higher poverty rates (10 percent) than whites (7 percent). Although unemployment rates are currently lower than that of whites, Asians have had higher unemployment rates in previous years (ibid.), and in 2010 they had the highest levels of long-term unemployment – being jobless for over half a year – than any other race (Kim, 2012).

Third, similar to Hispanics, Asians are not a uniform group. While those from Japan and India have higher education levels and higher earnings than white workers, those from other ancestral groups fare poorly. Asians from Cambodia, Laos, and Vietnam, and the Hmong and Native Hawaiians and Pacific Islanders have especially high unemployment and poverty rates and very low education levels (Mar, 2000, 2005; Kim and Mar, 2007). For example, one-fourth of Hmong families are poor, and one-third of Hmong children are poor (Kim, 2011). Unemployment rates for the Hmong are double those of all Asians, and the earnings of Hmong and Native Hawaiians and Pacific Islanders are one-third and three-fourths of Asian earnings, respectively (ibid.).

This heterogeneity among Asians, with those from some ancestries faring relatively well but others doing quite poorly, results in a bifurcated educational distribution when Asian Americans of all ancestries are examined as one group. Compared to whites, Asian Americans as a group are more likely to have college and graduate degrees, but they are also more likely to have failed to achieve a high school education, with 50 percent more Asians not obtaining a high school education compared to whites, as shown in Table 14.5. The bifurcation in education results in a similar pattern for jobs. Although Asians are more likely to work in management occupations than are white workers, they are also more likely to work in manufacturing (from Tables 14.1 and 14.2). Within Asian ancestries, Cambodians, Lao, Vietnamese, Hmong, Native Hawaiians and Pacific Islanders are more likely to work in these lower-paying manufacturing jobs (ibid.; see also Kim and Mar, 2007).

Fourth, many researchers have found evidence of a glass ceiling for Asian Americans. Although this population is perceived as competent technical workers, they are not viewed as leaders, and hence are not promoted to the same extent as similar white workers into higher management positions such as chief executive officers (CEOs) or other executive positions (Woo, 2000; Kim and Mar, 2007; Kim, 2009b). Finally, Asian Americans are more likely to suffer from discrimination at the top. Among those with higher levels of education, Asian Americans earn less than white workers (Duleep and Sanders, 1992; Sakamoto and Furuichi, 2002).

Table 14.5   The Asian American population

	White alone	Asian alone
Income		
Median family income	69,730	78,833
Per capita income	31,767	29,841
Educational attainment of population 25 years and older		
Less than high school	9.6	14.5
High school or GED	29.3	15.8
Some college	30.0	19.6
College degree	19.5	29.8
Graduate degree	11.6	20.4

Note: Data are for those who are 'White alone' and 'Asian alone'.

Source: US Census Bureau, American Community Survey, 2008–10, 3-year estimates.

IV   ACCOUNTING FOR RACIAL DIFFERENCES IN EMPLOYMENT AND EARNINGS

There is a lively debate among scholars regarding the cause of racial and ethnic differences in earnings, jobs, and income. Neoclassical economists claim that human capital, or productivity-enhancing characteristics such as education levels, work experience and training, is lower in racial and ethnic minorities, hence their lower earnings and income (see, for example, Abowd and Killingsworth, 1985; Heckman, 1998; O'Neill and O'Neill, 2005). Indeed, compared to whites, blacks and Hispanics are more likely to have lower levels of education and are less likely to have graduated from college (see also Trejo, 1997). Less than 20 percent of blacks and only 13 percent of Hispanics have college degrees, compared to over 30 percent of whites. Thirty-eight percent of Hispanics over the age of 24 do not hold high school degrees, compared to less than 10 percent of whites.[7]

Researchers typically use multiple regression analysis to examine the extent to which differences in human capital by race or gender can account for differences in employment. This technique predicts earnings while controlling for education, work experience, and other factors that account for differences in earnings (such as geographical dispersion or working in large urban areas that usually pay higher wages). Researchers then examine if one's race or gender has an effect on earnings once these have been accounted for. If so, race or gender could be exerting an effect on earnings apart from productivity-enhancing characteristics.

This research shows that lower education levels among black and Hispanic workers do partially account for the lower levels of earnings and income levels (Trejo, 1997, 2003; Joassart-Marcelli, 2009). Empirical research confirms that education levels, as well as other productivity characteristics such as work experience and age, account for some or (in some studies) all of the racial differences in earnings (O'Neill, 1990; Trejo, 1997, 2003; Antecol and Bedard, 2002; O'Neill and O'Neill, 2005; Abowd and Killingsworth, 1985).

Critics of neoclassical theory, however, argue that even when productivity-enhancing characteristics such as education level and work experience are taken into account, racial and ethnic minorities earn less than comparable white workers (Kim, 2007; Leicht, 2008; Smith, 2012). Studies by David Neumark (1999) and by Emilio Castilla (2011) find that even after accounting for job performance ratings, black and Hispanic workers are paid less than comparable white workers. In addition, job preferences cannot account for black workers' concentration in low-level jobs and their underrepresentation in high-paid ones (Gill, 2001). Finally, Catherine Weinberger (1998) finds that measures of ability, interests, and motivation, accounted for by one's grade point average, college attended, and college major, show that Asian and black men earn less than comparable white men. Thus, these critics argue that discrimination and racial bias are responsible for some of these earnings and occupational differences.

Research also shows the presence of racial wage disparities for women of color. Black women earn less than white women (Anderson and Shapiro, 1996; Farkas et al., 1997; Kim, 2009a; Mason, 2011), even when factors such as job performance (Neumark, 1999) and quantitative measures of aptitude (Blackburn, 2004) are taken into consideration. Studies of Asian women and Latinas find different results, depending on ancestral origin, nativity, and the econometric specification used (Farkas et al., 1997; Antecol and Bedard, 2002; Kim and Mar, 2007).[8] For example, women from Spain and Cuba are less likely to suffer from racial wage penalties, although those from South and Central America do (Reimers, 1985; Carlson and Swartz, 1988). Research finds mixed results for Mexican women (Reimers, 1985; Antecol and Bedard, 1992). Among Asians, research finds that women from India do not suffer from racial wage penalties, though Native Hawaiians and Pacific Islanders do. Studies on Japanese, Chinese, Filipino, Vietnamese, and Korean women have mixed results (Carlson and Swartz, 1988; Duleep and Sanders, 1992; Mar, 2002; Kim and Mar, 2007), with some studies showing evidence of discrimination, while others do not (see ibid., for a review of this literature).

An important issue for this type of analysis is what factors should be accounted for in the statistical models as legitimate attributes in determining earnings. One of the most controversial factors that can explain racial earnings differences are measurements of aptitude, intelligence, or other quantitative measures of ability. Economists (O'Neill, 1990; Neal and Johnson, 1996) have included the scores from the Armed Forces Qualifications Test (AFQT) when they examine the earnings of black workers. They argue that these scores measure aptitude, school quality, or ability. With these measures included, the racial earnings penalty for black workers and for Hispanic men disappears. The authors argue that because differences in earnings by race disappear once this measure is included, unmeasured ability, intelligence or school quality explains racial differences in earnings.

Measures of intelligence or ability are highly controversial, however, and many scholars have criticized the previous studies. Racial differences in earnings reappear once other factors are controlled for, such as age, years of education, or measures of psychological capital (Darity and Mason, 1998; Goldsmith et al., 1998; Blackburn, 2004). In addition, AFQT scores affect different workers in different ways, leading to skepticism among some about what they in fact measure. For example, higher math scores in the AFQT lead to higher earnings for white women but not for black women (Darity and Mason, 1998). Other critics believe that unmeasured characteristics, such as school quality, job performance, family, and neighborhood characteristics, may be causing differences in earnings that are attributable to racial differences (Heckman, 1998). Scholars try to account for these factors to see if racial or gender differences persist after these additional controls (see Neumark, 1999; Blackburn, 2004; Corcoran and Kunz, 2007).[9]

The outcome of the debate over what characteristics should and should not be accounted for in wage equations is critical because it has important policy implications. If education, skill levels, intelligence, and ability explain racial differences in earnings, discrimination is not necessarily a factor in determining job outcomes, income and one's economic well-being. Any government policy would be limited to ensuring access to education and training programs, and once access is equal, any racial differences that result are the outcomes of differences in skill levels. In contrast, if racial differences in earnings are caused in part by skill differentials but also from discrimination, government anti-discrimination efforts are needed, and earnings differences would reflect racial bias as well as differences in skills.

Critics of neoclassical theory point to audit and correspondence studies that examine whether or not racial minorities (or women) are less likely to be hired. Correspondence studies involve sending out equivalent résumés and cover letters of job applicants but with names that reveal one's race or ethnicity. These studies find that job applicants with non-Anglo-American names are less likely to be interviewed or hired, even with identical qualifications (Riach and Rich, 1991; Bertrand and Mullainathan, 2004). In addition, blacks and Hispanics with accents are less likely to receive job offers than similar white job applicants, and when offered jobs, the starting salaries for black workers are lower than those of whites (see Bergmann, 1996 for a survey of audit studies).

Studies on housing find that racial minorities are less likely to obtain housing compared to white workers (ibid.; Massey and Lundy, 2001; Turner et al., 2002; Fischer and Massey, 2004). They are also less likely to obtain mortgages and housing insurance (Munnell et al., 1996; Squires and Chadwick, 2006). Because of this, racial minorities are likely to remain outside of the better school districts, preventing them from obtaining quality educations.

V   THE DOUBLE BIND: GENDER AND RACE

The debate around gender differences in employment outcomes is similar to that with race. In addition to differences in productivity characteristics or human capital, neoclassical economists refer to different choices women make regarding the jobs they want and the hours they want to work (see Hegewisch and Liepmann, Chapter 13, this volume). For example, some argue that compared to men, women commit less time and energy to their careers, working less continuously because they take time off to care for their families (O'Neill, 1994; Blau and Kahn, 2007). Compared to men with young children, women with young children are more likely to work part-time (Bardasi and Gornick, 2008; US Department of Commerce, 2011), and to meet childcare needs, some women choose occupations that allow them flexibility in the hours they work, such as nursing and teaching.

Critics of these neoclassical explanations try to control for factors that can explain career aspirations and productivity differences, such as the number of hours worked, working part-time, having young children at home, and being married. These studies generally find that even with these controls, women earn less than men (see Blau and Kahn, 2007, for an overview of these; see also Joy, 2003; Graham and Smith, 2005; Leicht, 2008). In addition, even after controlling for job aspirations, occupational preferences and how they value money versus intrinsic rewards such as helping others, women earn less than men (Blau and Ferber, 1991; Solberg, 2004; Fortin, 2007).

Studies on particular workplaces, such as academia, find that women earn less than men, even when all areas of productivity, such as books, research articles, and grant money received are accounted for (Binder et al., 2010). Finally, to dispute the argument that women often major in less remunerative areas, such as the liberal arts rather than engineering or science, Catherine Weinberger and Lois Joy (2007) control for college major, the university attended, and college grade point average (GPA). They find that even when attending the same college and having the same college major and GPA, women earn less than men.

Because racial and ethnic minorities earn less than white workers, and because women earn less than men (even similarly qualified men), many scholars believe that women of color suffer from two sources of bias – that from their gender and their race. The majority of studies on gender and race in employment examine *either* the effects of race within gender *or* the effect of gender within race (Brewer et al., 2002). In other words, they examine how race affects women, such as how black and white women compare regarding occupations or earnings (Carlson and Swartz, 1988; Cunningham and Zalokar, 1992; Anderson and Shapiro, 1996; Farkas et al., 1997; Neumark, 1999; O'Neill and O'Neill, 2005; Kim, 2009a; Mason, 2011), or they examine the effect of gender within race – such as the gender wage gap for black and white workers (Brown et al., 1980; Green and Ferber, 2005; O'Neill and O'Neill, 2005). A few, however, compare the earnings of women of color to white men (Corcoran and Duncan, 1979; Carlson and Swartz, 1988; McGuire and Reskin, 1993), in order to discern the effects of both gender and race. Although these studies find that women of color are underpaid or under-rewarded compared to white men, whether this is due to their race or gender cannot be determined.

While few statistical studies do examine both gender and race-ethnicity, such studies are important because it is unclear how race and gender interact for women of color. Feminist scholars believe that gender and race interact in complex ways; as Deborah King (1995) states, the importance of gender or race varies depending on the circumstances and the reference group examined. In some areas, race will be the more predictive factor; in others, gender or class may be more important. The importance of each depends on the sociohistorical context and what is being examined, and this can change depending on the time period and geographical area as well as the jobs studied (ibid.; Browne and Misra, 2003). In other circumstances, the effect of gender and race can lead to unique outcomes (Bell et al., 2001; Browne and Kennelly, 1999).

Multicultural and multiracial feminist scholars believe that the way gender and race interplay depend on one's social location, of which gender and race play an important but not exclusive role. Women of color will experience race differently depending on their class, so that professional, managerial, and working-class women will have different experiences (Zinn and Dill, 1996; Brewer et al., 2002). In addition, one's sexuality will affect one's experiences and job outcomes (see Weichselbaumer, Chapter 15, this volume). A matrix of domination thus defines the relative power all men and women experience regarding their gender, race, class, sexuality, religion, and geographical area;

one's degree of marginalization, shaped by this matrix, will define the multiple ways one experiences gender, race, job, and life outcomes (Zinn and Dill, 1996; Brewer et al., 2002; Ruwanpura, 2008). One can thus be a member of a dominant group in some sense but a member of a minority group when other factors are considered, such as Latino immigrant men. Furthermore, a poor Buddhist Thai heterosexual woman living in Bangkok will have profoundly different employment experiences from a Jewish white lesbian middle-class woman in New York City (Zinn and Dill, 1996; Ruwanpura, 2008), and race and gender will affect each in different ways.

VI MODELING GENDER AND RACE

Various methods can be employed to examine the effects of race and gender. Among statistical studies, a common methodology is to use dummy variables for gender and race in a multiple regression. This has been performed in several ways. First, race and gender categories can be separate and in one equation (Reskin and Ross, 1992; Baldi and McBrier, 1997; Castilla, 2012). With this approach, the effect of gender can be estimated from the coefficients on the female variable, and the effects of race from the coefficients on the race variables. Interaction terms of key independent variables with race (or gender) dummy variables can help determine if key variables have lower payoff by race (or gender), but the effect on women of color, such as black women, still remains unclear.

Some researchers presume that the effect of race and gender is the sum of the race and gender variables. For example, one could examine the effect of being a black woman by adding the coefficient on the black dummy variable to the coefficient on the female dummy variable, and follow a similar approach to examine the effect on Asian women or Latina women. But many scholars do not believe that one can so easily add race and gender to understand effects on women of color (Brewer et al., 2002; Ruwanpura, 2008). Instead, gender and race may interact such that the combination of the effects of gender and race is either more or less than the sum of their separate parts (Bell et al., 1993; McGuire and Reskin, 1993; Kilbourne et al., 1994; King, 1995; Reskin and Charles, 1999; Ruwanpura, 2008). If more than the sum of their separate parts, there would be a negative interaction; for example, gender and race would be so odious that the combination of the two imparts a separate negative effect (Almquist, 1975). If the combination of gender and race is less than the sum of their parts, there is a positive interaction, and they may work in the same way, such as if both are prized for counting toward an employer's affirmative action goal (Bell et al., 1993).

Scholars have used various approaches to try to model interaction effects of race and gender. For example, in a study examining pay differences among academics in one university, Melissa Binder et al. (2010) use dummy variables for women, Hispanics, and a separate variable for Hispanic women, thus adding a variable interacting race and gender. A similar methodology entails including dummy variables in a single multiple regression equation for different combinations of race and gender; researchers have separate dummy variables for white women, black women, black men, Hispanic women, and Hispanic men, for example (see Blackburn, 2004; Weinberger and Joy, 2007; Weinberger, 1998; Smith, 2012). This specification can include each gender and race category, and unlike the first method, enables one to examine the specific effects on black,

Hispanic, and Asian women in comparison to white men, usually the omitted demographic group. Another approach is to have two separate multiple regression equations by gender, with dummy variables for race in each separate equation (see McGuire and Reskin, 1993; Neumark, 1999). One can then examine the coefficients on the independent variables to see how they vary by gender, and interpret the coefficient on the race variable to examine how race affects the dependent variable (the dependent variable can be earnings or another job outcome such as employment in a high-paid job). However, none of these approaches allows the coefficients on the independent variables to vary by gender or race. In the real world, of course, the effect of an additional year of education may be lower for Latina women born in Mexico than for white men born in the US.

The one methodology that does allow variables to vary by both gender and race is Blinder–Oaxaca decompositions. This method first runs separate human capital wage regressions for each gender/race group. For instance, researchers can run one multiple regression equation for black women, one for white women, one for white men, and one for black men, thus allowing the coefficients on the independent variables to vary by these four gender/race groups. The second step involves using the coefficients and the means of the variables obtained from these four regressions to analyze the extent to which one demographic group (such as black women) is underpaid because of human capital characteristics versus the returns (having different, often lower, coefficients) for these characteristics. The existence of the latter can be interpreted as evidence of discrimination or unmeasured variables.

Using the results of the separate wage regressions, this methodology allows one to examine the outcome for various race/gender groups if they had the same returns to their human capital characteristics as another group (such as white men).[10] By examining differences in the coefficients, this methodology also enables researchers to investigate whether key variables (for example, work experience or cognitive skills) work in the same way or if they differ by gender or race (see Reimers, 1985). One such study finds that black women are penalized more than white women for working in female jobs, that they are concentrated in jobs that require less cognitive skill, and that they receive lower relative salaries for these skills, resulting in lower earnings for black women (Kilbourne et al., 1994).

Only two empirical studies try to examine how race and gender interplay at various points of time, locations and among various workers. The first is by Gail McGuire and Barbara Reskin (1993), who calculate the earnings of white women, black women, and black men had they faced the same earnings structure and payoff to their characteristics as white men. They find that compared to black men and white women, black women lost more authority in their jobs and hence earnings because employers failed to reward their credentials in the same way they did white men's: 'receiving white men's rates of payoff for the independent variables would have increased Black women's earnings by over $7000 compared to $2050 for Black men and $6865 for white women' (p. 499). In this study, however, all wage penalties are calculated in comparison to white men. The authors thus estimate the race penalty by examining the wage differences of black men and white men, and the gender penalty by examining the wage difference between white men and white women. The race penalty for black women can differ from that of black men, however; likewise, the gender penalty for black women is not necessarily the same as that for white women.

An alternative approach I took (Kim, 2009a) uses Blinder–Oaxaca decompositions to estimate race, gender, and intersection penalties for black women by using black women as the reference point, rather than white men. I do not assume that the gender penalty for black women is the same as for white women, nor do I assume that the race penalty for black women is the same as for black men. Instead, I estimate the race penalty in earnings as the earnings difference between what black women earn and what they would earn had they faced the same wage structure as white women. (Note that unlike previous approaches, gender is held constant in this comparison.) Similarly, the gender penalty is the difference between what black women earn and their earnings had they faced the same wage structure as black men; in this decomposition, race is held constant. The total penalty of both race and gender is measured as the earnings difference between what black women earn and their earnings had they the wage structure of white men. The intersection of race and gender is then calculated as the difference between the total (race and gender) penalty and the sum of the separate race and gender penalties.

What I found was that in the United States, black women were underpaid 9 percent because of their race, 15 percent because of their gender, and 3 percent because of the intersection of both gender and race. In other words, black women suffered from three types of penalty: their gender, their race, and the combination of both, which imparted a separate penalty. Underlying this result are the jobs black women hold: black women were placed in jobs in the US that were the worst of women's occupational structure (in the service sector as were women, but in the lowest-paid service jobs), and they were omitted from the higher-paying industries of men. Thus, the interplay of gender and race was such that they occupied the lowest rungs of the job structure – not fit to be in white women's jobs and not fit for black men's either – which led to their lower pay.[11]

VII CONCLUDING THOUGHTS: THE CONSEQUENCES OF RACE AND ETHNICITY

Women of color face disparities in the labor market because of their gender and race. As we saw earlier, women of color earn less than their male (same race/ethnicity) counterparts, and they earn less than white women. Minority women have very high poverty rates for this reason. Racial and ethnic minorities are also more likely to have difficulty paying their rent or mortgage, and blacks and Hispanics report having inadequate incomes to pay their bills and are more likely to delay medical treatment because of insufficient income (*Washington Post* et al., 2001; Gallup, 2004).

Much debated is the source of these outcomes. Neoclassical economists argue that productivity differences and different preferences result in these economic disparities. Critics of this view, however, argue that women of color are underpaid and underadvanced in the labor market despite having the same productivity characteristics and career aspirations of white men. A limitation of most of this research is its exclusive focus either on gender or race. Given the implications for economic well-being, it is clear that more attention needs to be paid to the ways race and gender interact for minority women.

NOTES

1   Author's calculations from the American Community Survey, 2008–10, three-year estimates.
2.   Researchers may find US poverty information at http://www.census.gov/hhes/www/poverty/.
3.   The 2011 annual averages are from Table 24, 'Unemployed persons by marital status, race, Hispanic or Latino ethnicity, age, and sex', available at: www.bls.gov/opub/ee/2012/cps/annavg24_2011.pdf.
4.   See the US Census Bureau reports on poverty, found at the website referenced in note 2.
5.   Author's tabulations from the American Community Survey, 2008–10, 3-year estimates.
6.   Hispanics earn $15,000 and blacks, $18,000 per capita (author's tabulations from the American Community Survey, 2008–10).
7.   Author's calculations from the American Community Survey, 2008–10.
8.   Antecol and Bedard (2002) find evidence of earnings discrimination by race for Mexican women when they account for self-selection, but no evidence without these controls.
9.   Corcoran and Kunz (2007) find that racial wage penalties for black men disappear once family and neighborhood characteristics are accounted for. However, Blackburn (2004) finds racial penalties for blacks and Hispanics even after including these controls.
10.   This analysis helps to measure the extent to which race or gender alters economic outcomes because of receiving different (often lower) payoff amounts to the same characteristics compared to higher-paid workers of a different gender or race (see McGuire and Reskin, 1993; Kim, 2009a).
11.   Statistical analyses on occupations and the glass ceiling also confirm that women and racial minorities have a more difficult time attaining job categories with authority, including management jobs (Kanter, 1993; Ragins et al., 1998; Woo, 2000; see also Hirsh et al., Chapter 12, this volume).

REFERENCES

Abel, David (2010), 'Study finds use of food pantries soaring in Mass', *Boston Globe*, February 3, B4.
Abowd, John M. and Mark R. Killingsworth (1985), 'Employment, wages, and earnings of Hispanics in the federal and nonfederal sectors: methodological issues and their empirical consequences', in George J. Borjas and Marta Tienda (eds), *Hispanics in the US Economy*, Orlando, FL: Academic Press, pp. 77–124.
Almquist, Elizabeth M. (1975), 'Untangling the effects of race and sex: the disadvantaged status of black women', *Social Science Quarterly*, 56(2), 130–42.
Anderson, Deborah and David Shapiro (1996), 'Racial differences in access to high-paying jobs and the wage gap between black and white women', *Industrial and Labor Relations Review*, 49(2), 273–86.
Antecol, Heather and Kelly Bedard (2002), 'The relative earnings of young Mexican, black and white women', *Industrial Labor Relations Review*, 56(1), 122–35.
Baldi, Stephane and Debra Branch McBrier (1997), 'Do the determinants of promotion differ for blacks and whites?', *Work and Occupations*, 24(4), 478– 97.
Bardasi, Elena and Janet C. Gornick (2008), 'Working for less? Women's part-time wage penalties across countries', *Feminist Economics*, 14(1), 37–72.
Bell, Ella, L.J. Edmonson and Stella Nkomo (2001), *Our Separate Ways: Black and White Women and the Struggle for Professional Identity*, Cambridge, MA: Harvard Business School Press.
Bell, Ella, L.J. Edmonson, Toni C. Denton and Stella Nkomo (1993), 'Women of color in management: toward an inclusive analysis', in Ellen A. Fagenson (ed.), *Women in Management: Trends, Issues, and Challenges in Managerial Diversity*, Newbury Park, CA: Sage, pp. 105–30.
Bergmann, Barbara R. (1996), *In Defense of Affirmative Action*, New York: Basic Books.
Bertrand, Marianne and Sendhil Mullainathan (2004), 'Are Emily and Greg more employable than Lakisha and Jamal? A field experiment on labor market discrimination', *American Economic Review*, 94(4), 991–1013.
Binder, Melissa, Kate Krause, Janie Chermak, Jennifer Thacher and Julie Gilroy (2010), 'Same work, different pay? Evidence from a US public university', *Feminist Economics*, 16(4), 105–35.
Blackburn, McKinley L. (2004), 'The role of test scores in explaining race and gender differences in wages', *Economics of Education Review*, 23(6), 555–76.
Blau, Francine D. and Marianne A. Ferber (1991), 'Career plans and expectations of young women and men: the earnings gap and labor force participation', *Journal of Human Resources*, 26(4), 581–607.
Blau, Francine D. and Lawrence M. Kahn (2007), 'The gender pay gap: have women gone as far as they can?', *Academy of Management Perspectives*, 21(1), 7–23.
Brewer, Rose M., Cecilia A. Conrad and Mary C. King (2002), 'The complexities and potential of theorizing gender, caste, race and class', *Feminist Economics*, 8(2), 3–18.

Brown, Joel (2010), 'Job cuts pushing more out of homes', *Boston Globe*, July 15, p. 1.

Brown, Randall S., Marilyn Moon and Barbara S. Zoloth (1980), 'Incorporating occupational attainment in studies of male–female earnings differentials', *Journal of Human Resources*, **15**(1), 3–28.

Browne, Irene and Ivy Kennelly (1999), 'Stereotypes and realities: images of black women in the labor market', in Irene Browne (ed.), *Latinas and African American Women at Work: Race, Gender, and Economic Inequality*, New York: Russell Sage, pp. 302–26.

Browne, Irene and Joya Misra (2003), 'The intersection of gender and race in the labor market', *Annual Review of Sociology*, **29**, 487–513.

Carlson, Leonard A. and Caroline Swartz (1988), 'The earnings of women and ethnic minorities, 1959–1979', *Industrial and Labor Relations Review*, **41**(4), 530–46.

Castilla, Emilio J. (2012), 'Gender, race, and the new (merit-based) employment relationship', *Industrial Relations*, **51**(S1), 528–62.

Chan, Swein and Ann Huff Stevens (2001), 'Job loss and employment patterns of older workers', *Journal of Labor Economics*, **19**(2), 484–521.

Corcoran, Mary and Greg Duncan (1979), 'Work history, labor force attachment, and earnings differences between the races and sexes', *Journal of Human Resources*, **14**(1), 3–20.

Corcoran, Mary and James Kunz (2007), 'Do black and white children start out on an equal footing in the race for economic success?', in Marlene Kim (ed.), *Race and Economic Opportunity in the Twenty-First Century*, London: Routledge, pp. 186–204.

Cunningham, James S. and Nadja Zalokar (1992), 'The economic progress of black women, 1940–80: occupational distribution and relative wages', *Industrial and Labor Relations Review*, **45**(3), 540–55.

Darity, William A., Jr. and Patrick L. Mason (1998), 'Evidence of discrimination in employment: codes of color, codes of gender'', *Journal of Economic Perspectives*, **12**(2), 63–90.

Duleep, Harriet Orcutt and Seth Sanders (1992), 'Discrimination at the top: American-born Asian and white men', *Industrial Relations*, **31**(3), 416–32.

Farkas, George, Paula England, Kevin Vicknair and Barbara Stanek Kilbourne (1997), 'Cognitive skill, skill demands of jobs, earnings among young European American, African America, and Mexican American workers', *Social Forces*, **75**(3), 913–38.

Fischer, Mary J. and Douglas S. Massey (2004), 'The ecology of racial discrimination', *City and Community*, **3**(3), 221–41.

Fortin, Nicole M. (2007), 'The gender wage gap among young adults in the United States: the importance of money vs. people', University of British Columbia, Vancouver, unpublished paper.

Gallup Organization (2004), *Civil Rights and Race Relations*, Princeton, NJ: Gallup Organization.

Gill, Andrew M. (2001), 'Incorporating the causes of occupational differences in studies of racial wage differentials', *Journal of Human Resources*, **24**(1), 20–41.

Goldsmith, Arthur H., William A. Darity, Jr. and Jonathan R. Veum (1998), 'Race, cognitive skills, psychological capital and wages', *Review of Black Political Economy*, **26**(2), 9–21.

Goodman, Peter S. and Jack Healy (2009), 'Work losses hit mortgages seen as safe', *New York Times*, May 25, A1.

Graham, John and Steven Smith (2005), 'Gender differences in employment and earnings in science and engineering in the US', *Economics of Education Review*, **24**(3), 241–54.

Green, Carole A. and Marianne A. Ferber (2005), 'Do detailed work histories help to explain gender and race/ethnic wage differentials?', *Review of Social Economy*, **63**(1), 55–85.

Healy, Jack (2009), 'Unemployed driving up foreclosures', *New York Times*, May 29, B5.

Heckman, James J. (1998), 'Detecting discrimination', *Journal of Economic Perspectives*, **12**(2), 101–16.

Jacobson, Louis, Robert La Londe and Daniel Sullivan (1993), 'Earnings losses of displaced workers', *American Economic Review*, **83**(4), 685–709.

Joassart-Marcelli, Pascale (2009), 'The spatial determinants of wage inequality: evidence from recent Latina immigrants in Southern California', *Feminist Economics*, **15**(2), 33–72.

Joy, Lois (2003), 'Salaries of recent male and female college graduates: educational and labor market effects', *Industrial and Labor Relations Review*, **56**(4), 606–21.

Kanter, Rosabeth Moss (1993), *Men and Women of the Corporation*, New York: Basic Books.

Kilbourne, Barbara, Paula England and Kurt Beron (1994), 'Effects of individual, occupational and industrial characteristics on earnings: intersections of race and gender', *Social Forces*, **72**(2), 1149–76.

Kim, Marlene (2007), 'Racial economic differences in the twenty-first century', in Marlene Kim (ed.), *Race and Economic Opportunity in the Twenty-First Century*, London: Routledge, pp. 1–26.

Kim, Marlene (2009a), 'Race and gender differences in the earnings of black workers', *Industrial Relations*, **48**(3), 466–88.

Kim, Marlene (2009b), 'Glass ceiling', in Edith Wen-Chu and Grace J. Yoo (eds), *Encyclopedia of Contemporary Asian American Issues Today*, Santa Barbara, CA: Greenwood Press, pp. 107–10.

Kim, Marlene (2011), 'Asian Americans and Pacific Islanders: employment issues in the United States', *AAPI Nexus*, **9**(1), 58–69.

Kim, Marlene (2012), *Unfairly Disadvantaged: Asian Americans and Unemployment After the Great Recession*, Washington, DC: Economic Policy Institute.

Kim, Marlene and Don Mar (2007), 'The economic status of Asian Americans', in Marlene Kim (ed.), *Race and Economic Opportunity in the Twenty-First Century*, London: Routledge, pp. 148–84.

King, Deborah K. (1995), 'Multiple jeopardy, multiple consciousness: the context of a black feminist ideology', in Beverly Guy-Sheftall (ed.), *Words of Fire: An Anthology of African-American Feminist Thought*, New York: The New Press, pp. 294–317.

Leicht, Kevin T. (2008), 'Broken down by race and gender? Sociological explanations of new sources of earnings inequality', *Annual Review of Sociology*, **34**, 237–55.

Lopez, Mary (2012), 'Skilled immigrant women in the US and the double earnings penalty', *Feminist Economics*, **18**(1), 99–134.

Mar, Don (2000), 'Four decades of Asian American women's earnings: Japanese, Chinese and Filipino American women's earnings, 1960–1990', *Contemporary Economic Policy*, **18**(2), 228–37.

Mar, Don (2002), 'Asian women professionals: does discrimination exist?', San Francisco State University, San Francisco, CA, unpublished paper.

Mar, Don (2005), 'Asian Americans in the labor force: public policy issues', *AAPI Nexus*, **3**(2), 39–57.

Mason, Patrick (2011), 'Moments of disparate peaks: race–gender wage gaps among mature persons, 1965–2007', *Review of Radical Political Economics*, **38**(1), 1–25.

Massey, Douglas S. and Garvey Lundy (2001), 'Use of black English and racial discrimination in urban housing markets: new methods and findings', *Urban Affairs Review*, **36**(4), 452–69.

McGuire, Gail M. and Barbara F. Reskin (1993), 'Authority hierarchies at work: the impacts of race and sex', *Gender & Society*, **7**(4), 487–506.

Munnell, Alicia H., Geoffrey M.B. Tootell, Lynn E. Browne and James McEneaney (1996), 'Mortgage lending in Boston: interpreting HMDA data', *American Economic Review*, **86**(1), 25–53.

Neal, Derek A. and William J. Johnson (1996), 'The role of human capital in earnings differences between black and white men', *Journal of Political Economy*, **104**(5), 869–93.

Neumark, David (1999), 'Wage differentials by race and sex: the roles of taste discrimination and labor market information', *Industrial Relations*, **38**(3), 414–45.

O'Neill, June E. (1990), 'The role of human capital in earnings differences between black and white men', *Journal of Economic Perspectives*, **4**(4), 25–45.

O'Neill, June E. (1994), 'The gender gap in wages, circa 2000', *American Economic Review*, **93**(2), 309–14.

O'Neill, June E. and Dave M. O'Neill (2005), 'What do wage differentials tell us about labor market discrimination?', NBER Working Paper 11240, Cambridge, MA.

Ragins, Belle Rose, Bickley Townsend and Mary Mattis (1998), 'Gender gap in the executive suite: CEOs and female executives report on breaking the glass ceiling', *Academy of Management Executive*, **12** (February), 28–42.

Reimers, Cordelia (1985), 'A comparative analysis of the wages of Hispanics, blacks and non-Hispanic whites', in George J. Borjas and Marta Tienda (eds), *Hispanics in the US Economy*, New York: Academic Press, pp. 27–76.

Reskin, Barbara F. and Camille Z. Charles (1999), 'Now you see, 'em, now you don't: race, ethnicity, and gender in labor market research', in Irene Browne (ed.), *Latinas and African American Women at Work: Race, Gender and Economic Inequality*, New York: Russell Sage, pp. 380–406.

Reskin, Barbara F. and Catherine E. Ross (1992), 'Jobs, authority and earnings among managers', *Work and Occupations*, **19**(4), 342–65.

Riach, Peter A. and Judith Rich (1991), 'Testing for racial discrimination in the labour market', *Cambridge Journal of Economics*, **15**(3), 239–56.

Ruhm, Christopher J. (1991), 'Are workers permanently scarred by job displacements?', *American Economic Review*, **81**(1), 319–24.

Ruwanpura, Kanchana N. (2008), 'Multiple identities, multiple discrimination: a critical review', *Feminist Economics*, **14**(3), 77–105.

Sakamoto, Arthur and Satomi Furuichi (2002), 'The wages of native-born Asian Americans at the end of the twentieth century', *Asian American Policy Review*, **10**(1), 1–16.

Smith, Ryan (2012), 'Money, benefits and power: a test of the glass ceiling and glass escalator hypotheses', *Annals of the American Academic of Political and Social Science*, (639), 149–72.

Solberg, Eric J. (2004), 'Occupational assignment, hiring discrimination, and the gender pay gap', *Atlantic Economic Journal*, **32**(1), 11–27.

Squires, Gregory D. and Jan Chadwick (2006), 'Linguistic profiling: a tradition of the property insurance industry', *Urban Affairs Review*, **41**(3), 400–415.

Stevens, Ann Huff (1997), 'Persistent effects of job displacement: the importance of multiple job losses', *Journal of Labor Economics*, **15**(1), 165–88.

Sullivan, Daniel and Till von Wachter (2009), 'Job displacement and mortality: an analysis using administrative data', *Quarterly Journal of Economics*, **124**(3), 1265–306.

Trejo, Stephen J. (1997), 'Why do Mexican Americans earn low wages?', *Journal of Political Economy*, **105**(6), 1235–68.

Trejo, Stephen J. (2003), 'Intergenerational progress of Mexican-origin workers in the US labor market', *Journal of Human Resources*, **38**(3), 167–89.

Turner, Margery Austin, Stephen L. Ross, George C. Galster and John Yinger (2002), *Discrimination in Metropolitan Housing Markets*, Washington, DC: The Urban Institute.

United States Department of Commerce (2011), *Women in America: Economic Indicators of Social and Economic Well-Being*, Washington, DC: Department of Commerce, Economics and Statistics Administration and Executive Office of the President Office of Management and Budget.

von Wachter, Till, Jae Song and Joyce Manchester (2007), 'Long-term earnings losses due to job separation during the 1982 recession: an analysis using longitudinal administrative data from 1974–2004', Social Security Administration, Washington, DC.

Washington Post, Kaiser Family Foundation and Harvard University (2001), *Race and Ethnicity in 2001: Attitudes, Perceptions and Experiences*, Washington DC: Henry J. Kaiser Family Foundation.

Weinberger, Catherine (1998), 'Race and gender wage gaps in the market for recent college graduates', *Industrial Relations*, **37**(1), 67–84.

Weinberger, Catherine and Lois Joy (2007), 'Relative earnings of black college graduates', in Marlene Kim (ed.), *Race and Economic Opportunity in the Twenty-First Century*, London: Routledge, pp. 50–72.

Woo, Deborah (2000), *Glass Ceilings and Asian Americans: The New Face of Workplace Barriers*, New York: Alta Mira Press.

Zinn, Maxine Baca and Bonnie Thornton Dill (1996), 'Theorizing difference from multiracial feminism', *Feminist Studies*, **22**(2), 321–31.

15. Discrimination in gay and lesbian lives
Doris Weichselbaumer

I INTRODUCTION

Less than 15 years ago, in an article in *Feminist Economics*, Marieka Klawitter (1998) posed the timely question: 'Why aren't more economists doing research on sexual orientation?'. Indeed, before her article was published there were only two economic studies that examined issues of sexual orientation. Since her appeal, the economic literature on sexual orientation has grown substantially. A number of reasons may explain this development. First, there is a heightened awareness that discrimination against gays and lesbians is of great political concern. In 2000, the European Union introduced the Employment Equality Directive (2000/78/EC) that prohibits discrimination based on sexual orientation in the private and the public sector.[1] In the US, since the late 1990s various states and cities have introduced bans on employment discrimination of gays and lesbians. President Bill Clinton's 1998 Executive Order 13087 prohibited discrimination based on sexual orientation in civilian federal employment (Badgett, 2007). Since labor market discrimination against gays and lesbians has been on the political agenda, it is no surprise that this issue has gained particular prominence in the economic literature.

However, there may also be pragmatic reasons why economic research on sexual orientation has picked up only recently. More data sources are available that allow the identification of gays and lesbians because surveys increasingly ask questions on sexual orientation and behavior. In addition, experiments have become more popular in economic research and have been used to create 'data' on discrimination in spheres usually not available, such as housing.

Despite the increased political awareness, negative attitudes toward gays and lesbians are still lingering. According to a recent Gallup Poll (2010), 43 percent of Americans surveyed considered gay and lesbian relationships morally wrong and only 58 percent of respondents thought that gay or lesbian relations between consenting adults should be legal. Nonetheless, Americans' acceptance of gay and lesbian relations has steadily increased over the past few decades (Loftus, 2001; Gallup, 2010). In 1977 a significantly smaller fraction of the population, only 43 percent, believed that gay and lesbian relationships should be legal. Also, 56 percent of Americans then advocated equal rights in terms of job opportunities, but this fraction had risen to 86 percent by 2002 (Avery et al., 2007).

What is particularly interesting in the literature on prejudice is that there are some relatively consistent findings which suggest that attitudes may differ by sex. Psychologists have shown that men hold more negative attitudes toward 'homosexuals' than women, and gays are evaluated more negatively than lesbians. This result seems to be driven by a particular hostility of heterosexual men against gays (Kite and Whitley, 1996; LaMar and Kite, 1998; Herek, 2002), though it has been diminishing. Even though attitudes do not directly translate into discrimination, given the current gendered job distribution where men disproportionately occupy decision-making positions, these findings give reasons to speculate that gay men may be even more adversely affected by discrimination than lesbians.

Sexual identity is an important component of gender relations in society. It matters to people's lives and well-being. As a result, following an outline of the theoretical background (Section II), this chapter assesses the research on sexual orientation within economics, with particular attention to traditional multiple regressions of wages (Section III) as well as field and laboratory experiments with regard to hiring practices (Section IV). Because sexual orientation and gender identity are part of living a full life – not just the labor market – I also discuss research experiments on the impact of sexual orientation in shopping, housing, and receiving help or assistance (Section V). Section VI concludes with implications for policy and activism in the US and Europe.[2]

II THEORETICAL BACKGROUND

The most prominent theory of economic discrimination builds on negative attitudes toward minority group members. In his 'taste for discrimination' model, Nobel laureate Gary Becker (1971) argues that members of the dominant group may have a distaste to work with 'others'. If employers hold these distastes, they will be willing to hire minority group members only if they can pay them less – as a compensation for their decreased well-being caused by the interaction.[3] Customers or coworkers may also hold such discriminatory tastes and attitudes. Customers may not wish to be helped by a minority group member, and thus may switch to shops and businesses where they can interact with their own group. Coworkers may be less productive when minority members are introduced, or may not give minority group members the necessary training. If minority workers are excluded from information and networks or suffer from stress and anxiety caused by a hostile environment, this actually hampers their productivity given the same, or even higher, effort. Even a nondiscriminatory employer may worry about how productive a minority member can be given the social circumstances and only employ him or her at a lower wage, as a compensation for decreased productivity. Given the negative attitudes held toward gays and lesbians in many societies of the world, it is easy to imagine that discrimination based on Becker's theory occurs.

The second influential explanation of unfavorable treatment of minorities has been proposed by Edmund Phelps (1972) and Kenneth Arrow (1973) in their model of 'statistical discrimination'. They have argued that under incomplete (or imperfect) information, for example when hiring a new employee, individuals are judged on the basis of beliefs about group averages. If one minority group is considered less productive, on average, then a member of this group is expected to have a lower productivity and is offered a lower wage or is less likely to be hired. A typical example is the greater likelihood of women to drop out of the labor market, that is to interrupt their labor market participation, due to childbirth. This may cause statistical discrimination against women because they are expected to drop out based on group averages rather than knowing anything about the individual worker's labor market plans.

Neoclassical economics considers statistical discrimination to be rational because it can be cost efficient. However, with respect to gays and lesbians it is more difficult to think of how statistical discrimination may occur. After all, gays and lesbians are brought up within the majority culture (usually by heterosexual parents) and are socialized according to majority norms from birth on.[4] This should lead to identical productivity. Conventional economic theory, though, puts this into question. In his *Treatise of the Family*, Becker (1991) argued that in heterosexual households the rearing of children makes a division of labor between market and housework efficient and partners specialize in different work spheres. According to Becker, the fact that women give birth gives them a comparative advantage in childcare and housework, which, as a result, they specialize in. Men, consequentially, specialize in market work. As this division of labor in traditional households is anticipated, heterosexual men and women make different human capital investments already when young. Within Becker's model, specialization makes less sense for gay and lesbian couples, in part because they have fewer children and often no access to the institution of marriage or a comparable arrangement (civil unions, in particular) that insures the home provider. Without a legal basis that guarantees the home provider access to the income or wealth of the primary earner – to some degree also in the case of a breakup – specialization in household tasks is too risky.

Most importantly, for young gays and lesbians, their own sex cannot work as a sorting device for which human capital to invest in because it is not clear, *ex ante*, whether in a future relationship specialization will take place at all, and, if it does, which partner will specialize in which sector. According to Becker's household model, gay men should invest less into their human capital and work fewer hours than heterosexual men, while the contrary should be true for lesbians (Black et al., 2003, 2007). If such differences in human capital and effort would indeed occur, statistical discrimination is plausible. However, data consistently show that gays and lesbians have higher levels of education than heterosexuals. This fits the predictions of Becker's model for lesbians but contradicts those for gay men (Badgett, 2007; Black et al., 2007). Furthermore, information on the education of workers is usually easily observable. Only unobserved differences in human capital can lead to statistical discrimination. It is not obvious why gays, who have better observable human capital, should be doing worse in unobservable human capital characteristics and therefore suffer from statistical discrimination.[5] These issues will be further discussed when the existing evidence on gay and lesbian earnings is debated.

III   EVIDENCE ON EARNINGS

The economic literature on gay and lesbian earnings has been pioneered by a seminal study conducted by Lee Badgett (1995).[6] She examined pooled data from the General Social Survey (GSS), 1989–91, that includes questions on the number of same- and different-sex partners respondents have had. She found that after controlling for observable differences in human capital and other relevant characteristics,[7] gay and bisexual men suffered from a wage penalty of 11 to 27 percent. Similar results have been obtained for lesbians however these results have not been statistically significant. Later research that used additional waves of GSS data (occasionally complemented by data from the National Health and Social Life Survey) has confirmed the results for gay men (Badgett, 2001; Berg and Lien, 2002; Black et al., 2003; Blandford, 2003; Cushing-Daniels and

Yeung, 2009), but the lower wages of lesbians turned out to be specific to the limited 1989–91 sample. Studies including additional waves of the GSS systematically found higher wages for lesbians (11 to 30 percent), usually statistically significant.[8] Of course, these results are inconsistent with a simple theory of discrimination – at least with respect to lesbians. For example, differences in household specialization of lesbians and heterosexual women, as derived from Becker's household model, have been proposed to explain the findings. As will be discussed later, higher earnings of lesbians do not rule out the existence of discrimination against this group.

The US Census of Population provides another important database for the examination of gays' and lesbians' earnings, with a new category in 1990 that allowed household members to categorize themselves as 'unmarried partners'. As a result, the data allow the identification of those gays and lesbians who live as couples. Single gays and lesbians cannot be observed. The advantage is that even the 5 percent sample of the Public Use Microdata Set (PUMS) of the census data includes thousands of gays and lesbians, in contrast to sometimes less than a hundred that are present in the GSS.

Using the 1990 PUMS, Marieka Klawitter and Victor Flatt (1998) report that when examining individuals, married men earn higher incomes than gay and unmarried heterosexual men. In contrast, lesbians obtain higher earnings than unmarried women, who earn more than married heterosexual women. However, when looking at household income, the results look different as gay male and married heterosexual households enjoy a significantly higher joint income than lesbian couples (see also Ahmed et al., 2011a). Unmarried heterosexual partners, in these data, make the least joint income. Notably, the effect for individual lesbians vanishes when examining full-time workers only. Other authors examining the PUMS data report higher earnings for lesbian women in most age groups, and confirm the lower earnings for gay men (Clain and Leppel, 2001, for the 1990 PUMS; Antecol et al., 2008, for the 2000 PUMS). This wage penalty of gay men can partly be explained by the heterosexual 'marriage premium', as Sylvia Allegretto and Michelle Arthur (2001) have shown. Higher lesbian incomes are corroborated by Lisa Jepsen (2007), who, like Amanda Baumle (2009), finds that lesbians with children enjoy a particularly high income premium.

Alternative nationwide data sources have been applied to verify the results from the GSS and PUMS data. Scholars have confirmed higher wages for gay men (Carpenter, 2007), while there has not been a significant effect for lesbian women (Elmslie and Tebaldi, 2007). Christopher Carpenter (2005) examined the state of California and could detect no earnings differentials, either for gay men or for lesbians. This may be due to the relatively liberal attitudes prevalent in California.

Studies on differences in earnings caused by sexual orientation also exist for a number of other OECD countries, in particular for the Netherlands (Plug and Berkhout, 2004), the UK (Arabsheibani et al., 2004, 2005), Canada (Carpenter, 2008a) and Sweden (Ahmed and Hammarstedt, 2010; Ahmed et al., 2011a). All of these studies univocally confirm the familiar pattern of gay men's wage penalty and lesbians' wage premium.[9]

Only one study on Australia obtains different results. Carpenter (2008b) presents the only evidence for systematically lower earnings for lesbians in the literature. Interestingly, he explored data that provide information also on nonpecuniary economic outcomes. He finds that lesbians are three times more likely to report harassment at work than heterosexual women. Also, lesbians are more likely to have ever lost a job, to have had difficulty in finding a job, or to have had experienced periods of decreased income. According to this research, lesbian women are also less satisfied with work issues and report more stress in relation to work. These results are interesting as they indicate that lesbians also face problems in the labor market, that may not be obvious from the typical wage study.

Explanations for the Evidence from Earnings Studies

As the previous section illustrated, results from earnings studies suggest that gay men experience a wage penalty while lesbians earn more or the same as heterosexual women. Only one study finds a lesbian income penalty. While the results for gay men fit a theory of discrimination, the findings for lesbian women suggest that a more complex interpretation is necessary. Of course the particularly unfavorable attitudes toward gays (Kite and Whitley, 1996; Herek, 2002) may lead to especially severe discrimination against this group, but attitudes cannot explain the sometimes favorable results for lesbian women. How can these findings be reconciled?

Wage studies typically control for a whole battery of productivity-related characteristics. However, it is possible that there are unobserved characteristics that drive the results. Becker's specialization model outlined above has been cited most frequently in this context. This model allows speculation that lesbians invest more into market-specific human capital than heterosexual women (Black et al., 2003), for example, in increased on-the-job training (Clain and Leppel, 2001), which may not be observable in the data. They may also choose different hours of work (Klawitter and Flatt, 1998; Tebaldi and Elmslie, 2006) or different effort levels (Berg and Lien, 2002), as they do not have access to a – generally higher – male income. Also the fact that they are less likely to have children and the prime responsibility for household work may increase lesbians' productivity. Contrary to the hypothesis from the Becker model, Jepsen (2007) finds little support that differences in specialization across lesbian and straight households explain the lesbian wage premium. Indeed, lesbian mothers also enjoy an earnings premium.[10] Yet Heather Antecol and Michael Steinberger (2013) emphasize that specialization actually does take place within lesbian couples and needs to be accounted for.

There may also be unobserved heterogeneity with respect to other characteristics than specialization. In particular, gays and lesbians choose different occupations from heterosexuals, possibly to escape discrimination and harassment. Gay men are typically more likely to work in female-dominated jobs and are less present in male-dominated professions. The reverse is true for lesbians (Antecol et al., 2008). While most studies control for occupation, data may not be precise enough to capture all effects stemming from occupational distribution (Blandford, 2003). It has also been suggested that employers discriminate in favor of the personality characteristics of the stereotypical heterosexual male (Clain and Leppel, 2001). As lesbians are often believed to be more similar to heterosexual males, and gay men are considered to be more like heterosexual women (Kite and Deaux, 1987), a 'taste for masculinity' could explain the prevalent findings.

Finally, disclosure at the workplace is of course a precondition for labor market discrimination. Unlike sex or ethnicity, sexual orientation can be successfully hidden at the job to avoid harassment and other unfavorable labor market outcomes. However, studies on income differentials cannot account for whether gays or lesbians are 'out' on the job, as this information is not available in the data. If fewer people are out on the job than in the data, discrimination may be underestimated. Badgett (2001) presents some evidence that women may be less likely to out themselves, which may partly explain the different results for men and women. But disclosure to an interviewer is required to correctly assess the sexual orientation of an individual. If people with higher incomes are more likely to out themselves to an interviewer, wages of gays and lesbians will be overestimated.

As this discussion illustrates, there is ample uncertainty with respect to interpreting findings on earnings differentials. Indeed, the higher or equal wages that lesbians seem to earn according to these studies may simply be due to measurement problems and/or a higher labor market commitment unobservable in the data. The results are even compatible with the existence of labor market discrimination if the unobserved productivity advantage of lesbians is sufficiently large. Therefore, while interesting as such, wage regressions may not be suitable tools to examine discrimination against lesbian women.

IV   EXPERIMENTAL EVIDENCE

Experiments are often considered to provide the clearest and most convincing evidence for discrimination (Fix and Struyk, 1993). They have been conducted since the 1970s to examine, in particular, discrimination against ethnic minorities (Daniel, 1968; Jowell and Prescott-Clarke, 1970; Firth, 1981; Riach and Rich, 1991, 2002; Bertrand and Mullainathan, 2004) as well as women (Fidell, 1970; Levinson, 1975; Neumark et al., 1996; Weichselbaumer, 2004). The advantage of such experiments is that they allow a direct comparison of individuals, who are carefully matched in all characteristics but one that is suspected to cause discrimination. They are particularly useful for studying labor market discrimination based on sexual orientation as they allow the researcher to fully control information on sexual identity. Conventional data such as the GSS or PUMS usually allow the identification of gays and lesbians only through indirect routes (sexual behavior or cohabitation) and do not reveal whether gays and lesbians are 'out'. As a result, experiments can give a more accurate measure for the differential treatment of openly gay or lesbian individuals.

There are two main strands in the literature. Laboratory experiments on labor market discrimination are usually more popular with psychologists. They typically mimic hiring or evaluation scenarios, where officially invited study participants examine individuals with different demographic characteristics. The advantage of laboratory experiments is that the experimenter can fully control all aspects of the investigated situation. However, participants' behavior is probably more socially acceptable in the laboratory as they know that they are being observed; they will also be influenced by the fact that their 'decisions' have no real-life consequences. For that reason economists generally prefer field experiments that examine discrimination in real settings.

Here mainly two different procedures have been used. In 'audit' or 'situation tests', testers with different demographic backgrounds attend job interviews or apply for jobs in person or on the phone. However, it is difficult to find and sufficiently train suitable testers so that they are comparable in all dimensions apart from the one characteristic under investigation (Heckman and Siegelman, 1993). The technique of 'correspondence testing' avoids potentially problematic personal interactions. Here letters of applications of individuals with identical qualifications but different demographics are sent out to firms. If one individual is invited to interviews more often than the other, then this is ascribed to discrimination. Because of the clear control this design allows in a real-life setting, it has recently become popular also for examining discrimination based on sexual orientation. Table 15.1 gives an overview of existing labor market experiments on discrimination based on sexual orientation.

Field Experiments

The first field experiment examining discrimination against gays and lesbians in hiring was conducted by sociologist Barry Adam (1981). In a small-scale experiment on apprenticeship positions in law firms in Ontario, Canada, he sent out identical résumés for males and females, half of which included the line 'Active in Gay People's Alliance'.[11] While 17 percent of firms invited the presumably heterosexual male to an interview, this rate was only 10 percent for gay applicants. For women, the corresponding rates were 7 percent (lesbian) and 15 percent (heterosexual). However, the small sample size (about 40 observations per cell) and lack of any signification test limits the persuasiveness of the study.

Weichselbaumer (2003) represents the first large-scale correspondence test on sexual orientation discrimination. In this experiment, which examines discrimination against women in clerical jobs in the city of Vienna, both sexual orientation as well as gender identity were varied to also test the effect of gender conformity. While gender non-conformity is usually socially punished, the fact that masculinity is typically valued in labor markets may also work as an advantage for masculine women, including lesbians (often assumed to be more masculine). To indicate lesbian orientation, a former secondary occupation in the management of the local Gay and Lesbian Alliance was indicated in the application; the 'heterosexuals' had been active in other nonprofit organizations. The different gender types were constructed through gender-typed hobbies and masculine/feminine looks of the applicant as indicated in a photo, the inclusion of which is standard in Austria. While the heterosexual female was invited to an interview in 55 percent of the cases, the lesbian was successful in only 42 percent of the cases. This result proved the existence of labor market discrimination based on sexual orientation for the first time on a statistically significant level. (Interestingly, while sexual orientation did affect hiring chances, the gender identity of applicants did not.[12])

Since the 2003 study, a couple of researchers have conducted correspondence studies on sexual orientation discrimination in different countries. The highest discrimination has been found by Nick Drydakis (2009, 2011) for Greece. He reports levels of discrimination as high as 28 percentage points for lesbians (2011) and 26 percentage points for gay men (2009). This result may be due to particularly unfavorable attitudes toward homosexuality in Greece, but, to some degree, also to the low qualification of the applicants. Interestingly, Drydakis managed to identify the gender of a significant fraction of employers and found that gay men suffered a 35 percentage point lower chance to be invited to an interview if the employer was male (2009).[13] This fits with the results from

Table 15.1 Findings from studies on sexual orientation discrimination in hiring

Study	Location	Method	Jobs examined	Findings – gay men	Findings – lesbian women
Adam (1981)	Ontario, Canada	Correspondence test, $N = 163$	Apprenticeship in law firms	−7% invitation rate for gays	−8% invitation rate for lesbians
Weichselbaumer (2003)	Vienna, Austria	Correspondence test, $N = 1{,}226$	Clerical jobs (accountant, secretary)		−13% ($p < 0.01$)
Drydakis (2009)	Athens, Greece	Correspondence test, $N = 3{,}428$	*All occupations* Office jobs Industry jobs Restaurant and café Shop sales	−26% ($p < 0.01$) −31% ($p < 0.01$) −25% ($p < 0.01$) −21% ($p < 0.01$) −28% ($p < 0.01$)	
Drydakis (2011)	Athens, Greece	Correspondence test, $N = 2{,}114$	*All occupations* Office jobs Industry jobs Restaurant and café Shop sales		−28% ($p < 0.01$) −23% ($p < 0.01$) −24% ($p < 0.01$) −27% ($p < 0.01$) −37% ($p < 0.01$)
Ahmed et al. (2011b)	Sweden, nationwide	Correspondence test, $N = 3{,}996$	*All occupations* Shop sales assistant Construction worker Preschool teacher High school teacher Motor-vehicle driver Cleaner Restaurant worker Sales person Nurse Mechanic worker	−4% ($p = 0.07$) −8% ($p = 0.05$) −8% ($p = 0.24$) +2% ($p = 0.74$) −5% ($p = 0.56$) No effect No effect −8% ($p = 0.13$) −10% ($p = 0.10$) +5% ($p = 0.66$) −12% ($p = 0.06$)	−6% ($p < 0.01$) −5% ($p = 0.11$) −6% ($p = 0.33$) −10% ($p = 0.06$) −11% ($p = 0.19$) −10% ($p = 0.17$) −10% ($p = 0.02$) −8% ($p = 0.17$) No effect +4% ($p = 0.68$) No effect

Table 15.1 (continued)

Study	Location	Method	Jobs examined	Findings – gay men	Findings – lesbian women
Bailey et al. (2011)	Chicago Dallas Philadelphia San Francisco, US	Correspondence test, N = 4,608	Random jobs applied to by college graduates with major in business or psychology	No effect	No effect
Hebl et al. (2002)	Texas, US	Audit study, N = 84	Sales clerk	-13% ($p = 0.35$) of gays/lesbians have been told of job vacancies	
Van Hoye and Lievens (2003)	Flanders, Belgium	Laboratory experiment with personnel experts, N = 135	Human resource manager	No effect of sexual orientation on ratings of applicants	
Crow et al. (1998)	Metropolitan southern city, US	Laboratory experiment with full-time employees N = 4,384 (548 × 8)	Accountant	-37% ($p < 0.05$)	-39% ($p < 0.05$)
Horvath and Ryan (2003)	Midwestern university, US	Laboratory experiment with student population, N = 1,888	Technical writer	On a 100 point scale, the heterosexual man is evaluated most favorably (84.87 points), followed by the lesbian (80.76), the gay man (80.38), and the heterosexual woman (76.2)	

Note: % represents percentage points. N is the total number of résumés/applicants evaluated in a study irrespective of the number of evaluators (firms, subjects). In Crow et al. (1998), all résumés have not been rated, but 548 subjects decided which six candidates to hire out of eight. Results have been rounded and levels of significance are given where available in the original study. In contrast to other correspondence tests, the significance levels from Drydakis (2009, 2011) do not come from probit analyses, but from a Chi-squared test comparing the number of firms that have discriminated against the sexual minority applicant with the number of firms that preferred the gay/lesbian (when simultaneously also receiving résumés of a straight candidate).

psychologists that attest heterosexual males have more negative attitudes against sexual minorities than women (Kite and Whitley, 1996; LaMar and Kite, 1998).

The most comprehensive study thus far has been conducted by Ali Ahmed et al. (2011b) who examined the employment chances of both gays and lesbians for 10 different occupations in Sweden. This large number of jobs allows the authors to infer effects resulting from different gender shares of occupations. They find that discrimination against gay men tends to be higher in male-dominated jobs. In these, gay men have an overall 8 percentage point lower success rate with respect to invitations to interviews than heterosexual men, while there is no significant effect for female-dominated occupations. Conversely, discrimination against lesbians is more pronounced in female-dominated occupations (–7 percentage points versus no significant effect in male-dominated jobs). This result is interesting given that previous experiments showed that women are less successful in male-dominated jobs while men fare worse in female-dominated jobs (Riach and Rich, 2002; Weichselbaumer, 2004). It may be either that gays and lesbians are considered to be less gender congruent (Kite and Deaux, 1987) and therefore less suitable for jobs of their own sex type, or employers fear problems when mixing employees of the same sex with different sexual orientations. As Bernard Whitley (1988) has shown, heterosexual men and women fear advances from their own sex. In any case, this evidence helps to explain why gay men are overtly represented in female-dominated and lesbians in male-dominated occupations as illustrated by Antecol et al. (2008).

To my knowledge, only one correspondence test has been conducted in the US so far. A team of sociologists, John Bailey et al. (2011), has created résumés of college graduates (with a business-related or psychology major), indicating sexual orientation with information about activities in the university's Gay–Lesbian Association. The applications have been sent as response to advertisements for different jobs (from Administrative to Warehouse) from a popular job search website. The number of observations per job has been set in approximate proportion to their representation on the website. The data yield surprising results: in Philadelphia, gay men are the most successful group of applicants (invitation rate: 15.1 percent) while lesbians are the least successful (6.8 percent). The results for heterosexuals lie in between. This picture is exactly reversed in San Francisco. Despite the large number of observations, the findings reveal no discernible pattern on the city level. When the authors pool the data for the four cities investigated (Chicago, Dallas, Philadelphia, San Francisco), there is no significant difference between invitation rates to different candidates (in percent: lesbian, 12.4; gay, 13.9; heterosexual female, 12.4; heterosexual male, 11.9). These results may not prove the absence of discrimination in the US. As the authors note, the high (or over-)qualification of applicants may be responsible for this outcome, particularly since positions with lower educational requirements than college education were applied for. Also, mainly big firms were contacted, which are known to discriminate less (Kaas and Manger, 2012).[14] Finally, the pooling of different occupations may explain the lack of discrimination observed.

The only audit study on sexual orientation discrimination has also been carried out in the US, by Michelle Hebl et al. (2002). The scholars examine not only hiring chances but also interpersonal behavior. They have instructed students to enter different clothing stores of a mall in Texas to inquire about job openings. The testers followed a particular script with the goal to engage the person in charge, ideally the manager, in a conversation that could reveal potentially differential treatment based on sexual orientation also on an interpersonal level. To signal sexual orientation the authors randomly equipped the applicants with baseball hats either saying 'Gay and Proud' or 'Texan and Proud'.[15] The testers entered the stores themselves being unaware of the particular identity that they have been assigned. This is interesting as it eliminates the typical problem of audit studies that testers may subconsciously try to confirm the experimenters' expectations by adapting their behavior accordingly.

It turned out that 56 percent of the 'heterosexual' applicants but only 43 percent of the 'gays' or 'lesbians' were told about available jobs. However, probably due to the relatively small sample size, this effect is not significant. With respect to *ex post* job offers, 19 percent of the applicants were successful in the 'heterosexual' condition and 12 percent in the 'gay and lesbian' condition. Again, this difference is not statistically significant. In contrast to the employment-related success rates, the authors did identify significant effects concerning differences in interpersonal treatment: fewer words were spoken to 'gays and lesbians' and the testers – unaware of their own identity – reported higher levels of negativity received from the potential employer in the gay and lesbian condition.[16] This result suggests that formal discrimination with respect to job opportunities is only the tip of the iceberg: a lot of discrimination may occur through personal interaction.

The results from these field experiments are interesting in a number of ways. Significant employment discrimination based on sexual orientation has been found for Sweden, Austria, and Greece in ascending magnitude. This ranking exactly fits the order of countries with respect to their attitudes toward homosexuals from the World Value Survey 2000. Asked whether they find homosexuality justifiable (on a scale of 1–10 with 10 most justifiable), Swedes reveal the most tolerant attitudes (7.7), followed by Austrians (5.4), and Greeks (4.9). US respondents hold similar attitudes to Greeks (4.8). One can therefore only speculate whether insignificant results for the US are due to small sample size (likely for Hebl et al., 2002), particular features in the research design, or whether there is indeed no discrimination on the formal level. If the latter is the case, the fact that discrimination on the interpersonal level does exist (as illustrated by Hebl et al.) would indicate that despite unfavorable attitudes, there is sufficient awareness, possibly created by political debates, that employers want to avoid the stigma of being prejudiced.

The findings presented in this section are also interesting for other reasons. Some economists doubt the existence of labor market discrimination, which in neoclassical economics is considered irrational and suboptimal for profits. It has also been argued that wage regressions cannot prove discrimination against minorities because unobserved heterogeneity may drive the estimated lower incomes of one group (see Weichselbaumer and Winter-Ebmer, 2006, for a discussion). James Heckman (1998) has extended this criticism to experiments, arguing that it is impossible to experimentally control for all relevant productive characteristics, for example, when designing application material. As a result, employers confronted with résumés have to form expectations on unobservable characteristics and unequal treatment may simply be due to different endowments of different groups in these unobservable characteristics (for example, work commitment). This would lead to statistical discrimination, which is considered fair on average, but would not represent 'real discrimination'. However, Heckman's argument does not hold for the case of lesbians. As can be seen from the discussions on earnings, for lesbians it can only be that unobservable characteristics – should they matter – work in their favor. According to the specialization theory, lesbians should have a *higher* labor market commitment and should be less likely to take maternity leave. Consequently, if anything, they should be *favored* by employers due to their unobservables. This is not what we find in the experiments. Therefore, these indeed provide clear and convincing evidence for actual discrimination.

Laboratory Experiments

A few laboratory experiments have been carried out by psychologists and management scientists to examine sexual orientation discrimination in hiring. The first study of this type, Stephen Crow et al. (1998), examined which six out of eight applicants (differing in sex, sexual orientation, and race) subjects would choose for an accountant position when they were told that all affirmative action goals have already been met. The subject sample consisted of employees (predominantly managers and supervisors) from a metropolitan southern city of the US. The authors found that in general gays and lesbians were less likely to be selected; if they were black, their chances to be selected were even lower.

Another laboratory experiment on hiring discrimination in the US comes from Michael Horvath and Ann Marie Ryan (2003). They have asked students (white females were the majority) to evaluate résumés for technical writers. On a 100-point scale, the heterosexual male has received the highest score (84.87), followed by the lesbian (80.76), and the gay (80.38) applicant. The heterosexual woman was the least successful (76.2). As Badgett et al. (2007) have pointed out, these results resemble the findings from wage studies, where gays and lesbians are at a disadvantage in comparison to heterosexual men, but lesbians fare better than heterosexual women.

Greet Van Hoye and Filip Lievens (2003) have asked personnel experts in Flanders, Belgium, to rate male applicants of different sexual orientation (as indicated via statements concerning their family status). It turned out that sexual orientation did not have a significant impact on personnel experts' evaluations. Perhaps this is because personnel experts from consultancy firms or human resource departments have very standardized rules when evaluating candidates. They are usually aware of the merits of diversity management and the problem of discrimination, which they may try to avoid. These laboratory experiments have been useful, but recall what was pointed out earlier about their weaknesses; they may underestimate discrimination.

V FIELD EXPERIMENTS RELATED TO SHOPPING, SEARCHING FOR HOUSING AND HELPING BEHAVIOR

Interesting experiments on discrimination based on sexual orientation have also been executed in other areas, in particular with respect to discrimination against gay and lesbian customers and in helping behavior. Experiments on unfavorable treatment in product markets are generally less common, probably due to the belief that profit-maximizing firms would not turn away paying customers for their demographic characteristics. Nevertheless, previous studies on the effects of ethnicity did find significant discrimination in the insurance and car markets (Riach and Rich, 2002) as well as in the housing market (Yinger, 1986).

Of course, testing for the effect of sexual orientation presents some challenge in how to communicate sexual orientation in the experiment. In his study on the housing markets of Ontario, Canada, and Michigan, US, psychologist Stewart Page (1998) chose to have his callers say 'I guess it's only fair to tell you that I'm a gay (lesbian) person' when they inquired about the availability of a flat/apartment. The likelihood of a positive response was 46 percentage points lower (statistically significant) for the gay or lesbian person (no significant difference between the two, gay men and lesbians). However, the defensive statement in the phone call may actually induce landlords to think that gay or lesbian orientation was wrong and respond negatively. A team of economists, Ahmed et al. (2008) and Ali Ahmed and Mats Hammerstedt (2009), chose a more indirect route to indicate sexual orientation when they contacted Swedish landlords via emails in which the fictitious applicants described themselves as a couple. The sexual orientation became obvious through the couple's first names. The authors found that gay men were 12–14 percent less likely to get a call-back (ibid.), while there was no effect for lesbians (Ahmed et al., 2008). They explain this surprising difference with the fact that women are actually preferred in the Swedish housing market, which may work in favor of lesbians. Their result also fits the finding that gay men suffer from higher prejudice (LaMar and Kite, 1998; Herek, 2002). It cannot be explained by statistical discrimination based on expectations about the ability to pay rent. As research on earnings has shown, lesbian couples in Sweden have the lowest joint income of all partnered households (Ahmed et al., 2011a).

While there is some possibility that landlords worry about complaints from other tenants when renting to gays and lesbians, discrimination was even detected in very short-term interactions. For example, David Jones (1996) found in the US, same-sex couples were 14 percentage points less likely than different-sex couples to receive a reservation in a hotel when requesting a room with one bed. The effect was particularly pronounced for small hotels, which the author explains with a potentially higher identification of the owner with the premises and a greater likelihood of guests noticing each other. It corresponds with the common finding that small firms discriminate more than big ones (Kaas and Manger, 2012). The result also suggests that businesses are willing to forgo profits to discriminate against sexual minorities, which is often doubted by neoclassical economists.

Even with respect to the treatment of customers in shops, there is evidence that same-sex couples are attended less favorably than heterosexuals. Andrew Walters and Maria-Cristina Curran (1996) measured how long it took sales clerks to attend to customers and found that heterosexual couples (as indicated by holding hands) were helped within 82 seconds upon entering a store, while gay couples were attended only after 231 seconds and lesbians after 259 seconds. This means that heterosexuals were helped significantly more quickly than gays and lesbians, and lesbians had to wait for help even longer than gay men. An observer also rated staff behavior (on the dimensions staring, laughing, pointing, talking about, and being rude) and found that gay customers have been treated particularly unfavorably in these dimensions. While the staff behavior may not be in accordance with the rules of the management (as also suggested by *ex post* interviews), it indicates unfavorable treatment, even of paying customers. If employees discriminate against minority group customers, who they are supposed to kindly attend to, it makes the reverse even more likely: that majority customers can discriminate against minority staff. However, to my knowledge, no experiments exist to test customer discrimination directly.

Outside of the strictly economic sphere, experiments examine the helping behavior toward people of different sexual orientations. In the wrong number technique, testers call different phone numbers, apparently by mistake. Upon being informed by this mistake, the caller claims to run low on battery or not to have any credit left to make another call and asks the respondent for help by relaying an important message to his or her partner. The sexual orientation of the caller is revealed by the name of the partner. In a study from Berlin, Ute Gabriel and Rainer Banse (2006) found that heterosexual callers received significantly more help (83.5 percent) than gay (67.9 percent) and lesbian (66 percent) callers. Lesbians were discriminated similarly by men and women, while gay men were only discriminated by male respondents. Jason Ellis and Pauline Fox (2001) found that discrimination against gays and lesbians existed in the UK, but due to more favorable helping rates toward women, lesbians still received a similar amount of help as heterosexual men. Males discriminated against gays more heavily than against lesbians, while women offered similar help to lesbians and gay men. This result corresponds to other UK findings obtained by Amy Hendren and Hartmut Blank (2009) who used a different experimental design. Here, testers wore either a neutral T-shirt or one with a pro-gay slogan and asked for 10 pence for a parking meter.[17] In both of the last studies, gay men received the lowest and heterosexual women the highest amounts of help. Apart from proving discrimination against gays and lesbians, again these results suggest that gay men may suffer from particular antipathy (LaMar and Kite, 1998; Herek, 2002). However, the findings may also be due to the fact that social norms encourage helping women (Eagly and Crowley, 1986), which partly counteracts negative attitudes toward lesbians.

Of course, these experiments are not directly transferable to the work environment. However, help is also often needed from colleagues on the job. The presented results suggest it is likely that gays and lesbians receive less help also from coworkers on the job and in that way may suffer from coworkers' discrimination.

V   CONCLUSION

This chapter has illustrated how gays and lesbians are confronted with discriminatory practices in multiple spheres of life, and employment in particular. Wage regressions typically find lower earnings for gay men and equal or higher wages for lesbians when controlling for productivity-related characteristics. However, wage regressions are likely to suffer from various measurement problems, for example with respect to identifying 'out' gays and lesbians, and unobserved heterogeneity.

Experiments are therefore better suited to document sexual orientation discrimination as they allow a better control of productive characteristics and sexual identity. Indeed, experimental studies have documented that women suffer from employment discrimination once their sexual orientation is made explicit – for example in Austria, Greece, and Sweden. In the US, discrimination on an interpersonal level has been found for gays and lesbians looking for a job. Unfavorable treatment has also been established in the search for housing and help, as well as when shopping. Obviously, results of experiments strongly depend on the context studied as well as on the experimental design. Caution is therefore warranted from generalizing their results. For example, with respect to discrimination in hiring, experiments usually cannot cover highly qualified jobs that require lots of experience. In these jobs discrimination may be higher or lower than what is typically observed.

Of course, the experience of discrimination severely affects people's lives. It can hamper the job satisfaction of gays and lesbians as well as their overall happiness. Activists have therefore taken different measures to escape the discriminatory practices of markets. In Europe, queer activists, who reject the fixed identity construction implicit in the terms 'gay' and 'lesbian', have founded collectives for generating income (for example, bars and cafes) that also allow alternative ways of living. These collectively run projects usually do not only aim at fair and equal wages for queers, but also support anti-racist and anti-sexist goals. With respect to housing, queers who reject market liberalism as well as gentrification have squatted buildings and founded laagers (alternative trailer parks on otherwise empty urban compounds).[18] But also those who participate in conventional market structures have organized privately owned housing projects that protect them from immediate discrimination and allow living in a home largely free of harassment and looks from neighbors.

Not everyone may be able to engage in activism on this level, though. It is therefore essential to introduce legislation that protects all queers, gays, and lesbians from all forms of discrimination based on sexual orientation and gender identity.[19] In the US (unlike the European equality directive), only a limited number of states have introduced bans on sexual orientation discrimination. Thus, further legal protection is needed. However, prejudice is at the core of discrimination and may sustain even when formal discrimination has already been precluded. Indeed prejudice is at the roots of harassment and unfavorable treatment in all kinds of interactions. It can even lead to hate crimes committed against gays, lesbians, and 'genderqueers'. Policies that combat negative attitudes toward queers, gays, and lesbians are therefore fundamental for moving toward a more egalitarian society.

NOTES

1. The directive had to be incorporated into national law by the member states of the European Union by December 2, 2003 (see De Schutter, 2008, for details).
2. Often references on an apparent lack of rights of gays and lesbians in 'developing countries' are implicitly used as a rhetoric tool to demonstrate the 'backwardness' or 'barbarity' of non-western people while, for example, homophobe violence within western countries is ignored. A discussion of discrimination against gays and lesbians in Africa, Asia, and Latin America merits a study of its own and is beyond the scope of this chapter.
3. This implies that employers actually do not maximize profits but well-being. Because discriminatory firms hire majority workers of equal productivity for higher wages, neoclassical economists argue that in competitive markets discriminatory firms will be pushed out of business by nondiscriminatory, profit-maximizing firms who do not give majority workers such preferential treatment.
4. As Black et al. (2003) illustrate, there is also no systematic difference in family background of people with different sexual orientations.
5. If sexual orientation makes gay men invest more in their observable educational characteristics it seems unlikely that they invest less in unobservable productivity-related characteristics.

6. See Badgett (2007) and Badgett et al. (2007) for more detailed reviews on early income studies.
7. The studies presented typically control for age/experience, education, marital status, region of residence, occupation, and other variables of interest.
8. Cushing-Daniels and Yeung (2009) report lower wage differences for the more recent time.
9. Ahmed and Hammarstedt (2010), however, also report specifications with lower earnings for lesbians in nonmetropolitan areas.
10. Lesbians are more likely than heterosexual women to be in a relationship with a partner who works less than full-time and can help with household tasks. But also differences in spouses' market work cannot explain the lesbian wage premium. Only experience weights differently for lesbians, which may confirm that they invest more in on-the-job training during that time (Jespen, 2007).
11. Note that the other half did not provide any information about volunteer activities. This could actually be considered a negative signal as these applicants are less socially engaged. For the experiment this means that discrimination may be understated. However, if the local 'Gay People's Alliance' was a very political group, differences in treatment may also be driven by a distaste against political activism.
12. This suggests that masculinity in women, that is, gender nonconformity, does not necessarily lead to heightened discrimination, at least as long as this physical masculinity fits mainstream ideals of beauty. However, it also does not seem to improve labor market outcomes.
13. Respective results are not presented in the study for lesbians.
14. In their study on discrimination against migrants in Germany, Kaas and Manger (2012) have shown that it is the small firms (<50 employees) that discriminate the most.
15. In a small pretest, they confirmed that the saying 'Gay and Proud' was rated negatively while 'Texan and Proud' was rated neutrally. This suggests that the control group should not evoke effects, like local patriotism, in its own. However, given the relatively small sample size of the pretest, this cannot be totally ruled out.
16. This increased negativity was also confirmed by separate raters who assessed the taped conversations.
17. Of course, with this design it can be argued that discrimination may simply be directed against people wearing T-shirts with any political slogan.
18. I thank Sandra Stoll for pointing this out. An overview of the history of queer and feminist squatting in Germany can be found in amantine (2011).
19. As studied by economists, the relative effect of anti-discrimination law is yet unclear (Klawitter and Flatt, 1998; Gates, 2003; Leppel, 2008).

REFERENCES

Adam, Barry D. (1981), 'Stigma and employability: discrimination by sex and sexual orientation in the Ontario legal profession', *Canadian Review of Sociology and Anthropology*, **18**(2), 216–21.

Ahmed, Ali and Mats Hammarstedt (2009), 'Detecting discrimination against homosexuals: evidence from a field experiment on the Internet', *Economica*, **76**(303), 588–97.

Ahmed, Ali and Mats Hammarstedt (2010), 'Sexual orientation and earnings: a register data-based approach to identify homosexuals', *Journal of Population Economics*, **23**(3), 835–49.

Ahmed, Ali, Linda Andersson and Mats Hammarstedt (2008), 'Are lesbians discriminated in the rental housing market? Evidence from a correspondence testing experiment', *Journal of Housing Economics*, **17**(3), 234–38.

Ahmed, Ali, Lina Andersson and Mats Hammarstedt (2011a), 'Inter- and intra-household earnings differentials among homosexual and heterosexual couples', *British Journal of Industrial Relations*, **49**(S2), 258–78.

Ahmed, Ali, Lina Andersson and Mats Hammarstedt (2011b), 'Are gays and lesbians discriminated against in the hiring situation?', IFAU Working Paper 21, Uppsala.

Allegretto, Sylvia A. and Michelle M. Arthur (2001), 'An empirical analysis of homosexual/heterosexual male earnings differentials: unmarried and unequal?', *Industrial and Labor Relations Review*, **54**(3), 631–46.

amantine (2011), *Gender und Häuserkampf*, Münster: Unrast-Verlag.

Antecol, Heather and Michael D. Steinberger (2013), 'Female labor supply differences by sexual orientation: a semi-parametric decomposition approach', *Economic Inquiry*, **51**(1),783–805.

Antecol, Heather, Anneke Jong and Michael D. Steinberger (2008), 'The sexual orientation wage gap: the role of occupational sorting and human capital', *Industrial and Labor Relations Review*, **61**(4), 518–43.

Arabsheibani, G. Reza, Alan Marin and Jonathan Wadsworth (2004), 'In the pink: homosexual–heterosexual wage differentials in the UK', *International Journal of Manpower*, **25**(3/4), 343–54.

Arabsheibani, G. Reza, Alan Marin and Jonathan Wadworth (2005), 'Gay pay in the UK', *Economica*, **72**(286), 333–47.

Arrow, Kenneth (1973), 'The theory of discrimination', in Orley Ashenfelter and Albert Rees (eds), *Discrimination in Labor Markets*, Princeton, NJ: Princeton University Press, pp. 3–33.

Avery, Alison, Justin Chase, Linda Johansson, Samantha Litvak, Darrel Montero and Michael Wydra (2007), 'America's changing attitudes toward homosexuality, civil unions, and same-gender marriage: 1977–2004', *Social Work*, **52**(1), 71–9.

Badgett, M.V. Lee (1995), 'The wage effects of sexual orientation discrimination', *Industrial and Labor Relations Review*, **48**(4), 726–39.

Badgett, M.V. Lee (2001), *Money, Myths, and Change: The Economic Lives of Lesbians and Gay Men*, Chicago, IL and London: University of Chicago Press.

Badgett, M.V. Lee (2007), 'Discrimination based on sexual orientation. a review of the literature in economics and beyond', in M.V. Lee Badgett and Jefferson Frank (eds), *Sexual Orientation Discrimination: An International Perspective*, London: Routledge, pp. 19–43.

Badgett, M.V. Lee, Holning Lau, Brad Sears and Deborah Ho (2007), 'Bias in the workplace: consistent evidence of sexual orientation and gender identity discrimination', Discussion Paper, UCLA School of Law, Williams Institute, Los Angeles, CA.

Bailey, John, Michael Wallace and Bradley R.E. Wright (2011), 'Are gay men and lesbians discriminated against when applying for jobs? A four-city, internet-based field experiment', University of Michigan Working Paper, Ann Arbor, MI.

Baumle, Amanda K. (2009), 'The cost of parenthood: unraveling the effects of sexual orientation and gender on income', *Social Science Quarterly*, **90**(4), 983–1002.

Becker, Gary S. (1971), *The Economics of Discrimination*, Chicago, IL and London: University of Chicago Press.

Becker, Gary S. (1991), *Treatise on the Family*, Cambridge, MA: Harvard University Press.

Berg, Nathan and Donald Lien (2002), 'Measuring the effect of sexual orientation on income: evidence of discrimination?', *Contemporary Economic Policy*, **20**(4), 394–414.

Bertrand, Marianne and Sendhil Mullainathan (2004), 'Are Emily and Greg more employable than Lakisha and Jamal? A field experiment on labor market discrimination', *American Economic Review*, **94**(4), 991–1013.

Black, Dan A., Seth G. Sanders and Lowell J. Taylor (2007), 'The economics of lesbian and gay families', *Journal of Economic Perspectives*, **21**(2), 53–70.

Black, Dan A., Hoda R. Makar, Seth G. Sanders and Lowell J. Taylor (2003), 'The earnings effects of sexual orientation', *Industrial and Labor Relations Review*, **56**(3), 449–69.

Blandford, John M. (2003), 'The nexus of sexual orientation and gender in the determination of earnings', *Industrial and Labor Relations Review*, **56**(4), 622–42.

Carpenter, Christopher S. (2005), 'Self-reported sexual orientation and earnings: evidence from California', *Industrial and Labor Relations Review*, **58**(2), 258–73.

Carpenter, Christopher S. (2007), 'Revisiting the income penalty for behaviorally gay men: evidence from NHANES III', *Labour Economics*, **14**(1), 25–34.

Carpenter, Christopher S. (2008a), 'Sexual orientation, work, and income in Canada', *Canadian Journal of Economics*, **41**(4), 1239–61.

Carpenter, Christopher S. (2008b), 'Sexual orientation, income, and non-pecuniary economic outcomes: new evidence from young lesbians in Australia', *Review of Economics of the Household*, **6**(4), 391–408.

Clain, Suzanne Heller and Karen Leppel (2001), 'An investigation into sexual orientation discrimination as an explanation for wage differences', *Applied Economics*, **33**(1), 37–47.

Crow, Stephen M., Lillian Y. Fok and Sandra J. Hartman (1998), 'Who is at greatest risk of work-related discrimination – women, blacks, or homosexuals?', *Employee Responsibilities and Rights Journal*, **11**(1), 15–26.

Cushing-Daniels, Brendan and Tsz-Ying Yeung (2009), 'Wage penalties and sexual orientation: an update using the general social survey', *Contemporary Economic Policy*, **27**(2), 164–75.

Daniel, William W. (1968), *Racial Discrimination in England*, Hormondsworth, UK: Penguin Books.

De Schutter, Olivier (2008), *Homophobia and discrimination on grounds of sexual orientation in the EU Member States. Part I – Legal analysis*, Vienna: European Union Agency for Fundamental Rights.

Drydakis, Nick (2009), 'Sexual orientation discrimination in the labour market', *Labour Economics*, **16**(4), 364–72.

Drydakis, Nick (2011), 'Women's sexual orientation and labor market outcomes in Greece', *Feminist Economics*, **17**(1), 89–117.

Eagly, Alice H. and Maureen Crowley (1986), 'Gender and helping behavior: a meta-analytic review of the social psychological literature', *Psychological Bulletin*, **100**(3), 283–308.

Ellis, Jason and Pauline Fox (2001), 'The effect of self-identified sexual orientation on helping behavior in a British sample: are lesbians and gay men treated differently?', *Journal of Applied Social Psychology*, **31**(6), 1238–47.

Elsmslie, Bruce and Edinaldo Tebaldi (2007), 'Sexual orientation and labor market discrimination', *Journal of Labor Research*, **28**(3), 436–53.

Fidell, Linda S. (1970), 'Empirical verification of sex discrimination in hiring practices in psychology', *American Psychologist*, **25**(12), 1094–8.

Firth, Michael (1981), 'Racial discrimination in the British labour market', *Industrial and Labor Relations Review*, **34**(2), 265–72.

Fix, Michael and Raymond J. Struyk (eds) (1993), *Clear and Convincing Evidence: Measurement of Discrimination in America*, Washington, DC: The Urban Institute.

Gabriel, Ute and Rainer Banse (2006), 'Helping behavior as a subtle measure of discrimination against lesbians and gay men: German data and a comparison across countries', *Journal of Applied Social Psychology*, **36**(3), 690–707.

Gallup Organization (2010), 'Americans' acceptance of gay relations crosses 50% threshold', available at: http://www.gallup.com/poll/135764/americans-acceptance-gay-relations-crosses-threshold.aspx (accessed November 30, 2011).

Gates, Gary (2003), 'Workplace protection linked to higher earnings for less educated gay men, available at: http://www.urban.org/publications/900632.html (accessed December 18, 2011).

Hebl, Michelle R., Jessica B. Foster, Laura M. Mannix and John F. Dovidio (2002), 'Formal and interpersonal discrimination: a field study of bias toward homosexual applicants', *Personality and Social Psychology Bulletin*, **28**(6), 815–25.

Heckman, James (1998), 'Detecting discrimination', *Journal of Economic Perspectives*, **12**(2), 101–16.

Heckman, James and Peter Siegelman (1993), 'The Urban Institute audit studies: their methods and findings', in Fix and Struyk (eds.), pp. 271–5.

Hendren, Amy and Hartmut Blank (2009), 'Prejudiced behavior toward lesbians and gay men: a field experiment on everyday helping', *Social Psychology*, **40**(4), 234–8.

Herek, Gregory M. (2002), 'Gender gaps in public opinion about lesbians and gay men', *Public Opinion Quarterly*, **66**(1), 40–66.

Horvath, Michael and Ann Marie Ryan (2003), 'Antecedents and potential moderators of the relationship between attitudes and hiring discrimination on the basis of sexual orientation', *Sex Roles*, **48**(3/4), 115–30.

Jepsen, Lisa K. (2007), 'Comparing the earnings of cohabiting lesbians, cohabiting heterosexual women, and married women: evidence from the 2000 census', *Industrial Relations*, **46**(4), 699–727.

Jones, David A. (1996), 'Discrimination against same-sex couples in hotel reservation policies', *Journal of Homosexuality*, **31**(1–2), 153–9.

Jowell, Roger, and Patricia Prescott-Clarke (1970), 'Racial discrimination and whitecollar workers in Britain', *Race*, **11**(4), 397–417.

Kaas, Leo and Christian Manger (2012), 'Ethnic discrimination in Germany's labour market: a field experiment', *German Economic Review*, **13**(1), 1–20.

Kite, Mary E. and Kay Deaux (1987), 'Gender belief systems: homosexuality and the implicit inversion theory', *Psychology of Women Quarterly*, **11**(1), 83–96.

Kite, Mary E. and Bernard E. Whitley (1996), 'Sex differences in attitudes toward homosexual persons, behaviors, and civil rights: a meta-analysis', *Personality and Social Psychology Bulletin*, **22**(4), 336–53.

Klawitter, Marieka (1998), 'Why aren't more economists doing research on sexual orientation?', *Feminist Economics*, **4**(2), 55–9.

Klawitter, Marieka M. and Victor Flatt (1998), 'The effects of state and local antidiscrimination policies on earnings for gays and lesbians', *Journal of Policy Analysis and Management*, **17**(4), 658–86.

LaMar, Lisa and Mary E. Kite (1998), 'Sex differences in attitudes toward gay men and lesbians: a multidimensional perspective', *Journal of Sex Research*, **35**(2), 189–96.

Leppel, Karen (2008), 'Labour force status and sexual orientation', *Economica*, **76**(301), 197–207.

Levinson, Richard (1975), 'Sex discrimination and employment practices: an experiment with unconventional job inquiries', *Social Problems*, **22**(4), 533–43.

Loftus, Jeni (2001), 'America's liberalization in attitudes toward homosexuality, 1973 to 1998', *American Sociological Review*, **66**(5), 762–82.

Neumark, David, Roy J. Bank and Kyle D. Van Nort (1996), 'Sex discrimination in restaurant hiring: an audit study', *Quarterly Journal of Economics*, **111**(3), 915–41.

Page, Stewart (1998), 'Accepting the gay person: rental accommodation in the community', *Journal of Homosexuality*, **36**(2), 31–9.

Phelps, Edmund S. (1972), 'The statistical theory of racism and sexism', *American Economic Review*, **62**(4), 659–61.

Plug, Erik and Peter Berkhout (2004), 'Effects of sexual preferences on earnings in the Netherlands', *Journal of Population Economics*, **17**(1), 117–31.

Riach, Peter A. and Judith Rich (1991), 'Testing for racial discrimination in the labor market', *Cambridge Journal of Economics*, **15**(3), 239–59.

Riach, Peter A. and Judith Rich (2002), 'Field experiments of discrimination in the market place', *Economic Journal*, **112**(483), F480–F518.

Tebaldi, Edinaldo and Bruce Elmslie (2006), 'Sexual orientation and labour supply', *Applied Economics*, **38**(5), 549–62.
Van Hoye, Greet and Filip Lievens (2003), 'The effects of sexual orientation on hireability ratings: an experimental study', *Journal of Business and Psychology*, **18**(1), 15–30.
Walters, Andrew S. and Maria-Cristina Curran (1996), 'Excuse me, sir? May I help you and your boyfriend? Salespersons' differential treatment of homosexual and straight customers', *Journal of Homosexuality*, **31**(1–2), 135–52.
Weichselbaumer, Doris (2003), 'Sexual orientation discrimination in hiring', *Labour Economics*, **10**(6), 629–42.
Weichselbaumer, Doris (2004), 'Is it sex or personality? The impact of sex-stereotypes on discrimination in applicant selection', *Eastern Economic Journal*, **30**(2), 159–86.
Weichselbaumer, Doris and Rudolf Winter-Ebmer (2006), 'Rhetoric in economic research: the case of gender wage differentials', *Industrial Relations*, **45**(3), 416–36.
Whitley, Bernard E. (1988), 'Sex differences in heterosexuals' attitudes toward homosexuals: it depends upon what you ask', *Journal of Sex Research*, **24**(1–4), 287–91.
Yinger, John (1986), 'Measuring racial discrimination with fair housing audits: caught in the act', *American Economic Review*, **76**(5), 881–93.

PART IV

EMPLOYMENT POLICIES

16. Low-wage mothers on the edge in the US
Randy Albelda

I INTRODUCTION

A defining aspect of the study of gender in economic life is the exploration of the ways women's earnings and paid work opportunities have been circumscribed by the economic and social conventions surrounding their caregiving roles.[1] A key consistent empirical finding is that when the quintessential caregivers – mothers – do paid work, they work fewer hours and earn lower wages, even when adjusting for hours worked, than men and other women (see Budig and England, 2001; Anderson et al., 2003; Sigle-Rushton and Waldfogel, 2007). Mothers in low-wage work face the highest wage penalties (Budig and Hodges, 2010).

The role of mothers as caregivers and its counterpart of fathers as breadwinners have also shaped key US social protection policies, the set of programs that minimize any individual's risk associated with the loss of earnings income (Nelson, 1990; Orloff, 1993; Fraser, 1994; Lewis, 2002). In the United States, the 1930s brought key sets of federally legislated employment-based protections that included unemployment insurance and old-age and disability payments. The programs were developed to provide supplementary income to breadwinners (and by extension wives) when breadwinners' earnings are suspended (see Gordon, 1994). At the same time, a less generous and means-tested (income-based) anti-poverty policy emerged that targeted female caregivers without husbands. Both types of programs expanded through the early 1970s with employment-based policies mostly protecting workers in higher-paying, family-supporting jobs, while means-tested programs covered single mothers and others with little or no earnings.

Employment prospects and the low level of social protection make economic security for single-mother families particularly precarious. Historically, they have relied on a combination of a low level of earnings, kinship or community networks, and means-tested public supports (see Spalter-Roth et al., 1995; Edin and Lein, 1997). A changed political and policy terrain facing single mothers over the last three decades has not reduced their economic fragility much, but it has somewhat changed its form. Specifically, there are new presumptions about single mothers' wage-earning capacities as well as their use of public programs that have prompted the perceived desirability of employment, any employment, over receipt of cash assistance. This has resulted in a corresponding revamping of government support programs directed toward single mothers that promote or require employment, thereby establishing a new social compact between the government and single mothers.

However, this new compact has *not* been accompanied by much-needed reforms in the low-wage labor market, including extending employment-based social protection to these workers and establishing the sets of work–family policies that facilitate working parents. Further, because employment brings new costs and risks and because anti-poverty policies typically fail to cover low-wage workers, many employed single mothers are facing different types of resource dilemmas. Together, the new terrain requires rethinking the problems single-mother families face, the sets of resources they need, and the ways anti-poverty and employment policies might be reformed to better accommodate these changes. This chapter focuses on the economic situation of single mothers over the last 30 years, exploring the sets of dilemmas faced by low-income single mothers and arguing for a new social compact.

Section II provides an overview of the economic situation of single mothers over the last 30 years. Stepping back historically, Section III lays out the landscape of social policies in the US, especially for single-mother families beginning in the mid-1930s. The shift in these policies, in particular the move toward employment promotion, that comprise a new social compact is explored in Section IV, while Section V discusses the sets of dilemmas faced by low-income single mothers created by these changed policies. Section VI concludes by setting out directions for a new social compact that would improve the economic situation for low-wage single mothers.

II   ECONOMIC SITUATION OF SINGLE MOTHERS

When it comes to earnings, single mothers face what Albelda and Chris Tilly (1997) call a 'triple whammy'. First, as women they earn less than men. Second, as mothers they earn less than other women. Third, as single mothers they are both primary breadwinners and primary caregivers, limiting their employment capacities. Full-time breadwinning is typically not compatible with full-time caregiving; as such, single mothers have always found themselves in a bind.

Using data from the Annual Social and Economic (ASEC) Supplement of the Current Population Survey from March 1980 to 2010, Figures 16.1 and 16.2 provide some earnings and income trends for single and married mothers to illustrate the precarious economic position many single mothers face.[2] This includes the percentages of single

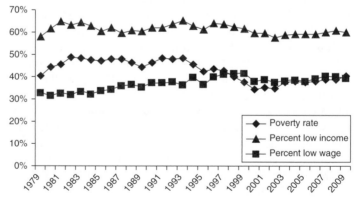

Source: Author's calculation using annual Social and Economic Supplement (ASEC) of the current population Survey, 1980–2010.

Figure 16.1   Single mothers' poverty rates, percent low income, percent low wage, 1979–2009

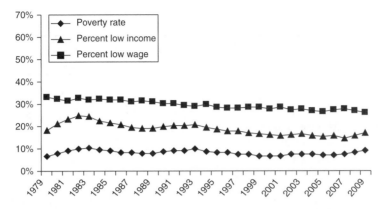

Source: Author's calculation using annual Social and Economic Supplement (ASEC) of the current population Survey, 1980–2010.

Figure 16.2   Married mothers' poverty rates, percent low income, percent low wage, 1979–2009

mothers who are poor, low income, and low wage. The percentage that is poor (the poverty rate) is the percent of all single (and married) mothers whose family income falls below poverty income thresholds defined by the Census Bureau. These levels were developed in the 1960s to measure how much income a family would need to meet very basic needs and as such, they differ by family size. Using 1950s budget data that assessed low-income families' needs and their spending patterns, the poverty income thresholds were originally based on the cost of a minimal food diet. These thresholds have been updated every year by increases in the cost of living as measured by the Consumer Price Index. While this measure has been criticized (see Citro and Michael, 1995; Blank, 2008), it has not been changed.[3]

In response to the inadequacy of the poverty thresholds to accurately measure minimal income needs, three different organizations calculate the actual cost of living for families of different sizes, ages of children, and area of the country. These 'family budgets' are based on average costs of housing, food, transportation, childcare (if needed), medical insurance, miscellaneous costs for necessities, and taxes (including refundable tax credits). All three organizations calculate these budgets for various regions within states.[4] While there is some small variation in levels of these budgets for any particular area, each of them find that the typical cost of living, especially for a single employed parent with children, is considerably higher than the federal poverty level. For example, each of the three organizations estimates the cost of living for a single parent and pre-schooler in the Jacksonville, Florida, area to be about $32,000 in 2007.[5] In that year the federal poverty income threshold for a family of two (one adult and one child) was $13,884 (US Bureau of the Census, 2011a).

Acknowledging that the Census Bureau's poverty definition does not do an adequate job at measuring the nation's poor, researchers, advocates, policy-makers and administrators increasingly have adopted the term 'low income' when talking about the populations that struggle to meet their needs. This term is typically defined as having family income below 200 percent of the poverty line. There is no agreed-upon definition of what

Table 16.1   Various definitions of low wage

Author (year)	Definition	Wage rate	Year applied	Percent workers low wage	Data used
Bernstein and Gittleman (2003)	2/3 median wage	$8.67	2001	22	National Compensation Survey
Schochet and Rangarajan (2004)	Hourly wage working 2080 hrs (YRFT) equal to the poverty line for family of four	$8.20	2000	25	1996 Panel of Survey of Income and Program Participation (SIPP)
Boushey et al. (2007)	2/3rd of male median wage	$11.11	2006	~33	Current Population Survey (CPS)
Acs and Nichols (2007)	150% of minimum wage	$7.73	2004	23	CPS
Gautié and Schmitt (2010)	2/3 median wage	(not provided)	2003–05	24	CPS (outgoing rotation)
Acs et al., (2010)	Hourly wage working 2080 hrs (YRFT) equal to the poverty line for family of four	$8.63	2001	25	2001 Panel of SIPP
Albelda and Carr 2011	2/3 state median wage	$11.06 (average across states)	2009	27	CPS

level of earnings constitutes low-wage work. Some authors (such as Acs et al., 2010) base it on the poverty income threshold level by determining the hourly wage it would require to earn poverty-level income for a family of four working full-time. But most analysts use a relative measure of wages, usually some portion of the median wage. Table 16.1 summarizes some recently used measures and estimates of the low-wage population. I also employ a relative wage measure, but to account for variation in regions and in minimum wage laws across the states I have calculated a low-wage-earner as receiving an hourly wage lower than two-thirds of state median hourly wages.[6]

As depicted in Figure 16.1, the percent of officially poor single mothers has fallen from just under 50 percent in the 1980s and first half of the 1990s to just under 40 percent in the 2000s. Figure 16.2 indicates that the poverty rate for married mothers is considerably lower, under 10 percent for most of the time period. And while the decline in poverty for single mothers represents an improvement, the percentage that is poor is still very high. Further, a majority of single mothers have been and are still low income – perhaps this is the better measure of being able to meet actual resource needs. Over the period, about three out of every five single mothers have a household income below 200 percent of the federal poverty line, compared to one out of every five married mothers. This percentage has not changed much over the last 20 years. Clearly, most single-mother families struggle to make ends meet.

Unlike the percentages of the poor and the low income, there is more similarity among the percentages of employed married mothers and single mothers who are low wage, though over time the trends diverge. The percentage of low-wage single mothers has slowly but steadily risen from 32 percent in the early 1980s to around 40 percent in the 2000s. In the late 1970s, the percent of married mothers who were low-wage was about 33 percent. That percentage has dropped slowly and steadily to 26 percent by 2009. And while the trends are opposite, substantial percentages of both types of mothers are in low-wage jobs. But, as evidenced by the vastly different poverty rates and percentage that are low income, the economic consequences of being low wage are very different for single mothers than they are for married mothers.

III   SINGLE MOTHERS AND THE TWO-TRACK SYSTEM OF SOCIAL PROTECTION

For many single mothers, means-tested public assistance, specifically government cash transfer programs and near-cash programs that help pay for housing, food, and medical care, have been an important lifeline. Typically men, often assumed to be breadwinners, have had access to social protections in the case of job loss through their employment status (see Nelson, 1990; Fraser, 1994). Specifically, the old-age, survivors, and disability insurance program (commonly referred to as Social Security) and unemployment insurance are based on employment history and were originally designed to cover jobs primarily held by white men (Gordon, 1994; Quadagno, 1994; Mettler, 1998). These programs are federally mandated and are paid for through payroll deductions (social insurance). Most women have had access to these programs through their status as wives of breadwinners.

While there is also a set of nonmandated (voluntary) employer-based benefits such as health insurance, retirement plans, and paid time off, low-wage jobs – the kind that many mothers and young workers tend to get – typically offer few or no voluntary employer benefits. For example, only 32 percent of workers at the bottom wage-earning quartile have access to paid sick leave, compared to 66 percent at the median (Gould et al., 2011). One estimate finds that 26 percent of all male workers and 32 percent of all female workers in the United States in 2006 make less than $17 per hour and have neither employer-sponsored health insurance nor a retirement plan (Schmitt, 2007).

Social protections for the long-term unemployed and those out of the workforce (or only tangentially tied to it) differ substantially from those for breadwinners just described. These low-income individuals may qualify for a set of federal-supported means-tested (income-based) programs. Historically, several government assistance programs were developed specifically to assist poor single-mother families (as well as the disabled and elders), recognizing that these families would not be able to support themselves through earnings or family networks. Many programs were enacted at a time when mothers – in particular white, native-born mothers – were not expected to be employed (Albelda, 2011). Especially important as a source of support for poor single mothers was the federal cash assistance program established in 1935, called Aid to Families with Children (which became Aid to Families with Dependent Children – AFDC – in 1962). But other programs have also been important to single mothers. These include Food Stamps (established in 1964, currently called Supplemental Nutritional Assistance Program – SNAP), the health insurance program Medicaid established in 1965, and housing assistance programs such as public housing (established in 1937) and the Section 8 Rental Assistance program established in 1974 (Albelda and Boushey, 2007).[7]

And as essential as these support programs were for single mothers, even before major changes to AFDC in the 1980s and 1990s, they were also fraught with problems. AFDC benefit levels were originally set low to discourage use (Gordon, 1994) and have remained very low.[8] AFDC eligibility rules initially discouraged marriage by only supporting one-parent families until the 1960s, and by keeping eligibility income levels so low that marrying even a marginally employed live-in boyfriend would boost family income to levels that might make one ineligible for assistance.[9] Food Stamp benefit levels were based on a very low-end diet that assumed food would be prepared from scratch (Mancino and Newman, 2007). Most important, AFDC, Food Stamps, and housing assistance provided disincentives for formal employment because benefits were reduced as reportable earnings increased. If receiving only a few of the benefits available, increased earnings could result in a large decrease in assistance; every dollar earned could and typically did result in a 66-cent reduction in AFDC, a 30-cent reduction in Food Stamps and a 33-cent reduction in housing assistance. Medicaid, AFDC, and Food Stamps disappeared altogether at income levels close to the federal poverty line. Finally, administrative requirements, including a great deal of face time at the welfare office, were time consuming, stigmatized, and often demeaning (see Edin and Lein, 1997; Dodson, 1998). But as undesirable as cash assistance was, the alternative of low-wage work coupled with finding appropriate care (including healthcare) for children was rarely much better until children were grown. Women without college degrees, then and now, find it hard to find a job with family-sustaining wages and health insurance.[10] But even for those with educational levels beyond a high school diploma, the constraints of taking care of young children make finding and keeping a good paying job difficult, as those types of jobs typically require a full-time commitment (Williams, 2001). As a result, some single mothers chose not to take long-term formal employment until children were old enough for them to find and keep steady employment, leaving most poor single mothers to package earnings and public supports and/or cycle from one to the other.

IV   WELFARE-TO-WORK: THE NEW SOCIAL COMPACT FOR SINGLE MOTHERS

The growth in married women's labor force participation, the decline in wage growth, and a misconceived understanding that AFDC served mostly unwed black mothers converged in the United States in the 1980s to help feed disdain for those receiving cash and other in-kind assistance.[11] There was increasing political pressure to overhaul and in some case dismantle the programs directed toward poor mothers, with the aim of moving them from welfare to paid work.[12] The Family Support Act of 1988 required states to implement work requirements, which could be fulfilled through education and training

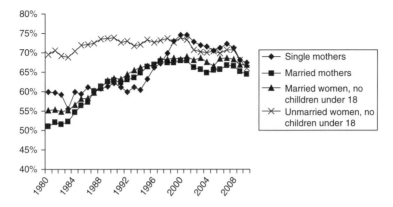

Source: Author's calculation using annual Social and Economic Supplement (ASEC) of the current population Survey, 1980–2010. Percent employed is the number of persons in each group ages 18–64 with employment in March of the survey year divided by total group population.

Figure 16.3   *Percent employed by marital status and presence of children for women ages 18–64, March 1980–March 2010*

programs, for mothers receiving AFDC. In the late 1980s and early 1990s, most states took advantage of federally provided waiver provisions to AFDC that allowed them to relinquish various legislative provisions; states experimented with different eligibility rules, doing this to make their programs more restrictive and to encourage employment. But the most significant changes to public support programs were ushered in with the Personal Responsibility and Work Opportunity Reconciliation Act (PRWORA) of 1996; this abolished the cash assistance program AFDC, replacing it with the Temporary Assistance to Needy Families (TANF) block grant and making significant changes to the Food Stamps program. These legislative efforts heavily discouraged receipt of cash supports and Food Stamps while employment was strongly promoted and often required. Political conservatives also persisted in including marriage-promotion language and provisions in the bill.

Recognizing that employment mandates would place many mothers into the low-wage labor market, some federal and state policies to help enable low-wage employment were expanded or created. By the mid-1990s, the minimum wage was increased, the refundable Earned Income Tax Credit (EITC) had expanded substantially, the State Child Health Insurance Program (SCHIP) was created, and funding for childcare had increased (Greenberg and Lower-Basch, 2008). Presumably a new social compact – the implicit relationship between government and single mothers – was drawn. Cash assistance would become a temporary and time-limited support for single mothers, while marriage and/or earnings would be the primary source of income. Government assistance programs would act as work supports until employment made single mothers self-sufficient.

By and large, single mothers lived up to their end of the compact. After passage of PRWORA, employment of single mothers rose dramatically. Figure 16.3 depicts the employment rates (number employed divided by the population) of single and married women ages 18–64, with and without children, over the 31-year period spanning from 1980 to 2010. The employment rates of married women with and without children under age 18 follow a similar pattern, rising steadily over the period from 51 percent for those with children and 55 percent for those without in 1980. Married women's employment rates peak in 2001 (at 68 percent for mothers with children under age 18 and 69 percent for those without children under age 18).

Rates fell slightly in the current recession to just over 64 percent for married mothers and 67 percent for married women without children. Unmarried women without children had consistently high employment rates of between 70 and 75 percent, until the recent recession when employment rates fell to 66 percent in 2010. Single mothers' employment starts out at 60 percent in 1980 (higher than married women's employment rates) and hovers at that level until the mid-1990s, when the rates jump almost 15 percentage points to just under 75 percent in 2001. Like other women, single mothers' employment rates decreased to 67 percent in 2010, but are currently equal to the employment rates of other single women and surpass those of married women (with and without children). As employment rates were increasing, the percentage of single mothers who were in low-wage work reached 40 percent (from Figure 16.1). Poverty rates did fall until the recession in the early 2000s, but the percent of single mothers who are low income stays persistently high.

V   LOW-WAGE WORK AND EMPLOYMENT SUPPORTS

Despite the increase in single mothers' employment, it is less clear that employers and the government have lived up to the other end of the compact by providing employed single mothers with the sets of wages, employment supports and time that allow them to adequately care for their families. The low-wage labor market has always been and remains a particularly bad fit for single mothers (Albelda, 2001). Low levels of pay and few employer benefits are at direct odds with single mothers' resource needs. But it is more than inadequate pay and benefits that make this a mismatch. Low-wage work often tends to provide employees with less scheduling flexibility than higher-waged work (Henly and Lambert 2005; McCrate, Chapter 17, this volume). Low-wage workers typically need to report to work at specific hours almost always determined by the employer. Attending a teacher meeting or doctor's appointment or taking care of minor emergencies (such as a missed school bus or picking up a sick child from school) requires a special arrangement with an employer, often resulting in missed work time. This can jeopardize work relations with employers and coworkers and result in docked pay. When work hours are not the same every week, as is often the case with retail and some service work, planning childcare arrangements becomes extremely difficult (Henly et al., 2006)

A paper summarizing findings from states that conducted federally funded research on those leaving welfare found that only half of those who secured employment were in jobs with employer-sponsored health insurance and no more than half had paid leave or employer-sponsored retirement plans (Acs and Loprest, 2001). In March of 2010, 53 percent of all employed single mothers indicated that they had employer-provided health insurance and 47 percent had an employer that sponsored a retirement plan, compared to 27 percent of all low-wage single mothers with employer-sponsored healthcare and 29 percent with an employer offering a retirement plan (author's calculations using the ASEC Supplement of the Current Population Survey).

While the dilemmas just described have always existed for single mothers, employment-promotion policies have reduced the option of suspending employment and exacerbated another less-explored dilemma: low-wage single mothers face a mismatch between low-wage employment and receipt of public supports. Many means-tested programs, despite the new sets of provisions to promote employment, do not support employment in at least three important ways. First, several of the programs are still administered as they were before employment promotion – ironically, as if the recipients were not working at jobs for long hours – by assuming that recipients have unlimited time to get and keep the supports. Low-income employed single mothers have always faced difficult tradeoffs in juggling time spent caring for their children versus time spent in the labor markets. But now they also must juggle the time it takes to apply for and keep public supports. Most of the programs available to poor and low-income single mothers are administered by state or local agencies, but often different ones. Each program has its own eligibility rules. This includes how income is defined, level of income to be eligible, costs that are deducted from eligibility, asset limits, immigrant status, and employment requirements.

Finally, each program typically has different documentation and reporting requirements. While states are moving toward more online information (including eligibility screening) about programs as well as electronic application processes, it is still difficult to determine if one is eligible (and for how much) and many states still require face-to-face visits. As of 2011, 19 states did not allow online application from SNAP, 25 did not have them for TANF, and 36 did not use online applications for childcare assistance (Center for Budget and Policy Priorities, 2011). Only 11 states have online eligibility screeners for all five major programs (SNAP, TANF, Medicaid, SCHIP, and childcare), while only 20 states allow recipients to update their information or complete renewal forms online (Center for Budget and Policy Priorities, 2011).[13] In addition to the time and effort to collect materials to prove eligibility, many single mothers must make repeated face-to-face visits to various agencies that may only be open during the times mothers also work. In short, getting and keeping public work supports can be a full-time job. The problem, of course, is that most single mothers already have two full-time jobs: their paid employment and taking care of their children.

Second, many programs phase out or stop at earnings levels that are far below what is required to make ends meet. The major support programs that poor single mothers have historically used were reformed to promote employment, but they were not reformed to support the type of employment many single mothers get. Income eligibility levels are as low (and in some cases lower) now as they were in the mid-1990s. In 2010, all the states set their income eligibility level for TANF below the federal poverty level (ibid.). Medicaid income eligibility for an employed parent varies from 17 percent of the federal poverty level in Arkansas to 215 percent in Minnesota, with 27 states setting the eligibility level at less than 75 percent of the poverty line in 2011 (Kaiser Family Foundation, 2011). To be eligible to receive any amount of Food Stamps, gross income must be below 130 percent of the federal poverty income threshold. TANF, Food Stamps, and housing assistance continue to phase out steeply as earnings increase.[14] Those who are able to get childcare assistance find that even at low levels of earnings they must make co-payments which then rise steeply with increased earnings. These high 'marginal tax rates' actually create work disincentives, especially for those whose income is between 100 and 200 percent of the federal poverty line (Albelda and Boushey, 2007; Holt and Romich, 2007).

Third, other key programs that facilitate employment, specifically childcare, are severely underfunded, leaving many single mothers eligible but unable to access them. With formal employment comes more income but also new needs and costs, such as transportation, clothing, and out-of-home food. Perhaps the most pressing need is to make sure children are safe and properly cared for when at work. All employed parents must make arrangements for getting children to and from childcare and school, but for a single parent with very limited income, this is difficult at best. And while PRWORA guarantees childcare funding for those leaving TANF (financed with TANF funds and Child Care Development Block Grants), because there has been a steep decline in the number of low-income mothers using TANF,[15] this means that fewer people are guaranteed these funds. Yet the demand for these funds is high and despite increases in funding since 1996, there is not enough to meet the need. Less than one-third (29 percent) of all eligible children and 40 percent of poor eligible children in 2005 were served by these funds (US Department of Health and Human Services, 2008b). Even with the expansion of new supports such as EITC and SCHIP, these are not always substitutes for public supports lost. The EITC (which is administratively much simpler and less stigmatized than other forms of support) is almost always taken as a 'lump-sum' payment, contributing little to ongoing expenses. And while covering children's health insurance is an important first step to universal coverage, it has not been accompanied by an expansion in coverage for adults.

The new employment promotion rules layered on the old anti-poverty programs have meant that employed, low-wage single parents still need public supports to get by but many just do not get them (Albelda and Boushey, 2007). While single mothers currently have little choice but to be breadwinners, they end up slipping between the cracks of employment-based social protections and means-tested program supports.

VI   WHAT'S TO BE DONE: DIRECTIONS FOR A NEW SOCIAL COMPACT

The 'safety net' for low-income mothers has changed rather significantly over the last several decades, as have our understanding and expectations of mothers' employment. However, single mothers face a low-wage labor market that shows little improvement in the employment opportunities for women without high levels of educational attainment. The difficulties associated with juggling employment and caring for children have changed little, while the sets of work supports intended to make this easier have not materialized. If anything, employment promotion has meant that low-income single mothers have less time for their families. This has taken place within a larger context of continued stagnation in wage levels at the bottom of the earnings distribution and a general decline in the provision of employer benefits (Gottschalk and Danziger, 2005; Bernhardt et al., 2008). The confluence of these trends has created enormous challenges for all families, but in particular for single-mother families and their advocates. The good news is that these challenges also create opportunities for shifting the debate by calling attention to some new contradictions that these dilemmas have generated. The interlocking relationship between mothers' time, earnings and employer benefits, and work supports paired with the shifting ground in mothers' employment and public supports suggests several directions for researchers and advocates.

We are only beginning to become aware of the nature of the intersection between the public supports available and the various means of accessing them and sustaining low-wage employment. Low-income mothers and the groups that serve them seem to be ahead of the researchers and policy-makers on these new sets of issues. Scholars are finding that even as single mothers gain employment and increase earnings, even over sustained periods of time, it has not necessarily meant economic security. Recent research is also revealing the link between low-wage work and poor educational and health outcomes for children (Johnson et al., 2010). This contradiction in some ways puts single mothers in the forefront in confronting this century's challenge that inequality and low-wage work have created: how to assure that all families have sufficient earnings and employer benefits, adequate time to care for themselves and their families, and the sets of public supports to meet their basic needs.

There are clearly a large number of single mothers that are in jobs without the earnings or employer-provided benefits that assure a sustainable living, and means-tested supports are not filling that gap. And it is not only single mothers who have that problem. Albelda and Boushey (2007) estimate that one in five persons in families with an earner cannot meet typical budget needs, even when including the sets of public supports they might receive. Repairing that gap promises to be very difficult in the face of political tides pushing for less government spending and emboldened employers (including state and local governments) that continue to retract employer-based supports. Still, there is a pressing need to improve earnings and employer supports for the bottom half of all workers and the role of government supports for those with limited income and earnings capacity can and should continue. The costs of not doing so are high and long-lasting.

What would help? It is clear that the United States needs to rethink its sets of social protection to include universal support for affordable healthcare coverage for all, quality early education and care programs, and nationally mandated employment standards for paid leave policies. Most industrialized countries have these (or at least most of these) so providing social protections will not reduce international competitiveness and might improve it, depending on how the programs are financed. While these programs do cost money, not providing is also costly, especially for communities and families in which workers lacking these supports live, but there are spillover costs associated with low-wage work and inequality for employers and the nation (see Wilkinson and Pickett, 2009).

The problems associated with low-wage work are as old as wage labor itself, but the configuration of families and expectations about who can and should work has changed. This complicates the ways in which workers, workers' organizations, governments, and employers might shape a set of policies to assure economic security. Only about half (51 percent) of all adults in the US in 2010 were married heads (or spouses) of households, while 32 percent were single adults (with and without children under 18), with the remainder living with other family members.[16] The prototypical married couple family is no longer typical. But our employment structure, childcare arrangements, and social protection system were built on a foundation of a married couple family with one (or even 1.5) employed adult. Rebuilding to take into account the varied household arrangements will be hard, but makes sense in light of the way we live. Proposals have surfaced over the last several decades to do just that. These include implementing a shorter work week (for example, 32 hours) to better accommodate family care; mandating employer benefits such as paid time off and retirement plans for all workers so as to re-secure social protection to employment; increasing minimum wages to assure a wage floor that can support at least a single worker; and expanding the safety net of means-tested benefits (for example, more funding plus higher eligibility thresholds that phase out more slowly). These all deserve attention and promotion but given the severe cost constraints all countries now face, it may make sense to research how they affect family types differently, and begin to target policies to specific populations.

While achieving a new social contract will be challenging, here are four ways to start framing the debate. First, there is a pressing moral argument to be made. If you 'play by the rules' by getting a job but are never quite able to succeed in garnering enough resources to adequately support a family, then the game is unfair. Second, the problem is structural, not the result of individual irresponsibility. The inability of so many families to meet their needs draws attention away from the supply side of the equation (the characteristics of individual workers, behavior of individual employers) and focuses it more on the demand side (the structure of employment and the public work support system as well as the absence of universal policies). The inability of employed single mothers to make ends meet demands a look at the rules of the game or the game itself, rather than the players. Third, a key discussion is what it takes to meet basic needs and how we best measure that. This calls attention to the outdated and inaccurate poverty income thresholds (or multiples of them) currently used as well as the fragmented and outdated sets of public support programs, that while necessary and useful, need to be totally restructured to reflect the fact that most parents are employed and do not have plentiful amounts of time to get and keep these supports. Finally, we should place responsibility on *all* major actors – workers, employers, and the public sector – and engage each in finding solutions.

Although this chapter assesses the challenges facing single mothers in the US, it has broader application. Other countries have been facing similar issues for single mothers, seeking labor activation policies that promote employment over socially provided benefits. Further, developed and developing nations rely extensively on labor markets to enable citizens to provision for themselves. In light of the recent global downturn, attention to both labor market regulations and social welfare policies will be increasingly important for mothers, children, and families across the globe. The United States' labor market structure and a relatively new welfare policy regime have managed to keep single mothers on the economic edge. It should serve as an important lesson for some things that policy-makers in other countries might want to avoid.

NOTES

1. Feminist economists have written extensively on this. For US-focused book-length historical treatments see Folbre (1994), Amott and Matthaei (1999) and Figart et al. (2002).
2. These extracts of the ASEC March supplement (with comparable variable definitions across all 31 years) were developed and made available by the Center for Economic Policy Research at www.ceprdata.org/cps.
3. Key criticisms include that thresholds are not adjusted for regional differences in cost of living or for families with employed members (whose costs are typically higher than those without any employed members); noncash income and taxes paid or tax credit received are not counted; and the budget data used are deeply outdated and flawed.
4. These include Economic Policy Institute's (2011) Basic Family Budget Calculator for all 50 states (614

areas) (data can be downloaded at http://www.epi.org/page/-/old/datazone/fambud/xls/epi_basic_family_budgets_rev200807b.xls); the National Center for Children in Poverty's (2011) Basic Needs Budget Calculator developed for various areas in 19 states; and Wider Opportunities for Women's (2010) Basic Economic Security budget developed for the entire US as well as various states and regions in states (data can be downloaded at http://www.wowonline.org/documents/USBESTAllFamiliesTables.xls).

5. Economic Policy Institute (2011) estimates the cost at $31,953; National Center for Children in Poverty (2011) estimates it to be $33,820, while the Wider Opportunity for Women (2007) estimate is $32,207.

6. Self-employed workers are not included in the calculations for low-wage workers as I am largely concerned with workers who are in more formal employment relationships. Self-employed workers represent 5.8 percent of all married mothers and 4.3 percent of single mothers with earnings in 2009. Annual hours worked are calculated by weeks worked last year multiplied by usual hours worked last year. Hourly wages are then determined by dividing annual earnings by annual hours. The typical hourly wage is of most interest here, so this measure works well even though weekly hours worked can vary considerably for some workers.

7. The refundable Earned Income Tax Credit, established in 1975, provided only a small amount of assistance until the mid-1990s. Similarly, small amounts of federal childcare assistance have been available since the 1930s, but are sorely underfunded and have been guaranteed only for those leaving AFDC for employment beginning in 1988 (Page and Larner, 1997).

8. For example, in 1996 on the eve of major federal changes to the program, the maximum monthly benefit for a family of three ranged from $120 in Mississippi to $923 in Alaska, with a mean of $397 and median payment of $377 (Schott and Finch, 2010, Appendix 1). In comparison, the annual federal poverty income threshold for a family of three in 1996 was $12,641, or $1,053 a month (US Bureau of the Census, 2011b).

9. A review of 1970s and 1980s research on family structure and receipt of AFDC mostly indicates this to be true (Moffitt, 1992).

10. The Economic Policy Institute (2010, Table 3.17) reports that women with a high school diploma had an inflation adjusted (in 2007 dollars) mean real hourly wage of around $12.00 an hour in the 1970s and 1980s. Through the 2000s it was about $13.00 an hour.

11. See, for example, authors in edited volumes by Albelda and Withorn (2002) and Schram et al. (2003).

12. For a sample of the public discourse on poverty, poor families and government policies toward the poor at the time, see Albelda and Folbre (1996) and Mink and Solinger (2003).

13. A Report by the Pew Research Center (Smith, 2010) finds that 45 percent of adults in households with income less than $30,000 use broadband internet services; 78 percent of all adults use the internet (Pew Internet, 2011).

14. States vary in their TANF disregards (percentage of cash grant you keep for every dollar earned), but 50 percent is not uncommon (that is, for every additional $1 earned, you lose 50 cents of the grant). For every additional dollar earned, a family typically loses about 30–33 cents of Food Stamps and of housing assistance. It is possible, then, if getting all three supports, to actually have fewer resources when earning more.

15. In 1995, there were 13 million AFDC/TANF recipients, representing 36.4 percent of the poverty population; by 2006, there were 4.5 million recipients, representing 12.5 percent of the poverty population (US Department of Health and Human Services, 2008a, Table TANF 2).

16. Author's calculations using the 2010 ASEC Supplement of the Current Population Survey.

REFERENCES

Acs, Gregory and Pamela Loprest (2001), *Final Synthesis Report of Findings from ASPE's 'Leavers' Grants*, Washington, DC: The Urban Institute, available at: http://www.urban.org/UploadedPDF/410809_welfare_leavers_synthesis.pdf (accessed August 2011).

Acs, Gregory and Austin Nichols (2007), *Low-Income Workers and Their Employers: Characteristics and Challenges*, Washington, DC: The Urban Institute.

Acs, Gregory, Pamela Loprest and Caroline Ratcliffe (2010), *Progress toward Self-Sufficiency for Low-Wage Workers*, Washington, DC: The Urban Institute.

Albelda, Randy (2001), 'Welfare-to-work, farewell to families? US welfare reform and work/family debates', *Feminist Economics*, **7**(1), 119–35.

Albelda, Randy (2011), 'Time binds: US antipoverty policies, poverty, and the well-being of single mothers', *Feminist Economics*, **17**(4), 189–214.

Albelda, Randy and Heather Boushey (2007), *Bridging the Gaps: A Picture of How Work Supports Work in*

Ten States, Washington, DC: Center for Economic and Policy Research and Boston, MA: Center for Social Policy, University of Massachusetts Boston, available at: http://www.bridgingthegaps.org/publications/nationalreport.pdf (accessed August 2011).

Albelda, Randy and Michael Carr (2011), 'Low-wage and low-income workers in the US: 1979–2009', working paper, Economics Department, University of Massachusetts Boston, Boston, MA.

Albelda, Randy and Nancy Folbre (1996), *The War on the Poor: A Defense Manual*, New York: New Press.

Albelda, Randy and Chris Tilly (1997), *Glass Ceilings and Bottomless Pits: Women's Work, Women's Poverty*, Boston, MA: South End Press.

Albelda, Randy and Ann Withorn (eds) (2002), *Lost Ground: Welfare Reform, Poverty and Beyond*, Boston, MA: South End Press.

Amott, Teresa L. and Julie A. Matthaei (1999), *Race, Gender, and Work: A Multicultural Economic History of Women in the United States*, rev. edn, Boston, MA: South End Press.

Anderson, Deborah J., Melissa Binder and Kate Krause (2003), 'The motherhood wage penalty revisited: experience, heterogeneity, work effort and work-schedule flexibility', *Industrial and Labor Relations Review*, **56**(2), 273–94.

Bernhardt, Annette, Heather Boushey, Laura Dresser and Chris Tilly (2008), 'An introduction to the "gloves-off economy"', in Annette Bernhardt, Heather Boushey, Laura Dresser and Chris Tilly (eds), *The Gloves-Off Economy: Workplace Standards at the Bottom of America's Labor Market*, Champaign, IL: Labor and Employment Relations Series, pp. 1–30.

Bernstein, Jared and Maury Gittleman (2003), 'Exploring low-wage labor with the National Compensation Survey', *Monthly Labor Review*, **126**(November/December), 3–12.

Blank, Rebecca (2008), 'How to improve poverty measurement in the United States', *Journal of Policy Analysis and Management*, **27**(2), 233–54.

Boushey, Heather, Shawn Fremstad, Rachel Gregg and Margy Waller (2007), *Understanding Low-wage Work in the United States*, Washington, DC: The Mobility Agenda and Center for Economic and Policy Research, available at: http://www.inclusionist.org/files/lowwagework.pdf (accessed August 2011).

Budig, Michelle J. and Paula England (2001), 'The wage penalty for motherhood', *American Sociological Review*, **66**(2), 204–25.

Budig, Michelle J. and Melissa J. Hodges (2010), 'Differences in disadvantage: variation in the motherhood penalty across white women's earnings distribution', *American Sociological Review*, **75**(5), 705–28.

Center for Budget and Policy Priorities (2011), *Online Services for Key Low-Income Benefit Programs*, Washington, DC: Center for Budget and Policy Priorities, available at: http://www.cbpp.org/files/1–14–04tanf.pdf (accessed August 2011).

Citro, Connie and Robert T. Michael (eds) (1995), *Measuring Poverty: A New Approach*, Washington, DC: National Academy Press.

Dodson, Lisa (1998), *Don't Call Us Out of Name: The Untold Lives of Women and Girls in Poor America*, Boston, MA: Beacon Press.

Economic Policy Institute (2010), 'Women's real hourly wage by education, 1973–2007', in *State of Working America 2008–2009*, Washington, DC, available at: http://www.epi.org/page/-/datazone2008/wage%20comp%20trends/wagebyed–w.xls (accessed August 2011).

Economic Policy Institute (2011), 'Basic Family Budget Calculator: introduction, methodology and data download', Washington, DC, available at: http://www.epi.org/pages/budget–calculator–intro/ (accessed August 2011).

Edin, Kathryn and Laura Lein (1997), *Making Ends Meet: How Single Mothers Survive Welfare and Low-wage Work*, New York: Russell Sage Foundation.

Figart, Deborah M., Ellen Mutari and Marilyn Power (2002), *Living Wages, Equal Wages: Gender and Labor Market Policies in the United States*, London and New York: Routledge.

Folbre, Nancy (1994), *Who Pays for the Kids? Gender and the Structures of Constraint*, London and New York: Routledge.

Fraser, Nancy (1994), 'After the family wage: gender equity and the welfare state', *Political Theory*, **22**(4), 591–618.

Gautie, Jerome and John Schmitt (eds) (2010), *Low-wage Work in the Wealthy World*, New York: Russell Sage Foundation.

Gordon, Linda (1994), *Pitied But Not Entitled: Single Mothers and the History of Welfare Reform*, New York: Free Press.

Gottschalk, Peter and Sheldon Danziger (2005), 'Inequality of wage rates, earnings and family income in the United States, 1975–2002', *Review of Income and Wealth*, **51**(2), 231–54.

Gould, Elise, Kai Falion and Andrew Green (2011), 'The Need for Paid Sick Days: The Lack of a Federal Policy Further Erodes Family Economic Security', briefing paper 319, Economic Policy Institute, Washington, DC: available at: http://w3.epi-data.org/temp2011/BriefingPaper319–2.pdf (accessed August 2011).

Greenberg, Mark and Elizabeth Lower-Basch (2008), 'Single mothers in the era of welfare reform', in Annette

Bernhardt, Heather Boushey, Laura Dresser and Chris Tilly (eds), *The Gloves-Off Economy: Workplace Standards at the Bottom of America's Labor Market,* Champaign, IL: Labor and Employment Relations Series, pp. 163–90.

Henly, Julia R. and Susan Lambert (2005), 'Nonstandard work and child care needs of low-income parents', in Suzanne M. Bianchi, Lynne M. Casper and Rosalind King (eds), *Work, Family, Health, and Well-being,* Mahwah, NJ: Lawrence Erlbaum Associates, pp. 473–492.

Henly, Julia R., H. Luke Shaefer and Elaine Waxman (2006), 'Nonstandard work schedules: employer – and employee-driven flexibility in retail jobs', *Social Service Review* (December), 609–34.

Holt, Stephen D. and Jennifer L. Romich (2007), 'Marginal tax rates facing low – and moderate-income workers who participate in means-tested transfer programs', *National Tax Journal,* **60**(2), 253–76.

Johnson, Rucker C., Ariel Kalil and Rachel E. Dunifon, with Barbara Ray (2010), *Mothers' Work and Children's Lives,* Kalamazoo, MI: W.E. Upjohn Institute for Employment Research.

Kaiser Family Foundation (2011), 'Income Eligibility Limits for Working Adults at Application as a Percent of the Federal Poverty Level (FPL) by Scope of Benefit Package', January, available at: http://www.statehealthfacts.org/comparereport.jsp?rep=54&cat=4 (accessed August 2011).

Lewis, Jane (2002), 'Gender and welfare state change', *European Societies,* **4**(4), 331–57.

Mancino, Lisa and Constance Newman (2007), 'Who Has Time To Cook? How Family Resources Influence Food Preparation', Economic Research Service, Report No. 40, US Department of Agriculture (USDA), Washington, DC.

Mettler, Suzanne (1998), *Dividing Citizens: Gender and Federalism in New Deal Public Policy,* Ithaca, NY: Cornell University Press.

Mink, Gwendolyn and Rickie Solinger (2003), *Welfare: A Documentary History of US Policy and Politics,* New York: New York University Press.

Moffitt, Robert (1992), 'Incentive effects of the US welfare system: a review', *Journal of Economic Literature,* **30**(1), 1–61.

National Center for Children in Poverty (2011), 'Basic Needs Budget Calculator', available at: http://www.nccp.org/tools/frs/budget.php (accessed August 2011).

Nelson, Barbara J. (1990), 'The origins of the two-channel welfare state: workmen's compensation and mothers' aid', in Linda Gordon (ed.), *Women, the State, and Welfare,* Madison, WI: University of Wisconsin Press, pp. 123–51.

Orloff, Ann (1993), 'Gender and the social rights of citizenship: The comparative analysis of gender relations and welfare states', *American Sociological* Review, **58**(3), 303–28.

Page, Stephen B. and Mary B. Larner (1997), 'Introduction to the AFDC program', *The Future of Children,* **7**(1), 20–27.

Pew Internet (2011), 'Demographics of internet users', Pew Internet and American Life Project, available at: http://www.pewinternet.org/Trend-Data/Whos-Online.aspx (accessed October 2011).

Quadagno, Jill (1994), *The Color of Welfare: How Racism Undermined the War on Poverty,* New York: Oxford University Press.

Schmitt, John (2007), *The Good, The Bad, and the Ugly: Job Quality in the United States over the Three Most Recent Business Cycles,* Washington, DC: Center for Economic and Policy Research.

Schochet, Peter and Anu Rangarajan (2004), 'Characteristics of Low-Wage Workers and Their Labor Market Experiences: Evidence from the Mid-to-Late 1990s', submitted by Mathematica Policy Research, Inc. to Office of the Assistant Secretary for Planning and Evaluation, Department of Health and Human Services.

Schott, Liz and Ife Finch (2010), *TANF Benefits are Low and Have not Kept Pace with Inflation,* Washington, DC: Center for Budget and Policy, available at: http://www.cbpp.org/cms/index.cfm?fa=view&id=3306 (accessed August 2011).

Schram, Sanford, Joe Soss and Richard Fording (eds) (2003), *Race and the Politics of Welfare Reform,* Ann Arbor, MI: University of Michigan Press.

Sigle-Rushton, Wendy and Jane Waldfogel (2007), 'Motherhood and women's earnings in Anglo-American, Continental European, and Nordic Countries', *Feminist Economics,* **13**(2), 55–91.

Smith, Aaron (2010), 'Home Broadband 2010', Pew Research Center, Washington, DC, available at: http://pewinrternet.org/~/media/Files/Reports/2010/Home%20broadband%202010.pdf (accessed October 2011).

Spalter-Roth, Roberta, Beverly Burr, Heidi Hartmann and Lois Shaw (1995), *Welfare that Works: The Working Lives of AFDC Recipients,* Washington, DC: Institute for Women's Policy Research.

US Bureau of the Census (2011a), 'Poverty Thresholds 2007', available at: http://www.census.gov/hhes/www/poverty/data/threshld/thresh07.html (accessed August 2011).

US Bureau of the Census (2011b), 'Poverty Thresholds 1996', available at: http://www.census.gov/hhes/www/poverty/data/threshld/thresh96.html (accessed August 2011).

US Department of Health and Human Service, Office of the Assistant Secretary for Planning and Evaluation (2008a), *Indicators of Welfare Dependence: Annual Report to Congress 2008,* Washington, DC, available at: http://aspe.hhs.gov/hsp/indicators08/ (accessed August 2011).

US Department of Health and Human Services, Office of the Assistant Secretary for Planning and Evaluation (2008b), 'Child Care Eligibility and Enrollment Estimates for Fiscal Year 2005', ASPE Issue Brief, Washington, DC, available at: http://aspe.hhs.gov/hsp/08/cc-eligibility/ib.htm (accessed August 2011).

Wider Opportunities for Women (2007), *Florida: The Self-Sufficiency Standard County by County*, Washington, DC: Wider Opportunities for Women: Table 16, available at: http://www.wowonline.org/ourprograms/fess/stateresources/documents/Countybycountytables2007.pdf (accessed August 2011).

Wider Opportunities for Women (2010), *The Basic Economic Security Tables for the United States*, Washington, DC: Wider Opportunities for Women, available at: http://www.wowonline.org/documents/BESTIndexforTheUnitedStates2010.pdf (accessed August 2011).

Wilkinson, Richard and Kate Pickett (2009), *The Spirit Level: Why Greater Equality Makes Societies Stronger*, New York, Berlin and London: Bloomsbury Press.

Williams, Joan C. (2001), *Unbending Gender: Why Family and Work Conflict and What To Do About It*, New York and Oxford: Oxford University Press.

17. Employer-oriented schedule flexibility, gender and family care
Elaine McCrate

I   INTRODUCTION

'Work schedule flexibility' means fundamentally different things to workers and employers. Schedules may adjust to the supply side of the labor market, responding to the needs or preferences of a worker, often a family caregiver, to adjust times at work. Alternatively, changes in product demand, absenteeism, and turnover may create pressure on workers to adjust their work times in order for employers to maximize profits. A great deal of recent evidence has suggested tremendous pent-up excess demand for worker-oriented flexibility in many affluent countries, particularly in outliers such as the United States that do not require even the most rudimentary forms of flexibility such as paid vacation days or sick leave (Heymann, 2000). At the same time, workers on schedules that are driven by employers' needs for flexibility often express tremendous frustration with the schedules (Baret, 2000; Henly and Lambert, 2005). As such, the two types of flexibility may be at odds.

Worker-oriented flexibility can complicate a production schedule or the delivery of services, and employer-initiated flexibility can make it very difficult to address personal contingencies, plan time away from work, adhere to a routine, or prevent the fragmentation of one's personal time. While this is likely to be disruptive for anyone who needs to synchronize their personal activities with others – hence the apt European notion of 'unsocial hours' – it is particularly problematic for those who have primary caregiving responsibilities. Moreover, when an hourly worker's total hours vary, her earnings become unstable. If she receives public transfers that are conditional on earnings or hours worked, these transfers also fluctuate, often accentuating rather than offsetting the irregularity of income due to lags in eligibility determination.

Workers have various instruments for flexibility, such as voluntary quits, formal provisions for sick, vacation and personal leave, formal flextime arrangements, accommodating supervisors, and absenteeism and turnover. Employers also have numerous tools for flexibility: layoffs, overtime, short-hours contracts, fixed-term employment, outsourcing, functional flexibility, and so forth. This chapter concentrates on the class of flexibility tools that most directly impact day-to-day scheduling and family care. While much previous research has viewed working time through the lens of total hours worked or nonstandard shifts, here I concentrated on variability in hours worked.

This chapter discusses schedule flexibility in a historical context. First, I describe the traditional relationship between gender and flexibility (Section II). In Section III, I summarize the extent of variable hours, particularly those not controlled by workers. Sections IV and V review the processes in Western Europe and North America (also, to some extent, in Japan) that have given rise to schedule flexibility, especially for employers, while considering the implications for gender and well-being. For the most part, I do not address flexibility in developing countries, where it is institutionally quite different, usually closely connected to large informal sectors, and involving home work. Section VI concludes.

II   GENDER AND FLEXIBILITY

The archetypal gender division of labor in capitalist economies has traditionally reconciled family needs with employer-driven flexibility by assuming the full-time female homemaker and the temporally unencumbered male worker. Men were expected to be categorically available for wage work, whether that meant long work days, evening, weekend, or holiday work, or a variable schedule. Young single childless women have also been valued as flexible workers (Liu and Chiu, 1999; Baret, 2000). However, marriage and childbearing have typically changed women's availability for employers. As wives and mothers, women have historically been caregivers of first and last resort, available to respond to any family needs, whether anticipated or not. Those exceptional caregivers who held jobs – often single mothers, immigrants, and members of subordinate racial groups – participated for the most part in a male-normative work world, and did not often have the flexibility they needed for family care. A prime example was the live-in servant in the US. Alternatively, employed mothers often crowded into marginalized jobs that were more compatible with family care, such as taking in laundry or boarders.

Although variability in working time seems to be a recent development, in fact the 'standard work schedule' – approximately 35–40 hours per week, mostly daytime, mostly Monday through Friday, mostly fixed hours, usually associated with a contract of indefinite duration and with full benefits and social protections for the worker and 'his' family – is primarily a post-World War I achievement (Cross, 1989) for a limited group of workers, mainly prime-age primary sector men in the industrialized countries. Before that, schedules varied enormously for workers (related both to supply- and demand-side factors). The standard workday, often won by unions (Hinrichs, 1991), was without doubt a significant achievement for workers to the extent that it promoted *regularity* by reserving some hours for the coordination of activities with families and communities. It contributed to broad solidarities based on common work times and common work rhythms (Supiot, 2001), albeit largely male work times and rhythms.

This norm of regularity was especially remarkable in that it required employers to assent: first to the exchange of a fixed hourly wage for a variable amount of work done, the amount of work actually done depending in part on the volume and timing of demand (Rubery et al., 2006); and second to the principle of accumulating costly inventory for periods of unexpectedly high demand. Statutory or collectively bargained mandates for the payment of overtime premia provided supporting incentives for the standard workday.

But this standard was founded on a radical gender division of labor, with men as unencumbered workers and women as the first and last line of responsibility for the family, so that the *rigidity* of the standard working day, and the loss of individual autonomy over working time, were initially less consequential than they could have been. Men also absorbed the majority of varying overtime hours. In the early years of mothers' rising labor force participation in the US, mothers initially were somewhat more likely to have jobs that made it easy to take time off (Filer, 1985), but as mothers began to enter the labor force in greater numbers in the twentieth century, their schedules became more similar to men's, and they were concentrated in 'feminine' jobs with schedules that were more stable and predictable, albeit rigid, such as clerical work in the US (McCrate, 2003, 2012).

Mothers were also concentrated in part-time work.[1] These patterns reflected both personal choices and constraints, and statistical discrimination by employers who expected mothers not to be productive with some kinds of work-time regimes. In this kind of situation, economic theory predicts self-fulfilling feedback loops. Because employers did not expect women to be available for long or irregular hours, they did not invest in developing women's skills; because women expected to be relegated to dead-end jobs, they did not invest in skills that would probably not pay off. Even in Sweden, which offers extensive life-cycle flexibility for working parents, working-time adjustments have been associated with reduced career and earnings development. As Dominique Anxo et al. note, 'In all countries, it is largely women who make these adjustments, and in part the penalty incurred in career and wage evolution is because it is a gender "signal" of women's deviation from the standard employment relationship' (2006, p. 116).

Similarly, in the Netherlands, where part-time work has been normalized to a great extent, part-timers still have fewer opportunities to advance (Fouarge and Baaijens, 2006). Part-time work is highly marginalized in the US where it is associated with large hourly wage penalties (Gornick and Meyers, 2003). In developing countries, part-time work is often concentrated in the informal sector (Lee et al., 2007). In Japan, 'part-time work' can entail full-time hours, but it often offers some control over days and times worked, as well as predictability, although with extremely low wages relative to full-time work and few opportunities for advancement (Ribault, 2000; Nagase, 2002). Another example of marginal part-time work is the German 'mini-job'. Since the mini-job entered the German taxation and social insurance system in 1998, it has featured lower social security contributions for employers, as well as tax advantages for married couples, provided that monthly pay does not exceed €400. But it provides no entitlement to the usual package of social insurance benefits for individual workers. Mini-jobs are disproportionately held by women and by students, and coexist uneasily with the intent (if not the word) of the European Union Directive on Part-Time Work (see below) (Bosch and Weinkopf, 2008).[2]

III THE DECLINE OF STANDARD WORKING HOURS

The standard work schedule began to erode in the late twentieth century for several reasons, reflecting variations in firms' competitive environment, market strategies and institutional constraints, and the segmentation of supply along the lines of race, gender, class, and skill level (Rubery, 2005). By the twenty-first century, that process was highly advanced.

McCrate (2012) found that the proportion of US workers (not self-employed, ages 18–65) who had variable starting or stopping times, but did not have the flexibility that would allow them to change their schedule, increased from 6.6 percent in 1997 to

11.5 percent in 2004. Men (12.6 percent), and especially black men (16.5 percent), were somewhat overrepresented in 2004 among these workers who lacked both control and stability. White married mothers were greatly underrepresented in, but hardly exempt from this type of schedule, at 7.7 percent. However, black single mothers, who might be expected to have the greatest need to control their schedules, were overrepresented at 11.8 percent. While this kind of schedule was concentrated in industries that cannot inventory output (transportation, services and retail trade), it was increasing everywhere except in public sector employment (McCrate, 2011). It was significantly more common among hourly employees than salaried workers (McCrate, 2012).

The extent of flexible scheduling and its correlation with gender probably vary a great deal from one country to another due to differences in labor force characteristics, industrial composition, and institutional specificities. Steffen Lehndorff and Dorothea Voss-Dahm (2005) mention the case of a European firm that manages changes in demand differently in each country in which it operates. Using a unique cross-country dataset of large and medium-size transnational European firms, Sebastian Schief (2010) found that, regardless of home country, establishments operating in the UK rely most heavily on overtime to respond to changes in demand. Those operating in Germany are more likely to use flexible working times (including working-time accounts), those in France to use external labor supply (including temporary agency workers), and those in Portugal to use recruitment and dismissal. The variance across countries was enormous; for example, the proportion of transnational companies using overtime ranged from 91 percent in the UK to 54 percent in Portugal, and the proportion using flexible working times varied from 80 percent in Germany to 20 percent in the UK. Schief concluded that transnational firms tend to adopt the flexibility conventions of the countries in which they operate. Furthermore, the heterogeneity of flexibility arrangements suggests that 'institutional arrangements . . . emerge out of historically determined power relationships between and within capital and labour' (Rubery, 2005, p. 263).

Notwithstanding the persistent influence of specific national institutions, working hours are becoming less stable across the industrialized world. The European Working Conditions Observatory (2005) reported that 42.6 percent of EU27 workers do not work the same number of hours each day, 39.3 percent do not have fixed starting and finishing hours, and 26.0 percent do not work the same number of days each week. This has increased: in 1995, 65 percent of EU workers had fixed work schedules, but only 61 percent did in 2005. Although this does not clarify whether the employee or the employer determined the schedule, a separate calculation in the same report shows that about 20 percent of EU27 workers not on shift schedules entirely determined their own working times, and about 54 percent had their schedules determined entirely by the employer, with no possibility for change. Workers in Northern European countries had the most autonomy with respect to scheduling, while Southern and Eastern European countries had the least. Furthermore, many European workers had unpredictable schedules: about one-fourth of European workers in 2000 said that their hours changed at least once a month, but only about half of these got more than one day's notice (Boulin et al., 2006).

Both demand- and supply-side processes are involved in the growth of variable hours. On the supply side, when mothers of young children began seeking full-time work in larger numbers, the male-normative standard workday began to look long. Although employed mothers have been performing less housework in most affluent countries, they have by several measures been spending about the same amount of time – or more – with children, at least in the US (Bianchi et al., 2006).

While the standard work schedule began to look long, it also began to look quite rigid. Fixed hours were not compatible with the contingencies of family care, such as breakdowns in childcare arrangements. In addition to regularity, and instead of rigidity, women sought flexibility on their own terms, and began to achieve it, especially professional workers (McCrate, 2007). In 2005, in about one-third of the 31 countries in the Fourth Annual European Survey of Working Conditions, approximately 40 percent of workers said that they could adapt their work times within certain limits (most fell into this category), choose between several fixed working schedules, or set their schedules entirely by themselves. The countries with the greatest incidence of worker-oriented flexibility were first, Scandinavian (Sweden, Denmark, Finland, Norway), and second, Central European (the Netherlands, Switzerland, Belgium, Austria, Luxembourg).

Gender differences in the likelihood of influencing one's schedule were mostly small, with men somewhat more likely to do so in about two-thirds of the countries surveyed. Sangheon Lee, Deirdre McCann and Jon Messenger (2007) reported a similar pattern among employees in Brazil, Hungary, Malaysia, and the Russian Federation, where the gender difference in the proportion of workers with children who said they could start work late or leave early, without losing pay, was small. The US falls approximately in the middle of the spectrum, with about 50 percent of workers saying that their employer alone decided on their working hours (McCrate, 2003). In the US, the gender difference is also slightly in men's favor, while blacks and immigrants have had much less control over their schedules than native-born whites (McCrate, 2003; OEDC, 2009).

Flexible schedules that are controlled to some extent by workers are associated with greater job satisfaction and mental health, especially when employees can frequently change their starting and stopping times (Fredriksen-Goldsen and Scharlach, 2001; Jang et al., 2011). Flexible schedules have facilitated the management of domestic responsibilities (Silver and Goldscheider, 1994). Fredriksen-Goldsen and Scharlach (2001) also found that job flexibility reduced role strain, physical strain, financial strain, and emotional strain for parents and caregivers of adults. However, Benjamin Gottlieb et al. (1998) noted the weak design and ambiguous results of many evaluations of flexible work.

Demand-side developments also began to destabilize the standard working day. The growth of services and retail trade in the affluent countries increased the exchange of products that cannot be inventoried, and that often require direct customer contact. Trade and service employers began to seek large numbers of part-time workers that could be scheduled during peak business hours only. In the 1980s, 'Employers saw part-time employment as a flexible, reversible and individual solution for work-sharing, and an alternative to the collective working time reduction desired by the trade unions' (Yerkes and Visser, 2006, p.242). Among the establishments surveyed in the 2004–05 European Establishment Survey on Working Time that employed part-time workers, 69 percent offered fixed hours every day, and 38 percent offered some other fixed hours arrangements (European Foundation for the Improvement of Living and Working Conditions, 2006). To some extent this matched many women's preferences for part-time work, given their responsibilities in the home.

IV   VARIABLE PART-TIME WORK AND ITS IMPACT ON WELL-BEING AND THE GENDER DIVISION OF LABOR

The increasing application of just-in-time principles to services and trade, and the proliferation of off-the-shelf regression-based software that aligns staffing with demand on an hourly basis, increased the proportion of part-time schedules that became variable, but to a great extent beyond workers' control – a fundamental problem for caregivers. Among the establishments surveyed in the 2004–05 European Establishment Survey on Working Time that used part-time arrangements, 27 percent used flexible hours on demand. The rate of on-demand part-time work was highest in the British Isles, and lowest in Central Europe, the Mediterranean, and Scandinavia (European Foundation for the Improvement of Living and Working Conditions, 2006).

Maximum availability of workers' time for employers has become perhaps the most important selection criterion for part-time employees in many services and retail trade, both in North America and Europe. Susan Lambert and Julia Henly (2012) found that front-line retail managers in the US used three strategies to meet the exacting cost targets of their firms: maintaining a large payroll, filling it disproportionately with part-time workers, and demanding maximum availability as a condition of employment. A small sample of Chicago area retail employers unanimously rated availability as an extremely influential factor affecting hiring (Henly et al., 2006). The combination of short hours and broad availability allows supervisors to construct different schedules from day to day and week to week, often at very short notice. In Germany, availability at short notice 'is becoming a more important criterion in the selection of sales staff in the retail food trade than vocational qualifications' acquired through the exemplary German training system (Kirsch et al., 2000, p. 81). In France, retail hiring agents prefer young women with few qualifications and no families, with reliable transportation and phones. Job interviewers have sometimes gone so far as to request details of applicants' personal lives, such as husbands' occupations and availability to look after young children, in order to ascertain applicants' availability for shifts (Baret, 2000). As one French retail food worker quoted by Christophe Baret (p. 49) observed, 'The principle's always the same with them – you have to make yourself available. You're not supposed to have a family life.'

Working times are not only variable, they are often unpredictable. In the German food retailing firms studied by Johannes Kirsch et al. (2000), rosters were typically established the Friday before the work week, and the longest advance notice was 14 days. Even that was subject to change at the last minute, often due to absenteeism. Extreme unpredictability is also common in France, where 43 percent of the economically active population did not know the next day's work schedule in 1998, 64 percent did not know the next week's schedule, and 27 percent did not know the next month's schedule. While this was somewhat concentrated among skilled and white-collar workers, the proportions of unskilled blue-collar workers in the same predicaments were 32, 59, and 25 percent, respectively (Gadrey et al., 2003). In the US, 42 percent of retail store employees in a Chicago area sample collected by Henly et al. (2006) reported three or more different start times in the previous week, and 47 percent reported three or more different finishing times. These authors also reported that one-half of sampled retail employees had one week or less advance notice of their schedules. Employers frequently called employees at home at the very last minute to request additional hours or to tell workers to stay home when demand changed unexpectedly. Although employers did provide means to request occasional planned absences, they did not reciprocate when employees had last-minute needs for flexibility; all of the employers sampled had formal sanctioning processes that could result in demerits when employees unexpectedly missed work, sometimes for any reason at all.

To the extent that women part-timers are assigned variable hours that they do not control, often at short notice, they are being asked to put jobs before families; that is, *employers are treating them as unencumbered.* When mothers – especially single mothers – hold jobs with erratic and often unpredictable hours, while maintaining the bulk of care-giving responsibility, it is extraordinarily difficult to plan childcare or to provide the spontaneous, unconditional ('drop everything now') availability that dependents often need. In this respect, the traditional gender division of labor has become a liability for many employers, even in traditionally feminized sectors. But because the traditional gender division of labor between home and market remains dominant virtually every-where, increasing employer demands for availability have two effects. First, they make jobs with erratic hours essentially off-limits for those mothers who have some choices or a decent fallback position. In the US, these are most often white married mothers, who take these jobs less frequently than other demographic groups. Second, for women with fewer choices and a more tenuous fallback position, such as African-American single mothers, these jobs are quietly undermining the historical basis of family care, usually without putting a secure substitute system into place (McCrate, 2012). In other coun-tries, such as Sweden and Denmark, where women's part-time jobs are less marginalized, and feature longer and more stable hours, employers have had to resort more to the youth labor market to fill variable part-time jobs (although young workers fill these jobs disproportionately everywhere) (Rubery, 2005).[3]

Nonstandard schedules have been associated with more strained family relationships (Presser, 2003). While early explorations of nonstandard schedules did not distinguish between worker- and employer-oriented flexibility, and had somewhat mixed effects for families, more recent work has made that distinction and underscored the problems that employer-driven flexibility creates for families. Thomas Haipeter (2006) found that health problems were associated with unstable and unpredictable schedules, although the workers he studied saw no alternative because of the scarcity of jobs. Isik Zeytinoglu et al. (2004) chronicled the stresses on Canadian retail employees with variable and unpre-dictable schedules. In a recent study of low-wage retail employees, Henly and Lambert (2010) found that work schedule unpredictability heightened work–family conflict and stress, and interfered with activities outside work. When workers had input into the total number and scheduling of their hours, these conflicts and stresses were somewhat attenuated. However, worker input into scheduling is constrained by the limited number of hours available, and their extreme fragmentation.

Working parents on unstable and unpredictable schedules were more likely to resort to multiple childcare arrangements and care of lower quality (Henly and Lambert, 2005). A study of the children of Michigan single mothers leaving welfare in the US found that the type of flexibility was critical for understanding the effects of welfare reform on families. The greater the number of cumulative years of fluctuating work hours, the greater the likelihood of school absenteeism and child behavioral problems, especially externalizing problems such as bullying. With models controlling for child fixed effects, a change from stable, predictable hours to fluctuating hours was associated with an increase in child problem behaviors (Johnson et al., 2010). The Organisation for Economic Co-operation and Development (2004) found that work–life conflict increased significantly when respondents worked variable hours and had short notice of schedule changes. In contrast, work–life conflict decreased significantly when workers had more control over their working hours.

The radical irregularity of these schedules tends to affect others besides the frontline worker. Salaried full-time store managers must often be available to oversee the operation of the store, to substitute in the event of absenteeism, and to compensate for deliberately lean staffing, with the result that they often put in extremely long and unpredictable hours (Baret, 2000; Beynon et al., 2002). While nonmanagerial full-time shopfloor workers in France are seldom required to work overtime because of the associated costs, in some supermarkets researchers observed full-timers working unpaid overtime (Baret, 2000). Researchers noted the same practice at German firms where working time was often neither recorded nor paid (Kirsch et al., 2000; Haipeter, 2006). Rubery et al. (2006, p. 126) further observed, 'When working time is fragmented or individualized, the opportunities for staff to develop customary norms relating to reasonable effort levels are reduced.'

Irregularity also spills over to the workers' own family, friends, and service providers. As women's schedules become more variable and unpredictable, the hours that they require childcare also become more contingent, extending working-time instability to service providers, or to family members who might be called upon to pitch in (Henly and Lambert, 2005).[4] Women who need to fit shopping and appointments in between their own unstable shifts contribute to firms' demand for irregular schedules in retail and services. Similarly, just-in-time procurement of inputs ensures that instability will spread backward through the supply chain.

Contingent part-time scheduling has also transformed the relationship between employers and workers in several ways. First, it has shifted the risk of low demand during certain hours or days to workers with seemingly secure contracts of open-ended duration. This new precariousness compounds the conventional risk of job loss. Second, it has blurred the 'bright line' between free time and working time (Supiot, 2001; McCrate, 2012). As such, it encroaches on personal and community time.

Third, contingent part-time schedules have the effect of increasing the average intensity of labor, by eliminating work during slack periods within a day or week (Supiot, 2001; Rubery et al., 2006). This is exacerbated by the common practice of employers demanding maximum availability *as a condition of* getting the job, the desired number of hours, desired shifts, incentive pay, or promotion opportunities (Jany-Catrice and Lehndorff, 2005; Lambert and Henly, 2012; McCrate, 2012).

The institutional incentives for employers to maintain regular schedules usually do not apply to part-timers. For example, governments that regulate overtime do not require premia for unusually long hours unless they exceed the *full-time* maximum; just as importantly, they rarely mandate a minimum number of hours; and until the European Union's directive on part-time work went into effect, part-time work usually did not get many pro-rated private or social benefits, either. In most countries part-timers are less likely to be covered by collective bargaining agreements. As such part-time work is a major tool of flexibility for employers: at low cost, it can be targeted at hours of peak demand, even when those change from week to week and day to day. While Americans often think that the major attraction of part-time work for employers is the lack of benefits such as health insurance, part-time work has also proliferated rapidly in other advanced economies with national health insurance. Since the European Union Directive on Part-Time Work, it has also flourished despite the broad equalization of wages and benefits for full-timers and part-timers required by the directive. A chief attraction for all employers across borders is its intrinsic flexibility – what Lehndorff and Voss-Dahm (2005, p. 306) call the 'flexibility for free syndrome'.

V   VARIABLE OVERTIME AND THE GENDER DIVISION OF LABOR

Exceptionally long hours for men have been part of the traditional gender division of labor which reserves men primarily for market work. While women (especially professionals) are certainly not exempt from long hours, overtime is a disproportionately male flexibility tool around the world (Lee et al., 2007). In Japan, predominantly male *seishain*, who work full-time on a contract of indefinite duration with attractive wages, fringe benefits, and opportunities for promotion, are expected to provide extensive availability for their employers, typically for overtime work with little advance notice (Ribault, 2000; Nagase, 2002). Huw Beynon et al. note that in Western Europe, 'Male workers primarily experience . . . longer hours combined with flexible scheduling, while female workers were more often affected by reductions in available hours combined with flexible scheduling' (2002, p. 225). One exception was women in supervisory and lower management jobs, who had to adjust to longer hours and flexible schedules. While the flexibility, and often the unpredictability, of overtime arrangements have been important for firms to respond to variations in demand, they have also been incompatible with gender-egalitarian family caregiving. Statutory or collectively bargained limits on overtime have been important for the reconciliation of work and family, especially for men. Stated more strongly, some limits on overtime – on its volume and unpredictability – are essential for changing the gender division of labor.

However, full-time workers have been increasingly pressured to tailor their hours to the ebb and flow of demand. In the 1980s, European manufacturers wanted to extend operating hours, in part to extend the use of physical capital, and in part to more closely match output with demand. The diffusion of just-in-time inventory control, which maintains minimal buffers of inventory, also contributed to the growth of variable hours in manufacturing. When demand grows, firms organized on just-in-time principles cannot draw down stocks of inputs or outputs. They either have to hire and train more (often using fixed-term workers), or they have to use overtime.

European employers increasingly called for 'flexibilization' to meet temporary spikes in demand in novel, low-cost forms. One such form is the conversion of full- to part-time jobs where employers can increase workers' hours without paying overtime (Beynon et al., 2002; Bosch and Lehndorff, 2005). Although the hourly wage rate is sometimes converted to a higher base rate upon conversion, there are no premia for evenings, weekends, or holidays. In other cases, employers simply extended hours while reducing overtime and unsocial hours premia.[5] For example, in Great Britain, where there was no statutory regulation of overtime prior to EU mandates in the 1990s (ILO, 2012), and increasingly strained unions were the only means to regulate overtime, supermarkets extended opening hours while reducing overtime and unsocial hours premia (Beynon et al., 2002).[6]

Another novel form of low-cost overtime is the working-time account through which employers secure flexibility without the payment of overtime premia. A working-time account allows the employer to use overtime while banking the excess hours in individual worker accounts, to be reimbursed to workers as time off when demand falls, within a specified time interval. Most working-time accounts allow employers to vary daily or weekly hours as long as the average equals regular full-time hours over a specified longer period, typically a month, a year, or more. Time in the accounts is drawn down at the regular wage rate, not the overtime rate.

According to Schief (2010), working-time accounts are now the most common instrument of flexibility in Germany (among the four instruments he considered), but they, and similar kinds of averaging agreements, are also found in other European countries, Canada, and some developing or transition countries, especially Brazil, China, the Czech Republic, and Hungary (Lee et al., 2007). For example, in British public sector healthcare, under the pressure of tighter budgets and the threat of outsourcing to the private sector, 'nursing staff were encouraged to sign on with "the [time] bank", to enable flexible overtime to be worked without premium rates' (Beynon et al., 2002, p. 208). Often European employers seek volunteers for overtime, sometimes it is simply assigned, and sometimes it is a combination of the two (European Foundation for the Improvement of Living and Working Conditions, 2006). In Germany, the share of workers with working-time accounts rose from 33 percent in 1998 to 48 percent in 2005 (Gross and Schwarz, 2007).

Some working-time accounts also provide flexibility for workers. Employees may accumulate hours in one period to draw down later when personal needs arise. These programs differ greatly in the amount of time that may be accumulated and the period in which banked hours may be redeemed (OECD, 2009). The 2004–05 European Establishment Survey on Working Time clearly asked employers to specify if they allowed variations in working time according to employees' wishes. In the EU21, 48 percent of personnel managers in firms with at least 10 employees reported some form of worker-led flexibility; of these, 25 percent allowed the use of accumulated hours for full days off, and 27.8 percent allowed the use of accumulated hours for longer periods of leave. Managers and employees in these firms agreed that worker-oriented flexibility schemes reduced paid overtime, allowed a better adaptation of hours to workload, reduced absenteeism, and *most often*, improved job satisfaction (European Foundation for the Improvement of Living and Working Conditions, 2006). These results are consistent with other research in suggesting that worker-oriented flexibility may be a win–win strategy for employers and workers.

Several parameters determine the degree of flexibility in working-time accounts: the maximum number of hours that may be accrued, the window of time in which hours must be drawn down or averaged, and the penalties imposed on employers for failing to draw down the accounts within the specified period. While the time limit for drawing down accrued time is often one year (so that this tool is also sometimes called 'annualization'), in Germany, the average window is 30 weeks, and the penalty for failure to compensate workers with time off within the window is payment for the accrued hours at the overtime premium rate[7] (Gross and Schwarz, 2007). However, because of excessive workloads, it can be difficult to draw down banked hours (Beynon et al., 2002), sometimes turning the working-time account into a de facto early retirement account (Haipeter, 2006). Other means of limiting long hours under averaging agreements include consultation with workers' representatives, or absolute limits on the number of excess hours per week (Lee et al., 2007).

Working-time accounts and hours averaging often were concessions accepted by European labor unions in exchange for fewer hours, so that averaging agreements have sometimes gone hand-in-hand with working time reduction. While France has reduced overall work hours to 35 per week, it still permits averaging, so that some workers can have significant variance around 35 hours (Gadrey et al., 2006). Similarly, in Belgium and Spain, some unions have negotiated an average annual work week of 35 hours, while permitting annualization (Bouffartigue and Bouteiller, 2006). The tradeoff between shorter total hours and increased employer-initiated flexibility has mixed implications for the gender division of labor. On the one hand, shorter hours increase the time available for families, especially among men who have been most likely to work long hours. On the other hand, when hours are assigned on demand, they exacerbate the instability and unpredictability of workers' schedules, which makes these jobs less available for caregivers who have the wherewithal to avoid them.

A common alternative, or complement, to working-time accounts in Europe is 'short-time working' or 'work sharing'. This tool gives employers flexibility over the business cycle by reducing the daily or weekly hours of employees, with government compensation to workers for some of the lost income. Unions tend to prefer work sharing to hours averaging because workers broadly share the cost of downturns and, for the most part, it does not entail unpaid flexibility. In the most recent economic crisis, German manufacturers have made extensive use of both work sharing and hours averaging (Burda and Hunt, 2011). Several countries have extended the length of work-sharing programs or the size of the government contribution. Other countries have introduced temporary work-sharing programs in this period (Arpaia et al., 2010).

Finally, salaried work offers enhanced opportunities for low-cost overtime. With salaried workers, there is often greater variability in working time and greater ambiguity over the control of working time. Consider the dilemma faced by software engineers, whose clients expect 24-hour availability. The effects have been summarized by Janneke Plantenga and Chantal Remery:

> Due to the opportunities for autonomous time management by employees, working hours become destandardised, generating flexibility for the employee, the employer and the client . . . this flexibility is generated against a background of long working hours. The result may therefore not necessarily be the flexibility to limit the workload but the flexibility to work at all times and in all places. (2005, p. 206)

Among professionals, considerable personal autonomy in work is often combined with heavy workloads and limited amounts of time and financial resources, resulting in a high volume of routine or variable overtime (Lehndorff and Voss-Dahm, 2005).

In Canada, the result of such processes was that 62.1 percent of employees who worked any paid or unpaid overtime learned about their overtime schedule less than one day in advance. (While men were more likely to work overtime, the gender difference in advance notice among overtime workers was small.) For this group with little advance notice (about half of whom were hourly workers), their average usual overtime per week was 6.6 hours (author's calculations from the 2005 Workplace and Employee Survey). In Canada, men have borne the brunt of long, unstable, and unpredictable hours, making them less available for family care, and rigidifying the gender division of labor.

VI   CONCLUSIONS AND POLICY IMPLICATIONS

While the modal job in most countries still features the rigid but stable work schedule, working-time variability has been rising to accommodate both firms' and workers' demands for flexibility. Volkswagen manager Peter Hartz best expressed firms' desire for flexibility with his metaphor of the factory that 'breathes' with the market (quoted in Haipeter, 2006, p. 323). Today many workers' schedules are at a crossroads, where they are somehow expected to breathe both with the market and with the rhythms of family life. The result of the incompatibility between workers' and employers' priorities in flexible scheduling in most countries (perhaps less so in the Scandinavian countries) may be the reification of men's traditional primary assignment to market work, and the unsettling of women's primary assignment to family care – the latter usually without accommodating arrangements in childcare, social security systems, and other work supports. There have been offsetting trends toward worker-oriented flexibility, particularly among white-collar workers, although often the degree of control they have over their schedules is sometimes compromised by their employers' expectations of flexibility and long hours. Employer-oriented working-time variability, especially when it is difficult to predict, has compromised the quality of family care, especially among low-wage workers.

Eviatar Zerubavel (1981) spoke of the need for regular sequential structures, durations, temporal locations, and rates of recurrence in daily life, in order for sociality to be possible at all. His conclusions need to be tempered by workers' needs for flexibility, albeit in a context of basically stable hours. The 2004–05 European Establishment Survey on Working Time suggests that some part-time and overtime arrangements facilitate flexibility for both workers and employers, particularly in Scandinavian countries. Flexibility for employers dominates in most western countries and overrides workers' interests in flexibility. Employers have increasingly imposed irregularity in all of Zerubavel's categories throughout the western world. While this has often been associated with high turnover, the fact that the incidence of employer-initiated irregular schedules is increasing suggests that many employers have found an adequate number of workers willing to settle for these conditions.

Workers' interests may be addressed through collective agreements. European unions initially sought to maintain the standard workday but showed little interest in worker-initiated flexibility. For example, when women in the Netherlands first pressured their unions to support part-time work, the unions initially opposed it because of its association with inferior working conditions (Yerkes and Visser, 2006). In response to high unemployment, trade unions instead sought general reductions in working time (eventually achieved in France), and the expansion of work sharing (which has been most successful in Germany). But because the high unemployment of the period made it easier for employers to shift the risk of variability to workers, employers got more of the flexibility they sought in the 1980s, while it would take a bit longer for unions to achieve any reduced hours, and to embrace women's interest in flexibility for family care. This eventually did happen. For example, the British Trades Union Congress (TUC) launched a campaign in the late 1990s called 'Changing Times' to encourage unions to negotiate working-time options for better work–family balance (Boulin et al., 2006).

Unions have had only modest success in regulating employer-oriented flexibility. Nurses' collective agreements in the US often specify methods for distributing flexible hours. An innovative agreement in Swedish call centers and telemarketing establishments regulated working-time flexibility (Dølvik and Waddington, 2005). But more often, unions have had a difficult time regulating employer-initiated scheduling flexibility, despite the fact that in some European countries, such as Germany and Great Britain, the unions rather than the state were the main force regulating work time before the statutory EU directives on working time. In countries with low rates of union density, it is even harder to respond to employer demands for nonstandard hours in ways that give workers more flexibility and allow better reconciliation of work with family responsibilities. This increases the significance of legislation.

The European Union has imposed some broad limits on both overtime and part-time work. The 1993 EU Directive on Working Time (Official Journal of the European Communities, 1993), mandatory for member countries, limited average work time for each seven-day period to 48 hours, including overtime.[8] Individual countries were instructed to implement the directive in their own way. The EU decision to allow employers to exclude salaried staff from the provisions of the Working Time Directive vitiated its effects (Beynon et al., 2002).

Another mandatory limit on employer flexibility imposed by the EU was its Directive on Part-Time Work (Official Journal of the European Communities, 1998). It prohibited discrimination against part-time workers, and required *pro rata* compensation with regard to quasi-fixed labor costs (pensions, and so on). Member states were permitted to exclude part-time casual workers from the terms of the agreement, and national law was permitted to 'make access to particular conditions of employment subject to a period of service, time worked or earnings qualification', the loophole that legitimates the German mini-job.

Most recently, the EU has tried to address the conflict between employer- and worker-led flexibility by encouraging 'flexicurity', which promises both flexibility and security. In principle, there can be solutions that achieve a higher level of at least one of these without reducing the other. But at least initially, as the OECD observed:

> The extent to which flexi-time practices help workers balance work and family life is co-determined by the extent to which workers have control over these arrangements. In practice, flexible working schemes are primarily designed to address employer needs in the production process, and their use as a reconciliation tool is determined by the extent to which employees can use these arrangements . . . to reflect their preferred working time schedule. (2009, p. 1)

Zeytinoglu et al. (2009) reached the same conclusion for Canada. Flexicurity with respect to scheduling seems to be most advanced in the Scandinavian countries, where employers and workers' representatives tended to agree on the beneficial outcomes of worker-oriented flexibility for both firms and employees (European Foundation for the Improvement of Living and Working Conditions, 2006).

The contemporary economic environment is not propitious for increased worker control over the variability of working time. Employees' acquiescence with temporal instability has been conditioned on meager social provision of alternatives for part-time workers, and high unemployment. Worker bargaining power is on the decline in much of Europe and North America. Even the European Union directives on working time contain important loopholes that facilitate irregular scheduling. Finally, irregularity begets irregularity, as workers on flexible or unstable shifts require services themselves at variable hours. For all of these reasons, despite the costs to employers in the form of higher turnover, these trends may continue; it does not bode well for the well-being of working women, men, or their families.

NOTES

1. In Eastern and Southern Europe the choice of hours is often more constrained to be one between full-time work and no work outside the home.
2. Similarly, the Japanese tax system creates incentives for part-time work by one member of a married couple (Ribault, 2000; Nagase, 2002).
3. Extended shop opening hours in Sweden have 'led to considerably less flexibilisation of individual working hours than in the UK . . . since the trade unions were able to push through new, collectively agreed protective provisions' (Bosch and Lehndorff, 2005, p. 20).
4. Employers do take limited measures to mitigate the problems caused by demanding maximum availability. Workers on these kinds of schedules can usually express their scheduling preferences and sometimes swap shifts with coworkers. But even so, case studies confirm that individual workers still have the responsibility to scramble to work assigned hours, and managers have the final say (Kirsch et al., 2000; Henly and Lambert, 2005).
5. In Western Europe, the idea of 'unsocial hours' generally refers to any kind of nonstandard hours that impinge upon hours historically set aside for workers' own activities, including activities with family, friends, and community.
6. In 2004–05, among those European establishments with overtime, 40 percent of employee representatives reported that management consulted with them before the use of overtime, 13 percent learned about the overtime after it had occurred, and 45 percent of employee representatives said they were not consulted (European Foundation for the Improvement of Living and Working Conditions, 2006, p. 17).
7. The German working-time accounts were negotiated by the employers' associations and the unions in the 1990s and 2000s; the unions conceded greater flexibility in return for less outsourcing and more training. Such accounts are more common at large firms, and they are overseen by works councils (Burda and Hunt, 2011).
8. The directive specified derogations for people with autonomous decision-making powers, for industries that require continuity such as security and healthcare, and for industries with foreseeable surges of demand, including agriculture, tourism, and the postal services. Council Directive 2000/34/EC amended the Working Time Directive to exclude transportation workers and doctors in training from the scope of the original directive.

REFERENCES

Anxo, Dominique, Jean-Yves Boulin and Colette Fagan (2006), 'Decent working time in a life course perspective', in Jean-Yves Boulin, Michel Lallement, Jon C. Messenger and François Michon (eds), *Decent Working Time: New Trends, New Issues*, Geneva: International Labour Office, pp. 93–122.

Arpaia, A., N. Curci, E. Meyermans, J. Peschner and F. Pierini (2010), 'Short time working arrangements as response to cyclical fluctuations', Occasional Papers 64, European Commission Directorate-General for Economic and Financial Affairs and Directorate-General for Employment, Social Affairs, and Equal Opportunity, Brussels.

Baret, Christophe (2000), 'The organization of working time in large French food retail firms', in Christophe Baret, Steffen Lehndorff and Leigh Sparks (eds), *Flexible Working in Food Retailing: A Comparison between France, Germany, the United Kingdom and Japan*, London and New York: Routledge, pp. 31–57.

Beynon, Huw, Damian Grimshaw, Jill Rubery and Kevin Ward (2002), *Managing Employment Change: The New Realities of Work*, Oxford: Oxford University Press.

Bianchi, Suzanne M., John P. Robinson and Melissa A. Milkie (2006), *Changing Rhythms of American Family Life*, New York: Russell Sage Foundation.

Bosch, Gerhard and Steffen Lehndorff (eds) (2005), *Working in the Service Sector: A Tale from Different Worlds*, London and New York: Routledge.

Bosch, Gerhard and Claudia Weinkopf (2008), *Low-Wage Work in Germany*, New York: Russell Sage Foundation.

Bouffartigue, Paul and Jacques Bouteiller (2006), 'Two occupational groups facing the challenge of temporal availability: hospital nurses and bank managerial staff in France, Belgium and Spain', in Jean-Yves Boulin, Michel Lallement, Jon C. Messenger and François Michon (eds), *Decent Working Time: New Trends, New Issues*, Geneva: International Labour Office, pp. 369–94.

Boulin, Jean-Yves, Michel Lallement and François Michon (2006), 'Decent working time in industrialized countries: issues, scopes and paradoxes,' in Jean-Yves Boulin, Michel Lallement, Jon C. Messenger and François Michon (eds), *Decent Working Time: New Trends, New Issues*, Geneva: International Labour Office, pp. 13–40.

Burda, Michael C. and Jennifer Hunt (2011), 'What explains the German labor market miracle in the great recession?', Working Paper 17187, National Bureau of Economic Research, Cambridge, MA.

Cross, Gary (1989), *A Quest for Time: The Reduction of Work in Britain and France, 1840–1940*, Berkeley, CA: University of California Press.

Dølvik, Jon Erik and Jeremy Waddington (2005), 'Can trade unions meet the challenge? Unionisation in the marketised services', in Bosch and Lehndorff (eds), pp. 316–41.

European Foundation for the Improvement of Living and Working Conditions (2006), 'Working Time and Work–Life Balance in European Companies', Dublin, available at: http://www.eurofound.europa.eu/pubdocs/2006/27/en/1/ef0627en.pdf (accessed November 2011).

European Working Conditions Observatory (2005), 'Fourth European Working Conditions Survey (2005)', available at: http://www.eurofound.europa.eu/surveys/ewcs/2005/ewcs2005individualchapters.htm (accessed November 2011).

Filer, Randall (1985), 'Male–female wage differences: the importance of compensating differentials', *Industrial and Labor Relations Review*, **38**(3), 426–37.

Fouarge, Didier and Christine Baaijens (2006), 'Labour supply preferences and job mobility of Dutch employees', in Jean-Yves Boulin, Michel Lallement, Jon C. Messenger and François Michon (eds), *Decent Working Time: New Trends, New Issues*, Geneva: International Labour Office, pp. 155–80.

Fredriksen-Goldsen, Karen I. and Andrew E. Scharlach (2001), *Families and Work: New Directions in the Twenty-First Century*, Oxford: Oxford University Press.

Gadrey, Nicole, Florence Jany-Catrice and Martine Pernod-Lemattre (2003), 'Les enjeux de la qualification des employés. Conditions de travail et competences des non qualifiés', Rapport pour la Ministère de l'emploi et de la solidarité – DARES, June.

Gadrey, Nicole, Florence Jany-Catrice and Martine Pernod-Lemattre (2006), 'The working conditions of blue-collar and white-collar workers in France compared: a question of time', in Jean-Yves Boulin, Michel Lallement, Jon C. Messenger and François Michon (eds), *Decent Working Time: New Trends, New Issues*, Geneva: International Labour Office, pp. 265–88.

Gornick, Janet C. and Marcia K. Meyers (2003), *Families That Work: Policies for Reconciling Parenthood and Employment*, New York: Russell Sage Foundation.

Gottlieb, Benjamin H., E. Kevin Kelloway and Elizabeth Barham (1998), *Flexible Working Arrangements: Managing the Work-Family Boundary*, Chichester: John Wiley & Sons.

Gross, Hermann and Michael Schwarz (2007), 'Betriebs- und Arbeitszeiten 2005: Ergebnisse einer repräsentativen Betriebsbefragung', *Beiträge aus der Forschung: Sozialforschungsstelle Dortmund*, **153**, 1–174.

Haipeter, Thomas (2006), 'Can norms survive market pressures? The practical effectiveness of new forms of working time regulation in a changing German economy', in Jean-Yves Boulin, Michel Lallement, Jon C. Messenger and François Michon (eds), *Decent Working Time: New Trends, New Issues*, Geneva: International Labour Office, pp. 319–42.

Henly, Julia R. and Susan J. Lambert (2005), 'Nonstandard work and childcare needs of low-income parents', in Suzanne M. Bianchi, Lynne M. Casper and Rosalind Berkowitz King (eds), *Work, Family, Health, and Well-Being*, Mahwah, NJ: Lawrence Erlbaum Associates, pp. 473–92.

Henly, Julia R. and Susan J. Lambert (2010), 'Schedule flexibility and unpredictability in retail: Implications for employee work–life outcomes', working paper, University of Chicago, IL.

Henly, Julia R., H. Luke Shaefer and Elaine Waxman (2006), 'Nonstandard work schedules: employer- and employee-driven flexibility in retail jobs', *Social Service Review*, **80**(4), 609–34.

Heymann, Jody (2000), *The Widening Gap: Why America's Working Families Are in Jeopardy, and What Can Be Done About It*, New York: Basic Books.

Hinrichs, Karl (1991), 'Working-time development in West Germany: departure to a new stage', in Karl Hinrichs, William Roche and Carmen Sirianni (eds), *Working Time in Transition: The Political Economy of Working Hours in Industrial Nations*, Philadelphia, PA: Temple University Press, pp. 27–60.

International Labour Organization (ILO) (2012), 'TRAVAIL: Conditions of Work and Employment Programme', available at: http://www.ilo.org/dyn/travail/travmain.sectionReport1?p_lang=en&p_structure= 2&p_sc_id=1045&p_sc_id=1161&p_countries=GB (accessed January 2012).

Jang, Soo Jung, Rhokeun Park and Allison Zippay (2011), 'The interaction effects of scheduling control and work–life balance programs on job satisfaction and mental health', *International Journal of Social Welfare*, **20**(2), 135–43.

Jany-Catrice, Florence and Steffen Lehndorff (2005), 'Work organisation and the importance of labour markets in the European retail trade', in Bosch and Lehndorff (eds), pp. 211–36.

Johnson, Rucker C., Ariel Kalil and Rachel E. Dunifon with Barbara Ray (2010), *Mothers' Work and Children's Lives: Low-Income Families after Welfare Reform*, Kalamazoo, MI: W.E. Upjohn Institute for Employment Research.

Kirsch, Johannes, Martina Klein, Steffen Lehndorff and Dorothea Voss-Dahm (2000), 'The organisation of working time in large German food retail firms', in Christophe Baret, Steffen Lehndorff and Leigh Sparks (eds), *Flexible Working in Food Retailing: A Comparison between France, Germany, the United Kingdom and Japan*, London and New York: Routledge, pp. 58–82.

Lambert, Susan and Julia Henly (2012), 'How frontline managers matter: labour flexibility practices and sustained employment in hourly retail jobs in the US', in Chris Warhurst, Françoise Carré, Patricia Findlay and Chris Tilly (eds), *Are Bad Jobs Inevitable? Trends, Determinants, and Responses to Job Quality in the Twenty-First Century*, London: Palgrave, pp. 143–59.

Lee, Sangheon, Deirdre McCann and Jon C. Messenger (2007), *Working Time Around the World: Trends in Working Hours, Laws and Policies in a Global Comparative Perspective*, London and New York: Palgrave.

Lehndorff, Steffen and Dorothea Voss-Dahm (2005), 'The delegation of uncertainty: flexibility and the role of the market in service work', in Bosch and Lehndorff (eds), pp. 289–315.

Liu, Tai-Lok and Tony Man-yiu Chiu (1999), 'Global restructuring and non-standard work in newly industrialised economies: the organisation of flexible production in Hong Kong and Taiwan', in Alan Felstead and Nick Jewson (eds), *Global Trends in Flexible Labour*, London: Macmillan, pp. 166–80.

McCrate, Elaine (2003), 'Working mothers in a double bind', Economic Policy Institute Briefing Paper 124, Washington DC: available at: http://www.epi.org/content.cfm/briefingpapers_124 (accessed January 2012).

McCrate, Elaine (2007), 'Flexible hours, workplace authority, and compensating wage differentials in the US', *Feminist Economics*, **11**(1), 11–40.

McCrate, Elaine (2011), 'Parents' work time in rural America: the growth of irregular schedules', in Kristin E. Smith and Ann R. Tickamyer (eds), *Economic Restructuring and Family Well-Being in Rural America*, University Park, PA: Pennsylvania State University Press, pp. 177–93.

McCrate, Elaine (2012), 'Flexibility for whom? Control over the work schedule variability in the US', *Feminist Economics*, **18**(1), 1–34.

Nagase, Nobuko (2002), 'Wife allowance and tax exemption behind low wages for part-time workers', *Japan Labor Bulletin*, **41**(9), 8–10, available at: http://www.jil.go.jp/jil/bulletin/year/2002/vol41-09.pdf (accessed February 2011).

Official Journal of the European Communities (1993), available at: http://eur-lex.europa.eu/LexUriServ/ LexUriServ.do?uri=OJ:L:1993:307:0018:0024:EN:PDF (accessed November 2011).

Official Journal of the European Communities (1998), available at: http://eur-lex.europa.eu/LexUriServ/ LexUriServ.do?uri=OJ:L:1998:014:0009:0014:EN:PDF (accessed November 2011).

Organisation for Economic Co-operation and Development (OECD) (2004), *OECD Employment Outlook*, Paris: OECD, available at: http://www.oecd.org/dataoecd/8/5/34846847.pdf (accessed February 2012).

Organisation for Economic Co-operation and Development (OECD) (2009), *LMF2.4: Family-Friendly Workplace Practices*, Social Policy Division, Directorate of Employment, Labour and Social Affairs, OECD, Paris, available at: http://www.oecd.org/dataoecd/1/52/43199600.pdf (accessed November 2011).

Plantenga, Janneke and Chantal Remery (2005), 'Work hard, play hard? Work in software engineering', in Bosch and Lehndorff (eds), pp. 189–210.

Presser, Harriet B. (2003), *Working in a 24/7 Economy: Challenges for American Families*, New York: Russell Sage Foundation.

Ribault, Thierry (2000), 'The organisation of working time in large Japanese food retail firms', in Christophe Baret, Steffen Lehndorff and Leigh Sparks (eds), *Flexible Working in Food Retailing: A Comparison between France, Germany, the United Kingdom and Japan*, London and New York: Routledge, pp. 114–42.

Rubery, Jill (2005), 'The shaping of work and working time in the service sector: a segmentation approach', in Bosch and Lehndorff (eds), pp. 261–88.

Rubery, Jill, Kevin Ward and Damian Grimshaw (2006), 'Time, work and pay: understanding the new relationships', in Jean-Yves Boulin, Michel Lallement, Jon C. Messenger and François Michon (eds), *Decent Working Time: New Trends, New Issues*, Geneva: International Labour Office, pp. 123–52.

Schief, Sebastian (2010), 'Does location matter? An empirical investigation of flexibility patterns in foreign and domestic companies in five European countries', *International Journal of Human Resource Management*, **21**(1), 1–16.

Silver, Hilary and Frances Goldscheider (1994), 'Flexible work and housework: work and family constraints on women's domestic labor', *Social Forces*, **72**(4), 1103–19.

Supiot, Alain (2001), *Beyond Employment: Changes in Work and the Future of Labour Law in Europe*, Oxford: Oxford University Press.

Yerkes, Mara and Jelle Visser (2006), 'Women's preferences or delineated policies? The development of part-time work in the Netherlands, Germany, and the United Kingdom', in Jean-Yves Boulin, Michel Lallement, Jon C. Messenger and François Michon (eds), *Decent Working Time: New Trends, New Issues*, Geneva: International Labour Office: pp. 235–62.

Zerubavel, Eviatar (1981), *Hidden Rhythms: Schedules and Calendars in Social Life*, Chicago, IL: University of Chicago Press.

Zeytinoglu, Isik U., Waheeda Lillevik, Bianca Seaton and Josefina Moruz (2004), 'Part-time and casual work in retail trade: stress and other factors affecting the workplace', *Relations Industrielles/Industrial Relations*, **59**(3), 516–44.

Zeytinoglu, Isik U., Gordon B. Cooke and Sara L. Mann (2009), 'Flexibility: whose choice is it anyway?', *Relations Industrielles/Industrial Relations*, **64**(4), 555–74.

18. Work–family reconciliation policies in Europe
Janneke Plantenga and Chantal Remery

I INTRODUCTION

Over recent decades, the reconciliation of work and family life has become one of the major topics of the European social agenda. The focus is mainly instrumental: reconciliation policies are likely to foster gender equality and to increase female labor force participation. A higher participation rate may improve economic growth and the sustainability of the present-day welfare state, especially in light of an aging population. It is exactly for this reason that the European 2020 strategy has set targets for the overall employment rate of 75 percent for the population aged 20–64 (EC, 2010a). Reconciliation policies might also increase fertility by making a child less costly in terms of income and career opportunities. At the level of the European Union (EU), a better work–life balance for women and men throughout the life-course is thus promoted in order to enhance gender equality, increase the female participation rate, and meet demographic challenges.

Yet, actual reconciliation policy differs widely among EU member states. Some countries have framed childcare as a social right, and focus strongly on the outsourcing of care. Others are much more focused on leave provisions or emphasize the importance of flexible working hours in order to make work more compatible with family life. This diversity in policy responses is often referred to as illustrating the highly diverse nature of European welfare states (for example, Gornick et al., 1997; Thevenon, 2011). Although the male breadwinner model has eroded in most European member states, only a few countries – with the Nordic EU member states as the best-known examples – have developed a system of leave and childcare arrangements that seems to be based on the assumption of both fathers and mothers being engaged in the labor market. In other countries, the actual policies are much more hesitant and may be focusing more on fostering family life than on increasing the participation rate of both men and women. National reconciliation policies are thus devised taking into account different national circumstances, and focusing on different policy issues.

This differentiated nature of the policies makes it difficult to compare countries on their actual policy design. National scores on the provision of childcare services, for example, may be difficult to interpret without also taking into account the parental leave system or the possibility of working part-time. In that respect, a comprehensive approach based on the actual policy mix seems to make much more sense. In addition, the differentiated nature of reconciliation policies makes it difficult to study the impact because the policy goal may differ from increasing female participation to improving social inclusion and from fostering gender equality to increasing the fertility rate.

Indeed, perhaps one of the most complicated challenges of European reconciliation policy refers to the fact that the policy objectives on participation, gender equity, and fertility are not always easily compatible and that the actual impact of reconciliation policy is rather unclear. Parental leave facilities, for example, might increase the fertility rate but lower the female participation rate. Part-time work arrangements, on the other hand, might increase the participation rate, but might have a rather negative impact on gender equality as it is most likely that women take up the part-time jobs. Only childcare services seem to escape the tradeoffs between facilitating care and stimulating labor supply, as there is strong evidence that the availability of good-quality childcare services has a positive impact on both. That does not imply, however, that the childcare issue is beyond debate. Even in countries where childcare is accepted (and does not meet major financial objections) as in the Nordic countries, every now and then 'good motherhood' and the well-being of children in childcare are topics of public debate. The outcome of these debates will to a large extent structure the actual design of reconciliation policies and the work and care patterns of young families.

Within this context, the purpose of this chapter is twofold. Section II provides a summary of the reconciliation policies in the different EU member states. Given the paradigmatic policy shift from a traditional breadwinner society toward an adult worker society (Lewis, 2001), we focus especially on measures that try to bridge work and family life (financial allowances will therefore not be taken into account). Instead we focus on childcare services, leave, part-time work, and flexible working-time arrangements. By combining the different scores into one reconciliation index, we are able to rank the countries on their policy efforts and to use this as an independent variable in the rest of the analysis. Section III then focuses on the impact of reconciliation policies. Both by a summary account of the available literature and by a simple cross-country correlation, we investigate the impact of reconciliation policies on five different fields: female labor force participation; fertility; perceived work–life balance; gender equality; and happiness. As such, the ambitions of this chapter are mainly descriptive: to provide an update on structure and impact of reconciliation policies within Europe. At the same time the approach is not exclusively descriptive. The variables that are used to monitor the impact of reconciliation measures are also intended as input into a more conceptual debate about the optimal design of reconciliation policy (see Plantenga, 2010). This is extremely important as an increasing number of women (and men) struggle to combine work and family life. As such, the results are interesting not only within the European context, but also from a global point of view. Section IV concludes.

II RECONCILIATION POLICIES WITHIN EU MEMBER STATES

Reconciliation policies are usually referred to as 'policies designed to ease the reconciliation of work and family life, including leave to care for sick children; maternity, paternity, parental, and career interruption leave; childcare facilities; and measures that better match working-time with school hours' (Evans, 2001, p. 6). In line with this definition, this section details the extent of childcare services, leave arrangements, part-time work, and flexible working-time arrangements. The availability of harmonized statistics enables an assessment of the current state of affairs in all EU member states and allows for a careful comparison of the measures taken. In addition, each subsection begins with an overview of European legislation.

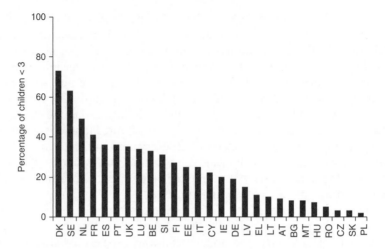

Source: Eurostat European Survey on Income and Living Conditions.

Figure 18.1   Use of formal childcare arrangements, 0–2 years old, 2009

Childcare Services

The importance of affordable and accessible quality childcare provision has been recognized by the European Council and the European Union at a rather early stage. In March, 1992, the Council of the EU passed a recommendation on childcare stating that member states 'should take and/or progressively encourage initiatives to enable women and men to reconcile their occupational, family and upbringing responsibilities arising for the care of children' (CEU, 1992). Ten years later, at the 2002 Barcelona summit, the aims were formulated more explicitly and targets were set with regard to childcare. Confirming the goal of full employment, the European Council agreed that member states should remove disincentives to female labor force participation and, taking into account the demand for childcare facilities and in line with national patterns of provisions, strive to provide childcare by 2010 for at least 90 percent of children between three years old and the mandatory school age and at least 33 percent of children under three years of age.

The Barcelona targets are set within the context of the European Employment Strategy. This means that the targets should be interpreted as an important goal for the near future. However, the targets are not obligatory; there is no sanction for noncompliance. In fact, most countries have not yet reached the Barcelona targets. The current state of affairs with regard to the youngest age category is summarized in Figure 18.1, the share of children under the age of three that are taken care of in a 'formal arrangement' in the EU member states. Formal arrangements in this context cover the following services: education at pre-school, education at compulsory school, childcare at center-based services and childcare at daycare center (see Eurostat, 2011a). Note that the differences in the EU are extensive. The highest coverage rate is found in Denmark (73 percent), followed by Sweden. In the Netherlands and France, the coverage rates are also relatively high (49 and 41 percent, respectively). Poland has the lowest share (2 percent), followed by Slovakia and the Czech Republic (3 percent).

It should also be noted that within EU countries, the younger the child, the more often it is cared for at home, especially by the parents, followed by other groups such as grandparents and/or other relatives. In Denmark, for example, the share of children under one year in a formal daycare center is rather low, as most parents have maternity and parental leave for about 11 months. After this period, however, the majority of children are taken care of in a childcare center. In addition, a more detailed analysis reveals that countries are highly diverse with regard to the number of hours these formal arrangements are used. In several countries, such as Denmark, Greece, Finland, Hungary, Latvia, Lithuania, Portugal, Slovenia, Slovakia, and Poland, the formal services are used for 30 hours or more per week. In other countries, however, part-time use is more common. Examples include Austria, the Czech Republic, Germany, Hungary, the Netherlands, and the United Kingdom (for more details, see Plantenga and Remery, 2009).

Leave Policies

Another important element of reconciliation policies is parental leave. Since June 1996, national policy in the field of leave arrangements has been underpinned by a directive of the European Council (a directive ensures that a certain minimum standard is guaranteed within the member states). The parental leave directive obliges member states to introduce legislation that will enable parents to care full-time for their child for a period of three months. In principle, this refers to an individual, nontransferable entitlement for both mothers and fathers. In 2010, the European Council decided that the individual entitlement will be extended to four months. In order to stimulate a more equal take up of leave by men and women, and as such promote equal opportunities, at least one of the four months will have to be nontransferable. This is an encouragement for fathers to take on more family responsibilities because the fourth month cannot be transferred to mothers and will be lost if not taken. Moreover, the directive states that member states and/or social partners have to take measures to ensure that workers returning from parental leave may request changes to their working hours and/or patterns for a set period of time. Employers should consider and respond to such requests, taking into account both employers' and workers' needs. The new directive has to be implemented in 2012 at the latest (CEU, 2010).

Over and above the European Directive, there is a broad range of national regulation with countries differing as to duration, payments, flexibility, and entitlement. The duration, for example, ranges from three months in some countries (Belgium, Cyprus, Ireland, and Malta) to the period until the child's third birthday (the Czech Republic, Estonia, Germany, France, Latvia, Lithuania, Poland, Slovakia, and Spain). Regarding the level of payment, in some countries the leave is unpaid whereas in others leave takers are compensated more or less for their loss of income. In addition, parental leave can be organized along family or individual lines. If the former is used as the basis, parents can decide who will make use of the parental leave allocated to the family. If both parents have an individual, nontransferable entitlement to parental leave, then both can claim a period of leave. If one parent does not take advantage of this entitlement, the right expires. Especially in the newest member states, parental leave is often framed as a family right.[1]

Given the large differentiation in leave arrangements, the best way to compare the

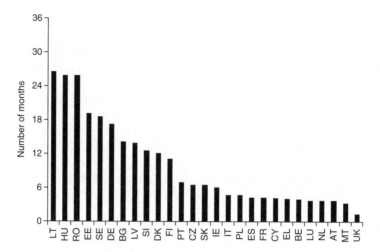

Source: Author's update of Table 18.M3 (EC, 2010b).

Figure 18.2   Total number of months of maternity, paternity, and parental leave with benefits replacing at least 2/3 of salary, 2009

national policies is on the basis of an indicator in which the length of the leave is weighted by the payment level. Such an indicator is provided by the European Commission within the context of the European Employment Strategy. This indicator gives the number of months of maternity, paternity and parental leave with benefits replacing at least two-thirds of salary, presented in Figure 18.2. Based on this indicator, the highest score is found in Lithuania, providing parents with a little more than 26 months of paid leave. Lithuania is followed by Hungary and Romania, both offering almost 26 months of paid leave. On the other end of the ranking is the United Kingdom. Here only six weeks of maternity leave is paid (offering 90 percent of women's average earnings); all other leave is unpaid.

Part-time Work

At the level of the EU, there is no generally binding regulation that entitles employees to part-time work, but Directive 97/81/EC calls upon the member states to ensure equal treatment of full-timers and part-timers unless there are objective reasons to treat them differently. The aim is to increase the quality of part-time jobs and to facilitate access to part-time work for men and women in order to prepare for retirement, reconcile professional and family life, and take up education and training opportunities to improve skills and career opportunities (CEU, 1998). Though it does not entitle all employees to part-time work, several countries have developed national legislation in this respect. In some countries such as Germany and the Netherlands, (the majority of) employees are entitled to work part-time. In other countries, including for example Estonia and Austria, entitlements are limited to those with care responsibilities (for an overview, see Plantenga and Remery, 2010).

Figure 18.3 shows the share of male and female employees working part-time.[2] The

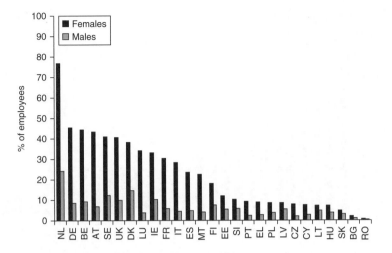

Source: Eurostat European Labour Force Survey.

Figure 18.3   Share of part-time employees by gender, 2009

highest part-time rate is found in the Netherlands, both for men and women (24 and 77 percent respectively). Germany, Belgium, Austria, Sweden, and the United Kingdom also have relatively high female part-time rates. The United Kingdom, Ireland, Sweden, and Denmark have relatively high part-time rates for men (10 percent or more). In 11 countries, all East or South European, the part-time rate for men and women is less than 10 percent, with the lowest rates being found in Romania, Bulgaria, and Slovakia; these labor markets appear to be rather traditionally organized around a 40-hour working week. Figure 18.3 also illustrates that part-time work is mainly used by women. In all EU countries, the female part-time rate is higher than the male part-time rate.

Flexible Working Hours

At the level of the EU, there is also no general binding entitlement to flexible working hours. According to the revised directive on parental leave, employees returning from leave may request flexible working hours, but there is no guarantee that the request will be met. In addition, the revised directive on maternity leave, as proposed by the European Commission in October 2008, regulates that employees having maternity leave or returning from maternity leave have a right to ask the employer to adapt their working patterns and hours to the new family situation. Employers are obliged to con-sider such a request (EC, 2008, p. 9). However, this proposal is still under discussion in Council and European Parliament (see Plantenga and Remery, 2010). This implies that in most European countries flexible working-time arrangements are settled at the level of the firm.

   Data on flexible working-time arrangements are not standardly available from Eurostat, the EU statistical agency. A European Labour Force Survey ad hoc module from 2004 does provide some data on flexible working-time schedules including: (i) staggered working hours; (ii) flexitime arrangements; and (iii) working-time banking.

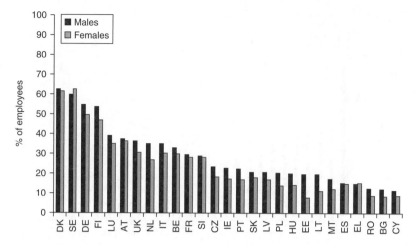

Source: Eurostat, European Labour Force Survey, ad hoc module (2004).

Figure 18.4   Share of employees having access to flexible working-time arrangements, 2004

Staggered hours employees have the opportunity to start and finish work at slightly different times, fixed by the employee or the employer. Flexitime arrangements include the option of a flexible start and end of the working day and the possibility to fully determine personal working schedules. Working-time banking refers to a system of accumulation and settlement of debit and credit hours around the standard number of weekly or monthly hours, that is, an employee can work more hours in exchange for taking the equivalent time off at some time in the future. Over a longer period, the average number of working hours is equal to the contractually agreed working time. Two options are further distinguished: working-time banking with the opportunity only to take hours off, and working-time banking with the possibility to take full days off (EC, 2006, p. 37).

The share of male and female employees having access to one of these forms of working-time flexibility is summarized in Figure 18.4. Denmark and Sweden have the highest share of employees with access to flexible working-time schedules (more than 60 percent). Also, in Germany, more than half of the employees have access to flexible working-time schedules. In Finland, more than half of the male employees have access to such schedules; among female employees it is a little lower, but still among the highest in the European Union. In all other countries of the EU, the majority of employees have fixed working times. In Romania, Bulgaria, and Cyprus, flexible working-time schedules are least common: around 10 percent of the employees have access.

It appears that the mix of flexible working-time schedules is rather different across countries. In Denmark, flexitime arrangements and (to a lesser extent) working-time banking are rather common whereas in Sweden staggered hours are an important form of flexible working-time schedules. Working-time banking is the main form of flexibility in Germany, which is also the country with the highest share of employees having access to this type of work schedule. In the countries with the lowest levels of flexibility in working time, notably the new member states and some South European countries, working-time banking is a less well-known concept. The limited flexibility mainly refers to staggered hours and flexibility in start and end times or determining personal working schedules. Overall, the gender differences in access to flexible working-time schedules are relatively small.

Toward a Reconciliation Index

Thus far we have illustrated that there are considerable differences in the country measures of the reviewed reconciliation policies. In order to get a more overall score on reconciliation policies, we calculate a 'reconciliation index'. This index is composed of country scores on the three elements of reconciliation policies: childcare services, leave arrangements, and flexibility of working time. As the indicators refer to different dimensions (with different scaling), first the z-scores of the individual country scores are calculated. This normalizes the data and transforms them into a new set with a mean of 0 and a standard deviation of 1. Negative z-scores imply that the observed country scores are below the sample average; positive z-scores imply that the countries perform above the sample average. Afterwards, an average 'reconciliation score' is calculated by adding the z-scores (for example, OECD, 2001). In order to avoid a higher weight of flexibility of working time in the index, we have recalculated an average score of the share of part-time employees and the share of employees having access to flexible working time.

Table 18.1 gives the z-scores on the different dimensions and the score on the reconciliation index. The ranking shows that Sweden has the highest score; Sweden scores above average on all three policy areas. The runner up is Denmark, which also performs above average on all three indicators. These high scores are not surprising as the countries are well known for their emphasis on gender equality (for example, Gornick et al., 1997; Bettio and Plantenga, 2004; Thevenon, 2011). High scores are also found for Germany and the Netherlands. On the other end of the ranking is a group that consists of new member states (Poland, the Czech Republic, and Slovakia) and southern countries (Greece, Malta, and Cyprus). These countries score below average on all three indicators of reconciliation.

All in all, this index provides us with a comprehensive measurement of national EU policy with regard to reconciliation. Of course, the methodology used implicitly assumes that the different dimensions are interchangeable; the index is calculated by simply adding the scores on the dimensions. This presumes perfect substitutability between the dimensions: a low score on one dimension can be compensated by a high score on the other. This may not be the case, however. Leave provisions especially may have a different impact on labor market behavior than childcare services and flexible work arrangements. Nevertheless, we will use the score on the index as a summary account of the national reconciliation policies and next assess the correlation between the reconciliation index and several macroeconomic outcomes.

III RECONCILIATION POLICIES: WHAT IS THE IMPACT?

Obviously, countries may invest in reconciliation policies for different reasons. Some countries may invest in childcare facilities in order to boost the female participation rate

Table 18.1   Z-scores of EU member states on reconciliation policies and reconciliation
index

Country	Flex	Childcare < 3	Leave	Reconciliation index
SE	1.97	2.12	1.13	5.22
DK	1.99	2.67	0.28	4.94
DE	1.57	−0.28	0.94	2.23
NL	1.66	1.36	−0.81	2.22
FI	0.93	0.16	0.14	1.23
LT	−0.78	−0.77	2.15	0.60
EE	−0.68	0.05	1.19	0.56
SI	−0.20	0.38	0.34	0.52
FR	0.24	0.92	−0.74	0.42
BE	0.68	0.49	−0.78	0.39
HU	−0.79	−0.93	2.06	0.34
LU	0.56	0.54	−0.81	0.30
UK	0.74	0.60	−1.11	0.22
RO	−1.26	−1.04	2.06	−0.24
IT	0.28	0.05	−0.69	−0.36
PT	−0.67	0.65	−0.38	−0.40
LV	−0.64	−0.50	0.51	−0.63
ES	−0.54	0.65	−0.74	−0.63
IE	0.03	−0.22	−0.51	−0.70
AT	0.84	−0.82	−0.81	−0.79
BG	−1.24	−0.88	0.54	−1.58
CY	−1.09	−0.11	−0.75	−1.95
CZ	−0.66	−1.15	−0.44	−2.25
MT	−0.57	−0.88	−0.87	−2.32
SK	−0.76	−1.15	−0.44	−2.36
EL	−0.87	−0.71	−0.77	−2.36
PL	−0.76	−1.20	−0.69	−2.65

Source: See Figures 18.1–18.4.

while others improve parental leave schemes in order to increase the fertility rate. At the most basic level, the assumption is that reconciliation policies facilitate the combination of work and private life and as such, have a positive impact on participation and/or fertility. In fact, the fertility and participation argument may be interpreted as two sides of the same coin. In the participation argument, the fertility rate is taken for granted and reconciliation services should facilitate the combination of care responsibilities with paid work. In the fertility argument, participation is taken for granted and reconciliation policies are presumed to facilitate the combination of paid work with care. We will therefore start our analysis with the relationship between reconciliation policies and participation and fertility.

Another reason for investing in reconciliation policies refers to gender equality. By introducing more flexible working hours, family-friendly leaves, and affordable childcare facilities, countries may reach a more equal distribution of paid and unpaid work and as such have higher scores in terms of gender equality. First, we will cover the relationship between reconciliation policies and gender equality. Then we will relate the score on reconciliation with the most general outcome variable: the extent of happiness. Of course these macro outcomes are not completely independent. For example, participation is one of the pillars of gender equality.[3] Nevertheless, we think that these three perspectives on the impact of reconciliation policies capture most of the policy debate.

Participation and Fertility

The relationship between reconciliation policies and the female employment rate has been studied extensively. The actual relationship may be rather complicated as the different elements of such policies have different incentives, costs, and benefits. Parental leave, for example, provides employment protection and as such contributes to higher participation rates and to more continuity in female employment. The period of leave, however, should not be too long as this reduces the probability that the (female) employee will return. From a labor market perspective, the leave entitlements should therefore be of moderate duration (Ruhm and Teague, 1995; Ruhm, 1998; Jaumotte, 2003; OECD, 2007, 2011). Formal childcare services imply an outsourcing of care, enabling parents to keep working. Indeed, numerous studies show that the availability of good-quality childcare services has a positive impact on the female participation rate (for overviews, see Blau and Currie, 2004; OECD, 2007; Hegewisch and Gornick, 2011). Flexibility in working time may also have a positive impact. Part-time work allows for unpaid (care) work and may translate into a higher participation rate. Generally, research confirms the positive relation between the presence of part-time work and the female employment rate (for example, O'Reilly and Fagan, 1998; Jaumotte, 2003). However, in several countries, part-time work is hardly an option for employees. Especially in these circumstances, the possibility to work flexible hours may facilitate a higher female participation rate.

The actual correlation between the reconciliation index and the participation rate is illustrated by Figure 18.5.[4] As it might be argued that reconciliation policies are particularly relevant for working mothers, the focus is on the female employment rate of the 25–49 age group, using harmonized data from the European Labour Force Survey. It appears that in countries with a higher score on the reconciliation index, the female participation rate is higher; the relationship is fairly strong (0.58; $p = 0.001$).

Reconciliation policies may also influence fertility rates. Researchers have traditionally argued that female employment has a negative effect on fertility rates. Due to higher educational levels of women, opportunity costs of children have increased and fertility has declined. However, since the early 1990s, this downward trend has reversed in several countries, particularly in countries with high female employment rates (D'Addio and d'Ercole, 2005; Thevenon and Gauthier, 2011). The availability of reconciliation policies, making a child less costly in terms of income and career opportunities, seems important in this respect. Research shows that the availability and affordability of childcare services indeed increases fertility rates (for example, Ermisch, 1989; Del Boca et al., 2003; D'Addio and d'Ercole, 2005; Hilgeman and Butts, 2009). With respect to leave, however, the results are mixed. Anna D'Addio and Marco d'Ercole (2005), find that a longer duration of parental leave has a negative impact on the fertility rate, whereas paid leave has a positive impact. Christin Hilgeman and Carter Butts (2009) find a negative impact of family leave on the fertility rate, but this effect is not significant. Finally, flexibility in working time, generally measured as part-time working hours, positively influences fertility rates, the argument being that in flexible labor markets the costs of leaving and re-entering the labor market are relatively low (Adsera, 2004a, 2004b; D'Addio and d'Ercole, 2005). The study of Frances Castles (2003) finds a positive impact of working flexitime on fertility but no impact of part-time hours.

Figure 18.6 illustrates the scores of the EU member states on the reconciliation index and total fertility rate, using harmonized data from population statistics of Eurostat.[5] In most countries with a low score on the reconciliation index, the total fertility rate is rather low and in the countries with the highest score on this index fertility rates are rather high. The correlation is not very high, though (0.34; $p = 0.044$). As such, the results seem to be in line with the (more sophisticated) empirical research, illustrating that the relationship between reconciliation policies and fertility is not very straightforward.

Work–Life Balance and Gender Equality

Another argument to invest in reconciliation measures is to increase gender equality. Reconciliation policies should support employees in combining work and private life and as such contribute to a better work–life balance. As women still spend most hours on care activities, they might benefit most from such policies (Bettio and Plantenga, 2004; Lewis et al., 2008). In a study comparing Britain, France, Finland, Norway, and Portugal, Rosemary Crompton and Claire Lyonette (2006) show that the level of work–life conflict is indeed lower in the countries that offer the most encompassing reconciliation policies (Finland and Norway). Reconciliation policies in this respect refer to the provision of public childcare and availability of leave facilities. Evidence on the impact of flexibility of working hours is more mixed. Agnès Parent-Thirion et al. (2007), for example, show that employees (and self-employed) working with fixed starting and finishing times are more satisfied on their work–life balance than employees with variable working times. This suggests that predictability is more important than flexibility. Regarding the length of working hours, however, the expected impact on work–life balance is found. On a general level, part-time workers, both male and female, are more satisfied with their work–life balance than full-time employees (Burchell et al., 2007). Based on a multivariate analysis, the authors conclude that the volume of working hours is the main dimension of working time that determines work–life balance. That is, 'the higher the number of hours worked, the more likely men and women are to report that their working hours are incompatible with family and other commitments' (ibid., p.49).

Figure 18.7 illustrates the cross-country correlation between the score on the reconciliation index and perceived work–life balance, based on harmonized data from the Eurobarometer (EC, 2008). The correlation is low and not significant (0.33; $p = 0.09$). Apparently, there is more in the perceived work–life balance than just the availability of reconciliation policies. The figure also suggests that different policies may have a comparable outcome in terms of perceived work–life balance. Finland and the Netherlands, for example, have a similar score on the perceived work–life balance, yet the actual policy packages are rather different. In the Netherlands, emphasis is on part-time in

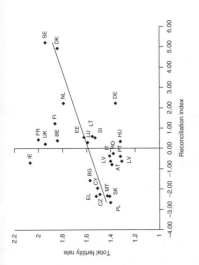

Sources: Table 18.1 for reconciliation index; Eurostat European Labour Force Survey for female employment rate.

Figure 18.5   Scores on the reconciliation index and female employment rate (age group 25–49)

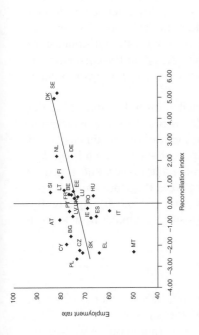

Sources: Table 18.1 for reconciliation index; Flash Eurobarometer (2008) for perceived work–life balance.

Figure 18.7   Scores on the reconciliation index and perceived work–life balance

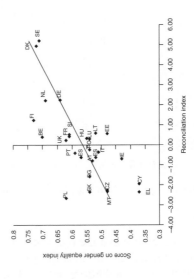

Sources: Table 18.1 for reconciliation index; Eurostat population database for fertility rate (2011b).

Figure 18.6   Scores on the reconciliation index and total fertility rate

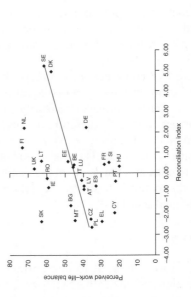

Sources: Table 18.1 for reconciliation index; author's update of Plantenga et al., (2009) for gender equality index.

Figure 18.8   Scores on the reconciliation index and EU gender equality index

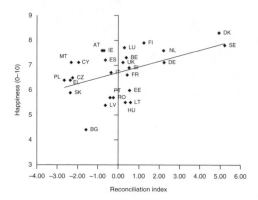

Sources: Table 18.1 for reconciliation index; Veenhoven (2011) for happiness.

Figure 18.9   Scores on the reconciliation index and happiness (scale 1–10)

combination with part-time use of childcare services, whereas in Finland leave facilities are more extended and more employees have access to flexible working hours.

In addition, reconciliation measures might favor one aspect of gender equality (participation rate), but be rather detrimental to another (wages level). Hadas Mandel and Moshe Semyonov (2005), for example, conclude that while 'mother-friendly' policies enable more women to participate in the labor market, they also result in more segregation and a higher gender wage gap. This is particularly clear for extended maternity leaves. Moreover, mother-friendly policies seem to reduce the chances of women to attain managerial positions (ibid.). Given this tradeoff between different dimensions of gender equality, it is also important to see what the cross-country correlation is between the reconciliation index and gender equality, measured in a more comprehensive way.

Figure 18.8 combines the country scores on the reconciliation index and the scores on the European Union gender equality index. This index is based on the assumption that a full concept of gender equality should take into account different dimensions of life. Gender equality is therefore defined as an equal sharing of assets, which is conceptualized as equal sharing of paid work, money, decision-making power, and time (see Plantenga et al., 2009). There is a clear positive relation between the score on the reconciliation index and the score on the gender equality index (0.63; $p = 0.000$). Apparently, on a cross-country basis reconciliation measures are positively linked with a more gender-equal society.

Happiness

Finally, we might want to concentrate on a more comprehensive outcome measure. As a critique to the rather narrow economic approach, Joseph Stiglitz et al. (2009), for example, argue that there should be more focus on measuring people's well-being. Therefore, as a final indicator, we analyze the relationship between reconciliation policies and the average level of happiness in countries. Research shows that, on the one hand, time spent on paid work and household work creates time pressure, which decreases happiness. On the other hand, however, time spent on both paid work and household work itself makes people happier (Pouwels, 2011). By mitigating the time pressure, reconciliation policies could contribute to increasing happiness. The number of studies on work and happiness is expanding (for example, Tesch-Römer et al., 2008; Boye, 2011). There are, however, hardly any comparative studies linking reconciliation policies and happiness. An exception is Alison Booth and Jan Van Ours (2009) who show that women's life satisfaction is higher when they work part-time. For men, the opposite is the case; their life satisfaction is higher when they work full-time.

Finally, in Figure 18.9, the scores on the reconciliation index are combined with average happiness scores of countries (measured on a scale from 1–10) using the World Database of Happiness (Veenhoven, 2011). Higher scores on reconciliation policies indeed combine with higher scores on happiness. The correlation is not very strong, though, and just below significance (0.38; $p = 0.054$). Obviously, the overall level of happiness in a country is influenced by many factors, among which (perhaps) is the extent of reconciliation policies.

IV   CONCLUSIONS

Reconciliation policies have become quite an established concept, both within social policy and in the academic literature. The overview provided in this chapter shows that throughout Europe the actual score on reconciliation policies varies extensively, ranging from a rather hesitant approach with policies offering only the minimum in terms of services and working-time flexibility to a comprehensive package offering full childcare coverage, generous leave facilities, and flexibility in working hours. Investments in reconciliation policies may be motivated by different factors, such as increasing participation rates, fertility rates, or gender equality. As such, it is likely that different packages have a different impact. We have assessed the impact of reconciliation policies on five outcome variables: the female employment rate; the fertility rate; the perceived work–life balance of female employees; gender equality; and happiness.

It appears that countries with more comprehensive packages also have a higher female employment rate, a higher fertility rate, and a higher score on the European Union gender equality index. In addition, the overall level of happiness is higher, though the correlation is just below significance. Obviously, the level of analysis is rather general and should stimulate further research in the field. As already indicated, the methodology applied in calculating the index presumes perfect substitutability between the dimensions: a low score on one dimension can be compensated by a high score on the other. It seems likely, however, that the three dimensions translate into different incentive schemes. Whereas childcare and flexibility in working hours clearly facilitate participation, extended periods of leave might have an opposite impact. Additional analyses between participation and a reconciliation index excluding leave facilities, however, do not show higher correlations. More sophisticated research focusing on different elements of reconciliation policy might further inform policy-makers on the optimal design of the actual policies within this area.

The results make it clear that reconciliation policies provide important support to working families and contribute to gender equality. The EU has been an important stimulus in this respect, even though the specific packages differ per member state. While the European Commission strives for further progress in this field as stated in the Strategy for Equality between Women and Men 2012–2015 (EC, 2010c), it is not clear if additional policies will be implemented. National developments may also be stimulated by other factors. In particular, the demographic changes may put some pressure on the specific design of the family policy for parents of young children. Countries that combine low employment rates with low fertility rates are particularly vulnerable to rising levels of old-age spending. In these cases, increasing the female employment rate, by creating a supportive infrastructure, may partly offset the costs of the pension system taken as a share of GDP.

Certainly more research is needed to determine the optimal packaging of reconciliation policies to exert the strongest possible impact on well-being and gender equality. Furthermore, we must not forget that although the issue of work–family balance is a global one, the solutions may be rather local: different regions may have very different 'optimal' reconciliation policy packages.

NOTES

1. For more details on leave entitlements, see Plantenga and Remery, 2005; Fagan and Hebson, 2006; Moss, 2011; see also Ray et al., 2010 on the extent to which policy designs are gender egalitarian.
2. The distinction between full-time and part-time work is made on the basis of the spontaneous answer given by respondents; a more exact differentiation is impossible due to variations in working hours between member states and branches of industry (Eurostat, 2007).
3. A correlation table of outcome variables is available from the authors.
4. Regarding Figures 18.5–9, an appendix with the actual values is available from the authors.
5. Total fertility rate refers to the mean number of children that would be born alive to a woman during her lifetime if she were to pass through her childbearing years conforming to the fertility rates by age of a given year (Eurostat, 2011b). This is a commonly (widely) used measure in studies on fertility.

REFERENCES

Adsera, Alícia (2004a), 'Changing fertility rates in developed markets: the impact of labor market institutions', *Journal of Population Economics*, **17**(1), 1–27.
Adsera, Alícia (2004b), *Where are the Babies? Labor Market Conditions and Fertility in Europe*, Chicago, IL: University of Chicago, Population Research Center.
Bettio, Francesca and Janneke Plantenga (2004), 'Comparing care regimes in Europe', *Feminist Economics*, **10**(1), 85–113.
Blau, David and Janet Currie (2004), 'Preschool, day care, and afterschool care: who's minding the kids?', NBER Working Paper 10670, National Bureau of Economic Research, Cambridge, MA.
Booth, Alison and Jan van Ours (2009), 'Hours of work and gender identity: does part-time work make the family happier?,' *Economica*, **76** (301), 176–96.
Boye, Katarina (2011), 'Work and well-being in a comparative perspective – the role of family policy', *European Sociological Review*, **27**(1), 16–30.
Burchell, Brendan, Colette Fagan, Catherine O'Brien and Mark Smith (2007), *Working Conditions in the European Union: The Gender Perspective*, Luxembourg: Office for Official Publications of the European Communities.
Castles, Frances (2003), 'The world turned upside down: below replacement fertility, changing preferences and family-friendly public policy in 21 OECD countries', *Journal of Europan Social Policy*, **13**(3), 209–27.

Council of the European Union (CEU) (1992), Council recommendation of 31 March 1992 on childcare (92/241/EEC), *Official Journal of the European Union*, 08–05–1992: L 123, 0016–0018.

Council of the European Union (CEU) (1998), Council Directive 97/81/EC of 15 December 1997 concerning the Framework Agreement on part-time work concluded by UNICE, CEEP and the ETUC, *Official Journal of the European Union*, 20–01–1998: L 14/9–L 14/14.

Council of the European Union (CEU) (2010), Council Directive 2010/18/EU of 8 March 2010 implementing the revised Framework Agreement on parental leave concluded by Business Europe, UEAPME, CEEP and ETUC and repealing Directive 96/34/EC, *Official Journal of the European Union*, 18–03–2010: L68/13–L68/20.

Crompton, Rosemary and Claire Lyonette (2006), 'Work–life "balance" in Europe', *Acta Sociologica*, **49**(4), 379–93.

D'Addio, Anna Christina and Marco Mira d'Ercole (2005), 'Trends and Determinants of Fertility Rates in OECD Countries: The Role of Policies', Social Employment and Migration Working Papers No. 27, OECD, Paris.

Del Boca, Daniela, Sylvia Pasqua and Chiara Pronzato (2003), *Analyzing Women's Employment and Fertility Rates in Europe: Differences and Similarities in Northern and Southern Europe*, Turin: Child.

Ermisch, John (1989), 'Purchased child care, optimal family size and mother's employment: theory and econometric analysis', *Journal of Population Economics*, **2**(2), 79–102.

European Commission (EC) (2006), *Final Report of the Task Force for Evaluating the 2004 LFS Ad Hoc Module on Work Organisation and Working Time Arrangements*, Luxembourg: Office for Official Publications of the European Communities.

European Commission (EC) (2008), *Proposal for a Directive of the European Parliament and of the Council Amending Council Directive 92/85/EEC on the Introduction of Measures to Encourage Improvements in the Safety and Health at Work of Pregnant Workers and Workers Who Have Recently Given Birth or are Breastfeeding*, Brussels: European Commission.

European Commission (EC) (2010a), *Europe 2020. A Strategy for Smart, Sustainable and Inclusive Growth*, COM(2010) 2020 final, Brussels: European Commission.

European Commission (EC) (2010b), *Indicators for Monitoring the Employment Guidelines including Indicators for Additional Employment Analysis 2010 Compendium* (update 20/07/2010), Brussels: European Commission.

European Commission (EC) (2010c), *Strategy for Equality between Women and Men 2010–2015*, Brussels: European Commission.

Eurostat (2007), *EU Labour Force Survey Database User Guide*, EC/Eurostat.

Eurostat (2011a), *Childcare Arrangements. Reference Metadata in Euro SDMX Metadata Structure (ESMS)*, available at: http://epp.eurostat.ec.europa.eu/cache/ITY_SDDS/en/ilc_ca_esms.htm (accessed November 2011).

Eurostat (2011b), EU population database, available at: http://epp.eurostat.ec.europa.eu/portal/page/portal/population/data/database/ (accessed November 2011).

Evans, John M. (2001), 'Firms' contribution to the reconciliation between work and family life', OECD Labour Market and Social Policy Occasional Papers, No. 48, OECD Paris, available at: http://dx.doi.org/10.1787/344836028454 (accessed November 2011).

Fagan, Colette and Gail Hebson (2006), *Making Work Pay: A Comparative Review of Some Recent Policy Reforms in Thirty European Countries*, Luxembourg: Office for Official Publications of the European Communities.

Flash Eurobarometer Report (2008), *Family Life and the Needs of an Ageing Population*, Flash EB Series 247, Hungary: The Gallup Organization.

Gornick, Janet, Marcia Meyers and Katherin Ross (1997), 'Supporting the employment of mothers: policy variation across fourteen welfare states', *Journal of European Social Policy*, **7**(10), 45–70.

Hegewisch, Ariane and Janet Gornick (2011), 'The impact of work–family policies on women's employment: a review of research from OECD countries', *Community, Work and Family*, **14**(2), 119–38.

Hilgeman, Christin and Carter Butts (2009), 'Women's employment and fertility: a welfare regime paradox', *Social Science Research*, **38**(1), 103–17.

Jaumotte, Florence (2003), *Female Labour Force Participation: Past Trends and Main Determinants in OECD Countries*, Paris: OECD.

Lewis, Jane (2001), 'The decline of the male breadwinner model: implications for work and care', *Social Politics*, **8**(2), 152–69.

Lewis, Jane, Mary Cambell and Carmen Huerta (2008), 'Patterns of paid and unpaid work in Western Europe: gender, commodification, preferences and the implications for policy', *Journal of European Social Policy*, **18**(1), 21–37.

Mandel, Hadas and Moshe Semyonov (2005), 'Family policies, wage structures and gender gaps: sources of earnings inequality in 20 countries', *American Sociological Review*, **70**(6), 949–67.

Mandel, Hadas and Moshe Semyonov (2006), 'A welfare state paradox: state interventions and women's employment in 22 countries', *American Journal of Sociology*, **111**(6), 1910–49.

Moss Peter (2011), 'International review of leave policies and related research 2011', Institute of Education, University London.

O'Reilly, Jacqueline and Colette Fagan (1998), *Part-time Prospects: An International Comparison of Part-time Work*, London: Routledge.

Organisation for Economic Co-operation and Development (OECD) (2001), 'Balancing work and family life: helping parents into paid employment', *Employment Outlook 2001*, Paris, OECD, pp. 129–66.

Organisation for Economic Co-operation and Development (OECD) (2007), *Babies and Bosses*, Paris: OECD.

Organisation for Economic Co-operation and Development (OECD) (2011), *Doing Better for Families*, Paris: OECD.

Parent-Thirion, Agnès, Enrique Fernández, John Hurley and Greet Vermeylen (2007), *Fourth European Working Conditions Survey*, Luxembourg: Office for Official Publications of the European Communities.

Plantenga, Janneke (2010), 'The rise of the adult worker model; balancing work and family life in Europe', in John B. Davis (ed.), *Global Social Economy*, London: Routledge, pp. 149–63.

Plantenga, Janneke and Chantal Remery (2005), *Reconciliation of Work and Private Life: A Comparative Review of Thirty European Countries*, Luxembourg: Office for Official Publications of the European Communities.

Plantenga, Janneke and Chantal Remery (2009), *The Provision of Childcare Services: A Comparative Review of Thirty European Countries*, Luxembourg: Office for Official Publications of the European Communities.

Plantenga, Janneke and Chantal Remery (2010), *Flexible Working Time Arrangements and Gender Equality: A Comparative Review of Thirty Countries*, Luxembourg: Office of Official Publications of the European Union.

Plantenga, Janneke, Chantal Remery, Hugo Figueiredo and Mark Smith (2009), 'Towards an EU gender equality index', *Journal of European Social Policy*, **19**(1), 19–33.

Pouwels, Babette (2011), 'Work, Family, and Happiness: Essays on Interdependencies within Families, Life Events, and Time Allocation Decisions', PhD thesis, Utrecht University.

Ray, Rebecca, Janet Gornick and John Schmitt (2010), 'Who cares? Assessing generosity and gender equality in parental leave policy designs in 21 countries', *Journal of European Social Policy*, **20**(3), 196–216.

Ruhm, Christopher (1998), 'The economic consequences of parental leave mandates: lessons from Europe', *Quarterly Journal of Economics*, **113**(1), 285–317.

Ruhm, Christopher and Jackqueline Teague (1995), 'Parental Leave Policies in Europe and North America', NBER Working Paper 5065, National Bureau of Economic Research, Cambridge, MA.

Stiglitz, Joseph, Amartya Sen and Jean-Paul Fitoussi (2009), 'Report by the Commission on the Measurement of Economic Performance and Social Progress', available at: www.stiglitz-sen-fitoussi.fr (accessed November 2011).

Tesch-Römer, Clemens, Andreas Motel-Klingebiel and Martin Tomasik (2008), 'Gender differences in subjective well-being: comparing societies with respect to gender equality', *Social Indicators Research*, **85**(2), 329–49.

Thevenon, Olivier (2011), 'Family policies in OECD countries: a comparative analysis', *Population and Development Review*, **37**(10), 57–87.

Thevenon, Olivier and Anne Gauthier (2011), 'Family policies in developed countries: a "fertility booster" with side-effects', *Community, Work & Family*, **14**(2), 197–216.

Veenhoven, Ruut (2011), 'World Database of Happiness', Erasmus University Rotterdam, available at: http://worlddatabaseofhappiness.eur.nl (accessed November 2011).

19. The role of the government in work–family conflict in the US

Heather Boushey

I INTRODUCTION AND HISTORICAL BACKGROUND

The United States stands apart as particularly weak on policies to address work–family conflict (see Heymann, 2000; Waldfogel, 2001; Gornick and Meyers, 2003; Ray et al., 2008). A key challenge is that, unlike in the European Union and OECD countries more generally, US policies that address working-time regulation and social insurance remain stuck in an early twentieth-century mindset about who works and who cares, one that no longer reflects the ways that American families work and live. Because policy-makers have not updated their concept of what the American family looks like, they have not prioritized policies to help families who are at work also be good caregivers. While employers have made some progress addressing these issues voluntarily, they have not filled in the gaps left by an outdated policy structure.

It was in the 1930s that President Franklin Roosevelt and Secretary of Labor Frances Perkins put in place the federal policies in the United States that continue to provide the framework for policies addressing the intersection of work and family in the United States. During that era, most families had a stay-at-home caregiver, usually a mother, who could provide full-time care for children, the aged, and the sick. Relative to today, few women worked outside the home, although some, disproportionately women of color and recent immigrants, always have had relatively high labor force participation (Amott and Matthaei, 1991). The laws in place that govern the intersection between work and family were enacted at a time when US culture presumed women were (or should be) full-time caregivers.

Today's reality is, of course, very different. Most women work, including most mothers, and workers often have family responsibilities that conflict with paid employment as it currently looks. Yet despite remarkable changes in the United States in both women's labor supply and family structure over the decades, especially since the 1970s, the wage-and-hours regulatory system and the social insurance infrastructure put in place by Roosevelt and Perkins have not been systematically expanded to address specifically the dual role that most workers play as workers and caregivers today, nor been extended to provide universal access to care services, such as childcare and elder care.

The 1938 Fair Labor Standards Act lays out the US regulatory wage-and-hours framework. Congress enacted the FLSA following earlier state action to limit hours worked by women and children. The law limited the hours of work for some workers and established the minimum wage, both of which affect the ability of workers to reserve time to care for families. Because the assumption underlying the FLSA is that workers who need government protection are employed full-time – at that time, commonly 10–12 hours each day – the law did not deal with part-time work or scheduling flexibility or predictability.

US policies around employment took a leap forward with the passage of the Civil Rights Act of 1964, which made it illegal to discriminate against workers based on their race or gender, among other things. Until the 1950s, for example, many employers refused to hire married women or mothers because women were presumed to belong in the home (Goldin, 1988). Title VII of the Civil Rights Act helps ensure that work performance, not a worker's personal characteristics, determined employment and pay; but large gaps remained – and remain still – for workers with care responsibilities.

The Social Security Act of 1935 established Old Age and Survivors Insurance, unemployment insurance, and income assistance to widows and children through the Aid to Dependent Families program. Because the law was grounded in the assumption that men were breadwinners and women were caretakers, it left a legacy of gaps in coverage and eligibility for today's families. Policy-makers have since tried to fill many of these gaps, but inequalities that affect caregivers remain, perhaps most notably the failure of the law to cover caregiving leave. In two states, California and New Jersey, state-level programs provide social insurance to workers for family leave, but the United States remains the only developed nation that does not provide some type of paid leave to new parents nationwide, nor are most workers able to take a job-protected day off to care for a sick child or family member (Ray et al., 2008; Commonwealth of Australia, 2009).

This chapter outlines how current US policies that address the interaction between employment and caring for family members are embedded in outdated notions of how families structure care and who is employed outside the home. Section II discusses the challenges involved in negotiating work–family balance and the need for employment flexibility, before focusing on the role (and limitations) of the Fair Labor Standards Act and the variety of strategies for workplace flexibility that employers have experimented with. In Section III, I focus on the legislative foundation for equal rights in the workplace, noting the advance made in anti-discrimination law over the past few decades while also highlighting growing evidence of discrimination against workers with care responsibilities. Section IV continues with an examination of the need for paid time off from work for caregiving. Each section concludes with ideas for how to move policy forward to recognize the realities facing twenty-first-century families in the United States. Section V concludes the chapter.

II   NEGOTIATING WORK AND FAMILY WITH FLEXIBILITY

The reality is that most American caregivers are also employed outside the home, which means most families no longer have a full-time stay-at-home parent or caregiver. In 2008, among mothers of children under age 18, 71 percent participated in the workforce; among all workers, both male and female, 42 percent reported that they had cared for an elderly person within the past five years (Galinsky et al., 2009; Aumann et al., 2010). Workers with care responsibilities may be able to perform their jobs fully, but may also need some flexibility from their employers to manage work–family conflicts. Such flexibility would include, for example, being allowed to negotiate, have input into, or control hours or location of work, without fear of discrimination or penalty. For professional workers and those subject to mandatory overtime, the problem is most often too much work; for low-wage workers, it is more often too few hours and unpredictable schedules. Many higher earners, whether they are professionals tied to their Blackberry devices or nurses struggling to comply with mandatory overtime on little or no notice, would like to work fewer hours, while many low-wage workers can find only part-time work, face irregular schedules, or have no work at all (Jacobs and Gerson, 2005; Swanberg, 2008; Williams and Boushey, 2010).

Although workers report needing and wanting some flexibility in terms of hours or location of work, the nation's wage-and-hours regulatory structure, based on outdated models of who works and who cares, provides little guidance to help employers deal with the realities of today's workforce. The FLSA, which lays out the national regulatory structure on hours, remains grounded in assumptions about work and family that are no longer valid – and in fact were never valid for large numbers of workers. Although many employers do address workplace flexibility issues, wide gaps exist regarding which workers have access to flexibility. Further, a growing body of research suggests that mothers and caregivers often experience explicit discrimination because of their roles as caregivers and their need for workplace flexibility (Boushey, 2009b; Bornstein, 2011).

The Fair Labor Standards Act

The 1938 Fair Labor Standards Act (FLSA), the foundation of the US regulatory structure governing hours of work, sets overtime thresholds by defining a regular workweek as being 40 hours and requiring that workers covered by the law be paid 150 percent of the usual hourly wage for any hours worked above that threshold. When the US Congress passed the FLSA, its intent was to encourage employers to curtail the long hours of their current employees and to put more people to work. The law specifies that workers who need protection in terms of hours of work are those employed full time at regular jobs. The legislation was passed following decades of state efforts to restrict excessive work hours, at least for women and children (Samuel, 2000; Mutari et al., 2002). The FLSA initially excluded some groups of workers, but was gradually extended from the 1940s through the 1980s to include almost every worker except employees of state and local government and small farms, as well as some domestic workers (US Department of Labor, Wage and Hour Division, 1988, 2008). In December 2011, President Barack Obama proposed changes to the FLSA that would extend minimum wage and overtime regulations to domestic workers providing in-home care to the elderly and people with disabilities (US Department of Labor, 2011).

The FLSA's overtime provisions do not apply to all workers; they cover only the six in 10 workers who are paid hourly wages (Bureau of Labor Statistics, 2009). Salaried workers who earn at least $23,600 a year, who are paid on a salary basis with a 'guaranteed minimum', and who perform exempt job duties (such as high-level management roles, professional occupations, outside sales positions, or operational positions) are not protected by the FLSA's overtime provisions (Code of Federal Regulations, 2011). No statutory limit governs the number of hours that salaried, 'exempt' employees can be asked to work in a given week. The FLSA's failure to provide universal coverage thus creates conditions of overwork for exempt employees and, because the FLSA was never targeted at the problem of underwork or scheduling predictability, it does not address part-time parity, sufficient hours of work, or issues around predictable or flexible scheduling.

The Market Response to the Need for Flexibility

The FLSA allows workers and employers great leeway in how and where hours are worked. Employers can allow any employee – whether covered by or exempt from the FLSA overtime provisions – to vary arrival and departure times, days worked, shift arrangements, or take time off during the day so long as covered workers put in no more than 40 hours in a given week if the employer wants to avoid paying overtime. Employers have even more flexibility regarding the hours of exempt workers. For example, exempt employees can have compressed workweeks over two-week intervals, working nine-hour days each week Monday through Thursday, then, every other Friday, alternating between working eight hours and taking the day off.

Firms that experiment with workplace flexibility often allow employees to make requests for flexibility, thus beginning a process of negotiation over how the schedule will help both employees and employers to meet their needs (Harrington and Ladge, 2009). Few workers, however, have access to workplace flexibility, and those that do are still too often 'mommy tracked'. Only about a quarter to a third of employees report having some kind of flexibility (McCrate, 2002; Galinsky et al., 2004; Golden, 2005; Council of Economic Advisers, 2010). But about half to most of all employers report offering flexibility of some kind (Benko and Weisberg, 2007). Workers with the least access to predictable work schedules are disproportionately low-wage workers, women, and workers of color (Boushey and O'Leary, 2010; McCrate, Chapter 17, this volume).

Some firms offer compensatory time, or 'comp time', to their salaried employees who are exempt from the overtime provisions of the FLSA. Although the specific policy varies by firm, the basic idea is that when employees work more than their usual hours, they can bank those extra hours and use them later to compensate for the extra work. In the private sector, this policy is available only to workers exempt from the FLSA's overtime provisions; about a third (36 percent) of employers offer comp time to some workers and one in five (18 percent) makes it available to all workers (Bond and Galinsky, 2006; Galinsky et al., 2010).

Firms that voluntarily implement flexibility do so because they see it as good for their bottom line. A growing body of empirical research suggests that these policies enhance productivity by improving retention and reducing turnover. In 2010, the President's Council of Economic Advisers reviewed evidence on the economic value of adopting workplace flexibility and concluded that the 'costs to firms of adopting these kinds of management practices can also be outweighed by reduced absenteeism, lower turnover, healthier workers, and increased productivity' (Council of Economic Advisers, 2010). In a review of research in *The Shriver Report*, Executive Director of the Boston College Center for Work & Family Brad Harrington and Northeastern University Assistant Professor of Management and Organizational Development Jamie Ladge (2009) cite several studies showing that when firms allow workers flexibility and managers implement it, the benefits are considerable.

However, whether comp time or flexibility programs are helpful for employees struggling to resolve work–family conflict hinges on how they are implemented. A review of litigation history found that even within the public sector where comp time is less contentious, employers limit their employees' ability to use comp time at their own discretion. In the private sector, which is less regulated and less unionized than the public sector, employees are likely to be even less able to make use of their comp time when it suits them (Walsh, 1999).

New Ideas for Workplace Flexibility

Federal, state, and local governments have experimented with several innovative programs to increase scheduling flexibility that could provide a model for policy-makers. Since the late 1970s, for example, federal employees have had some access to two kinds of alternative work schedules, a 'flexible work schedule' and a 'compressed work schedule'.[1] In 2010, the US Office of Personnel Management launched a pilot program called Results-Oriented Work Environment that allows employees to work whenever and wherever they want as long as they complete their tasks. Initial results from the evaluation of the federal pilot found greater employee satisfaction, a shift in focus among both employees and employers to output instead of hours worked, and improved perception of leadership (Foley, 2010; Ressler and Thompson, 2011).

State and local governments have also implemented alternative schedules. In 2008, Utah Governor Jon Huntsman moved most state employees, except key personnel, to a four-day workweek by executive order. Although the primary goal of the reform was to reduce energy expenses, it also reduced work–life conflict and improved productivity (Facer and Wadsworth, 2010). In 2006, Houston Mayor Bill White began a Flexible Workplace Initiative Program to encourage companies to implement flexible work-scheduling policies. In an annual Flex in the City program, participating Houston area employers 'adopt new flexible workplace policies for two weeks'. Although there are no studies of the impact on work–family conflict, city government surveys of both employees and employers found that the flexible scheduling reduced traffic congestion, lowered commute costs, and increased productivity (Lyons, 2006; Flexworks, 2010).

US policy-makers can also look to other nations for guidance on how to implement workplace flexibility. The United Kingdom, New Zealand, and Australia have all implemented policies that give workers the right to request a flexible schedule without fear of retaliation (Kornbluh, 2005; Levin-Epstein, 2006). Because many US workers are subject to being disciplined for even asking about flexibility or predictability, the right to request could be a very important addition to the US work–family policy framework (Boushey and O'Leary, 2010). These policies require employers to set up a process to discuss and negotiate workplace flexibility and permit them to turn down the requests only for certain business reasons. In the United Kingdom, for example, employers may refuse the request for flexibility only for such reasons as the burden of additional costs, negative effects on meeting customer demand or on business quality and performance, or the inability to reorganize the existing staff to make it work (Kornbluh, 2005; Levin-Epstein, 2006). Right-to-request legislation has increased the number of workers in the United Kingdom with flexible schedules (Holt and Grainger, 2005). Only 11 percent of requests were turned down in the two years between enactment in 2003 and 2005 (ibid.). And although the law applied originally only to workers with a child under the age of six, the business community joined with workers to lobby to extend it gradually to workers with caregiving responsibilities for disabled or ill adults or for children under age 18 by April 2011 (Local Government Employers, 2011).

In the United States, Congresswoman Carolyn Maloney and Senator Robert Casey introduced right-to-request legislation, in the form of the Working Families Flexibility Act, in the 111th Congress. While earlier versions of the bill passed the House in the 104th and 105th Congresses, it has not been voted on in subsequent years, although some version of the bill has been introduced in almost every year since. So far, New Hampshire is the only state where such legislation has been introduced (Boushey and O'Leary, 2010).

III   EQUAL RIGHTS IN THE WORKPLACE AND THE IMPLICATIONS FOR WORK–FAMILY RECONCILIATION

The foundation for equitable treatment at work in the United States is laid out in Title VII of the 1964 Civil Rights Act. As originally passed, Title VII protected individuals against employment discrimination on the basis of sex, race, color, national origin, and religion. (Other legislation has expanded the rights of the disabled.) Although the Act ensures that all employees have an equal opportunity within the existing structure, it does not require employers to make changes to their workplace structures to address specific protected class issues. And although having broad protections from unfair treatment certainly helps some caregivers address discrimination in the workplace, nevertheless, as Berkeley Law Professor Ann O'Leary and OECD Ambassador Karen Kornbluh (2009) note, 'Equal protection laws are only as good as the nature and quantity of benefits the employer provides to other workers' (p. 89).

In 1978, the Pregnancy Discrimination Act (PDA) amended Title VII to prohibit discrimination on the basis of pregnancy. The PDA has helped normalize a pregnant woman as a still functioning employee (Thornton, 2005), but it does not mandate that employers take any specific positive actions; they must only offer pregnant women the same benefits that they offer any other worker (O'Leary and Kornbluh, 2009). For example, a company may fire an employee for breast feeding too often, making the argument that breast feeding is part of childcare and not part of pregnancy (Barnard and Rapp, 2005). The Patient Protection and Affordable Care Act of 2010 now requires employers with more than 50 employees to provide appropriate breaks and locations so that working mothers covered by FLSA can pump breast milk. Under the law, employees must be given time and a private place that is not a bathroom to express breast milk for up to one year after they have given birth. Employers with fewer than 50 employees do not have to provide time and space for women to pump milk if it would cause 'undue hardship' (US Department of Labor, Wage and Hour Division, 2010; US House of Representatives, 2010).

The Americans with Disabilities Act (ADA) of 1990 prohibits discrimination on the basis of disability in employment, as well as in other areas such as public services, public accommodations, transportation, and telecommunications (Workplace Flexibility 2010, 2009). For employees with disabilities, the ADA provides workplace flexibility by requiring employers to provide 'reasonable accommodations' that enable employees to perform their jobs. An employer is not required by the ADA to provide a reasonable accommodation if doing so would create an 'undue hardship' – defined as 'significant difficulty or expense'. The ADA also covers caregivers for the disabled.

'Family Responsibility Discrimination'

Notwithstanding the advances made in anti-discrimination law over the past few decades, evidence is growing that workers with care responsibilities experience discrimination in the workplace and that government policy has a role in ensuring workplace equity. Joan Williams, Director of the Center for WorkLife Law at the University of California, Hastings College of the Law, has coined the phrase 'family responsibility discrimination' to describe disparate treatment at work of 'pregnant women, mothers and fathers of young children, and workers with aging parents or sick spouses or partners' (Center for WorkLife Law, 2008). She notes that these workers 'may be rejected for hire, passed over for promotion, demoted, harassed, or terminated – despite good performance – simply because their employers make personnel decisions based on stereotypical notions of how they will or should act given their family responsibilities' (ibid.). Shelley Correll et al. (2007) have found that among two groups of job candidates with identical credentials, the group identified as mothers are perceived to be less competent, less promotable, less likely to be recommended for management, and less likely to be recommended for hire, and that they have lower recommended starting salaries than non-mothers.

Employment discrimination is particularly problematic in the United States, where most workers have no explicit employment contract and thus can be fired for any reason not explicitly prohibited through judicial or statutory exceptions.[2] Workers with care responsibilities may need to request flexible work arrangements, but may have no job-protected mechanism even for asking their employer to help them resolve their work–family conflict. A policy such as the Working Families Flexibility Act would help to alleviate this problem, as it prohibits firing or discriminating against workers who request flexible work arrangements.

New Ideas to Address Family Responsibility Discrimination: Legal Protection

In 2007, the US Equal Employment Opportunity Commission (EEOC), the enforcement agency for the Civil Rights Act, laid out how the laws that establish workplace fairness also provide protections for workers with family responsibilities. Although no one law specifically addresses the dual role that most workers now play as workers and caregivers, a framework based on the growing body of case law is emerging. The EEOC's Caregiver Guidance outlines how, based on current law, workers cannot be subject to a hostile work environment or treated differently once they develop caregiver responsibilities, or be held to stricter standards (for example, about requesting leave or timeliness) than other workers. It also highlights difficulties in the workplace for minority women who are pregnant or have young children, as well as for men, when they request flexible schedules, and what treatment constitutes discrimination for them (EEOC, 2007). The guidance, however, does not provide a framework that would give workers the time and flexibility to take care of caregiving obligations and not be discriminated against as a result, and, as with the PDA, this does not give caregivers more right than other workers.

For the future, one possibility would be to transform the EEOC Caregiver Guidance into legislation. Australia has done something similar, implementing protection for employees against discrimination based on care responsibilities, and requiring employers to affirmatively provide reasonable, flexible work schedules unless doing so would cause them undue hardship (Workplace Flexibility 2010, 2006). In its Equal Treatment Directive, the European Union explicitly lays out that member states may promote employment of and protection for workers with caregiving responsibilities (European Union, 2012).

IV   TIME OFF TO CARE

Because the vast majority of American families now have no one at home to provide care, workers occasionally need paid time off from work to tend to loved ones with serious illnesses or to bond with a new child. Most families receive the bulk of their income from employment, making access to paid time off critical for family economic well-being. Families who earn less than $100,000 a year typically derive 80 percent of their income from employment, and few families have more than a few months' expenses saved up in case a breadwinner is unemployed.[3] In 2007, just before the onset of the Great Recession, less than a third (29.4 percent) of middle-class families had at least three months of income in savings (Weller and Logan, 2008). US social insurance programs provide income support when a family member cannot work because of retirement, unemployment, or disability, but they do not cover a worker's need for short-term or extended time off to provide care for a new child or a sick family member.

Two related, but conceptually separate, issues create work–family conflict in this area. The first is whether workers can take extended time off work to care for a seriously ill family member or to care for a new child. Such time off, which I call 'paid family and medical leave', can often but not always be planned in advance. The second issue is whether workers can miss up to a few days of work to care for an ill family member who has a relatively minor illness, such as a cold or flu. The need for this second type of leave, which I call 'paid sick days', is often unexpected.

The Social Security Act

The Social Security Act of 1935 established Old Age, Survivors, and Disability Insurance, commonly known as 'Social Security'. The law established social insurance, whereby workers pay into funds through payroll taxes and then, having demonstrated sufficient labor market attachment, become eligible for benefits upon retiring or becoming unemployed. The law also established a program of income support for women and children without a breadwinner. In 1954, the federal government added Social Security Disability Insurance for workers who become disabled; in 1972, it added Supplementary Security Income for disabled and blind people regardless of work history (US Social Security Administration, 2007). The income support program for women and children – called

Aid to Dependent Families in the original legislation – was designed for widows who had lost their male breadwinner and needed funds to help them support their children. The program is means-tested – that is, limited to mothers with income up to a certain limit – and reforms during the mid-1990s tied eligibility for benefits to work or job search activities (Fremstad, 2004; Albelda, Chapter 16, this volume).

Some of the fundamental assumptions underlying the Social Security Act were that individuals were either caregivers or breadwinners, but not both; that married couples typically stayed married for life; and that most families had a stay-at-home parent, usually a mother, to provide care for children, the sick, and the elderly. Eligibility for the retirement and disability benefits of Social Security depends on a history of employment and payment into the system by the recipient or his or her spouse if the recipient was primarily a full-time stay-at-home caregiver. Social Security resembles insurance, because workers' income risks are pooled and payments into the system (that is, insurance premiums) are paid based on expected benefit. To qualify for retirement benefits, a worker must accumulate at least 40 credits (approximately 10 years of work). Adults and younger people qualify for disability or survivor benefits with proportionally fewer credits appropriate to their age and potential labor market experience. Most Americans are eligible for both the retirement and disability benefits. In 2009, 89.7 percent of those aged 65 and older received Social Security benefits (Bureau of Labor Statistics, 2007, Table 7.2). Caregivers, however, are less likely to be eligible for benefits in their own right, because they are likely to have spent less time in the workforce. Spousal benefits provide a married woman as much as half of her husband's benefit if she has no work history. In 2008, 56 percent of women received Social Security benefits that depend wholly or in part on their husband's benefits (Hartmann, 2010).

The Social Security Act also established an unemployment insurance system that is administered by the states, but this system too leaves out some workers with care responsibilities. Although most workers are covered by the program, eligibility depends on reaching certain thresholds of earnings and hours worked in the four or five calendar quarters preceding unemployment. Up until 2009, much of the US unemployment insurance system did not cover part-time workers and did not allow workers to receive unemployment benefits if they quit their job because of problems with childcare or if they had to move because their spouse found a job in another location. Such rules made it less likely that caregivers would be able to receive unemployment benefits if they lost their job. Some of these issues were addressed in the Unemployment Insurance Modernization Act, which was implemented as a part of the American Recovery and Reinvestment Act in 2009, but not all states have implemented the reforms (National Employment Law Project, 2010). As of August 22, 2011 – the date by which states were required to apply for funding with the Department of Labor – 40 states had applied for and were granted at least a portion of the incentive funding, with 14 states and Puerto Rico being granted the full incentive amount. Of these, 32 states modified their unemployment insurance systems to allow those seeking or participating in part-time work to claim benefits and 28 states made changes to allow those who left a job for family or childcare reasons to claim benefits (US Department of Labor, 2011). In order to qualify, states had to have their laws certified to establish that they indeed comply with the unemployment insurance modernization provisions of the Recovery Act.

The Family and Medical Leave Act

By the 1980s, although increasingly fewer families had a stay-at-home caregiver, much of the social insurance infrastructure continued to assume that they did. The Family and Medical Leave Act (FMLA) signed into law in 1993 was the first piece of legislation in US history to give workers a right to job-protected leave for caregiving. The FMLA provides up to 12 weeks of unpaid leave a year for employees who need time off to care for a new child (newborn or adopted), to recover from a serious illness, or to care for a seriously ill family member. To be eligible for FMLA leave, an employee must put in at least 1,250 hours of work a year at a large company (one with 50 or more employees) and must have worked at that company for at least a year, although not necessarily consecutively.

The FMLA, however, has two major shortcomings. The first is that the leave it provides is unpaid. Unlike programs that offer leave for other reasons, such as a short-term disability or unemployment, the FMLA is not a social insurance program; rather, it provides job protection when workers take the leave. Unpaid leave, however, is not adequate to the needs of low- and moderate-income families. For them, the right to job-protected leave is nice, but not enough (Cantor et al., 2001). The second limitation is that it excludes a significant portion of the labor force. The FMLA gave approximately 44 million workers (out of a workforce of more than 128 million) the right to job-protected unpaid family and medical leave (Committee on Labor and Human Resources, 1993). By covering only workers in firms with 50 or more employees, the law leaves out about a third of all US workers – those who tend to earn less, and to be less likely to have access to paid benefits than their counterparts in larger companies (Boushey and Schmitt, 2007).

Furthermore, even workers in covered establishments are eligible for FMLA leave only if they meet other requirements that fit the traditional male model of employment – which no longer captures many of the realities of the modern workforce. Tying workers' eligibility to a minimum number of hours worked, for example, fails to acknowledge that many people work part time for caregiving reasons or that young workers are most likely job switching for career reasons. Among workers aged 18–25 with a small child at home, 43.3 percent of women, 31.2 percent of men, 38.5 percent of whites, 48.0 percent of blacks, and 31.5 percent of Hispanics have been at their job less than a year (ibid.).

The Market Response to the Need for Paid Time Off for Caregiving

Thus far, the market on its own has not filled the need for paid time off for caregiving. Employers do not typically offer extended leave to care for a new child or for an ill family member, and, when they do, they tend to offer it only to higher-wage, higher-status workers, thus flying in the face of the compensating-wages model. And employers who do provide paid leave, unlike those who offer pensions and health insurance, face no government requirements that policy be uniform within the firm.[4] Thus, even within a given firm, not all employees may have access to the same paid family and medical leave benefits. In a study of the Fortune 100 companies, the US Joint Economic Committee found that 'Many firms responded with a minimum and maximum number of weeks of paid leave, depending on the employee's job category or tenure or other requirements and our analysis provides measures of both the minimum and the maximum weeks provided' (Joint Economic Committee, 2008). In general, employees least likely to get family and medical leave are low-wage workers who are most likely to need workplace flexibility because they cannot afford paid help to care for loved ones (O'Leary, 2007). The US Census Bureau reports that 66 percent of new mothers with a bachelor's degree or higher received any kind of paid maternity leave, compared with only 19 percent of those without a high school degree (US Bureau of the Census, 2011).

Further, the leave that exists is a patchwork available to employees for their own illness or for childbirth with very little for caregiving or bonding with a new child. About 40 percent of all workers are covered by private temporary disability insurance programs that provide benefits for maternity and an employee's own illness (Workplace Flexibility 2010 and Urban Institute, 2009). Such insurance, however, does not address the work–family conflicts that arise when no stay-at-home family member is available to provide care for others who are ill or for a new child. New fathers, who are ineligible for disability leave for childbirth, are typically offered little or no paid leave, and employees who deplete their sick days must hope that they – or their new child – do not get sick later on. Further, because there is no government requirement that the programs be universally applied, many low-paid workers may not be offered the benefit even if higher-paid workers are.

The market has not on its own developed an effective system of paid sick days to provide care for a sick child or family member. In a recent National Opinion Research Center poll, 64 percent of US workers said they could access paid sick time for their own illness, while 47 percent said they had paid sick days that they could use both when they were ill and when they needed to care for a sick family member (Smith and Kim, 2010). Some observers, such as US Bureau of Labor Statistics economists Iris Diaz and Richard Wallick (2009), have argued that workers who have paid vacation or other personal leave are really 'covered' for sick time, but many workers cannot take such leave without giving their employer advance notice, making it impossible to use when a child wakes up with the flu or other urgent care needs arise. Other research found that nearly two-thirds (63 percent) of workers (both full-time and part-time) do not have access to paid sick leave to care for a sick child (Lovell, 2004). The share of employees without paid leave for their own or a child's illness rises to 84 percent in construction and nondurable manufacturing and to 94 percent in accommodations and food services, an industry that disproportionately employs women (ibid.).

New Ideas for Paid Time off for Caregiving: Paid Family and Medical Leave and Paid Sick Days

Most developed countries use the social insurance model to provide extended time off for family and medical leave (Gornick and Meyers, 2003; Ray et al., 2008). The American model – which is to rely on individual firms to pay for these leaves – disproportionately burdens firms that have staff who are prone to serious health problems, who have ailing family members who need their care, or who are of childbearing age.

US advocates have conducted campaigns targeted at all levels of government to require employers to provide their employees with job-protected paid sick days. As of 2012, workers who are sick have the right to job-protected paid leave in only three places: San Francisco (as of 2007), Washington, DC (as of 2008), and Connecticut (as of 2012).

The Seattle city council passed a paid-sick-days resolution in 2011 that will take effect in September 2012. Voters in Milwaukee passed a paid-sick-days ballot initiative in 2008, but it is being held up by a court injunction. The Healthy Families Act, introduced in the US House of Representatives by Congresswoman Rosa DeLauro, which would give workers the right to earn up to seven paid sick days a year, has been introduced in the last few Congresses.

In terms of paid family and medical leave, over the past decade, California and New Jersey both implemented state-level social insurance programs to cover caregiver leave for new parents or for workers who need to care for a seriously ill family member by building on a long-standing statewide Temporary Disability Insurance (TDI) program. California and New Jersey, along with Hawaii, New York, and Rhode Island, are the only five US states that have TDI programs that provide workers coverage for nonwork-related disabilities. In 2002, California extended its TDI program to offer six weeks of comprehensive insurance, covering everyone, but with only partial wage-replacement family leave, for which every private sector California worker is eligible (State of California Employment Development Department, 2010). New Jersey passed similar legislation in 2008.[5] In 2007, Washington became the first state to pass legislation establishing a new, stand-alone program for paid parental leave (although the financing mechanism remains to be worked out) (US Government Accountability Office, 2007; Economic Opportunity Institute, 2009).

This experimentation at the state level shows that paid family and medical leave can be a successful policy for both employers and employees and is a model for federal policy-making. Appelbaum and Milkman's (2011) evaluation of California's family leave insurance program found that, contrary to opponents' warnings, it was not a 'job killer' and in fact had no discernible effect on overall employment. Their survey of employers found that nearly all employers (89 percent) said the law had no effect or a positive effect on productivity and nearly all (87 percent) reported no increase in their costs. The survey of employees documents how important the legislation has been for family well-being and improved job tenure. In 2010, a quarter of paid family leave claims (26 percent) were filed by fathers to bond with a new child, up from a fifth (17 percent) when the program first began in 2004. Workers, especially low-wage workers who made use of the leave were more likely to transition back into their job: among workers in low-quality jobs, 82.7 percent of those who used the leave returned to their job, compared with 73.9 percent of those who did not use the leave. Individuals may not have used leave because they either did not know they were eligible or did not want to risk losing their job since the leave is paid, but not job protected for all workers.

A parallel to the success of the states using their TDI programs is for the federal government to implement paid family and medical leave nationwide as part of the Social Security Administration (Boushey, 2009a). Under this idea, individuals could pay into a new trust fund that would support paid family and medical leaves. This would be similar to the extensions to Social Security for long-term disabilities implemented in the 1950s. There are a variety of advantages to the approach: it would reduce startup costs for a new program; there is now near-universal coverage by Social Security, thus everyone would be covered; and the rules could use the lifetime employment rules of Disability Insurance for determining adequate employment history and benefit level, which has the advantage of covering young and intermittent workers.

V   CONCLUSION

Crafting a comprehensive government policy to ease work–family conflict requires rethinking the basic labor standards and social insurance models that the United States has had in place since the 1930s, when Frances Perkins presented President Roosevelt with the ideas that became the Fair Labor Standards Act and the Social Security Act. Her dual vision for workers included ensuring fair treatment for workers at work and ensuring income support, based on insurance principles, for workers when they could not work or find work (Downey, 2009). In developing these cornerstone pieces of legislation, Secretary Perkins did not foresee that just over half a century later, most American mothers would be either breadwinners or co-breadwinners and that most American families would need income support and flexibility when a family member needed to provide care. Updating the nation's basic labor standards and social insurance to address conflicts that arise between work and family today is the next step.

The United States has a long way to go to modernize and update basic labor standards and social insurance protections to meet the needs of twenty-first-century families. The federal government can look to the experimentation at the state level as well as the kinds of policies that have become common in other developed nations. The lack of modernization leaves workers and employers struggling on a daily basis to come to terms with the realities of conflicts between work and family that bring down our nation's productivity. Solving these issues would lead to a healthier economy, improve women's livelihood, and be an important step forward in securing the well-being of American households and families.

NOTES

1. Under the flexible work schedule, employees must work certain core hours and days. Beyond these designated times, employees may structure their schedule to accommodate their personal needs. Under a compressed work schedule, an employee's basic biweekly 80-hour work requirement is scheduled within less than the traditional 10 workdays. Federal employees are not exempt from the FLSA, although individuals may still be exempt based on whether they have a managerial or other exempt job. With respect to both programs, if employees are unionized, then the collective bargaining agreement must include language that allows the alternative work schedule program.
2. Although all 50 states honor employment-at-will, all but four (Florida, Georgia, Louisiana, and Rhode Island) have statutory exceptions to the at-will doctrine (Gibson and Lindley, 2009).
3. Author's analysis of Internal Revenue Service (2007).
4. The Employee Retirement Income Security Act of 1974 sets minimum standards for pension plans in private industry, requiring that an employer that provides a retirement plan to some employees must provide the same plan to employees generally.
5. Three other states (Hawaii, New York, and Rhode Island) have Temporary Disability Insurance programs, and in these states (as well as California and New Jersey), mothers are granted a minimum of six weeks of leave to recover from childbirth. Hawaii, New York, and Rhode Island offer mothers longer leaves as necessary to recover from childbirth. In New York, the length is capped at 26 weeks, and in Rhode Island the cap is 30 weeks.

REFERENCES

Amott, Teresa and Julie Matthaei (1991), *Race, Gender, and Work: A Multicultural Economic History of Women in the United States*, Boston, MA: South End Press.

Appelbaum, Eileen and Ruth Milkman (2011), *Leaves That Pay: Employer and Worker Experiences with Paid Family Leave in California*, Washington, DC: Center for Economic and Policy Research.

Aumann, Kerstin, Ellen Galinsky, Kelly Sakai, Melissa Brown and James T. Bond (2010), *The Elder Care Study: Everyday Realities and Wishes for Change*, New York: Families and Work Institute.

Barnard, Thomas H. and Adrienne L. Rapp (2005), 'The impact of the Pregnancy Discrimination Act on the workplace – from a legal and social perspective', *University of Memphis Law Review*, **36**(Fall), 93–144.

Benko, Cathleen and Anne Weisberg (2007), *Mass Career Customization*, Boston, MA: Harvard Business School Press.

Bond, James T. and Ellen Galinsky (2006), *What Workplace Flexibility is Available to Entry-Level, Hourly Employees?*, New York: Families and Work Institute.

Bornstein, Stephanie (2011), *Poor, Pregnant, and Fired: Caregiver Discrimination Against Low-Wage Workers*, San Francisco, CA: Center for WorkLife Law.

Boushey, Heather (2009a), *Helping Breadwinners When It Can't Wait: A Progressive Program for Family Leave Insurance*, Washington, DC: Center for American Progress.

Boushey, Heather (2009b), *Will Economic Trends Change Family Dynamics? CAP Action Testimony to the Equal Employment Opportunity Commission*, Washington, DC: Center for American Progress.

Boushey, Heather and Ann O'Leary (eds) (2009), *The Shriver Report: A Woman's Nation Changes Everything*, Washington, DC: Center for American Progress.

Boushey, Heather and Ann O'Leary (2010), *Our Working Nation: How Working Women Are Reshaping America's Families and Economy and What It Means for Policymakers*, Washington, DC: Center for American Progress.

Boushey, Heather and John Schmitt (2007), *Job Tenure and Firm Size Provisions Exclude Many Young Parents from Family and Medical Leave*, Washington, DC: Center for Economic and Policy Research.

Bureau of Labor Statistics (2007), *National Compensation Survey: Employee Benefits in Private Industry in the United States, March 2007*, Washington, DC: US Department of Labor.

Bureau of Labor Statistics (2009), 'Characteristics of minimum wage workers 2009, table 10', available at: http://www.bls.gov/cps/minwage2009tbls.htm#10 (accessed January 27, 2011).

Cantor, David, Jane Waldfogel, Jeff Kerwin, Mareena McKinley Wright, Kerry Levin, John Rauch, Tracey Hagerty and Martha Stapleton Kudela (2001), *Balancing the Needs of Families and Employers: Family and Medical Leave Surveys, 2000 Update*, Rockville, MD: Westat.

Center for WorkLife Law (2008), 'About FRD', available at: http://www.worklifelaw.org/AboutFRD.html (accessed February 10, 2011).

Code of Federal Regulations (2011), '29 CFR Part 541: Defining and delimiting the exemptions for executive, administrative, professional, computer and outside sales employees', available at: http://ecfr.gpoaccess.gov/cgi/t/text/text-idx?c=ecfr&sid=cfb344dae2db85c15fc55b68376f32c5&rgn=div5&view=text&node=29:3.1.1.1.22&idno=29 (accessed February 16, 2011).

Committee on Labor and Human Resources (1993), *Report on the Family and Medical Leave Act of 1993*, Washington, DC: US Senate.

Commonwealth of Australia (2009), *Australia's Paid Parental Leave Scheme: Supporting Working Australian Families*, Canberra: Australian Government.

Correll, Shelley J., Stephen Benard and In Paik (2007), 'Getting a job: is there a motherhood penalty?', *American Journal of Sociology*, **112**(5), 1297–338.

Council of Economic Advisers (2010), *Work–Life Balance and the Economics of Workplace Flexibility*, Washington, DC: The White House.

Diaz, Iris S. and Richard Wallick (2009), 'Leisure and illness leave: estimating benefits in combination', *Monthly Labor Review*, **132**(2), 28–34.

Downey, Kirstin (2009), *The Woman Behind the New Deal: The Life of Frances Perkins, FDR's Secretary of Labor and His Moral Conscience*, New York: Nan A. Talese.

Economic Opportunity Institute (2009), 'Our successes: family leave', available at: http://www.eoionline.org/about/success_stories/paid_family_leave_success.htm (accessed January 20, 2010).

Equal Employment Opportunity Commission (EEOC) (2007), 'Enforcement guidance: unlawful disparate treatment of workers with caregiving responsibilities', available at: http://www.eeoc.gov/policy/docs/caregiving.html (accessed February 22, 2010).

European Union (2012), 'Equal treatment in employment and occupation', available at: http://europa.eu/legislation_summaries/employment_and_social_policy/employment_rights_and_work_organisation/c10823_en.htm (accessed March 2, 2012).

Facer, Rex L. II and Lori Wadsworth (2010), 'Alternative work schedules and work–family balance: a research note', *Review of Public Personnel Administration*, **28**(2), 166–77.

Flexworks (2010), 'Flex in the city', available at: http://www.flexworks.org/fitc/index.shtml (accessed February 9, 2011).

Foley, Jonathan (2010), 'Statement of Jonathan Foley, Senior Advisor to the Director, US Office of Personnel Management', Office of Personnel Management, Washington, DC.

Fremstad, Shawn (2004), *Recent Welfare Reform Research Findings: Implications for TANF Reauthorization and State TANF Policies*, Washington, DC: Center on Budget and Policy Priorities.

Galinsky, Ellen, James T. Bond and E. Jeffrey Hill (2004), *When Work Works: A Status Report on Workplace Flexibility*, New York: Families and Work Institute.

Galinsky, Ellen, James T. Bond and Kelly Sakai (2009), *2008 National Study of Employers*, New York: Families and Work Institute.

Galinsky, Ellen, Kelly Sakai and Tyler Wigton (2010), *Workplace Flexibility Among Small Employers*, New York: Families and Work Institute.

Gibson, Jane W. and Lester Lindley (2009), *The Evolution of Employment-at-Will: Past, Present, and Future Predictions*, Las Vegas: Ninth Annual Institute for Business and Economic Research and College Teaching & Learning (TLC) Conference.

Golden, Lonnie (2005), 'Flexibility gaps: differential access to flexible work schedules and location in the US', in Isik Urla Zeytinoglu (ed.), *Flexibility in Workplaces: Effects on Workers, Work Environment and the Unions*, Geneva: IIRA/ILO, pp. 38–56.

Goldin, Claudia (1988), 'Marriage bars: discrimination against married women workers 1920's to 1950's', NBER Working Paper, Cambridge, MA.

Gornick, Janet C. and Marcia K. Meyers (2003), *Families that Work: Policies for Reconciling Parenthood and Employment*, New York: Russell Sage Foundation.

Harrington, Brad and Jamie J. Ladge (2009), 'Got talent? It isn't hard to find', in Boushey and O'Leary (eds), pp. 198–231.

Hartmann, Heidi (2010), *The Importance of Social Security Benefits to Women: Testimony before the National Commission on Fiscal Responsibility and Reform*, Washington, DC: Institute for Women's Policy Research.

Heymann, Jody (2000), *The Widening Gap: Why America's Working Families are in Jeopardy and What Can Be Done About It*, New York: Basic Books.

Holt, Heather and Heidi Grainger (2005), *Results of the Second Flexible Working Employee Survey*, London: United Kingdom Department of Trade and Industry.

Internal Revenue Service (2007), 'Table 1: Individual income tax, all returns: sources of incomes and adjustments', available at: http://www.irs.gov/pub/irs-soi/07in01ar.xls (accessed February 7, 2011).

Jacobs, Jerry A. and Kathleen Gerson (2005), *The Time Divide: Work, Family, and Gender Inequality*, Cambridge, MA: Harvard University Press.

Joint Economic Committee (2008), *Paid Family Leave at Fortune 100 Companies: A Basic Standard but Still Not the Gold Standard*, Washington, DC: Joint Economic Committee of the US Congress.

Kornbluh, Karen (2005), 'The joy of flex', *Washington Monthly*, December 1, available at: http://www.washingtonmonthly.com/features/2005/0512.kornbluh.html (accessed March 5, 2012).

Levin-Epstein, Jodie (2006), *Getting Punched: The Job and Family Clock – It's Time for Flexible Work for Workers of All Wages*, Washington, DC: Center for Law and Social Policy.

Local Government Employers (2011), 'Flexible working', available at: http://www.lge.gov.uk/lge/core/page.do?pageId=119703 (accessed February 14, 2011).

Lovell, Vicky (2004), *No Time to be Sick: Who Suffers When Workers Don't Have Sick Leave*, Washington, DC: Institute for Women's Policy Research.

Lyons, Webb (2006), *Flex in the City: The Story of a Mayor and His Vision*, Washington, DC: Center for Law and Social Policy.

McCrate, Elaine (2002), *Working Mothers in a Double Bind: Working Moms, Minorities Have the Most Rigid Schedules, and are Paid Less for the Sacrifice*, Washington, DC: Economic Policy Institute.

Mutari, Ellen, Marilyn Power and Deborah M. Figart (2002), 'Neither mothers nor breadwinners: African-American women's exclusion from the US minimum wage policies, 1912–1938', *Feminist Economics*, **8**(2), 37–61.

National Employment Law Project (2010), *Implementing the Unemployment Insurance Modernization Provisions of the Recovery Act in the States*, New York: National Employment Law Project.

O'Leary, Ann (2007), 'How family leave laws left out low-income workers', *Berkeley Journal of Employment and Labor Law*, **28**(1), 1–62.

O'Leary, Ann and Karen Kornbluh (2009), 'Family friendly for all families', in Boushey and O'Leary (eds), pp. 74–109.

Ray, Rebecca, Janet C. Gornick and John Schmitt (2008), *Parental Leave Policies in 21 Countries: Assessing Generosity and Gender Equality*, Washington, DC: Center for Economic and Policy Research.

Ressler, Cali and Jody Thompson (2011), 'OPM ROWE pilot update', available at: http://gorowe.com/2011/01/24/opm-rowe-pilot-update/ (accessed February 9, 2011).

Samuel, Howard D. (2000), 'Troubled passage: the labor movement and the Fair Labor Standards Act', *Monthly Labor Review*, **123**(12), 32–7.

Smith, Tom W. and Jibum Kim (2010), *Paid Sick Days: Attitudes and Experiences*, Chicago, IL: National Opinion Research Center.

State of California Employment Development Department (2010), 'Disability insurance: frequently asked questions', available at: http://www.edd.ca.gov/disability/FAQs.htm (accessed February 9, 2011).

Swanberg, Jennifer E. (2008), *Workplace Structure and its Impact on Hourly Workers and their Families*, Washington, DC: Working for Change: A Conversation on Workplace Flexibility, Georgetown Law School.

Thornton, Saranna (2005), 'Pregnancy Discrimination Act (2005)', available at: http://wfnetwork.bc.edu/encyclopedia_entry.php?id=272 (accessed February 2, 2011).

US Bureau of the Census (2011), *Maternity Leave and Employment Patterns of First-Time Mothers: 1961–2008*, Washington, DC: Department of Commerce.

US Department of Labor, Wage and Hour Division (1988), 'History of changes to the minimum wage law', available at: http://www.dol.gov/whd/minwage/coverage.htm (accessed February 9, 2011).

US Department of Labor (2011), 'DOL–ETA information related to the American Recovery and Reinvestment Act of 2009', available at: http://www.doleta.gov/recovery/ (accessed January 27, 2012).

US Department of Labor, Wage and Hour Division (2008), 'Fact Sheet #25: the home health care industry under the Fair Labor Standards Act (FLSA)', available at: http://www.dol.gov/whd/regs/compliance/whdfs25.pdf (accessed February 16, 2011).

US Department of Labor, Wage and Hour Division (2010), 'Fact Sheet #73: break time for nursing mothers under the FLSA', available at: http://www.dol.gov/whd/regs/compliance/whdfs73.pdf (accessed February 16, 2011).

US Government Accountability Office (2007), 'Assessment of dependent care needs', GAO, Washington, DC.

US House of Representatives (2010), *Patient Protection and Affordable Care Act*, 111th Congress, HR 3590.

US Social Security Administration (2007), *SSI: History of Provisions*, Baltimore, MD: Social Security Administration.

Waldfogel, Jane (2001), 'International policies toward parental leave and child care', *Future of Our Children*, **11**(1), 99–111.

Walsh, David (1999), 'The FLSA comp time controversy: fostering flexibility or diminishing worker rights?', *Journal of Employment and Law*, **20**(1), 74–137.

Weller, Christian E. and Amanda Logan (2008), *America's Middle Class Still Losing Ground*, Washington, DC: Center for American Progress.

Williams, Joan C. and Heather Boushey (2010), *The Three Faces of Work–Family Conflict: The Poor, the Privileged, and the Missing Middle*, Washington, DC: Center for American Progress and the Center for WorkLife Law, Hastings College of the Law, University of California.

Workplace Flexibility 2010 (2006), *The New South Wales Carers' Responsibilities Act*, Washington, DC: Georgetown Law.

Workplace Flexibility 2010 (2009), 'Americans with Disabilities Act', available at: http://workplaceflexibility2010.org/index.php/laws_impacting_flexibility/ADA (accessed February 2, 2011).

Workplace Flexibility 2010 and Urban Institute (2009), 'Fact sheet on extended time off (EXTO)', available at: http://workplaceflexibility2010.org/images/uploads/EXTO_Fact_Sheet.pdf (accessed February 16, 2011).

PART V

MACROECONOMIC POLICIES, FINANCE AND CREDIT

20. From micro-level gender relations to the macro economy and back again

Stephanie Seguino

I INTRODUCTION

Until recently, micro-level economic relations tended to be analyzed separately from macroeconomic outcomes, with little consideration of their interaction. The 'separate spheres' framework has come under challenge as a result of an expanding investigation into the effect of inequality on economic growth that gained momentum in the 1990s. The exploration of the two-way relationship between gender inequality and macroeconomic outcomes has contributed to the integration of microeconomics into the study of macroeconomics.[1]

The origins of the gender and macroeconomics research agenda can be traced to three strands of inquiry in the emerging field of feminist macroeconomics. One thread emerged in the 1980s, exploring the impact of macroeconomic policies in the form of structural adjustment programs on women's absolute and relative (to men) well-being. In this body of work, feminist scholars undertook a gender impact 'mapping' of macro-level policies, previously believed to be gender neutral.

A second line of inquiry that forms part of the gender and macroeconomics theoretical foundation explores the care economy, alternatively known as 'social reproduction'. Caring labor, often unpaid, is required to reproduce human beings and thus forms one pillar of a society's material resources essential for improving living standards and the quality of life. That caring labor has largely been performed by women in recent history and has long been ignored in national income accounts rendered it invisible with the women who performed it labeled 'unproductive'.

The third strand of feminist research has shed light on the 'black box' of intrahousehold resource allocation. Earlier mainstream theory had assumed the household to be a unitary system, with resources equitably distributed among household members. A large literature has now emerged, demonstrating that although households are cooperative enterprises, they also exhibit conflict and competition for resources with outcomes influenced by the relative power of household adults. This implies that macro-level policies that differentially benefit men or women also change power dynamics within the household, affecting the degree of gender equality in the performance of labor and in access to resources. Such studies find, too, that a determinant of children's well-being is the distribution of power between adults, with implications for long-run productivity growth.

These three research areas collectively led to a reconceptualization of the boundaries of economic activities, attention to the role of gender power differentials in influencing distribution, and recognition of the effect of gender norms, stereotypes, and roles in mediating the impact of macro-level policies. Beginning in the early 1990s, feminist economists began to explore the reverse causality, that is, the impact of changes in gender (in) equality on macroeconomic outcomes. This new subfield of macroeconomics is part of a broader research agenda that explores the relationship between intergroup inequality and the macro economy.

This chapter explores theoretical contributions of feminist economics to macroeconomic theory, exploring the two-way causality and discussing the implications for macroeconomic policy. Section II discusses the impact of gender on the macro economy. Section III lays out the pathways by which gender at the micro level affects macro-level outcomes. The reverse causality – the effect of macro-level policies on the degree of gender inequality – is examined in Section IV. Section V offers examples of policies that would be part of a gender-equitable inclusive macroeconomic framework. Section VI concludes.

II   THE IMPACT OF GENDER ON THE MACRO ECONOMY: CONCEPTUAL AND THEORETICAL ROOTS

The subfield of gender and macroeconomics is built upon new conceptual frameworks that categorize relevant gender inequalities. This framework has been applied to several traditional macro-theoretical frameworks, combining and expanding them in unique ways in order to trace gender effects on the macro economy.

The emphasis of gender and macroeconomic theorizing by feminist economists has been on women's *relative* well-being (as compared to simply their absolute well-being). A first step in exploring the effect of gender on the macro economy is to identify the domain in which we measure gender (in)equalities. This is essential since some types of gender inequality may have a negative effect on macro-level outcomes while other measures will have a positive effect. Moreover, some types of gender inequality impact the macro economy in the short run and others only have an effect with a lag.

Broadly speaking, the gender distribution of well-being can be grouped into three domains: capabilities, livelihoods, and empowerment/agency. The *capabilities* domain encompasses fundamental human abilities or functionings necessary to lead a good life (see Robeyns, 2005). These include education and measures of health (which encompasses life, captured by the ratio of females to males in the population), and are preconditions for self-expression and self-realization.[2]

The second domain, *livelihoods*, or access to and control over resources and opportunities, refers to the ability to use capabilities to generate a livelihood to support oneself and one's family. The relevant indicators of gender equality in this domain will differ by the structure of production in economies. For example, where there are well-developed labor markets, three representative measures are wage rates, employment, and annual income. Livelihood equality in agricultural economies characterized by widespread subsistence production may be better reflected by measures of land ownership, access to credit, and time spent in unpaid labor.

The third domain, *empowerment/agency*, measures gender differences in 'voice' – the ability of a group to shape decision-making in the productive sphere (for instance, in the workplace) and in the political process. The concept of empowerment, while intuitively appealing, is still operationally underdeveloped. It can be understood, however, as the ability of both individuals and the groups to which they belong to shape their environment. Thus gender equality in this domain would imply that women are equally *agentic* as men.[3] Women's share of professional and managerial positions, and of leadership positions in cooperatives, businesses, and governing bodies can be used as indicators.

Two schools of thought have influenced the development of feminist macroeconomic growth theory and analysis. The first, neoclassical thought, draws inspiration from the (Robert) Solow growth model, which assumes full employment and thus eschews the possibility of demand-side constraints that could lead to excess capacity and sustained unemployment.

While aspects of the neoclassical framework have been useful, the substantive architecture of feminist macroeconomics draws from a second theoretical perspective: heterodox macroeconomic theory. Post-Keynesians in the tradition of Michal Kalecki have developed a body of work that investigates how the functional distribution of income (between workers and capitalists) affects output, employment, and growth in demand-constrained economies. Feminists have adapted this framework to account for gender differences in income, thereby simultaneously exploring the effects of both *inter*class and *intra*class distribution.

In addition, feminist economists have drawn from structuralist macroeconomics, an approach that incorporates the stylized structural features of economies (market structure, the structure of production and trade and resulting price elasticities, and balance-of-payments constraints to growth) into macro models. This approach, which originated in Latin America, is primarily associated with Raúl Prebisch (1950) and Celso Furtado (1964).[4] Gendered macro models account for the specific key structural features of economies in question: the country's economic structure (agricultural, semi-industrialized, postindustrial), macro-level policies that influence relations with the rest of the world (rules governing trade and cross-border investment and finance), and the form and extent of gendered job segregation. The incorporation of the effects of household dynamics and caring labor also distinguishes gendered macro models from mainstream and heterodox approaches, enlarging the space in which we understand macroeconomies to operate. This work has been built on a strong foundation of empirical work that has helped to estimate the relative sizes of parameters used in the macroeconomic models.

III   FEMINIST THEORY ON THE ROLE OF GENDER IN THE MACRO ECONOMY

Feminist macro economists have contributed to the theoretical integration of gender into macro models, not as an add-on or special case but as an integral feature of economic systems that plays an important role in influencing the level of economic activity. In contrast to previous research, these models establish a conceptual distinction between sex, which is seen as biological or anatomical, and gender, which is socially constructed, and reflects social valuation of masculinity and femininity that contributes to power differences and therefore inequality between women and men.

Macroeconomic models of this genre make clear there is no one-size-fits-all effect of gender equality on the economy. The effect will depend on a variety of additional factors. For example, the effects of gender depend on whether we evaluate the short versus the long run, the country's stage of development and thus structure of production, and accompanying institutions such as those that influence wage bargaining. Gender effects

also depend on and interact with other forms of intergroup inequality. In ethnically heterogeneous societies, racial/ethnic minorities might bear a greater burden of stimulating
growth through low wages than women.

The form that gender job segregation takes affects labor market outcomes and social
provisioning, and will influence the macroeconomic effects of gender inequality. Further,
a country's balance-of-payments constraint depends not only on gender but also on the
characteristics of the products that are imported and exported. Finally, women's bargaining power *vis-à-vis* employers and their access to important resources such as jobs
and credit depend on other macro-level policies, including monetary and fiscal policies.
Despite the complexities and variations in modeling the role of gender, several key linkages form the basic architecture of these models. We describe them here, first considering
short-run models and then long-run models.

The Short Run

One of the key differences in neoclassical and heterodox efforts to engender macroeconomic theory is that the neoclassical approach ignores the short run. Emphasizing
the long run, neoclassical theorists focus on those forms of gender equality that have
delayed effects on the macro economy – such as educational equality and health
improvements. Keynesians and other heterodox economists would argue that the macro
economy, however, is itself made up of a series of short runs. Disequilibria that result
from demand-side shocks can produce long-lasting effects (Dutt and Ros, 2007). This
is especially true of countries that face balance-of-payments constraints, particularly
developing countries. Any shock that worsens the terms of trade or balance of payments
can trigger International Monetary Fund (IMF)-type austerity programs with long-term
negative effects on the productive capacity of the economy, as has been well-documented
by feminist economists (Elson, 1991; Benería and Feldman 1992; Çagatay et al., 1995).

What differentiates the short run is that the gender variables of interest are fast acting.
Two variables in this category are wages (and, depending on the circumstances, access
to credit and other inputs) and government spending. The latter could be targeted, for
example, to sectors that reduce women's care burden or to fund investments in women's
access to on-the-job training.

In the short run, output is demand determined. In common parlance, 'there are no
sellers if there are no buyers'. Therefore, if we want to understand what determines the
level of economic activity, we must look at the effect of gender equality via wages and
government spending on components of aggregate demand: consumption (and thus
saving), investment, exports, and imports. In a simple model, two conditions must be
met for macroeconomic equilibrium in an open economy – the equality of leakages with
injections, and balanced trade or:

$$S + T + M < I + G + X \tag{20.1}$$

$$NX = X - M, \tag{20.2}$$

where S is aggregate saving, T is tax revenues, M is the domestic currency value of
imports, I is business investment, G is government spending, X is exports, and NX is net

exports. An assessment of the effects of greater gender equality on macroeconomic and trade balance is arrived at by summing the net effects on each of the individual components of aggregate demand in equation 20.1 and net exports in equation 20.2.[5]

In the short run, gender equality could improve directly via a change in relative female/male wages or indirectly through government spending that differentially benefits females (such as investments in education, or public investment that reduces women's care burden). An increase in gender equality that results in injections exceeding leakages $(S + T + M = I + G + X)$ is expansionary. That is, a redistribution stimulates aggregate demand, leading to an increase in output and employment in the short run. A redistribution with this effect would be 'gender cooperative' – a redistribution to women maintains and even potentially increases men's absolute income, depending on the sectors that expand as a result of the redistribution. Conversely, of course, a contractionary increase in gender wage equality may harm both women and men through job losses and thus would be considered 'gender conflictive'.

I forgo discussion of the insights that can be obtained by analyzing the impact of a fiscal stimulus $(G > T)$ targeted to expenditures that promote gender equality. Suffice it to say that the macroeconomic evidence suggests that appropriately targeted expenditures can 'crowd in' private investment, exerting an unambiguously positive effect on output, employment, and growth. The critical question is whether such expenditures are fiscally sustainable. For more on that issue, I refer the interested reader to Diane Elson and Tonia Warnecke (2011) and Seguino (2012).

A more complex case is the effect of greater gender wage equality on each of the variables in the macroeconomic and net export equilibrium conditions. Here I focus on the impact of a narrowing of the wage gap by raising women's wages (holding the average male wage constant). This approach is heterodox. Unlike neoclassical theory, which assumes that wages reflect marginal productivities, heterodox theorists see wages determined as a result of social bargaining between employers and workers, where implicitly, power matters (Bowles and Gintis, 1990; Figart et al., 2002).

Increased gender wage equality might be achieved by raising the minimum wage or extending the right to organize to export-processing zones that employ primarily female labor. The net aggregate demand effect of higher relative female wages will depend on gender differences in saving propensities, the composition of women's and men's consumption expenditures (women and men may consume differential proportions of domestically produced goods, affecting the level of import demand and thus balance of payments, for example), the degree of firm mobility which determines the impact of higher female wages on investment, and the gender composition of the workforce in the export sector.

The size and sign of net effects will differ across countries, but we can make some generalizations based on modeling exercises and empirical studies. In semi-industrialized export-oriented economies (SIEs), women workers are concentrated in the export sector that produces labor-intensive manufactured goods, business services (call centers), and nontraditional agricultural exports. Because firms are mobile, or because these goods can be globally sourced by large buyers in developed countries along global commodity chains (Walmart and Tesco are two examples), higher female wages dampen both investment and exports, producing an economic contraction and worsening the balance of payments. In these countries, even if women's marginal propensity to save is less than men's (with higher female wages thus stimulating consumption), the expansionary effect of higher female wages is unlikely to be large enough to offset the negative investment and export effects.[6] This is because the labor-intensive firms that employ women tend to be mobile and because export demand for the goods women produce is price elastic.

In contrast, in low-income agricultural economies (LIAEs) where men are concentrated in natural resource or cash crop export production and women in the subsistence agriculture sector, greater gender wage equality can be a stimulus to output and employment. This is because women's wages from off-farm work may be reinvested in subsistence agriculture, raising productivity, expanding food production, and thus reducing macroeconomic leakages for food imports. Moreover, women's greater access to resources improves their bargaining power *vis-à-vis* husbands and male relatives, permitting them to reduce (or receive a better price for) the labor they provide on male crops, again with positive effects for domestic food production (Darity, 1995).

Other measures of gender equality that have short-run effects may be more salient in LIAEs, however. These include female property rights, access to credit, inputs, technology, and extension services. There is some theoretical and empirical evidence that greater gender equality in access to inputs can stimulate agricultural production, with a potentially positive effect on food production, and thus the balance of payments, due to a reduction in food imports. In Burkina Faso, for example, fertilizer is applied more heavily to male plots, resulting in their greater productivity relative to female plots, controlling for weather conditions and types and characteristics of plots (Udry, 1996). The implication is that equalization of inputs could raise yields on women's plots with household production potentially increasing by 6 percent (Blackden et al., 2007). Given that women's food production is largely for domestic consumption, the demand for food imports could fall as a result, though on this latter point, there is as yet no solid empirical evidence.

Women's lack of secure property rights in LIAEs, neoclassical scholars argue, inhibits access to agricultural credit and therefore productivity. The policy prescription proffered is to promote individualized land titling. While it is clear that women's productive activities are credit-constrained in ways that inhibit agricultural productivity, individualized control over land may not be sufficient or even necessary to promote gender equality. Some feminist scholars indeed are critical of the individualist and private property emphasis of the neoclassical literature that links gender equality in inputs and property rights with greater agricultural productivity (Whitehead and Kabeer, 2001; O'Laughlin, 2007; Razavi, 2009). Noting that households are not only the site of conflict but also cooperation, O'Laughlin points out:

> The feminist mandate is not trading oppression for isolation, providing women with resources so they can make it on their own, but redressing inequality within co-operative gender relations through reconstruction of the division of labour. This can only be a disruptive and broad political process that cuts across households and communities. (2007, p. 41)

Feminist scholars note that in the face of uncertain harvests and the market volatility induced by integration into the global economy, collective arrangements and community institutions offer an important alternative to enhance food security and sustainable use of resources – and promote gender equality (Agarwal, 2000; Whitehead and Kabeer, 2001).

Feminist scholars have devoted less attention to constructing macro models that explore how gender equality affects short-run macroeconomic outcomes in countries with structures resembling those of developed economies. Some models that can incorporate countries at different stages of development are, however, applicable to developed economies. Korkut Erturk and William Darity (2000) highlight the dual effects of increased female labor force participation. On the one hand, due to rigid gender roles, women's entry into paid labor reduces time spent on unpaid caring labor with negative impacts on the production of labor power. On the other, women's lower wages have a positive effect on profits and thus output. In developing economies with limited public services, the negative effect on the production of labor power is likely to dominate, but in developed economies with broader social spending, the second effect is likely to be more important.

Addressing the absence of attention to the care sector in macro models, Elissa Braunstein et al. (2011) develop a macro model with caring labor. They show that higher female wages, in addition to directly affecting production, could induce more investment at the household level in 'human capacities' that can raise labor productivity and reduce unit labor costs. In that case, the net effect of higher female wages on profits and thus investment may be positive or negative, depending on structural conditions. This promising work awaits empirical verification on the rapidity with which labor productivity responds to wage hikes.

The Long Run

The long run is characterized by the flexibility of all gender well-being variables. Thus, in addition to opportunities variables such as wages or access to credit, measures of capabilities and empowerment/agency are allowed to vary. The pathways by which these are hypothesized to affect the rate of economic growth depend on the theoretical framework.

Neoclassical growth theory, based on the workhorse Solow model, emphasizes the positive effect of increases in factor inputs (physical and human capital and labor supply) on economic growth, assuming exogenously determined productivity growth. In recent years, endogenous growth theory has attempted to give substance to the determinants of productivity growth, typically emphasizing the role of institutions, such as the rule of law and property rights. Assuming Say's Law (that is, that economies do not face demand-side constraints and thus problems of unemployment or underemployment), the supply side determines the rate of economic growth.

Gendered neoclassical accounts emphasize the positive effects of gender equality in capabilities (in particular, women's health and education). There are several pathways by which capabilities equality can raise economy-wide productivity. If innate abilities are similarly distributed across the genders, unequal educational investments in favor of boys lead to inefficiencies due to a selection distortion problem: overinvestment in less-qualified males and underinvestment in more-qualified females. This can lower economy-wide efficiency, implying that gender *equality* in educational investments can stimulate economic growth. Several studies provide empirical support for this hypothesis (Hill and King, 1995; Klasen and Lamanna, 2009).[7]

The benefits of greater educational equality for development and growth are also argued to operate through the impact on children's well-being. Whether due to greater bargaining power within the household or the enhanced ability to provide better care for children, women's increased educational attainment (relative to men's or absolutely) has been found to produce a positive effect on children's survival, health, and education (Blumberg, 1988; Morrison et al., 2007). One (indirect) pathway by which children's well-being may be enhanced is through the effect on fertility. As the opportunity cost of having children rises with more education, women's fertility declines, reducing the dependency ratio which permits larger investments in children.

Greater gender equality in terms of the unpaid labor burden is also argued to promote growth. Holding constant men's performance of unpaid labor, a reduction in time required for such tasks frees women to spend time in remunerative activities that can increase their bargaining power within the household, and reduce child labor. In some cases, it can also directly benefit girls' education if they are differentially relied on to assist in unpaid labor. Public investments in infrastructure can be a vehicle to reduce the time women must allocate to unpaid caring and other forms of reproductive labor (Agénor et al., 2010). To the extent that women's relative capabilities, incomes, and assets improve, their bargaining power within the household gives them greater control over their fertility.

Increases in female empowerment (for example, advances in women's political representation) can affect long-run growth via the effect on the composition and level of public expenditures. Although there is no guarantee that having more women in political decision-making will leverage gender-equitable policies, their experiences and interests are likely to be given greater visibility and attention. Raghabendra Chattopadyay and Esther Duflo (2004) find, for example, that a policy implemented in West Bengal that reserved one-third of village council seats for women resulted in public investments more responsive to women's priorities, such as water and roads.

Even without accession to positions of political power, women's increased labor force participation can influence voting patterns that reflect their greater interest in redistributive public spending to fund social safety nets (Iversen and Rosenbluth, 2006; Cavalcanti and Tavares, 2011). Although this does not imply a direct causal link to growth, if such public spending reduces care burdens and improves women's capacity to generate income, the effect on economic growth could be positive.

Another form of empowerment – women's share of managerial, supervisory, and professional jobs that influence decision-making in the workplace – can have a demonstration effect that changes gender norms and stereotypes, with a reduction in employers' propensity to discriminate based on gender. Reduced discrimination that leads to a narrower gender wage gap can then produce a positive effect on growth via the impact, as described above, on economy-wide labor productivity.

Neoclassical economists who explore gender effects on growth are inclined to emphasize the benefits of greater equality, primarily transmitted through effects on labor productivity, but fail to identify or give serious consideration to the potential costs. This striking vacuum in a discipline that emphasizes opportunity costs of decisions is perhaps influenced by the desire of mainstream economists in international institutions such as the World Bank to make the efficiency argument (or as some would call it, the 'business case') for gender equality (World Bank, 2012). The resulting lacuna is unfortunate since plotting a path toward a macroeconomic environment that is compatible with gender equality is hampered by failure to accurately assess the roadblocks along the way. As such, it is important to acknowledge that power and hierarchy can lead to inefficient but profitable production methods, making gender inequality a viable contributor to economic growth.

A heterodox approach differs in three key ways from neoclassical growth theory. First, it underscores that the growth of potential output (supply) must be matched by the growth of demand, itself influenced by the distribution of income. Second, the balance-of-payments constraint must be relaxed in order for growth to occur. And third, in addition to labor productivity, it is emphasized that potential output is stimulated by cost reductions that enhance profits and thus stimulate investment in physical capital.

The ability to hire women at low wages due to their weaker bargaining position *vis-à-vis* capitalists (relative to their productivity) can thus be a stimulus to investment and technological advancement. Moreover, in developing economies that rely on imported intermediate and capital goods to industrialize, low wages of women workers segregated in export industries can generate much-needed foreign exchange.

As a result, greater educational equality due to rising female educational attainment coupled with women's lack of bargaining power to translate productivity into higher wages can be a winning combination for employers. This is because unit labor costs are reduced, raising profits, stimulating export demand, and generating access to imported technologies. A stylized price equation demonstrates this relationship. Equation (20.3) gives a markup price equation with only one input, labor (this may seem unrealistic but think of the case of a call-center worker, ignoring for simplicity the capital equipment required for this type of work):

$$P_X = (1 + \tau)\, w_F b \qquad\qquad (20.3)$$

where P_X is the price of the exported good or service in a sector employing primarily female workers, τ is the mark-up rate over prime unit costs, w_F is the nominal female wage rate, and b is the labor coefficient – the amount of time required to produce one unit of a good or service. Greater educational equality, it is argued, will improve productivity, causing the size of the labor coefficient b to decrease.

Neoclassical theory posits that, at least in the longer run, women's wages would rise to reflect their increased productivity. Thus, the effect of greater educational equality on prices and profits (via the markup) is zero, with women capturing the full benefit of their improved productivity in higher wages (in equation [20.3], the decline in b is accompanied by a proportionate increase in w_F, such that P_X and τ are constant). However, heterodox feminist economists argue that women's weak bargaining power inhibits their ability to raise their wages. This creates the possibility that instead, P_X falls with women's increased educational attainment, stimulating export demand, and/or t rises, stimulating profitability and thus business investment. This implies that under some conditions, gender equality in education combined with gender wage *in*equality can be a stimulus to long-run growth.

The factors that shape that relationship depend on an economy's economic structure and other macro-level policies (see Seguino, 2010). The conditions just described are those present in SIEs. In LIAEs, the long-run growth effect of gender wage equality may differ substantially. Balance-of-payments effects are not likely to be as negative. In fact, as noted, improvements in women's control over income may enhance agricultural investments with benefits for on-farm productivity and a positive net effect on long-run growth. This implies that in LIAEs, both in the short and long run, gender equality may be a stimulus to growth.

I would caution readers that although gender equality may be more compatible with growth in LIAEs in an *economic* sense, it may be strenuously resisted both socially and politically. The required policy shifts in LIAEs (for example, women's more secure land rights and investments that improve women's livelihood outcomes) may face severe resistance from males in societies in which patriarchal norms are deeply embedded in cultural institutions (Morrisson and Jütting, 2005). Male rent-seeking behavior may impede the efforts to realize gender equality, leading to societal conflict in ways that impede growth (Braunstein, 2008).

This brief summary demonstrates advances in our knowledge of the effect of micro-level gender relations on macro-level outcomes, and in particular, the pathways by which equality may stimulate economic growth and potentially development, defined as broadly shared improvements in well-being. That said, this research agenda is far from complete and its boundaries have not been definitively drawn.

Further theoretical work is needed. For example, there has been little theorizing about the interactional effects of race and gender inequality in economies of any structure. Thus, while we have a better sense of the linkages and constraints to improving gender equality (more pronounced in SIEs than LIAEs), country-specific case studies would greatly benefit our understanding of these relationships. In addition, there has been little consideration of the societal effects of gender equality on norms of masculinity and, indeed, hyper-masculinity. Equality achieved at the expense of men's access to employment, given male breadwinner norms, can trigger socially dysfunctional backlash. Rhoda Reddock (2009) notes that in the Caribbean, men distance themselves from and reduce their contributions to children's upbringing as their male breadwinner role deteriorates. Moreover, loss of income to the family can result from men's reduced ability to control family surplus income (Braunstein and Folbre, 2001). In other words, gender equality can contribute to gender conflict as men's position or perceived position deteriorates. An exclusive focus on improvements in women's well-being misses this important and potentially corrosive dynamic.

IV HOW DO MACROECONOMIC POLICIES AFFECT THE DEGREE OF GENDER EQUALITY?

A question of great interest in feminist economics is whether economic growth can improve gender equality. Arguably, if growth is gender-equalizing, then simply adopting growth-inducing policies might allow us to avoid the difficulties of developing potentially conflictive gender-specific policies. Why might growth contribute to gender equality? Signaling rising per capita incomes, growth can generate more revenue for households to invest in female family members, closing the gender gap in well-being. Further, economic growth may generate increased state-level resources that can be differentially allocated to females, thus improving their relative well-being during the process of growth. Further, economic growth that expands livelihood opportunities raises the opportunity cost of unpaid labor, spurring women's integration into the paid economy, raising their access to income and bargaining power.

Several studies find positive effects of growth on gender equality as measured by life expectancy, educational attainment, and access to employment (Dollar and Gatti, 1999; Forsythe et al., 2000). A weakness of these earlier approaches is that they fail to account for the differential effect of various macroeconomic policies. In other words, some macro-level policies and growth may be gender-equalizing while others worsen gender inequality (see Seguino, 2002, 2007a; Berik et al., 2008). This is because, whether by design or not, macroeconomic policies almost inevitably have distributional effects. Understanding the impact of the macro economy on gender equality therefore requires us first to identify the specific policies in question and the measures of gender inequality we want to consider. With that in mind, I explore below several categories of macro-level policies and their impacts on gendered equality.

Monetary and Fiscal Policy

Two major tools at the disposal of the government to manage the macro economy are monetary policy (central bank interventions to influence the money supply, rate of interest, availability of credit, and exchange rate) and fiscal policy (government taxation and spending to control the level of expenditures in the economy and influence structural change).

Monetary policy, by affecting interest rates and credit availability, influences the level of unemployment. Measures to expand credit can expand the number of jobs, benefiting women directly with increased access to jobs so long as gender norms do not stand in the way. In recent years, however, countries have been more likely to adopt contractionary monetary policy. The reason is that central banks have been pressured to become more 'independent', such that they autonomously set policy goals independently of those the government may be pursuing. Central banks, for a variety of reasons and pressures, have discarded the policy goal of employment generation, adopting instead an almost exclusive focus on inflation targeting, that is, keeping inflation rates low and close to zero.

Conservative economists hold that inflation is harmful to growth because it creates conditions of uncertainty that dampen investment. In contrast to this view, evidence from a number of studies finds that inflation rates below 20 percent are not harmful for growth (Pollin and Zhu, 2006). Central banks' emphasis on low inflation has distributional consequences. Low inflation raises the real rate of return on investments, boosting the income of wealth holders. The cost, however, is measured in jobs. That is because tightening the money supply, which restricts credit availability, raises interest rates. Higher borrowing costs dampen business investment, and as a result employment growth.

Workers lose out with inflation targeting, as do small farmers whose access to credit is squeezed. Though the evidence is as yet sparse, research suggests that women suffer disproportionately from job loss when the money supply is tightened to fight inflation. This appears to occur in both developing countries and in some, though not all, developed countries (Braunstein and Heintz, 2008; Takhtamanova and Sierminska, 2009; Seguino and Heintz, 2012).

Fiscal policy can also affect employment opportunities. The rigidity of gender norms about the division of labor will affect who gets newly created jobs and thus gender differences in income. For example, public works projects typically generate 'male' jobs (for example, in construction and road work), thus disproportionately benefiting men. This is not universally so, as the case of India demonstrates. There, women hold a large share of public works jobs, suggesting that fiscal policies that promote such spending are gender-equalizing.

Despite the potential for public spending to promote job access, developing countries have been under great pressure to cut their public sector budgets. In part, this is the direct result of trade liberalization that has reduced revenues available to the state. It also is a result of financial liberalization and the veto power of financial markets (a tendency that has been dubbed 'bond market vigilantism') whose investors flee economies with public budget deficits. Their flight reflects a fear that such deficits might result in inflation, cutting into financial returns. The result has been that governments, especially in poor countries but now even in richer countries, have felt pressure to cut their budgets. The impact of these trends is evidenced by the decline in global public investment as a share of GDP, which fell from 2.1 percent in 1980 to 0.81 percent in 2000 (Rathin et al., 2009, p. 70).

Public sector budget cuts have received detailed scrutiny from a gender perspective, beginning in the 1980s, with the wide implementation of structural adjustment programs (SAPs) in developing countries (see Elson, 1991; Benería and Feldman, 1992; Sparr, 1994; Çagatay et al., 1995). These cuts affect women and men differently. When the public sector downsizes, women are often the first to lose their jobs for two reasons. Cuts may be in social sector jobs such as education and health, which employ a larger share of women than other sectors. Second, gender norms about who is most deserving of employment when jobs are scarce can lead women to be the first to be laid off.

Even when it is men's jobs that are eliminated, there are negative consequences for women. Many women are under pressure to engage in 'distress' sales of their labor to make up for lost family income as men are laid off. Women may, for example, take on makeshift jobs in the informal sector, such as street vendors. At least some of these jobs are best described as disguised unemployment; they increase women's labor burden but for very little pay, reflecting the distress conditions under which they sell their labor. In addition to the increase in time women must spend in paid work, there is evidence that their unpaid labor burden intensifies during times of economic austerity. Because the family is forced to reduce expenditures, it must rely more on home-produced goods, such as meals. While this care work could in principle be shared, the reality is that gender norms are very strong. Men see this work as women's responsibility and may find it emasculating. Therefore, women's unpaid labor burden increases.

Public sector budget cuts exacerbate the disproportionate sharing of care work. A reduction in infrastructure expenditures exacerbates women's work burden in countries where they have a responsibility for providing water and fuel and transporting goods to market. More generally, public sector cuts have made it difficult for states to provide an economic cushion even as globalization has made incomes more volatile. The burden for smoothing family income often rests on women's shoulders. The result is an increase in their unpaid labor burden as they try to shield their families from economic austerity measures. Together, the fiscal and monetary policies of the neoliberal era, dating from 1980 onward, create a deflationary bias that disproportionately harms low-income households, particularly women (Elson and Çagatay, 2000).

Trade and Investment Rules

Economists and policy-makers have only recently begun to recognize that national and international rules on trade, investment, and finance have gendered implications. This has been nowhere more evident than in the area of trade. Many countries have liberalized trade, reducing tariffs on imports and eliminating export subsidies and taxes. The World Bank and other free trade proponents have argued that this policy shift should lead to more employment opportunities for women. This is because women's significantly lower wages makes them a key source of labor in a liberalized investment and trade environment where cost competition makes low-wage labor attractive. Proponents hold that over time, the sustained demand for women's labor will drive up their wages relative to men's, leading to a narrowing of the gender wage gap.

There is evidence that trade and investment liberalization have led to women's increased employment opportunities although the effects are uneven (van Staveren et al., 2007). The female share of employment rises in the light manufacturing stage of export-led growth in SIEs, but their share of manufacturing jobs declines with industrial upgrading to the production of more capital-intensive goods (Tejani and Milberg, 2010). This occurs despite the substantial narrowing of gender educational gaps. The gender-equalizing employment effects of trade liberalization are further weakened due to the fact that the increase in one country's exports stimulated by hiring low-wage women may come at the cost of a decline in other countries' exports. As a result, job gains for women in some countries may be counteracted by women's job losses in others (Fussell, 2000; Bussolo and de Hoyos, 2009).[8]

Evidence of the impact of trade and investment liberalization for gender wage equality is also mixed. Some studies show that gender wage differentials have declined, in large part due to narrowing educational gaps. However, in several developing countries, including China and Vietnam, the discriminatory portion of gender wage gaps has increased (Maurer-Fazio et al., 1999; Liu, 2004; Berik et al., 2004; Weichselbaumer and Winter-Ebmer, 2005; Menon and Rodgers, 2009).

What might explain the failure of wage gaps to narrow, particularly in rapidly growing export-led economies that disproportionately employ women? With trade and investment liberalization, labor-intensive firms that employ primarily women have become increasingly mobile or 'footloose'. With weakened regulations on foreign direct investment and reduced communications and transport costs, firms find it less costly to relocate if local cost conditions do not meet their profit goals. There is evidence that the mobility of firms reduces the bargaining power of workers, and thus, holds down their wages (Choi, 2006; Seguino, 2007b). The rise of global commodity chains with lead firms outsourcing to subcontractors across the globe increases the bargaining power of employers, also holding down wage growth. (Though used in a different context, the term 'traumatized worker' effect – so dubbed by Alan Greenspan – captures this phenomenon.) Insofar as women's employment is concentrated in mobile industries, the possibility for trade and investment liberalization to improve gender equality is limited.

In addition to the problem of firm mobility that holds down wages, trade and investment liberalization has pushed firms to use flexible and informal work arrangements that are temporary, seasonal, casual, and based on unregulated labor contracts with women slotted for those jobs (Carr et al., 2000; Balakrishnan, 2002; Benería, 2007). In some countries, the process of labor 'informalization' has affected not only women but also men, leading to a downward harmonization of labor conditions. Thus, we see some evidence of greater gender equality because men's condition has worsened rather than women's improving (Kongar, 2007).

This illustrative review of gender effects of macro-level policy suggests that the soundness of macroeconomic policies should be evaluated not only for their impact on macroeconomic aggregates – employment, inflation, the trade balance, and GDP growth – but also for their gendered effects. Policies should also be assessed on the basis of their effectiveness at achieving social objectives, including the extent of broadly shared well-being. More generally, policy formulation requires awareness of the distributional effects by gender in order to avoid unintended negative effects.

V   A GENDER-EQUITABLE INCLUSIVE MACROECONOMIC FRAMEWORK

Under the right conditions, a more equitable gender distribution of income and opportunities can be a stimulus to growth, funding further investments in human development. Developing the policies to create those conditions is the central challenge for any gender-aware macroeconomic program. I briefly discuss here what a gender equity-led macroeconomic policy framework would look like, with suggestions for proposals to not only produce greater equality but also reduce economic instability, while stimulating rising living standards. The specifics of inclusive macroeconomic policy of necessity will be determined according to the structure of an economy. That said, we could outline the broad goals that any inclusive macroeconomic framework might want to achieve. I would identify three components as key: (i) full employment, (ii) gender, class, and ethnic equality, and (iii) economic stability and security.

The state, far from being superfluous, has a key role to play in facilitating a development strategy that is characterized by greater equality and economic stability. Our challenge lies in carefully redefining that role and in rethinking the relationship between the state and the market. A redefined role for the state requires an assessment of how we can use fiscal policy to achieve the three goals I have outlined. Fiscal policies broadly fall into two categories: (i) countercyclical policy and (ii) public investment. While the former is important, I would like to emphasize some new ways to think about the latter that are gender responsive. An understanding of gender relations should be integral to defining that public investment strategy. Both *physical* and *social* infrastructure public investment can improve gender equality and stimulate long-run growth by raising economy-wide productivity. In this sense, such investments are also anti-inflationary if targeted to address bottlenecks in the economy that drive up prices.

Research identifies a strong link between physical infrastructure expenditures and women's unpaid care burden. Targeted investments can reduce the time women spend in unpaid labor, freeing up time to spend in paid labor, with benefits for children's well-being and economy-wide long-run productivity growth. Improvements in mothers' health have been found to affect children's health *in utero* with evidence of long-term positive effects on children's cognitive skills. These linkages imply that public investments that reduce women's care burden and improve their health, in addition to promoting gender income equality, have long-term benefits to the economy in the form of a healthier, more educated and productive workforce.

Depending on the type of economy, public investments in both physical and social infrastructure can close gender gaps in job access and raise incomes. In agricultural economies, for example, targeted expenditures to women farmers can raise agricultural productivity. Women are credit-constrained due to lack of land rights but even this constraint can be overcome with appropriate monetary policy, a point I take up in more detail below.

Social infrastructure investment, a relatively new and underdeveloped concept, has important gender dimensions. These investments have a public goods quality with positive spillover effects for the rest of the economy, and can include, for example, investments in education and training of healthcare workers. The evidence that closing the education gap between boys and girls can raise per capita GDP growth rates suggests that expenditures of this type should not be classified as social welfare, but rather as investments that produce a stream of financial and human development returns into the future, thus generating the resources to pay down the debt incurred by the initial investment. Investments in social infrastructure tend to be especially beneficial for gender equality since women disproportionately work in the sector providing these goods and services and thus benefit from the job creation it implies.

Public investments in *physical infrastructure* (for example, roads, transportation, and irrigation) also stimulate job growth and expand the economy's productive capacity. These tend to create 'male' jobs, however. Countries can make such investments more gender responsive by ensuring women's equitable access to employment created by public infrastructure projects. On-site care facilities and ensuring access to work close to home would facilitate this.

What about *fiscal space*? Many countries might be construed as lacking sufficient fiscal space to undertake public investment, even if economically desirable. The degree of space is circumscribed by limits placed on a country's debt to GDP ratio. Debt ceilings that do not factor in the growth-expanding potential of public investments unduly constrain such investments, which by their very nature are longer term. Properly understood as a means to raise productivity, public investment can yield a flow of financial returns in the future, which can be used to pay down the debt incurred by the investment. The timeframe for this type of borrowing is about 10 years. Within that time, appropriate public investments will have begun to expand the productive base of the economy, generating (taxable) incomes with which to pay down the debt. Such investments then are both fiscally sound and sustainable. Key here is that gender-responsive investment itself *creates* fiscal space by adding to the productive base of the economy.

A new role for *central banks* is also required. Inflation targeting, which attempts to solve the problem of inflation by reducing aggregate demand, in many cases contributes to slower growth and higher unemployment. For many countries, however, inflationary pressures are related to low productivity due to widespread health problems such as HIV/AIDS, poor transportation networks, and constrained food supplies. This suggests that inflation might be more efficiently addressed with public investment rather than monetary policy.

In an alternative framework that emphasizes inclusive monetary policy, the central bank would identify a 'real' target – one that focuses on key social and economic problems to be addressed by policy. An obvious one is employment, with the central bank's policy goal shifting to employment targeting in place of inflation targeting. If a country has a particular problem with generating good jobs for women or marginalized ethnic groups, the real targeting approach can accommodate such needs.

An example of a policy to reach employment targets would be for the central bank to identify priority sectors or groups, and provide loan guarantees to banks that extend loans in these areas. In agricultural economies where women are subsistence farmers, small-scale agriculture is an obvious choice. Priority might also be given to small- and medium-sized businesses that are labor-intensive and disproportionately employ women. In this framework, the private sector would still provide the bulk of credit, but it would be characterized by low interest rates leveraged with government loan guarantees.

Much more intellectual work is needed to flesh out a viable gender-equitable macroeconomic framework. Policies to manage trade, investment, and financial flows will also be required in order to promote gender-equitable macroeconomic well-being. The basic challenge here is to rebalance the bargaining power of firms relative to workers, citizens, and governments in ways that contribute to greater wage equality and more-equitable tax burdens. As yet, there have been few gender-specific proposals in these areas.

Areas in which feminist economics could fruitfully develop specific policy prescriptions include controls on capital (such as a currency financial transaction tax with proposals on how to use those revenues), and industrial and agricultural development strategies that move countries out of the trap of low-wage low-productivity labor-intensive production. New thinking (and institutional reform at the World Trade Organization: WTO) is also needed on how to manage incentives of the private sector to induce innovation-enhancing investments that yield long-run benefits. This would act as an antidote to the current incentive framework which leads to a race to the bottom, based on weak wage compensation and a reduction in capital's share of the tax burden.

VI   CONCLUSION: THE CHALLENGE AND BENEFITS OF A FEMINIST MACROECONOMICS

Feminist economists have taken up the challenge of engendering macroeconomics and trade theory with laudable results. There is more work to do to fully elucidate the ways in which micro-level gender relations affect macroeconomic outcomes. Research on developing economies is more advanced than that on developed economies. Models have yet to fully integrate the implications of race and ethnicity or care work, with some noteworthy exceptions. Nevertheless, what is clear from the work that has already been done is that the role of gender in influencing macroeconomic performance is critical and its role differs according to a country's structural conditions and the policy regime.

One concern about the uses of the work that has been produced to date, however, is the tendency among feminist economists and international institutions to emphasize only the positive effects of gender equality on macroeconomic outcomes and growth.

This can be a dangerous and slippery slope. By emphasizing only the instrumental value of gender equality, we fail to acknowledge those cases where gender inequality is a stimulus to growth. Perhaps this is fueled by a concern that noting the growth-inducing effects of gender inequality will stimulate policy-makers to weaken commitment to gender equality, or even worse, promote gender inequality as a way to stimulate growth.

The evidence on East Asia has shown, however, that rapid growth in that region was in part fueled by gender wage and job discrimination (Braunstein, 2000; Seguino, 2000; Busse and Spielmann, 2006). This evidence contradicts the arguments that East Asian success is alternatively due to market deregulation, the role of the state in identifying strategic industries, or the equitable distribution of the benefits of growth. In contrast to the much-heralded success of East Asia and now China, the gender research highlights that the Asian model does not necessarily provide a roadmap for other countries, fueled as it is by gender inequality. Growth based on exploitation of a group may or may not be harmful to long-run growth. But it does fail in its goal of development, defined as broadly shared well-being.

A lesson to draw from the Asian case is that explicit policies must be adopted to make equity compatible with growth. Given that, a challenge for feminists is to define not only microeconomic but also more detailed macroeconomic policy proposals that promote gender, race/ethnic, and class equity in ways that also promote broadly shared improvements in living standards. This path can ensure that greater equity is self-sustaining.

NOTES

1. This approach contrasts with another trend that rests macroeconomic theory on microeconomic foundations of optimizing agents.
2. The UN Millennium Task Force (2005) identified *security* as a separate domain, with the argument that bodily integrity and freedom from violence are prerequisites for women and men to use their accumulated capabilities. While there may be some value in placing security in a separate domain, it is conceptually linked to *capabilities* and therefore I fold it into the first domain.
3. The term 'agentic' comes from social cognition theory and implies that individuals and groups are both producers as well as products of their social systems – that agents react to social norms but can in turn shape norms, and the gender system.
4. See also Taylor (2004) on structuralist macroeconomics.
5. We can think of this as a modified IS curve with the gender wage ratio (taking the place of the interest rate) plotted against output. A fully developed short-run model would also include a producer equilibrium curve that integrates the effect of the gender wage ratio on profits and prices. See Braunstein (2000) and Blecker and Seguino (2002) for models along these lines.
6. To date, there is only sparse empirical evidence on gender consumption propensities and patterns, so it is difficult to hypothesize about the effect of gender wage equality on consumption, saving, and imports. For developing countries, however, we can surmise that women are more likely to consume domestic goods, with men's expenditures including a larger share of luxury goods that tend to be imported (for example, cell phones, automobiles, and televisions).
7. Some studies explore effects on components of macroeconomic aggregates. For example, Busse and Nunnenkamp (2009) find that gender equality in education attracts foreign direct investment.
8. This may explain why, despite educational equality in the Caribbean, we observe that women's unemployment rates continue to be double those of men (Seguino, 2003).

REFERENCES

Agarwal, Bina (2000), 'Conceptualizing environmental collective action: why gender matters', *Cambridge Journal of Economics*, **24**(3), 283–310.

Agénor, Pierre-Richard, Otaviano Canuto and Luiz Pereira da Silva (2010), 'On gender and growth: the role of intergenerational health externalities and women's occupational constraints', World Bank Policy Research Working Paper No. 5492, World Bank Washington, DC.

Balakrishnan, Radhika (ed.) (2002), *The Hidden Assembly Line: Gender Dynamics in Subcontracted Work in a Global Economy*, Bloomfield, CT: Kumarian Press.

Benería, Lourdes (2007), 'Gender and the social construction of markets', in van Staveren et al. (eds), pp. 13–32.

Benería, Lourdes and Shelley Feldman (1992), *Unequal Burden: Economic Crises, Persistent Poverty and Women's Work*, Boulder, CO: Westview Press.

Berik, Günseli, Yana Rodgers and Ann Zammit (eds) (2008), *Social Justice and Gender Equality: Rethinking Development Strategies and Macroeconomic Policies*, London: Routledge.

Berik, Günseli, Yana Rodgers and Joseph Zveglich (2004), 'International trade and gender wage discrimination: evidence from East Asia', *Review of Development Economics*, **8**(2), 237–54.

Blackden, Mark, Sudharshan Canagarajah, Stephan Klasen and David Lawson (2007), 'Gender and growth in Africa: evidence and issues', in George Mavrotas and Anthony Shorrocks (eds), *Advancing Development: Core Themes in Global Economics*, London: Palgrave Macmillan, pp. 349–70.

Blecker, Robert and Stephanie Seguino (2002), 'Macroeconomic effects of reducing gender wage inequality in an export-oriented, semi-industrialized economy', *Review of Development Economics*, **6**(1), 103–19.

Blumberg, Rae Lesser (1988), 'Income under female versus male control: hypotheses from a theory of gender stratification and data from the third world', *Journal of Family Issues*, **9**(1), 51–84.

Bowles, Samuel and Herbert Gintis (1990), 'Contested exchange: new microfoundations for the political economy of capitalism', *Politics and Society*, **18**(2), 165–222.

Braunstein, Elissa (2000), 'Engendering foreign direct investment: household structures, labor markets, and the international mobility of capital', *World Development*, **28**(7), 1157–72.

Braunstein, Elissa (2008), 'The feminist political economy of the rent-seeking society', *Journal of Economic Issues*, **42**(4),1–21.

Braunstein, Elissa and Nancy Folbre (2001), 'To honor and obey: efficiency, inequality, and patriarchal property rights', *Feminist Economics*, **7**(1), 25–54.

Braunstein, Elissa and James Heintz (2008), 'Gender bias and central bank policy: employment and inflation reduction', *International Review of Applied Economics*, **22**(2), 173–86.

Braunstein, Elissa, Irene van Staveren and Daniele Tavani (2011), 'Embedding care and unpaid work in macroeconomic modeling: a structuralist approach', *Feminist Economics*, **17**(4), 5–31.

Busse, Mathias and Peter Nunnenkamp (2009), 'Gender disparity in education and the international competition for foreign direct investment', *Feminist Economics*, **15**(3), 61–90.

Busse, Matthias and Christian Spielmann (2006), 'Gender inequality and trade', *Review of International Economics*, **14**(3), 362–70.

Bussolo, Maurizio and Raphael de Hoyos (eds) (2009), *Gender Aspects of the Trade and Poverty Nexus: A Micro–Macro Approach*, London and Washington, DC: Palgrave Macmillan.

Çagatay, Nilufer, Diane Elson and Caren Grown (1995), 'Introduction', *World Development*, **23**(11), 1827–36.

Carr, Marilyn, Martha Chen and Jane Tate (2000), 'Globalization and home-based workers', *Feminist Economics*, **6**(3), 23–142.

Cavalcanti, Tiago and José Tavares (2011), 'Women prefer larger governments: female labor supply and public spending', *Economic Inquiry*, **49**(1), 155–71.

Chattopadhyay, Raghabendra and Esther Duflo (2004), 'Women as policy makers: evidence from a randomized policy experiment in India', *Econometrica*, **72**(5), 1409–43.

Choi, Minsik (2006), 'Threat effects of capital mobility on wage bargaining', in Pranab Bardhan, Samuel Bowles and Michael Wallerstein (eds), *Globalization and Egalitarian Redistribution*, Princeton, NJ: Princeton University Press, pp. 64–86.

Darity, William A., Jr. (1995), 'The formal structure of a gender-segregated low-income economy', *World Development*, **23**(11), 1963–68.

Dollar, David and Roberta Gatti (1999), 'Gender inequality, income, and growth: are good times good for women?', Policy Research Report on Gender and Development, World Bank Working Paper Series No. 1, World Bank, Washington, DC.

Dutt, Amitava and Jaime Ros (2007), 'Aggregate demand shocks and economic growth', *Structural Change and Economic Dynamics*, **18**(1), 75–99.

Elson, Diane (ed.) (1991), *Male Bias in the Development Process*, Manchester: Manchester University Press.

Elson, Diane and Nilufer Çagatay (2000), 'The social content of macroeconomic policies', *World Development*, **28**(7), 1347–64.

Elson, Diane and Tonia Warnecke (2011), 'IMF policies and gender orders: the case of the poverty reduction and growth facility', in Isabella Bakker, Diane Elson and Brigitte Young (eds), *Questioning Financial Governance from a Feminist Perspective*, London and New York: Routledge, pp. 110–31.

Erturk, Korkut and William A. Darity, Jr. (2000), 'Secular changes in the gender composition of employment and growth dynamics in the north and the south', *World Development*, **28**(7), 1231–38.

Figart, Deborah M., Ellen Mutari and Marilyn Power (2002), *Living Wages, Equal Wages: Gender and Labor Market Policies in the United States*, London: Routledge.

Forsythe, Nancy, Roberto Korzeniewicz and Valerie Durrant (2000), 'Gender inequality and economic growth: a longitudinal evaluation', *Economic Development and Cultural Change*, **48**(3), 573–617.

Furtado, Celso (1964), *Development and Underdevelopment*, Berkeley, CA: University of California Press.

Fussell, Elizabeth (2000), 'Making labour flexible: the recomposition of Tijuana's maquiladora female labour force', *Feminist Economics*, **6**(3), 59–79.

Hill, M. Anne and Elizabeth King (1995), 'Women's education and economic well-being', *Feminist Economics*, **1**(2), 21–46.

Iversen, Torben and Frances Rosenbluth (2006), 'The political economy of gender: explaining cross-national variation in the gender division of labor and the gender voting gap', *American Journal of Political Science*, **50**(1), 1–19.

Klasen, Stephan and Francesca Lamanna (2009), 'The impact of gender inequality in education and employment on economic growth: new evidence for a panel of countries', *Feminist Economics*, **15**(3), 91–132.

Kongar, Ebru (2007), 'Importing equality or exporting jobs? Competition and gender wage and employment differentials in US manufacturing', in van Staveren et al. (eds), pp. 215–36.

Liu, Amy (2004), 'Sectoral gender wage gap in Vietnam', *Oxford Development Studies*, **32**(2), 225–39.

Maurer-Fazio, Margaret, Thomas G. Rawski and Wei Zhang (1999), 'Inequality in the rewards for holding up half the sky: gender wage gaps in China's urban labour market, 1988–1994', *China Journal*, Issue 41, 55–88.

Menon, Nidhiya and Yana van der Meulen Rodgers (2009), 'International trade and the gender wage gap: new evidence from India's manufacturing sector', *World Development*, **37**(5), 965–981.

Morrison, Andrew, Dhushyanth Raju, and Nistha Sinha (2007), 'Gender equality, poverty, and economic growth', World Bank Policy Research Working Paper 4349, World Bank, Washington, DC.

Morrisson, Christian and Johannes Jütting (2005), 'The impact of social institutions on the economic role of women', *World Development*, **33**(7), 1065–81.

O'Laughlin, Bridget (2007), 'A bigger piece of a very small pie: intrahousehold resource allocation and poverty reduction in Africa', *Development and Change*, **38**(1), 21–44.

Pollin, Robert and Andong Zhu (2006), 'Inflation and economic growth: a cross-country nonlinear analysis', *Journal of Post Keynesian Economics*, **28**(4), 593–614.

Prebisch, Raúl (1950) *The Economic Development of Latin America and Its Principal Problems*, New York: United Nations.

Rathin, Roy, Antoine Heuty and Emmanuel Letouzé (2009), 'Fiscal space for public investment: towards a human development approach', in Roy Rathin and Antoine Heuty (eds), *Fiscal Space: Policy Options for Financing Human Development*, London and Sterling, VA: Earthscan, pp. 67–92.

Razavi, Shahra (2009), 'Engendering the political economy of agrarian change', *Journal of Peasant Studies*, **36**(1), 197–227.

Reddock, Rhoda (2009), 'What now for Caribbean people and their leaders? Reflections on the current economic and social crisis: a gender perspective', 10th W.G. Demas Memorial Lecture, University of West Indies, St. Augustine, Trinidad and Tobago, May 26.

Robeyns, Ingrid (2005), 'The capability approach: a theoretical survey', *Journal of Human Development*, **6**(1), 93–114.

Seguino, Stephanie (2000), 'Accounting for gender in Asian economic growth', *Feminist Economics*, **6**(3), 22–58.

Seguino, Stephanie (2002), 'Gender, quality of life, and growth in Asia 1970 to 1990', *The Pacific Review*, **15**(2), 245–77.

Seguino, Stephanie (2003), 'Why are women in the Caribbean so much more likely than men to be unemployed?', *Social and Economic Studies*, **52**(4), 83–120.

Seguino, Stephanie (2007a), 'The great equalizer? Globalization effects on gender equity in well-being in Latin America and the Caribbean', in Anwar Shaikh (ed.), *Globalization and the Myth of Free Trade*, London: Routledge, pp. 177–214.

Seguino, Stephanie (2007b), 'Is more mobility good? Firm mobility and the low-wage low-productivity trap', *Structural Change and Economic Dynamics*, **18**(1), 27–51.

Seguino, Stephanie (2010), 'Gender, distribution, and balance of payments constrained growth in developing countries', *Review of Political Economy*, **22**(3), 373–404.

Seguino, Stephanie (2012), 'Macroeconomics, human development, and distribution', *Journal of Human Development and Capabilities*, **13**(1), 59–83.

Seguino, Stephanie and James Heintz (2012), 'Monetary tightening and the dynamics of race and gender stratification in the US', *American Journal of Economics and Sociology*, **71**(3), 603–38.

Sparr, Pamela (1994), 'Feminist critiques of structural adjustment', in Pamela Sparr (ed.), *Mortgaging Women's Lives: Feminist Critiques of Structural Adjustment*, London: Zed Books, pp. 13–39.

Takhtamanova, Yelena and Eva Sierminska (2009), 'Gender, monetary policy, and employment: the case of nine OECD countries', *Feminist Economics*, **15**(3), 323–53.

Taylor, Lance (2004), *Reconstructing Macroeconomics: Structuralist Proposals and Critiques of the Mainstream*, Cambridge, MA: Harvard University Press.

Tejani, Sheba and Will Milberg (2010), 'Global defeminization? Industrial upgrading, occupational segregation, and manufacturing', SCEPA Working Paper 2010–1, Schwartz Center for Economic Policy Analysis New York.

Udry, Christopher (1996), 'Gender, agricultural production and the theory of the household', *Journal of Political Economy*, **104**(5), 1010–46.

UN Millennium Task Force (2005), *Taking Action: Achieving Gender Equality and Empowering Women*, London and Sterling, VA: Earthscan.

Van Staveren, Irene, Diane Elson, Caren Grown and Nilufer Çagatay (eds) (2007), *The Feminist Economics of Trade*, London and New York: Routledge.

Weichselbaumer, Doris and Rudolf Winter-Ebmer (2005), 'A meta-analysis of the international gender wage gap', *Journal of Economic Surveys*, **19**(3), 479–511.

Whitehead, Ann and Naila Kabeer (2001), 'Living with uncertainty: gender, livelihoods and pro-poor growth in rural Sub-Saharan Africa', IDS Working Paper 134, Institute of Development Studies, University of Sussex, Brighton.

World Bank (2012), *World Development Report 2012: Gender Equality and Development*, Washington, DC: World Bank.

21. Central bank policy and gender
Elissa Braunstein

I INTRODUCTION

The dominant policy position of most central banks is to maintain very low rates of inflation, without much consideration for how these restrictive policies impact the real economy – outcomes such as employment, investment, and economic growth. Although there is scant evidence that maintaining very low rates of inflation raises economic growth (see Epstein, 2003), such policies remain a key feature of mainstream or orthodox approaches to monetary policy. The ever-increasing financialization of the global economy contributes to this stance, as central banks feel pressure to maintain an attractive investment environment (one characterized by very low inflation and high interest rates) lest they run into balance-of-payments problems. This is particularly the case among developing and emerging market countries, where a central bank commitment to a (low) inflation target – to the exclusion of other targets such as employment – is perceived as an increasingly essential component of macroeconomic management. The result has been what many term the 'deflationary bias' of the global economy, where orthodox economic theory, combined with the policies deemed necessary to mollify highly mobile financial capital, result in sluggish economic growth and high unemployment.

Gerald Epstein and Juliet Schor argue that anti-inflation policy and orthodox approaches to central banking reflect the 'contested terrain' of central banks, the class and intra-class conflicts over the distribution of income and power in the macro economy (Epstein and Schor, 1990; Epstein, 2000). Their work underscores the importance of understanding monetary policy from a political perspective, as the distribution of the gains and costs of economic policy proffers insight into both a policy's genesis and its longer-term consequences. Class is one dimension of this contested terrain; gender is another.

This chapter will build on their analysis by considering the gendered aspects of central bank policy from an employment perspective. Section II gives a brief overview of current practices in central bank policy, their basis in economic theory, and the consequences for economic life. Section III reviews extant research on contractionary monetary policy and gendered employment outcomes. Section IV discusses the gendered political economy of central bank policy and some policy alternatives. Section V concludes.

II INFLATION TARGETING, UNEMPLOYMENT, AND WELL-BEING

Economists model the objectives of central bankers in terms of a social welfare function that includes inflation and unemployment (or output). Both inflation and unemployment are taken as social 'bads', so the task for central bankers conducting monetary policy is to balance the tradeoff between the two. This tradeoff was most famously proposed back in 1958, when economist A. William Phillips found a negative relationship between inflation and unemployment in the United Kingdom (Phillips, 1958), an observation that spurred a lot of similar research among industrialized country scholars.[1] Their collective work underlies the economic adage that lower unemployment is associated with higher inflation, and vice versa, at least in the short run. The reasoning is that lower unemployment and tighter labor markets strengthen workers' power to bargain for higher wages. In order to maintain profits, employers respond to higher wages by raising prices; this results in a general increase in the price level, or inflation. These observations emerged at a time in economic history when Keynesian approaches to economic management held sway. In terms of the inflation–unemployment tradeoff, the implication was that governments could use expansionary monetary and fiscal policies to generate employment, even though such actions might exact a cost in terms of some inflation.

The short-run nature of this relationship is based on the consequent work of orthodox economist Milton Friedman and others who argued that in the long run, workers and employers eventually build their inflation expectations into wage contracts, effectively neutralizing efforts to alter employment with monetary policy in any long-term sense (Friedman, 1968; Lucas, 1973). According to this logic, at some point the price increases spurred by expansionary monetary policy and increased aggregate demand induce calls for higher wages among workers, some of whom have recently been hired to meet increased aggregate demand. The reason is that workers have seen their real wages (wages divided by prices) decline as prices have gone up. As nominal wages increase, so do real wages, and workers become more expensive to employers, inducing some layoffs. Eventually, the story goes, this process continues until real wages and unemployment reach the same levels as before the expansionary monetary policy was introduced. The theoretical implication is that (in the long run) there exists some threshold unemployment rate (sometimes referred to as the 'natural rate of unemployment') below which inflation rises without generating more employment.[2]

Extended into the political arena, expansionary economic policy becomes associated with higher inflation, not more jobs. These Friedman-type arguments intellectually substantiate the type of conservative economic policies that have characterized the decidedly hawkish approach to inflation taken by most of the world's governments since the 1980s (Pollin, 1999). Economic research casts considerable doubt on the more extreme versions of Friedman's original argument, with most economists maintaining that the natural rate of unemployment varies over time based on the economic and institutional contexts (see ibid.), and that government policies can be effectively used to moderate cyclical changes in output and employment. Still, despite this evolution on the natural rate of unemployment, fear of any inflation at all is still an overriding concern for orthodox economic policy-makers.

For central bankers, the shift away from concerns about employment toward a nearly exclusive focus on inflation is manifested by the increasing popularity of inflation targeting (Epstein, 2007). Inflation targeting (IT) refers to a formal commitment by the central bank to maintain a target inflation rate and steering inflation toward that target. In practice, IT is associated not just with price stability, but also with keeping inflation extremely low, most commonly around 2 percent for advanced economies and less than 5 percent for developing economies (Blanchard et al., 2010). Committing to an inflation target means it is the central bank's exclusive policy objective. As of March 2012, 28 countries have adopted formal IT regimes (Jahan, 2012). About half are emerging and/ or low-income economies, with many more expressing an intention to move toward IT in the future (Allen et al., 2006). Further, a number of central banks in advanced econo- mies are also moving toward IT, including the European Central Bank, the US Federal Reserve, the Bank of Japan, and the Swiss National Bank (Roger, 2010, p. 46). Even if a formal IT policy is not adopted, it is certainly the case that central banks around the world are unwavering about the perils of inflation, and increasingly follow at least infor- mal IT regimes.[3]

The impetus behind this stance stems partly from a theoretical argument that links central bank credibility with inflation expectations. Recall the point made by ortho- dox economists that inflation expectations determine the effectiveness of expansionary economic policies. If indeed workers and employers incorporate inflation expectations into wage contracts and pricing behavior, actual inflation – the actual movement of the overall price level – will be driven by these expectations. This is where central bank credibility purportedly comes in. If central bankers weigh inflation more heavily than unemployment in their objective functions, and workers and employers know about it and believe in it (central bank credibility), then inflation expectations will be lower, as will actual inflation (Rogoff, 1985). The consequence, theoretically, is that the employ- ment cost of maintaining low inflation – what is called the 'sacrifice ratio' – will decline. Because everyone believes in the central bank's commitment to a low inflation target, they will revise their inflation expectations downward, creating more space for employ- ment to increase without accelerating inflation. The question now becomes whether this actually happens in practice. Empirical evidence does not support the contention that adopting IT enhances central bank credibility or lowers the sacrifice ratio (see Epstein, 2000; Ball and Sheridan, 2005; Heintz and Ndikumana, 2011). Central bankers tend to reduce inflation 'the old-fashioned way: by raising interest rates, causing recessions or slowing growth, and by throwing people out of work' (Epstein, 2007, p. 4).

Another argument for IT is that high and variable inflation hinders economic growth because it creates uncertainty for investors and consumers. But even though IT can be associated with a decline in the variability of inflation, there is no evidence that it is the best monetary policy tool to achieve such a goal, particularly if policy-makers are inter- ested in supporting growth and employment creation as well as price stability (Epstein, 2007). The very instruments used to keep inflation low, such as raising nominal interest rates or cutting government spending, also constrain economic growth (Pollin et al., 2009). There is no evidence that inflation rates of up to 20 percent have any predictable negative consequences on the real economy; they are not associated with lower growth, lower domestic or foreign investment, or any other significant real variable that has been studied (Epstein, 2007, p. 7).

These points are particularly important from a development perspective because of how IT impacts exchange rates, and how exchange rates, in turn, affect economic growth in developing economies. Low inflation and the policies used in IT, including raising short-term interest rates, can lead to appreciation of the real exchange rate. Most of us are more familiar with the nominal exchange rate (often referred to simply as the 'exchange rate'), the price at which one currency exchanges for another. But it is the real exchange rate that measures the value of one country's goods against its trading partners', and that thus reflects that country's trade competitiveness.[4] The link between IT and appreciated real exchange rates works as follows: when financial capital, attracted by the high interest rates of an IT regime, flows into a country, it leads to pressures for appreciation of the nominal (as opposed to real) exchange rate. How these pressures on the nominal exchange rate affect the real exchange rate depends on what is happening with domestic inflation. The higher interest rates associated with IT, by restraining economic activity and consequently keeping domestic inflation low, can counterbalance the pressures for real exchange rate appreciation introduced by nominal exchange rate appreciation.[5] However, there is the added problem of what is called 'pass-through': depreciated nominal exchange rates – which raise the domestic price of imports – will put upward pressure on the domestic price level and increase inflation. The net result is that IT often implies not just an inflation target, but also an (appreciated) real exchange rate target (Heintz, 2006). Appreciated real exchange rates tend to discourage exports and encourage imports, ultimately slowing down economic growth and employment creation (Frenkel and Taylor, 2006).

IT is also potentially problematic from a short-term, cyclical point of view because it constrains monetary policy choices in sometimes counterproductive ways. We tend to think of inflation most often as the demand–pull type associated with an overheating of the economy. But in the developing world, inflation is frequently the result of supply-side shocks such as global spikes in commodity prices, supply bottlenecks caused by things such as infrastructure failure or war, or exchange rate shocks stemming from external conditions in currency markets (Agénor et al., 2000). Under these circumstances, the standard inflation fighting tool – raising short-term interest rates – will only intensify the contractionary effects of the initial supply shock. In advanced economies, where inflation targets are around 2 percent, there is the problem of the 'liquidity trap': inflation and nominal interest rates are already so low that there is little room for expansionary monetary policy in case of a recession. This was the case in the economic crisis that began in 2008, when central banks quickly decreased policy interest rates to the nominal limit of zero, but probably needed to decrease them a lot more (for example, another 3–5 percent in the US case) (Blanchard et al., 2010, p. 8). The result was a turn to fiscal policy, with its associated political constraints, time lags, and assumption of debt. The liquidity trap issue even spurred the International Monetary Fund's (IMF) chief economist to suggest that inflation targets among advanced economies be raised to 4 percent (ibid., p. 11).

A common counterargument to these points from a social welfare perspective is a distributional one: inflation unduly harms the poor and those on fixed incomes because price increases eat away at the limited purchasing power that these groups do have. This point is an important one, but one needs to consider the tradeoffs. Studies that consider attitudes by income group suggest that the poor would gladly trade more inflation for a greater supply of jobs (Jayadev, 2006, 2008). A plethora of happiness and life satisfaction studies, where economists evaluate the statistical association between self-reported well-being and a variety of economic and demographic variables, consistently show that individuals care a lot more about aggregate unemployment than inflation, even in advanced economies with generous social welfare states and unemployment insurance. Estimates of the marginal rate of substitution between unemployment and inflation range between 1.6 (Di Tella et al., 2001; Blanchflower, 2007) and 4.7 (Wolfers, 2003) for advanced economies, to 8.0 for a sample of Latin American countries (Ruprah and Luengas, 2011). To give a sense of what this means: a marginal rate of substitution between unemployment and inflation of 1.6 indicates that a 1.0 percentage point increase in unemployment has the same (negative) impact on well-being as a 1.6 percentage point increase in inflation, a 60 percent difference based on the low-end estimates. From a well-being perspective, at least, overall unemployment is much more socially costly than inflation.

This indicates that many central bankers put a lot more weight on inflation relative to unemployment than is warranted by either the preferences of the public or the empirical evidence. To better understand the choices and consequences of IT-type central bank policy regimes, we will use a gender-aware analytical framework to explore how central bank policy shapes economic life, focusing in particular on its gendered employment costs.

III MONETARY POLICY AND GENDERED EMPLOYMENT

Gender is only rarely understood as a macroeconomic issue (see Seguino, Chapter 20, this volume, for a discussion). It is even less frequent that gender is linked with financial structures and outcomes in particular, partly because in orthodox economic models the role of money is merely to equilibrate macroeconomic imbalances, and thus finance does not have any long-term or qualitatively significant effects on the 'real' economy.[6] We can see this understanding reflected in orthodox approaches to monetary policy where central banks are encouraged (or required in the case of formal IT) to confine their activities to managing inflation. However, such a perspective contradicts a growing body of research that central bank policies adopted to target and maintain low inflation have real employment effects, and that these differ by race and gender.

Why might we expect central bank policy to have differential effects on women's versus men's unemployment? The short answer is that there are systematic gender differences on both the supply and demand sides of the labor market. On the supply side, differences in human capital are probably the most commonly considered, but the institutional, social, and material contexts in which workers live create fundamental differences in choice and opportunity by gender. On the demand side, gender segregation by industry and occupation means that women and men face systematically different rates of cyclical volatility at work. In emerging economies, labor-intensive export-oriented industries that tend to employ women are more cyclically volatile than men's industries, resulting in higher overall rates of unemployment for women relative to men (Howes and Singh, 1995; Braunstein and Heintz, 2008). In advanced economies, men's higher aggregate unemployment rates relative to women's in the most recent recession are reflected in popular tags such as 'man-cession' in the US and 'he-cession' in the UK, and were widely attributed to the fact that the sectors initially hardest hit by the recession (for example, construction and manufacturing) were male labor intensive.

However, closer analysis in the US shows that this portrayal is an oversimplification. Men are recouping jobs faster than women during the recovery, and the probability of unemployment among women increases significantly if one is less educated, a racial or ethnic minority, or a single parent (Grown and Tas, 2010; Boushey, 2011). This points to the fact that overt and more subtle forms of gender discrimination can also result in gender differences in unemployment. In terms of direct discrimination, the male breadwinner ideal – the presumption that men should and do bear the primary financial responsibility for provisioning families – has been linked with higher unemployment for women relative to men in OECD countries (Algan and Cahuc, 2006). Women get laid off first because employers presume that it is more important for men to be able to fulfill their traditional breadwinning responsibilities, or because men are perceived as simply more deserving of jobs when they are scarce (Seguino and Heintz, 2012). In light of these differences between women's and men's unemployment, we suspect that economic shocks such as those introduced or exacerbated by central bank efforts to combat inflation may have systematically different gender effects.

Much of the empirical work on the differential employment costs of monetary policy focuses on race or ethnicity in the US, most using some variant of vector autoregression (VAR) techniques.[7] The universal finding is that relative to whites, ethnic minorities face disproportionately larger declines in employment as a result of increases in interest rates (the main monetary policy instrument used to combat inflation), as do the less educated and less skilled. These results hold up to controls for industrial or occupational segregation, so the reasoning is not likely to be that ethnic minorities work in more cyclically volatile industries or occupations (Carpenter and Rodgers, 2005). One explanation is based on Olivier Blanchard's (1995) theoretical work on ladder effects: lower-income individuals, who also have fewer skills and less education, occupy the lower rungs of the labor market ladder and are thus more likely to face unemployment when aggregate demand declines as a consequence of contractionary monetary policy (see also Thorbecke, 2001). These types of studies tend to consider only the employment effects of contractionary policies, so the question of whether results are symmetrical – that is, whether ethnic minorities see their employment recover faster than whites when monetary policy is expansionary – is still an open one.

Turning to gender, we are aware of only three empirical studies that compare employment outcomes for women versus men in the context of monetary policy, one for a group of developing countries (Braunstein and Heintz, 2008), and two for advanced economies (Tachtamanova and Sierminksa 2009; Seguino and Heintz, 2012). Separating the discussion by level of development is important, as the relationship between monetary policy and gendered employment is likely to vary by economic structure, size, the significance of international trade to the domestic economy, and a host of other variables associated with per capita income.

Braunstein and James Heintz (2008) explore two broad questions for a group of low- and middle-income countries selected based on having at least 20 years of gender-disaggregated employment data between 1970 and 2003: (i) what is the impact of inflation reduction on employment, and is the impact different for women and men and (ii) how are monetary policy indicators as measured by real interest rates, real exchange rates, and the real money supply connected to deflationary episodes and gender-specific employment effects? The empirical approach is simple. After controlling for long-run trends in women's and men's employment (thus isolating cyclical changes), they evaluate how the ratio of female to male employment behaves during deflationary episodes, and whether this outcome varies based on monetary policy instrument.

The authors find that while periods of inflation decline are highly likely to be associated with employment losses for both women and men (they term these episodes 'contractionary inflation reduction'), women lose more employment than men in the vast majority of cases. In the fewer cases where inflation reduction is accompanied by employment expansion (termed 'expansionary inflation reduction'), the gender-specific impact is ambiguous. Looking at specific monetary policy instruments, higher real interest rates and declines in the real money supply are both associated with declines in employment overall, as well as disproportionate employment losses for women relative to men. Conversely, maintaining a competitive real exchange rate, a monetary policy option that essentially cheapens exports relative to imports, neutralizes the negative impact of contractionary inflation reduction on women's employment, with no clear pattern for men. This result is consistent with the observation that many developing and emerging economies with labor-intensive export-oriented sectors primarily employ women, so maintaining export competitiveness by keeping real exchange rates from appreciating can protect women's employment. (Recall that inflation targeting is often associated with appreciated real exchange rates.) Overall, then, the results suggest, at least for this group of countries, that contractionary monetary policy aimed at reducing inflation often has a disproportionately negative impact on women's employment, an effect that may be eased by maintaining a competitive real exchange rate.

The story in advanced economies is less conclusive. Yelena Tachtamanova and Eva Sierminsksa (2009) use both single-equation estimations and VAR on quarterly data for nine OECD countries between 1980 and 2004, where gender-specific employment is a function of short-term interest rates, exchange rates, and past employment. Taken together, the association between employment and interest rates is weak in their sample, with little evidence of differences between women and men, not surprising given the lack of a statistical association overall. For the VAR, there is evidence that the responsiveness of male employment to interest rate increases is higher than that of female employment in Canada, Finland, Japan, Spain, and the UK, but that female responsiveness is higher in the US. In all these cases, however, the gender differences in responsiveness are economically small.

A different conclusion comes from the work of Stephanie Seguino and Heintz (2012), who use US state-level panel data from 1979 to 2008 to assess how both gender and race determine the impact of central bank policy on employment. Their framework is unique in that they explore the interconnectedness between different types of inequality, as well as proffer an alternative to standard VAR techniques as the latter give no insight into the structural relationships among the variables studied. Using the ratios of female/white male and black/white unemployment rates as their baseline dependent variables, Seguino and Heintz consider (i) whether monetary policy, as measured by the federal funds rate, affects the unemployment of women or blacks differently from white men, and (ii) how black population density affects these relationships.[8]

Including black population density tests contending theories on how racial identity plays out economically. The basic question is how increased exposure of the dominant group (whites) to the subordinate group (blacks) – proxied by black population density – affects discrimination. One of these is threat theory, which posits that black population density induces whites to feel that their dominant group position is threatened, instigating more racialist identities, norms, and stereotypes among whites. Blacks thus suffer more discrimination and consequently bear a greater proportion of the burden of contractionary monetary policy as they are the first to get laid off and the last to be hired when jobs become more scarce. An alternative is contact theory, which counters that the more contact the dominant group has with the subordinate group, the more that damaging racialist stereotypes break down with concomitantly less discrimination.

After exploring a number of different specifications, including whether black population density exhibits threshold effects, Seguino and Heintz provide strong evidence for gender and racial bias in the distribution of the employment costs of contractionary central bank policy. Even after controlling for education and industry, they find that, relative to white men, both blacks and white women bear a heavier unemployment burden from contractionary monetary policy than white men, but blacks as a group fare worse than white women, with black women faring worst of all. They also find evidence for threat effects as black population density increases. When black population density is low, the burden of unemployment shifts to both white women and black men. As black population density rises, however, the unemployment burden shifts away from white women and toward blacks, both female and male. From a threat theory perspective, the interpretation is that discrimination based on race comes to dominate that based on gender as black population density rises: the dominant group, white men, facing increases in perceived threats to their dominant group position, increasingly identify with white women as part of the same identity group (white) rather than as part of a subordinate group (women).

Because Seguino and Heintz provide one of the few studies combining both expansionary and contractionary policies, we can interpret their results symmetrically. That is, the finding that blacks and white women bear a disproportionate unemployment burden from contractionary monetary policy implies that the opposite is also true: employment for blacks and white women recovers faster than white men's when monetary policy is expansionary. In future work, it would be important to differentiate between contractionary and expansionary monetary policy episodes, as it seems likely that job growth responds differently in the two cases. Still, however, the overall economic environment in the world today is deflationary, so emphasizing the differential unemployment effects of contractionary monetary policy is warranted.

Taken as a whole, Seguino and Heintz's insights are powerful because they precisely articulate how systems of inequality influence the allocation of the costs and benefits of central bank policy, challenging us to see how macroeconomic aggregates are not above the fray of social relationships. If, indeed, women or other subordinate groups – whether they be defined in terms of race or ethnicity, education, or skill – do bear a disproportionate share of the burden of contractionary monetary policy or IT regimes, we can use a gender-aware framework to better understand the economic consequences and political implications of these macroeconomic policies.

IV   THE GENDERED POLITICAL ECONOMY OF CENTRAL BANK POLICY

Focusing on the economic consequences of gender bias, it is important to note that the studies reviewed above address only the short-run gender-specific impacts on employment. The results say little about the long-run impact of different policy responses to inflation, such as raising interest rates versus reducing the money supply. Supporters of inflation targeting frequently acknowledge that short-run tradeoffs might exist, but the long-run benefits of low inflation for growth and development are more significant. This argument is problematic when transitory policy shocks have long-run consequences for real economic variables (Fontana and Palacio-Vera, 2005; Dutt and Ros, 2007). For example, an extended recession can inhibit investments in innovation, lowering the trajectory of productivity and income growth. Similarly, short-term gender-specific shocks can have long-run effects for a country's human and economic development.

A number of empirical studies suggest that gender-based inequality in employment and unemployment have implications for long-term development. For example, this body of research shows that a positive relationship exists between gender equality (measured most commonly as educational or labor force participation equality) and economic growth (Hill and King, 1995; Dollar and Gatti, 1999; Klasen, 1999; Klasen and Lamanna, 2009). Some of the effects are quite large. A recent study of the 1960–2000 period found that relative to East Asia, annual average growth rates in the Middle East and North Africa were 0.9 to 1.7 percentage points lower, and in South Asia 0.1 to 1.6 percentage points lower due to gender gaps in education and employment (ibid., p. 91). Investing in girls makes for a higher productivity workforce, but higher rates of unemployment and cyclical volatility in women's jobs will discourage these types of investments at both the individual and community levels.

In a related sense, lower incomes and higher-income volatility for women could lead to lower investments in human capital overall, thereby lowering long-term growth. Theory and evidence in the developing world have aptly demonstrated a higher coincidence between a mother's income and the family's basic needs than a father's income (Bénería and Roldán, 1987; Blumberg, 1991; Chant, 1991). Income that is controlled by women is more likely to be spent on children's health and nutrition (Dwyer and Bruce, 1988; Hoddinott et al., 1998). In many countries, a large proportion of fathers provide little or no economic support for their children (Folbre, 1994). But faced with cyclically higher rates of unemployment during disinflation, mothers will have fewer opportunities to invest in their children, compromising future labor force quality.

Moving beyond instrumental arguments, the finding that women or other subordinate groups may shoulder a disproportionate share of the costs of contractionary inflation reduction introduces an important political economy question into the discussion: what do the distribution of the costs and benefits of inflation reduction indicate about the contested terrain of monetary policy? One might simply respond 'not much', with an argument going something like the following. It is true that the empirical evidence indicates gender differences in labor supply and demand result in women's jobs being more cyclically volatile (at least on the economic downturn) than men's jobs in many developing economies, although the evidence is more mixed for advanced economies other than the US (Howes and Singh, 1995; Tachtamanova and Sierminksa, 2009). While central bank policies may have gender-differentiated impacts, these impacts reflect gender dynamics in the labor market, not in the central bank. Monetary policy-makers should not be tasked with addressing gender inequality; such issues are, and should properly remain, outside the purview of monetary management. Ultimately, the best thing (indeed perhaps the only thing) a central banker can do for gender equality is to keep inflation low and stable, as these policies provide the sort of macroeconomic stability essential for growth and income generation. Gender is only a matter of concern for social policy, the argument concludes.

As touched on at the beginning of this chapter, the reach of this argument is global in scope. Most central banks in developing countries are constrained by the reactions of international financial markets to their policy choices. This is particularly likely to be the case when capital markets have been liberalized and prudential capital controls have been eliminated. In addition, central banks in many low-income countries – including the heavily indebted poor countries (HIPC) – must still craft their policies under the auspices of IMF conditionalities.[9] Monetary policies enshrined in poverty reduction strategy papers reflect these biases (see UNRISD, 2010). Ironically, many of these development strategies claim to have incorporated a gendered analysis into their poverty reduction program. However, this gender-sensitive analysis does not spill over into the macro-economic realm.

A different sort of insight comes from thinking about what would happen if gender equality concerns were indeed incorporated into monetary policy from the start. Such a shift would most likely necessitate a move away from inflation targeting as it is currently practiced and could harm those invested in a low inflation, high interest rate environment – largely finance capital. Even the most brief perusal of central bank leaders and managers around the world shows that they are largely drawn from finance and banking, a pool that is also primarily male, especially at the upper echelons of management. For instance, in the US, women constitute 2.9 percent of chief executives in the finance industry, and 16.6 percent of its executive officers (Catalyst, 2011). Looking at central banks in particular, women constitute only 6.3 percent of the world's central bank governors, making for a total of 12 (Jordan, 2012).

Taken from this standpoint, one that acknowledges how gender, class, and nation shape our opinions of the appropriate or feasible reach of macroeconomic policy, resistance to seeing, much less incorporating, the social content of inflation targeting is clearly a political matter. It is not just that central bank policy has gender differentiated effects; it is also that the very structures of central banks and global financial markets and institutions, the permissible discourses on monetary policy, and the technical models used to illustrate them are themselves 'bearers of gender' (Elson, 1998, p. 198).

Another aspect of the gendered political economy of these empirical findings is the point that if women's labor force participation keeps unit labor costs and inflation lower than they would otherwise be, then a focus on gender equality within the context of sustainable levels of inflation could require other mechanisms for price control that are more consistent with long-run growth and development. Examples of such policies include incomes policies that constrain nominal wage growth or anti-monopoly policies to maintain price competition. Such a move might be resisted by those who benefit (perhaps only in the short run) from women's more precarious employment, for example, their employers and employed men. Understanding central bank policy in this way, one that queries which segments of society enjoy the benefits and bear the costs, uncovers both its social and political nature. Gender-biased central bank policy may help solve the political problems introduced by orthodox central bank policy in that gender bias concentrates the costs of these policies on a less powerful segment of society: women. Empirical evidence for this type of political content in terms of race and central bank policy in the US is proffered by Heintz and Seguino (2009), who find that the higher the black/white unemployment ratio (in other words, the more that blacks bear the brunt of unemployment in the economy), the less responsive is interest rate policy to unemployment. From this perspective, certain groups of workers defined in terms of gender or race constitute a reserve army of labor, one that enables capitalists to protect profit shares by dampening nominal wage increases while maintaining low inflation. Thus, inflation targeting and deflationary monetary policy must be considered in terms of their social content (for example, what are the social structures that underlie this policy) as well as their social impact (Elson and Çagatay, 2000).

V   CONCLUSION: GENDER-SENSITIVE CENTRAL BANK TARGETS

A number of progressive alternatives to the current dominant policy position among central banks of maintaining very low inflation rates – to the exclusion of other policy concerns – call for supplementing inflation targeting with other types of targets. These include but are not limited to exchange rate targets, capital controls, output or employment targets, incomes policies to directly limit inflation, and targeted credit programs to encourage employment-creating (rather than inflation-generating) investments (Epstein and Yeldan, 2009). All of these proposals would benefit from gender-aware construction and analysis.

Targeting employment generation alone, whether it be directly through employment targets or indirectly through exchange rate targets or credit programs, will not guarantee more gender-egalitarian outcomes if they fail to take into account the gender dynamics of employment. If and where employment or other targets are used to assess central bank policy, these indicators must be disaggregated by gender. In light of the tremendous growth of informal and contingent employment worldwide, these figures should include some measure of employment quality as well as quantity. Of course, data constraints may mean that this sort of labor force information is not available in a timely enough fashion to use in formulating and monitoring central bank policy. If indeed that is the case, it is important to research and formulate next-best options for tracking gender-specific employment effects.

From the perspective of central bank policy and economic life, it is important to remember that employment is not an end in and of itself. While employment has some direct human development implications (personal development, self-esteem, and so on), it is primarily a means to an end, a source of income that partly determines one's provisioning capacities and ultimately human development. Thus, it is important to also consider human development outcomes as actual targets as well. Timely, detailed information that could serve as the basis for formulating central bank policies might be too costly to collect relative to other indicators such as employment. Still, gender-specific indicators of human development could be used to monitor the broader impact of employment or other central bank targets.

A central issue here is the often implicit assumption that the reproductive or care economy will seamlessly follow shifts in the paid economy. This is reflected in the notion that standard macroeconomic theory does not treat the labor force or human capabilities as produced. Even though we have yet to see some measure of care, paid or unpaid, regularly used as an indicator of economic well-being, it would be essential to construct one for use as a human development target in the analysis of central bank policies. It is only by doing so that we can move beyond understanding central bank policy as simply a monetary or employment issue to gain a deeper sense of how it affects gender and economic life.

NOTES

1. In Phillips's original work, he linked unemployment to changes in money wages, not overall inflation.
2. A more cumbersome term, the non-accelerating inflation rate of unemployment, or NAIRU, is more the norm among economists.
3. For instance, in the US the Federal Reserve Act of 1913 tasks the central bank with achieving three goals: maximum employment, stable prices, and moderate long-term interest rates (Board of Governors, 2005, p. 15). However, despite demonstrating a willingness to use monetary policy to spur output growth in the most recent recession, concerns about inflation still dominate the monetary policy discussion in the US.
4. For those who want to get a bit more technical: the *nominal exchange rate* is defined as the amount of domestic currency needed to buy one unit of foreign currency. Therefore, an increase in the exchange rate reflects a depreciation (it takes more home currency to buy one unit of foreign currency), and a decline in the exchange rate reflects an appreciation (it takes less home currency to buy one unit of foreign currency). The *real exchange rate* is equal to the nominal exchange rate times the ratio of the price level of a country's trading partners to the domestic price level.
5. Note that higher interest rates can be inflationary if interest payments are passed on to consumers in the form of higher prices (Heintz, 2006).
6. The most extreme version of this argument is associated with real business cycle theorists.
7. See, for instance, Abell (1991), Carpenter and Rodgers (2005), Rodgers (2008), and Thorbecke (2001). A structural alternative to these approaches is Heintz and Seguino (2009). Also note that VAR refers to a statistical model used with time-series data where a variable is estimated as a function of its own lagged values as well as the lags of all the other variables in the model. All of the variables are treated as endogenous, and there are no structural frameworks required (a strength as well as a weakness).
8. At the same time, Seguino and Heintz (2012) statistically control for the relevant ratio of labor force participation rates to account for discouraged worker effects, state-level economic growth, state fixed effects, and, in a robustness check, occupational and educational differences in the groups studied.
9. Conditionalities are terms that borrowers must agree to in order to secure a loan from an international financial institution such as the IMF. One example of a conditionality is that the government must maintain a target inflation rate.

REFERENCES

Abell, John D. (1991), 'Distributional effects of monetary and fiscal policy: impacts on unemployment rates disaggregated by race and gender', *American Journal of Economics and Sociology*, **50**(3), 269–84.
Agénor, Pierre-Richard, C. John McDermott and Eswar S. Prasad (2000), 'Macroeconomic fluctuations in developing countries: some stylized facts', *World Bank Economic Review*, **14**(2), 251–85.
Algan, Yann and Pierre Cahuc (2006), 'Job protection: the macho hypothesis', *Oxford Review of Economic Policy*, **22**(3), 390–410.
Allen, Mark, Ulrich Baumgartner and Raghuram Rajan (2006), 'Inflation targeting and the IMF', Prepared by Monetary and Financial Systems Department, Policy and Development Review Department and Research Department, International Monetary Fund, Washington, DC.
Ball, Laurence and Niamh Sheridan (2005), 'Does inflation targeting matter?', in Ben S. Bernanke and Michael Woodford (eds), *The Inflation Targeting Debate*, Chicago, IL: University of Chicago Press, pp. 249–76.
Benería, Lourdes and Martha Roldán (1987), *The Crossroads of Class and Gender: Industrial Homework, Subcontracting, and Household Dynamics in Mexico City*, Chicago, IL and London: University of Chicago Press.
Blanchard, Olivier (1995), 'Macroeconomic implications of shifts in the relative demand for skills', *Economic Policy Review*, **1**(1), 48–53.
Blanchard, Olivier, Giovanni Dell'Ariccia and Paolo Mauro (2010), 'Rethinking macroeconomic policy', IMF Staff Position Note 10/03, Washington, DC.

Blanchflower, David G. (2007), 'Is unemployment more costly than inflation?', NBER Working Paper 13505, Cambridge, MA.

Blumberg, Rae Lesser (1991), 'Income under female versus male control', in Rae Blumberg (ed.), *Gender, Family and Economy: The Triple Overlap*, Newbury Park, CA: Sage, pp. 97–127.

Board of Governors of the Federal Reserve System (2005), *The Federal Reserve System Purposes & Functions*, 9th edn, Washington, DC: Board of Governors of the Federal Reserve System.

Boushey, Heather (2011), 'The end of the mancession', available at: http://www.slate.com/articles/double_x/doublex/2011/01/the_end_of_the_mancession.html (accessed on March 23, 2012).

Braunstein, Elissa and James Heintz (2008), 'Gender bias and central bank policy: employment and inflation reduction', *International Review of Applied Economics*, **22**(2), 173–86.

Carpenter, Seth B. and William M. Rodgers III (2005), 'The disparate labor market impacts of monetary policy', *Labor History*, **46**(1), 57–77.

Catalyst (2011), 'Women in US finance', available at: http://www.catalyst.org/publication/504/women-in-us-finance (accessed March 22, 2012).

Chant, Sylvia (1991), *Women and Survival in Mexican Cities: Perspectives on Gender, Labour Markets and Low-Income Households*, Manchester and New York: Manchester University Press.

Di Tella, Rafael, Robert J. MacCulloch and Andrew J. Oswald (2001), 'Preferences over inflation and unemployment: evidence from surveys of happiness', *American Economic Review*, **91**(1), 335–41.

Dollar, David and Roberta Gatti (1999), 'Gender inequality, income, and growth: are good times good for women?', World Bank Policy Research Report Working Paper Series No. 1, Washington, DC.

Dutt, Amitava and Jaime Ros (2007), 'Aggregate demand shocks and economic growth', *Structural Change and Economic Dynamics*, **18**(1), 75–99.

Dwyer, Daisy and Judith Bruce (1988), *A Home Divided: Women and Income in the Third World*, Stanford, CA: Stanford University Press.

Elson, Diane (1998), 'The economic, the political and the domestic: businesses, states and households in the organisation of production', *New Political Economy*, **3**(2), 189–208.

Elson, Diane and Nilufer Çagatay (2000), 'The social content of macroeconomic policies', *World Development*, **28**(7), 1347–64.

Epstein, Gerald (2000), 'Myth, Mendacity and Mischief in the Theory and Practice of Central Banking', unpublished manuscript, University of Massachusetts, Amherst, MA.

Epstein, Gerald (2003), 'Alternative to inflation targeting monetary policy for stable and egalitarian growth: a brief research summary', Working Paper No. 62, Political Economy Research Institute, Amherst, MA.

Epstein, Gerald (2007), 'Central banks as agents of employment creation', Working Paper No. 38, UNDESA (United Nations Department of Economic and Social Affairs), New York.

Epstein, Gerald and Juliet Schor (1990), 'Macropolicy in the rise and fall of the Golden Age', in Stephen Marglin and Juliet Schor (eds), *The Golden Age of Capitalism: Reinterpreting the Postwar Experience*, Oxford: Clarendon Press, pp. 126–52.

Epstein, Gerald and Erinc Yeldan (eds) (2009), *Beyond Inflation Targeting: Assessing the Impacts and Policy Alternatives*, Cheltenham, UK, and Northampton, MA, USA: Edward Elgar.

Folbre, Nancy (1994), *Who Pays for the Kids? Gender and the Structures of Constraint*, London and New York: Routledge.

Fontana, Giuseppe and Alfonso Palacio-Vera (2005), 'Are long-run price stability and short-run output stabilization all that monetary policy can aim for?', Working Paper No. 430, Levy Economics Institute, Annandale-on-Hudson, NY.

Frenkel, Roberto and Lance Taylor (2006), 'Real exchange rate, monetary policy and employment: economic development in a garden of forking paths', Working Paper No. 19, UNDESA (United Nations Department of Economic and Social Affairs), New York.

Friedman, Milton (1968), 'The role of monetary policy', *American Economic Review*, **68**(1), 1–17.

Grown, Caren and Emcet Tas (2010), 'Gender equality in the US labor markets in the "Great Recession" of 2007–2010', Working Paper, American University, Washington, DC.

Heintz, James (2006), 'Globalization, economic policy and employment: poverty and gender implications', Employment Strategy Paper 2006/3, International Labour Organization, Geneva.

Heintz, James and Léonce Ndikumana (2011), 'Is there a case for formal inflation targeting in Sub-Saharan Africa?', *Journal of African Economics*, 20(AERC Supplement 2), ii67–ii103.

Heintz, James and Stephanie Seguino (2009), 'Federal Reserve policy and inflation dynamics in the US: racial inequalities in unemployment decisions', unpublished ms, University of Massachusetts Political Economy Research Institute and University of Vermont.

Hill, M. Anne and Elizabeth M. King (1995), 'Women's education and economic well-being', *Feminist Economics*, **1**(2), 21–46.

Hoddinott, John, Harold Alderman and Lawrence Haddad (eds) (1998), *Intrahousehold Resource Allocation in Developing Countries: Methods, Models and Policy*, Baltimore, MD: Johns Hopkins University Press.

Howes, Candace and Ajit Singh (1995), 'Long-term trends in the world economy: the gender dimension', *World Development*, **23**(11), 1895–912.

Jahan, Sarwat (2012), 'Inflation targeting: holding the line', *Finance & Development*, available at: http://www.imf.org/external/pubs/ft/fandd/basics/target.htm (accessed March 27, 2012).

Jayadev, Arjun (2006), 'Different preferences between anti-inflation and anti-unemployment policy among the rich and the poor', *Economics Letters*, **91**(1), 67–71.

Jayadev, Arjun (2008), 'The class content of preferences: towards anti-inflation and anti-unemployment policies', *International Review of Applied Economics*, **22**(2), 161–72.

Jordan, Amy (2012), 'Central Bank Directory highlights rise in female central bank governors', available at: http://www.centralbanking.com/central-banking/news/2136248/2011-rise-female-central-bank-governors (accessed March 22, 2012).

Klasen, Stephen (1999), 'Does gender inequality reduce growth and development? Evidence from cross-country regressions', Working Paper Series No. 7, World Bank Policy Research Report on Gender and Development, Washington, DC.

Klasen, Stephen and Francesca Lamanna (2009), 'The impact of gender inequality in education and employment on economic growth: new evidence for a panel of countries', *Feminist Economics*, **15**(3), 91–132.

Lucas, Robert (1973), 'Some international evidence on output–inflation tradeoffs', *American Economic Review*, **63**(3), 326–34.

Phillips, A. William (1958), 'The relation between unemployment and the rate of change of money wage rates in the United Kingdom, 1861–1957', *Economica*, **25**(100), 283–99.

Pollin, Robert (1999), 'Class conflict and the "natural rate of unemployment"', *Challenge*, **42**(6), 103–11.

Pollin, Robert, Gerald Epstein and James Heintz (2009), 'Pro-growth alternatives for monetary and financial policies in Sub-Saharan Africa', in Terry McKinley (ed.), *Economic Alternatives for Growth, Employment and Poverty Reduction*, New York: Palgrave Macmillan for United Nations Development Programme, pp. 24–32.

Rodgers, William (2008), 'African American and white differences in the impacts of monetary policy on the duration of unemployment', *American Economic Review: Papers and Proceedings*, **98**(2), 382–86.

Roger, Scott (2010), 'Inflation targeting turns 20', *Finance & Development*, **47**(1), 46–49.

Rogoff, Kenneth (1985), 'The optimal degree of commitment to an intermediate monetary target', *Quarterly Journal of Economics*, **100**(4), 1169–89.

Ruprah, Inder J. and Pavel Luengas (2011), 'Monetary policy and happiness: preferences over inflation and unemployment in Latin America', *Journal of Socio-Economics*, **40**(1), 59–66.

Seguino, Stephanie and James Heintz (2012), 'Monetary tightening and the dynamics of US race and gender stratification', *American Journal of Economics and Sociology*, **71**(3), 603–38.

Tachtamanova, Yelena and Eva Sierminksa (2009), 'Gender, monetary policy, and employment: the case of nine OECD countries', *Feminist Economics*, **15**(3), 323–53.

Thorbecke, Willem (2001), 'Estimating the effects of disinflationary monetary policy on minorities', *Journal of Policy Modeling*, **23**(1), 51–66.

United Nations Research Institute for Social Development (UNRISD) (2010), *Combating Poverty and Inequality: Structural Change, Social Policy and Politics*, Geneva: UNRISD.

Wolfers, Justin (2003), 'Is business cycle volatility costly? Evidence from surveys of subjective wellbeing', *International Finance*, **6**(1), 1–26.

22. Credit and self-employment

Nidhiya Menon and Yana van der Meulen Rodgers

I INTRODUCTION

Around the globe, small-scale entrepreneurship provides an important vehicle for income generation for women and men. Some people start microenterprises because they need more flexibility in their terms of employment, they have innovative ideas that warrant starting a new business, or they seek upward mobility in the labor market. Other people, often those at the lower end of the income scale, have little choice but to engage in self-employment when paid employment opportunities are scarce. A substantial proportion of the poor around the world rely on self-employment as a source of income as they navigate a host of constraints that include a lack of affordable loans from formal sources, restricted access to reliable savings accounts, few formal sources of insurance, insecure land rights, and insufficient public infrastructure such as piped water and electricity. More broadly, diversification of economic activities, especially in the rural sector, and the growth of nonfarm self-employment endeavors, serves not only as a means of survival for the very poor, but can also contribute to poverty reduction.[1]

Access to roads and personal assets such as education and credit are critical for diversification into nonfarm sources of income generation such as self-employment (Escobal, 2001). Infrastructure and financial constraints can be particularly severe for rural areas in developing countries, where between 25 and 98 percent of households living in poverty report being self-employed in agriculture.[2] Moreover, self-employment allows parents, especially mothers, to combine labor market participation with childcare responsibilities. Even though household businesses tend to be small, such business ventures can employ a large share of the labor force, especially in developing countries with burgeoning informal sectors.

A growing body of evidence indicates that an effective policy intervention in promoting self-employment is the provision of credit through small-scale loans that are mediated via rural banking reforms and microfinance initiatives.[3] Such initiatives target individuals who have difficulty obtaining conventional loans through commercial banks. Women in particular have faced difficulties in accessing formal credit through commercial banks due to their lack of collateral, a problem that is exacerbated by weak or nonexistent property rights for women in many developing countries. Without access to formal loans, low-income individuals have often had to rely on informal sector money lenders and other expensive sources of credit. By offering a variety of pecuniary resources and financial services to the poor, both microfinance and rural banks have helped to lower poverty in a number of countries. In this way, increasing access to credit can promote income redistribution and macroeconomic growth.[4]

For example, India's government initiated a rural social banking program following the nationalization of banks in 1969 that opened new bank branches in previously unbanked rural locations. This state-led expansion of the banking sector contributed to a statistically significant reduction in poverty in rural India.[5] Bangladesh's innovative Grameen Bank – which targets the poor and uses peer monitoring and joint liability lending to replace traditional collateral requirements – has also been linked with lower poverty and improved well-being.[6] Success stories associated with the Grameen Bank have in turn contributed to the proliferation of microfinance initiatives across countries and regions throughout the world. Also contributing to this surge in microfinance activity were other fairly small, independent programs in Latin America and South Asia during the 1970s. Since then, this movement has provided approximately 65 million low-income individuals around the globe with access to small loans without collateral and with opportunities to acquire assets and purchase insurance.[7] This movement has also demonstrated the extent of the unmet need for credit among poor women and men and the potential for commercial banks to play a bigger role by improving access of marginalized individuals to formal credit. Microfinance, in turn, has contributed to a substantial increase in self-employment activities worldwide.

The remainder of this chapter explores how women's and men's employment decisions respond to credit, with a particular focus on self-employment (Sections II and III). We also assess how new opportunities for women to engage in self-employment can have positive spillover effects within the household, especially for women's bargaining power and the well-being of their children (Section IV). Understanding the reasons why women and men decide to engage in self-employment can help to develop new policies that better support workers and their families, stimulate employment generation in countries with rapid labor force growth, and promote innovative entrepreneurial activities (Section V).

II   PREVALENCE OF SELF-EMPLOYMENT

Across regions, a substantial proportion of men and women engage in self-employment in order to support themselves and their families. Self-employment rates vary across countries at different stages of development and with different institutional structures. To support this assertion, we performed a descriptive analysis of current self-employment shares across countries, varying by region and income group. In this assessment, we constructed self-employment shares for men and women using the International Labour Organization's (ILO) published data on employment status across all regions. For a country to be selected for this comparison, it needed to report employment status data at some point in the 1999–2008 period, and it needed to report employment status separately for men and women. These criteria resulted in a sample of 129 countries. For each country, we chose the most recent year of employment status data available.[8] Following the ILO definition, we classified as self-employed all individuals reported to be employers, own-account workers, unpaid family workers, or members of producers' cooperatives.[9] The self-employment share is thus self-employed individuals as a proportion of all employed individuals, and this share is constructed separately by gender. Finally, we grouped all countries according to four broad income groups: low-income economies, lower-middle-income economies, upper-middle-income economies, and high-income economies.[10] The results of this descriptive analysis are presented in Figures 22.1–22.3.

Figure 22.1, Panel A shows that self-employment shares are generally very high in low-income economies, especially in Sub-Saharan Africa. Moreover, in all countries but

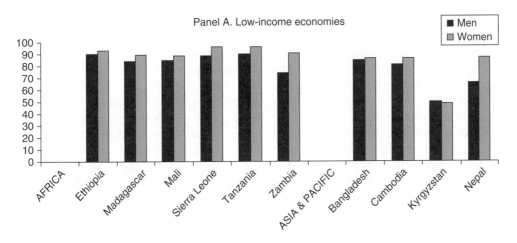

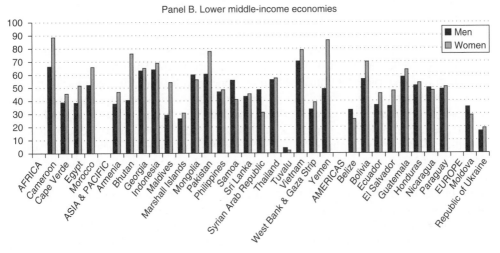

Note: For each country, the data are for the most recent year available between 1999 and 2008.

Source: Authors' calculations using data from ILO (2011)

Figure 22.1 *Self-employment shares by gender in low- and lower-middle-income economies, 1999–2008*

one (Kyrgyzstan), self-employment shares are noticeably higher for women than they are for men. On average in low-income economies, 86 percent of women are self-employed, compared to 79 percent of men. The highest rates of self-employment are found in Sierra Leone and Tanzania, where 96 percent of women are self-employed. Panel B shows that the conclusion regarding a greater incidence of self-employment among women compared to men also holds for lower-middle-income economies. However, the overall importance of self-employment as a source of employment declines markedly. On average, 52 percent of women and 46 percent of men in lower-middle-income economies are self-employed. Some of the highest rates of self-employment in this group of countries are observed for women in Cameroon, Yemen, and Vietnam. Overall among lower-middle-income economies, self-employment constitutes a larger source of employment among African countries as compared to other regions.

Not only does the importance of self-employment decline with overall income levels across countries, but the dominant form of self-employment also varies with the overall level of economic development. In particular, countries at the beginning stages of their structural transformation are characterized by 'survivalist' self-employment activities rooted in the traditional sector, while countries further along the development ladder have created the right conditions for 'opportunity-driven' entrepreneurship in the modern sector (Gries and Naudé, 2010).

As a specific example among the poorest developing countries, detailed household survey data for Nepal indicate that agricultural self-employment serves as the main source of employment for the vast majority of Nepal's female labor force. In 2006, the most recent year for which the household data were available, more than three-quarters of women workers in Nepal were engaged in agricultural self-employment.[11] Another 8 percent of women workers had jobs as paid farm workers. Only a small proportion of the female workforce (about 7 percent) worked in sales and services, with an even smaller percentage working as manual workers in the manufacturing sector. Moreover, about three-quarters of working women in Nepal have no cash earnings at all. The dominance of unpaid agricultural self-employment and the limited opportunities for more remunerative work have been associated with Nepal's persistent problems of high poverty rates and income inequality.[12] Moreover, a high proportion of women workers have little formal schooling and are restricted in their geographical mobility. In such a scenario, women are likely to be self-employed in agriculture or in 'female' trades such as spinners, weavers, and makers of tobacco products, which tend to be small scale and only marginally profitable. In this context, improved access to credit can provide the opportunity for women workers to move up the ladder of self-employment activities and to undertake more profitable work in larger-scale operations, thus facilitating the move toward poverty reduction.

As shown in Figure 22.2, self-employment shares are substantially lower in upper-middle-income economies relative to low-income and lower-middle-income economies, and they are also higher for men than for women. On average, 32 percent of men are self-employed in upper-middle-income economies, compared to 29 percent of women. Among this group of countries, some of the highest rates of self-employment for men are found in Azerbaijan, Colombia, and the Dominican Republic, and for women in Azerbaijan, Iran, Algeria, and Peru. Among broad regions, self-employment rates tend to be higher among upper-middle-income economies in Asia and the Pacific while they tend to be lower in Africa and Europe.

Finally, self-employment shares take a noticeable step downward for the high-income economies (see Figure 22.3). In addition, as in the upper-middle-income economies, men demonstrate a greater incidence of self-employment compared to women in the high-income economies. On average, 17 percent of men are self-employed, compared to just 10 percent of women. The variance across countries is also smaller among high-income economies compared to the other income groups, and only Korea and Greece have self-employment shares in excess of 30 percent. Among the regional groups, high-income countries in the Middle East (especially Kuwait, Qatar, and United Arab Emirates) have a very low incidence of self-employment.

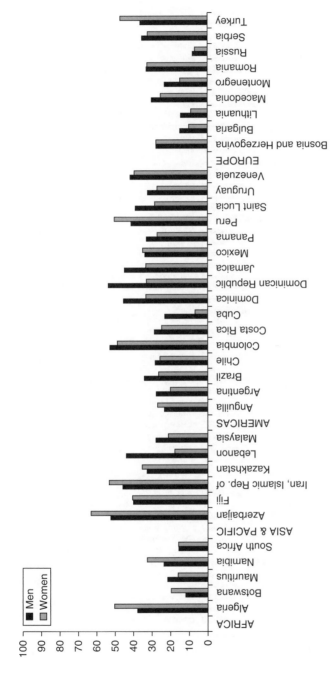

Note: For each country, the data are for the most recent year available between 1999 and 2008.

Source: Authors' calculations using data from ILO (2011).

Figure 22.2 Self-employment shares by gender in upper-middle-income economies, 1999–2008

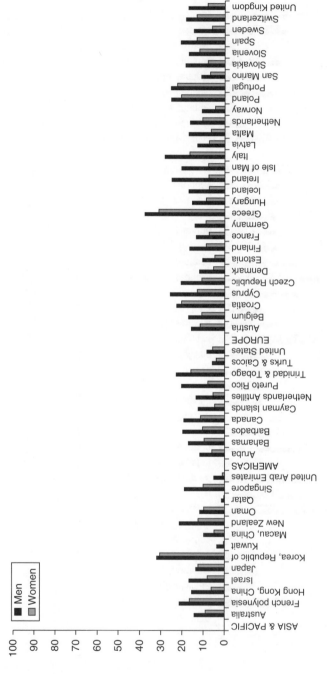

Note: For each country, the data are for the most recent year available between 1999 and 2008.

Source: Authors' calculations using data from ILO (2011).

Figure 22.3 Self-employment shares by gender in high-income economies, 1999–2008

These conclusions from the assessment of self-employment shares in the past decade are supported by earlier studies regarding general patterns in self-employment across countries at different stages of economic development. For example, using a sample of 64 developing countries and 19 industrialized countries from the 1960s to the 1990s, Carlo Pietrobelli et al. (2004) estimate a broadly negative relationship between self-employment and economic development. That is, self-employment rates decline with industrialization. However, this result is qualified with the observation that in some countries, innovative forms of entrepreneurship arise as a consequence of the existence of export manufacturing industries with high value-added. Moreover, primary education encourages self-employment whereas secondary education limits it. The authors argue that nothing conclusive can be said on the link between self-employment and economic and cultural factors such as financial sector development and women's labor force participation rates.

Even within advanced countries such as the United States, self-employment rates are not uniformly distributed across the population. Robert Fairlie and Bruce Meyer (1996) document very different self-employment rates among 60 ethnic and racial groups, and the differences persist even with controls for age, education, immigrant status, and time in the country. Further, the authors find that differences in self-employment rates are influenced by each ethnic/racial group's differential between average self-employment and wage and salary earnings. In particular, the more advantaged ethnic/racial groups (as measured by income) have the highest rates of self-employment. In another study of self-employment patterns in the United States, Magnus Lofstrom and Chunbei Wang (2006) argue that among Hispanics, the most rapidly increasing ethnic group in the United States, self-employment rates are low among Mexican-Hispanics but not among Hispanics from other countries. Moreover, education and access to financial assets are crucial to explaining differences in entrepreneurship trends. A reason put forth for low rates of self-employment among Mexican-Hispanics is their low rate of entry into high-barrier industries such as finance, insurance, and other professional fields with high human capital requirements.

Previous studies have also supported the findings from the descriptive assessment in Figures 22.1–22.3 on gender differences in self-employment shares across lower- and higher-income economies. In particular, the proportion of working men who report being self-employed exceeds the proportion of working women who are self-employed in higher-income countries such as Canada, the United States, Australia, Israel, and much of Western Europe (McManus, 2001). The consistency of lower self-employment rates for women as compared to men is striking given how different total self-employment rates are across these countries. Patricia McManus (2001) argues that a large part of the gender-differential in those reporting self-employment may be attributed to segregation in occupation, industry, and gender differences in business characteristics.

In addition to institutional factors, differences in self-employment rates by gender in higher-income countries may also be attributed to the manner in which individual workers react to various labor market characteristics. Using data from Germany, Yannis Georgellis and Howard Wall (2004) find that self-employment transition probabilities are influenced by the fact that men are more responsive to the wage differential between salaried employment and self-employed work. In addition, access to credit appears to be more binding for men as compared to women. The authors suggest that for women, self-employment appears to be a closer substitute for part-time work than it is for men.

In sum, within the population of self-employed workers, there are marked variations along gender lines. In contrast to higher-income countries, proportionately more women than men are self-employed in lower-income countries, with the implication that women have relatively less job security and more unstable incomes in these areas and thus turn to self-employment as a means of overcoming such obstacles. Moreover, in lower-income countries, self-employment commonly takes the form of a household enterprise, and women-owned household enterprises are often smaller in scale than those owned by men. The next section addresses how improved access to credit may help to generate more income stability by increasing the scale and scope of household enterprises.

III   ACCESS TO CREDIT AND SELF-EMPLOYMENT

Principally in developing countries, conventional sources of employment entail unstable income streams and no job security. Moreover, such livelihoods often remain uncovered by formal sector labor regulations. A key area of policy intervention to mitigate these risks and stimulate entrepreneurship is the provision of small-scale loans, especially to women, through microfinance and rural banks. This can be particularly beneficial in regions with limited paid-employment opportunities for women due to labor markets characterized by discrimination, imperfect information, or insufficient labor demand.[13] In these contexts, employment in home-based enterprises can reduce women's vulnerability, providing them with earnings potential and improving their social security and that of their households. When women do face constraints in finding sufficient opportunities for wage employment, they may be willing to borrow in order to start their own small business.

Previous research suggests that the targeted use of small loans can support and incentivize women's labor market activities and promote economic welfare. As the first microfinance program of its kind, Bangladesh's Grameen Bank has been the subject of numerous studies that have generally found positive results. For example, Mark Pitt and Shahid Khandker (1998) found that credit given to women participants through the Grameen Bank had a strong positive effect on women's labor supply, while income effects associated with the increased supply of credit reduced men's labor supply. Impacts of the same direction but smaller in magnitude were found for two other group-based lending programs in Bangladesh: the Bangladesh Rural Advancement Committee (BRAC) and the Bangladesh Rural Development Board's (BRDB) RD-12 program. Also assessing the impact of Bangladesh's largest microfinance programs, Syed Hashemi et al. (1996) conclude that loan recipients used the credit primarily for self-employment in small-scale activities ranging from animal husbandry to artisan crafts. Women reported that the credit they received helped to increase their control over finances, improve their economic and social standing, and raise their productivity in both paid and unpaid work. Other research has shown that credit and noncredit services made available by participation in Grameen programs has contributed to positive profits from self-employment in Bangladesh, and that the presence of village-level microfinance has boosted asset growth and occupational mobility in Thailand.[14]

Another important example is India's rural social banking program, which focused primarily on opening new bank branches in previously unbanked rural locations. Evidence in Nidhiya Menon and Yana Rodgers (2011a) indicates that India's rural banking reform program increased the likelihood of women engaging in gainful self-employment beyond unpaid family work, while having little effect on men's self-employment work as own-account workers. A likely explanation is that women have restricted access to formal employment in developing countries such as India, so when a household obtains a loan, it is rational for women to become self-employed and to earn a livelihood from their own trade or home-based business. These conclusions are supported by a recent study on women's mobility in India (Luke and Munshi, 2011) suggesting that historically disadvantaged groups are more likely to respond to new economic opportunities.

Moreover, the increase in women's self-employment in rural India appears to have occurred in more productive economic activities. Menon and Rodgers (2011a) report that increased access to credit facilitated the shift of women workers out of cultivation into other entrepreneurial activities including more capital-intensive livestock and dairy farming. Between 1983 and 2000, the proportion of women with credit who were employed as dairy and livestock farmers rose from about 25 percent in 1983 to 28 percent in 2000. These results concur with findings in S. Ramkumar et al. (2004) showing that women would rather be engaged in self-employment as cattle herders and dairy farmers as opposed to working in agricultural cultivation. They preferred self-employment in herding and dairy because it provided stronger financial security, gave the women more autonomy, allowed for a more flexible working schedule, and was physically less arduous.

The importance of credit in encouraging self-employment is also evident from studies in higher-income countries. David Evans and Boyan Jovanovic (1989) develop and test a model of entrepreneurial choice using data from the United States to show that capital constraints play a role in limiting entrepreneurship, and that conditional on education, experience, and demographic characteristics, the effect of assets on the likelihood of initiating a business is positive. Using information on windfall gains from the Swedish lottery and inheritances, Thomas Lindh and Henry Ohlsson (1996) find that the decision to become self-employed is curtailed by access to credit, and that the probability of becoming self-employed increases for recipients of lottery winnings and unanticipated inheritances. For Swedish women, the probability of self-employment is in general lower as compared to men. The study does not provide adequate information to answer whether the probability of self-employment increases more for women recipients of lottery winnings as compared to their male counterparts. Mark Taylor (2001) implements a comparable study for Britain and provides additional evidence that relaxing liquidity constraints can increase self-employment probabilities. Using lottery and inheritance data is a clever way to circumvent problems of self-selection that plague credit evaluation studies since those who choose to take credit may be systematically different from those who do not.[15]

Providing further evidence on the liquidity constraints that stand in the way of self-employment, Lindh and Ohlsson (1998) argue that self-employment rates should be higher in countries where the distribution of income is more unequal, because the number of people who are able to provide collateral for loans is higher in populations with unequal income distributions. This argument is supported with data from Sweden.

These results have implications for gender-differentiated distributions of income within industrialized countries and for the higher self-employment shares for men as compared to women. One possible explanation is that within an unequal income distribution, women tend to be at the lower end of the distribution whereas men are more likely to be at the higher end.

Not all previous research, however, has shined a favorable light on credit expansion, especially as embodied in microfinance and the widespread delivery of small-scale loans. Some have argued that because most microfinance schemes are not public programs, the proliferation of microfinance has shifted the burden of poverty reduction away from governments to the poor themselves, especially women. Moreover, the small loans provided by microfinance programs can act like a trap that prevents women entrepreneurs from raising their income levels beyond a poverty threshold. Another gender-related argument is that in some cases, husbands have taken control over the borrowed funds and the loans have contributed to increased domestic violence. Critics also argue that microfinance has become a magnet for large financial-sector firms who view the relatively high interest rates as profitable. This development can signal hardship for the poor and subvert the intended goal of poverty reduction.[16] Some of this criticism may be context specific as other studies have shown that even high interest consumer loans lead to improved welfare. For example, using data from South Africa, Dean Karlan and Jonathan Zinman (2010) show that individuals who borrowed consumer credit at rates as high as 200 per cent per annum benefited from doing so as compared to their next best alternative.

Others have argued that women's self-employment may be less responsive to new credit sources as compared to men's. For example, Suresh de Mel et al. (2008) demonstrated that small grants in the form of cash or in-kind support given to a randomly selected group of small businesses in Sri Lanka resulted in high rates of return for men, on the order of about 5 percent per month. Women-owned microenterprises, however, had rates of return that were essentially zero. Moreover, group-lending programs for women in northeast Thailand examined by Brett Coleman (1999) had no statistically significant impact on indicators of economic activity that included production, sales, and time spent working. Furthermore, Michael Kevane and Bruce Wydick (2001) showed that women entrepreneurs who borrowed from microenterprise lending institutions did not create new employment with their businesses, as compared to other entrepreneurs. Finally, David McKenzie's (2009) assessment of microenterprises and finance in developing countries concluded that simply providing greater access to capital is not sufficient to help microenterprises grow. Rather, additional policies that improve business training, offer business-development services, and assist in the shift toward more profitable activities were most effective in strengthening the impact of credit on microenterprises.

The argument that credit alone is not enough to stimulate productive self-employment is not new. This is evident in organizations such as the Self Employed Women's Association (SEWA) in India, which provides both credit and noncredit services. SEWA is a trade union for self-employed women from poor households that was founded in 1972. One of SEWA's main objectives has been to empower self-employed women through increased organization of individual disenfranchised women. Although savings and credit groups have played an integral role in SEWA's functions, SEWA has also provided services related to housing, trade, education, skill development, entrepreneurship training, political activism, and general insurance as well as community-based health insurance. SEWA increases the productivity of its members by providing integrated services that connect important aspects of business creation such as training, capital, and access to markets. For example, in addition to providing know-how on occupations as varied as dairy farming and handicrafts, SEWA also provides support services in infrastructure development financed through micro loans and disaster rehabilitation and relief (see Crowell, 2003). One motivation for SEWA's move to providing an integrated set of services was that the organization's clientele was composed of poor women with multiple informal sector occupations. This is common since women in the informal economy are often forced to take up more than one job in order to generate sufficient income. Thus, the provision of integrated services generated more value-added for such women who were not specialized. SEWA has gained the support of major multilateral agencies and donors given its broad-ranging impact on women's empowerment and poverty reduction.[17]

Other studies have also deemphasized the role of credit in furthering self-employment and they have stressed the importance of alternative determinants such as human capital. In a study of intergenerational links in self-employment using data from the United States, Thomas Dunn and Douglas Holtz-Eakin (1996) find that although financial assets of young men do exert a significant effect on the probability of being self-employed, the magnitude of the effect is quantitatively small. What appears to matter most is parents' human capital in self-employment, with a father's experience in self-employment having the largest impact.

Finally, reforms that enable increased asset ownership could have implications for self-employment even though they might not work by directly improving access to credit in the short run. For example, Quy-Toan Do and Lakshmi Iyer (2008) examine the economic impact of the 1993 Land Law of Vietnam that created a land market by giving households the power to exchange, lease, and mortgage their land-use rights. Using variation in the speed of implementation of the reform to identify effects, the authors find that as a consequence of the additional land rights, households increased their labor in nonfarm work. However, since household borrowing did not exhibit much variation during the period of analysis (1993–98), these effects are attributed mainly to the additional security of land tenure rather than increased access to credit. It is probable that a five-year window is too small to see the implications on access to credit from the creation of a land market. Long-run comparisons that use more recent waves of data could possibly show stronger implications on nonfarm work arising from the improved access to credit that land titling enabled.

IV   SELF-EMPLOYMENT, WOMEN'S AUTONOMY, AND CHILD HEALTH

Providing women with increased access to credit serves as a viable means of incentivizing the shift from low-paid work in marginally productive activities to more remunerative work in productive activities. Ultimately, the creation of productive self-employment and new wage-employment opportunities will increase women's cash earnings. Increased income in the hands of women, in turn, has beneficial impacts on women's autonomy and the well-being of their children.

The income that mothers earn impacts their children's well-being in different ways than the income that fathers earn, given women's tendency to allocate a greater portion of household budgets on children's educational, health, and nutritional needs. Raising women's control over income can contribute not only to greater expenditures on food, but also to expenditures on foods with improved nutritional content. Women's earnings can strengthen their bargaining power within the household by improving their fallback position. Greater autonomy for women and a shift in intrahousehold power dynamics toward the mother can have many useful consequences including greater utilization of antenatal care and vaccination programs for their children.

A growing body of work has substantiated the relationship between women's control over financial resources, greater expenditures on children, and improved child health.[18] For example, in Côte d'Ivoire, raising the share of household cash income controlled by the wife leads to a positive and statistically significant increase in the household budget share allocated to food and a decrease in the share allocated to adult-oriented items – even after controlling for household characteristics. In particular, doubling the share of household cash income controlled by wives caused a 1.9 percent decrease in the budget shares allocated to alcohol and cigarettes (Hoddinott and Haddad, 1995).

Evidence from Brazil (Thomas, 1997) indicates that the marginal effect of additional income in the hands of women on child survival is 20 times as large as that of additional income in the hands of the father, while the marginal effects on child wasting and stunting differ by factors of eight and four, respectively. Similar conclusions were also made for the case of Bangladesh, where credit allocated to women through the Grameen Bank and similar microfinance programs had stronger positive effects on children's nutritional status as measured by arm circumference and height-for-age as compared to credit allocated to men (Pitt et al., 2003). Research in Esther Duflo (2003) on the expansion of South Africa's pension program to the black population found improvements in weight-for-height of all girls and in height-for-age of younger girls. These effects were attributed entirely to the pensions received by women and not by men.

Improving control over assets such as land can have especially powerful consequences, as shown in Do and Iyer (2008). The availability of collateral facilitates additional borrowing, which may give households the capital required to finance home-based self-employment work. Evidence that supports this conclusion is provided by Keera Allendorf (2007) who finds that children are less likely to be underweight if their mother owns land. This relationship is attributed to the additional resources that women's ownership of land brings, and is not solely due to the empowering effect of land ownership.

The beneficial impact of endowing women with more control over resources via self-employment has implications on demographic behavior such as fertility and contraception as well. Ruhul Amin et al. (1995) document that women loan recipients of Bangladesh's Grameen, BRAC, and BRDB programs were more likely to use contraceptives, have fewer children, report an increase in the desire for no more children, and be more empowered (as measured by physical mobility, authority, and aspiration). Sidney Schuler and Hashemi (1994) find that participation in Grameen and BRAC programs has positive effects on empowerment as measured by economic security, political and legal awareness, and freedom from violence within the family. Focusing only on demographic behavior such as contraception and fertility, Pitt et al. (1999) use data from Grameen, BRAC, and BRDB to show that with a more rigorous control for heterogeneity bias, women's participation in group-based credit programs has no effect on contraception or fertility. Alternatively, male participation does reduce fertility and increase contraceptive use, although the latter effect is small in magnitude.

Hence a large body of developing country literature indicates that additional income controlled by men and women can contribute to improved own and child well-being, although the effects are not always indisputable. In the same vein, mothers' market-based work could reduce the quantity or quality of time spent caring for children, with potentially adverse effects on child health. Absence from children while working in the labor market could reduce the ability of mothers to engage in care practices that influence child development and health. Mothers may have less time to breastfeed, prepare nutritious foods, engage in preventive health-seeking practices, or take children to public services that improve child well-being.

Self-employment, however, may help to mitigate this tradeoff between increased income and reduced time for childcare if the self-employment conditions are compatible with childrearing. In such cases, women engage in market-based work with their children present although the pressures associated with this generally low-pay work, often on a piece-rate basis, may not allow mothers to have much high-quality interaction with their children. Work within or close to the home should be, in principle, more compatible with childcare, but the actual benefits to children may be tempered by the informality of such work and the lack of flexibility in the work requirements. Moreover, it may be inconvenient or unsafe for mothers to bring their children with them to work, or their work may involve intense pressure to complete a quota within a certain amount of time and thus prevent mothers from interacting meaningfully with their children. In countries where the agricultural sector still provides a large source of employment, women may bring their children with them to the field while they are farming in order to continue breastfeeding. Finally, mothers' direct time spent with children may not vary much with the type of labor market activity if they live in a household in which other family members, especially older siblings and grandparents, can care for young children.[19]

The empirical evidence on the compatibility of self-employment with healthy childcare practices is mixed. For example, Sirilaksana Chutikul's (1986) study of rural Thailand found that a mother's work in the informal sector had a positive impact on children's nutritional status while her work in the formal sector had a negative impact. In contrast, Peter Glick and David Sahn (1998) found that in urban Guinea, maternal working hours in self-employment and in wage-employment had negative effects of equal size on children's height-for-age, even after controlling for the mother's earnings brought in by her employment. The feasibility of combining employment with childcare was not strong enough to counteract the negative impact of maternal hours in market work. As another example, among low-income urban households in Chile, maternal employment had a net positive effect on infants' weight (Vial et al., 1989). However, this effect operated mostly through the additional income that mothers earned at work, rather than the type of work. Distance to work and type of employment did not serve as determining factors.

V   CONCLUSION AND CHALLENGES FOR RESEARCH

Household enterprises tend to rely on family labor which contributes to the tendency for such ventures to remain small in scale. Thus, policies that support the operations of household enterprises and help them expand their sales can transform them into stronger engines for job creation. By providing the means for initiating entrepreneurship or for increasing the scale of existing enterprises, improving access to credit can serve as the impetus to greater financial independence.

However, assessments of the impact of credit programs are fraught with endogeneity problems. These problems embody primarily two types – self-selection and nonrandom program placement.[20] Self-selection occurs when unmeasured individual-specific factors influence selection into the program and the outcome being studied. For example, it is possible that the most able women or those who have prior experience with self-employment are the first to join microfinance programs. Since ability is unmeasured, the researcher cannot control for its effects explicitly. Without such control, some part of the measured impact of credit will pick up the fact that the woman is able or very motivated, leading to misleading inferences on the true impact of loans. Pitt and Khandker (1998) controlled for such self-selection using a quasi-experimental framework. However, more recent evaluations have tried to randomize access to loans, thus inducing exogenous variations in which types of women receive a loan. Randomization is useful in that we can be confident that selection is not at work. But the results of a randomized study are particular only to that experiment, limiting its implications for wider policy analysis.

The second endogeneity problem deals with selection not at the individual level, but at the regional level. Nonrandom program placement implies that credit programs are not allocated exogenously to regions. For example, it is possible that the most vulnerable villages in Bangladesh were the first to receive a microfinance program because the need for credit was the highest in such areas. Alternatively, altruistic governments might choose to first locate public programs in the poorest districts. Not controlling for such motivations can also lead to misleading inferences on the impact of credit and programs. A structural solution would be the use of fixed-effects models, but these models need the strong assumption that the endogeneity is time invariant (see ibid.). On the other hand, randomly allocating regions to receive programs would help to circumvent this problem. But, as noted already, the broader implications of such randomization are limited in scope and remain constrained to the study at hand. In evaluating the impact of credit on self-employment or other outcomes, the challenge for the researcher is to think clearly about what the main aim of his or her work is, and then, ideally, construct a combination of structural and experimental methods that build on the strengths of each.

Having outlined the challenges for research in understanding the effect of credit access, we conclude by outlining best practices in this area. In particular, greater support for business owners to acquire training in accounting and management procedures would serve as useful mechanisms for enhancing the productivity of household businesses and for expanding their capacity to generate wage-based employment. The growth of wage-based employment, in turn, emphasizes the need for increasing employer compliance with labor market regulations that are consistent with fundamental worker rights, job security, and decent work. A high proportion of women in developing countries engage in low-paid jobs that remain uncovered by national labor standards. Measures such as safe workplace conditions, overtime pay, and paid benefits, although potentially costly to implement, promote lower turnover rates, improve well-being for workers, and contribute to extended firm-specific tenure. These measures need to be provided to a broader range of workers by removing exemptions, promoting awareness of benefit availability, and strengthening enforcement efforts.

Moreover, subsidies and targeted tax incentives can also assist small business owners in purchasing new profit-enhancing technologies. Public sector assistance to women entrepreneurs in marketing and selling their products can provide a valuable function in cases when women business owners face obstacles in accessing business networks. The Kenya Women's Finance Trust (KWFT) constitutes a good example along these lines. KWFT is the largest women-only financial organization in Africa, providing loans and know-how to entrepreneurs on different facets of their business.[21] It started 30 years ago in response to a growing recognition that women entrepreneurs had little to no access to financial assets as compared to the rest of the population.

Another good model is the Women Workers Employment and Entrepreneurship Development (WEED) program in the Philippines, which provides skills training, entrepreneurship development, and credit assistance to women who are underemployed, home based, and/or employed in the informal sector.[22] Programs such as WEED can facilitate a switch from low-paid work to work that yields greater returns. This program proved to be a particularly valuable component of the policy response by the Philippines' government to the global financial crisis of 2009 that led to a reduction in self-employment opportunities for women.[23] This setback for women arose because the economic crisis reduced demand for the small-scale products and services that women produce and sell, thus reinforcing the need for strengthening the social safety net for individuals who may slip through the cracks during times of crisis.

In closing, this chapter has assessed the prevalence of self-employment across lower-income and higher-income economies as well as gender differences in the tendency to engage in self-employment. It has also presented a synopsis of the current state of understanding on the interrelationship of credit and self-employment across countries at different stages of development. The discussion focused on the positive externalities of entrepreneurship income – especially income that is concentrated in the hands of women – on women's autonomy and child welfare. In general, there is an inverse relationship between self-employment shares and the economic development level of a country. Self-employment serves as a relatively larger source of employment for women in lower-income countries, while higher-income countries report a greater incidence of self-employment for men. Moreover, access to credit facilitates self-employment, but with qualifications. Enterprise productivity also depends on a variety of other factors including training and the provision of marketing expertise and business development support services. Standing to gain the most from publicly funded interventions that integrate training and best management practices are small-scale women-owned businesses that are credit constrained and isolated from business networks that provide information and sources of support. However, particularly in developing countries, the importance of credit in facilitating self-employment, a secure and stable source of income for the poor, cannot be overemphasized.

NOTES

1. This argument is supported with data from India in Lanjouw and Murgai (2009).
2. These numbers are from Banerjee and Duflo (2007).
3. See especially Hashemi et al. (1996), Pitt and Khandker (1998), McKernan (2002), and Kaboski and Townsend (2005).
4. This point about the benefits of expanding access to credit is made in Besley and Burgess (2003).
5. See Burgess and Pande (2005) for evidence linking India's rural banking reforms with poverty reduction.
6. See Pitt and Khandker (1998) and de Aghion and Morduch (2005) for empirical evidence of the impacts of the Grameen Bank.
7. See de Aghion and Morduch (2005) for more discussion of the background and prevalence of micro-finance programs.
8. A number of countries reported two sets of statistics on employment status: those based on population census data and those based on labor force surveys. In this situation, as a general rule we chose the data based on labor force surveys because they tended to be more recent. Several other countries reported two sets of employment status data, one for the entire country and one for just urban areas. In this latter situation, as a general rule we chose the data for the entire country.
9. This definition is found on the ILO's 'Main Statistics (Annual) Employment' webpage at http://laborsta.ilo.org/applv8/data/c2e.html.
10. The classification of countries follows the World Bank's definition of income groups, found at http://data.worldbank.org/about/country-classifications/country-and-lending-groups.
11. These averages on self-employment in Nepal are from Menon and Rodgers (2011b).
12. See especially Acharya (2008) on the generation of new employment opportunities in industry for women in Nepal.
13. See Karlan and Morduch (2009) for more discussion.
14. See especially results in McKernan (2002) and Kaboski and Townsend (2005).
15. Other studies for industrialized countries have also found that the decision to become self-employed is constrained by access to credit, and relief of those constraints through a loan or a windfall gain increases the probability of becoming or remaining self-employed. See especially Holtz-Eakin et al. (1994a, 1994b).
16. These arguments are explored further in Johnson (1998), Pollin et al. (2007), Berik and Rodgers (2009), and Seguino et al. (2010).
17. There is a large literature on the impacts of SEWA in India. See, for example, Datta (2003) and Chen et al. (2007).
18. See Blumberg (1988), Haddad et al. (1997), Quisumbing and Maluccio (2000), World Bank (2001), and Holvoet (2005).
19. See Bianchi (2000) for a review of studies supporting these arguments.
20. Omitted variables that are correlated with the outcomes of interest may also induce problems with estimating the impact of credit.
21. For more discussion of the KWFT, see Pollin et al. (2007).
22. This program is discussed in Manasan (2009).
23. This reduction in women's self-employment opportunities is documented in Rodgers and Menon (2010).

REFERENCES

Acharya, Sanjaya (2008), 'Poverty alleviation and the industrial employment of women (The Case of Nepal)', *Journal of International Development*, **20**(5), 670–85.

Allendorf, Keera (2007), 'Do women's land rights promote empowerment and child health in Nepal?', *World Development*, **35**(11), 1975–88.

Amin, Ruhul, Robert Hill and Yiping Li (1995), 'Poor women's participation in credit-based self-employment:

the impact on their empowerment, fertility, contraceptive use, and fertility desire in rural Bangladesh', *Pakistan Development Review*, **34**(2), 93–119.

Banerjee, Abhijit and Esther Duflo (2007), 'The economic lives of the poor', *Journal of Economic Perspectives*, **21**(1), 141–67.

Berik, Günseli and Yana Rodgers (2009), 'Engendering development strategies and macroeconomic policies: what's sound and sensible?', in Günseli Berik, Yana Rodgers and Ann Zammit (eds), *Social Justice and Gender Equality: Rethinking Development Strategies and Macroeconomic Policies*, New York and London: Routledge, pp. 1–43.

Besley, Timothy and Robin Burgess (2003), 'Halving global poverty', *Journal of Economic Perspectives*, **17**(3), 3–22.

Bianchi, Suzanne (2000), 'Maternal employment and time with children: dramatic change or surprising continuity?', *Demography*, **37**(4), 401–14.

Blumberg, Rae Lesser (1988), 'Income under female versus male control: hypotheses from a theory of gender stratification and data from the Third World', *Journal of Family Issues*, **9**(1), 51–84.

Burgess, Robin and Rohini Pande (2005), 'Do rural banks matter? Evidence from the Indian social banking experiment', *American Economic Review*, **95**(3), 780–95.

Chen, Martha, Renana Jhabvala, Ravi Kanbur and Carol Richards (eds) (2007), *Membership-Based Organizations of the Poor*, Oxford and New York: Routledge.

Chutikul, Sirilaksana (1986), 'Malnourished children: an economic approach to the causes and consequences in rural Thailand', Papers of the East West Population Institute, No. 102, East West Center, Honolulu, HI.

Coleman, Brett (1999), 'The impact of group lending in northeast Thailand', *Journal of Development Economics*, **60**(1), 105–41.

Crowell, Daniel (2003), *The SEWA Movement and Rural Development: The Banaskantha and Kutch Experience*, Thousand Oaks, CA: Sage.

Datta, Rekha (2003), 'From development to empowerment: the self-employed women's association in India', *International Journal of Politics, Culture, and Society*, **16**(3), 351–68.

de Aghion, Beatriz Armendariz and Jonathan Morduch (2005), *The Economics of Microfinance*, Cambridge, MA: MIT Press.

de Mel, Suresh, David McKenzie and Christopher Woodruff (2008), 'Returns to capital in microenterprises: evidence from a field experiment', *Quarterly Journal of Economics*, **123**(4), 1329–72.

Do, Quy-Toan and Lakshmi Iyer (2008), 'Land titling and rural transition in Vietnam', *Economic Development and Cultural Change*, **56**(3), 531–79.

Duflo, Esther (2003), 'Grandmothers and granddaughters: old-age pensions and intrahousehold allocation in South Africa', *World Bank Economic Review*, **17**(1), 1–25.

Dunn, Thomas and Douglas Holtz-Eakin (1996), 'Financial capital, human capital, and the transition to self-employment', National Bureau of Economic Research, NBER Working Paper No. 5622, Cambridge, MA.

Escobal, Javier (2001), 'The determinants of nonfarm income diversification in rural Peru', *World Development*, **29**(3), 497–508.

Evans, David and Boyan Jovanovic (1989), 'An estimated model of entrepreneurial choice under liquidity constraints', *Journal of Political Economy*, **97** (4), 808–27.

Fairlie, Robert and Bruce Meyer (1996), 'Ethnic and racial self-employment differences and possible explanations', *Journal of Human Resources*, **31**(4), 757–93.

Georgellis, Yannis and Howard Wall (2004), 'Gender differences in self-employment', The Federal Reserve Bank of St. Louis Working Paper Series 1999–008C.

Glick, Peter and David Sahn (1998), 'Maternal labour supply and child nutrition in West Africa', *Oxford Bulletin of Economics and Statistics*, **60**(3), 325–55.

Gries, Thomas and Wim Naudé (2010), 'Entrepreneurship and structural economic transformation', *Small Business Economics*, **34**(1), 13–29.

Haddad, Lawrence, John Hoddinott and Harold Alderman (eds) (1997), *Intrahousehold Resource Allocation in Developing Countries: Models, Methods, and Policy*, Baltimore, MD: Johns Hopkins University Press.

Hashemi, Syed, Sidney Ruth Schuler and Ann Riley (1996), 'Rural credit programs and women's empowerment in Bangladesh', *World Development*, **24**(4), 635–53.

Hoddinott, John and Lawrence Haddad (1995), 'Does female income share influence household expenditure patterns? Evidence from Côte d'Ivoire', *Oxford Bulletin of Economics and Statistics*, **57**(1), 77–96.

Holtz-Eakin, Douglas, David Joulfaian and Harvey Rosen (1994a), 'Entrepreneurial decisions and liquidity constraints', *Rand Journal of Economics*, **25**(2), 334–47.

Holtz-Eakin, Douglas, David Joulfaian and Harvey Rosen (1994b), 'Sticking it out: entrepreneurial survival and liquidity constraints', *Journal of Political Economy*, **102**(1), 53–75.

Holvoet, Nathalie (2005), 'Credit and women's group membership in South India: testing models of intrahousehold allocative behavior', *Feminist Economics*, **11**(3), 27–62.

International Labour Organization (ILO) (2011), *Labor Force Statistics Database*, Geneva: ILO, available at: http://laborsta.ilo.org.

Johnson, Susan (1998), 'Microfinance north and south: contrasting current debates', *Journal of International Development*, **10**(6), 799–809.

Kaboski, Joseph and Robert Townsend (2005), 'Policies and impact: an analysis of village-level microfinance institutions', *Journal of the European Economic Association*, **3**(1), 1–50.

Karlan, Dean and Jonathan Morduch (2009), 'Access to finance: credit markets, insurance, and saving', in Dani Rodrik and Mark Rosenzweig (eds), *Handbook of Development Economics*, Vol.5, Amsterdam: Elsevier Science & Technology, pp.4703–84.

Karlan, Dean and Jonathan Zinman (2010), 'Expanding credit access: using randomized supply decisions to estimate the impacts', *Review of Financial Studies*, **23**(1), 433–64.

Kevane, Michael and Bruce Wydick (2001), 'Microenterprise lending to female entrepreneurs: sacrificing economic growth for poverty alleviation?', *World Development*, **29**(7), 1225–36.

Lanjouw, Peter and Rinku Murgai (2009), 'Poverty decline, agricultural wages, and nonfarm employment in rural India: 1983–2004', *Agricultural Economics*, **40**(2), 243–63.

Lindh, Thomas and Henry Ohlsson (1996), 'Self-employment and windfall gains: evidence from the Swedish lottery', *Economic Journal*, **106**(439), 1515–26.

Lindh, Thomas and Henry Ohlsson (1998), 'Self-employment and wealth inequality', *Review of Income and Wealth*, **44**(1), 25–42.

Lofstrom, Magnus and Chunbei Wang (2006), 'Hispanic self-employment: a dynamic analysis of business ownership', IZA Discussion Paper No. 2101, Bonn.

Luke, Nancy and Kaivan Munshi (2011), 'Women as agents of change: female income and mobility in India', *Journal of Development Economics*, **94**(1), 1–17.

Manasan, Rosario (2009), 'Reforming social protection policy: responding to the global financial crisis and beyond', Discussion Paper No. 2009–22, Philippine Institute for Development Studies (PIDS), Makati City, Philippines.

McKenzie, David (2009), 'Impact assessments in finance and private sector development: what have we learned and what should we learn?', World Bank Policy Research Working Paper No. 4944, World Bank, Washington, DC.

McKernan, Signe-Mary (2002), 'The impact of microcredit programs on self-employment profits: so noncredit program aspects matter?', *Review of Economics and Statistics*, **84**(1), 93–115.

McManus, Patricia (2001), 'Women's participation in self-employment in western industrialized nations', *International Journal of Sociology*, **31**(2), 70–97.

Menon, Nidhiya and Yana Rodgers (2011a), 'How access to credit affects self-employment: differences by gender during India's rural banking reform', *Journal of Development Studies*, **47**(1), 48–69.

Menon, Nidhiya and Yana Rodgers (2011b), 'War and women's work: evidence from the conflict in Nepal', Report submitted to the World Bank, Washington, DC.

Pietrobelli, Carlo, Roberta Rabellotti and Matteo Aquilina (2004), 'An empirical study of the determinants of self-employment in developing countries', *Journal of International Development*, **16**(6), 803–20.

Pitt, Mark and Shahidur Khandker (1998), 'The impact of group-based credit programs on poor households in Bangladesh: does the gender of participants matter?', *Journal of Political Economy*, **106**(5), 958–96.

Pitt, Mark, Shahidur Khandker, Omar Chowdhury and Daniel Millimet (2003), 'Credit programs for the poor and the health status of children in rural Bangladesh', *International Economic Review*, **44**(1), 87–118.

Pitt, Mark, Shahid Khandker, Signe-Mary McKernan and M. Abdul Latif (1999), 'Credit programs for the poor and reproductive behavior in low income countries: are the reported causal relationships the result of heterogeneity bias?', *Demography*, **36**(1), 1–21.

Pollin, Robert, Mwangi wa Githinji and James Heinz (2007), *An Employment Targeted Economic Program for Kenya*, Brasilia, Brazil: International Poverty Centre.

Quisumbing, Agnes and John Maluccio (2000), 'Intrahousehold allocation and gender relations: new empirical evidence from four developing countries', FCND Discussion Paper No. 84, International Food Policy Research Institute, Washington, DC.

Ramkumar, S., S.V.N. Rao and Kevin Waldie (2004), 'Dairy cattle rearing by landless rural women in Pondicherry: a path to empowerment', *Indian Journal of Gender Studies*, **11**(2), 205–22.

Rodgers, Yana and Nidhiya Menon (2010), 'Impact of the 2008–2009 food, fuel, and financial crisis on the Philippine labor market', Report submitted to the World Bank, Washington, DC.

Schuler, Sidney and Syed Hashemi (1994), 'Credit programs, women's empowerment, and contraceptive use in rural Bangladesh', *Studies in Family Planning*, **25**(2), 65–76.

Seguino, Stephanie, Günseli Berik and Yana Rodgers (2010), 'An investment that pays off: promoting gender equality as a means to finance development', Friedrich Ebert Stiftung Occasional Paper, Friedrich Ebert Stiftung, Berlin, May.

Taylor, Mark (2001), 'Self-employment and windfall gains in Britain: evidence from panel data', *Economica*, **68**(272), 539–65.

Thomas, Duncan (1997), 'Incomes, expenditures, and health outcomes: evidence on intrahousehold resource allocation', in Haddad et al. (eds), pp. 142–64.

Vial, Isabel, Eugenia Munchnik and Francisco Mardones (1989), 'Women's market work, infant feeding practices, and infant nutrition among low-income women in Santiago, Chile', in Joanne Leslie and Michael Paolisso (eds), *Women, Work, and Child Welfare in the Third World*, Boulder, CO: Westview Press for the American Association for the Advancement of Science, pp. 131–59.

World Bank (2001), *Engendering Development: Through Gender Equality in Rights, Resources, and Voice*, Oxford: Oxford University Press.

23. Gender, debt and the housing/financial crisis
Brigitte Young

I INTRODUCTION

When financial crises occurred in Latin America, Russia, and Asia during the 1980s and 1990s, analysts could safely argue that the financial instabilities were not systemic, but were the result of shortcomings in the affected countries (Wade, 2008), meaning that these countries needed to clean up their crony capitalism and start dismantling their protective domestic barriers. The picture has changed dramatically since the emergence of the US subprime (loan) housing crisis in mid-2007, which led to a full-blown, systemic financial crisis with devastating impact on the real economy in both industrial and developing countries. Because the financial crisis had its epicentre on Wall Street, the collapse has undermined the confidence in the superiority of the American free market philosophy.

As discourse has shifted from the benefits of financial liberalization to the costs of fast and excessive financial liberalization (Semmler and Young, 2010), the efficient market hypothesis, the cornerstone of neoclassical economics, has largely been refuted as a myth (Stiglitz et al., 2006; Csaba, 2009). Even the representative voice of liberal international capital, *The Financial Times*, declared the era of deregulation begun under US President Ronald Reagan was officially dead after the collapse of the investment banks Lehman Brothers, Merrill Lynch and others, and the conversion of Morgan Stanley and Goldman Sachs into regular commercial banks (September 21, 2008).

A heated academic debate has now emerged among neoclassical and heterodox[1] economists on who is to blame for the crisis. Neoclassical economists continue to believe that the market is not to blame, but rather that the folly lies in what John Maynard Keynes has called the 'animal spirit'[2] of human behavior. Alan Greenspan, the former Federal Reserve Chairman, while agreeing that he made a mistake in presuming to rely on the 'banks' self-interest to protect the shareholders' (Greenspan, 2008, p. 524), nevertheless continues to believe in the philosophy of self-disciplinary markets. In contrast, heterodox economists challenge the belief in the perfect market and start from the more realistic assumption of imperfect capital markets, which need to be embedded in regulatory structures of supervision (Minsky, 1986; Stiglitz et al., 2006; Semmler and Young, 2010).

In the midst of this debate, several scholars have pointed out the multifaceted gendered effects of the recent crisis (Froud et al., 2010; Gill and Roberts, 2011; Starr, 2011). However, studies on how gender relations influence the very structure of how finance is organized and operates are relatively sparse (see Warnecke, 2006; Schuberth and Young, et al., 2011; Young et al., 2011;Young, 2012).[3] While this chapter makes no claim to fill the deficit in feminist financial theorizing, I focus on how 'credit becomes debt' (Langley, 2008) and how women and minorities were integrated into the ideology of the home ownership society (Bush, 2004) via private debt. In so doing, I illustrate how the (US) process of accessing loanable funds for a mortgage exacerbated pre-existing inequalities along race and gender lines.

In Section II, I discuss the social relations of money and its double purpose – functioning both as a claim (credit) and as a corresponding obligation (debt). The social role of money is important as it shows the specific dynamics of inclusion and exclusion of the poor to a money society based on the 'financialization of everyday activities' (Seabrooke, 2008, p. 6; see also Froud et al., 2010). Section III discusses how 'welfare as we know it'[4] was delegitimized starting with US President Ronald Reagan in the 1980s, and how privatized Keynesianism became a functional substitute for the publicly provided social insurance system (Crouch, 2009; Young, 2009). As Section IV shows, the subsequent proliferation of the home ownership society affected poor women and minorities; further, the subprime crisis is a case in point. Section V concludes that the tide of debt is not just rising – it is also increasingly gendered, and as such affects many aspects of daily life for women and their families. Though many demographic groups have recently suffered a stagnation of real income (hence increasing the incentive to carry more debt), this is particularly problematic for women, who generally earn less to start with. Most women not only experience a gender pay gap, but are also typically part-time or flexible workers with commensurate wage differentials, and they are responsible for the social reproduction of the care economy. This double or triple burden, combined with tighter debt constraints, is bound to have multiple feedback effects on household life, family time, and interpersonal relationships. This sheds new light on the idea that the financial risks of the homeownership society were foisted on those who can least afford it (Young and Schuberth, 2010; Gill and Roberts, 2011).

II   THE SOCIAL FORM OF MONEY: CREDITORS AND DEBTORS

The mainstream literature on financial market liberalization focuses mostly on the consequences for efficiency in terms of financial stability and economic growth. Missing in these neoclassical models is the fact that different regulatory regimes have distinct distributive effects that go far beyond the narrow scope of the financial sector itself (Mooslechner et al., 2006). These distributive effects are highly gendered.

Diane Elson (2002) has suggested that there are three gender biases built into the theories of macroeconomic policies, which from the point of view of women spread the financial risks to those who can least afford to shoulder them: (i) the *deflationary bias*, (ii) the *male-breadwinner bias*, and (iii) the *commodification* or *privatization bias*. Male breadwinner bias refers to public policies that prioritize the right of males to decent employment while relegating women to the status of secondary workers (part-time) with fewer rights, less pay and highly restricted access to state-provided social benefits. Although the majority of women participate in the paid labor force, either in the informal or formal sector of the economy, public policies in many countries still rely on the assumption that women's livelihoods are provided by the incomes earned by husbands and fathers.

This male-breadwinner bias is further enforced by a commodification or privatization bias, which occurs when public provisions are replaced by market-based, individualized entitlements for those who can afford them. 'Rather than pooling and sharing risks and resources, with scope for the solidarity of cross-subsidy, there is a separate insurance for specific contingencies' (ibid., p. 33), such as private pensions, private health insurance, private hospitals, private schools, private paid care for children and old people, and privatized utilities for energy and transport.

The deflationary bias is directly linked to the international financial governance processes and the interests they prioritize. The increasing power of capital on a global scale means that the financial markets exert pressure on governments to keep inflation, as well as taxation and expenditures low (see Elson and Warnecke, 2011). The benefits from such policies accrue overwhelmingly to owners of financial investments and exclude those who are mostly dependent on the 'labour society' (Altvater, 1997).

However, I would argue that there is an additional bias, which could be called 'creditor bias'. This bias goes to the heart of the functions and institutions of money (and thus the financial system) with quite different distributional impacts for women and men. Traditionally, the functions of money are defined as a store of value, as a medium of exchange, a unit of account, and a means of payment. The unit of account is the measurement in which values are stated and recorded, while the medium of exchange is the unit in which the exchange in the world of commodities is expressed (British pound, euro, US dollar, Japanese yen, and so on). The store of value, however, expresses the monetary value of the assets, that is, money as wealth, which implies a social relation establishing a system of incentives for those with wealth to gain access to resources, with the object of amassing further wealth. As Altvater has reminded us: 'Marx had already pointed out in the 19th century, the "wealth of nations" (Adam Smith) appears not only as a "huge collection of commodities" (Marx), but also in the form of monetary assets' (ibid., p. 48).

This monetary asset, in the form of money as money, expresses the social form of money and has a twofold function. On one side is the creditor (monetary asset) and on the other the debtor (corresponding obligation). While the relationship between debtor and creditor is not static, the increasing power of capital on a global scale has led the relationship between creditors and debtors to become highly asymmetrical (Gill, 1997). This is particularly visible in the subprime mortgage markets that collapsed in the United States in the summer of 2007, given the staggering amount of privatized debts of many women and minorities and the subsequent high rates of repayment problems, delinquencies, and foreclosures. The crisis illustrates how the nature of financial power at the micro level of the individual is linked to the macro financial global structure. When credit becomes debt, the borrower responsibility for outstanding obligations is increasingly enforced through market discipline and political pressure; this sustains the prevailing (gendered) forms of dominance/domination in the monetary asset regime (ibid., p. 73; see also Langley, 2008, p. 1; Gill and Roberts, 2011).

The process of normalizing the social relations of money is highly gendered in that it systematically includes and excludes individuals from the 'monetary society' and thus also from the symbols of economic and social citizenship (Altvater, 1997; Gill, 1997). While generally women and minorities were the last in and the first out in having access to the housing wealth, they often were not able to convert the housing wealth into other investments used to launch social mobility. Invariably, the money used in the refinancing resulted in cash pull-outs that were used by families to keep pace with rising costs and burgeoning debt to pay off credit card debts (Montgomerie, 2008). The integration of poor women into the financialization of everyday activity through subprime home ownership shows a disturbing disparity in the loan products for which women and minorities were able to get approval as opposed to loans obtained by similarly situated men. The same disparity can now also be seen in the process of deleveraging of subprime debt in that it has caused financial stress for many more women and minorities at the lower end of the economic ladder who are already struggling to make ends meet (Secor, 2007; Oliver and Shapiro, 2008).

III HOME OWNERSHIP AS 'WELFARE FOR THE MASSES'[5]: PRIVATIZED KEYNESIANISM

To understand the recent subprime crisis in the United States, it may help to situate home ownership within a specific US-American context before discussing how women became integrated into the model of residential capitalism. First of all, home ownership has historically been part of the American dream irrespective of class, race, and gender. Property ownership is deeply ingrained in US-American conservative values of individualism, freedom and self-responsibility. In contrast to most European countries in which the elderly rely on public pension systems for their income, US retirees' primary store of wealth is ownership of a house (Schwartz, 2008, p. 277).

In fact, Castles (1997) has argued that there is an inverse relationship between the level of home ownership and the degree of welfare state provision in industrial countries during the postwar period. Widespread home ownership may reduce the need for generous income maintenance for the aged and is believed to be a mechanism to redress the overall extent of inequality among the population. Unlike citizens in high-taxation countries, citizens in Anglo-Saxon states have engaged in a welfare tradeoff, 'where they have chosen to use residential property as means of storing wealth over the income life-cycle, while paying less tax and relying less on the state for social support' (Seabrooke, 2008, p. 11). Home-ownership and social service provisions are thus functional equivalents (Castles, 1997; Schwartz, 2008).

Given the positive values associated with property rights and at the same time the negative discourse on state-provided welfare, it is not surprising that US President G.W. Bush announced the moral superiority of an *ownership society* in 2004. The emphasis on a market-friendly ownership society is not just intended for domestic consumption; it also squares readily with the US hegemonic project to transport the values of individualism, democracy, and freedom around the globe. Similarly to the conservative tenets of the United Kingdom's Margaret Thatcher, who initiated the privatization of the British public council housing projects in the 1980s, G.W. Bush defined the pillars of the ownership society in a speech on June 17, 2004, as follows: 'If you own something, you have a vital stake in the future of our country. The more ownership there is in America, the more vitality there is in America, and the more people have a vital stake in the future of this country' (Bush, 2004).

In addition to the moral tenets associated with home ownership, an additional factor accounting for the development of the subprime market was the weak wage growth since the 1990s and the reforms of the New Deal welfare provisions (Reich, 2010). Since the rise of Margaret Thatcher in 1979 and Ronald Reagan in the 1980s, the pillars of the

Keynesian welfare state model have been challenged. These included the promise for full employment (pursued through state-guided demand management) and the availability of social policies with a strong welfare orientation to spread mass consumption to all national citizens, thereby favoring a growth dynamic based on a virtuous cycle of mass production and mass consumption. Within this matrix, as Bob Jessop pointed out, 'it was national states that were mainly held responsible for developing and guiding Keynesian full employment and welfare policies' (Jessop, 2006, p. 146).

Feminists have often criticized the male assumptions of this Fordist model[6] of industrial production, which was foremost a class compromise between capital and labor (McDowell, 1991). I will focus on only one aspect of this criticism: the need to differentiate among specific gender orders. The concept of gender order is used here to refer to institutionalized practices and forms of gendered systems of governance structures that are constituted as social ordering principles. Social norms, rules, regulations, and principles are not gender-neutral entities, but are inscribed with specific norms for the roles men and women are designed to play in the polity. The networks of overlapping social and cultural mores then become embedded in the institutional structures of the polity and relations of citizenship. The process of institutionalization creates conditions that tend to reproduce specific forms of practice and intersubjectivity (Bakker, 2003; Young, 2003; Maier, 2011).

A particular gender order (breadwinner model) emerged within the confines of the Fordist production model in industrial countries that is based upon a specific idealized model of workplace, home, and family. The family is seen as consisting of a male breadwinner who supports a dependent wife and children. The state, through the tax system and expenditure policies, is active in constructing a gender order and shaping social reproduction. For this model to work in reality, it requires the wife's unpaid domestic labor to provide the care services. The state, in turn, guarantees a 'family wage' through policies such as income transfers (for example, government child benefits, social welfare payments, and unemployment insurance).

However, research since at least the 1980s reveals a shift away from the Keynesian welfare state toward a system based on permanent innovation, enterprise, and flexibility focusing on the supply side of the economy in order to strengthen the competitiveness in global markets. In this Schumpeterian Workfare regime (Jessop, 2006, p. 145), the national state has largely retreated from the traditional demand management of the national economy, and the responsibility for social reproduction is subordinated to the demands of labor flexibility; combined with the declining resource allocation to public finance, this means that activities previously provided through the state have now shifted to the family (especially women) or to those (largely male or dominant class) individuals wealthy enough to afford private services (Standing, 1989).

The shift toward a Schumpeterian Workfare regime has accompanied a change in the gender order. No longer is the 'breadwinner model' the dominant order. Instead we see a tendency toward a more individualized gender order, with women trying to gain middle-class status by purchasing homes via subprime loans. We could call this emerging trend a 'home-ownership model'. Important in the American context is the fact that this model is not associated with the negative connotation of state welfare (Seabrooke, 2008, p. 12). Home ownership meant that the *wealth* accumulated in the home could be 'cashed-out' to meet consumer demands. The underlying assumption is that house prices will rise and thus owners could refinance to either reduce the interest rates payable on their loans, or release equity from their homes, so home ownership becomes an object of leveraged investment (Langley, 2008, p. 7; Schwartz, 2008; Watson, 2009). Of course, the system of leveraged home ownership could not have happened without the innovations in the financial markets over the past 30 years.[7]

In the present game of who is to blame for the subprime crisis, which turned into the banking and credit crisis and subsequently spilled over into the euro crisis, fingers are pointed to excessive leveraging, misrepresentation, insider conflict of rating agencies, lack of transparency, neglect of supervisory controls, and the 'triumph of engineered euphoria over evidence' (Kuttner, 2007; Csaba, 2009); however, one aspect has largely been overlooked. Easing the standards of lending had also to do with the desire to ensure that home ownership was accessible to households which had historically been underserved by mortgage lenders (Bank for International Settlements 2008, p. 5).

IV   THE FINANCIALIZATION OF THE OWNERSHIP SOCIETY THROUGH PRIVATE DEBT

The subprime sector was not an illicit mortgage market, but very much part of a legitimate and highly celebrated mass ownership society in the United States (Langley, 2008). While Fannie Mae[8] and Freddie Mac[9] competed in the private mortgage market, Ginnie Mae[10] dealt with the pure public market. The federal government's concern about access to affordable housing facilitated numerous legislative acts from the 1970s onward, aiming to empower low-income and minority borrowers (Seabrooke, 2008). Some of this legislation ensured that Freddie Mac and Fannie Mae catered not only to the middle class, but also to groups who had previously been denied access to affordable mortgage loans. The Equal Credit Opportunities Act of 1974 outlawed discrimination in credit sanctioning based on the characteristics of gender, marital status, race, national origin, religion, or income source. In 1989, an amendment to the Home Mortgage Disclosure Act (HMDA) of 1975 required mortgage lenders to collect information on who were denied loans, 'including information on income, gender, race, and location' (ibid., p. 8).

The development of the subprime sector thus needs to be seen through the lens of a rights-based discourse within the United States; home ownership and subprime lending became politically legitimized because it was seen as providing access to credit to marginalized communities. Still, the various legislative changes to make home ownership available to the poor by lowering the costs of home loans and allowing homeowners to deduct the interest on their mortgage[11] from their taxes are not regarded as state-supported welfare for the poor. Leveraged home ownership thus became an accepted form of 'welfare for the masses' (ibid., p. 8) and fitted with the cultural values of the American private ownership mentality. The *Wall Street Journal* (2006) reports that subprime lending helped to increase home ownership from 65 to 69 percent over the last 10 years.

Owning property and gaining assets through real estate thus became one of the few avenues open to women and minorities for social mobility and securing middle-class status. As Melvin Oliver and Thomas Shapiro (2008, p. 2) note, 'Income helps families get along, but assets help them get and stay ahead'. Indeed, since the 1980s the proportion of women heads of households who are home owners has increased from 48 percent to 53 percent (NCRW, 2008). Still, the gender order illustrated by the 'home-ownership model' did not enable women and minorities to enter the asset price regime on a level playing field. Access to affordable mortgage rates was highly skewed in that mortgage banks targeted women across the board as 'risk borrowers' in relation to men in similarly situated circumstances (Fishbein and Woodall, 2006; Donovan, 2011).

The vulnerability of women and minorities to unfair lending practices can best be shown in terms of the subprime market. The concept of subprime refers to loans to consumers who are unable to meet the approval standards of the prime lenders. Thus the interest rate associated with subprime loans is higher (125 basis points or 6.25 percent as opposed to 5 percent)[12] in order to compensate for the higher risks and higher loan processing fees that lenders assume when making these loans (*Futurist*, 2007; Secor, 2007). As a result, the additional costs of such subprime loans are substantial. For families that took out mortgages in 2005 (prior to the start of the present mortgage crisis), a subprime loan on a median price home would translate into an extra $235 per month and $85,000 more in total payments.[13] This helps to explain why the present housing crisis is particularly devastating for women and minorities.

Even though women have higher average credit scores than men (682 versus 675 on the FICO scale), women borrowers are more likely to receive subprime loans at every income level. Women with income levels twice the median income are 46.4 percent more likely to have to accept subprime loans than men with similar earnings (ibid.). A study by the National Council for Research on Women finds that women constitute 29 percent of borrowers for mortgages, but they are overrepresented among borrowers receiving subprime loans (women comprise 32 percent of these borrowers, but only 24 percent of borrowers receiving prime loans) (NCRW 2008, Graph 8).

While the mortgage industry claims that approval ratings are strictly on the merits of credit rating and financial standing, research shows just the opposite. Disparity is found across all home loans including home purchase, refinancing, and home improvements (Secor, 2007). At a US Senate Committee Hearing on Health, Education, Labor and Pensions (2008), evidence was given that women disproportionally receive subprime mortgages in comparison to men. Women are also found more often in the high-cost subprime market;[14] more than one in 10 (10.9 percent) female borrowers compared to about one in 13 (7.7 percent) male borrowers received high-cost subprime mortgage loans in 2005.

Minority women were the most likely to receive a subprime loan, regardless of income. While single women across ethnic lines have made strong inroads into home ownership, purchasing nearly one in five homes sold in 2005, it was African American and Latina women who actively sought out mortgage loans: 46.7 percent of female borrowers were African American women and 31.4 percent were Latina women (NCRW, 2008). Older women of color are particularly vulnerable to subprime loans because of their cumulative effect of lower wages, occupational segregation, and smaller retirement savings.

In fact, African Americans were twice as likely as whites to receive subprime loans in all income ranges. The only group less likely to receive subprime loans than whites was Asian Americans (ibid.). Housing wealth has been one of the most important avenues for African Americans to accumulate wealth. As Oliver and Shapiro (2008) point out in their study on the 'Sub-prime as a black catastrophe',[15] home equity is the most important reservoir of wealth for average American families and disproportionately so for African

Americans. According to the authors, home equity accounts for 63 percent of total average net worth for black households. In contrast, home equity represents only 38.5 percent of average white net worth. Especially in minority communities, home equity is used as collateral to finance retirement, start small business, pay for college education and rely on in times of hardship. Therefore, 'while home ownership reached historic highs, families today actually own a lesser share of their homes than at any previous times, because they have borrowed against their housing wealth' (ibid., p. 2).

Especially tragic is the timing of the subprime crisis for women and minorities. Just as women were making inroads into this critical avenue of wealth building, the integration of women via the subprime market has left them so much more vulnerable to indebtedness and even foreclosure (Gill and Roberts, 2011). Although subprime loans were only 13 percent of all mortgages, they represented 54 percent of all foreclosures in 2008 (US Senate Committee 2008, p. 8; see also Glaister and Bruce-Lockhart, 2008). Since the mortgage meltdown began in 2007, about 6 million homes have been lost to foreclosures (as of 2011); in 2011, another four million homes were estimated to be at some stage in the foreclosure process, with a rate of about two million a year. While the pace of new foreclosures seemed to ease in the third quarter of 2011 (from 8.44 percent in the second quarter to 7.99 in the third quarter), borrowers with subprime adjustable mortgages saw the biggest jump. Some 4.65 percent of those subprime loans entered the foreclosure process. This is an increase from 3.62 percent in the second quarter of 2011, a hefty 28 percent increase. The reason for the rise in subprime foreclosures was in part due to an increase in the number of loans that failed to get lender approval for modification. At the same time, some states ended their moratorium on foreclosures during the 3rd quarter (The Bottom Line, 2011).

In a keynote speech at the opening of the Museum of Modern Arts exhibit, 'Foreclosed: Buying into the "American Dream"', US Secretary of Housing and Urban Development, Shaun Donovan, told the audience that the foreclosure crisis disproportionally hit low-income and minority households in the suburbs. He noted how in some of these communities the majority of people receiving mortgages during the housing bubble were given subprime loans when many of them qualified for prime ones. And he cited a study that showed that Latinos lost two-thirds of their wealth between 2005 and 2009 (Donovan, 2011).

V   CONCLUSION

The subprime housing/credit/financial crisis is still unfolding and thus we do not know the full impact across the intersectionality of class, race, and gender. While not providing a theoretical framework for analyzing financial markets, this chapter suggests an analytical focus by expanding and redefining the functions of money. If money as wealth is seen as a social relation between creditor and debtor, in which the latter has to obey the logic of monetary rationality, then market discipline is the dominant disciplinary form to ensure that the risks of the creditor/debtor relationship shift to the individual debtor. The same logic does not seem to apply to the insolvent banks, which were largely able to immunize themselves from the disciplinary market measures and socialize the risks. The increasing power of capital on a global scale has not only changed the financial practices and operations of banks and investment houses, it has also altered 'the everyday routines, risk behaviors, and intersubjective understanding among the broader population' (Seabrooke, 2008, p. 6).

This can readily be observed in the present unfolding of subprime lending. At one level, subprime borrowers were integrated into the ownership society via privatized debt, a strategy that had the support of the political, financial, and business community. Leveraging one's home was praised by the economic journal *Forbes* in an article entitled 'Hock your house' in 2004 with the undertitle: 'Some advisors say to pay off your mortgage. We say leverage up and invest' (Forbes, 2004). Acquiring mortgages with virtually no assets (the NINJA loans – no income, no job and no assets) during the boom phase was legitimized as welfare for the masses. In fact, this shift entailed a change to a new gender order based on individualized home ownership rather than relying on the traditional gender order of a male breadwinner. However, as the subprime crisis spiraled into a financial crisis, the cultural politics of the response to the subprime crisis (Watson, 2009) has turned into a behavioral issue of constructing the poor as irresponsible mortgage borrowers. By discursively constructing the poor as irresponsible and lacking the necessary economic logic, the blame and the risks for the housing meltdown is shifted to the individual debtor.

The other side of the narrative is, as Robert Kuttner's 2007 testimony to the US House of Representatives has shown, that the securitization of mortgages benefited mostly the mortgage broker, the mortgage banker, the investment banker, and the bond-rating agencies, while the borrower was left with the fees and the systemic risks (Kuttner, 2007, p. 6). If we analyze the official response by the Treasury Department and the Federal Reserve to the financial crisis, it seems that lending institutions are largely sheltered from exposure to the market logic in their own business practices. Matthew Watson (2009) has argued that the pricing structure/regulation of financial instruments has remained outside the social control, while the subprime borrowers are fully subjected to the rationale of market discipline.

For women and minorities, there is the added impact that they have been integrated in this leveraged ownership society through discriminatory lending practices. Women across the income and racial spectrum were targeted more often for subprime loans than their male counterparts in similar financial situations. This means not only that they have been the last in, and the first out, but it also means that they have to bear much higher interest rates and fees. The challenge confronting women and minorities who are facing default, delinquency, and foreclosures is how to gain access to a modicum of state protection, and how in the future they are guaranteed a more level playing field in the mortgage market.

As we move forward, we must realize that (gendered) ideas and discourse influence the formulation of financial policies. Why must financial regulation favor the claims of financial capital? Why is the logic of finance based on abstract mathematical models instead of the real economy? Some have suggested that men themselves may be a culprit for the crisis:

> After all, it is men who dominate the financial system that got us into this mess; it is men, by and large, whose trading inflated the profits of banks to levels that now seem like the stuff of testosterone-fuelled fantasy; and it is men who pocketed most of the bulging bonuses that even Gordon Brown reckons were a key cause of the crisis. (*The Times*, September 30, 2008)

As this chapter has pointed out, financial crisis reinforces existing gender inequalities. What is needed is a financial architecture and an economic growth model which serves social values instead of privileging the financial sector. Both gender inequalities and income inequalities are the result of a certain group-think mentality of financial experts, which is exclusive and carries an outdated set of norms about women and men. The homogeneity of these norms disregards the complex interactions of the real world. The crisis provides now an opportunity to re-embed financial activities within society, thereby benefiting women and men globally.

NOTES

1. Heterodox economists represent different schools of thought such as neo-Keynesianism, Post Keynesianism, feminist economists, 'autistic' economics, Gramscian economics, and international political economics, who are united in their rejection of free-market orthodoxy and its belief that 'markets, private property and minimal government will achieve maximum welfare' (Hayes, 2007, p. 3).
2. Keynes referred to 'animal spirits' as the psychological forces driving the economy, such as fear or exuberance (Akerlof and Shiller, 2009).
3. As Seguino (Chapter 20, this volume) notes, the theoretical difficulty stems from the fact that the field of macroeconomics operates with aggregate variables, such as interest rates, currency rates, monetary policy, capital flows and investment rates, which appear 'gender neutral' on the surface. Unlike the field of micro- and meso-economics, where labor market segregation and/or the wage gap between women and men can be measured, the same is not true at the level of macroeconomics. The challenge for feminist economists is to make visible the gender assumptions that are inherent at both the epistemological and the ontological levels.
4. President Bill Clinton declared at his State of the Union Address before both Houses of Congress in 1993 that he would 'end welfare as a way of life and make it a path to independence and dignity' (White House, Press Release, 1993).
5. This term is from Seabrooke (2008, p. 8).
6. Fordism is a demand-driven economic system characterized by a complementarity between mass production and mass consumption. Wages are adjusted in accordance with productivity, and the state provides the necessary social insurance system and monetary stimulus to ensure an adequate demand level. In this class compromise, women are integrated in the social insurance system as dependents, and in the labor markets as part-time workers (McDowell, 1991; Young, 2001).
7. A range of legislative changes had been made in the early 1980s to deregulate the mortgage markets, which resulted in more responsive pricing, an extended supply of tailorized services, and ultimately broader access to mortgage credits (see Bank for International Settlements, 2008; IMF, 2008, p. 3; Schwartz, 2008; Young, 2009.
8. Fannie Mae was created in 1938 as a Federal National Mortgage Association in response to the massive foreclosures as a result of the depression. Fannie Mae was then privatized between 1968 and 1970, but was taken over by the Federal Housing Finance Agency (FHFA) on September 6, 2008 due to its horrendous losses.
9. Freddie Mac is a Federal Home Loan Mortgage Corporation and was created as part of the Emergency Finance Act in 1970. Similarly to Fannie Mae, Freddie Mac was privatized in 1989, but also taken over by the FHFA on September 6, 2008.
10. Ginnie Mae, created in 1968, is a government-sponsored enterprise meant to address the lending needs of low-income and minority borrowers.
11. Mortgage interest tax deductions go back to 1913.
12. Calculated on 100 basis points = 1 percent, thus 5 percent plus 1.25 is 6.25 percent.
13. A high-cost subprime loan could mean an extra $517 in payments each month and an extra $186,000 in total extra payments.
14. The high-cost subprime category is an even more risk-prone market and thus interest rates and fees for administration are even higher than in the subprime market.
15. Unfortunately, this article does not break down the data between African American women and men, but refers to African-American households.

REFERENCES

Akerlof, George A. and Robert J. Shiller (2009), *Animal Spirits*, Princeton, NJ and Oxford: Princeton University Press.

Altvater, Elmar (1997), 'Financial crises on the threshold of the 21st century', in Leo Panitch and Colin Leys (eds), *Socialist Register, World Market and Socialism*, London: Merlin, pp. 48–74.

Bakker, Isabella (2003), 'Neo-liberal governance and the reprivatization of social reproduction – social provisioning and shifting gender orders', in Isabella Bakker and Stephen Gill (eds), *Power, Production and Social Reproduction: Human In/Security in the Global Political Economy*, Basingstoke: Palgrave, pp. 66–82.

Bank for International Settlements (2008), 'The housing meltdown: why did it happen in the United States?', BIS Working Papers No. 259, Basel, available at: http://www.bis.org/publ/work259.pdf (accessed October 15, 2008).

Bottom Line, The (2011), 'Foreclosure crisis only about halfway over', available at: http://bottomline. msnbc.msn.com/_news/2011/11/17/8859967-foreclosure-crisis-only-about-halfway-over (accessed January 15, 2012).

Bush, George W. (2004), 'President Bush's policies to promote the ownership society', Office of the Press Secretary, White House, Washington, DC, June 17.

Castles, Francis G. (1997), 'The really big trade-off: home ownership and the welfare state in the New World and the Old', *Acta Politica*, **32**, 153–73.

Crouch, Colin (2009), 'Privatised Keynesianism: an unacknowledged policy regime', *British Journal of Politics and International Relations*, **11**, 382–99.

Csaba, László (2009), 'Orthodoxy, renewal and complexity in contemporary economics', *Zeitschrift für Staats – und Europawissenschaften*, **7**(1), 50–70.

Donovan, Shaun (2011), 'Foreclosed: Buying into the "American Dream"' Keynote speech, Museum of Modern Art, November 23, at *INSIDE/OUT* blog, Available at: http://www.moma.org/explore/multimedia/videos/182/1015 (accessed February 20, 2012).

Elson, Diane (2002), 'International financial architecture: a view from the kitchen', *femina politica*, **1**, 26–37.

Elson, Diane and Tonia Warnecke (2011), 'IMF policies and gender orders: the case of the poverty reduction and growth facility', in Young et al. (eds), pp. 110–31.

Financial Times (2008), 'It's mourning again for Americans', September 21.

Fishbein, Allen J. and Patrick Woodall (2006), *Women as Prime Targets for Subprime Lending: Women are Disproportionately Represented in High-Cost Mortgage Market*, Washington, DC: Consumer Federation of America.

Forbes (2004), 'Hock your house', December 13, available at: www.forbes.com/forbes/20004/1213/236.htm (accessed July 7, 2007).

Froud, Julie, Sukhdev Johal, Johnna Montgomerie and Karel Williams (2010), 'Escaping the tyranny of earned income? the failure of finance as social innovation', *New Political Economy*, **15**(1), 147–64.

Futurist (2007), 'Subprime lenders target women unfairly', May–June, available at: www.wfs.org (accessed November 20, 2008).

Gill, Stephen (1997), 'Finance, production and panopticism: inequality, risk and resistance in an era of disciplinary neo-liberalism', in Stephen Gill (ed.), *Globalization, Democratization and Multilateralism*, London: Macmillan, pp. 51–76.

Gill, Stephen and Adrienne Roberts (2011), 'Macroeconomic governance, gendered inequality, and global crisis', in Young et al. (eds), pp. 155–72.

Glaister, Can and Anna Bruce-Lockhart (2008), 'Subprime crisis: US foreclosures bring homelessness to the middle class', *The Guardian*, June 25, available at: www.guardian.co.uk (accessed November 20, 2008).

Greenspan, Alan (2008), *The Age of Turbulence*, London: Penguin Books.

Hayes, Christopher (2007), 'Hip heterodoxy', *The Nation*, June 11, available at: www.thenation.com/doc/20070611/hayes 12.6.2007 (accessed December 12, 2007).

International Monetary Fund (IMF) (2008), *World Economic Outlook, Housing and the Business Cycle*, April, available at: www.imf.org/external/pubs/ft/weo/2008/01/pdf/c3.pdf (accessed May 26, 2009).

Jessop, Bob (2006), 'State – and regulation-theoretical perspectives on the European Union and the failure of the Lisbon Agenda', *Competition & Change*, **10**(2), 141–61.

Kuttner, Robert (2007), 'Testimony before the Committee on Financial Services', October 2, US House of Representatives, Washington, DC, available at: www.house.gov/apps/list/hearing/financialsvcs_dem/testimony-kuttner.pdf (accessed May 15, 2008).

Langley, Paul (2008), 'When Credit Becomes Debt: Foreclosures and Forbearance in Sub-Prime Mortgages', paper presented at The Political Economy of the Subprime Crisis – The Economics, Politics and Ethics of Response workshop, Warwick University, UK, September 18–19.

Maier, Friederike (2011), 'Macroeconomic regimes in OECD countries and the interrelationship with gender orders', in Young et al. (eds), pp. 11–37.

McDowell, Linda (1991), 'Life without father and Ford: the new gender order of post-Fordism,' *Transactions of the British Institute of Geographers*, **16**(4), 400–19.

Minsky, Hyman P. (1986), *Stabilizing an Unstable Economy*, New Haven, CT: Yale University Press.

Montgomerie, Johnna (2008), 'Spectre of the subprime borrower beyond a credit score perspective', Centre for Research on Socio-Cultural Change (CRESC) Working Paper No. 58, available at: http://www.cresc.ac.uk/sites/default/files/wp58 (accessed February 15, 2010).

Mooslechner, Peter, Helene Schuberth and Beat Weber (2006), 'Financial market regulation and the dynamics of inclusion and exclusion', in Peter Mooslechner, Helene Schuberth and Beat Weber (eds), *The Political Economy of Financial Market Regulation. The Dynamics of Inclusion and Exclusion*, Cheltenham, UK and Northampton, MA, USA: Edward Elgar, pp. i–xvii.

National Council for Research on Women (NCRW) (2008), 'NCRW big five: women, homeownership, and sub-prime mortgages – a need for fair lending practices', available at: http://www.ncrw.org/sites/ncrw.org/files/Subprime%20mortgages.pdf (accessed March 19, 2012).

Oliver, Melvin L. and Thomas M. Shapiro (2008), 'Sub-prime as a black catastrophe', *The American Prospect*, September 22, available at: www.prospect.org/cs/article=sub-prime_as_a_black_castrophe (accessed December 20, 2008).

Reich, Robert B. (2010), *Aftershock: The Next Economy and America's Future*, New York: Vintage.

Schuberth, Helene and Brigitte Young (2011), 'The role of gender in governance of the financial sector', in Young et al. (eds), pp. 132–54.

Schwartz, Hermann (2008), 'Housing, global finance and American hegemony: building conservative politics one brick at a time', *Comparative European Politics*, **6**(3), 262–84.

Seabrooke, Leonard (2008), 'Embedded liberalism is dead, long live embedded liberalism: national welfare concerns and international policy responses to the sub-prime crisis, paper presented at The Political Economy of the Subprime Crisis – The Economics, Politics and Ethics of Response workshop, Warwick University, UK, September 18–19.

Secor, Sharon L. (2007), 'Sub-prime lending, women, and the foreclosure crisis', *American Chronicle*, October 26, available at: http://www.americanchronicle.com/articles/viewArticle.asp?articleID=41314 (accessed November 20, 2008).

Semmler, Willi and Brigitte Young (2010), 'Lost in temptation of risk: financial market liberalization, financial market meltdown and policy reactions', *Comparative European Politics*, **8**(3), 327–53.

Standing, Guy (1989), 'Global feminization through flexible labor,' *World Development*, **17**(7), 1077–95.

Starr, Martha A. (ed). (2011), *Consequences of Economic Downturn: Beyond the Usual Economics*, Basingstoke: Palgrave Macmillan.

Stiglitz, Joseph E., José Antonio Ocampo, Shari Spiegel, Racardo Ffrench-Davis and Deepak Nayyar (2006), *Stability with Growth: Macroeconomics, Liberalization, and Development*, Oxford: Oxford University Press.

The Times (2008), 'What caused the crunch? Men and testosterone', September 30, available at:www.women.timesonline.co.uk (accessed October 5, 2008).

US Senate Committee on Health, Education, Labor and Pensions (2008), 'Taking a toll: the effects of recession on women', April 18, available at: http://Kennedy.senate.gov/imo/media/doc/Taking%20a%20Toll--%20report%20on%20effects%20of%20recession%20on%20women1.pdf (accessed November 20, 2008).

Wade, Robert (2008), 'The First World debt crisis in global perspective', paper presented at The Political Economy of the Subprime Crisis – The Economics, Politics and Ethics of Response workshop, Warwick University, UK, September 18–19.

Wall Street Journal (2006), 'As home owners face strains, markets bet on loan defaults', October 30, available at: www.wsj.com (accessed June 20, 2008).

Warnecke, Tonia (2006), 'A gender-aware approach to international finance', in Betsy Jane Clary, Wilfred Dolfsma and Deborah Figart (eds), *Ethics and the Market – Insights from Social Economics*, New York: Routledge, pp. 175–90.

Watson, Matthew (2009), 'Headlong into the Polanyian dilemma: the impact of middle-class moral panic on the British government's response to the sub-prime crisis', *British Journal of Politics and International Relations*, **11**(3), 422–37.

White House (1993), 'Address by the President to the joint session of Congress', February 17, available at: www.ibiblio.org/pub/archives/whitehouse-papers/1993/ (accessed September 15, 2008).

Young, Brigitte (2001), 'Globalization and gender: a european perspective', in Rita Mae Kelly, Jane H. Bayes, Mary E. Hawkesworth and Brigitte Young (eds), *Gender, Globalization, and Democratization*, New York/Oxford: Rowman & Littlefield, pp. 27–47.

Young, Brigitte (2003), 'Financial crises and social reproduction: Asia, Argentina and Brazil', in Isabella Bakker and Stephen Gill (eds), *Power, Production and Social Reproduction*, Basingstohe and New York: Palgrave Macmillan, pp. 103–23.

Young, Brigitte (2009), 'Vom staatlichen zum *privatisierten Keynesianismus*: Der globale makroökonomische Kontext der Finanzkrise und der Privatverschuldung', *Zeitschrift für Internationale Beziehungen*, **2**, 141–59.
Young, Brigitte (2012), 'Structural power and the gender-biases of the technocratic network governance in finance', in Gülay Caglar, Elisabeth Prügl and Susanne Zwingel (eds), *Feminist Strategies in International Governance*, New York/London: Routledge, pp. 267–82.
Young, Brigitte, Isabella Bakker and Diane Elson (eds) (2011), *Questioning Financial Governance from a Feminist Perspective*, London and New York: Routledge.
Young, Brigitte and Helene Schuberth (2010), 'The global financial meltdown and the impact of financial governance on gender', GARNET Policy Brief, Science Po, Paris, available at: http://www.garneteu.org/fileadmin/documents/policy_briefs/Garnet_Policy_Brief_No_10.pdf (accessed February 10, 2013).

PART VI

HUMAN DEVELOPMENT, EDUCATION AND HEALTH

24. Measuring gender disparities in human development

Amie Gaye, Jeni Klugman, Milorad Kovacevic,
*Sarah Twigg and Eduardo Zambrano**

I INTRODUCTION

Gender equity is an intrinsic dimension of human development. There is much country-level evidence showing how investments in women and girls can be a vehicle to promote long-term prospects for growth and human development (see Permanyer, 2009). Further, equity is enshrined in the United Nations Charter and the 'promotion of gender equality and the empowerment of women' is the third Millennium Development Goal. In addition, several major international agreements have urged governments to take steps to ensure that both women and men enjoy equal rights, opportunities, and responsibilities, such as the Nairobi Forward Looking Strategy for Advancement of Women (in 1985) and the Beijing Platform for Action (in 1995).

Yet global, regional and national reports have investigated and exposed key dimensions of gender disparities. The influential 1995 United Nations Development Programme (UNDP) global *Human Development Report* (HDR) on gender highlighted areas of progress, but also noted that women still outnumbered men two-to-one in terms of illiteracy, and girls constituted around 60 percent of those without access to primary school. Globally, women and girls still fare badly on important fronts. Their labor force participation rate continues to hover around 51 percent compared with around 83 percent for males. Women's reproductive health needs are too often neglected. Many developing countries do not provide qualified birth attendants, good prenatal or postnatal care or emergency care during deliveries. Maternal mortality averages 400 deaths per 100,000 births globally (UNICEF, 2008), but ranges as high as 822 deaths per 100,000 births in low human development countries. And the global average for women in parliament is still only 16 percent. These are examples of just a few domains where gender inequalities persist.

In order to know whether progress is being made toward the policy objective of gender equality, calculation of relevant comparative indicators and their monitoring are needed. This is a difficult endeavor – in part because of conceptual complexities and deficient data, but also because some aspects do not readily lend themselves to quantitative measurement. Pioneering measures were developed and published by the UNDP, offshoots of the Human Development Index (HDI): the Gender Development Index (GDI) and the Gender Empowerment Measure (GEM), both published annually until 2009. The greater a country's gender disparity, the lower the GDI in comparison to the HDI. The GEM measures change in accordance with progress in women's economic and political status.

This chapter reviews the challenge of measuring and monitoring gender inequality.

Section II evaluates the GDI and GEM as well as the following indices: the Gender Equity Index (GEI); the Gender Gap Index (GGI); the Relative Status of Women Index (RSWI); the Social Institutions and Gender Index (SIGI); and the Women's Economic Opportunities Index (WEOI). Section III introduces the new index that was first presented in the 2010 HDR (UNDP, 2010): the Gender Inequality Index (GII). The GII is unique in its focus on critical issues of educational attainment, economic and political participation, and reproductive health issues and in accounting for overlapping inequalities at the national level. As such, it represents an important advance on existing global measures of gender equity. The GII is designed to reveal the extent to which the realization of a country's human development potential is curtailed by gender inequality, and provides empirical foundations for policy analysis and advocacy efforts. Selection of an appropriate index and maintaining it for cross-sectional and longitudinal comparisons is vital to both understanding the role of gender in society and improving the economic lives of women and girls. Section IV discusses the application of the GII, and Section V compares the results with other gender indices. Section VI concludes.

II   A REVIEW OF EXISTING MEASURES OF GENDER DISPARITIES

Measures of the disadvantages affecting women have played an important role in raising awareness of problems and helping to keep governments accountable. As a result of broad collective efforts, including on the part of the International Labour Organization, the World Bank, the Organization for Economic Cooperation and Development, and the World Economic Forum, the amount of data that incorporates a gender perspective has increased considerably since the early 1990s. Basic indicators that are systematically available on a gender-disaggregated basis include school enrollment, most health data, and employment in different sectors of the economy. Much better information is also available for specific issues, such as reproductive health (Abdullah, 2000; Ransom and Yinger, 2002) and violence against women (Kelly et al., 2008), although, as we see below, there are still large gaps. Yet one of the key challenges in evaluating progress in gender equality has been quantifying important dimensions. For example, the notion of women's empowerment is difficult to evaluate and measure (Benería and Permanyer, 2010). Time use is another area that may in principle be easier to measure, but in practice is very difficult. The same is true for asset ownership.

A number of composite measures of gender disparities are now available. The potential advantage of a composite index is that it provides a good summary of a complex multidimensional problem that is easily interpretable. This can help us understand the complexities of gender relations and facilitate comparisons across time and countries. This in turn can attract public interest and capture the attention of policy-makers. Single summary numbers also allow for national and subnational rankings that are useful for advocacy purposes and to motivate government policy responses.

The first global indices designed to reflect gender disparities were the GDI and GEM, which were launched in the UN's 1995 HDR (UNDP, 1995). Since their introduction, the two measures have been used as advocacy and monitoring tools by the UNDP and other developmental partners. To calculate the GDI, the Human Development Index

(HDI), a composite measure of well-being comprising achievements in health, education, and incomes, is penalized (lowered) if gender inequality exists in any of the three dimensions. Thus an advantage of the GDI is its clarity of purpose: developed to capture gender inequalities in an overall assessment of well-being. The more the GDI differs from the HDI, the larger the measured inequality. But because the GDI cannot be interpreted independently of the HDI, it cannot be interpreted on its own as an indicator of gender gaps in well-being. Because of this, some critics have called the GDI a 'false start' because it is not a true measure of gender inequality (see Dijkstra, 2006).

The GEM was introduced as a complementary measure of gender equality in political, economic, and decision-making power. The three dimensions included are (i) control over economic resources, measured by men and women's earned income; (ii) economic participation and decision-making, measured by women's and men's share of administrative, professional, managerial, and technical positions; and (iii) political participation and decision-making, measured by male and female shares of parliamentary seats. The measure usefully captures some aspects of female empowerment,[1] although it has been criticized as having an unclear conceptual basis and questioned as to the appropriateness of the indicators (Klasen, 2006).

These pioneering efforts gained some public visibility, supported by annual updates in the HDR, and signaled the importance of collecting and disaggregating data by gender in country-level analysis, including in national human development reports. A number of later indices have actually used aspects of the GDI and GEM, as we see below. But both indices also attracted critical debate about how to construct a valid and reliable index with gender-differentiated data. Overall, the GDI and GEM have not had nearly as much success as the HDI in academic or policy circles. Both measures have frequently been misunderstood, and both had conceptual problems in the underlying components as well as empirical problems relating to data availability (see Dijkstra, 2006; Klasen, 2006; Schüler, 2006; and Hawken and Munck, 2009 for good overviews of the critiques).

The key drawbacks can be summarized as follows:

- The measures combine absolute achievements alongside relative aspects. This means, among other things, that countries with low absolute levels of income (GDP) cannot approach gender equity, even if there is total parity in incomes. The GDI is very strongly correlated with the level of GDP, and income levels tend to dominate the GEM.
- The GDI is often misinterpreted as a measure of gender inequality whereas it is actually a measure of how much gender inequality reduces a given country's level of human development. While this shows the human development costs of gender inequalities in basic human development, it does not really measure the position of women as compared to men in society.
- The indicators do not always correspond to the underlying concept. For example, 'Legislators, Senior Officials and Managers' is used in the GEM to measure *economic* participation and decision-making instead of political participation and decision-making.
- Other issues, for example, the health component of the GDI – life expectancy at birth – raise questions of whether women's biological advantage in longevity should be considered as a gender gap, and whether the measure should consider

the 'potentially alive' in order to take into account 'missing girls' (see Klasen, 2004).

● Each of the indicators in the GEM arguably suffers from urban, elite bias. For example, the economic component is measured by female share of economic decision-making positions, which does not include agricultural or informal work, or work in the lower levels of the formal economy, nor does it measure the unpaid labor of care work. Similar criticisms exist for other indicators in the GEM.

● There is over-reliance on imputations for missing data. In particular, for the estimated income shares, data is frequently unavailable and thus ultimately required imputations for over three-quarters of the countries in the sample.

Partly as a result of these problems, a whole range of other gender-related well-being indices have proliferated. These tackle important aspects of gender inequality in different ways, although, as we argue below, none has been able to provide a comprehensive picture of the levels of gender inequality experienced within and across countries (Agarwal, 1994, 2003; Hawken and Munck, 2009; and Permanyer, 2009 provide excellent critiques).

Social Watch introduced a Gender Equity Index (GEI) that measures gender equity in education, participation in the economy, and empowerment. It has been published annually since 2004. Estimated for 104 countries in 2004, it has expanded to 156 countries by 2009. Its key conceptual innovation was the inclusion of the dimensions presented separately in the GDI and GEM. The education dimension is measured by adult literacy rate and primary-, secondary-, and tertiary-level enrollment. The economic participation dimension uses two indicators: percentage of women in nonagricultural paid jobs and gaps in estimated female and male incomes. And the empowerment dimension uses shares in professional and technical positions, administrative and managerial positions, as well as the share of parliamentary seats and ministerial positions held by women.

The GEI is constructed by first identifying gender gaps in three dimensions: education, the economy, and political empowerment. The index itself is the arithmetic average of the three dimensions. A ratio of female to male scores on each of 21 weighted indicators generates the index; the maximum value is 100 points, where the ratio of female to male scores would equal 100 percent. While the approach has the advantage of being simple and easy to understand, the ratios used only allow for comparison of the degree of inequality between countries without reflecting the absolute levels of gender inequality at the country level. This means that the GEI is basically a ranking exercise, and thus is less useful for tracking changes over time at the country level.

The World Economic Forum's Gender Gap Index (GGI), introduced in 2006, includes five dimensions of gender inequality: economic participation, economic opportunity, political empowerment, educational attainment and health, and well-being. These are measured using 14 indicators – the same indicators used in the GDI, GEM, and GEI – to which the sex ratio at birth is added. The GGI is calculated for 154 countries and is published annually. The index is calculated by converting data into male/female ratios, which are then truncated according to an 'equality benchmark' and a somewhat elaborate weighting procedure,[2] which makes interpretation of the index and comparisons over time difficult. The index originally used gender gaps as well as female-specific measures, such as the number of years a woman has been head of state. It has been revised over time to address criticisms, so that the GGI now takes into account only the ratios of achievement between women and men and no longer includes women-specific measures. This index also relies on the HDR's estimated earned incomes, which suffer various limitations as discussed above.

In 2000, A. Geske Dijkstra and Lucia C. Hanmer (2000) developed the Relative Status of Women Index (RSWI). This index focuses only on the relative scores between men and women by taking their arithmetic mean in the three components of health, education, and income (the same three as the HDI). Lourdes Benería and Inaki Permanyer (2010) describe the RSWI as one of the 'simplest and most appealing' indices presented in the literature thus so far. It has the advantage of measuring gender gaps without taking into account countries' overall development levels. The values of RSWI are also only weakly related to income levels, thus addressing one of the criticisms of the GDI. However, because the index allows for 'full compensation', higher achievement in one dimension can fully offset lower achievement in another, which may not be desirable if the different dimensions have different intrinsic value. Use of the arithmetic mean for the ratios of men's and women's achievements can also lead to nonintuitive results because it is an additive function, while the ratios are multiplicative. And, because the gender gaps favoring men and women are all combined in a single formula, it is not possible to identify the level of contribution of each of the three subcomponents to the overall levels of gender inequality (Permanyer, 2009).

The OECD's Social Institutions and Gender Index (SIGI), published in 2009, takes a different approach, focusing on critical societal norms and institutions that affect how women fare – using family code, physical integrity, son preference, civil liberties, and ownership rights. It has been applied to 102 non-OECD countries. The SIGI is built around the overarching concept of social institutions, and therefore is focused not on gendered outcomes but rather on gendered institutions and processes. Because of this, it encompasses a range of issues largely ignored by other indices. A key criticism of the index, similar to the GEI, is that confusion in interpretation can occur due to the combination of different sorts of indicators; some reflect a comparison of the positions of women and men and others focus on the restriction of the rights of girls and women while making no contrast to the situations of boys and men.

New in 2010 is the Economist Intelligence Unit's Women's Economic Opportunity Index (WEOI). The index involves both quantitative and qualitative indicators that measure specific attributes of the economic environment for women employees and entrepreneurs in 113 countries. There are five dimensions – labor policy and practice, women's economic opportunity, access to finance, education and training, women's legal and social status and the general business environment – which are made up of a total of 26 indicators. The overall results are the average of the scores across the five categories. As with the SIGI, the WEOI seeks to show the extent to which underlying institutions affect women's equality of access to opportunities.

Each of these gender indices makes valuable contributions to the understanding of gender disparities around the world. However, as described above, each suffers from inherent shortcomings in its empirical scope, methodology or execution. It is in this light that the UNDP has designed the new GII measure, first published in 2010. We participated in its development and design.

III   INTRODUCING THE GENDER INEQUALITY INDEX (GII)

For an index to serve as a synthetic measure of gender disparities, the point of departure must be conceptual clarity and meeting of basic methodological standards. Building on recent reviews that helpfully summarized and clarified the key critiques, we proposed a new way forward. The GII is designed to capture women's disadvantage in three dimensions – empowerment, economic activity, and reproductive health – for as many countries as data of reasonable quality allow. The GII shows the loss in human development due to inequality between female and male achievements in these dimensions. It was designed taking as its basis the association-sensitive welfare indices studied in Seth (2009), and modeled from use of harmonic and geometric means first proposed by Eduardo Zambrano (2010a, 2010b). In 2010, the global HRD estimated the GII for 138 countries. The GII captures aspects that were traditionally measured using separate empowerment and development indices. We argue, however, that the issues should be considered using a more holistic approach, and for this reason we propose one synthetic measure.

The GII usefully highlights a country's performance in the dimensions of reproductive health, empowerment, and economic participation. We selected indicators on the basis of their conceptual and practical relevance, data reliability, international comparability, reasonable country coverage, and frequency of availability. The norms, or ideals, are set at zero for the adverse reproductive health outcomes of adolescent fertility (defined as the number of births per 1,000 women ages 15–19) and maternal mortality rates, and at parity with male achievements on the education, economic, and political fronts. The score (between 0 and 1) can thus be interpreted as characterizing where a country lies in reference to normative ideals for key indicators of women's health, empowerment, and economic status. We now turn to explain the dimensions and indicators chosen for inclusion.

We carefully reviewed candidates for inclusion, bearing in mind some basic criteria for indicator selection (OECD, 2009):

- Conceptual relevance: strongly related to human development definitions and theory, so that the indicators measure what they are supposed to measure.
- Nonambiguity: simple to interpret and monotonic such that higher (lower) values of the indicator suggest better (worse) outcomes in the respective dimension.
- Reliability: based on data that have been standardized in terms of definitions, statistical quality, and processing, ideally by a single reputable organization.
- Value added: each indicator should clearly add new information not captured by the remaining indicators (should not be redundant).
- Power of discrimination: the distribution of each indicator should differentiate well between countries, especially to avoid bunching among those at the top or bottom of the distribution.

For a small number of indicators, missing values need to be modeled and imputed. In particular, while we have a better understanding of the importance of time use in thinking about well-being, and valuable data relating to this for some countries, this information is not generally available or regularly collected. The same is true of owner-

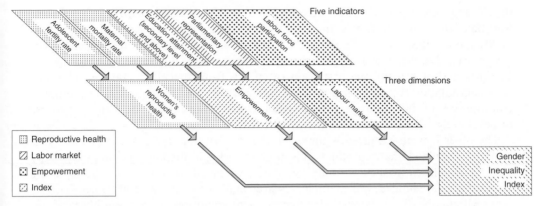

Note: The methodology of the index is presented in *Technical note 4*. The size of the boxes reflects the relative weights of the indicators and dimensions.

Source: HDRD (2010).

Figure 24.1   Components of the Gender Inequality Index

ship of economic assets by women, despite its crucial importance (see Agarwal, 1994, 2003). Another key dimension that is sadly both prevalent, but not well documented, is domestic violence. For participation in decision-making, some community level indicators would be valuable, but nothing comparable is available. Likewise, a gender breakdown of electoral turnout is available for only a handful of countries. Hence it remains very difficult to capture the political, economic and social freedoms that are inherent in women's human development. Figure 24.1 summarizes the indicators and their relative weights, all of which have reasonable country coverage (for more specifics, see Gaye et al., 2010). We then turn to a discussion and presentation of the indicators.

Reproductive Health

Two indicators are used to capture reproductive health situations. The *maternal mortality ratio* (MMR), which reflects the priority put on the well-being of women during childbirth, is a clear signal of women's status in the society. Current global estimates of maternal mortality – more than 500,000 women die each year because of complications related to childbirth – remain unacceptably high (UNICEF, 2008). The risk of death in childbirth, appallingly high in many countries around the world, could be reduced through the provision of basic education, access to contraceptives, the provision of antenatal health services, and skilled attendance at births. But such services are still denied to too many women. Many interventions that can decrease maternal mortality, such as providing women in childbirth with a trained birth attendant, are inexpensive. Some interventions, such as bans on female genital mutilation and discouraging teenage fertility and other harmful traditional practices, are less about spending and more about leadership in changing social norms. There is enormous variation in maternal mortality rates across societies, even at similar income levels. For example, Costa Rica and Iran both have a GNI (gross national income [PPP –

purchasing power parity]) of approximately $11,000, yet Iran's MMR is more than four times that of Costa Rica's. Indonesia's GNI (PPP) of $3,936 is slightly above that of Mongolia's ($3,594), yet Indonesia's MMR of 420 is more than nine times that of Mongolia's. Maternal mortality in the US is similar to Bulgaria and Lithuania and 11 times that of Ireland, the best country on this front. It is important to note that the maternal mortality ratio is a model-based estimate for the majority of developing countries where the vital registration system either is nonexistent or is in the process of developing.

The other indicator utilized is the *adolescent fertility rate* for 15–19-year-olds. This indicator highlights that reproduction is not only risky, it often begins too early. Many girls have children at such a young age that their health is compromised and future opportunities are limited. For example, research in Mexico among poor women suggests that early childbearing is associated with poor living conditions, lower monthly earnings, and decreased child nutrition (Buvinic, 1998; Greene, 2008).

Bearing a child while very young may reflect a lack of meaningful options outside of taking on the role of mother. Premature pregnancy and motherhood pose considerable health, economic, and social risks to teenage girls. Early childbearing tends to prevent them from achieving a higher level of education, and often destines them to low-skilled jobs at best. The younger a girl is when she becomes pregnant, the greater the health risks for herself and her baby. Maternal deaths related to pregnancy and childbirth are an important cause of mortality for girls aged 15–19 worldwide, accounting for nearly 70,000 deaths each year. The risk of death during childbirth is five times higher in teenage births, in part because their bodies are not yet fully developed (Rowbottom, 2007).

Empowerment

Education, especially higher levels of attainment, brings empowerment because it strengthens people's capacity to question, reflect and act on one's condition and increases access to the information needed to do so. Educated women are more likely to enjoy satisfying work, to use their voices in public debate, to be able to care for their own health and that of their family, and to take other initiatives. In this light, education is particularly important in strengthening the agency of women. Women's education also has instrumental importance for economic growth and children's health by fostering the capacity to absorb new information on health, nutrition, and hygiene, and to stimulate and facilitate children's learning (Desai, 2010). For example, a study in rural Zimbabwe revealed that education and paid work positively affected the likelihood that a woman will access contraception and antenatal care (Becker, 1997). The degree to which families decide to ensure that girls receive as much education as boys is affected by their perception of future job opportunities available for educated versus noneducated offspring (Clemens, 2004).

Our second indicator is the *share of female and male seats in parliament*. Women have traditionally been disadvantaged throughout the world in the political arena, at all levels of government. Unfortunately the measures available in this area are sparse. Estimates for parliamentary representation at the national level reflect women's visibility in political leadership and society more generally, and the extent to which women can hold high offices. While this measure has the broadest country coverage, it excludes political participation at the community and local levels.

There are other crucial elements of empowerment, but internationally comparable measures do not exist. For example, violence against women, both inside and outside the home, is an important and revealing issue, but it is not internationally measured with consistency and comparability. General insecurity, including strife, can also pose particular risks to women's physical safety as well as their participation in society, but here too we do not have the data.

Labor Market

In measuring economic activity, we decided to rely on *female and male labor force participation rates*. While some women choose not to participate in the formal labor market, or drop out to attend to unpaid family care responsibilities (care of children and/or elderly family members), relative labor force participation can be taken to reflect the degree of economic activity of women versus men. However, we know that much of women's work, especially in the home and in family businesses, is unpaid, and that women's informal work is undercounted, thus labor force participation does not accurately reflect women's work efforts. Further, it is well known that there are significant barriers to women's full participation in the economy. We also know, for example, that the gender wage gap persists at around 17 percent in OECD countries, ranging from 38 percent in South Korea to 9 percent in Belgium (OECD, 2009). Gender segregation in the workforce remains a daunting barrier to equality. Women's representation in occupations that have decision-making responsibilities – managers and analysts – falls well below that of men's. Women are also more likely to work in the service industry than men. In Latin America, 80 percent of women versus 45 percent of men work in services (Desai, 2010).

Labor force participation, as traditionally measured, ignores the important contributions of women in unpaid work and may perpetuate the undervaluing of these critical activities. Unfortunately data are too scarce to remedy these issues. Data on earned incomes and consumption are especially weak at the global level. Per capita consumption data, when available, do not account for inequalities in intrahousehold distribution of resources. The unemployment rate was considered but was ultimately dismissed due to the fact that this is not well measured and, in poor countries, is largely an urban phenomenon. Few rural women tend to be counted among the unemployed and the urban informal sector also tends to be excluded. Finally, we do recognize that some of the indicators will not have much intertemporal variation, in part due to infrequent measurement. In particular this is the case for the education indicators and maternal mortality ratios.

IV APPLICATION OF THE GENDER INEQUALITY INDEX

The GII is calculated for 138 countries around the world in the 2010 HDR, covering all regions and parts of the HDI spectrum. The results reveal that gender inequalities substantially erode human development achievements in all countries and regions, but with significant variation. Table 24.1 summarizes the regional and world average losses due to gender inequality and the losses experienced in some of the key dimensions measured by

Table 24.1 Regional losses due to gender inequality

	GII value	Maternal mortality ratio	Adolescent fertility rate	Seats in parliament, %	Labor force participation rate	
					Female	Male
Region						
Developed						
OECD	0.317	8	19.4	20.6	65.5	80.1
Non-OECD	0.376	16	11.2	18.1	58.2	82.3
Developing						
Arab states	0.699	238	42.6	8.7	27.0	78.2
East Asia & the Pacific	0.467	126	18.1	19.8	70.1	84.5
Europe & Central Asia	0.498	41	28.2	12.5	58.6	75.0
Latin America & the Caribbean	0.609	122	72.6	17.5	55.3	83.3
South Asia	0.739	454	65.0	10.4	37.2	84.2
Sub-Saharan Africa	0.735	881	122.3	17.3	63.8	82.3
2010 HDI Categories						
Very high	0.319	8	19.1	20.5	65.3	80.2
High	0.571	82	47.7	13.3	52.7	79.5
Medium	0.591	242	41.8	16.0	54.7	84.1
Low	0.748	822	108.9	14.4	61.3	83.4
Least developed	0.746	786	104.5	16.6	64.7	85.2
World	0.560	273	53.7	16.2	56.8	82.6

Note: The maternal mortality ratio is defined as deaths per 100,000 live births. The adolescent fertility rate is defined as the number of births per 1,000 women aged 15–19 years. The years for the data are 2008 for the GII, seats in parliament, and labor force participation. We use the latest available data for maternal mortality (2003–08) and adolescent fertility (1990–2008).

Source: Authors' calculations based on HDRs.

the GII.[3] The estimated global loss due to gender inequality is 56 percent, with the largest losses concentrated in South Asia, Sub-Saharan Africa and the Arab states. The group averages range from 32 percent in developed OECD countries to 74 percent in South Asia.

With an average loss due to gender inequality of 74 percent, South Asia has the worst losses of any region. Women lag behind men across each of the dimensions captured, and most notably in national parliamentary representation, education and labor force participation. Maternal mortality also tends to be high, with an average of 454 deaths per 100,000 live births. All the countries in the region perform poorly on the GII – most notably Afghanistan, Bangladesh, India, and Nepal – each with GII scores above 70 percent. The Maldives and Sri Lanka and perform somewhat better, with respective losses of 54 and 60 percent.

In Sub-Saharan Africa, significant gender disparities in education and high maternal mortality and adolescent fertility rates – which are the highest in the world – contribute to the region's 74 percent loss in potential human development due to gender inequality (only 0.4 percent less than the loss suffered in South Asia). The worst-performing countries are the Democratic Republic of Congo, Mali, and Niger (losses of 80–81 percent in each case) due to poor performance across each of the dimensions, most particularly reproductive health. The Democratic Republic of Congo has an MMR of 1,100 deaths and adolescent fertility rate (AFR) of 201 births; Niger has an MMR of 1,800 deaths and AFR of 158 births; and Mali has an MMR of 970 deaths and AFR of 170 births, compared to the regional average MMR of 881 deaths and AFR of 122 births. Mauritius and Burundi perform relatively better, with respective losses of 47 and 63 percent.

Women in the Arab states are affected by unequal labor force participation, which is only around half the global average, and poor educational attainment; less than one-third of women over the age of 25 have completed secondary education. Tertiary enrollment for women is relatively high, however, and with an increase of 45 percentage points since 1970, it now exceeds that of men in the Arab states; there are 132 females for every 100 males in tertiary education.

At the other end of the spectrum, the developed OECD countries top the list as being closer to gender equality, with eight countries registering less than 25 percent loss in human development due to gender inequality: the Netherlands, Denmark, Sweden, Switzerland, Norway, Belgium, Germany, and Finland. The gap in labor force participation remains marked, however, standing at about 66 percent for women as compared to 80 percent for men.

Countries in Europe and Central Asia have few women in parliament, though they are close to parity in educational attainment and employment, and they have low maternal mortality ratios. For example, in Lithuania, fewer than one in five parliamentarians are women, but the maternal mortality ratio is low (11 deaths per 100,000 births), secondary education rates are high, and two-thirds of women participate in the labor market compared with about three in four men.

Overall, regional patterns reveal that reproductive health is the largest contributor to gender inequality around the world. Women in Sub-Saharan Africa suffer the most in this dimension, followed by South Asia, the Arab states, Latin America, and the Caribbean. The Arab states and South Asia also exhibit relatively weak female empowerment and unequal labor force participation.

At the country level the GII ranges from 17 percent (Netherlands) to 85 percent

(Yemen). But tremendous variation in gender inequality exists. With a GII of 17 percent, the Netherlands is the country which is closest to gender equality. The country has very low maternal mortality (6 deaths per 100,000 births), among the world's lowest adolescent fertility rate (3.8 births per 1,000 women ages 15–19), and is close to parity in educational attainment, political participation, and employment. Yemen is the country at the other end of the spectrum, with a GII score of 85 percent. Only 20 percent of women in Yemen are in the labor force, women hold less than 1 percent of seats in parliament and only 8 percent of the female population have attended secondary school. The country also has a high maternal mortality ratio of 430 deaths per 100,000 births and an adolescent fertility rate of 68 births per 1,000 women.

The bottom 10 countries (in descending order) are Cameroon, Côte d'Ivoire, Liberia, Central African Republic, Papua New Guinea, Afghanistan, Mali, Niger, the Democratic Republic of Congo, and Yemen, with an average GII of 0.79. Saudi Arabia is another country with high gender inequality, and which is an interesting case. The country shows high human development, with a global HDI ranking of 55, an HDI of 0.75 and income per capita of nearly $25,000. However, despite good female educational attainment, women are nearly absent from parliament, and female labor force participation rates are only one-fourth those for men, giving the country a GII value of 0.76, and a ranking of 128 out of 138 countries. For the bottom 20 countries, the average maternal mortality ratio is about 915 deaths per 100,000 live births and the adolescent fertility rate is 111 births per 1,000 women ages 15–19, both well above the global averages of 273 deaths and 54 births. Moreover, there is only one woman for every eight men in parliament.

It is also interesting to compare the results to the inequality-adjusted HDI. In doing so, we find a strong correlation (0.87) between gender inequality and the loss due to inequality in the distribution of the HDI, suggesting that countries experiencing unequal distribution of human development also experience high inequality between men and women and vice versa (though there are exceptions). Eight of the 10 best-performing countries in terms of gender equality are also among the 20 countries that experience the smallest losses in human development due to inequality.

V   COMPARING RESULTS WITH OTHER GENDER INDICES

As noted above, the various gender indices measure gender inequality in different ways, and because the underlying conceptual frameworks differ, so too do the results. Still, given the commonality of objectives, it is interesting to review and contrast the results and pictures which emerge. We do this for the GDI and GEM, GGI, GEI, SIGI, and WEOI. There are 93 countries for which the GII, GDI, and GEM are calculated and we find very little rank-order correlation between the three indices – only 0.4. The different method of aggregation, which reduces the extent to which a high achievement in one dimension can compensate for a low achievement in another, partly explains this lack of correlation.

The comparison of GDI rank and GII rank shows some interesting results, shown in Figure 24.2. For example, the Republic of Moldova gains 41 places, China 29 places and Vietnam 23 places on the GII as compared to the GDI. The gain results mainly from relatively low maternal mortality and adolescent fertility rates combined with high levels

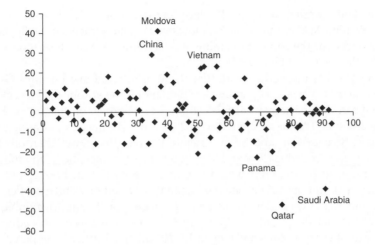

Source: Authors' computation based on data from the 2009 and 2010 HDRs.

Figure 24.2 Difference of GDI and GII ranks

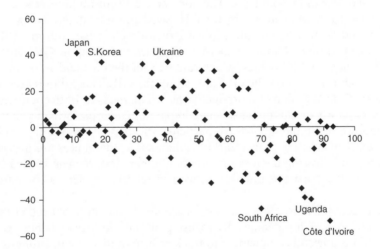

Source: Authors' computation based on data from the 2009 and 2010 HDRs.

Figure 24.3 Difference of GEM and GII ranks

of female labor force participation. Also, Qatar and Saudi Arabia lose 47 and 39 places, respectively. The huge loss is largely explained by relatively low female labor force participation rates and the absence of females in parliament. Absence of income from the measure also erodes advantages these countries had previously on the income dimension of the GDI.

In contrast, different rankings emerge relative to the GEM, due to more variation, arrayed in Figure 24.3. Côte d'Ivoire, South Africa, and Uganda fare poorly worse on the GII, losing 52, 45, and 40 places in rank, respectively. But Japan gains 41 places and

South Korea and Ukraine each gain 36 places in rank. Both Côte d'Ivoire and Uganda have relatively high MMR and AFR; and low female achievements in higher education. The reverse is true for the countries gaining in rank. South Africa's loss in rank is mainly explained by the relatively high MMR.

In looking at other measures, recall that the World Economic Forum's GGI differs from the GII in that it measures gender gaps but ignores the absolute achievements. This is useful, but can also be somewhat misleading. For example, on this index, Lesotho is in eighth position of 128 (as compared to 102 on the GII), ahead of, among others, the United States, Switzerland, and Spain, despite the fact that fewer than one-fourth of women have secondary education and almost one in 10 women die in childbirth. Hence the picture revealed by the GGI would appear to be partial, at best. Similarly South Africa comes in at number 12, despite the fact that only half of women participate in the labor force and one in every 250 women will die in childbirth; and Mozambique, at 22, regardless of the fact that less than 2 percent of women have secondary education and almost 150 out of every 1,000 women aged 15–19 will give birth, as compared to 82 and 111, respectively, on the GII.

The GEI provides a comparison of gender equity across countries, but as noted above the objective is to provide a ranking and not to capture the absolute levels of gender inequality within countries. The top- and bottom-ranking countries on the GEI are similar to those identified by the GII: Sweden, Finland, and Norway are all in the top five, and Yemen, Benin, and Côte d'Ivoire are all in the bottom 10. There are, however, some surprises: Rwanda ranks 5 on the GEI, but 83 on the GII. Other notable differences include the Philippines, which ranks 13 on the GEI and 78 on the GII, and Colombia which ranks 18 on the GEI and 95 on the GII. These differences appear to arise because of the inclusion of reproductive health on the GII. Both countries perform relatively very poorly on this dimension as compared to their performance in the dimensions of empowerment and labor force participation. It is also useful to recall that the GII is association sensitive. This clearly highlights that the indices are measuring different things, one showing the loss to potential human development caused by gender inequality, and the other the situation of women relative to men as compared across countries.

The SIGI, as noted above, does not assess gendered outcomes, but rather the institutions that influence such outcomes. By focusing on the root causes behind gender inequalities, SIGI is a useful complement to track reforms and social institutions affecting the gender-based inequalities measured by the GII. In 2009, the top five SIGI countries (out of 102 non-OECD countries) suffering the lowest discrimination in social institutions were Paraguay, Croatia, Kazakhstan, Argentina, and Costa Rica; in contrast, these country rankings on the GII are 85, 30, 67, 60, and 51, respectively. Such contrasting results underline the need to examine why countries making strong institutional and policy efforts to promote gender equity still experience significant losses in human development due to gender inequality. This may raise issues around implementation, cultural and other constraints, as well as questions about the time needed for reforms to take effect.

Finally, the recently released WEOI, like the SIGI, focuses on the institutions that affect women's participation, in this case relating to women's economic opportunities. Specifically, the WEOI considers the laws, regulations, practices, customs, and attitudes that allow women to participate in the workforce under conditions roughly equal to men, whether as wage-earning employees or as owners of a business. One data-related constraint is that the focus is limited to the formal sector, which means that the measure likely provides better insights for developed countries and urban elites in developing countries than for developing countries more generally. Nonetheless it is notable that the top five ranked countries on the WEOI (Sweden, Belgium, Norway, Finland, and Germany) are also in the top 10 on the GII. And four of the bottom five (Togo, Côte d'Ivoire, Yemen, and Sudan) also score poorly on the GII, with rankings of 115, 130, 138, and 106, respectively.

VI CONCLUSION

Significant progress has been made in measuring women's status and well-being. However, substantial challenges remain. First, there is a lack of gender-disaggregated data for many important aspects of women's status and well-being. Second, even when there are measures available for many countries, they may not be available for those countries where gender is a particularly salient issue. Third, time-series data for indicators measured consistently are usually not available. Finally, in order for international comparisons to be meaningful, consistent measures are needed. Some of the more interesting aspects of gender – including property ownership, participation in community life and decision-making, seats on boards, and gender-based violence – are not included in any of the indices.

The GII is unique in that it focuses on critical issues of educational attainment, economic and political participation, as well as female-specific health issues. None of the pre-existing gender gap measures incorporates a reproductive health indicator, which is very pertinent to the other choices women can make. Adolescent fertility raises important questions of whether young women have access to contraceptives and to sex education to help them make informed choices. The GII methodology thus allows us to combine issues where women's status is considered in relation to men's with issues where a male counterpart does not exist, namely reproductive health. In sum, by casting important light on gender disparities in health, empowerment, and labor market participation across countries, the GII yields new and important insights. It shows that some societies disadvantage women in critical dimensions, thereby pointing to the need for more proactive public policies. By looking at the component indicators, the GII shines a spotlight on areas needing critical policy intervention, thereby enhancing economic life and well-being.

In her study comparing major cross-country gender indices, Irene Van Staveren (2014) found high correlation between pairs of several indices (correlation cofficients of all pairs). There are indeed distinct parallels. Yet when it comes to choosing specific measures to be included in an index, the overlap is relatively low. This means that, as we have shown, there is some consistency in evaluating outcomes in regard to gender disparity. But it also means that policy-makers need to take care in their choice of index for policy analysis.

NOTES

* This chapter is excerpted and revised from a longer United Nations Development Programme (UNDP) study: 'Measuring key disparities in human development: the Gender Inequality Index', by Amie Gaye, Jeni Klugman, Milorad Kovacevic, Sarah Twigg and Eduardo Zambrano, Human Development and Research Paper 10/46 Washington, DC: (2010). For more on the methodology of the Gender Inequality Index and other country specifies, readers should consult the original source.

1. There are generally four dimensions of women's empowerment identified in the literature: economic, human and social, political, and cultural. (For a discussion, see Kabeer, 2005; Ibrahim and Alkire, 2007; and Luttrell et al., 2009.)

2. For example, the GGI's data driven weighting scheme assigns higher weights to indicators with lower standard deviations relative to those of other indicators of the same conceptual dimension, and the weighting scheme calculated for the 2006 index is used in subsequent versions of the index. But it is unclear, for example, why a ban on women holding seats in parliament in a certain country should be considered less of a problem simply because many other countries also have a similar ban (see Hawken and Munck, 2009).

3. Country classifications are based on HDI quartiles. A country is in the very high group if its HDI is in the top quartile, in the high group if its HDI is in percentiles 51–75, in the medium group if its HDI is in percentiles 26–50 and in the low group if its HDI is in the bottom quartile.

REFERENCES

Abdullah, Rashida (2000), *A Framework on Indicators for Action on Women's Health Needs and Rights after Beijing*, Kuala Lumpur, Malaysia: Asian-Pacific Resource and Research Centre for Women.

Agarwal, Bina (1994), 'Gender and command over property: a critical gap in economic analysis and policy in South Asia', *Journal World Development*, **22**(10), 1455–78.

Agarwal, Bina (2003), 'Gender and land rights revisited: exploring new prospects via the state, family and market', *Journal of Agrarian Change*, **3**(1/2), 184–224.

Becker, Stan (1997), 'Incorporating women's empowerment in studies of reproductive health: an example from Zimbabwe', paper presented at the Seminar on Female Empowerment and Demographic Processes, Lund, Sweden, April, 20–24.

Benería, Lourdes and Inaki Permanyer (2010), 'The measurement of socio-economic gender inequality revisited', *Development and Change*, **41**(3), 375–99.

Buvinic, Mayra (1998), 'The costs of adolescent childbearing: evidence from Chile, Barbados, Guatemala, and Mexico', *Studies in Family Planning*, **29**(2), 201–9.

Clemens, Michael A. (2004), 'The long walk to school: international education goals in historical perspective', Working Paper 37, Center for Global Development, Washington, DC.

Desai, Manisha (2010), 'Hope in hard times: women's empowerment and human development', Human Development Research Paper 14, United Nations Development Programme, Human Development Report Office, New York.

Dijkstra, A. Geske (2006), 'Towards a fresh start in measuring gender inequality: a contribution to the debate', *Journal of Human Development*, **7**(2), 275–83.

Dijkstra, A. Geske and Lucia C. Hanmer (2000), 'Measuring socio-economic gender inequality: alternative to the UNDP Gender-related Development Index', *Feminist Economics*, **6**(2), 41–75.

Gaye, Amie, Jeni Klugman, Milorad Kovasevic, Sarah Twigg and Eduardo Zambrano (2010), 'Measuring key disparities in human development: the Gender Development Index', Research Paper 2010/46, UNDP, New York.

Greene, Margaret E. (2008), 'Poor health, poor women. How reproductive health affects poverty', Woodrow Wilson International Center for Scholars, *Focus*, Issue 16, Washington, DC.

Hawken, Angela and Gerardo L. Munck (2009), 'Cross-national indices with gender-differentiated data: what do they measure? How valid are they?', Technical background paper for Asia Pacific Human Development Report on Gender, New York.

Ibrahim, Solava and Sabina Alkire (2007), 'Agency and empowerment: a proposal for internationally comparable indicators', OPHI Working Paper, University of Oxford, Oxford.

Kabeer, Naila (2005), 'Gender equality and women's empowerment: a critical analysis of the third millennium development goal', *Gender and Development*, **13**(1), 13–24.

Kelly, Liz, Lorna Kennedy and Miranda Horvath (2008), 'The next step: developing transnational indicators on violence against women', in Yakin Ertürk (ed.), *Addendum to the Report of the Special Rapporteur on*

Violence Against Women, its Causes and Consequences, New York: UN: General Assembly, p. A/HRC/7/6/ Add.5.

Klasen, Stephan (2004), 'Gender related indicators of well-being', UNU-WIDER Research Paper, World Institute for Development Economic Research, Helsinki.

Klasen, Stephan (2006), 'UNDP's gender-related measures: some conceptual problems and possible solutions', *Journal of Human Development and Capabilities*, **7**(2), 243–74.

Luttrell, Cecilia and Sitna Quiroz, with Claire Scrutton and Kate Bird (2009), 'Understanding and operationalising empowerment', Working Paper 308, Overseas Development Institute, London.

Organisation for Economic Co-operation and Development (OECD) (2009), *Country Profiles: Gender Equality and Social Indicators*, Paris: OECD Development Centre.

Permanyer, Inaki (2009), 'The measurement of multidimensional gender inequality: continuing the debate', *Journal of Social Indicators Research*, online ISSN 1573–02921.

Ransom, Elizabeth I. and Nancy V. Yinger (2002), *Making Motherhood Safer: Overcoming Obstacles on the Pathway to Care*, Washington, DC: Population Reference Bureau.

Rowbottom, Sara (2007), *Giving Girls Today and Tomorrow: Breaking the Cycle of Adolescent Pregnancy*, New York: United Nations Population Fund.

Schüler, Dana (2006), 'The uses and misuses of the gender-related development index and gender empowerment measures: a review of the literature', *Journal of Human Development*, **7**(2), 161–81.

Seth, Suman (2009), 'Inequality, interactions and human development', *Journal of Human Development and Capabilities*, **10**(3), 375–96.

United Nations Children's Fund (UNICEF) (2008), *Progress for Children: A Report Card on Maternal Mortality*, New York: UNICEF.

United Nations Development Programme (UNDP) (1995), *Human Development Report 1995: Gender and Human Development*, New York: UNDP.

United Nations Development Programme (UNDP) (2010), *Human Development Report 2010. The Real Wealth of Nations: Pathways to Human Development*, New York: UNDP.

Van Staveren, Irene (2014), 'To measure is to know? A comparative analysis of gender indices', *Review of Social Economy*, forthcoming.

Zambrano, Eduardo (2010a), 'Gender Inequality Do's and Don'ts', Economics Department Working Paper, California Polytechnic State University, San Luis Obispo, CA.

Zambrano, Eduardo (2010b), 'On the Measurement of Gender Inequality', Economics Department Working Paper, California Polytechnic State University, San Luis Obispo, CA.

25. Girls' schooling and the global education and development agenda
*Elaine Unterhalter and Amy North**

I INTRODUCTION

At the turn of the millennium, the project of infusing a women's rights perspective on gender and education into the global education and development agenda seemed particularly promising. However, despite economic growth, high-level political concern with the question of girls' schooling, and unprecedented levels of women's networking on gender issues, making progress on education through a framework concerned with women's rights and gender equity has been difficult.

The place of girls' schooling in the global education and development agenda suggests both an opening and a closure. There is an opening because of the emphasis given to girls' education in key frameworks, such as the Millennium Development Goals (MDGs) and the 2000 'Dakar Framework for Action – Education for All: Meeting Our Collective Commitments' (Dakar Framework, 2000; UNGEI, 2010). This means that resources and skill can be allocated to this area. Institutions can be adapted to support girls to enter school, progress, and attain well. However, there is also closure in that working to increase girls' enrollment has been seen as the only way in which a government, multilateral organization, or nongovernmental organization (NGO) might engage with gender and education issues. This limited perspective often rules out any advance of larger feminist concerns about the multidimensionality of gendered exclusion, exploitation, and subjection to violence in interconnected sites, or the development of visions of gender justice, equality, or empowerment.

This chapter shows how conceptualizations of gender equity in education have changed over the last couple of decades. Beginning with the pre-2000 focus on 'Education for All', we first discuss the problems with using access to education or parity as a measure (Section II). We then evaluate alternative indicators (Section III). In so doing, we can see that approaches to gender equity in education have evolved alongside the broader development agenda, itself a product of change. Although it highlights the struggles of translating theory to policy, our story also makes clear the importance of reconceptualizing educational policy 'success' to ensure the most benefit to girls and women around the world. Section IV concludes.

II MOVING BEYOND 'EDUCATION FOR ALL'

A major focus of the international development agenda up to 2000 was to ensure girls' access to school (see King and Hill, 1993; Chabbott, 2003; Chapman and Miske, 2007; Vaughan, 2010). In 2000, a positive, sweeping change in approach took place, partly associated with the mobilization of governments, multilateral and bilateral organizations, and many NGOs in support of the MDGs and the Dakar Framework for Action (Mundy, 2007; Unterhalter, 2007). The global policy framework associated with both the MDGs and the Dakar Framework moved beyond gender parity, though the meanings of gender that were invoked remained limited. At the same time, a parallel process associated with the 1995 Beijing Declaration and Platform for Action led to many organizations trying to use gender mainstreaming to link ideas and action (Verloo, 2007; Unterhalter et al., 2010b). Gender mainstreaming is an organizational strategy developed to prevent or overcome the neglect, or side-streaming, of women's issues, and to ensure that these become the concern of whole organizations that set out to structure their major goals around gender equality (Rai, 2008). This promised a more expansive engagement with questions of empowerment; but this transformational approach was very difficult to realize in practice, partly because of entrenched and exclusionary power in organizations, partly because of weak links with organizations concerned with women's rights and gender justice, and partly because ideas about gender appeared easily co-optable to agendas particularly concerned with maintaining the status quo.

The literature that discusses global gender-policy frameworks in action highlights a number of problems. First, there is the problem of purpose and realizability. Do global frameworks, even those fully engaged with questions of rights and gender justice, adequately distill the wide range of issues that feminist activists raise? Given that the gender and education global frameworks are much narrower than those dealing with gender and women's rights, can the existing frameworks be used as a stepping stone to a more substantive discussion of gender equality, or are they inherently flawed and compromised? Furthermore, do what is measured, the indicators selected, and the forms of value these bestow limit the use of these frameworks to realize substantive equality?

In addition to these questions related to purpose and realizability is a second problem highlighted by many authors – namely, the problem of multiple actors and diffuse conceptual resources. This means, in practice, that work on gender and education often fails to deliver on a feminist project. Third, there is a problem of existing global power formations, which means that very limited resources have been committed to work on gender equality in education, in contrast to those expended, for example, on war or the support of profligate financial institutions. The enormous optimism associated with the Beijing conference and the benefit of the doubt that a number of feminists accorded the MDGs were subject to considerable pressure after 2001, as global political agendas focused on issues of security, national growth, and the financial crisis, with scant attention to women's rights.

The question of the purpose and realizability of global frameworks on gender equality and education has generated sharp debate. From 2000 onward, commentators on women's rights have looked critically at the MDGs and Education for All (EFA) for what was left out, while, at the same time, some have acknowledged that they provide a platform to take forward elements of the vision of the Beijing Platform for Action (Antrobus, 2004; Aikman and Unterhalter, 2005; Kabeer, 2005; Grown et al., 2006; Unterhalter, 2007). For a number of writers, the very idea of the frameworks was flawed, distracting attention from the grassroots work that needed to be done (Antrobus, 2004; Cornwall et al., 2007). For others, the rigidity of the directives and lack of space for local processes were problematic. The MDG framework as a whole might be read as an example of what Frances Vavrus (2003) has called a view of the 'feminist modern', 'who takes an active role in controlling her fertility, practicing safe sex, and protecting the environment' (p.41). In problematizing this view of empowered, educated women, she points out that '[d]espite the desirability of such a scenario, however, women's choices about childbearing, reproductive health, and environmental conservation are shaped by social and political–economic considerations that the independent figure of the feminist modern does not take into account' (p.41).

At the heart of this critique is the notion that global development agendas are too far away from local conditions. They provide little guidance in negotiating the specifics of gender inequalities and affirming the localized elements of equality. As Obioma Nnaemeka (2003) argues with regard to feminism in Africa, one needs to understand the complexity and nuance of local spaces in order to realize forms of gender equality. She delineates what she terms 'Nego-feminism', which she sees emerging from a cultural and political space, a 'terrain that allows for the interplay of resistances and realizations' (p.377). Her account talks about 'when, where and how to negotiate with patriarchy' (p.377), and suggests ways in which her idea about negotiation may resonate with ideas about empowerment. But at the heart of the analysis is a conviction that the global development agenda is quite out of key with local politics and practice.

Among those who have argued for a strategic engagement with the MDGs and EFA, there are also criticisms and concerns (for example, Vandemootele, 2004; Unterhalter, 2005b). For instance, MDG2 aims to achieve universal primary education; its target entails that by 2015 all children will have completed primary school. The indicators comprise net enrollment ratios in primary school, the proportion of children who complete a primary cycle, and the literacy rate of 15–24-year-old women and men (UN, 2010). MDG3 aims to promote gender equality and empower women; its associated target is to eliminate gender disparity at all levels of education. The indicators are the ratio of girls to boys in primary, secondary, and tertiary education (gender parity), the share of women in wage employment in the nonagricultural sector, and the proportion of seats held by women in national parliaments (ibid.). The Dakar Framework for Action (2000) provided for a wider engagement with gender equity in education than the MDGs, in that together, its six goals draw attention to a range of sites of gender inequality, from the lack of provision of early childhood education, to low levels of adult literacy, to the nature of learning. However, the specific gender goal is cast in terms of gender parity in primary and secondary education. The limitations of the indicator frameworks associated with global gender and education policy of the MDGs and EFA have been an area of intense discussion around questions of strategic engagement and whether shifts can occur in the rather narrow conceptions of gender equality that the frameworks articulate (Subrahamanian, 2005; Unterhalter, 2007; Connell, 2010).

Gender parity in enrollment, attendance, or completion is easy to measure, even though it may be based on bogus numbers. Figures on this are relatively easily generated from attendance registers or exam results, although these may bear little relation to the numbers of children actually at school and completing a grade or cycle. For example, in Ghana, where schools receive a capitation fee based on the number of children attending, they regularly record more than 100 percent attendance, and it is recognized by the government that these statistics are not meaningful. Gender parity is thus the most ubiquitous indicator, but focusing on measuring the levels of gender parity in schooling obscures the importance of measuring more complex forms of gender inequality in school and beyond (Unterhalter et al., 2005, 2010a; Unterhalter, 2007). Gender parity in school enrollment, as many commentators acknowledge, is not the same as gender equality, which entails wider concerns with rights in and through education (Subrahamanian, 2005; Unterhalter, 2005a; Dunne, 2009; Para-Mallam, 2010).

A further critique is that the minimal thresholds in schooling required by the MDGs are too limited; focusing only on all children completing primary schooling or the improved proportions of young adults achieving literacy leaves major areas of inadequate education provision unaddressed. There is no threshold with regard to adult literacy, for example, although the majority of the world's population who lack adequate education are women over age 24 (UNESCO, 2010). No indicator is concerned with learning in conditions that are free from gender-based violence, even though this is a significant feature constraining girls' dignity and achievement (Leach and Mitchell, 2006; Parkes and Chege, 2010). With only the very limited concern of increasing the numbers of women in secondary and tertiary education suggested by the indicators for MDG3, there is very little incentive to mobilize global collaboration to increase gender equality in secondary education. Although the very first review by a UN task team of MDG3 suggested a revision of indicators to track girls' progression to secondary school (Birdsall et al., 2005), this was not incorporated into the general MDG framework.

The lack of attention to increasing women's access to secondary and tertiary education places limits on what can be achieved in the other MDGs; for example, the achievement of many of the health MDGs requires higher levels of education for the population, but there was no process within the MDG framework to encourage synergies across sectors (Waage et al., 2010). Similarly, the MDG indicator documenting women's share of wage employment in the nonagricultural sector misses major areas of women's work in the informal and care economy, so it is not a particularly good proxy for measuring empowerment through education (Kabeer, 2005). Furthermore, women's share of seats in national parliaments might indicate opportunities for particular elites and provide little information on whether or not women participate in decision-making in other sites (ibid.). Thus, the indicator frameworks, in specifying minimal levels, miss important dimensions of gender equality and women's rights and fail to realize the connection between education and other areas of social and political development.

The Dakar Framework does not suggest these minimum thresholds in education, but by focusing only on education, it failed to make important connections to a wider social-development agenda and alliances with other women's rights activists. In reflecting on what achieving the vision of the Dakar Framework would mean, Sheila Aikman and Elaine Unterhalter (2005) suggested that this entailed, at a minimum, schooling for all children. However, they went on to argue that the links between improved education quality and gender equality will be made only in part, because attention will be focused on the formal education system, to the exclusion of wider societal considerations. Schools may receive resources to implement education reforms, and school–community relations may be improved through the work of school councils and by enhanced training for teachers in gender equality, as well as increased numbers of female teachers. But the vital linkages across and between sectors will remain fragile.

In the 10 years since the Dakar 2000 conference, a number of studies have confirmed this assessment and some of the effects of a lack of integrated work. The UNESCO

Global Monitoring Report in 2010 drew attention to some of the gender issues associated with a focus on the aggregate expansion of enrollments with inadequate attention to regional and other inequalities. For example, in Pakistan in 2006, girls accounted for 60 percent of the children out of school; being a girl from a rural area in one of Cambodia's hill provinces increased the chance of not attending school by a factor of five; and in Nigeria, only 12 percent of poor Hausa girls from rural areas attended school. Ethnic discrimination might play a key part in understanding the social exclusion of girls from school, argued Maureen Lewis and Marlaine Lockheed (2007), although the details of how ethnicity is accounted for at the local level raise many questions and point to a need for refined work in policy and practice (Aikman and Unterhalter, 2013). Limited policy and completely inadequate professional training for teachers, civil servants, and NGO workers to understand the particular dynamics of poverty and gender in relation to schooling have been a significant hurdle in realizing EFA (Rose and Dyer, 2008; Unterhalter, 2012). The lack of policy attention to gender-based violence, despite its significance for schooling as highlighted in a range of studies, was a matter of concern (Leach and Mitchell, 2006; Dunne, 2009; Parkes and Chege, 2010). Additionally, there were reduced synergies between different phases of education, because the expansion of provision for women in universities took place without adequate attention to sexual harassment and rape or to features of exclusion associated with age, disability, or socio-economic status (Morley et al., 2009). Thus, the Dakar Framework expanded some elements of the narrow MDG education and gender agenda, but it did not touch key areas of women's rights and gender justice.

III   EVALUATING ALTERNATIVE MEASURES

In response to some of the critiques of purpose and realizability associated with the MDGs and EFA, a number of additional measures that go beyond gender parity have been developed. The Education for All Development Index (EDI) formulated for the UNESCO *Global Monitoring Report* in 2004 set the parity measure in a wider context that related to the four most easily quantifiable EFA goals: universal primary education, adult literacy, gender equality, and education quality. The gender component of the EDI and the gender-specific EFA index (GEI) were calculated by averaging the gender-parity indices (GPIs) of the gross enrollment ratios (GERs) at the primary and secondary levels and the gender-parity measure for adult literacy. Although the 2010 *Global Monitoring Report* recognizes that the GEI, as it stands, 'does not sufficiently reflect the equality aspect of the EFA gender goal' (UNESCO, 2010, p. 283), it does go a little beyond straight measures of gender parity at a particular school level as an indicator of equality.

In 2010, the *Global Monitoring Report* team developed the Deprivation and Marginalization in Education (DME) dataset, which allows for a much more nuanced understanding of intersecting inequalities. It documents some different dimensions of marginalization using a number of measures, including education poverty and extreme education poverty, and there is some capacity to look at gender, although the major focus is on girls and not the relational dynamic (UNESCO, 2010). Thus, the *Global Monitoring Report* has continued to comment on the gender aspects of education framed by the concerns of the Dakar Framework, looking at women teachers, the representation of girls in textbooks, and the numbers of girls and boys progressing through school, but in a limited fashion, not exploring the complexity of gender relations in school and beyond – or, as Joan DeJaeghere and Soo Kyong Lee (2011) point out, the complexity of discriminatory norms and conditions that perpetuate marginality. In developing an innovative scorecard on gender equality in education in seven countries in South Asia, Swati Narayan et al. (2010) graded countries using a number of indicators relating to five domains, which were identified as being important for securing gender equality in education: political will; transparency in governance; capabilities for basic education; education infrastructure, inputs, and incentives; and the overall gender-equality environment. While these expanded measures take account of some of the criticisms of measuring only what is easy, they do not address the critiques of education measures being detached from other areas of gender discrimination and social development.

Outside the education research community, a number of authors have worked on composite gender indicators in an attempt to respond to the multiple ways in which gender inequalities structure work, care, leisure, and status. Interestingly, however, the more developed their understanding of sites of gender inequalities, the less they appear to take account of education. Janneke Plantenga et al. (2009) developed a European Gender Equality Index with dimensions for equal sharing of paid work (labor force participation and unemployment), equal sharing of money (pay and income), equal sharing of decision-making (gender gaps in parliaments and in ranked occupations), and equal sharing of time in caring for children and leisure. However, education is not one of the selected dimensions. Similarly, the Organization for Economic Cooperation and Development's (OECD, 2009) Social Institutions and Gender Index (SIGI) assesses each country in relation to 12 social-institution variables, which do not include education. The Global Gender Gap Index does benchmark national gender gaps on economic, political, education, and health criteria (Hausmann et al., 2006) and country rankings allow for comparisons across time, regions, and income groups. The methodology intends to capture gaps in outcome rather than input variables. Educational attainment gaps are expressed through ratios of women to men in primary, secondary, and tertiary enrollments, and the ratio of the female-to-male literacy rate. However, as enrollment is not a very good measure of educational outcome, the education gender gap in this index is quite markedly understated. These more complex measures suggest a fruitful area for further work on gender and education indicators, but the global gender and education community has been slow to engage with this field.

This reluctance has some difficult consequences. Relatively straightforward forms of measurement associated with the MDGs and the Dakar Framework have meant that more complex relationships of inequality have not been addressed, and approaches to redress gender injustice have been allocated little value. It appears that a widely endorsed view is that the more limited the purpose of the global framework, the easier it is deemed to realize goals and measure impact (Gore, 2009). However, easy measures have meant that many substantive questions relating to equality and justice have been left behind.

A second set of issues that critical commentators raise are that even apparently simple frameworks to increase the numbers of girls in school and realize a form of gender equity have not been easy to realize. Competing conceptualizations and the elasticity of the word 'gender' mean that governments or organizations might have in mind only limited aims to enroll girls in school, despite giving rhetorical endorsement to frameworks concerned with rights (Unterhalter, 2007; Greany, 2008; Unterhalter and North, 2011). The challenge of multiple actors and contrasting conceptual and policy languages means that realizability is often more elusive than real; for instance, the difficulties that education departments encounter when they work with other social-development departments have been highlighted in a number of countries (Rose, 2005; Chapman and Miske, 2007; Karlsson, 2010). In addition, employment opportunities for women teachers have expanded, but realizing wider gender-equality rights remains challenging (Kirk, 2009). Girls might attend school, but often they encounter forms of violence associated with gender-inequitable family and community relationships (Parkes and Chege, 2010).

Many studies document similar challenges of realizability, because of the multiple actors and discourses engaged in social reform (for some collections see Robinson-Pant, 2004; Fennell and Arnot, 2007; Maslak, 2007; Kirk, 2009). It is impossible to draw out all the threads of analysis, but recurring themes concern the difficulties of realizing ambitious aims for gender equality in schools and communities where wider inequalities are reproduced and where there is limited support for change. Conversely, a number of studies show how alliances are built to challenge gender inequality in school, but many of these report on small-scale initiatives (Doggett, 2005; Gordon, 2008; Stromquist and Fischman, 2009). Even governments that have a strong commitment to gender-equality policy find it difficult to affect change in every school (Unterhalter, 2012).

However, the difficulties of implementation appear to have generated work that is neither cynical nor evades political confrontations, but is rather concerned to develop feminist visions in education that take account of empowerment (Monkman, 2011), different forms of equity (Unterhalter, 2009), the significance of affect and care (Lynch, 2007; Lynch et al., 2009) gender justice (Molyneux and Razavi, 2002; Mukhopapadhyay and Singh, 2007), and, particularly, located experiences in classrooms and schools (Nnaemeka, 2003; Salo, 2011).

A third group of critical commentaries has looked at the global political economy and the ways that existing power relations undermine the advancement of gender equality in education. The dynamics of the global security agenda and concern to protect global capitalism very often undermine the access to school that girls and women have achieved (Mohanty, 2003; Novelli and Lopes Cardoza, 2008; Griffin, 2010). It is often enormously difficult to advance and secure specific aid or government expenditure for gender projects unless they coincide with broader geopolitical or economic objectives of large donor nations, such as the United States and the United Kingdom (Jensen et al., 2006; de la Cruz, 2009; UNESCO, 2011). Often, high-profile media 'stars' in the global North simplify the message about girls' access to school and fail to take on a wider gender-equality agenda or work with women's rights activists by associating, instead, with campaigns to promote particular products or public relations.

IV   CONCLUSION

The literature highlights problems in the form, content, and process of realizing a global gender and education development agenda, and conceptual disconnections amplify difficulties with policy and practice. However, in contrast to the situation of the early 1990s, we currently have a rich array of policy instruments, conceptual vocabularies, and research approaches to draw on. Given this, why does progress continue to be elusive?

We note that some of the difficulties are associated with disconnections among different sites of action and silences, particularly regarding violence and the attenuation of transformational agendas in the wake of global crises (Unterhalter et al., 2010b), but these difficulties are not hard-edged limits. There is considerable political and conceptual energy to take forward a new phase of gender equity and justice in a global development agenda. However, the next decade will need to attend more strongly to politics and practice. The global climate might be more difficult, but we think we understand better the kind of strategic work that needs to take place to build the alliances, understanding, and critical reflection that can take ideas into action.

NOTE

* This chapter is based on Elaine Unterhalter and Amy North (2011), 'Girls' schooling, gender equity, and the global education and development agenda: conceptual disconnections, political struggles, and the difficulties of practice', *Feminist Formations*, **23** (3), 1–22©2011 Feminist Formations. Revised and reprinted with permission of the Johns Hopkins Press. Used with permission. The journal article reported on research conducted for The Gender, Education and Global Poverty Reduction Initiatives (GEGPRI) project. Funding, received from the UK Economic and Social Research Council (ESRC) Award no. RES 167–25–260 under a partnership with the UK Department for International Development (DFID), is gratefully acknowledged.

REFERENCES

Aikman, Sheila and Elaine Unterhalter (eds) (2005), *Beyond Access: Developing Gender Equality in Education*, Oxford: Oxfam.

Aikman, Sheila and Elaine Unterhalter (2013), 'Gender equality, capabilities and the terrain of quality education', in Leon Tikly and Angela Barrett (eds), *Education Quality and Social Justice in the South: Challenges for Policy, Practice and Research*, London: Routledge.

Antrobus, Peggy (2004), *The Global Women's Movement: Origins, Issues and Strategies*, London: Zed Books, pp. 25–39.

Birdsall, Nancy, Ruth Levine and Amina Ibrahim (2005), *Toward Universal Primary Education: Investments, Incentives and Institutions*, London: Earthscan.

Chabbott, Colette (2003), *Constructing Education for Development: International Organizations and Education for All*, London: Routledge.

Chapman, David and Shirley Miske (2007), 'Promoting girls' education in Africa: evidence from the field between 1996 and 2003', in Maslak (ed.), pp. 87–106.

Connell, Raewyn (2010), 'Kartini's children: on the need for thinking gender and education together on a world scale', *Gender and Education*, **22**(6), 603–15.

Cornwall, Andrea, Elizabeth Harrison and Ann Whitehead (eds) (2007), *Feminisms in Development: Contradictions, Contestations and Challenges*, London: Zed Books.

Dakar Framework (2000), 'Dakar Framework for Action – Education for All: Meeting Our Collective Commitments', available at: http://unesdoc.unesco.org/images/0012/001211/121147e.pdf (accessed January 7, 2011).

de la Cruz, Carmen (2009), 'Financing for Development and Women's Rights: A Critical Review', Trans. Alejandra Mantecón and Rosanna Thomson, WIDE, Globalising Gender Equality and Social Justice, Brussels, available at: http://62.149.193.10/wide/download/financingfordevelopment2009translationcarmendelacruz.pdf?id=995 (accessed January 7, 2011).

DeJaeghere, Joan and Soo Kyong Lee (2011), 'What matters for marginalized girls and boys in Bangladesh: a capabilities approach for understanding educational well-being and empowerment', *Research in Comparative and International Education*, **6**(1), 27–42.

Doggett, Ruth (2005), 'Enabling education for girls: the Loreto Day School, Sealdah, India', in Aikman and Unterhalter (eds), pp. 227–44.

Dunne, Máiréad (ed.) (2009), *Gender, Sexuality and Development*, Rotterdam: Sense.

Fennell, Shailaja and Madeleine Arnot (eds) (2007), *Gender Education and Equality in a Global Context: Conceptual Frameworks and Policy Perspectives*, London: Routledge.

Gordon, Gill (2008), '"One finger cannot kill a louse" – working with schools on gender, sexuality, and HIV in rural Zambia', in Sheila Aikman, Elaine Unterhalter and Tania Boler (eds), *Gender Equality, HIV, and AIDS: A Challenge for the Education Sector*, Oxford: Oxfam, pp. 129–49.

Gore, Charles (2009), 'The global development cycle, MDGs and the future of poverty reduction', paper presented at the After 2015: Promoting Pro-Poor Policy After the MDGs Conference, Brussels, June 23, available at: http://www.eadi.org/fileadmin/MDG_2015_Publications/Gore_PAPER.pdf (accessed December 1, 2010).

Greany, Kate (2008), 'Rhetoric versus reality: exploring the rights-based approach to girls' education in rural Niger', *Compare: A Journal of Comparative and International Education*, **38**(5), 555–68.

Griffin, Penny (2010), 'Gender, governance and the global political economy', *Australian Journal of International Affairs*, **64**(1), 86–104.

Grown, Caren, Chandrika Bahadur, Jessie Handbury and Diane Elson (2006), 'The financial requirements of achieving gender equality and women's empowerment', paper prepared for the World Bank, Levy Economics Institute of Bard College Working Paper no. 467, available at: http://siteresources.worldbank.org/INTGENDER/Resources/GrownBahadurHandburyElsonFinancialRequirements.pdf (accessed December 1, 2010).

Hausmann, Ricardo, Laura D. Tyson and Saadia Zahidi (2006), *The Global Gender Gap Report 2006*, Geneva: World Economic Forum, available at: http://www.tripalium.com/actu/telechargement/wef.pdf (accessed January 7, 2011).

Jensen, Rikke Ingrid et al. (2006), 'Evaluation of DFID's policy and practice in support of gender equality and women's empowerment', Department for International Development report, EVSUM EV669, London, available at: http://www.dfid.gov.uk/Documents/publications1/evaluation/ev669-summary-report.pdf (accessed January 17, 2011).

Kabeer, Naila (2005), 'Gender equality and women's empowerment: a critical analysis of the Third Millennium Development Goal', *Gender and Development*, **13**(1), 13–24.

Karlsson, Jenni (2010), 'Gender mainstreaming in a South African provincial education department: a transformative shift or technical fix for oppressive gender relations?', *Compare: A Journal of Comparative and International Education*, **40**(4), 497–514.

King, Elizabeth M. and M. Anne Hill (1993), *Women's Education in Developing Countries: Barriers, Benefits, and Policies*, Baltimore, MD: Johns Hopkins University Press.

Kirk, Jackie (2009), *Women Teaching in South Asia*, New Delhi: Sage Publications India.

Leach, Fiona and Claudia Mitchell (eds) (2006), *Combating Gender Violence in and around Schools*, Stoke-on-Trent, UK: Trentham.

Lewis, Maureen A. and Marlaine Lockheed (eds) (2007), *Exclusion, Gender, and Education: Case Studies from the Developing World*, Washington, DC: Center for Global Development.

Lynch, Kathleen (2007), 'Love labor as a distinct and non-commodifiable form of care labor', *Sociological Review*, **55**(3), 550–70.

Lynch, Kathleen, John Baker and Maureen Lyons (2009), *Affective Equality: Love, Care and Injustice*, London: Palgrave Macmillan.

Maslak, Mary Ann (ed.) (2007), *The Structure and Agency of Women's Education*, Albany, NY: State University of New York Press.

Mohanty, Chandra Talpade (2003), *Feminism without Borders: Decolonizing Theory, Practicing Solidarity*, Durham, NC: Duke University Press.

Molyneux, Maxine and Shahra Razavi (eds) (2002), *Gender Justice, Development and Rights*, Oxford: Oxford University Press.

Monkman, Karen (2011), 'Introduction: framing gender, education and empowerment research', *Research in Comparative & International Education*, **6**(1), 1–3.

Morley, Louise, Fiona Leach and Rosemary Lugg (2009), 'Democratizing higher education in Ghana and Tanzania: opportunity structures and social inequalities', *International Journal of Educational Development*, **29**(1), 56–64.

Mukhopadhyay, Maitrayee and Navsharan Singh (eds) (2007), *Gender Justice, Citizenship and Development*, New Delhi: Zubaan.

Mundy, Karen (2007), 'Global governance, educational change', *Comparative Education*, **43**(3), 339–57.

Narayan, Swati, Nitya Rao and Maria Lourdes Khan (2010), *Gender, Equality and Education: A Report Card on South Asia*, Mumbai: ASPBAE.

Nnaemeka, Obioma (2003), 'Nego-Feminism: Theorizing, practicing, pruning Africa's way', *Signs: Journal of Women in Culture and Society*, **29**(2), 357–85.

Novelli, Mario and Mieke T.A. Lopes Cardoza (2008), 'Conflict, education and the global south: new critical directions', *International Journal of Educational Development*, **28**(4), 473–88.

Organisation for Economic Co-operation and Development (OECD) (2009), 'The OECD Social Institutions and Gender Index (SIGI)', available at: http://www.oecd.org/document/39/0,3343, en_2649_33935_42274663_1_1_1_1,00.htm (accessed February 23, 2010).

Para-Mallam, Funmi (2010), 'Promoting gender equality in the context of Nigerian cultural and religious expression: beyond increasing female access to education', *Compare: A Journal of Comparative and International Education*, **40**(4), 459–77.

Parkes, Jenny and Fatuma Chege (2010), 'Girls' education and violence: reflections on the first decade of the twenty-first century', paper presented at the UNGEI Conference Education and Empowerment, Dakar, Senegal, May 17–20, available at: http://www.e4conference.org/wp-content/uploads/2010/04/09en. pdf (accessed December 1, 2010).

Plantenga, Janneke, Chantal Remery, Hugo Figueiredo and Mark Smith (2009), 'Towards a European Union gender equality index', *Journal of European Social Policy*, **19**(1), 19–33.

Rai, Shireen (2008), *The Gender Politics of Development*, London: Zed Books.

Robinson-Pant, Anna (2004), *Women, Literacy, and Development: Alternative Perspectives*, London: Routledge.

Rose, Pauline (2005), 'Is there a "fast-track" to achieving education for all?', *International Journal of Educational Development*, **25**(4), 381–94.

Rose, Pauline and Caroline Dyer (2008), 'Chronic poverty and education: a review of the literature', background paper for the *Second Chronic Poverty Report*, Chronic Poverty Research Centre (CPRC), available from Dr C. Dyer, University of Leeds c.dyer@leeds.ac.uk.

Salo, Elaine (2011), 'South African viewpoint', *Equals*, **27**, 8.

Stromquist, Nelly P. and Gustavo E. Fischman (2009), 'Introduction – from denouncing gender inequities to undoing gender in education: practices and programmes toward change in the social relations of gender', *International Review of Education*, **55**(5), 463–82.

Subrahamanian, Ramya (2005), 'Gender equality in education: definitions and measurements', *International Journal of Educational Development*, **25**(4), 395–407.

United Nations (2010), *The Millennium Development Goals Report 2010*, available at: http://www.un.org/ millenniumgoals/pdf/MDG%20Report%202010%20En%20r15%20-low%20res%2020100615%20-.pdf (accessed December 1, 2010).

United Nations Educational, Scientific and Cultural Organization (UNESCO) (2010), *Global Monitoring Report 2010: Reaching the Marginalized*, Paris: UNESCO/Oxford University Press.

United Nations Educational, Scientific and Cultural Organization (UNESCO) (2011), *Global Monitoring Report 2011: The Hidden Crisis: Armed Conflict and Education*, Paris: UNESCO/Oxford University Press.

United Nations Girls' Education Initiative (UNGEI) (2010), 'Dakar declaration on accelerating girls' education and gender equality', available at: http://www.ungei.org/index_2527.html (accessed December 1, 2010).

Unterhalter, Elaine (2005a), 'Fragmented frameworks? Researching women, gender, education and development', in Aikman and Unterhalter (eds), pp. 15–35.

Unterhalter, Elaine (2005b), 'Global inequality, capabilities, social justice and the Millennium Development Goal for gender equality in education', *International Journal of Education and Development*, **25**(2), 111–22.

Unterhalter, Elaine (2007), *Gender, Schooling and Global Social Justice*, London: Routledge.

Unterhalter, Elaine (2009), 'What is equity in education? Reflections from the capability approach', *Studies in the Philosophy of Education*, **28**(5), 415–24.

Unterhalter, Elaine (2012), 'Silences, stereotypes and local selection: negotiating policy and practice to implement the MDGs and EFA', in Antoni Verger, Hulya Kosar Altinyelken and Mario Novelli (eds), *Global Education Policy and International Development: New Agendas, Issues and Policies*, London: Continuum, pp. 79–100.

Unterhalter, Elaine and Amy North (2011), 'Responding to the gender and education Millennium Development Goals in South Africa and Kenya: reflections on education rights, gender equality, capabilities and global justice', *Compare: A Journal of Comparative and International Education*, **41**(4), 495–511.

Unterhalter, Elaine, Chloe Challender and Rajee Rajagopalan (2005), 'Measuring gender equality in education', in Aikman and Unterhalter (eds), pp. 60–82.

Unterhalter, Elaine, Sonia Exley and Amy North (2010a), 'Measuring gender equality in education', paper presented at the Twenty Years of Human Development Workshop, Von Hugel Institute, St. Edmunds College, Cambridge, UK, January 25.

Unterhalter, Elaine, Amy North and Jenny Parkes (2010b), 'Gender equality and women and girls' education, 1995–2010: how much is there a space for hope?', paper for UNESCO's 15-year review of the Beijing Platform of Action.

Vandemootele, Jan (2004), 'Are the Millennium Development Goals feasible?', in Richard Black and Howard White (eds), *Targeting Development*, London: Routledge, pp. 124–44.

Vaughan, Rosie Peppin (2010), *E4 Conference Engendering Empowerment: Education and Equality: Conference Report*, New York: UNGEI/Institute of Education, available at: http://www.ungei.org/files/E4_Conference_Report.pdf (accessed January 14, 2011).

Vavrus, Frances K. (2003), *Desire and Decline: Schooling Amid Crisis in Tanzania*, New York: Peter Lang.

Verloo, Meike (ed.) (2007), *Multiple Meanings of Gender Equality: A Critical Frame Analysis of Gender Policies in Europe*, Budapest: CPS Books.

Waage, Jeff, Rukmini Banerji, Oona Campbell, Ephraim Chirwa, Guy Collender, Veerle Dieltiens, Andrew Dorward *et al.* (2010), 'The Millennium Development Goals: a cross-sectoral analysis and principles for goal setting after 2015', *The Lancet*, **376**(9745), 991–1023.

26. Intersecting sources of education inequality
*Elizabeth M. King and Vy T. Nguyen**

I INTRODUCTION

Thanks to a combination of policies and sustained investments in education by governments, communities and families, developing countries today have unprecedented numbers of schools, classrooms, teachers – and students. Compared with two decades ago, many more children are entering school, completing primary schooling, and continuing to secondary and tertiary education. In low-income countries, average net enrollment rates in primary education have surged upwards of 80 percent and completion rates up to 68 percent (UNESCO, 2010). Remarkable accomplishments have also been made toward achieving gender equality at all levels of education (see World Bank, 2010a). Since 1990, the ratio of girls to boys enrolled has increased most at the primary level in Sub-Saharan Africa and South Asia. At the secondary level, the ratio has risen substantially in East Asia and Latin America and the Caribbean. In tertiary education, Eastern European countries show the most progress.

Addressing gender inequality in education requires an approach that takes into account multiple, intersecting sources of disadvantage that include income poverty, place of residence, ethnicity, and linguistic background. Broad education reforms that expand access to schooling for everyone, such as removal of fees and more better-equipped schools, have been successful in raising enrollment rates in low-income countries, but sharper, more targeted interventions are needed to spur faster progress for girls from the poorest families, those who live in rural areas, and those who belong to ethnic and linguistic minority groups.

This chapter presents an overview of gender inequality in education across the globe, highlighting existing gaps and the importance of ensuring equal access and achievement of education for all children (Section II). Evidence indicates that gender inequality is better understood when it is considered together with other socioeconomic factors (Section III). We analyze the role of development policies and programs in their interaction with households and societal institutions and highlight good practices that have been successful in addressing disparity in education by gender (Section IV). Education is critical to women's empowerment and has a substantial impact on their ability to provide for themselves and their families. Section V concludes.

II EDUCATION: ITS IMPORTANCE AND GENDER GAPS

Why is it imperative that the world's 3.4 billion girls and women have the same chances to gain an education as boys and men? Basic education is a human right that is enshrined in the Universal Declaration of Human Rights and the Convention on the Rights of the Child. These declarations represent a global recognition that education allows people to live fuller, healthier, more satisfying lives. For societies and economies as a whole, education is also a strategic investment to improve their prospects for development. The human mind makes possible all other achievements, from health advances and technological innovations to infrastructure construction and cultural development. For all countries, educating all their people, not just half of them, makes the most sense for future progress.

Systematic disadvantage in access to schools for girls translates into a less-educated workforce, inefficient allocation of labor, lost productivity, and consequently diminished progress of economic development. Empirical research findings suggest that more gender equality in developing countries is associated with higher economic growth (Barro and Lee, 1994; Dollar and Gatti, 1999; Morrison et al., 2007). Using 1960–2000 country-level data, Stephan Klasen and Francesca Lamanna (2009) find that the combined gender inequality in education and employment in the Middle East and North Africa and in South Asia explains 0.9–1.7 and 0.1–1.6 percentage point slower growth, respectively, compared to East Asia. In addition, average human capital is 12 percent less and growth is 0.3 percent lower when boys receive more education than girls at the ratio of 70:30, compared with countries where there is more gender equality. Dina Abu-Ghaida and Klasen (2004) conclude that countries can benefit marginally more from educating women than men in terms of faster economic growth. Countries with more gender equality also have lower poverty rates (Morrison et al., 2007).

It is now also well recognized that the benefits from women's education go beyond both higher productivity for them[1] and economic growth. Women with more education tend to be healthier, have fewer children, and secure better healthcare and education for their children. These benefits transmit to their communities at large and cascade across generations. For example, it has been estimated that half of the 8.2 million fewer deaths among children under age five between 1970 and 2009 can be attributed to increases in the education of women of reproductive age (Gakidou et al., 2010). A recent study also concludes that countries with more-educated women have coped with extreme weather conditions better than countries with less-educated women (Blankespoor et al., 2010). Indeed, many more studies have found empirical evidence that demonstrates why investing in girls' education is smart policy.[2]

In the last two decades, there has been progress toward achieving gender equity in education. Enrollment rates are higher for both girls and boys, increasing gender equality at all levels of education. Since 1991, girls' gross enrollment rates have risen fastest in Sub-Saharan Africa and South Asia, especially at the primary level, by about 30 percentage points; in South Asia, girls' enrollment rates at the secondary level rose almost as fast. In the other regions where girls' enrollment rate at the primary level was already very high, the rate at the secondary and tertiary levels showed impressive increases (see Figure 26.1).

Despite this progress, millions of school-age children remain out of school. For reasons including poverty and inadequate schools, many children never enter and many leave well before completing even the primary level. Three-fourths of the countries that are the furthest from meeting the education Millennium Development Goal (MDG) on primary completion are in Sub-Saharan Africa, and nearly half of those are unlikely to meet the gender equality goal (World Bank, 2011). Using the ratio of girls' to boys' enrollment rates as an indicator of gender equality, many more countries are supposed

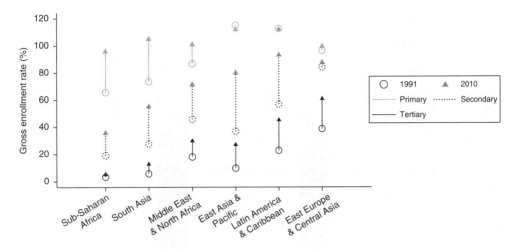

Note: Due to limited data availability at the tertiary level, the earliest year refers to 1999 instead of 1991 for tertiary gross enrollment rate.

Source: UNESCO Institute for Statistics (2012).

Figure 26.1   Improvements in girls' enrollment, 1991–2010, by world region

to meet the MDG on gender equality. But as Monica Grant and Jere Behrman (2010) point out, the changes between 1990–99 and 2000–06 reveal a more complex pattern in gender gaps than this indicator reveals, with boys being more likely than girls to ever attend school, except in Latin America and Southeast Asia, but that once enrolled girls are more likely to remain in school and to complete more years of schooling. Therefore, improving girls' education worldwide requires overcoming initial barriers to schooling and providing girls with opportunities to set foot in school. Broad reforms to address barriers to schooling for all children, such as removal of fees and better-equipped schools, have improved education outcomes, but for some groups of children it will take sharper, more targeted interventions to close gender gaps.

While gender accounts for observed disparities in education, poverty persists as the most important and pervasive factor for education inequality. Multivariate analyses support this conclusion; differences in educational attainment are more highly associated with economic status than with gender, orphanhood or rural residence in poor countries (Filmer, 2008b). Our calculations based on individual data from Demographic and Health Surveys (DHS) in 24 low-income countries support this even in the poorest countries. On average, only 34 percent of girls in the poorest-quintile households in these countries complete primary school, compared with 72 percent of girls in the richest-quintile households, a difference of 38 percentage points due to income poverty alone (see Figure 26.2). In comparison, controlling for income, the gap between the poorest girls and the poorest boys is about 10 percentage points, and that between the richest girls and the richest boys is 12 percentage points.

These simple statistics showing that disparities due to income poverty greatly exceed the differences due to gender do not diminish the need to pay attention to why gender makes any difference. For instance, in the low-income countries for which DHS data

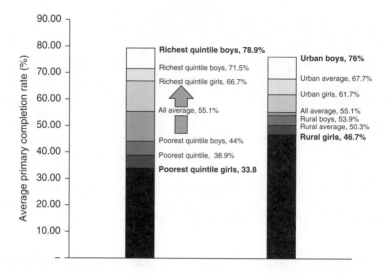

Note: Aggregates for low-income countries are averages of 24 low-income countries for wealth disaggregates and for urban/rural disaggregates weighted by primary school age population.

Source: Authors' calculations using latest available data from the World Bank Demographic and Health Surveys (DHS) project, 2000–2011.

Figure 26.2   Multiple sources of disadvantage: poverty, gender, and rural residence in low-income countries

are available, gender inequality is not wider among the poor than among the rich; on the contrary, the education gender gap among the poorest households may be narrower than among the richest households. In the following section, we examine factors other than income poverty and show that gender patterns are not so simply summarized as commonly used indicators such as the MDG measures would suggest.

III   BEYOND GENDER AND POVERTY: MULTIPLE INEQUALITIES IN EDUCATION

Distinguishing among groups further, we find evidence that education lags most significantly among people who face multiple sources of disadvantage, not only income poverty, but also place of residence, disability and/or ethno-linguistic background.[3] Using place of residence as an aggregate (though far from perfect) measure of economic development and the availability of schools, on average urban children fare much better in terms of school enrollment and completion rate, compared with children in rural areas (68 versus 50 percent). In fact, the primary completion rate of urban girls is 15 percentage points higher than that of rural girls and 7 percentage points higher than that of rural boys, indicating that gender is not the full story behind observed disparities. However, urban boys have the highest completion rate, exceeding that of urban girls by nearly 15 percentage points and that of rural girls by 30 percentage points (see Figure 26.2).

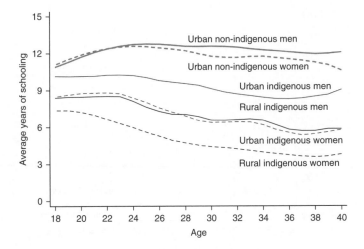

Note: Non-indigenous population is defined as those people whose native language is Spanish; the indigenous population is defined as those whose native language is Quechua, Aymara, Guarani, or other native languages. A STATA smoothing function has been applied to extract the time trend in the data.

Source: Authors' calculation using Bolivia DHS (2008).

Figure 26.3 Schooling inequality in Bolivia

Adding ethnic and linguistic background to place of residence, we see from three low-income countries across the globe that gender inequality is indeed a more complex story. In Bolivia, for example, the gender gap in completed years of schooling among the non-indigenous population, even at the age groups that correspond to secondary and tertiary education, has disappeared, as shown by the overlapping curves for the non-indigenous groups in Figure 26.3. However, among the indigenous populations, the gender pattern depends on place of residence: urban men have approximately two more years of schooling than urban women at age 18, but urban women have as many years of schooling as rural men. It is rural indigenous women who have the least schooling, about seven years at age 18. We note also that the total gap between urban, non-indigenous men and rural, indigenous women has narrowed dramatically across age cohorts, from nine years among the 40-year-olds to three years among the 18-year-olds.

The pattern of urban–rural differences accentuating gender differences is evident also in the Lao People's Democratic Republic, and those gender differences are magnified further by ethno-linguistic background. Lao PDR's population has four broad ethno-linguistic families: the Lao-Tai (67 percent of the population), the Mon-Khmer (21 percent), Hmong-Lu Mien (8 percent), and the Chine-Tibetan (3 percent); broad ethnic categories further subsume 49 distinct ethnicities and some 200 ethnic subgroups (King and van de Walle, 2007). In urban areas, ethnic majority Lao-Tai women have been catching up with Lao-Tai men in terms of completed years of schooling. In Figure 26.4, the lines for the urban Lao-Tai men and women have converged at the youngest ages, and those for the rural Lao-Tai males and females have come closer. In fact, over the years, urban Lao-Tai women have consistently advanced

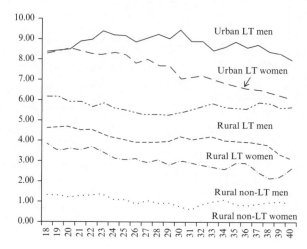

Note: LT stands for the ethnic majority Lao-Tai.

Source: King and van de Walle (2007).

Figure 26.4 Schooling inequality in Lao PDR

relative to rural Lao-Tai men. However, among the non-Lao-Tai groups gender disparity remains large across age cohorts. On average, an 18-year-old non-Lao-Tai girl in a rural area completes fewer than two years of schooling, compared with almost five years for an 18-year-old rural, Lao-Tai woman and about four years of schooling for a rural non-Lao-Tai man.[4]

In Mozambique, one of the poorest countries in Africa, urban–rural differences are also large (as in Bolivia and Lao PDR) but these differences have closed dramatically for the youngest cohorts. Adding language to place of residence, in urban areas lusophone (or Portuguese-speaking) and non-lusophone women have closed the gap in years of schooling with urban men, although this is relatively recent progress, as shown in Figure 26.5. Moreover, urban lusophone women appear to have overtaken urban non-lusophone men. In rural areas, however, among the non-lusophone groups, women have not gained on men across the years and generations. Yet the total gap in the population – between urban, lusophone men and rural, non-lusophone women – has closed to three years among the 18-year-olds from 10 years among the 40-year-olds.

Clearly, gender is not the only factor that explains inequalities in schooling, but among population groups that already suffer from other sources of disadvantage, gender widens that gap further. These country examples demonstrate that to understand the degree of gender inequality, it is not enough to use country-level averages. The very low level of education and large deficit for groups facing multiple sources of disadvantage suggest that the barriers they face are great even at the most basic levels, and that extraordinary efforts in policy and investments are needed to break down those barriers.

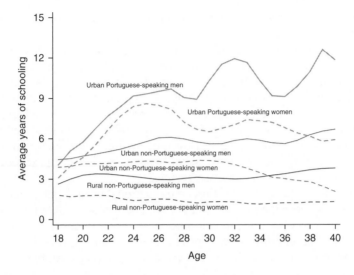

Note: The curves for the lusophone (or Portuguese-speaking) groups fluctuate more than the other curves, even after applying a STATA smoothing function to extract the time trend, because they represent small populations compared to the other groups.

Source: Authors' calculation using Mozambique DHS 2003–04.

Figure 26.5 Schooling inequality in Mozambique

IV STRATEGIES TO ADDRESS GENDER DISPARITIES

What policies and investments are likely to increase the education of girls and women? To what extent can broad education reforms benefit girls and women and thus close gender gaps? Are specially targeted interventions essential to close gender gaps?

Economic and development policies can improve or worsen gender disparities. Some are deliberately unequal (for example, affirmative action policies) and others, despite appearing gender neutral, have unintended consequences on those gender differences. The extent and nature of gender inequality differ across countries and, within countries, differ across communities. Thus, decisions about whether to intervene and about which interventions to undertake should be based on an understanding of the local context.

Societal institutions (that is, social norms, customs, rights, laws), together with economic institutions such as labor markets, shape and reinforce the roles and relationships between men and women and determine their opportunities and life prospects. Like policies, decisions within households – about the allocation of resources between men and women, or assignment of tasks and autonomy levels – can reinforce or mitigate gender disparities.[5] So can dissimilar expectations for sons and daughters. Individuals take these contextual aspects into account in shaping their own aspirations and behaviors, as well as their ability to afford the investments in education. Addressing gender inequality therefore requires interventions at all levels – households, the economy, markets, and institutions – to level the field of opportunities between men and women. It also requires promoting equal access to assets, markets, and services and giving women greater political voice, more security and greater control over household decisions (King and Mason, 2001).

Governments and nongovernmental organizations, including civil society groups and the private sector, have experimented with a variety of measures that attempt to address the multitude of factors that influence schooling (see, for example, the surveys by Herz and Sperling, 2004; Lloyd and Young, 2009). Constraints on the demand side can be addressed by reducing the cost of schooling through abolishing school fees and offering (conditional) cash transfers, targeted scholarships and vouchers that enable poor students to attend private educational institutions, or improving safety and mobility of girls. On the supply side, the number of schools can be expanded and school quality can be improved, both of which can increase demand.

The potential impacts of some of these interventions on enrollment and school continuation rates have been the subject of analytical and evaluative research. We cite a few specific examples below, focusing more on demand- rather than supply-side policies and programs. Following on our observations from the previous section, a topic for further research would be to estimate differential impacts on specific groups of girls and women.

Enhancing Demand for Education through Targeted Programs

Current research suggests that in places where girls receive less schooling than boys, especially in Sub-Saharan Africa and South Asia and in the rural areas of many countries, girls' schooling is more responsive to shifts in income and prices than boys' schooling. Measures to reduce the cost of schooling have been shown to promote girls' enrollment. These costs include both direct costs, such as fees for tuition, exams and textbooks, and the opportunity cost of schooling – that is, the foregone contribution to household income and labor (World Bank, 2011).

Mexico's PROGRESA/Oportunidades program is a well-known example of a program that addresses the problem of affordability of school attendance. It provides bimonthly subsidies to poor families with children between 7 and 18 years old, on the condition of a minimum school attendance rate of 85 percent. The program gives larger grants at higher grades and for females at the secondary level because the opportunity cost for girls and for higher levels of education is recognized as higher. The program increased secondary education enrollment by 7.1 percent for boys and 5.2 percent for girls and schooling attainment for the poor by 0.7 grades. It also raised the progression rate from primary to lower secondary education by 11.1 percent, of which the effects are larger for girls than boys, with 14.8 and 6.5 percent respectively (Schultz, 2004).

Another initiative that lowers the cost of schooling is the girls' scholarship program in Cambodia, a low-income country with average per capita gross domestic product of just $550 (constant 2000 prices) in 2010. The program awarded $45 to every girl in school for three years beginning in 2003, provided that she was enrolled, maintained a passing grade, and was absent for fewer than 10 days a year. These scholarships raised the school participation of recipients by approximately 30 percentage points, with the larger effect, 43 percent, for girls from low socio-economic status (Filmer and Schady, 2008).

Similarly successful is a long-running Female Secondary School Stipend Project in Bangladesh which compensates parents for the cost of girls' schooling, provided that specific conditions are fulfilled. Under the project, girls in grades 6 to 10 in rural districts have received a stipend that covers as much as 50 percent of the cost of textbooks, uniforms, stationery, transportation, and exam fees, on the condition that the girls attend 75 percent of school days, attain at least 45 percent marks on the annual exams, and remain unmarried. The result was an 8 percent increase in girls' enrollment for each additional year of exposure to the program (Khandker et al., 2003).

In Malawi, ongoing research finds that among girls and young women aged 13 to 22, an average cash transfer of only $10 per month can lead to significant increases in school enrollment, attendance, and grade attainment. It also has led to modest test score improvements in mathematics, English reading comprehension, and cognitive skills (Baird et al., 2010a, 2010b). In addition, the transfer program appears to have reduced teen marriage and pregnancy, brought measurable improvements in mental health, delayed the onset of sexual activity, and reduced risky sexual activity. An impressive decline of more than 60 percent in the prevalence of HIV and genital herpes was reported. Unconditional transfers were found to be more effective in reducing teen marriage and pregnancy and in improving mental health, while conditional transfers were more effective in improving learning in mathematics and reading comprehension. Smaller transfer amounts were generally as effective as higher amounts (Baird et al., 2010a, 2010b).

Can these programs actually sustain improvements for girls beyond their initial impact on enrollment? A stipend initiative for girls in Pakistan introduces incentives for girls to spend more time in school and less time at work (Alam et al., 2011). An evaluation found that in the short term, enrollment rates went up by almost 9 percentage points; five years hence, the program seems to have also increased transition rates from middle to secondary school and completion rates at grade 9.

Enhancing Demand for Education through Untargeted Programs

Targeted measures can be more costly to implement because of the administrative costs usually associated with targeting, so it is useful to examine also the potential impact of untargeted interventions. These have been as effective as targeted interventions in some environments, since the demand for girls' schooling seems more responsive to changes in costs, distance to school, and school characteristics. The abolition of primary school fees in Uganda, for example, raised the primary enrollment rates of girls by 6 percent compared to boys among children aged 9 to 12 and by 25 percent among adolescents aged 12 to 18 based on household survey data in 1992 and 1999. It also increased girls' secondary attendance rates by 14 percent (Deininger, 2003).

One example of a large, untargeted education reform is India's Sarva Shiksha Abhiyan program, which is supporting government efforts to put out-of-school children into primary school, including girls, first-generation learners from minority communities, and children with special needs. It is the largest ongoing Education for All program in the world. Initiated in 2001, it calls for locating primary school facilities within one kilometer of all habitations, and provides alternative education programs and 'bridge' courses for out-of-school children and dropouts. It also supports teacher recruitment and training, helps develop teaching materials and monitors learning outcomes. Villages identify out-of-school children, get them enrolled, organize themselves to manage school resources and construct classrooms and school buildings (World Bank, 2008). Since the project was launched, nearly 20 million more out-of-school children have enrolled in school, many of them girls. In 2009, 94 girls were enrolled for every 100 boys, compared to 90 in the early 2000s. In April 2010, India also enacted the right to education, prescribing and ensuring free and compulsory education for all children between ages 6 and 14 (World Bank, 2010b).

In Yemen, three education projects have supported a number of strategies to address gender disparities, including conditional cash transfers to raise girls' enrollment, an improved teaching force, and greater participation by communities and parents in school matters. In part due to these efforts, the gross enrollment ratio for girls in grades 1–6 increased from 51 percent in 1999–2001 to 76 percent in 2007–08. In 2008, Yemen also abolished school fees for girls in grades 1–6 and for boys in grades 1–3, and 1,000 new female teachers were contracted and trained. A systematic analysis of the impact of these various measures is still to be undertaken, but anecdotal evidence suggests that contracting more female teachers is attracting more girls to school (World Bank, 2009).

Other changes in schools can enhance the experience of girls within the classroom and deserve some mention. These 'supply-side' policies and interventions (for example, single-sex schools, latrines in schools, same-sex teachers) account for a large share of the literature on gender in schools, but evidence of their impact has not always established causality. For example, a girl's learning outcome may depend not only on whether a school is available in the community but also on whether female teachers are available; however, the evidence on whether learning is influenced by whether the student and the teacher are of the same sex is mixed. To cite just two studies, a quasi-experimental study in the US (Dee, 2007) finds that in middle schools same-sex teachers benefit both boys and girls, but a longitudinal study in Germany does not find any significant effect (Neugebauer et al., 2011). More higher-quality evidence on these 'supply-side' policies and practices, especially as they affect different socioeconomic and ethnic groups of girls, would help inform and sharpen relevant policy and investment choices.

V   CONCLUSION

Policy-makers will face special challenges in the coming decade. The youth bulge in many developing countries implies a tremendous need for new schools, especially in rural areas. In the absence of sufficient fiscal resources, governments may need to involve all actors – from private providers and civil society organizations to communities, families, students, and trainees – to help build and manage schools. For example, in urban areas of Pakistan provision of new private schools was found to be effective using a three-year government subsidy based on the number of girls enrolled (Alderman et al., 2001). Alternatively, in certain rural areas, village education committees were assigned with procuring or constructing schools, recruiting teachers, and monitoring school operations; the government provides teacher training and school supplies. As a result, girls' enrollment has increased by 43 percent and boys' enrollment by 38 percent (Alderman et al., 2003).

Past interventions and impact evaluations of those programs have given development actors more knowledge about the effectiveness of providing targeted scholarships, vouchers or conditional cash transfers and removing tuition fees, as well as their impact on the demand for girls' education. It has become clear that making more people aware of the benefits of girls' education, measuring gender inequalities, and rallying more voices to speak about those inequalities are powerful ways to remind people of this critical development issue.

But significant knowledge gaps remain with respect to addressing the full range of obstacles. There seems to be no shortage of ideas about interventions to promote gender equality. The 10 actions recommended by Cynthia Lloyd and Juliet Young's (2009) review of more than 300 programs are far-ranging: scholarships for girls, recruitment and training of female teachers, girl-friendly curricula, pedagogical approaches that enhance learning and employment, after-school tutoring and greater support for non-formal education. But the key challenge for policy-makers and the development community is to identify the smartest solutions, those reforms and programs which bring the largest benefit for gender equality for the least resources. Without hard facts and hard-headed analyses, financial and social resources are wasted on solutions that seem promising but are neither effective nor sustainable.

Finally, the quality of education remains an unfinished agenda because enrollment rates, not learning, have been the focus of past interventions. Yet improving the quality of education may have a larger impact on girls' enrollment and completion rates than on boys'. When schooling is not perceived to lead to higher productivity and better employment prospects, the demand for girls' schooling is likely to be weaker because girls' productivity in alternative (but unpaid home) work is usually higher than boys'. Better schools as well as the promise of future jobs and fair returns to educated women thus are incredibly important incentives for families to send their daughters to school.

Educating girls is a fundamental part of the development challenge. To achieve it, it is imperative to identify where educational disparities are widest and to expand the menu of interventions toward reducing gender gaps. As argued above, addressing gender inequality requires an approach that takes into account intersecting sources of disadvantage that include income poverty, place of residence, ethnicity, and linguistic background. Broad education reforms that expand access to schooling for everyone have been successful in raising enrollment rates even in low-income countries, but more is needed to spur faster progress for girls from the poorest families, those who live in rural areas, and those who belong to ethnic and linguistic minority groups. This means, among other things, ensuring equal access to schooling by providing a safe and healthy school environment for girls and improving the economic returns to female education by raising education quality, together with removing sources of gender-based labor market discrimination.

NOTES

*   This chapter is drawn from Elizabeth M. King and Vy T. Nguyen, 'Gender, poverty and institutions: intersecting sources of education inequality', in *Engineering Empowerment: Education and Inequality. A Companion Volume to the E4 Conferences*, by United Nations Girls' Education Initiative, 21–34, New York: United Nations Girls' Education Iniative, 2012.
1. Focusing on the evidence in just one country, Durasaimy (2002) concludes that investment in women's education in India, particularly at the middle, lower secondary and higher secondary levels, has been more profitable than that for men in 1983 and also in 1993–94. And while the returns to women's primary and middle levels of education have declined, those to secondary and college levels have increased during the decade 1983–94.

2. See the evidence reviewed in the *World Development Report* (World Bank, 2012), which focuses on gender issues in development.
3. See, for example, the summaries and citations in Hall and Patrinos (2012), Lewis and Lockheed (2006a, 2006b), and UNESCO (2010). Disability is also strongly associated with lower education rates, and this correlation is stronger than those with gender or other socioeconomic factors (Filmer, 2008b). Also see Filmer (2008a) and Posarac and Peffley (2011) on the negative impact of disability on schooling attainment.
4. These ethnic differences appear in many other countries. In Cameroon, for example, Fali girls complete 0.8 year of schooling, on average, compared with 1.2 years for Fali boys and 8.2 years for Bamilike-central boys and girls, the ethnic majority in the Cameroon (Authors' calculations using DHS Cameroon, 2004). The 2010 Global Monitoring Report (UNESCO, 2010) also shows strikingly large gender differences in completed years of schooling among income and ethnic groups in Nigeria.
5. See Kingdon (2005) for a concise and clear discussion of measurement issues that make it difficult to establish gender bias in educational expenditures within the household.

REFERENCES

Abu-Ghaida, Dina and Stephan Klasen (2004), 'The costs of missing the Millennium Development Goal on gender equity', *World Development*, **32**(7), 1075–07.
Alam, Andaleeb, Javier E. Baez and V. Del Carpio (2011), 'Does cash for school influence young women's behavior in the longer term? Evidence from Pakistan', Policy Research Working Papers, World Bank, Washington, DC.
Alderman, Harold, Jooseop Kim and Peter F. Orazem (2003), 'Design, evaluation, and sustainability of private schools for the poor: the Pakistan urban and rural fellowship school experiments', *Economics of Education Review*, **22**(3), 265–74.
Alderman, Harold, Peter F. Orazem and Elizabeth M. Paterno (2001), 'School quality, school cost, and the public/private school choices of low-income households in Pakistan', *Journal of Human Resources*, **36**(2), 304–26.
Baird, Sarah, Craig McIntosh and Berk Ozler (2010a), 'Cash or condition? evidence from a randomized cash transfer program', Policy Research Working Papers, World Bank, Washington, DC.
Baird, Sarah, Craig McIntosh and Berk Ozler (2010b), 'The short-term impacts of a schooling conditional cash transfer program on the sexual behavior of young women', *Health Economics*, **19**(S1), 55–68.
Barro, Robert J. and Jong-Wha Lee (1994), 'Sources of economic growth', *Carnegie-Rochester Conference Series on Public Policy*, **40**(June), 1–46.
Blankespoor, Brian, Susmita Dasgupta, Benoit Laplante and David Wheeler (2010), 'Adaptation to climate extremes in developing countries: the role of education', The Policy Research Working Papers, World Bank, Washington, DC.
Dee, Thomas S. (2007), 'Teachers and the gender gaps in student achievement', *Journal of Human Resources*, **42**(30), 528–54.
Deininger, Klaus (2003), 'Does cost of schooling affect enrollment by the poor? Universal primary education in Uganda', *Economics of Education Review*, **22**(3), 291–305.
Dollar, David and Roberta Gatti (1999), 'Gender inequality, income, and growth: are good times good for women?', Policy Research Report on Women in Development, Policy Paper Series, No. 1, World Bank, Washington, DC.
Durasaimy, Palanigounder (2002), 'Changes in returns to education in India, 1983–94: by gender, age-cohort and location', *Economics of Education Review*, **21**(6), 609–22.
Filmer, Deon (2008a), 'Disability, poverty and schooling in developing countries: results from 14 household surveys', *World Bank Economic Review*, **22**(1), 141–63.
Filmer, Deon (2008b), 'Inequalities in education: effects of gender, poverty, orphanhood, and disability', in Mercy Tembon and Lucia Fort (eds), *Girls' Education in the 21st Century*, Washington, DC: World Bank, pp. 95–114.
Filmer, Deon and Norbert Schady (2008), 'Getting girls into school: evidence from a scholarship program in Cambodia', *Economic Development and Cultural Change*, **56**(3), 581–617.
Gakidou, Emmanuela, Krycia Cowling, Rafael Lozano and Christopher J.L. Murray (2010), 'Increased educational attainment and its effect on child mortality in 175 countries between 1970 and 2009: a systematic analysis', *The Lancet*, **376**(9745), 959–74.
Grant, Monica J. and Jere R. Behrman (2010), 'Gender gaps in educational attainment in less developed countries', *Population and Development Review*, **36**(1), 71–89.

Hall, Gillette and Harry Anthony Patrinos (2012), *Indigenous peoples, poverty and development*, New York: Cambridge University Press.

Herz, Barbara and Gene B. Sperling (2004), *What Works in Girls' Education (Evidence and Policies in the Developing World)*, Washington, DC: Council on Foreign Relations Inc.

Khandker, Shahidur, Mark Pitt and Nobuhiko Fuwa (2003), 'Subsidy to promote girls' secondary education: the female stipend program in Bangladesh', MPRA Paper 23688, University Library of Munich, Munich.

King, Elizabeth M. and Andrew D. Mason (2001), *Engendering Development: Through Gender Equality in Rights, Resources, and Voice*, New York: Oxford University Press.

King, Elizabeth M. and Dominique van de Walle (2006), 'Girls in Lao PDR: ethnic affiliation, poverty, and location', in Lewis and Lockheed, (eds), pp. 31–70.

Kingdon, Geeta Gandhi (2005), 'Where has all the bias gone? Detecting bias in the intrahousehold allocation of educational expenditure', *Economic Development and Cultural Change*, **53**(2), 409–51.

Klasen, Stephan and Francesca Lamanna (2009), 'The impact of gender inequality in education and employment on economic growth: new evidence for a panel of countries', *Feminist Economics*, **15**(3), 91–32.

Lewis, Maureen A. and Marlaine E. Lockheed (eds) (2006a), *Exclusion, Gender and Education: Case Studies from the Developing World*, Washington, DC: Center for Global Development.

Lewis, Maureen A. and Marlaine E. Lockheed (eds) (2006b), *Inexcusable Absence: Why 60 Million Girls Still Aren't in School and What to do About It*, Washington, DC: Center for Global Development.

Lloyd, Cynthia B. and Juliet Young (2009), *New Lessons: The Power of Educating Adolescent Girls – A Girls Count Report on Adolescent Girls*, New York: The Population Council.

Morrison, Andrew, Dhushyanth Raju and Nistha Sinha (2007), *Gender Equality, Poverty and Economic Growth*, Washington, DC: World Bank.

Neugebauer, Martin, Marcel Helbig and Andreas Landmann (2011), 'Unmasking the myth of the same-sex teacher advantage', *European Sociological Review*, **27**(5), 669–89.

Posarac, Aleksandra and Karen Peffley (2011), 'Childhood disability, education and school health', in Donald Bundy (ed.), *Rethinking School Health: A Key Component of Education for All*, Washington, DC: World Bank, pp. 116–58.

Schultz, T. Paul (2004), 'School subsidies for the poor: evaluating the Mexican Progresa poverty program', *Journal of Development Economics*, **74**(1), 199–250.

UNESCO (2010), *Education For All: Global Monitoring Report 2010*, Paris: UNESCO.

UNESCO Institute for Statistics (2012), Data Centre, available at: http://www.uis.unesco.org/pages/default.aspx?&SPSLanguage=EN (accessed July 2012).

World Bank (2008), *Implementation Completion and Results Report for the Republic of India Elementary Education Project I (Sarva Shiksha Abhiyan)*, Washington, DC: World Bank.

World Bank (2009), 'IDA at Work: Yemen. Educating More Girls to Reach Universal Goals', September, available at: http://web.worldbank.org/WBSITE/EXTERNAL/EXTABOUTUS/IDA/0,,contentMDK:22341550~menuPK:3266877~pagePK:51236175~piPK:437394~theSitePK:73154,00.html (accessed August 4, 2011).

World Bank (2010a), *Equal Opportunities, Better Lives. Gender in Africa: Using Knowledge to Reduce Gender Inequality through World Bank Activities*, Washington, DC: World Bank.

World Bank (2010b), 'India: Delivering on the Promise of Education for All', September 13, available at: http://web.worldbank.org/WBSITE/EXTERNAL/PROJECTS/0,,contentMDK:22699660~menuPK:64282137~pagePK:41367~piPK:279616~theSitePK:40941,00.html (accessed August 4, 2011).

World Bank (2011), *Learning for All: Investing in People's Knowledge and Skills to Promote Development*, Washington, DC: World Bank, World Bank Group Education Strategy 2020.

World Bank (2012), *The 2012 World Development Report on Gender Equality and Development*, Washington, DC: World Bank.

27. The health of the world's women
Purnima Madhivanan and Karl Krupp*

I INTRODUCTION

When Paul Farmer described a parallel universe with 'no relation between the massive accumulation of wealth in one part of the world and abject misery in another', he was speaking about the inequality in resources between developed and developing worlds (Kidder, 2011, p. 218). He could as easily have been describing the disparities in health between men and women. Each year millions of females are lost to sex-selective abortion and hundreds of thousands to pregnancy-related causes. In Sub-Saharan Africa, more women than men are affected by HIV and uncounted numbers continue to die from unsafe abortions. In almost every case, being female is associated with disproportionately bad health outcomes.

Not surprisingly, already wide disparities are even wider in developing parts of the world. Some diseases that have largely disappeared from richer countries continue to take thousands of women's lives in poorer nations. Most women diagnosed with cervical cancer, for instance, live in India and China. A growing number of diabetes cases also occur in these rapidly developing countries. There are a few notable exceptions, of course. Breast cancer and cardiovascular disease continue to be afflictions found mostly in affluent nations. Even this may be changing. The greatest increases in chronic disease incidence over the last decade have been in low-income regions of the world. Whether this is the result of higher disease incidence or an artifact of improved case-finding is still unknown.

While the death of women has garnered the greatest amount of interest, chronic disease and disability have received less attention. Each year, millions of women suffer disabling illnesses from childbirth. Many suffer lifelong problems such as severe anemia, incontinence, damage to their reproductive or nervous systems, chronic pain, and infertility that go largely unnoticed. Uncounted numbers also suffer from conditions such as pelvic inflammatory disease that put them at future risk for ectopic pregnancy and infertility. According to one analysis, reproductive age women living in low-income regions lose more disability-adjusted life years (DALYs) during maternity than to any other cause except HIV/AIDS. The picture is even more complicated than it seems since the reasons why women die and suffer disability change over time. Declining mortality from infectious diseases has been replaced by mortality from chronic diseases. The effect is striking in developing countries, where respiratory illness, acute infectious diseases, and tuberculosis are quickly being replaced as leading causes of death by heart disease, cancer, and cerebrovascular diseases.

This chapter will examine the dynamic nature of women's health across both affluent and low-income regions of the world. Exploring each stage of life, it will show that although reasons for the death and disability of women are changing, disparities remain. Even in the richest countries, where new drugs and technologies promise a panacea for all, a disproportionate number of women – usually the poor, the very young, and the old – continue to suffer and die from treatable causes. The reasons for these disparities are complex. Evidence suggests that many are social and structural factors that determine how individuals and populations interact with issues of health and healthcare. Others stem from deeply embedded social preferences for males over females. How these issues play out depends on the stage of a woman's life: many 'go missing' before birth as the result of sex-selective abortions; others die from treatable illnesses and childbirth; and still others, uncounted millions, suffer preventable disabilities from deliberate neglect or abuse. Ultimately, it will take a wide range of solutions even to begin to address this multi-factorial problem. Without doubt it will also require the engagement of a large number of actors including government, civil society, and individuals to facilitate not only solutions to specific problems, but also systemic issues that influence the health of women everywhere.

While there are many useful ways in which a topic such as this might be covered, we have chosen to organize our discussion around the different periods of a woman's life span. We do this because the type of mortality and morbidity women face varies widely during different stages of their lives. In 'Conception to Adolescence' (Section II) we discuss the impact of sex-selective abortion, inadequate healthcare, poor nutrition and youth marriages. 'Adolescence' (Section III) focuses on how youth pregnancy, sexually transmitted infections, infectious diseases, and nutrition affect young women. In 'The Childbearing Years' (Section IV), we show how maternal mortality and morbidity continue to plague women of not only developing, but also developed countries. In 'The Middle Years' (Section V) we focus attention on what in our judgment is a sadly neglected period in women's lives, sandwiched somewhere between youth and old age. This period, from 40 to 60 years, will become increasingly important as dramatic demographic trends transform many societies. In 'Old Age' (Section VI) we cover the growing challenges facing older women who are living longer but not always better lives. Section VII discusses other threats to women's health, and Section VIII concludes.

II CONCEPTION TO ADOLESCENCE

Judy Yung (1997) wrote 'It is hard to be born a woman but hopeless to be born a Chinese woman' (p. 66). Demographers would agree. In 2010, China had a sex ratio of 118 males to 100 females, suggesting that as many as 1.2 million females did not survive through childbirth or suffered infanticide (Hudson, 2011). China is not alone. According to a 2011 census, India had a sex ratio of 914 girls aged 0–6 years for every 1,000 boys the same age – signifying a loss of 7.1 million girls before age 6 (*The Economist* online, 2011). Even affluent countries such as Taiwan and South Korea have severe sex imbalances. Taiwan's gender ratio at birth has ranged from 108 to 112 males for every 100 females, placing it behind only China in the severity of its gender imbalance. In 2010, it was estimated that Taiwanese women had between 300 and 500 thousand abortions, while only 166,000 babies were born (Baklinski, 2011). South Korea's sex ratio at 107.4 boys for every 100 girls is slightly less extreme, although it is down from a peak of 116.5 boys born for every 100 girls in 1990 (Sand-Hun, 2007).

How does male gender preference affect the health of women? First, there is strong evidence that couples unable to control family composition tend to have higher numbers of children as they continue trying to have a male child (Clark, 2000). In addition, surveys show that in larger families, particularly those in low-income countries such as India, girls are less likely to receive healthcare, hospital care, and adequate nutrition (Sen, 1992; Westley and Kim, 2007). Even in the absence of more children, a male preference appears to impact survival of girls. In industrialized countries, mortality among female children is 20 percent lower than male children, while in China, where small family sizes are mandated, mortality among girls is still 33 percent higher than among boys (WHO, 2003). How an eventual shortage of women will affect family formation is unknown. Christophe Guilmoto (2007) has suggested that fewer women may lead to marriage at younger ages, and a larger number of women withdrawing from the workforce. Even more pessimistic, Valerie Hudson and Andrea den Boer (2004) have suggested that social masculinization may lead to higher rates of gender-based violence, sex work, and human trafficking. The best hope is that reduced numbers of females may enhance the status of women and contribute to a greater social investment in women across the life span.

III   ADOLESCENCE

Adolescence can be a period of discovery as young women build new interpersonal relationships, take on greater responsibility, and experiment with adult roles. It is also a period of heightened risk, particularly among females. These dangers are greatest for the 85 percent of girls living in developing countries where violence, sexual abuse, and HIV are often endemic (United Nations Population Fund, 2005). Adolescent girls in lower-income countries are often subject to discrimination in education and healthcare, and are frequently forced into child marriages and early pregnancies. Mothers aged 15 to 19 are twice as likely as their older counterparts to suffer maternal death (Population Resource Center, 2001). Their children are also 50 percent more likely to die than the children of women in their 20s (Mayor, 2004). A study in Bangladesh found that mothers aged 10 to 14 were five times more likely to die of pregnancy related causes than mothers aged 20 to 24 (Chen et al., 1974). Indralal De Silva summarized the problem well when she observed that 'for large number of girls, adolescence can be best defined as the period which starts with the premature end of education and ends with the premature start of pregnancy and childbearing or even death' (1998, p. 5).

Infectious disease also plays a disproportionate role in the death of young women worldwide. According to an analysis of data from the 2004 Global Burden of Disease Study, more than one in five young females aged 10 to 24 years die from lower respiratory infections, HIV/AIDS, tuberculosis, and meningitis (Patton et al., 2009). Other important causes of mortality included suicide (6.2 percent), road traffic accidents (5 percent), fire-related deaths (4.3 percent), and drowning (2.5 percent). The most shocking feature of these causes is their preventable nature. For instance, lower respiratory illness, a top infectious killer of adolescents worldwide, claimed less than 300 adolescent lives in the US in 2004 compared with an estimated 153,000 in the developing world (ibid.; American Lung Association, 2010). Other major causes such as maternal mortality could be greatly reduced through provision to prevent unwanted pregnancies and access to basic maternal health services.

Another pervasive problem affecting adolescent females is the high rate of sexual and physical abuse. Worldwide, about four in every 10 rapes and sexual assaults are perpetrated against girls 15 years or younger (Heise, 1993). Studies in Uganda showed that one in every two sexually active primary school girls reported forced sexual intercourse (Noble et al., 1996). Research in Zimbabwe found that half of reported rape cases involved girls under 15 years of age (Njovana and Watts, 1996). Even in higher-income countries, rape is prevalent among young women. In 2009, 7 percent of all US students in grades 9 through 12 reported rape at some time in their lives, and 11 percent of female students said they had been raped during that year (CDC, 2010). The impact of rape in adolescence can have devastating and lifelong consequences. Victimized teenagers initiate intercourse earlier, are more likely to use drugs and alcohol, and experience teenage pregnancy more frequently (Boyer and Fine, 1992). Some studies also suggest a strong association between physical and sexual abuse and reproductive health in adulthood. A Scandinavian study showed that victims of physical and sexual abuse were more likely to suffer gynecological problems including vaginal bleeding, pain during intercourse, chronic pelvic pain, urinary tract infections, and pelvic inflammatory disease (Schei and Bakketeig, 1989; Schei, 1990).

It is also impossible to overestimate the impact of two decades of the HIV/AIDS epidemic on the health of young women. By 2010, about 1.8 million females aged 15–24 were living with HIV worldwide (UNAIDS, 2011). It is estimated that by 2017 more than 14 million will have been infected (Global Fund Updated, 2006). In Sub-Saharan Africa, HIV prevalence among women in this age group is at least three times that of young men (AMFAR, 2010). There are multiple factors for this increased vulnerability: in many cultures gender norms encourage men to have more sexual partners and to have sexual relations with younger women (WHO, 2008a). This means older HIV-infected males are often infecting younger and more inexperienced women. In addition, females have a substantially higher biological risk for HIV acquisition. Transmission from a man to a woman is two to eight times more efficient than from a woman to a man; women have greater mucous membrane exposure during sex and younger females with immature cervixes are more prone to HIV infection (Cummins and Dezzutti, 2000). Finally, rape and sexual violence in many countries are exposing girls and young women to the HIV virus. A study in South Africa showed that nearly one in seven cases of young women acquiring HIV could have been prevented if the women had not been subjected to intimate partner violence (AMFAR, 2010).

Substance abuse and mental illness are also important and growing problems among adolescent women. The 2007 US National Survey on Drug Use and Health found that compared with their male counterparts, adolescent females reported significantly higher rates of past month illicit drug use other than marijuana (Substance Abuse and Mental Health Services Administration, 2007). They also had higher rates of current alcohol, cigarette, and nonmedical pain reliever use and were more likely to report depression and alcohol dependence in the last year. Additionally, a majority (60 percent) reported that they first engaged in illicit substance abuse between the ages of 12 and 14.

The reasons for these differences are largely unexplored. Some researchers posit that women may be differentially affected by depression and parental and peer influences (Windle et al., 1989). Others suggest that many cultures create greater stress for females than males as a result of the societal view of females as subordinate and inferior to males (Rutter et al., 1970). Whatever the reasons, drug and alcohol abuse is a growing problem for women. Globally, while women have been shown less likely than men to use illicit drugs, they are at higher risk for abusing legal medications (Boyer and Fine, 1992; United Nations Office on Drugs and Crime, 2011). The gap between males and females also appears to be closing: younger women are more likely to use both prescription and illicit drugs, and the ratio of males to females abusing all drugs is shrinking (Degenhardt et al., 2008).

IV   THE CHILDBEARING YEARS

At the time Honoré de Balzac said 'Chance, my dear, is the sovereign deity in childbearing', he could have been observing how difficult it was to predict conception, or how often forecasts about the day of a child's birth were wrong. More likely he was talking about whether a woman would survive pregnancy and delivery – something unknowable in the eighteenth century. It would not be until the 1900s that women would have access to dependable contraception to space births, and 1975 before they could legally seek an abortion in France, Balzac's home country (Allison, 1994; Jütte, 2008). During his lifetime, as many as 970 deliveries in every 100,000 would end in maternal death (Caselli et al., 2005). Given his famous optimism, he would likely have been surprised that two centuries later there would still be countries such as Afghanistan, Burundi, Chad, Guinea-Bissau, Liberia, Sierra Leone, and Somalia, to name a few, that would have maternal mortality ratios equal to or greater than France in his time (World Bank, 2008).

Maternal death as defined by the World Health Organization (WHO) is 'the death of a woman while pregnant or within 42 days of termination of pregnancy, irrespective of the duration and site of the pregnancy' (WHO, n.d.). This definition includes deaths related to a variety of pregnancy outcomes including induced abortion, miscarriage, stillbirth, and live births. It also encompasses indirect causes such as malaria, anemia, HIV/AIDS, and cardiovascular disease that complicate pregnancy or are aggravated by it and lead to the death of a mother. Finally, it also includes maternal deaths after delivery. In many developing countries, more than 60 percent of mortality occurs in the postpartum period; about 45 percent within one day of delivery, 65 percent within the first week, and 80 percent within two weeks.

The death of mothers in pregnancy is largely concentrated in the developing world. In the year 2000, a woman living in Sub-Saharan Africa faced a one in a hundred risk of dying in childbirth. That hazard was halved in South Asia, and halved again in Latin America or the Caribbean. During that same year mothers in developed countries had a 50 times lower risk of mortality as the result of pregnancy with the lowest lifetime risk in Sweden, where only one in 30,000 women died (Ronsmans and Graham, 2006). In the last 70 years, maternal mortality has declined by fifty-fold but has barely declined at all in some African countries (Commission on Macroeconomics and Health, 2001). This great divide between the industrial and developing countries has been called the largest discrepancy of all public health statistics (Graham et al., 2006).

Successful efforts to address maternal death must also include interventions to address unsafe abortion. Of the 42 million pregnancies that are terminated worldwide each year, about 20 million put women's lives at unnecessary risk (Guttmacher Institute, 2009).

Statistics show that in 2008, almost all abortions in Africa, Latin America, and Eastern Asia were unsafe, while only about 65 percent would be considered so in South Central Asia (Grimes et al., 2006). In contrast, almost all countries offering legal abortion services reaching the poorest and most vulnerable populations have a high percentage of safe abortion services. For instance, in the Caribbean, there are only a negligible number of unsafe abortions because of liberal laws and availability of high-quality medical care. Unfortunately, about 40 percent of all abortions occur in areas where abortion is either illegal or highly restricted (S. Singh, 2010). With one in 8 pregnancies ending in an unsafe abortion, it is not surprising that deaths during abortions represent a significant source of maternal mortality (Guttmacher Institute, 2009, p. 3).

That maternal mortality can be successfully prevented is undeniable. Deaths among mothers in Europe and North America have largely been eliminated; women living in industrial countries have only a one in 1,800 lifetime risk of dying as the result of maternal causes compared with a one in 48 chance in developing countries (Commission on Macroeconomics and Health, 2001). While the cost of preventing these maternal deaths varies widely, intervention in developing countries is significantly more economical than similar programs in the United States or Europe. It is estimated that the cost of a normal delivery with a skilled attendant can range from $2 to $15 in Africa and Latin America. Normal deliveries conducted at a medical center cost between $10 and $35, and cesarean sections and complicated deliveries from $50–$100. When the cost of health system strengthening and provision of skilled birth attendance for all deliveries is included, the estimated costs per maternal and perinatal death averted range from $1,000–$3,000 (ibid.).

Developing countries are not the only places where maternal deaths are a growing problem. During the last several decades, maternal deaths have almost doubled in the United States (7.1 deaths per 100,000 births to 13.3 deaths per 100,000 births), an irony given the country's position as the largest funder of maternal health programs in the world (Council on Foreign Relations, 2008). As of 2005, the United States ranked 41 in maternity mortality out of 171 countries with one in 4,800 US women dying from complications of pregnancy or childbirth, the same as Belarus and just slightly better than Serbia, where one in 4,500 women die (WHO, 2005a). Not surprisingly, the death of mothers is concentrated among the poor and among ethnic minorities: black women die at a rate of 26.5 deaths per 100,000 live births, almost three times the maternal mortality rate (MMR) for Caucasian women (10/100,000). Data from 2005–07 also showed high rates among American Indians/Alaska Natives (16.9/100,000), Asian/Pacific Islanders (11/100,000), and Hispanics (9.6/100,000) (G. Singh, 2010).

Reducing the current estimated death toll of about 343,000 maternal deaths each year – both in developing and developed settings – will require a broad range of solutions. Investment in both community and clinic-level interventions will be necessary. While a large percentage of deaths occur in rural settings where mothers have low access to medical care, available data also indicate that a large number of maternal deaths still occur in medical facilities (Magadi et al., 2001; Oladapo et al., 2009). In addition, there is a critical need to translate what is already known into interventions. Misoprostol, a widely available and inexpensive drug used to terminate a pregnancy by starting labor, is recognized as an essential lifesaving tool to prevent mortality from obstetrical hemorrhage, particularly in low-income countries. A number of other interventions have been tested and proven but will involve international investment for health system strengthening. Only a strong commitment at all levels will address the scope of the problem worldwide.

V   THE MIDDLE YEARS

Middle age is a period largely overlooked and sandwiched between youth, so prized in the developed world, and maturity, which is venerated in traditional societies. Bernice Neugarten and Nancy Datan have suggested that this stage is often characterized as 'a plateau with little of significance occurring until old age' (Neugarten and Datan, 1996). While the period between 40 and 60 years is typically a time of relatively good health, some researchers have demonstrated that it may play a more important role in setting the stage for both mental and physical problems in old age (Siegler, 1997). For instance, the Nurses' Health Study being carried out by Harvard School of Public Health and the Brigham and Women's Hospital in Boston found that women who gained at least 22 pounds by the time they turned 50 had less chance of being healthy over 70 than those whose weight remained steady (Sun et al., 2009). The same study also showed that women who were physically active at midlife were less likely to experience mental health problems, cancer, diabetes, major heart disease, stroke, kidney failure, and chronic obstructive pulmonary disease.

The middle years do present women with a unique set of challenges. In high-income countries, heart disease and breast cancer are major killers. Other risks include obesity and its complications including Type-2 diabetes mellitus, hypertension, and dyslipidaemia (Caterson, 2009), and conditions related to menopausal hormonal imbalances such as osteoarthritis and osteoporosis. Women in developing world settings face an even broader set of risks. Poverty-related conditions such as inadequate nutrition, chronic anemia, and exposure to polluted water, agricultural pesticides, and indoor air pollution are often determinants of ill health in later life (WHO, 2000). Nutritional deficits also frequently manifest as chronic diseases such as osteoporosis, osteomalacia, thyroid deficiency, colorectal cancer, and cardiovascular illness (Tulchinsky, 2010). Collectively, poverty-related factors significantly reduce life expectancy. A 60-year-old woman in Cambodia can expect to live another six years while her counterpart in more affluent South Korea will likely live another 23 (Central Intelligence Agency, 2012). Unfortunately, those women living to older ages also face the same chronic diseases more common in developed settings.

Coronary heart disease (CHD) and other cardiovascular illnesses are the most common causes of death in middle age for women in the industrial world (Hayes, 2006) and the second leading cause of mortality in low- and middle-income countries (WHO, 2009). In higher-income regions of the world, interventions designed to reduce risk for CHD have resulted in an age-adjusted decline in CHD-related mortality. In the past, the disease was mainly concentrated among middle-age women. Today about 80 percent of deaths in the industrial countries occur among females over the age of 60 compared with 42 percent in low- and middle-income countries (Lopez et al., 2006). Rates of CHD have been increasing in low-income regions of the world. Age-adjusted CHD mortality increased almost 40 percent among women aged 35 to 74 years between 1984 and 1999.

Incidence of CHD has also increased by 1.2 percent annually in women (Wu et al., 2001). It is predicted that by 2030, mortality from ischemic heart disease (a coronary condition caused by a buildup of plaque in the arteries to the heart) and stroke will increase by 300 percent in Latin America, the Middle East, and Sub-Saharan Africa (Yach et al., 2004). Most of those deaths will be related to lifestyle factors including obesity, smoking, and lack of physical activity among women (see Alwan, 1997).

Cancer is a leading cause of death in industrial countries and the second leading cause of mortality in developing countries (WHO, 2008b). Breast cancer is the most frequently diagnosed of these cancers and the leading cause of cancer death among females, accounting for about a quarter of total cancer cases, and 14 percent of the cancer deaths (Jemal et al., 2011). About two-thirds of these cases develop in women aged 50 and older, both in lower- and higher-income countries (Phend, 2011).

The picture is considerably more skewed for cervical cancer. Of the approximately 530,000 new cases and 275,000 cervical cancer deaths, about 80 percent occur in low- and middle-income countries, where women have limited access to screening and early treatment (WHO, 2009; Sahasrabuddhe et al., 2011). Lung cancer is also a major source of mortality among women: about the same number of females in developing countries die from cancer of the lungs as from cervical cancer, with each accounting for 11 percent of female cancer deaths (Jemal et al., 2011). Worldwide, the number of new cancer cases is expected to top 15 million annually, and deaths may reach 12 million by 2020. At least 70 percent of these deaths will be in economically developing countries, where survival rates are often much lower than in the industrial world (Peedell, 2005).

Women in their middle years in both developed and developing countries also face an increasing risk for mental illness. In the United States, for instance, a study showed that increases in the overall suicide rate between 1999 and 2005 were due in part to larger numbers of 40–64-year-old women taking their own lives (Johns Hopkins University, 2008). Similarly, in low-income countries suicide rates for women peak in middle age and decline thereafter (Ruzicka, 1976). Women across the world also suffer from high rates of emotional disorders. A UK study showed that one in four English women aged 45 to 64 suffered some form of mental health problem, an increase of 20 percent in the last 15 years. Women in middle age are also suffering a greater decline in mental health than any other age group (NHS Information Centre, 2007). Mental health issues are not unique to industrial societies. A World Bank report shows that women in low-income countries also suffer considerable morbidity from psychiatric problems. Estimates place the number of DALYs lost among women at 8.6 million due to higher prevalence of depressive disorders and dementias including Alzheimer's disease (Young, 1994).

VI   OLD AGE

Due to their longevity compared with men, aging women represent one of the fastest-growing population groups worldwide. The sex ratio in the oldest groups is so skewed that they comprise primarily women. In 2007, according to the United Nations (UN Department of Economic and Social Affairs, 2008), the global sex ratio for men and women age 60 and over was 82 males per hundred females. In other words, there were approximately 70 million more women in that category than there were men. Since female mortality rates are lower than male rates in every category, the proportion of women in the population increases with age. In 2007, the ratio of women to men was 4:3 at 65 years and above and 2:1 at 80 and above. With income and longevity increasing in developing countries, chronic diseases are becoming the major source of mortality for older women. Globally, cardiovascular disease and chronic obstructive pulmonary disease account for 45 percent of deaths among women 60 years and over. A further 15 percent die as the result of cancers, mainly of the breast, lung and colon (WHO, 2009). The remaining mortality is attributed to infectious diseases. Many of the chronic illnesses are the result of risk factors during adolescence and adulthood such as smoking, excessive alcohol use, obesity, or unhealthy diet (ibid.). A study in China using data from 1999 and 2000 found that the five leading causes of death among older women were diseases of the heart, cerebrovascular illness, cancer, pneumonia and influenza, and infectious diseases, in that order (He et al., 2005). Causes of death for older women in high-income regions such as the European Union are surprisingly similar. The major causes of death include cardiovascular disease, killing almost 39 percent of older women, followed by stroke at 18 percent, and cancer at 17 percent (Carron, 2010).

While women have a longer life expectancy, they also experience significant morbidity as they age. Female infants at birth in upper-income countries can be expected to live 86 percent of their lives without any significant degree of disability at all, but then are likely to have serious disability in the last four years of their lives (Doll, 1995). A survey of health expectancy for women over 65 years of age in eight developing countries (six in Asia and two in North Africa) showed that women are expected to live without restriction in activities including eating, caring for one's own well-being, shopping, cooking, and so on (United Nations, 2000). Major causes of morbidity among older women include loss of visual acuity and hearing, osteoporosis, malnutrition, and anemia (Young, 1994). In some low-income countries such as India, diabetes has emerged as a leading cause of morbidity among older women (ibid.). In many higher-income countries, fall-related injuries are a leading cause of disabilities among women aged 65 and over. About half of those women hospitalized for hip fractures never regain their former level of function (Stevens and Olson, 2000).

As women reach the oldest age groups, they too often face other challenges such as elder abuse and neglect (Sherman et al., 2008). A study in the United Kingdom found that 2.6 percent of people (3.8 and 1.1 percent of women and men, respectively) over age 66 and living in private households, or about one in 40 of the older population, reported that they had experienced mistreatment involving a family member, friend, or care worker during the past year (O'Keeffe et al., 2007). A 2006 systematic review of studies of elder abuse and neglect in both developing and developed countries found a wide range in reported abuse (3.2–27.5 percent), suggesting that cultural differences may play a large role in both treatment of elders and in elders' perceptions of what constitutes abuse and neglect. Over 6 percent of seniors reported being abused in the last month, and one in 20 older couples reported physical violence in the last year. About one in four elders said that they had suffered psychological abuse, and one in five reported neglect. In addition, about a third of family caretakers reported perpetrating abuse. These studies indicate that abuse against older people is a worldwide phenomenon and that some elders suffer significant abuse and neglect (Cooper et al., 2008).

Mental illnesses are also a major issue among elderly women. Untreated mental health

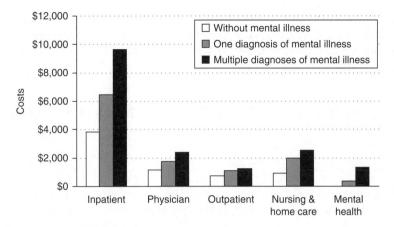

Source: Husaini et al. (2000).

Figure 27.1 *Healthcare costs for a Tennessee sample of elderly Medicare beneficiaries with and without mental illness*

problems lead to lower quality of life, and complicate treatment for other illnesses. While women and men suffer at about the same rate from severe mental disorders such as schizophrenia and bipolar disorder, they differ significantly in the prevalence of more common affective disorders (WHO, 2001). Worldwide, depressive disorders account for more than four of every 10 psychiatric disorders and anxiety for about one in 10 among elderly women (Brenes et al., 2005a; WHO, 2008b). Other leading mental health problems among elderly females include organic brain syndromes and dementia (WHO, 2001).

Depression and anxiety are about twice as common among older women than men (Husaini et al., 2004; Rahman, 2006). According to research, both depression and anxiety are significant predictors of disability (Lenze et al., 2001; Brenes et al., 2005b). Women suffering from these disorders are often unable to carry on the most basic activities such as social interaction and activities of daily living including feeding oneself, dressing, bathing, toileting, and mobility. The cost of these disorders in independence and quality of life among elderly patients is obvious and significant. As shown in Figure 27.1, one US study carried out among Medicare recipients showed that the total cost of care for elderly individuals with a diagnosis for mental illness was more than twice the cost of caring for an individual without mental illness.

Dementia is also a common mental health problem among the oldest women. Research shows that all-cause dementia 'almost doubles with every five years of age and prevalence of dementia rises from approximately 2 percent to 3 percent in those 65 to 75 years to 35 percent in those 85 years and older' (Yaffe et al., 2011, p. 631). Clinically identified Alzheimer's disease and mixed dementia were most common, with both accounting for 80 percent of cases. Amnesiac multiple domain and nonamnesiac single domain accounted for 33.9 and 28.9 percent of cases, respectively. Perhaps not surprisingly, cognitive impairment was more common among women 90 years or older (compared with those 85 to 89 years) and was more common in women with less education, a history of stroke, and prevalent depression (Yaffe et al., 2011). Currently, 60 percent of people with dementia live in developing countries. In India, China, and other Asian and Pacific countries, the prevalence of dementia is expected to increase by over 300 percent by 2040 (Murphy and Smith, 2009).

VII   OTHER THREATS TO WOMEN'S HEALTH ACROSS THE LIFE SPAN

Thus far we have shown how women over the course of the life cycle are statistically prone to and affected by certain illnesses, diseases, and related health issues. If societies across the globe are concerned about improving women's well-being, then health should be considered key to socioeconomic status and movements for gender equity. In this section, we briefly discuss four additional health risks for women that span age groups: violence against women; HIV/AIDS; sexually transmitted infections; and obesity.

Violence against Women

Violence against women, including intimate partner violence (IPV), is a major public health problem that impacts women at every age. The incidence is portrayed in Figure 27.2. It has been shown to be a contributor to mortality and morbidity in young girls, adolescents, pregnant women, and the elderly (Noble et al., 1996; Cooper et al., 2008; Salari and Nakhaee, 2008). Worldwide, IPV has been associated with physical injuries and homicides, unwanted pregnancies, abortions, miscarriages, and increased risk for HIV and other sexually transmitted infections (Gilbert, 1996; Bailey et al., 1997; Shackelford and Mouzos, 2005; Silverman et al., 2007; Decker et al., 2009; Dude, 2011). The women most at risk for violence are also the most vulnerable: typically they are younger in age (Jewkes et al., 2002; Burazeri et al., 2005), unemployed (Jewkes et al., 2002), poorer (Castro et al., 2003; Rivera-Rivera et al., 2004), and less educated (Jewkes et al., 2002; Salari and Nakhaee, 2008).

The economic cost of partner violence against women is staggering. Using figures from 1998, the US Centers for Disease Control and Prevention estimated the annual economic cost of violence against women in the US at $5.8 billion. This figure included the direct cost of treatment for injuries and mental health problems and the indirect cost of lost productivity for both paid and unpaid work (US Department of Health and Human Services, 2003). Other countries and regions have reported similar figures. It is estimated that in Canada, even with its relatively small population, violence against women costs US$6.98 billion each year or about US$13,312 per woman (University of British Columbia, 2011). The annual cost of violence against women for the 47 countries in the Council of Europe has been estimated as high as US$45 billion (European Policy Action Centre on Violence Against Women, 2012). While there is not sufficient data to assess the global economic impact of violence against women, it is presumed to be large. According to the UN, women provide 70 percent of the unpaid time spent in caring for family members, the value of which is estimated at US$11 trillion per year – one-third of global GDP (Geneva Centre for the Democratic Control of Armed Forces, 2005).

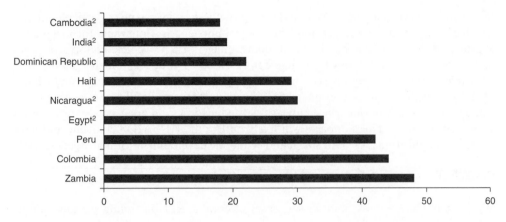

Notes:
1. In most surveys, 'ever beaten' includes having been hit, slapped, kicked, or physically hurt;
2. Cambodia, India, Nicaragua, and Egypt include only ever-married women.

Source: Husaini et al. (2000).

Figure 27.2   Percent of women ages 15–49 ever beaten[1] by an intimate partner, selected countries

HIV/AIDS

Women represent about one in every two people living with HIV/AIDS worldwide, and about 60 percent of HIV-infected individuals in Sub-Saharan Africa (Henry J. Kaiser Family Foundation, 2010). Young women are at even greater risk for infection, particularly in some areas of Africa, where they outnumber young men by as much as two to one. As stated above, the reasons include gender and income inequalities, rape and violence against women, poor access to healthcare and reproductive health services, and woman's biological susceptibility to HIV infection. Not surprisingly, women living with HIV also are disadvantaged in accessing antiretroviral therapy. A national study of insurance records for 24 large employers in the US showed that while about 71 percent of men with HIV received antiretroviral therapy, only about 39 percent of their female counterparts accessed those same services (Hellinger and Encinosa, 2004). The distribution of HIV worldwide and within countries gives proof to the conviction of Peter Piot, former Executive Director of UNAIDS, that 'gender inequality, discrimination and stigma, marginalization of vulnerable groups, and violation of human rights' are the underlying drivers of the HIV epidemic (Boesten and Poku, 2009, p. 9).

What social and economic impacts will emerge from the loss of so many reproductive age women to the HIV epidemic? A demographic analysis by the Economic Commission for Africa raises many chilling possibilities. Among Sub-Saharan countries most affected by the epidemic, mortality from HIV/AIDS is producing 'population pyramids that have never been seen before' (Economic Commission for Africa, 2003). The impact of these changes on families, communities, and even countries is unclear. Not only are many of the countries, including Botswana, Lesotho, Mozambique, South Africa, and

Swaziland, experiencing negative population growth, the winnowing of particular demographic groups is having larger and larger social impacts. In Botswana, for instance, it is projected that there will be more men than women in each five-year cohort from ages 15 to 44. Ominously, this may result in older men seeking younger women in all the marriageable cohorts, driving up HIV rates since age is a proxy for HIV exposure (ibid.). Moreover, as the result of ingrained social inequalities women will face declining living standards as the result of earlier marriage, less education, and great power differentials with their partners. These impacts will likely outlive the HIV/AIDS epidemic and have profound implications for both social and economic development for many generations.

Sexually Transmitted Infections (STIs)

Worldwide, there are 448 million new cases of curable STIs including syphilis, gonorrhea, chlamydia, and trichomoniasis each year. Untreated, they can have significant negative implications for reproductive, maternal, and newborn health. In a large number of studies, STIs have been associated with spontaneous abortion, stillbirth, prematurity, low birth weight, and postpartum endometritis. STIs have also been found to contribute to postinfection tubal damage, which is responsible for about one-third of female infertility (Mullick et al., 2005). Among pregnant women with untreated early syphilis, one in four cases ends in stillbirth. More than a third of pregnancies among women with gonorrhea result in spontaneous abortions (ibid.). It is ironic that many of these infections are easily treatable but expensive to diagnose. Investments in interventions and technology to detect STIs have the potential to save hundreds of thousands of women from death or long-term disability.

According to figures from the World Bank, STIs and HIV are responsible for a 6 percent loss in healthy years of life among women 14 to 44 years (Guttmacher Institute, 1997). In developing countries, poor health seeking and poor access to healthcare are major obstacles to STI control (Bailey et al., 1997). Even if women seek healthcare, many practitioners have limited capacity for accurate diagnosis and treatment (Aral et al., 2006). Other challenges include the asymptomatic nature of many infections, low knowledge and awareness about STIs, and stigma associated with genital symptoms leading to failure in health seeking (CDC, 2008). Despite the large number of infections worldwide, control efforts have also been underfunded and ineffective. For example, an estimated 1,640,000 pregnant women with syphilis in Sub-Saharan Africa go undiagnosed each year (Population Action International, 2006).

Obesity

Today, according to the WHO (2009), 65 percent of the world's population lives in countries where overweight and obesity kill more people than underweight. Worldwide, the number of individuals classified as obese has more than doubled since 1980 (WHO, 2011). In developing countries, where most people assume that starvation is ubiquitous, obesity now coexists with malnutrition. In India for instance, a survey of 83,000 women found that 33 percent were malnourished, and 12 percent were overweight. The same incongruity can be found across the world. In 2008, it was estimated that nearly 300 million women globally were obese (ibid.). This dramatic increase in adiposity among women has wide-ranging public health implications. First, it heightens risk for metabolic syndrome, a group of co-occurring risk factors that predispose females to coronary artery disease, stroke, and type 2 diabetes. It also substantially increases the risk for breast, endometrial, colorectal, esophageal, and pancreatic cancers. Obesity has been associated with negative economic outcomes, so the social consequences of the trend may be farther reaching. For example, there is substantial evidence from high-income countries of an inverse relationship between body weight and socioeconomic status. Women appear to suffer significant socioeconomic disadvantage if they are obese compared with their leaner counterparts (Sobal and Stunkard, 1989). Additionally, overweight adolescent girls are more likely to engage in risky sexual behavior than their normal-weight peers, according to research presented at the American Congress of Obstetricians and Gynecologists (CDC, 2011).

A number of studies have attempted to quantify the social and economic costs of obesity. One suggested that the economic costs of the condition were about $300 billion per year in the US and Canada. Researchers included direct costs for additional medical care and indirect costs for the loss of economic productivity resulting from excess mortality and disability among obese people (Behan et al., 2010). A systematic review of the costs of obesity worldwide also found substantial costs attached to the condition. According to one study, obesity was estimated to account for between 0.7 and 2.8 percent of a country's total healthcare expenditures. Furthermore, obese individuals were found to have medical costs that were approximately 30 percent greater than those of their normal weight peers (Withrow and Alter, 2011). The lesson is straightforward: preventing obesity in women is a more cost-effective strategy than providing the required medical and social services later in life. One study found that maintaining healthy weight in one 70-year-old in the US could save as much as $39,000 in healthcare costs for the remainder of that person's life (Lakdawalla et al., 2005).

VIII CONCLUSION

Women have been disproportionately affected by many of the risk factors associated with poor health. Despite increased longevity, they often have less income, less power, more social burdens, and higher risks for morbidity than men. Those in developed countries are clearly advantaged, living longer lives with less morbidity. Yet women from wealthier countries are subject to many of the same problems as their poorer counterparts: increasingly, the quality of their lives is affected by chronic illnesses such as diabetes, heart disease, and cancer. Improving outcomes for women will require more than advanced drugs and medical care. According to the World Health Organization (2005b), the causes are systemic and include widespread and persistent inequities in access to health services, the heavy burden of violence and victimization, inadequate reproductive health services, and mental illnesses that are frequently undiagnosed or untreated. In developing countries, social conditions including early or forced marriages; disempowerment at the level of family and community; and victimization lead to bad health outcomes. Whether these conditions change will depend largely on a realization among policy-makers that the cost of poor health among women is greater than any advantage gained from disempowerment or oppression.

How do we go about addressing health disparities between men and women in both the developed and developing worlds? First and foremost, inequalities in access to healthcare present the single largest barrier to the health of women. Across the world they are less likely to have health insurance or to be able to afford care when they are ill (Dodd and Munck, 2003). It should be no surprise that those able to access skilled care for deliveries and illnesses have better outcomes. Sadly, this is not a problem unique to the developing world. In the United States in 2010, for example, more than 27 million women went without health insurance for at least part of the last year (Commonwealth Fund, 2011). Other reasons for disparate health outcomes between men and women are more insidious. They are reflected in fewer opportunities for education and work; and norms of behavior, codes of conduct, and laws that perpetuate health disparities affecting women. These factors are shaped by history and the politics of place and time.

While each society confronts unique obstacles, the similarities are more striking than the differences. Gita Sen and Piroska Östlin (2007, p. 7) framed the challenge well in a report to the WHO Commission on Social Determinants of Health:

> Where biological sex differences interact with social determinants to define different needs for women and men in health (the most obvious being maternity), gender equity will require different treatment of women and men that is sensitive to these needs. On the other hand, where no plausible biological reason exists for different health outcomes, social discrimination should be considered a prime suspect for different and inequitable health outcomes. Health equity in the latter case will require policies that encourage equal outcomes, including differential treatment to overcome historical discrimination.

Although we face many challenges, the benefits of reducing gender inequalities in health (and the costs of not doing so) make this too important to neglect, not only for fostering economic growth and development, but also for improving the quality of everyday life for millions of girls and women around the world.

NOTE

*   For her generous assistance on this chapter, the authors would like to thank Kelly Winter from Florida International University for providing technical support and helpful suggestions.

REFERENCES

Allison, Maggie (1994), 'The right to choose: abortion in France', *Parliamentary Affairs*, **47**(2), 222–37.
Alwan Ala'din (1997), 'Noncommunicable diseases: a major challenge to public health in the Region', *Eastern Mediterranean Health Journal*, **3**(1), 6–16.
American Lung Association (2010), 'Trends in pneumonia and influenza morbidity and mortality', available at: http://www.lung.org/finding-cures/our-research/trend-reports/pitrend-report.pdf (accessed May 12, 2012).
AMFAR (2010), 'Statistics: Women and HIV/AIDS', available at: http://www.amfar.org/content.aspx?id=3594 (accessed April 4, 2012).
Aral, Sevgi O., Mead Over, Lisa Manhart and King K. Holmes (2006), 'Sexually transmitted infections', ch. 17 in Dean T. Jamison, Joel G. Brema, Anthoy R. Measham, George Alleyne, Mariam Claeson, David B. Evans, Prabhat Jha, Anne Mills and Philip Musgrove (eds), *Disease Control Priorities in Developing Countries*, 2nd edn, Washington, DC: World Bank, pp. 311–30.

Bailey, James E., Arthur L. Kellermann, Grant W. Somes, Joyce G. Banton, Frederick P. Rivara and Norman Rushforth (1997), 'Risk factors for violent death of women in the home', *Archives of Internal Medicine*, **157**(7), 777–82.

Baklinski, Thaddeus (2011), 'Sex-selective abortion causing massive gender imbalance in Taiwan', LifeSiteNews, available at: http://www.lifesite.net/news/sex-selective-abortion-causing-massive-gender-imbalance-in-taiwan (accessed March 14, 2012).

Behan, Donald F., Samuel H. Cox, Yijia Lin, Jeffrey Pai, Hal W. Pedersen and Ming Yi (2010), 'Obesity and its Relation to Mortality and Morbidity Costs', Committee on Life Insurance Research & Society of Actuaries, available at: http://www.soa.org/files/pdf/research-2011-obesity-relation-mortality.pdf (accessed January 11, 2012).

Boesten, Jelke and Nana K. Poku (2009), *Gender and HIV/AIDS: Critical Perspectives from the Developing World*, New York: Ashgate.

Boyer, Debra and David Fine (1992), 'Sexual abuse as a factor in adolescent pregnancy and child maltreatment', *Family Planning Perspectives*, **24**(1), 4–11, 19.

Brenes, Gretchen A., Jack M. Guralnik, Jeff Williamson, Linda P. Fried and Brenda W.J.H. Pennenix (2005a), 'Correlates of anxiety symptoms in physically disabled older women', *American Journal of Geriatric Psychiatry*, **13**(1), 15–22.

Brenes, Gretchen A., Jack M. Guralnik, Jeff Williamson, Linda P. Fried, Crystal Simpson, Eleanor M. Simonsick and Brenda W.J.H. Pennenix (2005b), 'The influence of anxiety on the progression of disability', *Journal of the American Geriatrics Society*, **53**(1), 34–9.

Burazeri, Genc, Enver Roshi, Rachel Jewkes, Susanne Jordan, Vesna Bjegovic and Ulrich Laaser (2005), 'Factors associated with spousal physical violence in Albania: cross sectional study', *British Medical Journal*, **331**(7510), 197–201.

Carron, Simone (2010), 'Emerging Trends in European Women's Health Imaging Market', available at: http://www.frost.com/prod/servlet/market-insight-top.pag?docid=211960207 (accessed May 14, 2012).

Caselli, Graziella, Jacques Vallin and Guillame Wunsch (2005), *Demography: Analysis and Synthesis, Four Volume Set: A Treatise in Population*, New York: Academic Press.

Castro, Roberto, Corinne Peek-Asa and Augustin Ruiz (2003), 'Violence against women in Mexico: a study of abuse before and during pregnancy', *American Journal of Public Health*, **93**(7), 1110–16.

Caterson, Ian D. (2009), 'Medical management of obesity and its complications', *Annals, Academy of Medicine, Singapore*, **38**(1), 22–7.

Centers for Disease Control and Prevention (CDC) (2008), 'Sexually transmitted infections in developing countries: current concepts and strategies on improving STI prevention, treatment, and control', available at: http://siteresources.worldbank.org/INTPRH/Resources/STINoteFINAL26Feb08.pdf (accessed May 21, 2012).

Centers for Disease Control and Prevention (CDC) (2010), 'Youth risk behavior surveillance – United States, 2009', *MMWR: Morbidity and Mortality Weekly Report*, **59**(SS5), Table 12, June 4.

Centers for Disease control and Prevention (CDC) (2011), 'Sexual Identity, Sex of Sexual Contacts, and Health-Risk Behaviors Among Students in Grades 9–12 – Youth Risk Behavior', available at: http://www.cdc.gov/mmwr/pdf/ss/ss60e0606.pdf (accessed October 4, 2011).

Central Intelligence Agency (2012), 'Life Expectancy at Birth', available at: https://www.cia.gov/library/publications/the-world-factbook/fields/2102.html (accessed October 4, 2011).

Chen, Lincoln C., Shamsa Ahmed, Melita Gesche and William Henry (1974), 'A prospective study of birth interval dynamics in rural Bangladesh', *Population Studies: A Journal of Demography*, **28**(2), 277–97.

Clark, Shelley (2000), 'Son preference and sex composition of children: evidence from India', *Demography*, **37**(1), 95–108.

Commission on Macroeconomics and Health (2001), 'The Evidence Base for Interventions to Reduce Maternal and Neonatal Mortality in Low and Middle-Income Countries', WG5 Paper No. 5, World Health Organization, Geneva.

Commonwealth Fund (2011), 'Realizing Health Reform's Potential: Women at Risk: Why Increasing Numbers of Women Are Failing to Get the Health Care They Need and How the Affordable Care Act Will Help', available at: http://www.commonwealthfund.org/~/media/Files/Publications/Issue%20Brief/2011/May/1502_Robertson_women_at_risk_reform_brief_v3.pdf (accessed September 15, 2012).

Cooper, Claudia, Amber Selwood and Gill Livingston (2008), 'The prevalence of elder abuse and neglect: a systematic review', *Age and Ageing*, **37**(2), 151–60.

Council on Foreign Relations (2008), 'CFR Symposium: Rethinking Maternal Health: Maternal Health and U.S. Foreign Policy (Session 3)', available at: http://www.cfr.org/projects/world/cfr-symposium-on-rethinking-maternal-health/pr1368 (accessed November 18, 2011).

Cummins, James E. and Charlene S. Dezzutti (2000) 'HIV-1 transmission and mucosal defense mechanisms', *AIDS Reviews*, **2**, 144–54.

De Silva, W. Indralal (1998), 'Emerging reproductive health issues among adolescents in Asia', available at: http://www.hsph.harvard.edu/research/takemi/files/rp139.pdf (accessed July 23, 2011).

Decker, Michele R., George R. Seage, David Hemenway, Anita Raj, Niranjan Saggurti, Danta Balaiah and Jay G. Silverman (2009), 'Intimate partner violence functions as both a risk marker and risk factor for women's HIV infection: findings from Indian husband–wife dyads', *Journal of Acquired Immune Deficiency Syndromes*, **51**(5), 593–600.

Degenhardt, Luisa, Wai-Tat Chiu, Nancy Sampson, Ronald C. Kessler, James C. Anthony, Matthias Angermeyer et al. (2008), 'Toward a global view of alcohol, tobacco, cannabis, and cocaine use: findings from the WHO World Mental Health Surveys', *PLoS Medicine*, **5**(7), e141.

Dodd, Rebecca and Lise Munck (2003), 'Dying for Change: Poor People's Experience of Health and Ill-health', available at: www.who.int/hdp/publications/dying_change.pdf (accessed May 12, 2011).

Doll, Richard (1995), 'Chronic and degenerative disease: major causes of morbidity and death', *American Journal of Clinical Nutrition*, **62**(6 Suppl), 1301S–5S.

Dude, Annie M. (2011), 'Spousal intimate partner violence is associated with HIV and other STIs among married Rwandan women', *AIDS and Behavior*, **15**(1), 142–52.

Economic Commission for Africa (2003), 'Africa: The Socio-Economic Impact of HIV/AIDS', available at: http://www.uneca.org/chga/maputo/SOCIO_ECO_IMPACT.pdf (accessed May 12, 2011).

Economist, The, online (2011), 'India's sex ratio: sons and daughters', April 4, available at: http://www.economist.com/blogs/dailychart/2011/04/indias_sex_ratio (accessed April 5, 2011).

European Policy Action Centre on Violence Against Women (2012), 'Women's NGOs call on the Council of Europe to move towards a strong instrument on violence against women', available at: http://www.coe.int/t/dghl/standardsetting/violence/STATEMENT-270409.pdf (accessed March 2, 2012).

Geneva Centre for the Democratic Control of Armed Forces (2005), 'Women in an Insecure World', available at: http://www.unicef.org/emerg/files/women_insecure_world.pdf (accessed March 2, 2012).

Gilbert, Leah (1996), 'Urban violence and health – South Africa 1995', *Social Science and Medicine*, **43**(5), 873–86.

Global Fund Updated (2006), 'HIV situation in the world', available at: http://www.gfaids.az/?i_id=116&do=hivsit&lang=e (accessed October 17, 2011).

Graham, Wendy J., John Cairns, Sohinee Bhattacharya, Colin H.W. Bullough, Zahidul Quayyum and Khama Rog (2006), 'Maternal and perinatal conditions', ch. 26 in Dean T. Jamison, Joel G. Brema, Anthoy R. Measham, George Alleyne, Mariam Claeson, David B. Evans, Prabhat Jha, Anne Mills and Philip Musgrove (eds), *Disease Control Priorities in Developing Countries*, 2nd edn, Washington, DC: World Bank, pp. 449–529.

Grimes, David A., Janie Benson, Susheela Singh, Mariana Romero, Bela Ganatra, Friday E. Okonofua and Iqbal H. Shah (2006), 'Unsafe abortion: the preventable pandemic', *Lancet*, **368**(9550), 1908–19.

Guilmoto, Christophe Z. (2007), *Sex–ratio Imbalance in Asia: Trends, Consequences, and Policy Responses*, Paris: United Nations Population Fund.

Guttmacher Institute (1997), 'Sexually Transmitted Diseases Hamper Development Efforts', available at: http://www.guttmacher.org/pubs/ib_std.html (accessed May 1, 2012).

Guttmacher Institute (2009), 'Facts and consequences: legality, incidence and safety of abortion worldwide', *Guttmacher Policy Review*, **12**(4), 3.

Hayes, Sharonne N. (2006), 'Preventing cardiovascular disease in women', *American Family Physician*, **74**(8), 1331–40.

He, Jiang, Dongfeng Gu, Xigui Wu, Kristi Reynolds, Xiufang Duan, Chonghua Yao et al. (2005), 'Major causes of death among men and women in China', *New England Journal of Medicine*, **353**(11), 1124–34.

Heise, Lori (1993), 'Violence against women: the hidden health burden', *World Health Statistics Quarterly*, **46**(1), 78–85.

Hellinger, Fred J. and William E. Encinosa (2004), 'Antiretroviral therapy and health care utilization: a study of privately insured men and women with HIV disease', *Health Services Research*, **39**(4P1), 949–67.

Henry J. Kaiser Family Foundation (2010), 'The Global HIV/AIDS Epidemic', available at: http://www.kff.org/hivaids/upload/3030–15.pdf (accessed October 18, 2011).

Hudson, Valerie (2011), *China's Census: The One-Child Policy's Gender-Ratio Failure*, Washington, DC: World Politics Review.

Hudson, Valerie M. and Andrea M. den Boer (2004), *Bare Branches: The Security Implications of Asia's Surplus Male Population*, Boston, MA: MIT Press.

Husaini, Baqar A., Sherry Cummings, Barbara Kilbourne, Howard Roback, Darren Sherkat, Robert Levine and Van A. Cain (2004), 'Group therapy for depressed elderly women', *International Journal of Group Psychotherapy*, **54**(3), 295–319.

Husaini, Baqar A., Robert Levine, Thomas Summerfelt, Charles Holzer, Robert Newbrough, Richard Bragg, Van A. Cain and Deborah Pitts (2000), 'Economic grand rounds: prevalence and cost of treating mental disorders among elderly recipients of Medicare services', *Psychiatric Services*, **51**(10), 1245–7.

Jemal, Ahmedin, Freddie Bray, Melissa M. Center, Jacques Ferlay, Elizabeth Ward and David Forman (2011), 'Global cancer statistics', *CA: A Cancer Journal for Clinicians*, **61**(2), 69–90.

Jewkes, Rachel, Jonathan Levin and Loveday Penn-Kekana (2002), 'Risk factors for domestic violence: findings from a South African cross-sectional study', *Social Science & Medicine*, **55**(9), 1603–17.

Johns Hopkins University Bloomberg School of Public Health (2008), 'U.S. Suicide Rate Increasing; Largest Increase Seen In Middle-aged White Women', October 21, available at: http://www.jhsph.edu/public healthnews/press_releases/2008/baker_suicide.html (accessed April 15, 2011).

Jütte, Robert (2008), *Contraception: A History*, New York: Polity.

Kidder, Tracy (2011), *Mountains Beyond Mountains: One Doctor's Quest to Heal the World*, London: Profile Books.

Lakdawalla, Darius N., Dana P. Goldman and Baoping Shang (2005), 'The health and cost consequences of obesity among the future elderly', *Health Affairs*, web exclusive, available at: http://works.bepress.com/dana_goldman/49/ (accessed February 12, 2011).

Lenze, Eric J., Joan C. Rogers, Lynn M. Martire, Benoit H. Mulsant, Bruce L. Rollman, Mary Amanda Dew et al. (2001), 'The association of late-life depression and anxiety with physical disability: a review of the literature and prospectus for future research', *American Journal of Geriatric Psychiatry*, **9**(2), 113–35.

Lopez, Alan D., Colin D. Mathers, Majid Ezzati, Dean T. Jamison and Christopher J.L. Murray (2006), *Global Burden of Disease and Risk Factors*, New York: World Bank and Oxford University Press.

Magadi, Monica, Ian Diamond and Nyonvani Madise (2001), 'Analysis of factors associated with maternal mortality in Kenyan hospitals', *Journal of Biosocial Sciences*, **33**(3), 375–89.

Mayor, Susan (2004), 'Pregnancy and childbirth are leading causes of death in teenage girls in developing countries', *British Medical Journal*, **328**(7449), 1152.

Mullick, Saiqa, Deborah Watson-Jones, M. Beksinska and David Mabey (2005), 'Sexually transmitted infections in pregnancy: prevalence, impact on pregnancy outcomes, and approach to treatment in developing countries', *Sexually Transmitted Infections*, **81**(4), 294–302.

Murphy, Padmini and Clyde Lanford Smith (2009), *Women's Global Health and Human Rights*, Burlington, MA: Jones & Bartlett Learning.

Neugarten, Bernice Levin and Nancy Datan (1996), 'Sociological perspectives on the life cycle', in Bernice Levin Neugarten and Dail Ann Neugarten (eds), *The Meanings of Age*, Chicago, IL: University of Chicago Press, pp.96–113.

NHS Information Centre (2007), 'Adult psychiatric morbidity in England, 2007: results of a household survey', National Centre for Social Research and the University of Leicester, Leicester, UK.

Njovana, Eunice and Charlotte Watts (1996), 'Gender violence in Zimbabwe: a need for collaborative action', *Reproductive Health Matters*, **4**(7), 46–55.

Noble, Jeanne, Jane Cover and Machiko Yanagishita (1996), *The World's Youth*, Washington, DC: Population Reference Bureau.

O'Keeffe, Madeleine, Amy Hills, Melanie Doyle, Claudine McCreadie, Shaun Scholes, Rebecca Constantine, Anthea Tinker, Jill Manthrope, Simon Biggs and Bob Erens (2007), *UK Study of Abuse and Neglect of Older People: Prevalence Survey Report*, London: National Centre for Social Research.

Oladapo, Olufemi T., Olalekan O. Adetoro, Oluwarotimi Fakeye, Bissallah A. Ekele, Adeniran O. Fawole, Aniekan Abasiattai, Oluwafemi Kuti, Jamilu Tukur, Adedapo B.A. Ande, Olukayode A. Dada for the Nigerian Network for Reproductive Health Research and Training (2009), 'National data system on near miss and maternal death: shifting from maternal risk to public health impact in Nigeria', *Reproductive Health*, **6**(8), 1–11.

Patton, George C., Carolyn Coffey, Susan M. Sawyer, Russell M. Viner, Dagmar M. Haller, Krishna Bose, Thea Vos, Jane Ferguson and Colin D. Mathers (2009), 'Global patterns of mortality in young people: a systematic analysis of population health data', *Lancet*, **374**(9693), 881–92.

Peedell, Clive (2005), *Concise Clinical Oncology*, Philadelphia, PA: Elsevier.

Phend, Crystal (2011), 'Breast, cervical cancers kill 625,000 women each year', available at: http://www.medpagetoday.com/HematologyOncology/BreastCancer/28519 (accessed February 12, 2012).

Population Action International (2006), 'Unsafe sex destroys lives and decimates societies', available at: http://209.68.15.158/Publications/Reports/Measure_of_Survival/sec2.shtml (accessed March 10, 2012).

Population Resource Center (2001), 'Executive Summary – Maternal Mortality and Morbidity', available at: http://www.prcdc.org/files/Maternal_Mortality.pdf (accessed May 1, 2012).

Rahman, Tomer Taha Abdel (2006), 'Anxiety and Depression in Lone Elderly Living at Their Own Homes & Going to Geriatric Clubs Versus Those Living at Geriatric Homes', available at: http://www.globalaging.org/health/world/2006/egyptelderly.pdf (accessed July 20, 2011).

Rivera-Rivera, Leonor, Eduardo Lazcano-Ponce, Jorge Salmerón-Castro, Eduardo Salazar-Martínez, Roberto Castro and Mauricio Hernández-Avila (2004), 'Prevalence and determinants of male partner violence against Mexican women: a population-based study', *Salud Publica Mexico*, **46**(2), 113–22.

Ronsmans, Carine and Wendy J. Graham (2006), 'Maternal mortality: who, when, where, and why', *Lancet*, **368**(9542), 1189–200.

Rutter, Michael, Jack Tizard and Kingsley Whitmore (1970), *Education, Health and Behaviour*, London: Longmans (reprinted, 1981, Melbourne, FL: Krieger).

Ruzicka, Lado Theodor (1976), 'Suicide, 1950–71', *World Health Statistics Report*, **29**, 396–413.

Sahasrabuddhe, Vikrant V., Groesbeck P. Parham, Mulindi H. Mwanahamuntu and Sten H. Vermund (2011), 'Cervical cancer prevention in low – and middle-income countries: feasible, affordable, essential', *Cancer Prevention Research*, **5**(1), 11–17.

Salari, Zohree and Nouzar Nakhaee (2008), 'Identifying types of domestic violence and its associated risk factors in a pregnant population in Kerman hospitals, Iran Republic', *Asia-Pacific Journal of Public Health*, **20**(1), 49–55.

Sand-Hun, Choe (2007), 'Where Boys Were Kings, a Shift Toward Baby Girls', *New York Times*, December 23, available at: http://www.nytimes.com/2007/12/23/world/asia/23skorea.html?pagewanted=all (accessed December 30, 2007).

Schei, Berit (1990), 'Psycho-social factors in pelvic pain: a controlled study of women living in physically abusive relationships', *ACTA Obstetrica et Gynecologica Scandinavia*, **69**(1), 67–71.

Schei, Berit and Leiv S. Bakketeig (1989), 'Gynaecological impact of sexual and physical abuse by spouse: a study of a random sample of Norwegian women', *BJOG: An International Journal of Obstetrics Gynaecology*, **96**(12), 1379–83.

Sen, Amartya (1992), 'Missing women', *British Medical Journal*, **304**(6827), 587–8.

Sen, Gita and Piroska Östlin (2007), 'Unequal, Unfair, Ineffective and Inefficient, Gender Inequity in Health: Why it Exists and How We Can Change It', Final Report to the WHO Commission on Social Determinants of Health, available at: www.who.int/social_determinants/resources/csdh_media/wgekn_final_report_07.pdf (accessed March 2, 2009).

Shackelford, Todd K. and Jenny Mouzos (2005), 'Partner killing by men in cohabiting and marital relationships: a comparative, cross-national analysis of data from Australia and the United States', *Journal of Interpersonal Violence*, **20**(10), 1310–24.

Sherman, Carey Wexler, Dorrie E. Rosenblatt and Toni C. Antonucci (2008), 'Elder abuse and mistreatment: a life span and cultural context', *Indian Journal of Gerontology*, **22**(3&4), 319–39.

Siegler, Ilene C. (1997), 'Promoting health and minimizing stress in mid-life', in Margie Lachman and Jacqueline Boone James (eds), *Multiple Paths of Mid-life Development*, Chicago, IL: University of Chicago Press, pp. 241–56.

Silverman, Jay G., Jhumka Gupta, Michele R. Decker, Nitin Kapur and Anita Raj (2007), 'Intimate partner violence and unwanted pregnancy, miscarriage, induced abortion, and stillbirth among a national sample of Bangladeshi women', *BJOG: An International Journal of Obstetrics Gynaecology*, **114**(10), 1246–52.

Singh, Gopal K. (2010), *Maternal Mortality in the United States, 1935–2007: Substantial Racial/Ethnic, Socioeconomic, and Geographic Disparities Persist*, Rockville, MD: US Department of Health and Human Services.

Singh, Susheela (2010), 'Global consequences of unsafe abortion', *Women's Health*, **6**(6), 849–60.

Sobal, Jeffrey and Albert J. Stunkard (1989), 'Socioeconomic status and obesity: a review of the literature', *Psychological Bulletin*, **105**(2), 260–75.

Stevens, Judy A. and Sarah Olson (2000, March 31), 'Reducing falls and resulting hip fractures among older women', *Morbidity and Mortality Weekly Report*, **49**(RR02), available at: http://www.cdc.gov/mmwr/preview/mmwrhtml/rr4902a2.htm (accessed June 3, 2010).

Substance Abuse and Mental Health Services Administration (2007), 'National Survey on Drug Use and Health', available at: http://oas.samhsa.gov/nsduh/2k7nsduh/2k7results.cfm (accessed June 3, 2010).

Sun, Qi, Mary K. Townsend, Olivia I. Okereke, Oscar H. Franco, Frank B. Hu and Francine Grodstein (2009), 'Adiposity and weight change in mid-life in relation to healthy survival after age 70 in women: prospective cohort study', *British Medical Journal*, **339**, b3796.

Tulchinsky, Theodore H. (2010), 'Micronutrient deficiency conditions: global health issues', *Public Health Reviews*, **32**(1), 243–55.

UNAIDS (2011), 'Global HIV/AIDS response: epidemic update and health sector progress towards universal access: progress report 2011', World Health Organization, Geneva.

United Nations (2000), 'The world's women 2000: trends and statistics', available at: http://unstats.un.org/unsd/demographic/products/indwm/wwpub2000.htm (accessed March 12, 2012).

United Nations Department of Economic and Social Affairs, Population Division (2008), 'Demographic profile of the older population', in *World Population Ageing*, New York: United Nations, pp. 23–7.

United Nations Office on Drugs and Crime (2011), 'The Role of C4D in addressing drug use amongst adolescent girls: draft background paper for the 12th UNRT on C4D', United Nations, New York.

United Nations Population Fund (2005), 'Adolescents fact sheet', available at: http://www.unfpa.org/swp/2005/presskit/factsheets/facts_adolescents.htm (accessed April 13, 2008).

University of British Columbia (2011), 'Annual cost of violence pegged at $6.9B after women leave abusive partners: UBC research', available at: http://www.publicaffairs.ubc.ca/2011/10/11/annual-cost-of-violence-pegged-at-6–9b-after-women-leave-abusive-partners-ubc-research/ (accessed March 15, 2012).

Westley, Sidney B. and Choe Minja Kim (2007), 'How does son preference affect populations in Asia?', East-West Center, 84, available at: http://www.eastwestcenter.org/sites/default/files/private/api084.pdf (accessed June 6, 2012).

Windle, Michael, Grace M. Barnes and John Welte (1989), 'Causal models of adolescent substance use: an examination of gender differences using distribution-free estimators', *Journal of Personality and Social Psychology*, **56**(1), 132–42.

Withrow, David and David Alter (2011), 'The economic burden of obesity worldwide: a systematic review of the direct costs of obesity', *Obesity Reviews*, **12**(2), 131–41.

World Bank (2008), 'Maternal mortality ratio (modeled estimate, per 100,000 live births)', available at: http://data.worldbank.org/indicator/SH.STA.MMRT (accessed December 6, 2010).

World Health Organization (WHO) (2000), 'Fact sheet no. 252: women, ageing and health', available at: https://apps.who.int/inf-fs/en/fact252.html (accessed March 1, 2012).

World Health Organization (WHO) (2001), 'Gender Disparities in Mental Health', available at: http://www.who.int/mental_health/prevention/genderwomen/en/ (accessed March 1, 2012).

World Health Organization (WHO) (2003), 'The World Health Report 2003', available at: http://www.who.int/whr/2003/en/ (accessed March 1, 2012).

World Health Organization (WHO) (2005a), 'Maternal Mortality in 2005: Estimates developed by WHO, UNICEF, UNFPA, and the World Bank', available at: www.who.int/whosis/mme_2005.pdf (accessed March 1, 2012).

World Health Organization (WHO) (2005b), 'The World Health Report 2005 – Make Every Mother and Child Count', available at: http://www.who.int/entity/whr/2005/whr2005_en.pdf (accessed March 1, 2012).

World Health Organization (WHO) (2008a), 'Gender inequalities and HIV', available at: http://www.who.int/gender/hiv_aids/en/ (accessed March 2, 2012).

World Health Organization (WHO) (2008b), *The Global Burden of Disease: 2004 Update*, Geneva: WHO, pp. 1–146.

World Health Organization (WHO) (2009), 'Fact sheet no. 334: women's health', available at: http://www.who.int/mediacentre/factsheets/fs334/en/index.html (accessed March 2, 2012).

World Health Organization (WHO) (2011), 'Fact sheet no. 311: obesity and overweight', available at: http://www.who.int/mediacentre/factsheets/fs311/en/ (accessed March 1, 2012).

World Health Organization (WHO) (n.d.), 'Health statistics and health information systems', available at: http://www.who.int/healthinfo/statistics/indmaternalmortality/en/index.html (accessed February 24, 2012).

Wu, Zhaosu, Chonghua Yao, Dong Zhao, Guixian Wu, Wei Wang, Jing Liu, Zhechun Zeng and Yingkai Wu (2001), 'Sino-MONICA project: a collaborative study on trends and determinants in cardiovascular diseases in China, Part I: morbidity and mortality monitoring', *Circulation*, **103**(3), 462–8.

Yach, Derek, Corina Hawkes, Linn Gould and Karen J. Hofman (2004), 'The global burden of chronic diseases: overcoming impediments to prevention and control,' *JAMA: The Journal of the American Medical Association*, **291**(21), 2616–22.

Yaffe, Kristine, Laura E. Middleton, Li-Yung Lui, Adam P. Spira, Katie Stone, Caroline Racine, Kristine E. Ensrud and Joel H. Kramer (2011), 'Mild cognitive impairment, dementia, and their subtypes in oldest old women', *Archives of Neurology*, **68**(5), 631–6.

Young, Mary Eming (1994), 'Health problems and policies for older women: an emerging issue in developing countries', HRO Working Papers, World Bank, Washington, DC.

Yung, Judy (1997), 'It is hard to be born a woman but hopeless to be born a Chinese: the life and times of Flora Belle Jan', *Frontiers: A Journal of Women's Studies*, **18**(3), 66–91.

28. A case of gendered hazards and health effects for ultra-poor women
*Rita Watterson, Lynn McIntyre and Krista Rondeau**

I INTRODUCTION

Gender inequality and unfairness reflected in power, resources, entitlements, norms and values, organizational structure, and programming disproportionately shape the health and well-being of women across the globe (Moss, 2002; CSDH, 2008). In 1995, it was estimated that 70 percent of the world's poor were women (UNDP, 1995). Since then, more complex analyses of poverty and gender have shown significant gender gaps in some countries based on intrahousehold income distribution by sex, type of household (for example, female- versus male-headed households with young children), control over household resources, as well as disparities in inheritance and property rights (UNSD, 2010).

Many of these gendered differences exist because of inequalities in the labor market (Chen et al., 2004). Since 1990, women's participation rate in the labor market world-wide has averaged 52 percent and remains below that of men (81 percent in 1990 and 77 percent in 2010) (UNSD, 2010). On a regional level, women's participation in the labor force is more variable: in 2010, rates were below 30 percent in Northern Africa and Western Asia, below 40 percent in Southern Asia, and below 50 percent in the Caribbean and Central America (ibid.). In addition to unequal labor force participation, a gendered pay gap between 70 and 90 percent of men's wages exists worldwide (ibid.).[1] At the same time, women in all regions of the world continue to carry a disproportionate burden of a household's unpaid labor and responsibilities, that is, childcare, housework, preparing meals, and caring for dependent others (Moss, 2002; UNSD, 2010).

While these statistics are sobering, efforts to address gender inequalities are occurring, such as the adoption of the Third Millennium Development Goal (MDG3) in 2000. MDG3 aims to facilitate and promote women's equality and empowerment, such as increased autonomy, freedom, choice, and responsibility that allows greater control over one's life (Mahmud et al., 2011, p. 611).[2] Efforts are being directed toward increasing female enrollment in education; increasing employment in nonagricultural sectors; and enhancing women's participation in national politics, with the intention that empowerment and equality are essential to the achievement of better health (WHO, 2012). Initial progress in these fundamental areas has been made, but improvements have slowed considerably following the global economic recession of 2008–09.[3]

As a consequence of asymmetrical trade and labor markets, the economic life of women and men living in lower- and middle-income countries (LMICs) is vastly different from that which exists in the formal, regulated markets of higher-income countries. Globalization may be contributing to LMICs downsizing their formal economies because of the 'race to the bottom' that has resulted from a shift toward neoliberal thinking in global economic policy (Benach et al., 2007, p. 16). This shift toward neoliberal policies is directed toward increasing free markets and subsequently pushes countries to move production where it is cheapest. As a result, markets have effectively been forced to limit costs in an effort to compete on the world stage, a phenomenon that has also been occurring in higher-income countries (Moss, 2002). As individuals seek to escape unemployment, informal and vulnerable employment has grown and now dominates the work sector in LMICs (Chen et al., 2004; CSDH, 2008).[4] Employment in this sector, especially as informal wage earners, exacts perverse effects on its workers, ranging from low wages to lack of or limited social benefits and powerlessness. These jobs are 'unstable, unprotected and . . . unable to sustain individuals and families' (Benach et al., 2007, p. 56), with subsequent implications for health and well-being. In 2009, for developing regions overall, 60 percent of workers were employed in the informal sector and in some LMICs, the prevalence rose to 80 percent (UN, 2011). Women in LMICs are overrepresented in the informal sector, which places them in poor working conditions with little to no security or safety net (Benach et al., 2007; UN, 2010; UNSD, 2010).

Given unhealthy work conditions, it is no surprise that workers engaged in informal markets typically have poor health indicators (Marmot, 2007), including higher mortality rates and negative mental health outcomes (CSDH, 2008). Labor market inequality is strongly associated with unfavorable population health outcomes, including a higher probability of dying for both women and men, higher mortality rates in children under five and pregnant women, and a greater number of deaths from cancer and injury (Benach et al., 2007). Occupational hazards associated with substandard working conditions in unhealthy and unsafe environments directly affect the health and safety of workers and the economic status of their families, and vulnerable employment in particular is associated with adverse health effects that are mediated through 'material or social deprivation and hazardous work environments' (ibid., p. 17).

While this research is clear, our understanding of the informal sector and its relationship to gender and health inequalities is lacking (Benach et al., 2007; Menéndez et al., 2007), especially within the context of LMICs, where the informal economy is extensive and information regarding this heterogeneous assortment of occupations is methodologically difficult to obtain. Given women's disproportionate representation in the informal economy, there is a need to understand more systematically how informal and vulnerable employment constitutes an occupational determinant of health in women. Certainly, there are 'fundamental causes of health differences . . . among women . . . that are rooted in the economic, political, historical, and social arrangements that structure how women live' (Moss, 2002, p. 653). Benach and colleagues (2007) have described two structural frameworks that reflect the relationship between employment and health inequalities at the macro and micro levels. While the macrostructural framework places employment relations and their subsequent health inequalities within their larger institutional context, the microstructural framework considers physical, chemical, ergonomic, and psychosocial factors while acknowledging that 'cross-cutting axes' such as gender (as well as social class and ethnicity/race) result in differential exposure to risk (ibid., pp. 31–2).

This chapter is offered as a gender-informed response to the research challenge of the World Health Organization Commission on the Social Determinants of Health (CSDH) to better understand how social factors, including gender, interact with the current work environment to influence health. We will primarily examine the intersection of gender, health, occupation, and the informal market from a microstructural perspective, although this is not to diminish the role that macrostructural factors, such as power relations, labor regulations and industrial relations, growing political conservatism and neoliberal policies, have on health inequalities (for further information on this, see Benach et al., 2007). We will draw on the employment experiences of 43 ultra-poor Bangladeshi women who were the sole financial earner for their households to produce new insights and new lines of inquiry on the intersection of gender, health, and occupation (see also Moss, 2002, p. 658). A separate, in-depth analysis of these data is presented here based on the labor experiences of the 43 women along with relevant literature to support our findings.

In Section II, we offer an overview of the empirical study that provides insights on the intersection of gender, health, and occupation for 43 ultra-poor female heads of household in Bangladesh. Sections III through V further elaborate the themes of the analytical framework derived from women's employment experiences. Finally, Section VI explores the implications of our finding – in particular, women's inability to advance and make positive economic gains that would benefit themselves and their families – and concludes with insights regarding new lines of inquiry that are required to address the development needs of this group of women.

II　OVERVIEW OF THE EMPIRICAL STUDY

In order to examine the relationship among health, occupation, and the informal market, we draw on existing literature and theory as well as insights from a secondary analysis of in-depth ethnographic interviews that focused on the food provisioning experiences of 43 ultra-poor female heads of household in Bangladesh; ultra-poor refers to living on less than US$1.25 per day (see McIntyre et al., 2011). In this study, women with dependent children were purposively sampled based on occupation (garment workers, urban and rural petty traders, subsistence agriculturalists) and place of residence (rural or urban). In addition, the sample included 10 Garo women, a marginalized indigenous population, who were employed in various occupations within the informal sector.[5] Women were the sole responsible financial earner for the household, despite the presence of other adults or children. The interviews were digitally recorded and translated using a multistep process to ensure accuracy. A complete description of the methodology and results of the food provisioning inquiry are available elsewhere (ibid.). Coding and analysis were conducted on fragments of text where women discussed their work. These extracts were elicited from the question that asked women to chronicle their typical day, as well as probes regarding their work, health, and family life.

The authors conferred regularly on emergent themes as all interviews were analyzed using techniques such as memoing, immersion/crystallization, thematic network analysis, and peer debriefing (Borkan, 1999; Attride-Stirling, 2001; Bryman, 2004). The final thematic analysis was confirmed with recoding. We have created a visual depiction of our thematic analysis in Figure 28.1. The resultant thematic framework of the women's experiences from the viewpoint of their occupation revealed that gendered hazards, negative health effects (both occupation specific and generalized ill health), and the perverse market economy in which women worked resulted in an overwhelming inability for women to

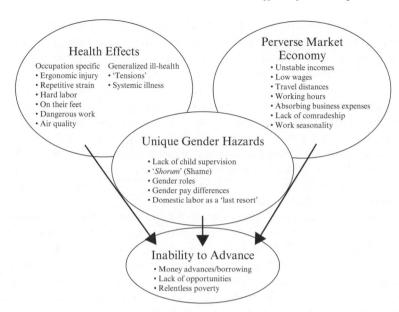

Figure 28.1   Analysis of ultra-poor Bangladeshi female heads of household experiences
from the viewpoint of occupation

advance from a socioeconomic perspective. These four components frame the discussion below. We will draw on these themes and the women's reflections to augment the literature in each of the four thematic constructs. Note that women's reflections are qualified with a pseudonym and their occupation in the presentation of findings and discussion below.

III   FRAMEWORK THEME 1: GENDERED HAZARDS WITHIN THE EMPLOYMENT EXPERIENCE

Our current understanding of how gender shapes the interaction of women within informal employment is limited, although we know that gender places women at particular risk for vulnerable employment and its associated risks and adverse health effects in LMICs and high-income countries (Menéndez et al., 2007). Indeed, 'in the current era, the *new* forms of gender-related historical factors such as patriarchy, end up damaging women's health more than men's' (ibid., p. 779, emphasis in original). Our analysis revealed that a number of resultant hazards are unique to women (outlined in Figure 28.1); we will expand on two themes on the subject that are prominently discussed in the literature – the patriarchal gender segregation of jobs and gendered roles of social reproduction. In addition, we examine further exploration of the gendered health hazards by occupation.

Gendered Segregation of Jobs

According to the 'breadwinner ideology', the patriarchal power structures that dominate market sectors in high-, low- and middle-income countries greatly affect the type of work in which women can participate. Within LMICs, men dominate the formal market while women are increasingly being pushed toward precarious, part-time, and nonstandard work arrangements that typically have less regulation and lower standards, that is, vulnerable work (Menéndez et al., 2007). Rheka Mehra and Sarah Gammage (1999) have argued that this shift is not transitory or temporary, and instead reflects long-term differences attributable to education, skill levels, poverty, and reproductive roles. As a result, gender segregation forces women into specific occupational niches (Menéndez et al., 2007) and women are pushed into jobs that are typically considered safe, but are associated with lower pay, lower prestige, and lower decision-making power (Meleis and Lindgren, 2002). For example, garment work was initially promoted as a socially accept-able form of employment for women who were poorer but could not engage in other forms of employment (Ahmed, 2004).

Even when women do enter more formal occupations, gender differences remain apparent. The most obvious indicator of inequality is income, with women persistently earning less than men (UNDP, 2005). Some researchers suggest that this is in part due to the differences in education, experience, and segmentation of the workforce (for example, Mehra and Gammage, 1999). However, a study in Latin America by George Psachoropoulos and Zafiris Tzannatos (1992) showed that men earned on average 30 percent more than women, but when education, job experience, and hours were accounted for, only 20 percent of the difference in earnings was explained by these factors; the remainder was thus attributed to gender discrimination. These concerns held true in our research findings: a woman working as an agricultural worker stated that women were paid a wage that was three-quarters of that earned by men who performed the same tasks. One woman employed in petty trading recounted that her product was sold at a higher price when her father sold the items than when she sold them. Furthermore, some traders reported that they accepted lower prices for their goods because they wanted to sell their items quickly – they feared being harassed in the bazaar.

Gendered Roles of Social Reproduction

Women's work extends beyond their economic roles and can be classified in three ways: social reproduction, social capital, and financial capital, which arise from both the paid and unpaid employment in which women participate (Meleis and Lindgren, 2002). Unpaid labor is seen as an extension of gender norms including the cultural roles, duties, and tasks of women and is typically devalued relative to men's paid labor (ibid.). In resource-poor settings, women carry the burden of maintaining the family and home, and their cultural roles and duties include cooking, cleaning, and raising and caring for the children. This is especially true for women who are the sole financial earners for their households and whose absence is therefore felt more acutely. For example, in our study, many women were unable to pay for their children's schooling. They also frequently lacked support from a husband or relative for childcare. Petty traders, garment workers, and any woman who had to travel long distances for work were required to leave their children unsupervised for extended periods of time during the day and sometimes into the night.

As a result, many expressed *shorum* (shame) regarding their inability to adequately meet their cultural gender roles of provider, mother, and worker. The women expressed that they were ashamed of themselves and the lives that they provided for their family. Their shame, however, extended beyond their job and extended to being without the support of a husband and thus forced into work that they disdained. Bhavani (agriculturalist) stated, 'I feel ashamed to go out of the house . . . [A]s I said earlier I wasn't used to live in this environment. I'm in this condition because of my fate.' The psychological effects and social exclusion of 'shameful' work in the informal sector have been widely reported in the literature (for example, Chen et al., 2004; Benach et al., 2007; Menéndez et al., 2007), but gender discrimination that is entrenched in cultural norms and practices provides an additional layer of burden for women who struggle with socially constructed identities.

Thus, by virtue of being female, women find themselves within the informal labor market, working in jobs or occupational niches with low power and prestige. Gender affects not only the types of jobs women get, but how much pay they receive, typically lower than men for the same or comparable work. These are gendered hazards because they are not attributable to differences in education or experience. The hazards emerge in large part because of gender-prescribed responsibilities in the household/family. Additionally, since these women must work because they are the sole earner in the household, they experience considerable shame. Next we consider women's negative health effects resulting from the informal labor market.

IV   FRAMEWORK THEME 2: NEGATIVE GENDERED HEALTH EFFECTS FROM EMPLOYMENT EXPERIENCES

This second theme within the thematic framework considers the occupation-specific and generalized negative health effects experienced within the specific employment experiences of ultra-poor women. Research that examines women, occupational hazards in precarious and informal markets, and the health effects of these hazards is limited. Traditional occupational health research has focused on the physical conditions of work at the point of production and the subsequent risk to its employees. In countries with a large informal market sector, there is a positive correlation between disability-adjusted life years (DALYS) lost for all diseases (Benach et al., 2007). This is in part due to the more hazardous work conditions to which employees are exposed, including painful positions, loud noises, repetitive movements, less freedom to take leave, and limited opportunities to be a part of health and safety commissions (ibid.). Work is also more strenuous and monotonous (Doyal, 2004). Although the specific effects of occupation are largely understudied, some occupations pertinent to women have been linked to specific negative health outcomes. For example, several studies have connected women's poor health to the exposure of pesticides and other environmental chemicals (ibid.), and lung disease in some women has been linked to constant exposure to poor air quality from cooking stoves (Mishra et al., 1999; Sims and Butter, 2002; Doyal, 2004). Others have described how environmental degradation in particular has created a situation in which women are required to walk further than in the past to find wood and water (Awumbila and Momsen, 1995; Davidson and Freudenburg, 1996; Doyal, 2004).

Early theoretical approaches that sought to better understand the relationship between the health of women and employment status in the United States and the United

Kingdom tended to adopt two broad approaches: the *role enhancement model*, in which paid employment yields positive health effects, and the *role overload model*, in which paid employment yields negative health effects (Bartley et al., 1992). The relationship between health and paid employment is now understood to be more complex and accounts for differences in how employment status and health are defined, the role of socioeconomic status, how health status selects for employment, and domestic responsibilities distinct from (but in addition to) the presence of children (for example, meal preparation, chores) (ibid.; Rose et al., 2004). Factors such as salary, promotions, access to jobs, control and decision-making power are also considered (O'Campo et al., 2004; Caplan and Schooler, 2007).

Less research has examined the gendered health effects of work in the informal sector in either high- or low- and middle-income countries. Recent research on job insecurity and temporal contracts/nonpermanent work, which is characterized by decreased workers' rights and protection and limited control, may provide some indication of the health effects of informal work. In general, nonstandard/precarious work arrangements in high-income countries have been associated with worsening physical and mental health, increased job dissatisfaction, increased alcohol-related deaths and smoking-related cancer, and increased participation in risky behaviors in both men and women (Menéndez et al., 2007). Two small cross-sectional surveys of households in impoverished areas of Brazil found a correlation between informal work and mental health outcomes (Santana et al., 1997; Ludermir and Lewis, 2003).

Thus, adequate frameworks and theories that connect gender, ill health, and occupation in the informal sector are lacking (Benach et al., 2007; Menéndez et al., 2007). Joyce Avotri and Vivienne Walters (1999) suggest that the focus on women's health has primarily been on their reproductive roles, neglecting their roles as workers. In part, this is a result of research defined by experts such as healthcare professionals, academics, and policy-makers, who do not privilege the lived experience of women (ibid.).

Similar to the findings of Avotri and Walters regarding Ghanaian women, our research suggests that women experience pervasive general ill health above and beyond occupation-specific hazard as a result of heavy workloads, financial worries, and the responsibilities they have to their children. Indeed, poor working conditions, minimal pay, long hours, and socially prescribed gender roles in the home created significant 'tensions' and stress for the women we interviewed: 'Usually I have to wake up at 4am. The train leaves at the time of *Fazar Azan* [the call for the first prayer of the day]. I have told you that if I think too much about my problems at night, I can't sleep well at that night. So, when I fall asleep late, I can't wake up in time in the morning' (Jayashri, agriculturalist). Research suggests that these are 'forms of distress that are linked with the material and social circumstances of [women's] lives' (ibid., p. 1125). The women in our study described work linked to tiredness, worrying, losing weight, and headaches. Experienced over months, tensions would build and many described complete exhaustion that required an extended break from work, which had deleterious impacts on their families' well-being: 'I take bed-rest, maybe for about 1 month or 15 days. I join the work when I feel better. I face much difficulty when I don't get any money' (Devangi, garment worker).

Our research also highlighted distinct negative health outcomes more typical of traditional occupational health studies that were associated with specific types of work.

Garment workers suffered from musculoskeletal pain and headaches from being in strained positions and poorly aerated work areas, respectively. Petty traders described ill health related to traveling long distances with their goods resting on their heads and asthma from working on the streets. The grueling work of agricultural workers is reflected in Promita's (agriculturalist) statement: '[I] lost almost all of my hairs by the scratches of the basket that I have to carry on my head while I do my work.' The Garo women faced additional danger from border guards because they had to cross the Indian border to collect firewood to sell. When Mitali (Garo) was asked about security concerns when she crossed the border to receive money from her sister who lived in India, she answered, 'I have to go even though I am scared to go cross the border.' These examples demonstrate the overwhelming chronic stress the women must go through to ensure the livelihood and survival of their family.

V   FRAMEWORK THEME 3: PERVERSE EFFECTS OF THE INFORMAL MARKET

As discussed in Section III, ultra-poor women find themselves employed primarily in the informal sector due to patriarchal gender segregation of jobs and gendered roles of social reproduction. In this section, we consider the perverse effects of the informal market on women once they are employed in this sector. Informal and vulnerable employment has emerged from political shifts and policies that have transformed the standard forms of work (Chen et al., 2004). For vulnerable employment, the erosion of worker protection and employment contraction has fostered the idea of the more 'flexible' work space (Menéndez et al., 2007, p. 776; see also Moss, 2002). Poor women in countries that provide limited wage employment and few social safety nets 'have little choice but to work – no matter how low or irregular their earnings' (Chen et al., 2004, p. 12). However, a characterization of these markets as flexible and entrepreneurial fails to recognize their entrenchment and does not adequately reflect their perverse effects, particularly on LMIC women workers. Liarae (garment worker), who is mandated to work overtime at the factory, explained, 'If there was any chance to avoid overtime, who would have done the overtime with such hardship till 10 pm of the night? If I had that option, I would come home a little bit early to take some rest.' Others have noted that the shift toward vulnerable and informal employment and the dominance of women within this sector signals the need for additional recognition to be given to the informal sector in both research and policy (Mehra and Gammage, 1999).

Informal and vulnerable employment is characterized by four main qualities: (i) high job insecurity; (ii) low wage level; (iii) lack of limited social benefits; and (iv) powerlessness (Benach et al., 2007). Each factor was well-articulated by the women in our study as they were uniformly exposed to unstable and inadequate income, long workdays both from travel to and from work and extended work days, an expectation to assume all additional business expenses, competiveness rather than camaraderie among similarly occupied workers, and work seasonality. Unlike Mexican-origin women working in fruit and vegetable canneries in California in the 1960s, the ultra-poor Bangladeshi women did not experience a culture of camaraderie that 'promoted close ties among women workers that often spilled into the organization and maintenance of the household'

(Moss, 2002, p. 654). Examining each occupation highlights the precariousness and subsequent ill effects for women.

The garment workers' days were dictated and constrained by the rules of their factory. Women had no say in their work life (they were 'compliant workers' (Ahmed, 2004, p. 37)) and had no awareness or understanding of the power structures within the company. As Fauzia Ahmed (2004) has articulated, 'becoming a garment worker and keeping your job is synonymous with losing collective voice and staying mute' (p. 41). Devangi (garment worker) affirmed this reality: 'The day before yesterday when my son became sick, I talked with my fellow operators and asked to the authority for leave; but they didn't grant me leave. If we push too much, they sack us. We can't speak too much.'

Petty traders experienced gender-based discrimination and all made little to no profit to sustain themselves and their family beyond the day. As a result, they frequently borrowed money or food to feed their family or to buy more products to supply their business. Furthermore, because these women were detached from the formal market, they were unable to buy their products from wholesalers; they were forced to access their products from the retail market and subsequently price them with little to no profit in order to compete. These types of production constraints on poor women are common and transform potentially productive self-employment opportunities into 'dead-end survival activities' (Mehra and Gammage, 1999, p. 542).

Sharecroppers bore all the risk and expenses (for example, seeds, fertilizer, and equipment) of raising crops and were then required to hand over 50 percent of their total proceeds to the landowner. When selling their crop at market, some lowered their prices so that they could sell their product as fast as possible because they did not like being in public view. Debjani (agriculturalist) explained, 'How will I get the right price, as I'm a woman?'. As mentioned earlier, female seasonal agricultural laborers were consistently paid less than men and many were required to take an advance on their wage in order to sustain their families when fieldwork was not available, creating a situation where they were indentured to work at a lower than market wage when called in.

The Garo women were the most vulnerable group of women, as they were disconnected from both the formal and informal markets due to geographical isolation and marginalization that forced them to live landless in rural areas. The women reported a variety of opportunistic jobs interspersed with prolonged periods of devastating unemployment that resulted from changes in the market, weather fluctuations, and employers' changing demands. The inability to buffer income loss from lack of work was explained by Rani (Garo): 'I have no savings. I have to use all that money that I earn on my survival. I can't even save 1 taka (local currency, 70 taka = US$1)'.

VI   INABILITY TO ADVANCE: IMPLICATIONS AND CONCLUSIONS

As illustrated in Figure 28.1, the result of the confluence of the gendered hazards and health effects of their work within a perverse market economy is that women were unable to advance and make positive economic gains that would benefit themselves and their families; they were trapped in a situation of relentless poverty with no discernible prospect for a better situation, let alone empowerment. This is a common outcome for all women, regardless of occupation, and is best summarized by Chumi (garment worker), who stated, 'Garment work is very hard; there is nothing without hardship in this life.' This phenomenon has also been observed in Mexican immigrant women who 'found employment as domestic servants, janitors, or low-wage workers in electronic and garment industries, work that is often isolating and demeaning, and offers no opportunity for advancement' (Moss, 2002, p. 654). As Martha Chen and colleagues have found, 'While the vast majority of the poor work, few are able to work their way out of poverty' (2004, p. 13).

As illustrated in this chapter, the economic lives and subsequent well-being of ultra-poor female heads of household and their families are shaped by micro- and macro-level structures. At the micro level, cultural norms, values and expectations shape the way women interact with work. These factors not only affect the type of employment in which women participate, but they permeate the daily work experience of women and expose them to discrimination (Mehra and Gammage, 1999). In LMICs, NGOs, communities, and regional and national governments also have a significant role in shaping the work environment.

At the macro level, women in LMICs are affected by international policy, trade agreements, and globalization that have shifted the way the international community invests and conducts business (Forastieri, 1999; Doyal, 2004). One of the significant sources of this change is Structural Adjustment Programmes, economic policies for low-income countries that have been promoted by the World Bank or International Monetary Fund since the 1980s (Avotri and Walters, 1999; WHO, 2011). The aid or payments have had conditions associated with them that generally prescribe the adoption of a free market structure within a global economy, which subsequently forces domestic markets to decrease the diversity of domestic products in order to remain competitive in the global market, among other economic and social outcomes.[6] Such changes also lead workers within LMICs to be driven to an expanding informal sector. Furthermore, 'because structural adjustment usually imposed user fees on health services, schools, transportation, among other services, the burden often fell disproportionally on women' (Moss, 2002, p. 650). As described, women are often forced to enter these nonstandard fields and are placed in vulnerable and hazardous work environments (Avotri and Walters, 1999).

In exploring the intersection of gender, health, and work for a diverse group of ultra-poor women who are heads of household in Bangladesh, we have highlighted a need for further research on the informal and formal market sectors and their effects on poverty alleviation, working conditions, and health inequalities. Current framing considers poverty alleviation, working conditions, and empowerment along the axes of wages/employers and micro-entrepreneur/self-employed. For example, the Final Report to the Commission on the Social Determinants of Health suggests that there are four main types of employment (micro-entrepreneurs; full-time regular wage earners; part-time, contract, casual, irregular wage earners; and informal wage earners), which have differing degrees of placement with respect to income, precariousness, and the formal versus informal market (Benach et al., 2007). In this schema, micro-entrepreneurs are shown to have the highest income level, and full-time regular wage earners have the lowest level of precariousness. In contrast, another framework (Chen et al., 2005) uses a pyramid structure to depict unpaid family workers earning the lowest income and employers and informal wage workers earning the highest income. Not only are these two frameworks contradictory, but they are unhelpful in understanding how perverse markets destabilize income and health for the numerous women who find themselves within this sector.

Our analysis revealed that regardless of occupation, all women employed in vulnerable employment in the informal sector experienced significant financial and job insecurity. For example, although seeming to have more stable work, garment workers were forced to work overtime, did not receive sick benefits, and were paid only once a month, which made borrowing a necessity. Petty traders acquired money daily, instead of monthly, which, if they earned even a modest income, could make their position less precarious; however, sick days and other calamities led to immediate penury.

The implications are significant when one considers that 'informal employment [including self-employment and wage employment] comprises one half to three quarters of non-agricultural employment in developing countries' (Chen et al., 2004, p. 13). For women living in conditions of severe disadvantage, employment may not be aligned with empowerment and poverty reduction given that they are typically engaged in 'precarious' or informal employment (Menéndez et al., 2007, p. 777). As Chen and colleagues (2004) point out, 'an increase in women's wage employment (both non-agricultural and agricultural) is likely to be associated with an increase in flexible or informal employment arrangements: that is, in employment without rights, protection or voice' (p. 17).

Given the interconnections between health and employment in the informal sector, the best way to effect change would be to support gender-sensitive and context-specific policies that would promote earning opportunities (including the provision of social and health services to women), secure workers' rights, protect informal workers, and build and recognize their voice (see ibid., p. 15; see also Mehra and Gammage, 1999). In addition, there may be a role for trade unions that help self-employed women organize for full employment (for example, the Self-Employed Women's Association, SEWA, in India) that includes work, income, food, and social security; however, as we have seen in this chapter, for women who are firmly entrenched within the informal and precarious labor markets that restrict advancement, the ability to organize is severely restricted and will likely remain so until structural factors that perpetuate this entrenchment are addressed.[7] In fact, research has shown that the ultra-poor in Bangladesh are generally excluded from social programs and policies (for example, Walker and Matin, 2006). Indeed, the women who participated in this study did not participate in any development program, except for one woman who received a widow's pension payment on one occasion.

The intent of this chapter was to discuss the unique gendered concerns of the informal market and vulnerable employment with insights provided from the narratives of ultra-poor female heads of household. Women's experiences augment a gender-neutral discussion of occupation and health that is usually concerned with physical hazards and exposures. A gender-based consideration of occupation from the narratives of ultra-poor Bangladeshi women heads of household reveals that the health impacts of work extend beyond their type of work. If poor women and their families are to benefit from the Third Millennium Development Goal, which seeks equality and empowerment of women with an explicit progress indicator of nonagricultural waged employment, we must acknowledge and address both gender inequity and the macro- and micro-level economic conditions that create a perverse market for informal and vulnerable workers.

NOTES

* Funding for this study was provided by the Canadian Institutes of Health Research (CIHR) Seed Grant in Globalization and Health and the CIHR Global Health and Knowledge Exchange Planning, Dissemination and Meetings Grant. We thank the women who participated.
1. Gender pay gap represents 'the ratio of women's average earnings to men's average earnings, expressed per 100' (UNSD, 2010, p. 96).
2. Further information on the Millennium Development Goals can be found at http://www.un.org/millenniumgoals/.
3. For women experiencing significant disempowerment, education and employment alone do not necessarily guarantee increased control over one's life (Menéndez et al., 2007, p. 777), especially when employment opportunities are most often precarious or informal and there are limited opportunities to put basic education to use (White and Ellison, 2007). Although MDG3 suggests that education and employment are critical indicators for the empowerment of women and the subsequent reduction of inequalities, other indicators such as participation in decision-making, financial independence, freedom of movement, as well as less tangible indicators such as self-esteem and attitudes toward discrimination provide a more complete picture of women's empowerment and consequent movement toward equality (Mahmud et al., 2011).
4. According to Benach et al. (2007), '[The] informal economy comprises a wide range of production and distribution of goods and services characterized by being out of State control. Firms from the informal economy are unregulated, unregistered and have low level of organization' (p. 61). The UN characterizes vulnerable employment by 'informal working arrangements, lack of adequate social protection, low pay and difficult working conditions' (UN, 2011, p. 9). Detailed information on the definition and measurement of informal employment can be found in Hussmanns (2002). An overview of vulnerable employment, informal employment, and the informal sector can also be found in UNSD (2010, pp. 86–8).
5. Further information on the Garo can be found in Bal (2007a, 2007b).
6. Further information on structural adjustment programs and the economic and social outcomes for lower- and middle-income countries can be found in WHO (2011).
7. Further information on SEWA can be found at http://www.sewa.org/index.asp.

REFERENCES

Ahmed, Fauzia Erfan (2004), 'The rise of the Bangladesh garment industry: globalization, women workers, and voice', *NWSA Journal*, **16**(2), 34–45.

Attride-Stirling, Jennifer (2001), 'Thematic networks: an analytical tool for qualitative research', *Qualitative Research*, **1**(3), 385–405.

Avotri, Joyce Yaa and Vivienne Walters (1999), 'You just look at our work and see if you have any freedom on earth: Ghanaian women's accounts of their work and their health', *Social Science & Medicine*, **48**(9), 1123–33.

Awumbila, Mariama and Janet Henshall Momsen (1995), 'Gender and the environment: women's time use as a measure of environmental change', *Global and Environmental Change*, **5**(4), 337–46.

Bal, Ellen (2007a), *They Ask if We Eat Frogs: Garo Ethnicity in Bangladesh*, Singapore: Institute of Southeast Asian Studies.

Bal, Ellen (2007b), 'Becoming the Garos of Bangladesh: policies of exclusion and the ethnicisation of a "tribal" minority', *South Asia: Journal of South Asian Studies*, **30**(3), 439–55.

Bartley, Mel, Jennie Popay and Ian Plewis (1992), 'Domestic conditions, paid employment and women's experience of ill-health', *Sociology of Health and Illness*, **14**(3), 313–43.

Benach, Joan, Carles Muntaner and Vilma Santana (2007), 'Employment conditions and health: final report to the WHO commission on social determinants of health (CSDH)', available at: http://www.who.int/social_determinants/resources/articles/emconet_who_report.pdf (accessed May 14, 2012).

Borkan, Jeffrey (1999), 'Immersion/crystallization', in Benjamin F. Crabtree and William L. Miller (eds), *Doing Qualitative Research*, Thousand Oaks, CA: Sage, pp. 179–94.

Bryman, Alan (2004), *Social Research Methods*, Oxford: Oxford University Press.

Caplan, Leslie J. and Carmi Schooler (2007), 'Socioeconomic status and financial coping strategies: the mediating role of perceived control', *Social Psychology Quarterly*, **70**(1), 43–58.

Chen, Martha Alter, Joann Vanek and Marilyn Carr (2004), 'Mainstreaming informal employment and gender in poverty reduction', Commonwealth Secretariat/IDRC, available at: http://wiego.org/sites/wiego.org/files/publications/files/Chen-Mainstreaming-Informal-Employment-and-Gender.pdf (accessed May 14, 2012).

Chen, Martha, Joann Vanek, Francie Lund, James Heintz, Renana Jhabvala and Christine Bonner (2005), 'Women, work and poverty', available at: http://www.un-ngls.org/orf/women-2005.pdf (accessed May 14, 2012).

Commission on Social Determinants of Health (CSDH) (2008), 'Closing the gap in a generation: health equity through action on the social determinants of health. Final report of the Commission on Social Determinants of Health', available at: http://whqlibdoc.who.int/publications/2008/9789241563703_eng.pdf (accessed May 14, 2012).

Davidson, Debra J. and Wiluam R. Freudenburg (1996), 'Gender and environmental risk concerns: a review of available research', *Environment and Behaviour*, **28**(3), 302–39.

Doyal, Lesley (2004), 'Women, health and global restructuring: setting the scene', *Development*, **47**(2), 18–23.

Forastieri, Valentina (1999), 'Improvement of working conditions and environment in the informal sector through safety and health measures', available at: http://www.ilo.org/safework/info/publications/WCMS_110306/lang--en/index.htm (accessed December 14, 2012).

Hussmanns, Ralf (2002), 'Defining and measuring informal employment', available at: http://www.ilo.org/public/english/bureau/stat/download/papers/meas.pdf (accessed May 14, 2012).

Ludermir, Ana Bernarda and Glyn Lewis (2003), 'Informal work and common mental disorders', *Social Psychiatry Psychiatric Epidemiology*, **38**(9), 485–89.

Mahmud, Simeen, Nirali M. Shah and Stan Becker (2011), 'Measurement of women's empowerment in rural Bangladesh', *World Development*, **40**(3), 610–19.

Marmot, Michael (2007), 'Achieving health equity: from root causes to fair outcomes', *Lancet*, **370**(9593), 1153–63.

McIntyre, Lynn, Krista Rondeau, Sharon Kirkpatrick, Jennifer Hatfield, Khaled S. Islam and Syed N. Huda (2011), 'Food provisioning experiences of ultra poor female heads of household living in Bangladesh', *Social Science & Medicine*, **72**(6), 969–76.

Mehra, Rheka and Sarah Gammage (1999), 'Trends, countertrends, and gaps in women's employment', *World Development*, **27**(3), 533–50.

Meleis, Afaf I. and Teri G. Lindgren (2002), 'Man works from sun to sun, but woman's work is never done: insights on research and policy', *Health Care for Women International*, **23**(6–7), 742–53.

Menéndez, María, Joan Benach, Carles Muntaner, Marcelo Amable and Patricia O'Campo (2007), 'Is precarious employment more damaging to women's health than men's?', *Social Science & Medicine*, **64**(4), 776–81.

Mishra, Vinod K., Robert D. Retherford and Kirk R. Smith (1999), 'Biomass cooking fuels and prevalence of tuberculosis in India', *International Journal of Infectious Diseases*, **3**(3), 119–29.

Moss, Nancy E. (2002), 'Gender equity and socioeconomic inequality: a framework for the patterning of women's health', *Social Science & Medicine*, **54**(5), 649–61.

O'Campo, Patricia, William W. Eaton and Carles Muntaner (2004), 'Labor market experience, work organization, gender inequalities and health status: results from a prospective analysis of US employed women', *Social Science & Medicine*, **58**(3), 585–94.

Psachoropoulos, George and Zafiris Tzannatos (1992), *Women's Employment and Pay in Latin America: Overview and Methodology*, Washington, DC: World Bank.

Rose, Kathryn M., April P. Carson, Diane Catellier, Ana V. Diez Roux, Carles Muntaner, Herman A. Tyroler and Sharon B. Wyatt (2004), 'Women's employment status and mortality: the arthrosclerosis risk in communities study', *Journal of Women's Health*, **13**(10), 1108–18.

Santana, Vilma S, Dana Loomis, Beth Newman and Siobán D. Harlow (1997), 'Informal jobs: another occupational hazard for women's mental health?', *International Journal of Epidemiology*, **26**(6), 1236–42.

Sims, Jacqueline and Maureen Butter (2002), 'Health and environment: moving beyond conventional paradigms', in Gita Sen, Asha George and Piroska Östlin (eds), *Engendering International Health: The Challenge of Equity*, Cambridge, MA: Massachusetts Institute of Technology, pp. 195–220.

United Nations (2010), 'The Millennium Development Goals Report 2010', available at: http://www.un.org/millenniumgoals/ (accessed May 14, 2012).

United Nations (2011), 'The Millennium Development Goals Report 2011', available at: http://www.un.org/millenniumgoals/ (accessed May 14, 2012).

United Nations Development Programme (UNDP) (1995), 'Human development report 1995', available at: http://hdr.undp.org/en/reports/global/hdr1995/chapters/ (accessed May 14, 2012).

United Nations Development Programme (UNDP) (2005), 'Human development report 2005', available at: http://hdr.undp.org/en/media/HDR05_complete.pdf (accessed May 14, 2012).

United Nations Statistics Division (UNSP) (2010), 'The world's women 2010: trends and statistics', available at: http://unstats.un.org/unsd/demographic/products/Worldswomen/WW_full%20report_color.pdf (accessed May 14, 2012).

Walker, Sarah and Imran Matin (2006), 'Changes in the lives of the ultra poor: an exploratory study', *Development in Practice*, **16**(1), 80–84.

White, Sarah and Mark Ellison (2007), 'Wellbeing, livelihoods and resources in social practice', in Ian Gough and J. Allister McGregor (eds.), *Wellbeing in Developing Countries*, Cambridge: Cambridge University Press, pp. 157–75.

World Health Organization (WHO) (2011), 'Structural adjustment programmes (SAPs)', available at: http://www.who.int/trade/glossary/story084/en/index.html (accessed May 14, 2012).

World Health Organization (WHO) (2012), 'MDG 3: promote gender equality and empower women', available at: http://www.who.int/topics/millennium_development_goals/gender/en/index.html (accessed May 14, 2012).

29. Gender and food security
Anandita Philipose and Mishka Saffar

I INTRODUCTION

The challenge of addressing food insecurity has been a focus of renewed international development efforts in recent years in light of the food, fuel, and financial crises in 2008–09 and the more recent famine in the Horn of Africa. Food security goes beyond the mere supply of food to encompass the entire chain of availability, access and utilization of food by all people – a chain that has been coined 'from farm to plate', a phrase used by the United Nations Food and Agriculture Organization (FAO), the International Fund for Agricultural Development (IFAD) and the World Bank. People can be chronically food insecure (never have sufficient quality food) or seasonally food insecure (those whose diet is conditioned by seasonality) or transitorily food insecure (those who are normally food secure but become food insecure in situations of economic, climatic, or civil shocks).

Research, policy responses, and programmatic interventions have been focused on how to ensure that millions of people do not continue to go hungry in a world of diminishing resources. However, these responses will not be effective if the gendered impacts of food insecurity are not understood and integrated into the responses. Gender considerations are central to attaining development goals and the ones related to food security are no exception. Unfortunately, however, this realization has not yet translated into a widespread and consistent integration of gender aspects in policy and program design and implementation. Considering the key roles that women play in agriculture and the well-documented evidence on women's roles in providing food and nutrition security to family members, gender considerations have to be taken into account in any policies and programs that seek to improve food security for men, women, boys, and girls. Changing gender dynamics can substantially influence the allocation, distribution and use of resources at national, district, and household levels (see Quisumbing and McClafferty, 2006).

This chapter focuses on two aspects of gender considerations in food security. The first is to provide an understanding of the important roles that women play in agriculture and thus how to better design programs and interventions that can support them in these roles. The second examines intrahousehold allocations as well as differences between male- and female-headed households[1] when it comes to food production, access and utilization. Food security is often measured at a national level, yet it is imperative that it is also analyzed at a household level as that is the only way to understand how sociocultural norms and gender inequalities impinge on people's ability to be food secure and to have an adequate nutritional intake.

The chapter integrates theoretical analysis of the links between gender and food security with programmatic aspects addressing those links – specifically, features in programs and policies around the world that aim to integrate gender issues meaningfully into practice. It should, however, be noted that while the importance of gender has been highlighted in research on food security since the 1980s, it is only in the last decade that real attempts have been made to design and implement gender-responsive programs and projects that have both food security and gender equality as twin goals. Moreover, different programs and projects address different aspects of gender and food security, which in combination with the great variations between the countries where they are implemented, provides little basis for generalization about gender-responsive[2] food security interventions. Despite these limitations, we seek to identify features in specific interventions that were fully or partially successful in meeting these goals. Starting at a macro level and moving toward a micro level, the sections below first analyze women's role in agriculture and food production and then focus on household dynamics and the access and utilization aspects of food insecurity.

The rest of this chapter is structured as follows. In section II, the barriers women face in relation to agricultural productivity and food security are identified through an analysis of women's limited access to land and to financial services for agricultural purposes. Other structural barriers such as women's illiteracy and their vulnerability to HIV and AIDS are also covered in this section. Section III examines food security and gender dynamics at the household level, including intrahousehold bargaining, vulnerabilities of female-headed households, and women's coping strategies within households. Section IV illustrates some examples of programs aimed at improving food security by influencing gendered household dynamics: through the delivery of food aid to women; improving children's nutritional status through cash transfers to mothers; and, reducing child malnutrition rates by investing in women's education. Section V summarizes the various gender issues within the food security framework and highlights the importance of understanding and integrating gendered impacts of food insecurity in policy and programs in order to improve the food security of entire households and by extension, global food security.

II WOMEN'S BARRIERS TO AGRICULTURAL PRODUCTIVITY AND FOOD SECURITY

Women have always played a critical role in agriculture, comprising nearly half – about 43 percent – of the world's farmers and contributing even more to the global agricultural output through their roles in growing, raising or harvesting food. This varies considerably between regions and within regions, with women accounting for 20 percent of the agricultural labor force in Latin America and about 50 percent in Eastern Asia and Sub-Saharan Africa (UNFAO, 2011). However, there is still a widespread 'perception bias' of women's role in agriculture being minor and secondary to the one occupied by men (Mogues et al., 2009; UNFAO and ILO, 2010; World Bank and International Food Policy Research Institute, 2010). Women are often not considered farmers despite the number of farming-specific activities they contribute to. Women continue to face significant barriers in owning, accessing, and controlling agricultural assets, inputs, and services, which adversely impacts their food production and in turn, their food security. They also are much less likely to use credit and are less likely to have access to extension services.

It is estimated that if women had equal access to agricultural inputs alone, they could increase yields on their farms by 20–30 percent (UNFAO, 2011). The proportional global benefits are huge; an estimated 925 million people were undernourished in 2010 and an increased yield could ensure that an additional 100–150 million people are pulled out of hunger (ibid.). Consequently, the FAO's current strategic framework (2010–19) identifies gender equity as one of the organization's key objectives for this decade. Gender equity is also deemed essential to implementing the decisions of the World Summit on Food Security held in Rome in November 2009, including a renewed commitment from countries to eradicate hunger: 'to work to reverse the decline in domestic and international funding for agriculture and promote new investment in the sector, to improve governance of global food issues in partnership with relevant stakeholders from the public and private sector, and to proactively face the challenges of climate change to food security' (World Summit on Food Security, 2012).

Land and Other Assets

Access to and control over good quality land is a key asset for households that make their livelihoods from agriculture. Research finds that good-quality land is a protective factor against food price shocks, thus making a strong case for strengthening land rights of women, particularly poor women (see Kumar and Quisumbing, 2011). However, women continue to face considerable barriers in owning and controlling good-quality land. Even in cases where laws and policies have been put in place to provide women rights to inherit and own land, there is often a discord between those rights conferred by law and customary practices. In many African countries for example, including Ethiopia, Malawi, Zimbabwe, and Senegal, customary law poses a major obstacle for women despite their legal rights to own land. In these countries, as in many others, women's security of tenure depends as much on addressing social assumptions as on enacting legal reforms. Often, women do not have direct ownership of land and cannot claim their legal rights to it except through their husbands or other male family members (UNFAO, 2004). This is mainly due to the fact that traditionally it was the household as an entity that was considered for land distribution and only heads of households were registered as members of the peasant associations. Consequently, land, people, and cattle are usually considered men's property. As for divorced women or widows, the land they live on is not accessible to them unless they live and farm with the husband's family. Cultural norms determine what a married woman can own and the advancement of girls and women in relation to inheritance of property is hindered by norms that regard boys and men as more permanent and important members of households (Paradza, 2011a, 2011b).

The example of Senegal can shed light on the mechanisms of customary law and some of the ways people are working together to effect a change. In Senegal, about 75 percent of the economically active women work in agriculture, and the 2001 Constitution states that men and women have equal access to land and natural resources. However, the patriarchal tradition holds its grip on the private sphere of the family, where most decisions related to land are taken. According to the 2001 Constitution, the wife and children of a deceased male head of household can claim their right to inheritance of the land at rural councils, but in reality the heads of household often identify their brothers or other male relatives as heirs. In the few cases when a woman approaches the rural council to claim her rights of access to the land, the councils, usually comprising local (male) heads of households, tend to favor the family decision, that is, the decision of the deceased husband (Budlender and Alma, 2011; Guénette, 2011).

The discrepancy between statutory and customary law underlines the importance of raising awareness of women's legal access to land and other agricultural resources as well as enforcing statutory laws. In Senegal, one problem illustrated by a 2011 survey is that a significant proportion of both men (42 percent) and women (38 percent) think that equal access to land is not necessary. Others believed that religion was the obstacle to women's access to land in Senegal, a country where about 90 percent of the population is of the Muslim faith (ibid). Facing these types of obstacles, Senegalese civil society organizations and researchers in cooperation with producers' organizations, religious leaders, and decision-makers are testing measures that could contribute to a change in the society and an improvement of women's situation. Consequently, Islamic religious leaders researched the question of land ownership and declared that Islam allows women to own land. By sharing this information with other religious leaders and encouraging them to address the issue in religious ceremonies, a collective effort was made to overcome a popular and misguided belief that put women at a disadvantage. The research results were spread to other rural communities in order to raise the awareness of women and men (ibid.).

Research indicates that raising awareness and encouraging women to take part in decision-making at different levels can help break the vicious circle in which they often are caught. Raising awareness about religious codes and customs is one way of doing that. Another way is to educate women about their legal rights. In Senegal, this has been done by translating legal documents into local languages in some parts of the country, thereby making these laws accessible to women. Different organizations and associations in collaboration with women leaders also offer training on women's land rights and community leadership. Encouraging women's civic and political participation is also important, as research has shown that civic engagement and women's access to land go hand in hand (Budlender and Alma, 2011; Guénette, 2011).

Countries in other regions face similar issues when it comes to women inheriting or having legal rights over land. In South Asian countries such as Bangladesh and India, even though women have equal rights as men to land under their constitutions, the multiplicity of personal laws based on religion and custom often favors men and boys and denies women the same inheritance and land ownership rights as men (UNFAO, 2012b). Thus, women's land access in many parts of South Asia continues to be insecure as their ability to negotiate for land depends on a variety of factors such as marital status, age, and childbearing status. Many women heads of households are single parents, widows, divorcees, wives of migrant workers, older women, or women with disabilities, who face additional challenges in having access or legal control over their land. According to the FAO (UNFAO, 2010), an international comparative analysis of agricultural census data indicates that less than 20 percent of landholders are women, specifically:

> The situation is particularly grim in Western and Central Africa as well as the Near East and North Africa where generally less than 10% of landholders are women. Numbers are only slightly higher in Asia. In Eastern and Southern Africa and in parts of Latin America, women seem to have somewhat better access to land. In some countries up to 30% of individual land

titles are held by women. Only in a few countries land is almost equally divided between women and men. Latvia and Lithuania top the list with more than 45% of land titles being held by women. Women's low access to land thus prevails across countries with different social, cultural and economic backgrounds. Indeed, differences are often greater within regions than between them. (p. 1)

Globally, even in cases where women do own land, the land holdings are usually smaller and of lower quality than those held by men. In addition, women face challenges in accessing other important agricultural resources needed to increase productivity. The FAO's State of Food and Agriculture 2010–2011 report shows that women face systematic gender inequalities in ownership of large farm animals such as cows and horses, and often find it more difficult to mobilize additional labor to assist on their farms.

Furthermore, women in agriculture are usually responsible for multiple spheres of activity – caregiving, household and childrearing – that detract from their ability to spend time farming the land while increasing the strain on their own health and well-being. Despite studies that have shown how poor health and nutrition constrain women's agricultural productivity (for example, Behrman et al., 2004), this point is rarely acknowledged in policy circles (Quisumbing and Pandolfelli, 2010). For female-headed households (usually consisting of fewer members but more dependents), women face additional time burdens but often do not have the resources or the ability to draw on additional labor to assist them. In such cases, women might lease out their land for sharecropping and do so from a weak negotiating position that further limits their productivity.

Extension and Financial Services

Another hindrance to women's access to land is related to technical knowledge, capital equipment, and credit. Research finds that women are less likely to have access to credit, technological inputs for agriculture, and extension services and training (Mehra and Rojas, 2008; World Bank, UNFAO and IFAD, 2009; Quisumbing and Pandolfelli 2010; UNFAO, 2011). Extension services are aimed at ensuring that farmers receive updated accurate information on the latest technologies and innovations in the field of agriculture and can lead to significant yield increases. However, extension services remain low in most developing countries and studies have shown that less than 5 percent of this is aimed at women. Further, less than 15 percent of all extension workers are women, something that poses a huge challenge in many countries where women are only comfortable approaching or talking to female extension workers (ibid.). Women might be further hampered by their lack of education or their time constraints at home, which could limit their ability to engage in training that uses written material or requires learning visits outside their villages.

Women also face considerable barriers in accessing finances for their work in agriculture. Despite making up almost 50 percent of the workforce in agriculture in Africa, it has been estimated that women receive less than 10 percent of the credit provided to smallholders and less than 1 percent of the total credit provided to the agriculture sector (Mehra and Rojas, 2008). Increasing women's access to credit supply, while important, is not enough. The amount of credit and the investment opportunities need to be carefully planned to ensure that women are able to gain from their credit and not be trapped into a loss-making venture and unable to pay back the loan.

Nigeria is an example of a country that has experimented with different agricultural development strategies, with varying implications for rural women. In the 1970s, World Bank-supported Agricultural Development Projects (ADPs) were initiated in several Nigerian states and were soon replicated across the country. Extension services and technology development were major components of the programs. By the end of the 1980s, it was acknowledged that although rural women had an important role in production, they were basically excluded from the ADP agenda. Consequently, a specific Women in Agriculture unit, with female extension staff, was established in every ADP throughout the country. The goal of these units was to identify the technical and information needs of rural women and to assist them to become more productive through training and technology dissemination offered by trained and qualified female agents working with women's groups. The Women in Agriculture unit experiment in Nigeria integrated women's needs successfully into the ongoing national agricultural development strategy despite limitations such as gaps in the skills of many female agents, difficulties to access women in many areas, and women's limited involvement in the selection and design of technology (UNFAO, 1997, ch. 9; Ogunlela and Mukhtar, 2009).

Other Barriers: Illiteracy, HIV and AIDS

Research has shown that there are a number of other factors that hamper women's ability to engage in agriculture. These include, among others, high levels of illiteracy among women engaged in the agricultural sector as well as external factors, such as HIV and AIDS, which disrupt labor patterns and productivity. A careful and thorough gender analysis of agriculture will have to take into account these factors, depending on the country/regional context.

We begin with education. The lowest literacy rates in the world are among countries in Sub-Saharan Africa, and in South and West Asia. In these world regions, according to the United Nations Educational, Scientific and Cultural Organization (UNESCO), about one-third of the men and half the women are illiterate (UNESCO, 2011). The high levels of illiteracy among women – who make up over 60 percent of the world's illiterates – further hamper their ability to access these support services and their ability to adopt new technologies. Investment in women's education can lead to huge increases in agricultural productivity. Simulations using data from women farmers in Kenya show that yields could potentially be increased by 25 percent if all women attended primary school (IFPRI, 2005).

Moving on to HIV and AIDS, it is acknowledged that gender inequality is one of the key driving forces of the HIV/AIDS epidemic as men continue to hold a disproportionate amount of power that affects women's ability to negotiate safer sex and access reproductive health services. Research in Uganda and other high HIV prevalence countries in East and Southern Africa shows that the socioeconomic burden of HIV and AIDS is disproportionately affecting rural women and that an increasing number of households is headed by widows. Achieving food security is more difficult in such high HIV prevalence countries (World Bank et al., 2007). Specifically, HIV and AIDS affects people's physical ability to produce and utilize food, changes labor dynamics within a household, leads to lower income generation and increases the work and care burden on women and girls (Philipose, 2007). HIV- and AIDS-related stigma and discrimination, coupled with gender discrimination, means that widows lose access to land, labor, inputs, credit, and support services; this brings their households into a downward spiral of increasing dependency ratios, poorer nutrition and health, and more food shortages (Izumi, 2006a, 2006b). In a particularly vicious cycle, individuals who are food insecure are more likely to engage in risky food-provisioning strategies and behaviors, including engaging in transactional sex, which further increases their risk of HIV infection (Gillespie and Kadiyala, 2005).

We offer two representative examples – one community driven and one government led – of programmatic interventions that sought to address the intersections of gender inequality, HIV/AIDS, and food insecurity. In Swaziland, a country with the highest HIV prevalence in the world according to the *Global Report on the AIDS Pandemic 2010* (UNAIDS, 2010), community engagement activities seek to address the specific vulnerabilities that HIV positive women face in food provisioning, among other challenges. In 2001, five HIV positive Swazi women experiencing stigma and discrimination by their relatives and members of their community organized SWAPOL (Swaziland for Positive Living). Starting as a support group to empower families of HIV positive people to cope, accept and deal with HIV, the group gradually evolved first into a professional organization and later transformed into a nongovernmental organization (NGO). In response to the precarious food security situation of many of its members, SWAPOL established agricultural cooperatives to promote food security for HIV-affected households (see SWAPOL 2012).

In Zambia, the government-led Agricultural Support Programme (ASP) (2003–08) aimed to contribute toward improving the livelihoods of small-scale farmer households through improved food and nutrition security and increased income through sale of agricultural products and services. It operated in four provinces and included two phases, with the first targeting 20,000 poor households interested in taking up 'farming as a business' and the second targeting an additional 24,000 households. A secondary target group included government, NGOs and the private sector providing services and activities enabling small-scale farmers to participate in the market economy (Bishop-Sambrook and Wonani, 2008). This program had a clear policy of integrating gender into all program activities to help attain gender equality. Both male- and female-headed households reported greater food security through their involvement in ASP, which also included training in coping strategies (that is, labor-saving technologies) to minimize the impact of HIV and AIDS on food security (Farnworth and Munachonga, 2010).

This section has described a number of obstacles that hamper women's agricultural productivity and negatively impact their food security as well as the food security of their families, their communities and by extension, their countries. Despite women's extensive engagement in the field of agriculture, they continue to face significant barriers in owning land and other assets as well as in accessing extension and financial services, and they continue to be constrained by the impacts of illiteracy and HIV/AIDS. Therefore, any serious efforts to effectively improve food security will necessarily have to overcome these barriers.

III   FOOD SECURITY AND GENDER DYNAMICS AT THE HOUSEHOLD LEVEL

Women are crucial for ensuring food security through the stages of availability, access and utilization. Beyond the key roles they play as farmers, women are also generally responsible for food selection, preparation, and feeding of children, so they can ensure that their households are not just food secure but nutritionally secure as well. It is thus critical to analyze food insecurity at the household level through a gender lens, both within a household and between male- and female-headed households.

Intrahousehold Bargaining

Intrahousehold resource allocation is the process by which resources are allocated among individuals in a household as well as the outcomes of this process (Quisumbing, 2003). Intrahousehold bargaining and resource allocation have been the focus of much research over the past three decades. Policy-makers and program leaders sought to understand the nuances of household dynamics in influencing a wide range of factors, including development factors such as health, nutrition, and education.

There are huge regional variations in women's status in the household – usually defined by decision-making power within the household and societal gender inequality. Women typically have lower levels of education and fewer assets relative to men, which then weakens their bargaining position within a household and within a community (Holmes and Jones, 2011). This has clear implications for gender dynamics within a male-headed household. Yet numerous studies have shown that women prioritize the use of the household income on food and education for the children; this means that improvements in women's status and increases in the resources controlled by a woman within a household lead to long-term development advantages (see Smith and Haddad, 2000; Smith et al., 2003; Basu and Stephenson, 2004; Hadley et al., 2007). An interesting and important outcome of research conducted by Agnes Quisumbing and Bonnie McClafferty (2006) is that the improvement of women's status and decision-making powers has a relatively stronger positive impact on child nutritional status in poorer households than rich ones, underlining the importance of making policies and programs targeted toward poor households more gender responsive.

In terms of regional differences, women are found to have the lowest status in South Asia, followed by Sub-Saharan Africa and then Latin America and the Caribbean (Smith et al., 2003). South Asia also has the world's highest levels and the highest numbers, by far, of malnourished children in the world (UNICEF, 2008). Referring to the 'South Asian enigma', studies have tried to pinpoint the reasons for such high levels of child malnutrition in South Asian countries in contrast with countries in Sub-Saharan Africa that are poorer but have higher levels of child nutritional status (Smith and Haddad, 2000; Smith et al., 2003). A persuasive argument is that the entrenched gender inequalities in South Asia prevent women and girls from being food and nutritionally secure, limit their decision-making abilities about fertility and child-raising and hinder their access to health services – all directly (and negatively) impacting child nutrition. A study by Lisa Smith et al. (2003) supports this hypothesis by showing that women's low status, which has a stronger influence in South Asia than in Sub-Saharan Africa, is a significant factor in explaining the high levels of child malnutrition in the South Asia region.

Vulnerabilities of Female-headed Households

Nobuhiko Fuwa (2000) posits that women heading households suffer from a triple burden: they are disadvantaged in the labor market; they are 'activity-burdened', being responsible both for household and productive duties; and they have more dependents on a sole income. Globally, female-headed households differ from male-headed households in a number of ways. Female household heads often are older and less educated than their male counterparts, and this gender disparity holds for the households as a whole, too, with the levels of education within female-headed households being lower than those within male-headed households (Quisumbing and McClafferty, 2006). Female-headed households tend to spend a larger proportion of income on education and food; despite this, they continue to face difficulties meeting their household's food and consumption needs, largely due to significant constraints outlined in the above sections in accessing and utilizing financial, technical, and human resources for farming and food production.

A study conducted on resource allocation among rural households in Nigeria (Babatunde et al., 2008) showed that gender-based disparities in allocation – ownership and control of production resources – resulted in female-headed households being more food insecure than male-headed households. Pre-school children in female-headed households were more likely to have wasting (or low weight for height) and stunting (or low height for age) compared with those in male-headed households, which implies that female-headed households have less access to food, among other resources.

Women's Coping Strategies within Households

Since female-headed households have fewer resources, these households are more likely to have food shortages (Zezza et al., 2009). Shocks such as HIV and AIDS, climate change or conflict can intensify pressure on rural households in particular, exacerbating food insecurity. When food prices spike, female-headed households suffer proportionally greater losses in welfare than male-headed households. This holds true in all countries at the national level, in urban and rural areas, even when female-headed households are not overrepresented among the poorest (UNFAO, 2011). Female-headed households have less response capacity, partly due to female household heads spending a greater percentage of household income on food, but also because women face gender-specific barriers that limit their ability to produce food.

Food price shocks can lead to asset-stripping, when households are driven to sell their already-meager assets (including livestock and other essential items) to survive (Zezza et al., 2009). In many cases, these households are more vulnerable to asset-stripping than male-headed households (Holmes and Jones, 2011). This leads to a vicious cycle by which female-headed households become even more resource poor and more food insecure, which leads to further cutbacks in household expenditure on food (and education).

Even when there is no food crisis, female-headed households are more likely to experience loss of income, consumption, or assets as well as a widening of the 'food gap' – that is, they reduce the number of meals consumed in good months and are more likely to consume less preferred foods. In times of food crises, women employ coping strategies such as reducing their own consumption to absorb the price shock and leave more food for other members of the household. Even in situations where both parents sacrifice food for their children, there are gender biases perceived in the level of food insecurity experienced by the children. A study of food insecurity among adolescents in Ethiopia found that while boys and girls are equally likely to live in food insecure households, girls were more food insecure, especially in severely food insecure households (Hadley et al., 2007).

Furthermore, as households cut back on both the quantity and quality of food, women and girls are more likely to develop micronutrient deficiencies due to lower food intake and less-diversified diets (see Holmes et al., 2009). In some cases, substituting rice and maize with cheaper starches such as millet and cassava increases the amount of time and energy women spend in processing and cooking these foods, which in turn cuts into their time for other productive activities as well as their time for rest. Pregnant and lactating mothers are most at risk during food crises, which has severe implications for their own health and nutritional status as well as the long-term productivity, health, and nutrition status of their child. According to the United Nations Children's Fund (UNICEF), malnutrition makes pregnant women more susceptible to infection, miscarriage, and premature labor and it increases the likelihood of HIV positive women transmitting their virus to their children (UNICEF, 2009).

IV PROGRAMS TO IMPROVE FOOD SECURITY BY INFLUENCING GENDERED HOUSEHOLD DYNAMICS

Despite the wealth of research on gender inequality being at the heart of intrahousehold dynamics and its long-term development consequences, it is very difficult to address these intrahousehold disparities through programs and projects. The private nature of this sphere makes it more difficult to access and to monitor, and is therefore one of the most challenging aspects of development interventions. Nevertheless, examining intrahousehold food distribution is relevant to the design of targeted interventions, that is, the choice between targeting at the household level or at the individual level.

Appropriate targeting ensures not only cost-effectiveness but also reduces the chance that the vulnerable groups are excluded from the intervention. Individual targeting is partly intended to bypass possible distributional inequity within the household. However, even if the targeting is successful, the benefits themselves are questionable. The beneficiary may subsequently choose to redistribute the benefits received to other household members or may be forced to redistribute the benefits to other household members with greater decision-making power, which serves to reinforce household power dynamics rather than changing them. If assistance is provided in the form of food, there are at least two ways to try to ensure that the intended beneficiary actually consumes it. One method is to monitor in-home consumption, while the other is to distribute for immediate consumption outside the home. Naturally both of these methods are very difficult to implement.

Food Aid to Women

One example of an operational policy that aims at addressing this problem is the United Nations World Food Programme's (WFP) commitment to make women the food entitlement holders. This means that in times of food crises, women are the ones who are entitled to receive food assistance on behalf of the household, no matter whether it is provided in the form of direct food distribution or food vouchers. According to an evaluation made by WFP, women's access to food has increased considerably as a result of this policy (WFP, 2008; see also UNFAO, 2009, 2012a):

> The baseline and follow-up show some marked accomplishments: increasing consultations with women on locations of food distribution points from 46.6% to 66.7% of decisions, and on distribution in insecure areas from 56.5% to 84.6%, along with increased mention of women on ration cards from 67.5% to 86.7% and separate cards for each polygamous wife from 56.2% to 87.1%. The increased focus on women in such settings has been a major accomplishment. (WFP, 2008, p. 32)

However, the evaluation also highlights the challenging aspects of this policy, mentioning among other things the challenge for women to carry the 50kg bags of grain (which is one of the food items they receive) while often carrying their babies on their back and other items such as tins of oil, salt, and pulses at the same time. The evaluation states that WFP staff and partners 'expressed concerns about the time and physical burdens on women, as well as noting that the focus on women seems to relieve men of some work and responsibilities' (ibid., p. 32 and annex E). It is however worth mentioning that WFP's Gender Policy of 2003–07, which the WFP community commonly calls the 'Enhanced Commitments to Women' (ECW) calls upon WFP to consider women's burdens and safety when establishing food distribution points (FDPs) and to determine whether special packaging is needed to enable women to carry food rations themselves.

Making women the holders of entitlements has also led to safety concerns, due to women's relatively increased exposure to violence and abuse in the process of collecting food aid. In order to address these challenges, WFP (2009) has identified additional areas in its operations in order to improve the protection of women and girls, including:

1. using food assistance to engage men and boys to foster understanding of the links between gender inequality and hunger and involve them in activities to protect women and children from violence, reduce burdens on women, and share childcare responsibilities;
2. making WFP distribution sites safe for women and girls; and
3. using WFP's field presence and national staff to encourage local initiatives aimed at ending violence against women and girls.

The end-of-term evaluation of WFP's gender policy (2003–07) highlights the importance of effective protection of women and girls and an understanding of the threats that generate protection issues (WFP, 2008). Consequently, the current gender policy aims to continue making women the food entitlement holders and ensure that they are not put at risk of abuse or violence as a result of this policy.

Improving Children's Nutritional Status by Providing Cash Transfers to Mothers

Conditional cash transfer programs aim to reduce extreme poverty and break the inter-generational cycle of poverty and food insecurity by requiring active participation from beneficiaries who need to fulfill certain conditions. These conditions may include school enrollment of children, health checks and other investments in human capital (European Report on Development, 2010).

An example of such a program is Oportunidades, a government social assistance program in Mexico founded in 2002, based on a previous program called Progresa, created in 1997 (Oportunidades/Progresa, 2012). The program was initiated with the aim of reducing extreme poverty in rural areas of Mexico by offering an integrated package of education, nutrition and health services to poor households in exchange for their active participation. The Mexican program had several gender-targeting aspects. The one specific to food security was a package comprising free preventive interventions (such as nutritional supplements); monetary transfers for the purchase of food, which were conditional on mandatory healthcare visits to public clinics; and education on hygiene and nutrition. This component of the program targeted children under the age of five and pregnant and lactating women. Nutritional supplements were given to children aged four months to two years and to pregnant and breastfeeding women, as well as to children aged two to five years showing signs of malnutrition. The nutritional conditions of beneficiaries were regularly monitored, with a higher frequency for children under the age of five and pregnant and lactating women. During each clinical visit, women and children were measured for wasting, stunting, and weight-for-age ratios.

A unique feature of this nationwide development program is its specific focus on mothers as recipients of cash transfers. The conscious decision to offer cash transfers directly to the mother was based on the aforementioned research showing that resources controlled by women are more likely to result in greater improvements in child health and nutrition than resources controlled by men. As Quisumbing and McClafferty note:

> The concentration and value of this transfer in the hands of the mother and the enormous scale of the [Oportunidades] program – 2.6 million families in extreme poverty as of the end of 1999 or almost 40 percent of all rural families in Mexico – suggest that the likely impact of the program in altering the balance of power within Mexican families is significant. (2006, p. 49)

Moreover, access to resources, even small resources, can boost women's bargaining power in the household–and their confidence, self-esteem and sense of control over changes in life circumstances (European Report on Development, 2010, p. 81). The success of the Oportunidades/Progresa program underlines the important role of women for children's nutritional status and household food security and confirms the positive effects of gender targeting in conditional cash transfer programs. The Mexican program has served as a model for programs across Latin America in countries such as Argentina, Brazil, Colombia, Honduras, and Nicaragua (Quisumbing and McClafferty, 2006), as well as in other parts of the world, including countries such as Malawi and Zambia (Nigenda and González-Robledo, 2005). The program was even the inspiration behind a pilot program in New York City, the 'Opportunity NYC', which was launched in 2007 and ended in 2010 (City of New York press release, 2007; *New York Times*, 2006; see also www.opportunitynyc.org).

Reducing Child Malnutrition Rates by Increasing Women's Education

Investment in women's education also has far-reaching impacts. Smith and Haddad (2000) found that increases in women's education in 63 developing countries made the biggest contribution to reducing child malnutrition, accounting for 43 percent of the total reduction, with improvements in food availability coming in second, contributing to 26 percent of the reduction rate. One explanation for this is that girls acquire skills in school that later allow them to understand health messages and access modern health services. Research conducted in India by Alaka Basu and Rob Stephenson (2004) found that even a little education for a woman (such as a few years of primary schooling) resulted in higher rates of child survival, though the same study cautioned against a limited focus on primary education for women; it is only with more years of schooling that women can be truly empowered enough to make independent decisions and change the balance of power in a household. Similar findings can be found in research on women's intrahousehold status relative to men in Pakistan. One study showed that the higher a woman's education and earning capacity was relative to the male head of household, the better the long-term nutritional status of the children (Guha-Khasnobis and Hazarika, 2006).

Efforts to close the education gender gap are believed to be strongly associated with household food security in female-headed households as well as in male-headed households. The facilitation of women's access to education not only increases their own self-knowledge but also knowledge about nutrition and health matters related to the household, thereby contributing to the improvement of the household's welfare.

V   CONCLUSIONS

With the growing volume of evidence-based research highlighting women's crucial roles in and contributions to food security, it is increasingly acknowledged that women are key players in the fight against hunger. The research clearly shows that women play central roles in agriculture and that targeted interventions to improve their access to land, productive resources and financial services can greatly increase overall agricultural productivity and go a long way toward achieving food security. Suggested interventions include giving women rights to land both through legal and customary laws; supporting resource allocations to women farmers and women heads of households; providing credit and other financial services to women involved in agriculture; and, increasing the number of female extension workers so that women are more comfortable in reaching out to them for the latest technologies and innovations that can improve their productivity.

Equally important is the need to examine household dynamics and take into consideration gender and power dynamics between and within households in designing appropriate gender-responsive interventions. While the research has been unambiguous in pointing out the multiple health, nutrition, and education benefits of women having greater decision-making power and greater control over household income and resources, it is extremely complex to influence intrahousehold dynamics through external interventions due to the range of factors – societal, economic, cultural, religious – that come into play.

While there are clear parallels in the gendered dynamics between men and women within a household as well as between male- and female-headed households, the policy and programmatic interventions required to address these separate situations are considerably different. For example, it is relatively easier to target female-headed households than it is to target women within male-headed households, and interventions targeting female-headed households are increasingly common, especially among those that target poorer households. However, researchers have warned that this singular focus on female-headed households risks overlooking the majority of women within male-headed households where household productivity can easily be increased, at no extra cost, if there would be a reallocation of resources to women within the households (see Mehra and Rojas, 2008).

If programs and projects do not pay specific attention to gender issues within the framework of food security, they are not only unlikely to address the problem in an adequate way but even run the risk of reinforcing inequalities between women and men, further exacerbating imbalances. A single individual project will not be able to fundamentally change these inequalities in the short term, but a range of interventions seeking to improve gender equality across different spheres can have a ripple impact and contribute to a process which closes the gender gap in food security as well as in other areas, thereby improving the lives and livelihoods of women, men, and children.

NOTES

1. Female-headed households are defined as encompassing both de facto female-headed households where the male head of the house is absent for the majority of the time and de jure female-headed households which are headed by divorced, separated, widowed or unmarried women (see Fuwa, 2000).
2. For the purposes of this chapter, gender-responsive interventions are largely women-targeted interventions that seek to address current gender inequalities and barriers to better food and nutritional security among men, women, girls, and boys. However, it is important to involve men and boys in efforts to change entrenched gender dynamics, both within the agricultural sphere as well as at a household and community level.

REFERENCES

Babatunde, Raphael Olarewaju, Olubunmi Abayomi Omotesho, Eniola Oluwatoyin Olorunsanya and Gbenga Mathew Owotoki (2008), 'Determinants of vulnerability to food insecurity: a gender-based analysis of farming households in Nigeria', *Indian Journal of Agricultural Economics*, **63**(1), 116–25.

Basu, Alaka and Rob Stephenson (2004), 'Low levels of maternal education and the proximate determinants of childhood mortality: a little learning is not a dangerous thing', *Social Science & Medicine*, **60**(9), 2011–23.

Behrman, Jere R., Harold Alderman and John Hoddinott (2004), 'Hunger and malnutrition', paper for the Copenhagen Consensus – Challenges & Opportunities, February 19, available at: http://plasma-nrg.com/PDF/Hunger_and_Malnutrition.pdf (accessed May 6, 2012).

Bishop-Sambrook, Clare and Charlotte Wonani (2008), 'The household approach as an effective tool for gender empowerment: a review of the policy, process and impact of gender mainstreaming in the agricultural support programme in Zambia', March, available at: http://asp.ramboll.se/Docs/stcs/GenderStudy.pdf (accessed March 2012).

Budlender, Debbie and Eileen Alma (2011), *Women and Land – Securing Rights for Better Lives*, Washington, DC: International Development Research Centre.

City of New York, News from the Blue Room (2007), 'Mayor Bloomberg releases incentives schedule for *Opportunity NYC*, aimed at helping New Yorkers break the cycle of poverty – families, adults, and children to receive incentives around health, education and adult workforce development', June 18, available at: nyc. org (accessed June 5 2012).

European Report on Development (2010), *Social Protection for Inclusive Development – A New Perspective in EU Cooperation with Africa*, San Domenico di Fiesole, Italy: Robert Schuman Centre for Advanced Studies, European University Institute.

Farnworth, Cathy R. and Monica Munachonga (2010), 'Gender approaches in agricultural programmes – Zambia country report', UTV Working Paper, Swedish International Development Cooperation Agency, Stockholm.

Fuwa, Nobuhiko (2000), 'The poverty and heterogeneity among female-headed households revisited: the case of Panama', *World Development*, **28**(8), 1515–42.

Gillespie, Stuart and Suneeta Kadiyala (2005), 'HIV/AIDS and Food and Nutrition Security: From Evidence to Action, Food Policy Review 7', available at: http://www.ifpri.org/sites/default/files/pubs/pubs/fpreview/pv07/pv07.pdf (accessed May 6, 2012).

Guénette, Louise (2011), 'Equality: a collective effort in Senegal: a case study in women and land – securing rights for better lives', International Development Research Centre, Ottawa.

Guha-Khasnobis, Basudeb and Gautam Hazarika (2006), 'Women's status and children's food security in Pakistan', Discussion Paper. 2006/03, United Nations University, World Institute for Development Economics Research, Helsinki, Finland, June.

Hadley, Craig, David Lindstrom, Fasil Tessera and Tefara Belachew (2007), 'Gender bias in the food insecurity experience of Ethiopian adolescents', *Social Science & Medicine*, **66**(2), 427–38.

Holmes, Rebecca and Nicola Jones (2011), 'Gender inequality, risk and vulnerability in the rural economy: refocusing the public works agenda to take account of economic and social risks', Overseas Development Institute, London, February.

Holmes, Rebecca, Nicola Jones and Hannah Marsden (2009 Background Notes,), 'Gender vulnerabilities, food price shocks and social protection responses', Overseas Development Institute, London August.

International Food Policy Research Institute (IFPRI) (2005), *Women – Still the Key to Food and Nutrition Security*, Washington, DC: International Food Policy Research Institute.

Izumi, Kaori (ed.) (2006a), *The Land and Property Rights of Women and Orphans in the Context of HIV and AIDS – Case Study from Swaziland*, Cape Town: Human Sciences Research Council Press.

Izumi, Kaori (ed.) (2006b), *Reclaiming Our Lives – HIV and AIDS, Women's Land and Property Rights, and Livelihood in Southern and East Africa*, Cape Town: Human Sciences Research Council Press.

Kumar, Neha and Agnes Quisumbing (2011), 'Gendered impacts of the 2007–08 food price crisis: evidence using panel data from rural Ethiopia', International Food Policy Research Institute, Washington, DC, June.

Mehra, Rekha and Mary Hill Rojas (2008), *Women, Food Security and Agriculture in a Global Marketplace*, New Delhi and Washington DC: International Center for Research on Women.

Mogues, Tewodaj, Marc J. Cohen, Regina Birner, Mamusha Lemma, Josee Randriamamonjy, Fanaye Tadesse and Zelekawork Paulos (2009), 'Agricultural extension in Ethiopia through a gender and governance lens', International Food Policy Research Institute and the Ethiopian Development Research Institute, Addis Ababa and Washington, DC, October, available at: http://www.ifpri.org/sites/default/files/publications/esspdp07.pdf (accessed May 6, 2012).

New York Times (2006), Editorial: 'Paying for better parenting', October 17, available at: http://www.nytimes.com/2006/10/17/opinion/17tues4.html (accessed June 5 2012).

Nigenda, Gustavo and Luz María González-Robledo (2005), 'Lessons offered by Latin American cash transfer programmes, Mexico's *Oportunidades* and Nicaragua's SPN. Implications for African Countries', Department for International Development (DFID), London, June.

Ogunlela, Yemisi I. and Aisha A. Mukhtar (2009), 'Gender issues in agriculture and rural development in Nigeria: the role of women', *Humanity & Social Sciences Journal*, **4**(1), 19–30.

Oportunidades/ (2012), 'Oportunidades', available at: http://www.oportunidades.gob.mx/Portal/wb/Web/english (accessed May 3, 2012).

Paradza, Gaynor (2011a), 'A synthesis report of action-research projects on women's access to land from Eastern Africa', International Land Coalition, Rome.

Paradza, Gaynor (2011b), 'A synthesis report of action-research projects on women's access to land from Southern Africa', International Land Coalition, Rome.

Philipose, Anandita (2007), 'HIV/AIDS, gender and food security in Sub-Saharan Africa', in Per-Pinstrup Anderson and Fuzhi Cheng (eds), *Food Policy for Developing Countries*, available at: http://cip.cornell.edu/dns.gfs/1200428152 (accessed March 2012).

Quisumbing, Agnes (ed.) (2003), 'Household decisions, gender and development: a synthesis of recent research,' International Food Policy Research Institute, Washington, DC.

Quisumbing, Agnes and Bonnie McClafferty (2006), *Food Security in Practice – Using Gender Research in Development*, Washington, DC: International Food Policy Research Institute.

Quisumbing, Agnes and Lauren Pandolfelli (2010), 'Promising approaches to address the needs of poor female farmers: resources, constraints and interventions', *World Development*, **38**(4), April 581–92.

Smith, Lisa C. and Lawrence Haddad (2000), 'Explaining child malnutrition in developing countries: a cross-country analysis', Research Report No. 111, International Food Policy Research Institute, Washington, DC.

Smith, Lisa C., Usha Ramakrishnan, Aida Ndiaye, Lawrence Haddad and Reynaldo Martorell (2003), 'The importance of women's status on child nutrition in developing countries', Research Report 131, International Food Policy Research Institute, Washington, DC, available at: http://www.ifpri.org/sites/default/files/pubs/pubs/abstract/131/rr131.pdf (accessed May 6, 2012).

Swaziland for Positive Living (SWAPOL) (2012), 'SWAPOL: Swaziland for positive living', available at: http://www.swapol.net/ (accessed March 2012).

UNAIDS (Joint United Nations Programme on HIV/AIDS) (2010), *Global Report on the AIDS Pandemic 2010*, available at: http://www.unaids.org/globalreport/Global_report.htm (accessed March 2012).

UNESCO (United Nations Educational, Scientific and Cultural Organization) (2011), *Global Education Digest 2011*, available at: http://www.uis.unesco.org/ (accessed March 2012).

UNFAO (UN Food and Agriculture Organization) (1997), *Improving Agricultural Extension. A Reference Manual*, Rome: FAO, available: at http://www.fao.org/docrep/W5830E/w5830e00.htm#Contents (accessed May 3, 2012).

UNFAO (2004), 'Rural women's access to land and property in selected countries', FAO, International Fund for Agricultural Development and the International Land Coalition, Rome, June.

UNFAO (2009), 'Strategic Framework 2010–2019', FAO, Rome, November 18–23.

UNFAO (2010), 'Gender and land rights – understanding complexities; adjusting policies', Policy Brief 8: Economic and Social Perspectives, March.

UNFAO (2011), *The State of Food and Agriculture 2010–2011. Women in Agriculture: Closing the Gender Gap for Development*, Rome: FAO.

UNFAO (2012a), 'Food program: food security', available at: http://www.fao.org/gender/gender-home/gender-programme/gender-food/en/ (accessed May 3, 2012).

UNFAO (2012b), 'Gender and Land Rights Database', available at: http://www.fao.org/gender/landrights/en/ (accessed March 2012).

UNFAO and International Labour Office (ILO) (2010), 'Gender dimensions of agricultural and rural employment: differentiated pathways out of poverty', FAO, Rome.

UNICEF (United Nations Children's Fund) (2008), *The State of Asia-Pacific's Children 2008. Child Survival*, New York: UNICEF.

UNICEF (United Nations Children's Fund) (2009), *The State of the World's Children 2009. Maternal and Newborn Health*, New York: UNICEF.

World Bank, UN Food and Agricultural Organization (FAO) and the International Fund for Agricultural Development (IFAD) (2009), *Module 1: Gender and Food Security. Gender and Agriculture Sourcebook*, Washington, DC: International Bank for Reconstruction and Development/World Bank.

World Bank, WFP, WHO, UNAIDS, UNHCR, USAID, AED, PATH and IFPRI (2007), *HIV/AIDS, Nutrition and Food Security: What We Can Do. A Synthesis of International Guidance*, Washington, DC: International Bank for Reconstruction and Development/World Bank.

World Bank and International Food Policy Research Institute (IFPRI) (2010), *Gender and Governance in Rural Services: Insights from India, Ghana and Ethiopia*, Washington, DC: International Bank for Reconstruction and Development/World Bank.

World Food Programme (WFP) (2008), 'Full Report of the End-of-Term Evaluation of WFP's Gender Policy (2003–2007): Enhanced Commitments to Women to Ensure Food Security', WFP, Rome, August.

World Food Programme (WFP) (2009), 'WFP gender policy and strategy', Rome, January 16.

World Summit on Food Security (2012), Rome, November 16–18 available at: http://www.fao.org/wsfs/world-summit/en/ (accessed March 2012).

Zezza, Alberto, Benjamin Davis, Carlo Azzarri, Katia Covarrubias, Luca Tasciotti and Gustavo Anriquez (2009), 'The impact of rising food prices on the poor', FAO, Rome, June, available at: http://1.umn.edu/bitstream/51696/2/Zezza%20et%20al%20IAAE-2.pdf (accessed May 6 2012).

PART VII

CONTEMPORARY GLOBAL ISSUES

30. Family migration in the US
Nina Banks

I INTRODUCTION

Until recently, scholars assumed that male migration experiences were typical and therefore were sufficient for explaining the migration process. Researchers contributed to this assumption by conducting empirical studies primarily on male migrants. However, nearly half of all 200 million international migrants are women. Since the 1980s, the feminization of migration has led feminist scholars to develop more appropriate studies by analyzing the various ways in which gender affects motivations for and patterns of migration, household decision-making, networks, family relations, macroeconomic policies, labor market outcomes, relocation adjustments, and so on. Feminist theories of migration do not view gender as the primary factor influencing female migrants. Rather, gender is understood through the lens of intersectionality since gender is constituted by social class, race-ethnicity, nationality, citizenship, religion, age, and sexuality. Patricia Pressar (1999) says that the process of 'engendering' migration studies involves analyzing the ways in which changing political and economic conditions affect male and female migrants differently as well as the role played by mediating institutions, such as households, in international migration.

Moreover, migration is often a disruptive process that affects a migrant's sense of self, group identity, and family roles. After relocation, migrants must learn to negotiate new social systems, institutions, and meaning systems (Lansford et al., 2007). Migration between the US and Mexico is often described as 'transnational' since migrants tend to maintain strong familial and cultural ties to Mexico but are also involved in and connected to institutions and practices within the United States. As such, Mexican transnational migration has created shifting identities and racial and gender subjectivities among migrants and their nonmigrating kin as they negotiate the realities of everyday life.

This chapter focuses on one of the most vulnerable groups of immigrants in the US, unauthorized immigrants from Mexico, and the work performed that reproduces families in both the US and Mexico. It uses an intersectional framework for discussing the ways in which gender, race, ethnicity, social class, and citizenship overlap to position immigrant women as providers of social reproduction in a global network of care. Mexican women's reproductive labor within the United States is embedded within historical relations and processes that have devalued and undermined racial-ethnic families and ensured that the labor of women of color would be available to perform work that is devalued in the racial and gender division of labor (see Dill, 1988; Glenn, 2000). Therefore, an important consideration for feminist understandings of family life is the relational aspect of social position that enables some groups of women to obtain benefits on the basis of other women's exploitation and exclusion (see Baca Zinn, 1994; Gordon, 1995).

The chapter builds on Eleonore Kofman's (2010) assertion that scholars must examine connections between social reproduction within private households and commercial establishments outside of the household within the context of state policies. Three sites of social reproduction that are largely 'invisible' in the US public mind are examined: reproductive labor within private households, reproductive labor in transnational households of Mexican immigrants, and reproductive labor in commercial establishments.[1] I argue that US state policies and employer practices have undermined Mexican migrants' ability to provide social reproduction for their own families but have facilitated this process for US employers and families by 'externalizing' costs of social reproduction. An analysis of the work performed by Mexican immigrants and their nonmigrating kin is indicative of the contribution low-wage immigrants and their families back home make to the US economy regardless of the country of origin. This work is not without cost to migrant workers and their families given the emotional and material hardships that it entails.

Section II discusses Mexican migration to the United States and the division of labor that links countries in the global South and North. Section III examines this link within the context of global care chains in the performance of reproductive labor. It focuses on reproductive labor performed by private household workers in the US and their exploitative working conditions. Section IV discusses transnational parenting and the reproductive labor performed by women in Mexico which helps to sustain migration to the US. Section V analyzes labor practices and public policies and sentiment that undermine unauthorized Mexican immigrants' ability to provide social reproduction for their families in Mexico. The chapter concludes by arguing for an extension of family workplace policies to address work performed in US private households and in nonmigrating households in Mexico.

II   MIGRATION FROM MEXICO TO THE UNITED STATES

Mexico and the United States have always had migration flows across their border but the US discouraged permanent Mexican settlement during most of the twentieth century. The Pew Hispanic Center (Taylor et al., 2011) estimates that there are 10.2 million unauthorized adult immigrants in the United States and that two-thirds have lived in this country for at least 10 years. Forty-six percent have minor children. Overall, approximately 11.2 million unauthorized immigrants, including children under age 18, live in the US. Approximately 6.5 million (58 percent) of the unauthorized immigrants in the US are from Mexico. The number of unauthorized immigrants peaked at 12 million in 2007 but has since decreased, due to a reduction in the number of immigrants from Mexico because of a worsening US economy and tougher border controls.

Nonetheless, a substantial portion of Mexico's population lives in the US. One-fifth of Mexican-born men aged 30 to 44 live in the US and 15 percent of Mexican-born women in the same age group reside in the US (Pew Hispanic Research Center, 2011). It is difficult to know the precise number of undocumented Mexican women in the US, but it is estimated that 35 to 45 percent of unauthorized border crossings are by women and that this percentage has increased from 20 percent two decades ago (Alvarez and Broder, 2006). Women migrating from Mexico have traditionally come to join husbands but the number of single women migrants has also increased. Moreover, many Mexicanas make the difficult decision to leave children behind so that they can earn more money in order to better support their children.

The increase in the number of Mexicanas immigrating to the US is part of the overall global increase in the number of women who are migrating across international borders. The increase in migration of women to the United States and other countries in the global North is tied to a number of structural, social, and demographic factors. Global economic restructuring has affected women globally and has led to an increase in women's migration. In particular, economic restructuring has entailed deindustrialization and the growth of the service sector, capital flight to low income countries, transnational corporations' subcontracting out work, and structural adjustment policies (Augustin, 2005).

Saskia Sassen's (1991) pathbreaking research has called attention to conditions that have created a 'global division of labor' between countries in the global North and South. This division of labor is tied to an increased demand for and supply of low-wage, low-skilled workers from rich and poor countries, respectively. In response to the debt crisis, low-and middle-income countries have restructured their economies through trade liberalization and reductions in government spending. Governments have cut spending on healthcare, education, and consumer food subsidies with the result that women and children have been hurt the most (Lugalla, 1995, p. 47). Women have tended to respond to economic restructuring by increasing their earnings through participation in the formal sector, in the informal economy, or through home production. Their increased labor force participation has revealed how important women's earnings are to the household and challenged the notion that men are the breadwinners and heads of households, a result that has often aggravated family tensions (Safa, 1995; Gamburd, 2002). Since structural adjustment reforms have contributed to an increase in poverty, unemployment, and small business failures, women have also resorted to internal and international migration as a survival strategy (Sassen, 2002).

In the global North, the increased demand for low-skilled, low-wage laborers–many of whom are women from lower-income countries – is tied to both the location of corporate headquarters in global cities such as New York and Los Angeles, where it is expensive for firms to operate, and to the increase in two-income professional households living in these cities (ibid.). When top corporations locate their corporate headquarters in global cities, it means that these companies not only hire highly educated and skilled workers, but also low-wage, low-skilled workers to do clerical, cleaning, and maintenance work for their offices. There has also been a growth in luxury service establishments which rely on low-wage laborers to cater to the needs of highly paid workers in global cities (ibid.).

Additionally, the increase in the labor force participation of married women with children has not been accompanied by state-sponsored programs which would enable mothers, the primary caregivers, to balance care for their children with their work outside of the household. Reliance on migrant labor to provide care for children in private homes enables parents living in global cities to have the flexibility that they lack in their own jobs, since migrant domestics often work irregular hours on behalf of their employers. Moreover, two-income earning households in global cities increasingly rely on the market to purchase goods and services previously performed at home by wives. The commodification of this work has led to the growth of commercial services in the areas of food preparation and service, childcare, healthcare services, and recreational services (Glenn, 2000; Folbre and Nelson, 2003). The global division of labor, however, has a racial and gender hierarchy embedded within. In describing American urban centers of production, Cynthia Cranford (2007) says that valued, professional, corporate jobs are typically done by men and women who are white and citizens whereas devalued service jobs – either in private households or commercial establishments – are typically done by people of color, especially women migrants from Latin America.

In the case of Mexico, economic and social changes since the 1970s have led to increased migration of men and women to the US. These changes include regional integration from the North American Free Trade Agreement (NAFTA), the growth of service sector jobs in both countries, and the increased need for low-wage, flexible labor in the United States (Segura and Zavella, 2007). Changes in Mexican cultural understandings of gender have also affected migration patterns. Mexican families have experienced a decline in patriarchal values and relations since the 1970s as families have responded to the effects of economic crisis and neoliberal policies through women's increased participation in paid labor, through migration, and through feminist organizing (Nehring and Alvarado, 2008–09).

III   MIGRANT LABOR AND SOCIAL REPRODUCTION IN PRIVATE HOUSEHOLDS

Feminists use the term 'social reproduction' to describe the activities and social relations that sustain and reproduce people over a period of time. In Karl Marx's analysis of capitalist production, he reasoned that the reproduction of an economic system requires both the labor that is involved in production of goods and services by employers and the labor performed at home that helps to sustain and reproduce the worker and the worker's family at a customary standard of living. Reproductive labor today has come to be understood more broadly than Marx conceived it and it includes household activities that involve biological reproduction, childrearing, nurturing, discipline, emotional care, and socialization of future workers. Families are also maintained and reproduced through the performance of physical labor within and around the household, such as cooking, cleaning, and gardening. Reproductive labor in capitalist economic systems benefits bosses by reproducing the conditions of existence of the working class. Employers pay wages that sustain workers and their families in order to replenish the workforce.

Reproductive labor benefits males directly and indirectly. Within households, men benefit directly from the work that women perform on their behalf. In labor markets, men also benefit from women having primary responsibility for performing reproductive labor at home, since it puts women at a disadvantage in paid labor markets relative to men because of the need for women to take time off from paid work in order to care for sick family members. Having primary responsibility for performing household services also means that women are burdened by having to work a second shift of unpaid labor at home (see Hartmann, 1981; Duffy, 2007). With less responsibility for performing reproductive work within the household, men have more freedom than women do to participate in a wide variety of economic and noneconomic pursuits.

Research by multicultural feminists has pointed to the important role that race and gender have played throughout US history in structuring the type of productive and reproductive work that women have performed. Studies by Evelyn Nakano Glenn (1985), Bonnie Thornton Dill (1988), Teresa Amott and Julie Matthaei (1996), and Nina Banks (2006) analyze differences in the reproductive labor performed by middle-class white women compared to that of women of color and working-class white women in the United States. Their research examines the racial hierarchy of jobs among women and the ways in which the reproductive labor of racial-ethnic men and women have benefited whites, including white women. Racial-ethnic women have historically worked in the homes of white families as domestic servants, alleviating white women of the responsibility for cleaning and caring for their children. Rather than challenge the unfair gender division of labor in their own homes, some white women have shifted their reproductive work onto women with less power by ignoring or undermining these women's material and familial needs (Glenn, 2000; see also Ehrenreich, 2002; Kofman, 2010). Grace Chang (2000) states that many middle- and upper-class women in the United States are able to pursue salaried, professional work and avoid the second shift at home precisely because they rely on unauthorized immigrant women who are low paid. Here, immigrant women's *lack* of citizenship rights enables native-born women to fully participate as citizens in paid, political, and cultural work (Kofman, 2010).

Arlie Russell Hochschild (2000) developed the term 'global care chains' to explain the links between countries in the north and south with respect to reproductive labor. The increased labor force participation of women with children in the global North has led to a process whereby their children are cared for by migrant women from the south who are unable to provide care for their own children. Instead, migrant women must leave their children in their home communities where they are likely to be cared for by women relatives. In both parts of the global care chain, men have not taken on the increased responsibility for reproduction within their own homes.

Presently, there are approximately 1.8 million domestic workers in the US (Excluded Workers Congress, 2011). There are no reliable estimates of the number of undocumented immigrants who work as private household workers. Private household workers include housekeepers, nannies, cooks, cleaners, elderly and disabled caregivers, babysitters, and baby nurses. Thus, paid reproductive labor within private households includes work that involves caregiving and work that does not, such as house cleaning and laundry. Both types of work are devalued because they are performed primarily by women or subordinate groups of men. Since the nineteenth century, however, with the rise of middle-class white households and Victorian gender ideals, household work involving cleaning and drudgery has typically been performed by women of color or immigrants rather than middle-class, native-born white women (Palmer, 1983).

As with any labor process, reproductive labor involves social relations of production between a boss and a worker. Bridget Anderson (2002) notes that the relation between the boss and the domestic worker is not just a contractual relation; it is a relation characterized by power. The employers' power over migrant domestic workers increases when they are undocumented. It also increases when women are live-in domestic workers. The practice of having domestic workers live in the homes of their employers generally died out during the World War I Great Migration era, as African American women replaced European immigrants as domestics in the homes of white Americans in northern and midwestern parts of the country. White families in these regions preferred not to have black women domestics staying overnight in their homes (Katzman, 1978).

Furthermore, black women domestics preferred day work over live-in work since day work enabled them to spend more time with their own families and provided them with greater freedom away from the watchful eyes of employers.

The return to the live-in domestic work arrangement is connected to abusive working conditions to which migrant domestics have been subjected. The fundamental characteristics of domestic work within private households are unpleasant. The work is low status, lacks privacy, and is typically performed in isolation from comparable workers. Domestic workers often work long and irregular hours at low pay and this is magnified for domestic workers who are live-in and are 'on call' throughout the day and night. Domestic workers are also vulnerable to verbal, physical, and sexual abuse (Vellos, 1997; Romero, 2000; Ehrenreich, 2002). Undocumented domestic workers face threats of deportation if they refuse to submit to long hours, extremely low wages, and other degrading circumstances such as debt-peonage (Chang, 2000). Ironically, unauthorized immigrants often choose work in private households because they view it as a safer workplace compared to more public spaces where detection by immigration officials is more likely.

Domestic workers who provide caregiving are sometimes taken advantage of by being viewed as 'one of the family'. Employers take advantage of domestic workers' loyalty to the family by expecting them to work longer hours than agreed and by not providing these workers with regular pay. As Fiona Williams (2010) states, the notion of 'one of the family' blurs the boundary between privacy and work. It blurs the lines between domestic workers' status as employees and as members of a private family unit. Thus, it enables migrant domestics to be exploited both as employees and as household caregivers assumed to be beyond the regulations of the state (Labadie-Jackson, 2008). The claim that migrants are 'part of the family' belies the reality of their status as caregivers who can be made to work long hours because they are separated from their own children (Anderson, 2001). Interestingly, Maria de La Luz Ibarra (2007, p. 304) found that Mexicanas working in domestic labor in the Santa Barbara region of California preferred housekeeping over human care work, since the latter is more emotionally taxing because it 'leaves its mark on the body and mind'. These women report that caregiving work involves psychic pain that stems from having emotional attachments to the people for whom they provide care.

Survey results from New York City (Domestic Workers United & Data Center, 2006) confirm the extensive use of immigrant and racial-ethnic women as private household workers in US global cities and their vulnerability to exploitative working conditions. The study found that 99 percent of the city's 200,000 domestic workers are foreign-born. Ninety-five percent of the city's domestic workers are people of color and 93 percent are women. Most workers reported working overtime but 67 percent stated that they did not receive overtime pay. In 2002, the Data Center (Mujeres Unidas, 2007) joined forces with two California organizations in order to research working conditions of the largely immigrant and undocumented domestic workers in the state. They interviewed private household workers over several years in the economically prosperous San Francisco Bay area. Survey results were similar to those in New York. Ninety-four percent of respondents were Latinas and 99 percent of respondents were born outside of the US. Three-quarters (72 percent) were supporting family in their home countries and 54 percent were the primary income earners for their families. And yet, 67 percent earned wages that were insufficient to sustain basic needs (defined as 'low wages' or wages below the poverty line).[2] Ninety-three percent of domestic workers said that they had difficulty meeting their own living expenses such as rent, childcare, groceries, and utilities. These women also experienced various forms of mistreatment and reported working for overtime without pay.

These data reveal the contradictions involved in the struggles that migrant domestic workers experience in trying to provide for their own and their families' social reproduction while they help to perform this function for families for whom they work. The pay that Mexicana and other racial-ethnic private household workers receive is too low to provide the necessities that their own families need for social reproduction, especially as intact families (see Dill, 1988). It is on this basis, however, that their employers extract work from them.

IV SOCIAL REPRODUCTION AND TRANSNATIONAL HOUSEHOLDS

An important aspect of migrant families and social reproduction is the impact of migration on nonmigrating family members and the role of nonmigrants in sustaining the migration process.[3] Reproductive labor performed in households reproduces workers and their families over time. When wages are too low for the workers to support themselves and their families, migrants often make the difficult decision to migrate without spouses and children. Nonmigrant family members remain a part of the process of social reproduction, but their geographical separation from migrants means that employers push some of the costs of reproducing their labor supply onto households in the global South.

The difficulty that unauthorized migrants have in bringing spouses and children with them to host countries have led to binational families and transnational parenting practices. Binational or split-household families include those that are formed when migrants leave spouses in source communities.[4] In the US, split-household formations are more common among Mexican male than female migrants for reasons that will be discussed soon. Women migrants, however, are often involved in transnational mothering. Transnational motherhood refers to mothering practices of immigrant women whose children remain in their country of origin while mothers work abroad and send money home to provide for their children.[5] Pierrette Hondagneu-Sotelo and Ernestine Avila (1997) developed the concept of 'transnational mothering' and they link the practice to a long history of people of color being drawn into coercive labor systems that disregard the rights and needs of their own families.

In a pioneering study of Latina migrant domestic workers in Los Angeles, California, Hondagneu-Sotelo and Avila analyzed work–family arrangements of women who worked as independent household cleaners, as live-out domestics, or as live-in domestics. Forty percent of the mothers in their survey had at least one child living back home. Women who worked as live-in domestics were the least likely to have their children in the US with them; 82 percent had at least one of their children living in their home country. The long working hours and low pay undermined their ability to care for their own children even if they also lived in the United States. When migrants brought their children to live with them in the homes where they worked, children were often treated poorly by members of the family.

Rhacel Parrenas (2005), one of the first scholars to analyze differences in caregiving between transnational mothers and fathers, revealed the continuities in gender inequities in caregiving that are maintained across transnational households. For Filipino/a transnational families, when males migrate and leave wives behind, nonmigrating mothers attend to the emotional and disciplinary needs of their children whereas when mothers migrate and leave husbands behind, husbands often relegate childrearing responsibilities to another female relative who is likely to have her own care responsibilities. Avila (2008) confirmed this pattern for transnational Mexican mothers and fathers. She also noted that transnational mothers encounter greater criticism than fathers do for leaving their children in Mexico because of cultural notions about the proper role of mothers as emotional caretakers and the acceptance of fathers as providers rather than as caregivers. Transnational mothers from Mexico tend to be unmarried and are stigmatized for leaving children behind and in the care of grandmothers or aunts. This is viewed unfavorably because traditional Mexican families idealize motherhood as a situation that involves mothers tending to their children by staying at home and not engaging in paid employment.

With economic restructuring, however, this has become less feasible for Mexican women. Despite the stigma, Rosa Maria Sternberg's (2010) interviews with transnational Mexican mothers revealed that they migrated to the US without their children because they were facing extreme poverty from lack of jobs and/or abandoned spouses, and were unable to meet their family's basic material needs. Avila's (2008) study describes the profound sense of pain felt by transnational mothers who had to care for other people's children while feeling the emotional loss of not being able to be with their own children. Paid domestic work intensifies their emotional pain through the reproductive work that they perform for other women's children.

Transnational mothers cope with the physical separation from their children by maintaining regular communication with them and their caregivers in order to sustain family ties, as well as to remain an authority figure in the lives of their children. Hondagneu-Sotelo and Avila (1997) note that Mexican migrant women who are engaged in transnational mothering are challenging Mexican cultural understandings of good mothering by redefining it to include the provision of financial and other support for children while leaving them in the care of a trusted, well-paid caregiver such as a grandmother. Good mothering means sending money home in order to improve their children's access to good nutrition, housing, quality education, and better clothing.

Historically, most migrants from Mexico to the US have been male temporary workers based on a combination of US policy preferences and patriarchal gender norms within Mexico. US immigrant labor recruitment policies have targeted Mexican men to work in the agricultural sector. Unauthorized Mexican men migrate to the US without their wives and children because they typically do not earn enough money to support families in the US. Migrating without family also enables migrants to have greater mobility to relocate to longer distances.

Women who remain in Mexico are central to the process of sustaining migration across national borders and enabling male migrants to periodically return home. The labor of nonmigrating kin also helps to reproduce migrant workers in their destinations.

They are, according to Shawn Kanaiaupuni (2000), the 'invisible' backbone that has facilitated transnational migration from Mexico to the US for over a century through their earnings as well as through their efforts to maintain a sense of family cohesion. As such, nonmigrating women in Mexico bear most of the cost of migration within their communities. When husbands migrate, it increases the work of nonmigrating wives since they often take on paid work in the informal sector or piecework within their households so that they can combine these activities with childcare responsibilities. This enables employers in the United States to pay migrant workers wages that are below subsistence levels. As such, nonmigrating households subsidize the low wages of migrants and US employers transfer some of the cost of reproducing its labor supply to labor processes in Mexico. This has the effect of maintaining a cheap supply of labor for US employers, especially since nonmigrating households are dependent on remittances.

In the absence of husbands, women assume responsibilities previously performed by men but must do so in a way that does not risk social disapproval within the community for overstepping gender boundaries. Children sometimes quit school in order to help support their families. Given women's limited work opportunities in Mexico, they are especially vulnerable to decreases in men's remittances since it puts the family at risk of hunger. Kanaiaupuni's research on nonmigrating families found that, given irregular remittances and women's low earnings, women often sustained and indebted themselves through small loans and in-kind supports from friends, neighbors, and kin within their origin network based on norms of reciprocity.

Nonmigrating mothers, as caregivers, try to maintain ties between their children and migrant husbands through phone calls, letters, and computers if they have access to them. However, when migrants have difficulty sending remittances home, they often decrease communication with family members out of concern that they will not understand and this puts a strain on family relations (Orellana et al., 2001). In addition to economic hardship, family separation has an emotional aspect on nonmigrants and migrants that involves feelings of isolation and estrangement, fear of infidelity and abandonment, and concerns over the well-being of family members. Although the reproductive tasks undertaken within nonmigrating Mexican households help to sustain migrant workers to the benefit of their employers, it is work that is largely invisible to people who live within the US.

V   UNDERMINING THE REPRODUCTION OF MEXICAN FAMILIES

As reported earlier, the process of social reproduction is carried out not only within households in the US and in Mexico but also within commercial service establishments in the paid labor market. This work, however, is also marked by invisibility since it is often performed in low-wage, 'back-room' spaces by unauthorized immigrants and by US racial-ethnic men and women. Race and gender continue to play a role in structuring access to both nurturing and non-nurturing (for example, 'dirty') reproductive work. As such, a hierarchy of jobs exists that is organized by race-ethnicity and nationality (Glenn, 2000; Duffy, 2007).[6] Specifically, white females are likely to be in more-skilled jobs, including registered nursing, and Asian, black, and Latina women are overrepresented in the lower-end jobs within professional care industries that involve cleaning rather than nurturing. US racial-ethnic and immigrant men, as racially subordinate men, are also likely to be employed in professional service industries and overrepresented in low-wage, non-nurturing service jobs.

The degree to which immigrants aged 16 years and over are overrepresented in service jobs can be ascertained from census data from the US Current Population Survey (CPS). One-third (29.6 percent) of noncitizens living in the United States work in a service occupation compared to 16.2 percent of native-born US citizens. About 15 percent (14.6 percent) of workers in service occupations are noncitizens (author's calculation of CPS data). Noncitizen males are equally distributed between service occupations and construction, extraction, and maintenance occupations: 22.7 percent work in service occupations and 23.7 percent work in construction, extraction, and maintenance occupations. Among noncitizen females, 41.8 percent work in service occupations. This amounts to 13 percent of all service workers (author's calculation using CPS data).

CPS data for the working-age population in 2010 also provide information on foreign-born Mexican immigrants in the US, both legal and unauthorized workers. Again, service occupations represent the most common occupational category with 32.2 percent working in services. One-third (29.5 percent) of foreign-born male immigrants from Mexico report working in construction, extraction, and maintenance occupations, followed by 25.4 percent who work in service occupations. Nearly half of all foreign-born Mexican females (46.5 percent) are employed in service occupations. Within service occupations, 9.8 percent of Hispanics of Mexican origin are concentrated in building and grounds cleaning and maintenance and 9.5 percent are in food preparation and serving related occupations (author's calculations of US BLS household data). Moreover, BLS household data for 2010 indicate that occupations in which unauthorized immigrants are overrepresented are low paid. Workers in food preparation and service had a mean hourly pay of $9.02 ($21,240 yearly) and 'Personal care and services' had a mean hourly wage of $11.82 ($24,590 yearly). Within the latter category, personal care aides earned $9.82 ($20,420 yearly) and childcare workers' mean hourly pay was $10.15 ($21,110 yearly).

Compared to other immigrants, Mexican immigrants are especially low paid. Median 2009 earnings for Mexican immigrants 15 years and older for full-time, year-round work is lower than the median earnings for all foreign-born workers in the US (US Census Bureau CPS, 2010). Mexican immigrants had median earnings of $24,389 for both males and females, compared to $32,932 overall foreign-born median earnings. Median earnings for Mexican-born males is $25,737 compared to $35,814 median earnings for foreign-born males overall, and for Mexican-born females median earnings are $21,308 compared to female foreign-born median overall earnings of $31,022.

Given their low pay, Mexican-born families living in the US, whether authorized or not, have high poverty rates and struggle to provide subsistence for household members. Analysis by the Pew Hispanic Research Center (2009) indicates the extent to which these families experience poverty. For 2009, the latest year for which data are available, 30.7 percent of families born in Mexico and living in the US lived below the poverty threshold. Of these families, 25.7 percent of married couples lived below the poverty line, 25.3 percent of male householders with no spouse present, and 51.9 percent of female householders with no spouse present lived below the poverty threshold. These data include both unauthorized immigrants and those who have legal status in the US. The high poverty rates for Mexican immigrants have consequences for their children. Analysis by Mark Lopez and Gabriel Velasco (2011) reveals that over two-thirds (4.1 million) of the 6.1 million Latino/a children living in poverty in the US are the children of immigrant parents. Latino/a children in the US now constitute the largest number of poor children: 37.3 percent of poor children in 2010 were Latino/a, 30.5 percent were white and 26.6 percent were black. The concentration of Mexican immigrants into low-wage service occupations impinges upon their ability to socially reproduce their families.

Although Mexican immigrants perform social reproduction work within the US, state policies of exclusion have undermined undocumented Mexicans' attempts to sustain their own families. These policies, therefore, increase migrants' reliance on support from nonmigrating family members. In doing so, they have externalized the cost of reproducing the labor force in the US to local economies in Mexico (Burawoy, 1976). Policies that prevent Mexican immigrants from receiving social goods have perpetuated unequal social relations based on race, ethnicity, gender, and citizen status. They have maintained a system of capitalist production that is dependent on the use of low-wage migrant laborers to reproduce the US labor force in those regions where unauthorized immigrants work.

Reproductive labor performed by Mexicana domestics within private households is intensified not only because of their immigration status but also because this category of work is excluded from various US labor protections. As such, the abuses that unauthorized private household workers experience are tied to the general lack of legal protections provided for private household, domestic workers compared to other categories of workers. Domestic workers, disproportionately women of color, are excluded from the right to organize and engage in collective bargaining under the National Labor Relations Act, they are excluded from the protections in the Occupational Safety and Health Act, and they are excluded from most state-level minimum wage laws and statutes for worker's compensation and unemployment benefits (Labadie-Jackson, 2008). This leaves this category of workers susceptible to abuse within private households, and this tendency is magnified when private household workers are undocumented.

Moreover, the migration of unauthorized immigrants from Mexico and other parts of Latin American has been accompanied by a rise in racial and ethnic antagonism within the US. Lynn Fujiwara (2008) characterizes the backlash against immigrant communities in the US at the end of the twentieth century as the 'New Nativism'. New Nativism is tied to a number of factors: racial anxiety on the part of whites fearful of loss of majority status as the number of immigrants from Asia and Latin America increases, economic insecurity over declining global competitiveness and job loss, and transnational migrants who maintain ties to their homeland rather than fully assimilating into the United States.

As more women have emigrated from Mexico, gender has been a key element in state policies aimed at preventing Mexican migrants' social reproduction. The issue of Latina reproduction has been central to nativist discourses. Nativist discourses based on gendered and racialized beliefs about Mexicans as a drain on the US economy are part of the ideological apparatus that buttress state-level restrictions against undocumented immigrants. This has been carried out as an attempt to prevent the reproduction of immigrant families and communities by denying them access to social services, since the assumption is that brown women come to the US to have babies and rely on welfare.[7]

Chang (2000) argues that Immigration and Naturalization Service (INS) policies misapplied the Immigration Reform and Control Act (IRCA) of 1986 by preventing undocumented women workers from becoming naturalized citizens if any of their citizen children received public assistance (to which they were legally entitled) and made women wait five years after applying for amnesty in order to receive public assistance for children. This policy discriminated against women since women – rather than men – typically receive aid for children. As such, it discouraged women from applying for amnesty. Instead, they continued to work in the shadows for low wages and long hours. The INS's interpretation of the IRCA undermined migrant women's ability to care for their families and move out of poverty and into regular jobs with higher pay and benefits. This policy is consistent with state regulations that have historically discouraged poor women of color from receiving public assistance and encouraged their labor to be available at very low wages for local businesses and private white households (Glenn, 1985; Chang, 2000).

The popular notion of high Latina fertility as a threat to Californians was central to the Save Our State initiative that culminated in the passage of Proposition 187 (Chavez, 2007). Proposition 187 denied unauthorized immigrants from receiving access to public education, nonemergency healthcare, and other social services.[8] The emphasis placed on high fertility rates of Mexican-born women in the US compared to the national average, however, overlooks the decline in fertility rates for second- and third-generation Mexican-Americans as well as the trend toward lower fertility rates in Mexico (ibid.). However, cast differently, the higher fertility rates of immigrants from Latin America compared to the US average has helped to sustain the United States' population growth and replenishment rate given the problem of low birth rates of native-born women in meeting US demands for labor (Nehring and Alvarado, 2008–09). This has important implications for maintaining productivity rates, wage levels, and retirement benefits in the United States.

New Nativism resulted in the convergence of immigration and welfare policies that stripped noncitizens of benefits for which they had previously been entitled (Fujiwara, 2008). By 1996, animosity against welfare recipients and immigrants in the US led to the passage of the Personal Responsibility and Work Opportunity Reconciliation Act (PRWORA) and Illegal Immigration Reform and Immigrant Responsibility Act (IIRIRA).[9] The PRWORA made citizenship a condition for receiving welfare benefits. Legal residents were no longer eligible for Supplemental Security Income (SSI), Food Stamps, and it was left up to states to determine if legal residents could receive Temporary Assistance to Needy Families (TANF) and Medicaid. Immigrants were also barred from receiving means-tested programs for five years after arrival in the US, if they arrived after 1996. Congress restored some of the SSI and Food Stamp benefits but it still remained up to states to determine permanent residents' eligibility for TANF and Medicaid. Although undocumented workers had not been entitled to receive these benefits, their US-born children are entitled. More than two-thirds (73 percent) of children of unauthorized immigrants are US citizens by birth and approximately 4 million children under age 18 live in mixed-status families where one parent is unauthorized (Passel and Cohn, 2008). Although these children are entitled to welfare benefits, their parents are often reluctant to obtain benefits for fear of immigration status detection.

In the past few years, several states have circumvented federal control of immigration enforcement by enacting harsh legislation that penalizes undocumented workers. In 2010, the State of Arizona passed a law that required that immigrants carry their alien registration documents at all times and also required that police check the immigration status of people whom they suspect are unauthorized immigrants.[10] Another state, Alabama, enacted a law in 2011 that requires, among other things, that police officers check the papers of people they suspect are undocumented, public schools check the legal status of students, and undocumented workers possess registration papers. The law has generated tremendous fear in families who are terrified that if they are detected, detained, and deported, they will lose custody of their children.

The US Justice Department has legally challenged these laws for violating the federal government's exclusive right to enforce immigration law. Some of the key provisions of these laws have been halted by federal judges and appeals courts. Nonetheless, the presidential administration of Barack Obama has deported immigrants at an unprecedented level. In 2011, approximately 400,000 immigrants were deported and nearly half of these had no criminal record. A recent report on 'Shattered Families' found that the administration's deportation of undocumented immigrants has resulted in approximately 5,100 children being placed in US foster homes (Wessler, 2011). One out of every four people deported are parents of US children.[11] The study also revealed that deportations have led to long family separations and some deported parents have had their parental rights terminated by child welfare agencies and juvenile court systems.

VI CONCLUDING REMARKS

This chapter has examined the conditions under which unauthorized Mexican immigrants perform reproductive labor in private households, in transnational households, and in paid commercial service enterprises. Reproductive labor is indispensible to the functioning of the US economy because it enables the replenishment of the labor force. And yet, the labor force that performs paid reproductive work is compensated at wages that undermine their ability to provide caregiving and non-nurturing services for their own families. US employers, whether in private households or public sites, have passed on the cost of reproducing labor power to paid household workers and their nonmigrating kin in Mexico. In addition to low wages, transnational families cope with the emotional strain of physical separation from loved ones.

Research suggests that feminists need to broaden our discussion of family workplace policies beyond the formal, public sector and, instead, link it to the private household sector by analyzing the ways in which these family work relations are shaped by class, race/ethnicity, and citizenship rights. With the phenomenon of transnational families, this discussion must also include the links between work in the US public sector, the private household, and the non-migrant household in Mexico. Thus far, state policies in the US have failed to provide sufficient public supports for families that would enable them to balance paid work with responsibilities for caring for people who are too young, elderly, or ill to care for themselves.

Instead, state policies have facilitated the exploitation of low-wage women and men for the benefit of private, middle-class households and US businesses. Nowhere is this more so than in the case of unauthorized immigrants. Currently, there is no clear legal pathway for unauthorized immigrants to become naturalized citizens.[12] US immigration restrictions mean that undocumented migrant women continue to remain poor, and therefore a source of cheap labor available to care for middle-class children, while the policies simultaneously undermine Mexican immigrants' ability to provide consistent care for their own children (Chang, 2000). These laws also help to ensure that migrant women and men are pushed into low-wage work in other industries, including professional service, electronics, and apparel. This analysis broadens our understanding of both global care chains and the racial-gender division of global labor by discussing the process by which employers in the global North externalize the cost of reproducing their labor force onto migrant families and their nonmigrating kin in the global South.

NOTES

1. Although it is beyond the scope of this study, these areas are also sites of contestation as migrants challenge working conditions and state policies that undermine their ability to sustain their own families.
2. Specifically, 23 percent of respondents earned wages that were below the poverty line ($6.75–$9.06) and 44 percent earned 'low wages' ($9.07–$14.26), insufficient to provide for basic needs according to the Self-Sufficiency Standard for California 2003. Self-sufficiency wages were defined as hourly wages of $14.27 and higher – required by a two-adult, two-child working family to pay for the basic needs of rent, food, childcare, healthcare, transportation, miscellaneous costs, and taxes in San Francisco County in 2003 (see Mujeres Unidas, 2007).
3. There is a growing literature examining the impact of migration on children who remain in sending countries and children who migrate (see Parrenas, 2005; Lansford et al., 2007).
4. For an analysis of transborder families living in the U.S.–Mexico border region, see Ojeda de La Pena (2007).
5. Kofman (2010) notes that the emphasis in migration literature on transnational mothering, to the exclusion of other familial relations, encompasses hetero-normative assumptions by neglecting gays, lesbians, and single heterosexual women.
6. Immigrant and racial ethnic workers who work for janitorial services, for example, work during the night shift when the building is empty. Within food service, immigrant workers are often found in dishwashing.
7. This notion is captured by the concept of 'anchor babies'.
8. The initiative was passed by California voters in 1994 but was later declared unconstitutional.
9. US welfare policies have always separated the poor into the categories of deserving versus undeserving. For an excellent history, see Linda Gordon (1995).
10. In October 2010, National Public Radio (NPR) reported on the findings of their investigation into Arizona's anti-immigration legislation. Their investigation found that the private prison industry in the state was the impetus behind the legislation since, if enacted, the law would lead to an increase in the arrest and incarceration of Mexicans. The report is available at: http://www.npr.org/2010/10/28/130833741/prison-economics-help-drive-ariz-immigration-law.
11. The Pew Hispanic Research Center (Taylor et al., 2011) estimates that there are 1 million unauthorized immigrant children living in the US and an additional 4.5 million children under 18 who were born in the US to at least one unauthorized immigrant parent. Moreover, some 400,000 of these unauthorized immigrant children have siblings who are US citizens.
12. Enforcement of workers' rights and protections is too often tied to citizenship status so citizenship status perpetuates inequalities among workers. Justice for Janitors, however, waged a successful campaign for living wages and family health insurance in Los Angeles by organizing both legal and unauthorized immigrants.

REFERENCES

Alvarez, Lizette and John Broder (2006), 'More and more, women risk all to enter U.S.', *New York Times*, January 10.

Amott, Teresa and Julie Matthaei (1996), *Race, Gender, and Work: A Multicultural Economic History of Women in the United States*, Boston, MA: South End Press.

Anderson, Bridget (2001), 'Reproductive labour and migration', paper delivered at Sixth Metropolis Conference, Rotterdam, The Netherlands, November.

Anderson, Bridget (2002), 'Just another job? The commodification of domestic labor', in Barbara Ehrenreich and Arlie Hochschild (eds), *Global Woman: Nannies, Maids, and Sex Workers in the New Economy*, New York: Henry Holt & Company, pp. 104–14.

Augustin, Laura (2005), 'Migrants in the mistress's house: other voices in the "trafficking" debate', *Social Politics: International Studies in Gender, State and Society*, **12**(1), 96–117.

Avila, Ernestine M. (2008), 'Transnational Motherhood and Fatherhood: Gendered Challenges and Coping', dissertation, University of Southern California, August.

Baca Zinn, Maxine (1994), 'Feminist rethinking from racial-ethnic families', in Maxine Baca Zinn and Bonnie Thorton Dill (eds), *Women of Color in U.S. Society*, Philadelphia, PA: Temple University Press, pp. 18–26.

Banks, Nina (2006), 'Uplifting the race through domesticity: capitalism, African American migration, and the household economy in the Great Migration Era of 1916–1930', *Feminist Economics*, **12**(4), 599–624.

Burawoy, Michael (1976), 'The functions and reproduction of migrant labor: comparative material from Southern Africa and the United States', *American Journal of Sociology*, **82**(5), 1050–87.

Chang, Grace (2000), *Disposable Domestics: Immigrant Women Workers in the Global Economy*, Cambridge, MA: South End Press.

Chavez, Leo (2007), 'A glass half empty: Latina reproduction and public discourse', in Segura and Zavella, (eds), pp. 67–91.

Cranford, Cynthia (2007), '"¡Aqui estamos y no nos vamos!" justice for janitors in Los Angeles and new citizenship claims', in Segura and Zavella (eds), pp. 306–24.

Dill, Bonnie Thorton (1988), 'Our mother's grief: racial-ethnic women and the maintenance of families', *Journal of Family History*, **13**(1), 415–31.

Domestic Workers United & Data Center (2006), 'Home Is Where the Work Is: Inside New York's Domestic Work Industry', July, available at: http://www.datacenter.org/wp-content/uploads/homeiswheretheworkis.pdf (accessed December 2011).

Duffy, Mignon (2007), 'Doing the dirty work: gender, race, and reproductive labor in historical perspective', *Gender & Society*, **21**(3), 313–36.

Ehrenreich, Barbara (2002), 'Maid to order', in Barbara Ehrenreich and Arlie Russell Hochschild (eds), *Global Woman: Nannies, Maids, and Sex Workers in the New Economy*, New York: Henry Holt & Company, pp. 85–103.

Excluded Workers Congress (2011), 'Domestic Workers', The Excluded Workers Congress, New York available at: http://www.excludedworkerscongress.org/domestic-workers (accessed December 2011).

Folbre, Nancy and Julie A. Nelson (2003), 'For love or money – or both?', in Ellen Mutari and Deborah M. Figart (eds), *Women and the Economy: A Reader*, Armonk, NY: M.E. Sharpe, pp. 108–23.

Fujiwara, Lynn (2008), *Mothers without Citizenship: Asian Immigrant Families and the Consequences of Welfare Reform*, Minneapolis, MN: University of Minnesota Press.

Gamburd, Michele (2002), 'Breadwinner no more', in Barbara Ehrenreich and Arlie Russell Hochschild (eds), *Global Woman: Nannies, Maids, and Sex Workers in the New Economy*, New York: Henry Holt & Company, pp. 190–206.

Glenn, Evelyn Nakano (1985), 'Racial ethnic women's labor: the intersection of race, gender and class oppression', *Review of Radical Political Economics*, **17**(3), 86–108.

Glenn, Evelyn Nakano (2000), 'From servitude to service work: historical continuities in the racial division of paid reproductive labor', in Vicki Ruiz and Ellen Carol DuBois (eds), *Unequal Sisters: A Multicultural Reader of U.S. Women's History*, London and New York: Routledge, pp. 436–65.

Gordon, Linda (1995), *Pitied but Not Entitled: Single Mothers and the History of Welfare 1890–1935*, Cambridge, MA: Harvard University Press.

Hartmann, Heidi (1981), 'The unhappy marriage of Marxism and feminism: towards a more progressive union', in Lydia Sargent (ed.), *Women and Revolution*, Boston, MA: South End Press, pp. 1–41.

Hochschild, Arlie Russell (2000), 'Global care chains and emotional surplus value', in Will Hutton and Anthony Giddens (eds), *Global Capitalism*, London: Jonathan Cape, pp. 130–46.

Hondagneu-Sotelo, Pierrette and Ernestine Avila (1997), 'I'm here, but I'm there: the meaning of Latina transitional motherhood', *Gender & Society*, **11**(5), 548–71.

Ibarra, Maria de La Luz (2007), 'Mexican immigrant women and the new domestic labor', in Segura and Zavella (eds), pp. 286–305.

Kanaiaupuni, Shawn Malia (2000), 'Sustaining families and communities: nonmigrant women and Mexico–U.S. migration processes', CDE Working Paper No. 2000–13, Center for Demography and Ecology, University of Wisconsin-Madison.

Katzman, David M. (1978), *Seven Days a Week: Women and Domestic Service in Industrializing America*, New York: Oxford University Press.

Kofman, Eleonore (2010), 'Gendered migrations and the globalisation of social reproduction and care: new dialogues and directions', in Marlou Schrover and Eileen Yeo (eds), *Gender, Migration and the Public Sphere, 1850–2005*, New York: Routledge, pp. 118–39.

Labadie-Jackson, Glenda (2008), 'Reflections on domestic work and the feminization of migration', *Campbell Law Review*, **31**(1), 67–90.

Lansford, Jennifer E., Kirby Deater-Deckard and Marc H. Bornstein (eds) (2007), *Immigrant Families in Contemporary Society*, New York: Guilford Press.

Lopez, Mark Hugo and Gabriel Velasco (2011), 'The toll of the Great Recession: childhood poverty among Hispanics sets record, leads nation', Pew Hispanic Center, Washington, DC, available at: http://www.pewhispanic.org/2011/09/28/childhood-poverty-among-hispanics-sets-record-leads-nation/ (accessed December 2011).

Lugalla, Joe L.P. (1995), 'The impact of structural adjustment policies on women's and children's health in Tanzania', *Review of African Political Economy*, **22**(63), 43–53.

Mujeres Unidas y Activas, the Day Labor Program Women's Collective of La Raza Centro Legal, and the DataCenter (2007), 'Behind closed doors: working conditions of California household workers', March, available at: http://www.datacenter.org/wp-content/uploads/behindcloseddoors.pdf

Nehring, Daniel and Emmanuel Alvarado (2008–09), 'Intimacy and reproduction: the role of Hispanic groups in American fertility', *Florida Atlantic Comparative Studies Journal*, **11**(1), 41–56.

Ojeda de la Peña, Norma (2007), 'Transborder families and gendered trajectories of migration and work', in Segura and Zavella (eds), pp. 327–40.

Orellana, Marjorie Faulstich, Barrie Thorne, Anna Chee and Wan Shun Eva Lam (2001),'Transnational child-hoods: the participation of children in processes of family migration', *Social Problems*, **48**(4), 572–91.

Palmer, Phyllis Marynick (1983), 'White women/black women: the dualism of female identity and experience in the United States', *Feminist Studies*, **9**(Spring), 151–70.

Parrenas, Rhacel Salazar (2005), *Children of Global Migration: Transnational Families and Gendered Woes*, Stanford, CA: Stanford University Press.

Passel, Jeffrey S. and D'Vera Cohn (2008), 'Trends in Unauthorized Immigration:Undocumented Inflow Now Trails Legal Inflow', DC: Pew Hispanic Research Center, Washington, October.

Pew Hispanic Research Center (2009), 'Poverty Status among Foreign-Born Families by Family Type and World Region of Birth of the Householder', Pew Hispanic Research Center, Washington, DC.

Pew Hispanic Research Center (2011), 'The Mexican–American Boom: Births Overtake Immigration', Pew Hispanic Research Center, Washington, DC, July 14, available at: http://www.pewhispanic.org/2011/07/14/the-mexican-american-boom-brbirths-overtake-immigration/ (accessed December 2011).

Pressar, Patricia (1999), 'Engendering migration studies: the case of new immigrants in the United States', *American Behavioral Scientist*, **42**(4), 577–600.

Romero, Mary (2000), 'Bursting the foundational myths of reproductive labor under capitalism', *Journal of Gender, Social Policy & the Law*, **8**(1), 177–95.

Safa, Helen (1995), 'Economic restructuring and gender subordination', *Latin American Perspectives*, **22**(2), 32–50.

Sassen, Saskia (1991), *The Global City: New York, Tokyo, London*, Princeton, NJ: Princeton University Press.

Sassen, Saskia (2002), 'Global cities and survival circuits', in Barbara Ehrenreich and Arlie Russell Hochschild (eds), *Global Woman: Nannies, Maids, and Sex Workers in the New Economy*, New York: Henry Holt & Company, pp. 254–74.

Segura, Denise A. and Patricia Zavella (eds) (2007), *Women and Migration in the U.S–Mexico Borderlands*, Durham, NC: Duke University Press.

Sternberg, Rosa Maria (2010), 'The plight of transnational Latina mothers: mothering from a distance', *Field Actions Science Reports*, Special Issue 2, online available at: http://factsreports.revues.org/486 (accessed November 2011).

Taylor, Paul, Mark Hugo Lopez, Jeffrey Passel and Seth Motel (2011), 'Unauthorized Immigrants: Length of Residency, Patterns of Parenthood', Pew Hispanic Research Center, Washington, DC, December 1, available at: http://www.pewhispanic.org/2011/12/01/unauthorized-immigrants-length-of-residency-patterns-of-parenthood/?ReportID=148&src=global-footer (accessed December 2011).

US Bureau of Labor Statistics, Household Data Annual Averages (2010), 'Employed Hispanic or Latino workers by sex, occupation, class of worker, full – or part-time status, and detailed ethnic group', Washington, DC, available at: http://www.bls.gov/cps/cpsaat13.pdf (accessed December 2011).

US Census Bureau, Current Population Survey, Annual Social and Economic Supplement, 2010: Table 1.7: Occupation of Employed Civilian Workers 16 Years and Over by Sex, Nativity, and U.S. Citizenship Status: 2010, available at: http://www.census.gov/population/foreign/data/cps2010.html (accessed December 2011).

US Census Bureau, Current Population Survey, Annual Social and Economic Supplement, 2010: Table 3.7:

Occupation of Employed Foreign-Born Civilian Workers 16 Years and Over by Sex and World Region of Birth: 2010, available at: http://www.census.gov/population/foreign/data/cps2010.html (accessed December 2011).

US Census Bureau, Current Population Survey, Annual Social and Economic Supplement, 2010: Table 3.11: Total Earnings of Full-Time, Year-Round, Foreign-Born Workers 15 Years and Over with Earnings by Sex and World Region of Birth: 2009, available at: http://www.census.gov/population/foreign/data/cps2010. html (accessed December 2011).

Vellos, Diana (1997), 'Immigrant Latina domestic workers and sexual harassment', *American University Journal of Gender and the Law*, **5**(Spring), 407–32.

Wessler, Seth Freed (2011), *Shattered Families: The Perilous Intersection of Immigration Enforcement and the Child Welfare System*, The Applied Research Center, New York, November, available at: http://arc.org/ shatteredfamilies (accessed December 2011).

Williams, Fiona (2010), 'Review article. Migration and care: themes, concepts, and challenges', *Social Policy & Society*, **9**(3), 385–96.

31. Environmental activism and gender
*Patricia E. Perkins**

I INTRODUCTION

Environmental activism merits an important place in a contemporary analysis of gender and economic life. In the first place, most environmental activists are, and apparently always have been, women – and this is at least partly related to gendered roles in the socio-economy. Because women's roles tend to involve food provision and preparation, healthcare, childcare, and in many places, agriculture, and because many environmental hazards manifest themselves as reproductive hazards, women are usually the first to know about environmental degradation, and are often more affected than men, both physically and socio-economically. This motivates women's activism and leadership on environmental issues. Moreover, because it leads to constructive change, women activists' work and leadership has crucial, valuable social and economic implications.

Further, in a theoretical sense, the economics of environmental degradation are closely related to the economics of gender. Both women's work and environmental goods and services tend to be 'externalized' by neoclassical economics, taken for granted, unaccounted for, and/or unpaid. This interrelationship among women's work and the environment offers important theoretical insights about how to build more sustainable socio-economies. Finally, when we stretch beyond the traditional framework of neoclassical economics to consider provisioning, well-being, social reproduction, nonmarket value, and sustainable economic futures, the process of activism is an economically relevant force for ongoing reconstruction and progressive improvements in society. In the following sections, this chapter discusses and provides a number of examples from around the world to illustrate each of these aspects of environmental activism and gender – the empirical, theoretical, and dynamic – ending with a few concluding remarks.[1]

Throughout the chapter, I have attempted to include data, voices, and views on environmental activism and gender from a variety of locations and perspectives. By 'activism', I mean the organizing and practice of direct vigorous action or campaigning to bring about political, economic, or social change. It is activists working in conditions of poverty and marginalization (for very logical reasons) who are most adept and efficient at organizing, articulating priorities, and developing effective movements, and who have a great deal to teach and share. Though the details of local environmental situations and activism vary widely, I believe that there is a great deal of commonality in the basic processes of organizing and activism across the global North and South.

Following a short discussion in Section II on the limited empirical evidence related to women's leadership in environmental activism, Section III then examines historical and theoretical frameworks for understanding women's activism, taking up in turn the themes of unpaid work and ecological services, valuation and collective decision-making, skills transmission for sustainability, relationships and exchange, local economies, interpersonal well-being and community, commons and property ownership, and feminist ecological economics contributions toward building equitable and sustainable societies.

II WOMEN AS ENVIRONMENTAL ACTIVISTS

Across the world, women are leaders in environmental activism. As Darlene Clover states,

> Throughout history, it has invariably been women who have blown the whistle on the negative impacts of environmental degradation and human manipulation of the environment. In fact they are at the forefront of major environmental initiatives, struggles and actions worldwide and the virtual 'backbone' of many an environmental group. (2002, p. 315)

Empirical research consistently shows a strong link between female gender and environmental concerns. In a range of studies conducted since 1960, women are significantly more concerned than men about environmental risks to their health and safety (see, for example, Blocker and Eckberg, 1989; Flynn et al., 1994; Davidson and Freudenburg, 1996). Women are also consistently more concerned than men about environmental issues at the local level (see Blocker and Eckberg, 1989), which may in turn be related to the recognizable health and safety concerns caused by detrimental local conditions and policies (Caiazza, 2003). Further, data from North America (Gould and Hosey, 2007) indicate that women are more likely to:

- rate the environment as a high priority;
- cast ballots around environmental issues;
- volunteer for and give money to environmental causes, especially related to public health;
- support environmental activists; and
- have more concern that government is not doing enough for the environment and therefore support increased government spending for the environment (while men favor spending cuts).

Cross-national studies also underscore the prevalence of women's environmental concern and behaviors (Zelezny et al., 2000; Hunter et al., 2004; Stein, 2004).

The vast list of individual women whose environmental activism has brought about progressive economic change, and whose leadership has inspired and motivated others, includes women from around the world: 2004 Nobel Peace Prize laureate Wangari Maathai, Rachel Carson, Vandana Shiva, Love Canal activist Lois Gibbs, US environmental justice activists Florenza Moore Grant, Beverly Wright, and Hazel Johnson, German Green Party founder Petra Kelly, Chernobyl and Bhopal investigator Rosalie Bertell, Chilean ecofeminist Rayen Quiroga, Josephine Mandamin (Beedawsige) and the other First Nations women of the Mother Earth Water Walk around the Great Lakes, Chinese environmental activist Man Si-Wai, toxicologist Theodora Colborn, Australian anti-nuclear activist Helen Caldicott, Brazilian ecofeminists Moema Viezzer and Miriam Duailibi, and so many others (UNEP, 2006). Their foremothers include Jeanne Baret, a French naturalist who travelled around the world in 1767–74 (Ridley, 2010) as well as Hildegard of Bingen and countless other European, Asian, American, and African women herbalists, naturalists, medicine women, and environmental defenders throughout human history (LeBourdais, 1991; Rosenberg, 1995; Shtier, 1996; Taylor, 2002; Spears, 2009; Brown, 2011).

With so much historical and anecdotal evidence, it is surprising that little specific data exists on the proportion of environmental activists who are women in any jurisdiction or time period.[2] What studies there are seem to indicate that, at least in North America, women's activism and leadership may be somewhat limited by time constraints given their double or triple workday, and that women tend to focus their environmental activism on local, health-related environmental problems rather than on the broad politics of environmental protection (Mohai, 1992; Tindall et al., 2003). Nonetheless, from the Chipko and Green Belt movements to the 1991 First National (US) People of Color Environmental Leadership Summit and the 1992 Women's Congress for a Healthy Planet, as well as many others, environmental activist movements begun and led by women have transformed local and global politics, forestalled ecological disasters, conserved resources, prevented the rapid externalization of environmental costs onto powerless people, and maintained traditions of environmental protection and stewardship (see Basset, 1991; Bullard and Johnson, 2000).[3] As political scientist Paul Wapner notes:

> When people change their buying habits, voluntarily recycle garbage, boycott certain products, and work to preserve species, it is not necessarily because governments are breathing down their necks. Rather, they are acting out of a belief that the environmental problems involved are severe, and they wish to contribute to alleviating them. They are being 'stung', as it were, by an ecological sensibility. This sting is a type of governance. It represents a mechanism of authority that can shape widespread human behavior. (1995, p. 326)

III   THEORETICAL INTERCONNECTIONS BETWEEN GENDER AND SOCIO-ENVIRONMENTAL ECONOMICS

With regard to the reasons and motivations for women's environmental activism, there is a huge literature that traces and debates the links between women and the environment, over time and space. Carolyn Merchant, one of the major theorists of ecofeminism, has stated that there are complex cultural reasons for why nature has been 'gendered' as female over the past 2,500 years throughout the world, and these factors are closely related to women's motivations 'to act to preserve both nonhuman nature and themselves' (1996, p. xi).

Economists and feminists extending back at least to Friedrich Engels, Emma Goldman, and Charlotte Perkins Gilman have documented how women always lead the ranks of the economically vulnerable and marginalized, and bear the brunt of economic and health problems caused by degraded environments (Engels, 1884 [2010]; Gilman, 1898 [1997]; Goldman, 1972). Goldman famously said, 'Woman is the worker's worker', highlighting the double exploitation of women in comparison with men of the same social class. Unsafe work conditions, including pollution, pesticides, industrial chemicals, and other ecological hazards, disproportionately affect women forced to accept dangerous jobs due to poverty, which is largely feminized in both the global North and South. Gendered work roles encompass both paid and unpaid labor in women's public and private lives. Responsible for the care and feeding of the young, aged and ill, women worldwide have to seek ways of sustaining themselves and their families even in times of environmental and political crisis. They have always done so by building and maintaining social structures that provide a modicum of resilience. Key strategies include developing local ecological knowledge to use and try to protect natural sources of food, water, fuel, and shelter, and transmitting wisdom intergenerationally that tends to involve a healthy skepticism about technicist, male-dominated and market-oriented structures.

Feminist ecological economics focuses on such subjects as unpaid work and ecological services; valuation, collective decision-making, and equity; skills transmission; relationships and exchange; local economies; interpersonal well-being and community; institution-building, commons and property ownership; and human/nonhuman continua, biological time, and future generations (Perkins, 1997; Kuiper and Perkins, 2005). *Feminist ecosocialism or ecofeminist socialism* is a related area of academic and activist work; some of the important writers in this field include Maria Mies, Vandana Shiva, Mary Mellor, and Ariel Salleh (Mellor, 1992, 1997a; Mies and Shiva, 1993; Shiva, 1994, 2010; Salleh, 1997, 2009; Mies, 1999; Mies and Bennholdt-Thomsen, 1999). Many thinkers and activists who call themselves ecofeminists live in the global North, but the most stark and inspiring stories of ecological activism and change led by women generally come from the global South.

I use the term 'ecofeminist' to include all those whose work demonstrates the connections between women and environment and their common exploitation by patriarchal, market-based political–economic systems. Also, feminist ecological and/or ecofeminist work is theoretically pluralist or heterodox, to a greater or lesser degree. That is, it envisions economic and political realities and processes in unconventional ways and actively challenges status quo disciplines, institutions, and assumptions. The following subsections discuss important themes that are addressed in the interrelated literatures on ecofeminism, feminist ecological economics, and feminist ecosocialism, summarizing how these themes relate to gender and economic lives and livelihoods.

Unpaid Work and Ecological Services: A Central Concern

For women, especially, there is much more to life than the market economy. The overlapping and mutually reinforcing ways in which unpaid work (mainly women's work) and unpaid ecological services are exploited by growth-driven economies is the central concern of feminist ecological economics. There are structural reasons for the 'externalization' of both the natural environment and gendered, unpaid work within economic theories and systems. All economic productivity depends on the productivity of women and 'nature', which provides workers and raw materials for capitalist economies, calling these factors 'free' (see Mellor, 1992, 1997a, 1997b; Mies, 1998; Langley and Mellor, 2002; Perkins, 2007). As Mies states, 'The characteristic of (capitalism) is that those who control the production processes and the products are not themselves producers, but appropriators. Their so-called productivity presupposes the existence and the subjection of other – and in the last analysis, female – producers' (1998, p. 71). This is both socially and ecologically unsustainable (see Folbre, 1994, pp. 254–5).

Finding new ways of recognizing and compensating the value of unpaid women's work as well as ecosystem services is crucially important. Nancy Folbre and many other feminist economists have grappled with how to value unpaid work and the difficulty of measuring it in monetary terms alone (Waring, 1989, 2009; Nelson, 1997; Himmelweit, 2003; Jochimsen, 2003); how to account for multitasking and multiple functions (Waring, 1989; Nelson, 2003); how to address underlying economic assumptions and fairly integrate the interests of market actors from different social locations (Henderson, 1978, 1980, 1983, 1992; Zein-Elabdin, 1996; Jochimsen and Knobloch, 1997; Todorova, 2005); and how to escape or pose alternatives to the market as the only site for economic transactions (Kennedy, 1987; Agarwal, 2000; Raddon, 2002; Jochimsen, 2003; Vaughan, 2004).

A further difficulty is that any conversion of unpaid work to paid work, besides being very costly – unpaid work is estimated to equal roughly 60 percent of GDP in the global North (Pietilä, 1997, 2007), and probably even more in the global South – could also potentially heighten ecologically damaging consumption and accelerate material throughput in the economy, as formerly unpaid workers' incomes rise. Another issue is the potential tradeoff of sorts between ecological and gender dimensions of economic activity if gender roles remain unchanged. Many aspects of more-sustainable living require increased labor inputs close to home (for example, composting waste, separating recyclables, participating in local food co-ops, doing errands by bike rather than driving, eating less packaged food, using cloth instead of disposable diapers, and so on). As long as these tasks are seen as mainly women's work, the responsibility for living more sustainably is shifted to women's shoulders. One important conclusion from this is that economic models and policies should be compared and judged by how well they 'treat the interaction of production and social reproduction' (Elson, 1998, p. 167), and also how they mediate the interaction of economic and ecological activity.

The economy and the market cannot possibly handle or compensate all the vital functions and productive work of women and nature. At the very least, the economy must be prevented from destroying and undermining the 'sustaining services' (O'Hara, 1997b) on which human society and subsistence depend. When poverty, combined with a breakdown in social institutions, forces people to deplete environmental resources in order to survive, this is symptomatic of how economic pressures can effectively destroy long-standing sustainable sociocultural systems. From a development perspective, Rayén Quiroga-Martinez and others have highlighted the pernicious effects of ignoring non-marketed goods and services; because they are outside of government statistics, policies may blindly harm both women and 'nature' (Quiroga-Martinez and van Hauwermeiren, 1996; Quiroga-Martinez et al., 2005).

To address these kinds of problems and build more sustainable economic systems that create just and democratic opportunities for people to pursue sustainable livelihoods, women's activism and leadership are crucial. This includes the creation of governance institutions, sustainable resource management processes capable of resisting the pressures of globalized markets, and structures which recognize and mediate both unpaid work and ecological services. Hilkka Pietilä, for instance, envisions a reversal of market priorities, which she says is in women's hands, since women can decide how much of their labor and skills to sell to the market economy:

> The entire picture of the human economy should be turned the right side up: the industrial and commercial economy should be seen only as auxiliary, serving the needs of families and individuals instead of using them as means of production and consumption . . . we have to denounce

the values and rules on which the neoliberal economy operates, such as constant economic growth, conspicuous consumption, maximization of profits and competition. (2007, p. 10)

Activist women are already taking steps in this direction. For example, every day for 15 years, Mexican women in the village of La Patrona, Veracruz have provided free food for migrant workers they do not know who are heading to the US on trains that run through their village (Las Patronas, 2011). They do this because they know it is important, not for money. Women around the world build, maintain, and rely on microcredit and informal loan pools to support subsistence production and small-scale economic initiatives. From Asia to Latin America, women build and use alternative community-based economic structures to invest in ecological supports for subsistence (Mies and Shiva, 1993; Bennholdt-Thomsen, 2001; SEWA, 2011). These are powerful examples, but in fact every community depends on work done for free by 'volunteers' who realize the importance of what they are doing, despite its nonrecognition by the market. They gain respect from others in the community and give hope by helping sustain the needy while creating community, and global, resilience through their work.

Valuation, Collective Decision-making, and Equity

Ecofeminists have contributed many ideas about alternative ways of valuing ecological services and unpaid work for the purposes of political decision-making. As economic processes become more complex and trade makes them less understandable and controllable at the local level, the need for alternative valuation methods becomes more pressing, since the value of unmarketed goods and services is contextual and socially or communally mediated.

The literature on 'discourse-based valuation' and other collective valuation systems meshes equity-enhancing identity-grounded discussions with political–economic decision-making (O'Hara, 1997a; Perkins, 2001; Wilson and Howarth, 2002). The essence of these proposals is that valuation and decision-making about what is to be produced and how, resource and energy allocation, incentives for economic change, and local/global distribution must involve the considered weighing of views from all members of the society (one person, one vote), not just those with economic interests/abilities in the market economy (one dollar, one vote). Discourse-based valuation legitimates social and discussion-centered valuation processes while calling into question market-derived, centralized, and rootless valuation systems, allowing local governments to reduce expenditures on circuitous economic valuation techniques while streamlining the political decision and public approval process. It is consistent with local democratization initiatives in response to neoliberal globalization, and while it is no panacea, it represents a step toward more diverse and equitable public decision-making. Brazilian and Venezuelan activists are at the forefront of exploring how this can work in practice (Luchmann, 2008; Martinez et al., 2010).

Skills Transmission

While technological change makes necessary the constant acquisition of new (individual) skills, scientific progress is a high price to pay when this comes at the expense of losing traditional (individual and also social) knowledge of how to live sustainably within the limits of local ecosystems. Childrearing and socialization, including skills transmission and early formal education as well as community service, are in most cultures done largely by women and are undervalued/underrecognized/underpaid. Thus it is not surprising that they have become endangered (van den Hove, 2006; Garmendia and Stagl, 2010; Swartling et al., 2010).

Ecofeminist attempts to combat social deskilling include the movements to reintroduce farmers' markets and facilitate direct links between food producers and consumers (Foodshare, 2011; The Stop Community Food Centre, 2011; Evergreen Brick Works Farmers' Market, 2011); harvest urban fruit (Not Far from the Tree, 2011); cultivate bees (Malach, 2010); link apartment-dwellers with urban householders who are willing to share garden space in their backyards (Yes in My Backyard, 2011); and provide communal cooking and childcare classes (Foodshare, 2011; The Stop Community Food Centre, 2011).

Ecosocial community organizations run a range of participatory ecological community-building programs. In a marginalized region at the western edge of Guanabara Bay near Rio de Janeiro, Brazil, Agua Doce People's Services works creatively with local people at the interface of social, economic, and ecological development; their goal is 'expanding human consciousness toward the development of sustainable communities and the emergence of a globalization that preserves the planet's community of life, guarantees the minimal social needs to all and promotes an efficient and human economy' (Centro Clima, 2005, p. 58). Such initiatives have the mutually reinforcing outcomes of contributing to community well-being, increasing trust and building social networks in marginalized areas, which can lead to increased political engagement and, ultimately, economic redistribution – extending far beyond the market economy while developing social resilience.

Relationships and Exchange

Partly because of the valuation problems mentioned above, ecofeminists have long been attracted to alternatives to money and nonmonetary exchange systems such as Local Exchange Trading Systems (LETS)[4] and other forms of community currencies (Kennedy, 1987; Raddon, 2002; Mellor, 2009). The essence of ecofeminist alternatives to money systems as they exist at present is their emphasis on the need to acknowledge and encourage the relationships among people – the true basis of material exchange (Perkins, 2002). As Mary Mellor eloquently states, 'A provisioning economy would start from the embodiment and embeddedness of human lives, from the life of the body and the ecosystem, from women's work and the vitality of the natural world. Priorities would be determined by the most vulnerable members of the community, not its 'natural' leaders as defined by economic dominance' (2009, p. 264). Mellor adds that making money subject to democratic control is essential to begin the process of building a nongendered, egalitarian and ecologically sustainable provisioning economy.

Genevieve Vaughan (2007) views the 'gift paradigm' as encapsulating the perspective that is needed for transforming competitive market-based economies into nurturing systems for life enhancement. Exchange, in her view, which creates and requires scarcity, needs to be replaced by free gift-giving as a general social value. Earlier, she commented: 'Indeed we could begin to take nurturing as the creative norm and recognize exchange as the distortion which is causing a de-evolution and a danger to the human species as well as all other species on the planet' (Vaughan, 2004). While this perspective offers hope about humanity's ability to change and improve upon the past, some other ecofeminists find it needs more coherence, detail, and safeguards before it can offer pragmatic signposts towards a better future (Fournier, 2005). Quiroga-Martinez et al. (2005), drawing from the 'matristic' philosophy of Humberto Maturana Romesin and Gerda Verden-Zöller (2008), call for a paradigm shift toward mutual care and interpersonal support as the foundation of a sustainable socioeconomic future.

Local Economies

Another central theme in ecofeminist visions of sustainable economic alternatives is that localization is more likely to generate caring and ecologically sustainable human communities than rampant globalization. That is, when people interact at human scales – producing, exchanging, consuming, dealing with pollution, and so on, without drawing inputs from or sending wastes to faraway places – this is the essence of healthy provisioning (Henderson, 1992; Nozick, 1992; Perkins, 1995, 1996). There are many reasons for this emphasis. First, people in local economies are forced to live sustainably within their means. When they know each other they are more likely to jointly solve problems and share assets. They will protect and preserve their ecological surroundings. And, finally, they will learn and transmit the knowledge necessary for making the best use of their local conditions.

Critics charge that in a globalized world, advocating localization is a rejection of the fundamental principles of economies of scale as well as quality-of-life-enhancing technical progress. This is not necessarily the case. The degrowth movement and local food movements are showing that consumption can shift significantly toward locally produced products and services within a market context (Perkins, 2010). But if all economies or many areas in the global North were to 'go local', what would be the mechanism driving redistribution at a global scale? Centuries of colonialism, now exacerbated by climate change, have produced extreme disparities in people's rights and access to resources which must urgently be addressed (Moyo, 2009). To these concerns we add the problems with a local economic bias. Local economies can be parochial and repressive to women, gays, and minority groups. They can allow 'bullies and thugs' to gain or retain power.

Recognizing these shortcomings, an important contribution of feminist work on local economies is the way its focus on equity highlights the pitfalls of aiming single-mindedly for local sustainability. Historical and current injustices, and mechanisms for addressing inequitable distribution, must be part of economic restructuring. The ecosocial sophistication of local subsistence strategies is demonstrated by ancient gravity-fed irrigation systems that are still in use in western Kenya (Adams and Carter, 1987; Turner, 1994; Watson et al., 1998), southern India (Shenoy, 2009), and other places. Such systems depend on socially mediated maintenance work and periodic reallocation of water and other resources within the community, creating the conditions for sustainable survival over very long periods of time.

Interpersonal Well-being and Community

Even neoclassical economists recognize that human well-being depends much more on relationships and relative positions in society than on actual levels of consumption or affluence. This is a powerful motivator for equity-enhancing policies: spreading resources around more fairly will make voters happy (Wilkinson and Pickett, 2010). Happiness can be measured, although governments tend not to measure it; alternative economic indicators include a range of proposals for community-derived, participatory measures of what is important (for example, Calvert-Henderson Quality of Life Indicators, 2006; Waring, 2009). Academic and activist collaborators meet regularly to discuss this at conferences on Gross National Happiness, inaugurated and led by the King of Bhutan (Gross National Happiness Commission, 2011). Participatory governance, including accurate statistical indicators of socioeconomic success and human well-being, will become ever more crucial for social resilience and stability.

Ecofeminists have not only highlighted the connections between interpersonal relationships, ecological health, community strength, and human well-being (Nozick, 1992; Perkins, 1995, 1996, 2002, 2003; Salleh, 1997; Bennholdt-Thomsen, 2001; Waring, 2009). They have also demonstrated and tested methods of measuring, fostering and nurturing these interconnected benefits for society (Forsey, 1993; Gibson-Graham, 1996; Eichler et al., 2002). As Ivone Gebara says:

> In Latin America we want to be part of a national and international movement for the globalization of social justice . . . A new national and international order is our goal. An ecofeminism as an echo of feminism takes this as its goal without forgetting the special commitment for all women, without forgetting the importance of local education for a better world for everybody. (2003, p. 97)

The dynamic and growing World Social Forum movement, initiated in Brazil in 2001, brings together global activists who are working similarly to build equitable ecosocial alternatives in the midst of and as an alternative to unsustainable existing institutions (see World Social Forum Charter of Principles, 2002).

Countless women have led valiant and inspirational struggles for political and economic rights and community access to land, water, and the products of their local ecosystems as a matter of subsistence. For all that are well-known – Chipko, las Madres de la Plaza de Mayo, Wangari Maathai and the Green Belt Movement – there are hundreds more whose struggles are no less important: Man Si-Wai in China, the Kenyan women of Freedom Corner (Tibbetts, 1994), and many others.

Institution-building, Commons and Property Ownership

Functioning equitable social systems grounded in institutions that foster mutual respect, which are required for common property systems to operate sustainably (Hardin, 1968), are intertwined with commons themselves as sources of community resilience. The awarding of the 2010 Nobel Prize in Economics to Elinor Ostrom, whose work focuses on commons, underscores the growing recognition of the problems with traditional economic rigidity regarding private property ownership. The International Association for the Study of the Commons (IASC) and its journal connect a growing network of scholars and activists who see promise in community-based mechanisms for holding, protecting, and using land and ecological resources collectively (Berkes and Davidson-Hunt, 2009). They advocate open sharing of artistic and intellectual resources, too, through mechanisms such as the Creative Commons (n.d.). Even financial savings can be held and used collectively for the greatest community benefit (Podlashuc, 2009), in the context of institutions which include mechanisms of equitable and flexible social self-governance.

Globally, women have a critical role in defending commons from enclosure and reestablishing commons management systems, in order to protect their own subsistence livelihoods and the sociocultural institutions which undergird them. As Terisa Turner and Leigh Brownhill state: 'Subsistence political economy is the world of commoners . . . The ecofeminist politics of counterplanning stands against the (usually, but not exclusively, white male) leftist prejudice denigrating the agency and revolutionary capacities of the unwaged, in general, and of housewives, indigenous peoples, peasants, students, and rural Third World women, in particular' (2006, p. 95).

Ana Isla's analyses of the tragic effects of enclosures of commons for the survival and subsistence of local people in Latin America (2002, 2005, 2009), along with those of Vandana Shiva citing situations in South Asia and elsewhere (1994, 2010), demonstrate the terrible costs of the global economic system in human terms. This scholarship shows how a commons framework can explain desperate conflicts that a market-based approach leaves mysterious; it also sheds light on potential solutions to intransigent ecological and political problems of globalization, through renewed social development of commons. One example is the overlapping forms of land tenure now being employed in Kenya, which in effect introduce land reform intertemporally over two generations, by allowing landless people access to unused land that is nominally owned by large landholders, and then granting the title to their children through usufruct rights (Brownhill, 2009). Similarly, using powers enshrined in Brazil's 1988 constitution, Landless Movement activists plan occupations and take possession of unused land needed for subsistence production (Movimento Sem-Terra, 2011).

Water commons, and common access to water, is another area where ecofeminist activists have demonstrated the practicality of shared ownership, overlapping access, and community-organized stewardship. For example, earth dams for water reservoirs in South India, traditionally built by women, were replaced in the colonial era by 'modern' British irrigation systems which soon silted up; the earthworks systems are now being reclaimed. Since 2003, a group of First Nations women and their supporters has been gradually walking around all the Great Lakes in North America to call attention to the importance and sacredness of fresh water, a commons of significance for millions (Mother Earth Water Walk, 2011). Womens' activism on water privatization and access to water is an example of the intertwined nature of commons, gendered economic roles, subsistence, and the need for progressive political change (Perkins and Moraes, 2007).

Human/Nonhuman Continua, Biological Time, and Future Generations

Human links with the biosphere involve far more than people's use of animals and plants as economic resources. When we see humanity as part of the web of life, it is easier to understand how our own health and well-being are intricately interwoven with those of the more-than-human world. Ecofeminist authors and activists have long explored these connections (Carson, 1962; Warren, 1987, 1997; Colborn et al., 1997; Noske, 1997; Steingraber, 1997 [2010]; Hawthorne 2002, 2009). Feminist animal care theory calls on humans to extend ethical reasoning to relationships with animals, especially domestic and agricultural animals that are associated with feminine energy in western cultures and also provide the economic basis for many people's livelihoods (Davis, 1995; Donovan, 2006). Ecofeminist animal sanctuary activists are exploring ways of rehabilitating and caring for abused animals, developing skills of empathy and social communication (Efrati, 2005; Jones, 2006; Herzog, 2010). Care for animals, plants, and ecosystems is a vital component of preserving the earth's diversity into the future.

Women's reproductive health, environmental hazards, all living beings, and future generations are connected in what Barbara Adam (1998) calls 'socio-environmental time'. 'Biological time' – the uncontrollable and often unpredictable amounts of time it takes for caring and for more-than-human processes such as growth and healing to run their course – is another concept that both Adam and Mary Mellor (1997b) have developed to point out the contradictions between this and 'economic time'. Mellor says, 'The exclusion of biological time means that economic systems are no longer rooted in the physical reality of human existence . . . If we are to be in tune with ecological time, the time-scale of ecological sustainability, the socially created time of economic systems will have to be abandoned' (ibid., pp. 137–8). Ursula Huws (2003), in describing how time and work have progressively become commodified, focuses on the concomitant loss of control that modern people have over our time. She also shows why 'the "knowledge" economy is not dissolving material (goods) into thin air but, on the contrary, generating new physical commodities that make voracious demands on the earth's resources' (p. 22). Far from relying on the dematerialization of the growing service-based global economy as a potential solution to the sustainability challenge, we must engage with and change the interpersonal, political dynamics driving human society in unsustainable directions. Indigenous peoples' practices of thinking ahead to the seventh generation illustrate the wisdom of situating current human decisions and actions in a timeframe long enough to allow biological time and socio-environmental time to merge, where economic time is the strange outlier.

IV　CONCLUSIONS: ACTIVIST PROCESSES IN SOCIOECONOMIC CHANGE

What are the key results and challenges related to gender and activism for broader aspects of gender and economic life: provisioning, social reproduction, well-being, value, climate change, sustainable futures? Fortunately, the structures and institutions that humans develop to manage their affairs are mutable and evolve to address challenges as they arise. Criteria for judging these institutions and their evolution include how well they facilitate the interpersonal transmission of skills for sustainability; how flexibly they permit different groups to develop their own culturally and ecologically appropriate systems of provisioning; and how well they mediate the boundaries between production and reproduction, among people of different ethnicities, genders and classes, and between human and more-than-human access to Earth's solar-fueled bounty.

One principle central to ecofeminist thought is that both theory and action are collective, collaborative, and based on relationships among diverse people who speak from, and share with each other, their situated knowledges. This happens best in a climate of respect, where justice for all is the goal. Sustainable social systems must foster equitable sharing of opportunity, work, power, and compensation, and must create democratic forums and multiple occasions for community-building. Moreover, production – or purposeful human action of any kind – cannot take place without a huge support system of reproduction, care, and interactions with the more-than-human world over long stretches of uncontrollable time. Humility, environmental caution, and mutual aid are fundamental.

These principles are expressed in ecofeminist visions and models of sustainable socio-economic dynamics. For example, Pietilä's (1997) model of the human economy (functioning within, and dependent upon, its environmental matrix) is a series of concentric circles centered on the home and local community, the area of freely given and exchanged human enterprise; surrounding this is the realm of monetized, market exchange; and finally the 'fettered' realm of global market constraints and controlled trade.

Quebec activists have recently proposed abandoning the dual public–private conception of economic activity in favor of a quadripartite model composed of

- a *social economy* composed of social and nonprofit enterprises and community, collective or cooperative organizations which render innumerable services to the people;
- an essential *domestic economy* based on the services provided in the family, by caregivers (primarily women) as well as free or volunteer services for which we seek means of recognizing socially and accounting for at their fair value;
- a *public, state and parastatal economy*, whose importance and social role should be enhanced in equitably providing accessible services to the entire population; and
- a *private economy* composed of private enterprises whose purpose is to sell products and services white functioning in compliance with the collective (social, environmental, and so on) rules that society establishes (see Fidler, 2011).

Most of the examples of sustainable livelihood strategies mentioned above were generated through processes involving diverse people's knowledge and varied contributions to social well-being, based in interpersonal skills, respectful communication and power-sharing. These are the kinds of processes we must keep envisioning and creating, even (especially) in times of political and ecological crisis.

Feminist ecological economics has built on and evolved from a cogent and compelling critique of the unstable and unsustainable capitalist status quo. Feminist ecological economists and political ecologists have described the economic importance of women's environmental and community development activism, the importance for women's work and health of ecological processes, and the fundamental economic significance of the myriad unmarketed services provided by women and nature. They have documented women's crucial role in subsistence production and in protecting and preserving ecosystems, as well as their leadership in political struggles over the natural environment and commons. This is contributing to new research and activism on nonmarket valuation methodologies and human well-being, quality-of-life indicators, links between health and the environment, local economic systems, trade and globalization, commons, and many other topics. Heightened by global climate change and other crises, there is also new pressure on public authorities to measure, monitor, and report on physical, ecological, health, and gender indicators as well as more traditional economic ones, to broaden the scope of what is called 'economic' data for use in designing progressive policies and preventing gendered social and ecological destruction.

Ecofeminism adds to this list of policy challenges a wisdom born in experiential understanding of inequities, provisioning and care for others and for earth systems. Ariel Salleh (2009) calls this an 'embodied materialism' that is capable of replacing 'metabolic rift' (Foster, 1999) with 'metabolic fit'. Women's environmental activism, feminist ecological economics, and ecofeminist theory and praxis are contributing to more sophisticated, nuanced, green, diverse, and equitable ways of understanding the processes of production and reproduction, distribution, consumption, waste generation and avoidance, materials cycles, and human well-being. The aim of both theory and praxis is to greatly improve gender relations and economic livelihoods.

NOTES

*   Many thanks to Ana Tavares Leary for research assistance and help with the references.
1.   At the outset, I would like to acknowledge my standpoint: I write as a white female academic and environmental activist, living on territory in Toronto which was violently taken from aboriginal peoples. I have also lived for several periods of time in the global South (Brazil, Mozambique) where power and economic privilege also distort social relations. Some of my activist work, especially around climate justice, is global in focus and reflects collaborations with partners and colleagues in many places. I welcome critiques of assumptions, omissions, and bias that readers may find in this very short summary of a very complicated story.
2.   This is an example of the kind of data gaps which often hamper studies of women's economic impact as well as feminist economics generally.
3.   The modern Chipko Movement began in the early 1970s in Uttarakhand, India, where grassroots women activists practiced the Gandhian nonviolent resistance method of satyagraha by hugging trees to prevent their being felled. Chipko also involves reforestation to protect marginalized people's livelihoods. The Green Belt Movement, started in 1977 by (the late) Kenyan activist and 2004 Nobel Prize winner Wangari Maathai, organizes women to plant trees, combat deforestation, stop soil erosion, and earn income while preserving their lands and resources. The environmental justice movement addresses the racism inherent in the fact that communities of color, often poor, are much more likely to live and work in polluted environments. The 1991 Women's World Congress for a Healthy Planet, organized by the Women's Environment and Development Organization (WEDO), adopted Women's Action Agenda 21 and led to women's strong participation in the UN Conference on Environment and Development in Rio de Janeiro in 1992, as well as a range of subsequent international women's environment meetings and actions.
4.   Local Exchange Trading Systems (LETS), are locally initiated, not-for-profit community enterprises that facilitate the exchange of goods and services among members by recording and crediting transactions, thus creating a local currency of LETS Credits. They may also be called Local Employment and Trading Systems or Local Energy Transfer Systems.

REFERENCES

Adam, Barbara (1998), *Timescapes of Modernity: The Environment and Invisible Hazards*, London and New York: Routledge.
Adams, William M. and Richard C. Carter (1987), 'Small-scale irrigation in Sub-Saharan Africa', *Physical Geography*, **11**(1), 1–27.
Agarwal, Bina (2000), 'Conceptualising environmental collective action: why gender matters', *Cambridge Journal of Economics*, **24**(3), 283–310.

Bassett, Libby (1991), 'Women activists and Eco '92', *In Context – A Quarterly of Humane Sustainable Culture*, Spring, **8**, available at: http://www.context.org/ICLIB/IC28/BasetPls.htm (accessed January 2, 2012).

Bennholdt-Thomsen, Veronika (2001), 'What really keeps our cities alive, money or subsistence?', in Veronika Bennholdt-Thomsen, Nicholas Faraclas and Claudia Von Werlhof (eds), *There Is an Alternative: Subsistence and Worldwide Resistance to Corporate Globalization*, London and New York: Zed Books; Melbourne: Spinifex Press, pp. 217–31.

Berkes, Fikret and Iain J. Davidson-Hunt (2009), 'Innovating through commons use: community-based enterprises', *International Journal of the Commons*, **4**(1), available at: http://www.thecommonsjournal.org/index.php/ijc/article/viewArticle/206/107 (accessed March 27, 2011).

Blocker, T. Jean and Douglas L. Eckberg (1989), 'Environmental issues as women's issues: general concerns and local hazards', *Social Science Quarterly*, **70**(3), 586–93.

Brown, Faye (2011), 'Walking for water', available at: http://onthecommons.org/walking-water (accessed January 2, 2012).

Brownhill, Leigh (2009), *Land, Food, Freedom: Struggles for the Gendered Commons in Kenya, 1870–2007*, Trenton, NJ: Africa World Press.

Bullard, Robert D. and Glenn S. Johnson (2000), 'Environmental justice: grassroots activism and its impact on public policy decision making', *Journal of Social Issues*, **56**(3), 555–78.

Caiazza, Amy (2003), 'Using research to amplify women's voices: IWPR's study on women's engagement in environmental issues', *Institute for Women's Policy Research Quarterly Newsletter*, Fall, Washington, DC, available at: http://www.iwpr.org/publications/publications-finder (accessed January 2, 2012).

Calvert-Henderson Quality of Life Indicators (2006), available at: http://www.calvert-henderson.com/ (accessed April 18, 2011).

Carson, Rachel (1962), *Silent Spring*, New York: Houghton Mifflin.

Centro Clima (2005), *The South–South–North (SSN) Project Country Study: Brazil*, Rio de Janeiro: Centro Clima, available at: http://www.southsouthnorth.org/download.asp?name=SSN2_Report_Adaptation%20Context_%20final4.pdf&size=4814863&file=documents/SSN2_Report_Adaptation%20Context_%20final4.pdf (accessed March 27, 2011).

Clover, Darlene (2002), 'Traversing the gap: concientization, educative-activism in environmental adult education', *Environmental Education Research*, **8**(3), 315–23.

Colborn, Theo, Dianne Dumanoski and J.P. Myers (1997), *Our Stolen Future: How We Are Threatening our Fertility, Intelligence and Survival*, New York: Plume/Penguin.

Creative Commons (n.d.), 'About', available at: http://creativecommons.org/about (accessed January 2, 2012).

Davidson, Debra J. and William Freudenburg (1996), 'Gender and environmental risk concerns: a review and analysis of available research', *Environment and Behavior*, **28**(3), 302–39.

Davis, Karen (1995), 'Thinking like a chicken: farm animals and the feminine connection', in Carol J. Adams and Josephine Donovan (eds), *Animals and Women: Feminist Theoretical Explorations*, Durham, NC: Duke University Press, pp. 192–212.

Donovan, Josephine (2006), 'Feminism and the treatment of animals: from care to dialogue', *Signs*, **31**(2), 305–29.

Efrati, Amir (2005), 'When bad chickens come home to roost, results can be good', *Wall Street Journal*, July 15, available at: http://www.dawnwatch.com/7-05_Animal_Media_Alerts.htm (accessed April 18, 2011).

Eichler, Margrit, June Larkin and Sheila Neysmith (eds) (2002), *Feminist Utopias: Re-Visioning Our Futures*, Toronto: Inanna Publications and Education.

Elson, Diane (1998), 'Talking to the boys: gender and economic growth models', in Cecile Jackson and Ruth Pearson (eds), *Feminist Visions of Development: Gender Analysis and Policy*, London and New York: Routledge, pp. 156–71.

Engels, Friedrich (1884 [2010]), *The Origin of the Family, Private Property and the State*, available at: http://www.gutenberg.org/ebooks/33111 (accessed January 18, 2012).

Evergreen Brick Works Farmers' Market (2011), available at: http://ebw.evergreen.ca/whats-on/farmers-market/ (accessed January 2, 2012).

Fidler, Richard (2011), 'Beyond capitalism? Québec Solidaire launches debate on its program for social transformation', *The Bullet*, E-Bulletin N. 491, available at: http://www.socialistproject.ca/bullet/491.php#continue (accessed April 18, 2011).

Flynn, James, Paul Slovic and C.K. Mertz (1994), 'Gender, race, and perception of environmental health risks', *Risk Analysis*, **14**(6), 1101–8.

Folbre, Nancy (1994), *Who Pays for the Kids? Gender and the Structures of Constraint*, London and New York: Routledge.

Foodshare (2011), available at: http://www.foodshare.net/index.htm (accessed April 18, 2011).

Forsey, Helen (ed.) (1993), *Circles of Strength: Community Alternatives to Alienation*, Philadelphia, PA and Gabriola Island: New Society Publishers.

Foster, John Bellamy (1999), 'Marx's theory of metabolic rift: classical foundation for environmental sociology', *American Journal of Sociology*, **105**(2), 366–405.

Fournier, Valerie (2005), 'Gift, she said', *Ephemera: Theory and Politics in Organization*, **5**(4), 655–61, available at: www.ephemeraweb.org/journal/5-4/5-4fournier.pdf (accessed March 27, 2011).

Garmendia, Eneko and Sigrid Stagl (2010), 'Public participation for sustainability and social learning: concepts and lessons from three case studies in Europe', *Ecological Economics*, **69**(8), 1712–22.

Gebara, Ivone (2003), 'Ecofeminism: a Latin American perspective', *Cross Currents*, **53**(1), 93–103.

Gibson-Graham, J.K. (1996), *The End of Capitalism (As We Knew It): A Feminist Critique of Political Economy*, Malden, MA and Oxford, UK: Blackwell.

Gilman, Charlotte Perkins (1898 [1997]), *Women and Economics*, North Chelmsford, MA: Courier Dover Publications, available at: http://digital.library.upenn.edu/women/gilman/economics/economics.html (accessed January 18, 2012).

Goldman, Emma (1972), *Red Emma Speaks: Selected Writings and Speeches*, New York: Random House.

Gould, Kira and Lance Hosey (2007), 'Is the environmental movement losing its feminine side?', available at: http://www.grist.org/article/gould_hosey (accessed January 2, 2012).

Gross National Happiness Commission (2011), available at: http://www.gnhc.gov.bt/; http://www.grossnationalhappiness.com/ (accessed April 18, 2011).

Hardin, Garrett (1968), 'The tragedy of the commons', *Science*, **162**(3859), 1243–48.

Hawthorne, Susan (2002), *Wild Politics*, Melbourne: Spinifex Press.

Hawthorne, Susan (2009), 'The diversity matrix: relationship and complexity', in Salleh (ed.), pp. 87–108.

Henderson, Hazel (1978), *Creating Alternative Futures*, New York: Perigee Books.

Henderson, Hazel (1980), *The Politics of the Solar Age*, New York: Knowledge Systems.

Henderson, Hazel (1983), 'The warp and the weft: the coming synthesis of eco-philosophy and eco-feminism', in Leonie Caldecott and Stephanie Leland (eds), *Reclaim the Earth*, London: The Women's Press, pp. 203–14.

Henderson, Hazel (1992), *Paradigms in Progress: Life Beyond Economics*, Indianapolis, IN: Knowledge Systems.

Herzog, Hal (2010), 'In the eyes of the beholder: the comparative cruelty of cockfights and happy meals', in Hal Herzog (ed.), *Some We Love, Some We Hate, Some We Eat: Why It's So Hard to Think Straight About Animals*, New York: HarperCollins, pp. 149–74.

Himmelweit, Susan (2003), 'An evolutionary approach to feminist economics: two different models of caring', in Drucilla K. Barker and Edith Kuiper (eds), *Toward a Feminist Philosophy of Economics*, London: Routledge, pp. 247–65.

Hunter, Lori M., Alison Hatch and Aaron Johnson (2004), 'Cross-national gender variation in environmental behaviors', *Social Science Quarterly*, **85**(3), 677–94.

Huws, Ursula (2003), *The Making of a Cybertariat: Virtual Work in a Real World*, New York: Monthly Review Press.

Isla, Ana (2002), 'A struggle for clean water and livelihood: Canadian mining in Costa Rica in the era of globalization', *Canadian Woman Studies*, **21/22**(4), 148–54.

Isla, Ana (2005), 'Conservation as enclosure: an eco-feminist perspective on sustainable development and biopiracy in Costa Rica', *Capitalism Nature Socialism*, **16**(3), 49–61.

Isla, Ana (2009), 'Who pays for the Kyoto protocol?', in Salleh (ed.), pp. 199–217.

Jochimsen, Maren A. (2003), 'Integrating vulnerability: on the impact of caring on economic theorizing', in Drucilla K. Barker and Edith Kuiper (eds), *Toward a Feminist Philosophy of Economics*, London: Routledge, pp. 231–46.

Jochimsen, Maren and Ulrike Knobloch (1997), 'Making the hidden visible: the importance of caring activities and their principles for any economy', *Ecological Economics*, **20**(2), 107–12.

Jones, Pattrice (2006), 'Rehabilitating fighting roosters: an ecofeminist project', available at: http://sanctuary.bravebirds.org/wp-content/uploads/2009/05/rehab2.pdf (accessed January 2, 2012).

Kennedy, Margrit (1987), 'Interest and Inflation-free Money: Creating an Exchange Medium that Works for Everybody and Protects the Earth', Seva International, available at: www.margritkennedy.de/pdf/BUE_ENG_Interest.pdf (accessed March 25, 2011).

Kuiper, Edith and Patricia E. Perkins (2005), 'Explorations: feminist ecological economics', *Feminist Economics*, **11**(3), 107–50.

Langley, Paul and Mary Mellor (2002), 'Economy, sustainability and sites of transformative space', *New Political Economy*, **7**(1), 49–65.

Las Patronas (2011), '"Las Patronas" coletivo de apoyo a los migrantes centroamericanos', available at: http://www.youtube.com/watch?v=DIq28UfEzuE (accessed April 18, 2011).

LeBourdais, Linda (1991), 'Women and environmental activity', *Women and Environments International*, **13**(2), 4–5.

Luchmann, Ligia (2008), 'Political participation, social inequalities and new institutionalities in Brazil', York University Brazilian Studies lecture series.

Malach, Sabrina (2010), 'Learn the buzz on pollination at International Pollinator Week', *Yfile*, June 3, available at: http://www.yorku.ca/yfile/archive/index.asp?Article=14952 (accessed March 26, 2011).

Martinez, Carlos, Michael Fox and JoJo Farrell (2010), *Venezuela Speaks! Voices from the Grassroots*, Oakland, CA: PM Press.

Maturana Romesin, Humberto and Gerda Verden-Zöller (2008), *The Origins of Humanness in the Biology of Love*, Exeter, UK: Imprint Academic.

Mellor, Mary (1992), *Breaking the Boundaries: Toward a Feminist Green Socialism*, London: Virago.

Mellor, Mary (1997a), *Feminism and Ecology*, New York: New York University Press.

Mellor, Mary (1997b), 'Women, nature, and the social construction of 'economic man'', *Ecological Economics*, **20**(2), 129–40.

Mellor, Mary (2009), 'Ecofeminist political economy and the politics of money', in Salleh (ed.), pp. 251–67.

Merchant, Carolyn (1996), *Earthcare: Women and the Environment*, New York: Routledge.

Mies, Maria (1998), *Patriarchy and Accumulation on a World Scale*, 2nd edn, London and New York: Zed Books; Melbourne: Spinifex Press. Republished London: Palgrave Macmillan, 1999.

Mies, Maria and Veronika Bennholdt-Thomsen (1999), *The Subsistence Perspective: Beyond the Globalized Economy*, London: Zed Books; Melbourne: Spinifex Press.

Mies, Maria and Vandana Shiva (1993), *Ecofeminism*, London: Zed Books.

Mohai, Paul (1992), 'Men, women, and the environment: an examination of the gender gap in environmental concern and activism', *Society and Natural Resources*, **5**(1), 1–19.

Mother Earth Water Walk (2011), available at: http://www.motherearthwaterwalk.com (accessed March 27, 2011).

Movimento Sem-Terra [Landless Movement] (2011), available at: http://www.mstbrazil.org/about-mst/agrarian-reform-need-basis (accessed March 27, 2011).

Moyo, Dambisa (2009), *Dead Aid: Why Aid Is Not Working and How There is a Better Way for Africa*, New York: Farrar, Strauss & Giroux.

Nelson, Julie (1997), 'Feminism, ecology, and the philosophy of economics', *Ecological Economics*, **20**(2), 155–62.

Nelson, Julie (2003), 'How did the "moral" get split from the "economic"', in Drucilla K. Barker and Edith Kuiper (eds), *Toward a Feminist Philosophy of Economics*, London: Routledge, pp. 132–42.

Noske, Barbara (1997), *Beyond Boundaries: Humans and Animals*, Montreal: Black Rose Books.

Not Far from the Tree (2011), available at: http://www.notfarfromthetree.org/about (accessed April 18, 2011).

Nozick, Marcia (1992), *No Place Like Home*, Ottawa: Canadian Council on Social Development.

O'Hara, Sabine (1997a), 'Discourse-based valuation: design of a community-based valuation process of development scenarios in the Hamilton Harbour Watershed', Sustainable Futures, Toronto and Hamilton, Ontario.

O'Hara, Sabine (1997b), 'Toward a sustaining production theory', *Ecological Economics*, **20**(2), 141–54.

Perkins, Patricia E. (1995), 'Social diversity and the sustainability of community economies', paper presented to the Seventh Annual International Conference on Socio-Economics, Washington, DC, April 7–9.

Perkins, Patricia E. (1996), 'Building communities to limit trade: following the example of women's initiatives', *Alternatives*, **22**(1), 10–15.

Perkins, Patricia E. (1997), 'Introduction: women, ecology, and economics: new models and theories', Special issue on Women, Ecology and Economics, *Ecological Economics*, **20**(2), 105–6.

Perkins, Patricia E. (2001), 'Discourse-based valuation and ecological economics', paper presented at the CANSEE conference, McGill University, Montreal, August 23–25.

Perkins, Patricia E. (2002), 'Feminist understandings of productivity', in Eichler et al. (eds), pp. 201–12.

Perkins, Patricia E. (2003), 'Social diversity, globalization and sustainability in community-based economies', *Canadian Woman Studies*, **23**(1), 38–46.

Perkins, Patricia E. (2007), 'Feminist ecological economics and sustainability', *Journal of Bioeconomics*, **9**(3), 227–44.

Perkins, Patricia E. (2010), 'Equitable, ecological degrowth: feminist contributions', in *2nd Conference on Economic Degrowth for Ecological Sustainability and Social Equity, Barcelona 2010*, Conference Proceedings, available at: http://www.barcelona.degrowth.org/fileadmin/content/documents/Proceedings/Perkins.pdf (accessed January 5, 2012).

Perkins, Patricia E. and Andrea Moraes (2007), 'Women and participatory water management', *International Feminist Journal of Politics*, Special Issue on Women and Water, **9**(4), 485–93.

Pietilä, Hilkka (1997), 'The triangle of the human economy: household–cultivation–industrial production. An attempt at making visible the human economy in toto', *Ecological Economics*, **20**(2), 113–27.

Pietilä, Hilkka (2007), 'The unpaid work in households – a counterforce to market globalization', paper presented at Matriarchy and the Mountain VII Conference, Trento, Italy, December, available at: http://www.hilkkapietila.net/articles/en/economy/Trento_paper.doc (accessed March 25, 2011).

Podlashuc, Leo (2009), 'Saving women: saving the commons', in Salleh (ed.), pp. 268–90.

Quiroga-Martinez, Rayén and Saar van Hauwermeiren (1996), *The Tiger Without a Jungle: Environmental Consequences of the Economic Transformation of Chile*, Santiago: Institute of Political Ecology. English translation of *El Tigre sin Selva: Consequencias Ambientales de la Transformacion Economica de Chile, 1974–1993*, Santiago: Instituto de Ecologia Politica.

Quiroga-Martinez, Rayén, Ellie Perkins, Edith Kuiper, Terisa Turner, Leigh Brownhill, Mary Mellor, Zdravka Todorova, Maren Jochimsen and Martha McMahon (2005), 'Exploring feminist ecological economics: gender, development, and sustainability from a Latin American perspective', *Feminist Economics*, **11**(3), 110–18.

Raddon, Mary-Beth (2002), *Community and Money: Men and Women Making Change*, Montreal: Black Rose Books.

Ridley, Glynis (2010), *The Discovery of Jeanne Baret, a Story of Science, the High Seas, and the First Woman to Circumnavigate the Globe*, New York: Crown Publishers.

Rosenberg, Harriet (1995), 'From trash to treasure: housewife activists and the environmental justice movement', in Jane Schneider and Rayna Rapp (eds), *Articulating Hidden Histories: Exploring the Influence of Eric Wolf*, Berkeley, CA: University of California Press, pp. 190–204.

Salleh, Ariel (1997), *Ecofeminism as Politics: Nature, Marx and the Postmodern*, New York and London: Zed Books.

Salleh, Ariel (2009), *Eco-sufficiency and Global Justice: Women Write Political Economy*, New York, London and Melbourne: Pluto Press and Spinifex Press.

Self-Employed Women's Association (SEWA) (2009), 'About Us', available at: http://www.sewa.org/ (accessed April 18, 2011).

Shenoy K, Narayana (2009), 'Traditional water harvesting methods of India', *Organiser*, **62** (6), August 16, 22–3, available at: http://www.organiser.org/dynamic/modules.php?name=Content&pa=showpage&pid=304&page=22 (accessed April 18, 2011).

Shiva, Vandana (1994), *Close to Home: Women Reconnect Ecology, Health and Development Worldwide*, London: Earthscan.

Shiva, Vandana (2010), *Staying Alive: Women, Ecology and Development*, New York: South End Press.

Shtier, Ann B. (1996), *Cultivating Women, Cultivating Science: Flora's Daughters and Botany in England, 1760–1860*, Baltimore, MD: Johns Hopkins University Press.

Spears, Ellen (2009), 'Ecofeminism: an old movement new to many ears', Women's News and Narratives, Emory University, Spring, available at: http://www.womenscenter.emory.edu/Women_News_and_Narratives/WNN_SP09/ecofeminism.htm (accessed January 2, 2012).

Stein, Rachel (2004), *New Perspectives on Environmental Justice: Gender, Sexuality, and Activism*, New Brunswick, NJ: Rutgers University Press.

Steingraber, Sandra (1997 [2010]), *Living Downstream: An Ecologist Looks at Cancer and the Environment*, New York and Cambridge, MA: Da Capo Press.

Swartling, Asa G., Cecilia Lundholm, Ryan Plummer and Derek Armitage (2010), 'Social Learning and Sustainability: Exploring Critical Issues in Relation to Environmental Change and Governance', Workshop proceedings, Stockholm Resilience Centre, Stockholm Environment Institute, Sweden, June 1–2, available at: www.sei-international.org (accessed March 25, 2011).

Taylor, Dorceta (2002), 'Race, Class, Gender and American Environmentalism', Forest Service, Pacific Northwest Research Station, General Technical Report PNW-GTR-534, US Department of Agriculture, Washington, DC, April.

The Stop Community Food Centre (2011), available at: http://www.thestop.org/ (accessed April 18, 2011).

Tibbetts, Alexandra (1994), 'Mamas fighting for freedom in Kenya', *Africa Today*, **41**(4), 27–48.

Tindall, D.B., Scott Davies and Celine Mauboules (2003), 'Activism and conservation behavior in an environmental movement: the contradictory effects of gender', *Society and Natural Resources*, **16**(10), 909–32.

Todorova, Zdravka (2005), 'Habits of thought, agency and transformation: an institutional approach to feminist ecological economics', *Feminist Economics*, **11**(3), 120–26.

Turner, Beryl (1994), 'Small-scale irrigation in developing countries', *Land Use Policy*, **11**(4), 251–61.

Turner, Terisa E. and Leigh Brownhill (2006), 'Ecofeminism as gendered, ethnicized class struggle', *Capitalism Nature Socialism*, **17**(4), 87–98.

United Nations Environment Programme (UNEP) (2006), 'Who's who of women and the environment', available at: http://www.unep.org/women_env/ (accessed January 2, 2012).

van den Hove, Sybille (2006), 'Between consensus and compromise: acknowledging the negotiation dimension in participatory approaches', *Land Use Policy*, **23**(1), 10–17.

Vaughan, Genevieve (2004), 'Introduction to the gift economy', available at: http://www.gift-economy.com/theory.html (accessed March 27, 2011).

Vaughan, Genevieve (2007), *Women and the Gift Economy: A Radically Different Worldview is Possible*, Toronto: Inanna Publications.

Wapner, Paul (1995), 'Politics beyond the state: environmental activism and world civic politics', *World Politics*, **47**(3), 311–40.

Waring, Marilyn (1989), *If Women Counted*, London: Macmillan.

Waring, Marilyn (2009), 'Policy and the measure of woman', in Salleh (ed.), pp. 165–79.

Warren, Karen (1987), 'Feminism and ecology: making the connections', *Environmental Ethics*, **9**(1), 3–20.

Warren, Karen (1997), *Ecofeminism: Women, Culture, Nature*, Indianapolis, IN: Indiana University Press.

Watson, Elizabeth E., William M. Adams and Samuel K. Mutiso (1998), 'Indigenous irrigation, agriculture and development, Marakwet, Kenya', *The Geographical Journal*, March 1, available at: http://findarticles.com/p/articles/mi_go2454/is_n1_v164/ai_n28703791/?tag=content;col1 (accessed April 18, 2011).

Wilkinson, Richard and Kate Pickett (2010), *The Spirit Level: Why Equality is Better for Everyone*, London: Penguin.

Wilson, Matthew A. and Richard B. Howarth (2002), 'Discourse-based valuation of ecosystem services: establishing fair outcomes through group deliberation', *Ecological Economics*, **41**(3), 431–43.

World Social Forum Charter of Principles (2002), available at: http://www.forumsocialmundial.org.br/main.php?id_menu=4&cd_language=2 (accessed March 27, 2011).

Yes in My Backyard (2011), available at: http://www.thestop.org/yes-in-my-back-yard (accessed January 2, 2012).

Zein-Elabdin, Eiman (1996), 'Development, gender and the environment: theoretical or contextual link? Toward an institutional analysis of gender', *Journal of Economic Issues*, **30**(4), 929–47.

Zelezny, Lynnette C., Poh-Pheng Chua and Christina Aldrich (2000), 'Elaborating on gender differences in environmentalism', *Journal of Social Issues*, **56**(3), 443–57.

32. Engendering peace, conflict and violence
Cilja Harders*

I INTRODUCTION

Why is it important to understand the gendered dimensions of war and peace? The reason is simple and profound: even though it is quite possible to make formal peace without including women and looking at gender relations, the *transformation* of violent conflict is impossible without using these gendered lenses. I therefore want to argue that there are compelling empirical, theoretical, and normative reasons to include gender as a main category of analysis.

Violence merits an important place in a contemporary analysis of gender and economic life. First, on an empirical level, societies organize the access to and use of different types of violence in a gendered way. For example, the world's armed forces are still a male domain even though women are entering the military to a certain degree. Heads of state, diplomats, foreign and defense ministers, and the world's richest persons are predominantly men. Women enter this picture mostly as exceptions to the rule or as victims of violence. Accepting this allocation of roles as a given and restricting one's research to just one realm would imply disregarding the experiences and actions of 50 percent of the population.

Second, on a more conceptual level, if war and peace involve both men and women in specific ways, we need to broaden our theoretical understanding of the state, peace, war, security, and democracy in order to adequately tackle these specific mechanisms of gendered inclusion and exclusion. This involves both the material and the symbolic or discursive levels of power relations, the gendered practices of states, and the construction of masculinities and femininities. Unless we take these into account, the root causes of violent conflict and their social and political contexts can be neither understood nor addressed in a transformative way.

Third, seen from a normative perspective, the lack of participation and representation of women in the domestic and international institutions of war and peace – such as parliaments, governments, foreign and defense ministries, armies, peacekeeping missions, or the United Nations – constitutes a severe democratic deficit (Harders, 2005). Consequently, the potential of gender-democratic politics and polities for achieving sustainable peace and development is left unexplored. In addition, no democratic state can accept high levels of individual or collective violence against some groups in that society, for example, domestic violence against women and children, or public violence and other human rights violations against vulnerable minorities.

These empirical, theoretical, and normative arguments have been analyzed in more detail in a rich body of literature, which can again be divided into empirically, conceptually, and normatively oriented studies. The first group focuses on 'blind spots', asking the questions: where are the women, where are the men, and why is this so? The authors are interested in 'engendering' their given fields, whether they be peace missions, the army, NGO work, humanitarian aid interventions, or conflict and development (Enloe, 1990; Rehn and Sirleaf, 2002; Eifler and Seifert, 2009). The second group of studies takes issue with the theoretical mainstream of political science, bringing to the fore the implicit gender dimensions in definitions of 'national security', 'international politics' and 'war'. For example, they shed light on the relationship between the gendered concepts of the nation-state, the military, and citizenship (Ruppert, 1998; Yuval-Davis, 2003). The third, normative group of studies deals with peace in theory and practice. They often relate to historical or current women's and peace movements and develop visions of a more peaceful and just world. Many consider unjust patriarchal gender relations to be a root cause of violence (Reardon, 1985; Peterson and Runyan, 1993; Holland, 2006).

This chapter discusses the relevance of gender for violence and conflict transformation, summarizing the state of the art of the academic debate and linking it to some of the challenges of gender-sensitive practice. It is based on the assumption that war and peace mark extremes on a gendered 'continuum of violence' (Cockburn, 2004), which links private and public, collective and individual, physical and structural, or symbolic violence. This approach stresses the interconnectedness of structures such as state institutions, gendered identity constructions and violence on the one hand and individual agency on the other. In Section II, I discuss the main concepts used and specifically address two sets of questions. First, how are conflict, violence, war and peace linked and gendered? And second, how can gender and gender relations be understood and how are they being shaped and sustained? In Section III, I explore the relationship between gender and violence, most notably the relation between masculinities, femininities, and violence. This approach introduces a method of interrogating what we see when looking through a gendered lens (Enloe, 2004), which can then be applied to other time – and context-bound examples. In Section IV, I offer some suggestions of how to apply this perspective in the practice of conflict transformation, asking how conflicts can be transformed in a gender-sensitive way. The conclusion, finally, discusses several dilemmas of doing gendered conflict transformation work, an important effort to enhance women's global well-being.

II GENDER CONCEPTS OF VIOLENCE, CONFLICT, WAR, AND PEACE

Human beings are dependent on bonding and relationships, which renders them vulnerable and gives them the power to violate others. But this essential human vulnerability only leads to victimization and violence under certain circumstances. Societies take precautions: they institutionalize, regulate, civilize, or unleash collective or personal violence within institutionalized power relations. They define 'legitimate' and 'illegitimate' violence and create institutions in order to enforce the formal or informal rules that apply to the use or prevention of violence. These processes are culturally and historically diverse. The gendered orders of violence are built through institutions such as the state, the military, the bureaucracy, the educational system, and the family (Sauer, 2009; see also Enloe, 1990). They are enshrined in religious beliefs, language, and symbolic orders. They are dynamic and they are organized along the lines of gender, class, race, and other identities.

Peace and conflict researchers use many approaches, ranging from international law to (social) psychology. They analyze the causes, developments, and characteristics of violent conflicts; ways of preventing violence and ways of overcoming violence's causes and consequences. Peace research focuses furthermore on the preconditions, barriers to and practices of peace (Senghaas, 1995; Adolf, 2009). Not surprisingly, the breadth of perspectives and disciplines is reflected in a host of different terms used in the field: conflict resolution, conflict settlement, conflict management, conflict prevention, conflict transformation, peace alliances, peacekeeping, peacemaking, peacebuilding – to name but a few.

Yet in dealing with (violent) conflict, two basic perspectives can be distinguished: an operational and a transformative way of seeking conflict resolution. Conflict management focuses on the state and formal actors, using formal instruments (early warning, preventive diplomacy, sanctions, coercive action, and so on). Conflict transformation aims to address the social root causes of collective violence by creating human security, catering to basic human needs and supporting justice and reconciliation (Reimann, 2004).

The idea of conflict management as a state-centered operative approach is closely connected to a realist and neo-realist theory of international relations (IR). This theory has been criticized for its implicit androcentrism and focus on the state (Tickner, 2001), which it models more or less explicitly along the lines of classical male role models: states (and men) search for autonomy, they use power to reach their aims and the ultimate means of power is the capacity to use violence. As a consequence, classical ways of dealing with conflict tend to rely heavily on military or other sources of hard power.

Conflict resolution (for some, transformation) as a strategy to address basic needs was developed by John Burton (1990) and avoids some of the pitfalls of conflict management described above. The basic needs approach is people-centered, rather than state-centered. It addresses the root causes of violence rather than managing it via formal diplomatic means. In terms of gender, however, it long used an 'add women and stir' approach[1] rather than incorporating gender issues because of a deep understanding that they are closely linked to conflict dynamics and the escalation and de-escalation of violence (Reimann, 2004).

Feminists and gender researchers have challenged these mainstream debates by questioning narrow concepts of war(making) and/or peace(building) and especially by stressing the interconnectedness of different types of violence. Focusing on the micro level of personal experience and starting from the so-called private sphere, gender scholars have discussed, for example, the highly ambivalent role of the state as the producer of 'public' security and 'private' insecurity. There might well be a state of peace between states, but if a state cannot provide for the security of all citizens – for example, if the degree of domestic violence or the degree of violence against minorities is very high – violence is 'privatized' and security is only provided for some parts of a society (Zwingel, 2002; Holland, 2006).

This, in turn, has implications for our understanding of 'war' and the relation between different types of violence. War (or violence), in this perspective, is not limited to enduring collective violence between states or organized groups. War should rather be framed as a specific type of collective violence, which is shaped by social dynamics of escalation and de-escalation (Elwert et al., 1999, p. 10). It then represents only one of many forms of violence. Wars are a product of social interaction, as human beings engage in dynamics of escalation. Furthermore, societies develop intricate material and symbolic structures, which 'allow' the use of violence on an individual level. Violence can indeed be used as a means of enacting individuality. All of these structures and practices are deeply gendered. For example, in most societies, the ability to use violence is attributed to the male gender. 'Manliness' thus becomes visible when men use violence. At the same time, they are judged along these lines – hence the many demeaning words describing men who do not wish to use violence. For example, men in administrative jobs in the army are called 'suppo-weenies' or 'sissies' (Eifler and Seifert, 1999; Apelt and Dittmer, 2009).

There is generally little consensus about the root causes of violent conflict among researchers, as men and women have produced a rich and controversial body of thought about the causes of war throughout history (Sahm et al., 2002; Daase, 2003, p.176; Adolf, 2009). There are several strands to this debate. First, wars, as understood in IR theory, can be seen as products of systemic asymmetry and anarchy. In this conception, states are the main actors and the structure of the international system is the main cause of war. Second, anthropological approaches may explain war with the human potential for aggression. Often, they build on biology and even genetics. Third, some actor-oriented approaches propose that human interest in securing power, fighting for political ideologies and economic gain, or fighting social injustice is an important driver of violent conflict. Fourth, a domestic politics argument (by which the internal structure and relations of a state strongly influence its external affairs) expects undemocratic or weak states to be the causes of war.

Feminist thinking has contributed a great deal of interesting insight in particular to this fourth perspective, based on analyses of the gendered deficits in the realm of participation and representation, the organization of the welfare state, or the philosophical foundations of democracy (see Pateman, 1988; Sauer, 2009). Current scholarship supports these arguments with quantitative data. Mary Caprioli (2005) and Erik Melander (2005), for example, analyzed the relationship between state behavior, gender justice, and democracy. They sustained the feminist claim that the private and the political spheres are as deeply linked as the domestic and the international spheres, and that peaceful domestic gender relations have a positive impact on external state behavior (Clasen and Zwingel, 2009).

A feminist perspective thus systematically links the domestic and the international realm and addresses unjust gender relations as a root cause of violence:

> [T]he achievement of peace, economic justice, and ecological sustainability is inseparable from overcoming social relations of domination and subordination; genuine security requires not only the absence of war but also the elimination of unjust social relations, including unequal gender relations. (Tickner, 1992, p.128)

In the content of our discussion, violence is mostly thought of in two ways: first, as direct physical violence. The absence of such violence (and the absence of any imminent threat of it) has been called negative peace. Second, there is a much broader range of violence, including structural, symbolic, and cultural violence (Hagemann-White, 2001). Johan Galtung (1972) holds that structural violence exists whenever the potential development of an individual or group is diminished, for example, by uneven distribution of power and resources (see also Confortini, 2006). The absence of these more indirect, nonphysical types of violence is a precondition for realizing comprehensive visions of 'positive peace'.

Within peace research there has been a long and diverse debate about the usefulness and necessity of broader or narrower conceptions of violence (and peace), which cannot be examined in detail here (see Brock, 1995; Senghaas, 1995; Moser and Clark, 2001). British peace activist and sociologist Cynthia Cockburn (2004) suggests thinking of violence as a continuum:

> Gender links violence at different points on a scale reaching from the personal to the international, from the home to the back street to the manoeuvres of the tank column and the sortie of the stealth bomber: battering and marital rape, confinement, 'dowry' burnings, honour killings, and genital mutilation in peacetime; military rape, sequestration, prostitutions, and sexualized torture in war. (p. 43)

The idea of a continuum of violence poses some conceptual and practical problems for those aiming to stop or transform it. Where to start? What are the most urgent types of violence to be addressed? How to define thresholds between different types and degrees of violence? Are there legitimate types of violence? And if so, how can they possibly be legitimized?

Some preliminary suggestions can be made using Clasen's 'Gendered Peace Index' (Clasen, 2006). The Gendered Peace Index measures the degree of peacefulness of a society based on a process-oriented conception of peace. This means that peace is not a given status or defined aim, but has to be continuously created through social processes which are open to change. Clasen defines three conditions for positive peace, which represent a progression from negative peace (that is, the absence of war) to a culture of peace. First, a secure physical existence for all men and women (*Existenzerhaltung*) forms the minimum requirement for peace. This can be measured by a balanced sex ratio, a low degree of domestic violence, and a low degree of public violence. Second, the possibility to live a good life (*Existenzentfaltung*) must be secured. This can be measured by the degree of gender justice in a society in terms of life expectancy, literacy, schooling, fertility, and economic and political participation of women. Third, and most important for conflict transformation, a plurality of lifestyles and roles (*Rollenpluralismus*) forms the last major step toward a culture of peace. This can be measured, for example, by looking at the discrimination of minorities, especially homosexuals, in a society.

In light of the discussion so far, it appears that what we need is a multicausal and multidimensional model of root causes of violence, which is sensitive to the gendered links between different types of violence and different stages of escalation. Collective and individual violence must be seen as products of gendered social processes and interactions. Thus, a gendered theory of society and the state is needed in order to understand (and change) the various social, political, and symbolic orders of violence.

Sex, Gender, Gender Relations

Gender matters. Being a man or a woman globally entails a difference in access to material and symbolic resources and rights, as the yearly global Gender Gap Report documents from the World Economic Forum (2009). But apart from this rather simple (and simplistic) truth there has been a long and controversial discussion about the concept of gender and its implications. Judith Lorber (2008, p. 538) defines gender as 'a social institution based on three structural principles: the division of people in two social groups, 'men' and 'women'; the social construction of perceptible differences between them; and their differential treatment, legitimated by socially produced differences'. I speak of gender relations in order to stress that gender is a relational category. In most societies this concerns the relations of 'men' and 'women', as already indicated by Lorber. It also implies that – as an institution – gender has a structural dimension and a process dimension. This means that the social, economic, cultural, linguistic, and religious systems we live in tend to be very stable. They deeply affect our individual behavior and beliefs. Individuals and groups act within these structures, and through their actions they shape and change the structures they live in. How the structural and process-related dimensions of gender interact, though, has been a matter of ongoing discussion in social and feminist theory.

The first debate in this context focuses on the difference between sex and gender. It starts from the assumption that biological sex can be distinguished from socially constructed gender. Conventional wisdom has it that the male and female sexes differ greatly: they have different genes, and different physical capabilities and bodily abilities (like being able to give birth). But even though female and male bodies do differ, intergroup differences are much bigger than the average difference between men and women.[2] Furthermore, the meanings we attach to these physical differences are not natural; they are the product of social processes. Post-structuralist theorizing has drawn our attention to the fact that both sex and gender are socially produced categories within a 'heterosexual matrix' that imposes the idea of two sexes (Knapp, 2001). Very often these processes of giving gendered meaning to bodies, behavior and experiences tend to be linked back to nature. This renders invisible the multilayered, constant individual and collective efforts that are needed to produce properly gendered women and men. Cross-cultural research on gender diversity, on the other hand, shows 'that there is no simple, universal, inevitable, or 'correct' correspondence between sex and gender and that the Euro-American privileging of biological sex (anatomy) is not universal' (Nanda, 2000, p. 2; Tuider, 2007).

The second debate focuses on the relationship between agency and structure, between 'doing gender' and 'gender being done'. Doing gender stresses the agency dimension. It means that while we talk, eat, dress, laugh, sing, pursue a career, raise a child or go to the doctor we also reproduce gender relations, consciously or unconsciously, willingly or unwillingly. These processes are context specific and time bound. Talking about gender being done refers to the symbolically, materially, and culturally diverse structures that shape our actions and perceptions despite individual preferences. This includes the institutional and structural side of the social organization of gender relations, such as state institutions. For example, most women gained their full political rights over 200 years later than men did. Or take the labor market, which is segregated along gender lines in terms of wages, representation of women in management positions, and access to wealth. Welfare services reproduce a certain model of the family, including gender roles (see Albelda, Chapter 16, this volume).

The third debate is the so-called 'intersectionality debate'. I have pointed out that gender is a relational category and that differentiation is a relational process: 'female' cannot be understood without 'male', 'poor' not without 'rich', 'black' not without 'white'. Obviously, there is differentiation between men and women, but there is also differentiation within each group. Thus, there is a homosocial and a heterosocial 'axis of difference' (Knapp, 2001). 'Homosocial differences' are those between a businesswoman and the nanny she employs. In addition to the class differences between the two women, there might be racial or ethnic differences, for example, between black and white women but also between immigrants and members of the dominant social group. 'Heterosocial differentiation' describes the differences between men and women. Here, too, other categories such as class, ethnic origin, religion, age, disabilities, sexual orientation, and individual choices interact. This complex web of categories of difference has been called 'intersectionality' (McCall, 2001; Klinger and Knapp, 2008).

Throughout these debates there has been major disagreement about the political implications of the various conceptions of gender relations. Should women pursue identity politics as women based on their shared gender? Or do such strategies lead to the exclusion of men and other women? Should feminist peace politics thus rather be based on universal human rights or on a politics of difference?

Using an intersectional conception of gender – as a power relation in which 'masculinities' and 'femininities' have ascribed and shifting meanings rather than essential qualities – has important practical implications. It helps us to analyze the durability and stability of unjust gender and social orders, including the use of violence by men against other men, women and children, without taking the connection between 'violence' and 'masculinity' as something natural or unchangeable. Rather, it allows us to question gendered stereotypes and to inquire about the possible functions of related structures. Sarah Clasen and Susanne Zwingel (2009) show, for example, that in order to understand the very high degree of murderous violence against women in Guatemala, we need to look at the history of a long and extremely violent civil war, which is rooted in the colonial experience and a class struggle. These led to the establishment of a culture of violence and, at the same time, to poverty and the destruction of families and traditional livelihoods. We also need to look at US-American immigration policies that led to the development of urban youth gangs, which were then forced back to Guatemala and reorganized as 'maras'. And we need to look at the current economic situation of lower-class boys and men in Guatemala (see also Luciak and Olmos, 2005).

Understanding the Relationship between Structure and Agency

One of the core questions of modern critical social and feminist theory is how gendered differentiation is converted into a system of gendered devaluation and hierarchy, and how such an unjust system is sustained. There is a host of different answers. As indicated above, the relationship between agency and structure – between individual will and decision-making and those structures that are outside our reach – is of central importance. French sociologist Pierre Bourdieu developed the concepts of 'habitus' and 'social field' in order to understand this relationship. Habitus is described as a 'system of durable, transposable dispositions, structured structures predisposed to function as structuring structures' (Bourdieu, 1977, p. 73). Thus habitus is the link between durable social structures and different individual agents with their choices, convictions, dreams, and perceptions.

Bourdieu stresses that the habitus of a person is at the same time deeply gendered and gendering (ibid., p. 94; Bourdieu, 2001). Again, habitus links individual agency (for example, the decision to behave like a 'good woman/man') and social and political structures (including education, experience in the social realm, state institutions, symbols, and norms about being a 'good woman/man'). Furthermore, according to Bourdieu, habitus is shaped through experience and interaction in a 'social field'; also, it is a bodily affair as it is incorporated in a very physical sense (Bourdieu, 1977, p. 76). We see habitus as 'natural' because it is literally 'embodied' in us from an early age. Joshua Goldstein (2001), for example, argues that gendered differences in children's education – especially the toughening up of boys – may be the most important factor for creating men and women who are willing to go to war.

Gendered habitus is a generating principle of masculinities and femininities (Meuser, 1998, p. 115). And although there have been great variations in the conceptions and practices of masculine and feminine habitus around the world throughout history, there are also dominant features of the gender habitus: shared expectations about appropriate behavior, language, and bodies. With respect to masculinities, these very specific dominant types have been called 'hegemonic masculinity' (Connell, 1995). The concept stresses differences among men as well as differences between men and women. Hegemony, in the Gramscian sense, implies the power of being able to dominate without using raw force as the main or only means of domination. Applied to gender relations this means that the powerful privileging of some types of masculinity in relation to women, as well as subordinate men, is mostly based on consent and voluntary subordination in 'a cultural dynamic by which a group claims and sustains a leading position in social life' (ibid., 1995, p. 77). The partial empowerment of some women may be a precondition for consent, as the discussion about intersectionality above has shown. Deniz Kandiyoti (1988) aptly named this the 'patriarchal bargain' offered to women. Within this social contract, women gain security and protection in the framework of family roles as mothers, daughters, and mothers-in-law. In turn, they impose the rules of a patriarchal order on younger and dependent women.

Male dominance is enacted heterosocially toward women and homosocially toward non-hegemonic masculinities such as poor, homosexual, or minority men. Still, all men, even those confined to subordinate or complicit masculinities, may benefit from 'patriarchal dividends'. These are structural benefits, which accrue to men regardless of their individual behavior and perceptions (Connell, 1995; Connell and Messerschmidt, 2005).[3] For example, a gender-segregated labor market allows employers to offer worse pay to women than to most men in the same position.

Even though hegemonic masculinity and femininity represent models which are not fully lived by most men and women (that is, they do not fully reflect the complexity of most men's and women's lives), they are embodied in the male and female habitus and, on the structural side, in the institutions of the state and of society. Birgit Sauer (2009) describes this as the 'masculinity' of the state. She argues that the ways in which states organize inclusion and exclusion – for example access to education, health, jobs, welfare services, housing or political participation – is both patriarchal and violent at the same time (p. 61).

Based on a feminist reading of political theories of the state, Sauer and others show that the civilization of collective violence in a monopoly of power/force held by the state has always been incomplete. The 'fraternal contract' is a sexual contract, as Carole

Pateman (1988) argues. It offers peace and participation to a society of brothers in a public sphere, while leaving the domestic sphere unregulated and women, children, and minorities in a state of patriarchal dependency and vulnerability. The monopoly of power, which in a democratic polity is regulated and controlled by law, has only lately been extended to this private sphere, as the difficulties in enacting and enforcing laws against domestic violence show.

Using a broad conception of violence, Sauer (2009) thus argues that state–society relations are gendered relations of violence, which are embodied in economic, social, reproductive, and political insecurity. This includes discourses and constructions of femininity and masculinity. Masculinities in many cultures are linked to the 'power of violation' whereas femininities are 'open to vulnerability'. Thus, gender relations are (latent) relations of violence as they systematically (re)produce the 'vulnerability' of women.

The concept of gendered habitus has important practical implications. It helps us to understand the durability and stability of unjust gender and social orders – including the use of violence – without claiming that there is a natural or unchangeable connection between violence and masculinity. Moreover, it allows us to question the gendered stereotypes regarding the use of violence and to inquire into the possible functions of such structures.

III GENDER RELATIONS AND VIOLENCE

Gendered Perceptions of Violence

Gendered beliefs about violence are quite similar cross-culturally and over time, as Goldstein's comprehensive study about gender and war proves. They imply that men fight and women don't (Goldstein, 2001; see also Elshtain, 1987). This is not to say that women do not want to fight or that they never have done it. They have always participated in collective violence throughout history, from the days of the Greek amazons to the American civil war and up to today's armed conflicts. Still, it is true that the majority of women do not take up weapons and that contemporary armies, as well as guerrilla groups or transnational terrorist networks, tend to be predominantly male. Thus, the gendered habitus produces two distinct, yet connected perceptions and practices: an aggressive, active, life-taking and violent masculine character versus a life-giving, passive, peaceful and caring feminine character. As relational concepts, they depend on each other (Harders, 2004).

Jean Elshtain (1987), in her important study about fighting women, suggested two opposite features of the female habitus: the 'beautiful soul' and the 'spartan mother'. The beautiful soul depicts women as better human beings, distanced from the dirt and brutality of the world – the caring and nonviolent mother and wife. The spartan mother by contrast encourages men to fight, or wishes to fight herself, and actively supports war. War propaganda has always used these perceptions, by honoring the mothers who gave birth to future soldiers, by encouraging women to work in the military sector or recruiting them for combat. Women are thus assigned a very important role on the home front.

On the male side of this equation, we find the male citizen and the soldier. Both roles are related to the use of violence, as the creation of the modern nation-state went hand in hand with the development of huge armies and general conscription. At the same time, women – who always had been a more or less formal part of military institutions and practices – were systematically excluded politically (Frevert, 2001). Paradoxically, the warring soldier as a symbol of powerful masculinity is at the same time feminized: soldiers cook, clean, iron, and take up other tasks that are often assigned to women. For example, a German soldier stated in a recent study that he never took better care of his clothing and cleanliness than during his time in the army (Apelt and Dittmer, 2009). Through military hierarchies, the power of violation and vulnerabilities are redistributed in a new way, which differs from civilian life. New recruits in particular undergo a harsh regime of bodily and physical training and hierarchical submission. These processes are deeply gendered, since they rely on gender stereotypes and at the same time create and reproduce certain types of masculinity and femininity (Dittmer, 2009). In this context, feminization is meant to devalue. This systematically leads to incidents of (sexualized) violence against women and men in almost all armies in the world (ibid., 2009; Scheub, 2010).

In addition, the soldier has to be willing to die for his or her comrades and ideologies. Again, the willingness to die for rather abstract concepts such as the nation or religion is not 'natural', and nor is the willingness to apply violence as means of social interaction. The military plays a crucial role in the (re)production of hegemonic masculinities which are open to the use of violence. Goldstein (2001, p. 331) argues:

> Cultures need to coax and trick soldiers into participating in combat . . . and gender presents a handy means to do so by linking attainment of manhood to performance in battle. In addition, cultures directly mould boys from an early age to suppress emotions in order to function more effectively in battle. This system, supported in various ways by women, produces men capable of fighting wars, but emotionally impaired. The militarized masculinity of men who fight war is reinforced by women's symbolic embodiment of 'normal' life and by women's witnessing of male bravery.

These gendered perceptions are as hierarchical as gender relations are. Even though the beautiful soul is as important for a militarized culture as the soldier, in patriarchal structures the female is devalued. Thus, constructs of femininity are rather contradictory: feminization is applied to dissenting men from the same group such as conscientious objectors, deserters, or homosexual men. Feminization discourses often coalesce with homophobia. They are also often linked to hypernationalism, racism, religious fervor, and other radicalized identities. At the same time, the 'male enemy' can be effectively portrayed as a beast by blaming him for exceptionally cruel deeds against women and children of the own group. Hence, the construction of an 'aggressive male' produces the idea of a threatened passive 'femininity' which is in need of protection.

These discourses can serve as the basis for a discursive and practical escalation of violence. For example, in many cases alleged or actual rape by one group provokes violence by the other. Thus, the stereotypes of peaceful, passive, and defenseless women are intimately connected with the active, aggressive, and defending men. As such, these discourses shape the male and female habitus and they create the power to violate, as well as creating vulnerability.

Masculinities and Violence

Empirically, men run a high risk of experiencing (physical) violence ranging from private domestic violence (for example, by parents against their children), to public criminal violence (for example, in youth gangs), or sexualized violence (for example, in prisons or as means of torture). Most violent crimes accounted for are perpetrated among men. Many acts of violent crime during times of peace are committed exclusively within male groups (Farr and Gebre-Wold, 2002). As a consequence, the overwhelming majority of prison inmates today are male. Most soldiers are men, as are most military victims of war. And in ethnopolitical conflicts, young civilian men frequently become victims of massacres because they are anticipated to be the 'future soldiers of the enemy' (for Rwanda, see Zdunnek, 2002; for Bosnia, see Cockburn and Zarkov, 2002).

In terms of agency, violence can nevertheless be understood as an identity resource for men. This is linked to the idea that the male habitus is constituted and shaped by serious games of competition among men. Homosocial institutions – the military, youth groups and gangs, prisons, boys' schools, sports, and some professions – are extremely important symbolic and material spaces for these games of competition. The military often functions as the 'school of the nation' by embodying a model of masculinity which is linked to physical power and strength, discipline, order, and the ability to fight. Militarized masculinity is a product of overemphasizing the idea of violence as a 'natural' part of masculinity. Competition and (group) solidarity are tightly linked (Meuser, 2007). Through competition between men, masculinities are shaped, experienced, and accomplished.

In addition, 'the experience of violence, for example in violent conflict, can cause the incorporation and habituation of violent practices' (Streicher, 2010, p. 26). These can in turn lead to a normalization of violence in the sense that violence becomes an integral part of an individual and collective habitus of certain men. Violence can also be a significant resource for reestablishing male domination and identity in a situation of crisis and devaluing traditional conceptions of masculinity. This kind of crisis can be provoked by an individual loss of autonomy, as studies about (sexualized) violence among men in prisons show. These studies argue that the use of violence and the fear of being victimized constitute an important dynamic in reestablishing masculinities (Toch, 1992; Bowker, 1998; Bereswill, 2006).

Reasserting masculine identities after individual or collective crisis is also one potent explanation for the usually high level of domestic violence in postwar societies, where demobilized and unemployed ex-combatants use violence in order to reestablish their position in the family and the household (see Zarkov, 2005 for ex-Yugoslavia; Dolan, 2002 and Schäfer, 2008 for Africa; Scheub, 2010 for a comprehensive debate). Ruth Streicher, in her study about youth gangs in East Timor, shows how gender, violence, age, class, and the legacy of a bloody civil war interact in producing masculinities. Youth gang members perceive themselves as protectors of their communities. They use violence in a ritualized form against other males and thus as a resource for identity building and competition. At the same time they are deeply insecure about their role as 'proper men' because they cannot live up to the role model of being a male breadwinner. European and US-American development aid agencies have played a role in introducing these models in the first place, as part of their humanitarian agenda (Streicher, 2010).

To summarize, the capacity to use violence is – in many societies and throughout much of history – an integral part of the male habitus. The use of physical or structural, collective, and/or individual violence against other men, women, and children can serve different social and individual functions, as demonstrated above. This does not mean that the use of violence is natural or that all men use violence. On the contrary, men have resisted public and private pressure to use violence throughout history. Young men have evaded conscription to the army or fled from fighting, as the history of 'traitors', 'cowards' and 'deserters' – names they have been called in order to stigmatize them – shows. Men have chosen not to join the guerrilla or militia and they have refrained from using violence in the domestic sphere. Men have also been actively supporting peace and nonviolent movements at all times. Furthermore, in order to sustain a culture of violence, both genders have to contribute.

Femininities and Violence

The 'feminine face' of war (Wasmuht, 2002, p. 88) is as diverse as the male one. In terms of intersectionality, for example, female members of the dominant ethnopolitical or social class may have as much interest in the escalation and the maintenance of violence as men. Like men, they may be driven by greed and grievance, by the belief in ideologies or the struggle for personal gains in power and money. Women may be active or passive supporters of militarized masculinities and therefore involved in maintaining a violent conflict culture. As soldiers, nurses, suppliers, weapon producers, and smugglers, women also actively sustain armed conflict. Even marginalized women may profit economically from a violent conflict by supplying the troops as merchants.

Women have not only been fighters in armies or guerrilla groups (Hagemann and Schüler-Springorum, 2002). They have also played a major role in the execution of collective violence in totalitarian and genocidal systems, as evident in Rwanda where women were heavily involved in violence (Zdunnek, 2002; McKelvey, 2007) and in Nazi Germany. Anette Kretzer (2009), in her study about the Ravensbrück women's concentration camp in Germany, shows how female perpetrators acted in a militarized and patriarchal system of violence, which was based on the institutionalized dominance of the male Nazi organizations. Within this system of patriarchal subordination, female concentration camp guards enjoyed and used a high degree of autonomy in the use of violence, torture, abuse, and murder. Even though there is no doubt about their role as active perpetrators, the postwar allied prosecuting authorities, as well as the German public, mostly framed their brutal deeds in terms of female deviation and excess. This can be explained by the deep-rooted gendered perceptions of the legitimate use of violence. For the purpose of our discussion here, it can be noted that – as perpetrators or fellows in crime, and as supporters of a violent conflict culture – women contribute to the escalation and de-escalation of conflicts just as much as men do.

At the same time, though, the gendered habitus, which assigns caring and less violent roles to women, has an important impact on the practices of peace activism. Women are often an important part of local peace alliances, and they often (and for longer) actively maintain social networks and connections with groups or individuals considered as 'the enemy'. Carolyn Nordstrom shows how dedicated and courageous women keep up medical care for civilians in war zones and thus produce islands of peace in an ocean of violence (Nordstrom, 2004). Often, they are the first to reconnect and return after violent conflicts (Cockburn, 2001). It is the assumed 'private' nature of their micro-level social interactions which allows them to cross lines of conflict and combat.

Women's entry into the political and public spheres for reasons of peacemaking or democratic transformation, on the other hand, often constitutes a rupture with traditional gender roles. It requires special justification. Women frequently use 'maternal' patterns of legitimization. Women thus may relate to their traditional gender roles when demonstrating for peace in order to protect their soldier sons, as this activist from the Philippines states:

> [It is] perhaps because of [women's] very lack of exposure to the way traditional politics has been played in this country and the way power has been used, there is in their attitude – not because it's in our genes but because it is in our experience and culture – much less of a kind of 'ego-involvement' that has to be overcome in dealing with the consensus building that needs to be done in forging a peace for a people that has been so divided. (International Alert, 1999, p. 13)

Many female activists utilize positive concepts of femininity and maternity for their peace work. But there is some tension between the political community of 'we, the women' and the real-life social, economic, and political inequalities between women, as well as those between women and men. The construction of an allegedly homogeneous identity (albeit as peace-promoting mothers) can stabilize rigid identity perceptions (Knapp, 2001, p. 43). As a case in point, many nationalist ideologies build on maternalism and thus restrict women to the role of mother and nurturer. This in turn often contributes to the legitimization of militaristic masculinities. It also contradicts the argument presented above that the possibility of living a plurality of gendered practices and roles is fundamental for sustaining a culture of peace. Thus, the line between essentialist exclusions and the maternal pragmatism of peace policies and practice is very narrow indeed.

IV   GENDER RELATIONS AND CONFLICT TRANSFORMATION: CONNECTING THEORY AND PRACTICE

How then can the complex theoretical considerations presented above serve those who are engaged in the practical politics of conflict transformation? This section suggests some general implications for gender-sensitive conflict transformation. Yet they always have to be put into the specific cultural, political, religious, and historical context of the projects concerned.

The difficult, conflict-prone, and diverse contexts of transformation work demand a substantial level of self-reflexivity. Practitioners of conflict transformation themselves are products of the gendered habitus and gender regimes that have shaped their lives. Practitioners and those they wish to support are constantly involved in doing gender and whatever they do is part of a structure in which gender is being done. The gendered lens proposed here can be applied to all societies, as nearly all societies experience some form of violence. Changing these deep-rooted beliefs and practices does involve long-term work and it can create severe tensions and conflicts. Nevertheless, self-reflexivity on the level of personal experience and beliefs, the levels of interaction and of professional concepts and actions is crucial.

All measures of conflict transformation work must be investigated and improved along the lines of gender indicators (Reimann, 2001, p. 32). Today, there is a host of literature about gender mainstreaming, gendered evaluations, and gender benchmarks, which suggests coherent ways of making the gendered dimensions of peace and conflict visible. These should be combined with measures that are sensitive to intersectionality, depending on the relevance of specific categories of differentiation for understanding a certain conflict dynamic. This includes collecting data that are disaggregated according to sex, race, and age, and securing the participation and empowerment of those who have previously been marginalized (women or men, old or young, minority groups according to race, religion or other ascribed identities).

Gender issues are a useful and empirically hard measure for testing social escalation, as they are closely connected to militarized constructs of masculinity. Thus, a narrowing down of women's social roles to mothers and growing public and private violence against women and unmanly men (for example, homosexuals, nonmilitaristic men, dissenters, peace activists) constitute major early-warning indicators (Hill, 2003). On the other hand, the possibility of living a plurality of roles and identities for men and women is a major indicator of a peaceful society (Clasen, 2006). Indicators like the ones suggested for the Gendered Peace Index should be systematically included in civil conflict transformation. This kind of data collection could serve as a baseline for situation assessments in observer missions, NGOs, or state institutions.

Conflict transformation activities need to address different types of violence simultaneously. Understanding the link between different types of violence sheds light on the gendered root causes of violence. The creation of negative peace is then just a precondition for further work. As a next step, practitioners have to ensure that restoring security in a postwar situation includes protection against sexualized violence and changes the culture of violence in all spheres of society.

Feminists, gender activists, and peace activists all over the world have made enormous efforts in order to publicize and politicize the nexus between gendered injustices and collective and individual violence. A growing body of international law has been the result and can now be used as a point of reference. Notable are the Universal Declaration of Human Rights and the Convention on the Elimination of All Forms of Discrimination Against Women (CEDAW). In addition, resolutions 1325 (2000) and 1820 (2008) of the UN Security Council highlight the new international and institutional visibility of gender issues in the field of peace and conflict. While development agencies and NGOs have been receptive to these new insights, governments and academia in their more mainstream approaches have been less so. Thus, many gender-sensitive policies are not implemented due to lack of political will and/or resources. Still too often, gender issues are perceived as women's issues, thus neglecting the male dimension of gender relations.

To begin to change this, awareness has to be raised more broadly still. In postwar contexts, for example, the police have to be trained, the awareness of judges needs to be heightened, safe spaces and hotlines must be made available for those who fall victim to violence. External actors and civil conflict resolution practitioners can support the development of a broader understanding of security, by supporting testimonies against perpetrators and by stressing the urgency of protecting and legitimizing human rights.

Most importantly, laws have to be passed for the prosecution of different types of violence, including domestic violence, as criminal acts. Finally, all local initiatives taking up this touchy issue should be supported, as it needs to be addressed in an appropriate cultural and political manner.

Any project which envisions building a culture of peace and mutual respect has to address the constructions and practices of masculinity in a given society. After war, this includes work with traumatized combatants, members of the military, police, and security forces. In other situations, fighting domestic violence and rape might be a priority. The goal should be to 'develop gender practices for men that shift gender relations in a democratic direction. Democratic gender relations are those that move towards equality, non violence, and mutual respect between people of different genders, sexualities, ethnicities, and generations' (Connell, 2001, p. 16). As a start, more men have to be won over to act decidedly against violence in everyday culture. Fortunately, men all over the world are already doing so. For example, the African campaign against violence 'real men don't rape' has triggered support in many African countries and around the globe (Schäfer, 2008; GTZ, 2009). MenEngage was founded in 2004 and constitutes a global and growing network of emancipatory men's organizations, which work to promote the engagement of men and boys in achieving gender equality (Scheub, 2010).

Changing gender relations and gendered role perceptions that enhance violence is as important as offering spaces for men and women to voice their concerns. This can be done by supporting men to work on war trauma, supporting gay, lesbian, and transgender groups, and supporting spaces in which the ambivalence of being a victim and a perpetrator at the same time can be voiced (Schroer, 2010). But sometimes, men – especially male members of minorities under pressure – rely heavily on games of competition and the degradation of women and femininity. They may lack noncompetitive, nonmilitarized alternative male identity roles, which have to be slowly and carefully created and promoted, as changes in gender roles may create tension and even cause violence (UN, 2008).

In times of war, women often gain access to new economic, familial, vocational, and social fields of action. These gains are, however, mostly of limited duration:

> The historical records confirm that societies neither defend the spaces women create during struggle nor acknowledge the indigenous way in which women bear new and additional responsibilities. ... [W]omen's activism in managing survival and community level agency is predictably devalued as accidental activism and marginalised post-conflict, as politics become more structured and hierarchical. (Meintjes et al., 2001, p. 9)

Postwar restorative tendencies can be traced back to a variety of causes, even though women take up numerous important tasks in reconstruction. Crucially, war and the gender relations it produced are collectively processed as an exceptional circumstance. The desired 'restoration of normalcy' is manifested by reestablishing the status quo of gender relations. In predominantly agrarian societies, the older generation has a strong interest in restoring their control over family reproduction, as they rely on the younger generation for survival (Meintjes et al., 2001). Men seek to reestablish their control over women, family structures, and decisions (GTZ, 2009). Similar setbacks can be witnessed on the political institutional level. Again, there are various reasons. One seems to be that women themselves do not internalize those transformations, and that men and women prefer the return to normalcy even at the price of social and economic losses (Meintjes et al. 2001, p. 12). For women, newly won access to the labor market and economic independence seem to be the easiest gains to hold on to. Changes in family roles and decision-making structures are more difficult to maintain.

A different but related issue concerns the demobilization of female combatants. Even though women have taken and still are taking part in conflicts as combatants, they are often ignored during phases of demobilization and reintegration (Dietrich Ortega, 2009; GTZ, 2009). They receive little or none of the appreciation given to men, are not incorporated into programs of demobilization and receive less compensation to build a new civil life. Female combatants face additional difficulties on the social level, being frequently stigmatized by their home communities, who refuse to reintegrate them (Bop, 2001). Following anti-colonial combat initiated by leftist nationalist groups in Algeria, Eritrea, and Nicaragua, women were also unsuccessful in retaining their obtained equality (Meintjes et al. 2001, p. 11).

Conflict transformation should take care not to directly or indirectly facilitate a return to the former (discriminatory) situation. Moreover, it should support processes of raising awareness that restoration does not have to mean a return to the status quo. It has to further encourage those organizations that are promoting concrete steps toward gender equality, and toward creating manifold livelihoods and perspectives for men and women.

V   CONCLUSION: DILEMMAS AND PERSPECTIVES

The complexities of a gendered conflict transformation strategy are great, as are its challenges. It is by no means obvious how to deal politically with the inequalities and injustices produced by intersecting differences along the lines of gender, race, class, or age. Changing gender relations, after all, might create new tensions. In war-torn societies, which have experienced violence and social upheaval, this might in turn lead to new forms of private and public violence. Feminism has developed three major strategies, which today are implicitly or explicitly adapted in most policy fields, from labor policies to development aid. They include equality and quota policies, affirmative action, and identity politics. German sociologist and feminist Gudrun-Axeli Knapp (2001, p. 44) points to at least three problematic dimensions of these strategies. The 'dilemma of equality' implies that ignoring difference by employing 'equality policies' actually leads to inequality being maintained. Most 'one-size-fits-all' approaches lead to such problems, because they ignore the very different resources and capabilities that different people have. The 'dilemma of difference' means that the disparate treatment of differences leads to the maintenance of discrimination. For example, affirmative action policies tend to recreate the categories of discrimination they actually set out to fight and dissolve. The 'dilemma of identity' points to the fact that substantial group identities always produce exclusions of the nonidentical. For example, peace politics based on an assumption of the general peacefulness of women exclude all those men who might share such a habitus and severely underestimates the importance of women's agency for war systems.

Another complicating factor is a perceived 'clash of cultures': those women and men who struggle for social change, peace, and gender justice in their societies often feel neglected and threatened by 'western' activism at the same time. Cultural relativism on the part of western actors gives oppressive regimes leeway to hide human rights violations behind 'traditions'. On the other hand, universalist projections of rights, gender roles, and modernity have constantly and rightly provoked criticism because of the paternalism and neglect of local experiences related to such unilateral projects of emancipation.

While there are no easy solutions to these dilemmas, there is some good advice. Cynthia Cockburn (2004, p. 29) argues:

> An assumption of equality and similarity should prevail except when those liable to suffer from differentiation (women in this case) say that difference should be taken into account. . . . When should women be treated as 'mothers', as 'dependents', as 'vulnerable'? When on the contrary, should they be disinterred from 'the family', from 'women and children' . . . and seen as themselves, women – people, even. Ask the women in question. They will know.

Thus, successful conflict transformation should be geared toward supporting and initiating those social processes that are necessary for producing context-specific answers to these dilemmas. This implies a participatory approach and a willingness to learn on the part of those who might come from the outside in order to support local conflict transformation. Knowledge transfer should always be a voluntary, two-way process. International concepts need to be adapted to the local context in a dialogue with those women and men who dare to challenge the gendered rules and restrictions of their societies. Very often, the local activists can suggest sustainable answers to the dilemmas of cultural context sensitivity and cultural relativism. While the path ahead is by no means clear, a focus on gender-sensitive conflict transformation matters for the quality of women's and men's lives and livelihoods around the world.

NOTES

*   This chapter is a slightly revised version of the following, reprinted with permission of the Berghof Foundation: 'Gender relations, violence and conflict transformation', Berghof *Handbook on Conflict Transformation*, available at: http://www.berghof-handbook.net/profile/. I thank Sarah Clasen, Ruth Streicher, Beatrix Austin and Martina Fischer for their valuable comments and discussion on earlier drafts of this chapter.
1. This ironic phrase was first used in critical development studies. It means that nongender-sensitive approaches include women without rethinking their (deeply gendered) concepts of conflict, violence, and so on.
2. See Goldstein (2001) for a very detailed discussion on the biological dimensions of warfare.
3. It is important to note, though, that intersectionality often contradicts these simple hierarchies of power, as power is also distributed along the lines of class and 'race'.

REFERENCES

Adolf, Antony (2009), *Peace: A World History*, Cambridge: Polity Press.
Apelt, Maja and Cordula Dittmer (2009), 'Under pressure – Militärische Männlichkeiten im Zeichen Neuer Kriege und veränderter Geschlechterverhältnisse', in Mechthild Bereswill, Michael Meuser and Sylka Scholz (eds), *Dimensionen der Kategorie Geschlecht. Der Fall Männlichkeit*, Münster: Westfälisches Dampfboot, pp. 68–83.
Bereswill, Mechthild (2006), 'Männlichkeit und Gewalt. Empirische Einsichten und theoretische Reflexionen über Gewalt zwischen Männern in Gefängnissen', *Feministische Studien*, **24**(2), 242–255.
Bop, Codou (2001), 'Women in conflicts: their gains and their losses', in Meintjes et al. pp. 19–34.

Bourdieu, Pierre (1977), *Outline of a Theory of Practice*, Cambridge: Cambridge University Press.
Bourdieu, Pierre (2001), *Masculine Domination*, Stanford, CA: Stanford University Press.
Bowker, Lee Harrington (ed.) (1998), *Masculinities and Violence*, London, New Delhi: Sage.
Brock, Lothar (1995), 'Frieden. Überlegungen zur Theoriebildung', in Dieter Senghaas (ed.), *Den Frieden denken. Si Vis Pacem, Para Pacem*, Frankfurt a.M.: Suhrkamp, pp. 317–40.
Burton, John (1990), *Conflict: Resolution and Prevention*, Basingstoke, UK: Macmillan.
Campa, Pamela, Alessandra Casarico and Paola Profeta (2009), Gender Culture and Gender Gap in Employment', Working Paper No. 143, Econpubblica Centre for Research on the Public Sector, Milan.
Caprioli, Mary (2005), 'Primed for violence: the role of gender inequality in predicting internal conflict', *International Studies Quarterly*, **49**(2), 161–78.
Clasen, Sarah (2006), 'Engendering Peace. Eine gendersensitive Weiterentwicklung des Czempielschen Friedensmodells', Institut für Politikwissenschaft, unpublished master's thesis, Universität Tübingen.
Clasen, Sarah and Susanne Zwingel (2009), 'Geschlechterverhältnisse und Gewalteskalation', in *PVS Sonderheft*, Nr. 43 Identität, Institution und Ökonomie, Ursachen innenpolitischer Gewalt, pp. 128–49.
Cockburn, Cynthia (2001), *The Space Between Us: Negotiating Gender and National Identities in Conflict*, London and New York: Zed Books.
Cockburn, Cynthia (2004), 'The continuum of violence', in Wenona Giles and Jennifer Hyndman (eds), *Sites of Violence, Gender and Conflict Zones*, Berkeley, CA: University of California Press, pp. 24–44.
Cockburn, Cynthia and Dubravka Zarkov (eds) (2002), *The Postwar Moment: Militaries, Masculinities and International Peacekeeping: Bosnia and the Netherlands*, London: Lawrence & Wishart.
Confortini, Catia C. (2006), 'Galtung, violence and gender: the case for a peace studies/feminism alliance', *Peace and Change*, **31**(3), 333–67.
Connell, R.W. (1995), *Masculinities*, Berkeley, CA, London: University of California Press.
Connell, R.W. (2001), 'Masculinities, violence, and peacemaking', *Peace News*, **2443**, 14–16.
Connell, R.W. and James W. Messerschmidt (2005), 'Hegemonic masculinity: rethinking the concept', *Gender & Society*, **19**(6), 829–59.
Daase, Christopher (2003), 'Krieg und Politische Gewalt. Konzeptionelle Innovation und Theoretischer Fortschritt', in Gunther Hellmann, Klaus Dieter Wolf and Michael Zürn (eds), *Forschungsstand und Perspektiven der Internationalen Beziehungen in Deutschland*, Baden-Baden: Nomos, pp. 161–208.
Dietrich Ortega, Luisa Maria (2009), 'Transitional justice and female ex-combatants: lessons learned from international experience', in Ana Cutter Patel, Pablo de Greiff and Lars Waldorf (eds), *Disarming the Past. Transitional Justice and Ex-Combatants*, New York: Social Science Research Council & International Center for Transitional Justice, pp. 158–88.
Dittmer, Cordula (2009), 'Gender Trouble in der Bundeswehr. Eine Studie zu Identitätskonstruktionen und Geschlechterordnungen unter besonderer Berücksichtigung von Auslandseinsätzen', transcript, Bielefeld.
Dolan, Chris (2002), 'Collapsing masculinities and weak states – a case study of northern Uganda', in Frances Cleaver (ed.), *Masculinities Matter! Men, Gender and Development*, London: Zed Books, pp. 57–83.
Eifler, Christine and Ruth Seifert (eds) (1999), *Soziale Konstruktion. Militär und Geschlechterverhältnis*, Münster: Westfälisches Dampfboot.
Eifler, Christine and Ruth Seifert (eds) (2009), *Gender Dynamics. Post-Conflict Reconstruction*, Frankfurt a.M.: Peter Lang.
Elshtain, Jean Bethke (1987), *Women and War*, Chicago, IL: Harvester Press.
Elwert, Georg, Stephan Feuchtwang and Dieter Neubert (1999), 'The dynamics of collective violence. An introduction', *SOCIOLOGUS*, **1**(supplement), 9–31.
Enloe, Cynthia (1990), *Bananas, Beaches and Bases: Making Feminist Sense of International Politics*, Berkeley, CA: University of California Press.
Enloe, Cynthia (2004), *The Curious Feminist: Searching for Women in The New Age of Empire*, Berkeley, CA and London: University of California Press.
Farr, Vanessa and Kiflemariam Gebre-Wold (eds) (2002), *Gender Perspectives on Small Arms and Light Weapons, Regional and International Concerns*, Bonn: Bonn International Center for Conversion.
Frevert, Ute (2001), *Die Kasernierte Nation. Militärdienst und Zivilgesellschaft in Deutschland,* München: C.H. Beck.
Galtung, Johan (1972), 'Gewalt, Frieden und Friedensforschung', in Dieter Senghaas (ed.), *Kritische Friedensforschung*, Frankfurt a.M.: Suhrkamp, pp. 55–104.
Gesellschaft für Technische Zusammenarbeit (GTZ) (ed.) (2009), *Masculinity and Civil Wars in Africa. New Approaches to Overcoming Sexual Violence in War*, Bonn: GTZ.
Goldstein, Joshua S. (2001), *War and Gender*, Cambridge: Cambridge University Press.
Hagemann, Karen and Stefanie Schüler-Springorum (eds) (2002), *Heimat-Front*, Frankfurt a.M. and New York: Campus Verlag.
Hagemann-White, Carol (2001), 'European research on the prevalence of violence against women', *Violence against Women*, **7**(7), 731–59.

Harders, Cilja (2004), 'Neue Kriegerinnen', in Lynndie England and Jessica Lynch (eds), *Blätter für deutsche und internationale Politik*, 9/2004, pp. 1101–11.

Harders, Cilja (2005), 'Geschlecht und Gewaltminderung: Konfliktbearbeitung durch veränderung von Machtverhältnissen', in Sahm et al. pp. 495–518.

Hill, Felicity (2003), 'Women's contribution to conflict prevention, early warning and disarmament', *Disarmament Forum*, 4, 17–24, available at: www.unidir.ch/bdd/fiche-article.php?ref_article=1994 (accessed September 24, 2010).

Holland, Jack (2006), *Misogyny: The World's Oldest Prejudice*, London: Robinson.

International Alert (IA) (1999), *Mainstreaming Gender in Peacebuilding: A Framework for Action*, London: International Alert, available at: http://www.cities-localgovernments.org/uclg/upload/docs/mainstreamingg enderinpeacebuilding-aframeworkforaction.pdf (accessed September 17, 2012).

Kandiyoti, Deniz (1988), 'The partiarchal bargain', *Gender & Society*, **2**(3), 274–90.

Klinger, Cornelia and Gudrun-Axeli Knapp (2008), *Überkreuzungen. Fremdheit, Ungleichheit, Differenz*, Münster: Westfälisches Dampfboot.

Knapp, Gudrun-Axeli (2001), 'Dezentriert und viel riskiert. Anmerkungen zur These vom Bedeutungsverslust der Kategorie Geschlecht', in Gudrun-Axeli Knapp and Angelika Wetterer (eds), *Soziale Verortung der Geschlechter*, Münster: Westfälisches Dampfboot, pp. 15–62.

Kretzer, Anette (2009), *NS-Täterschaft und Geschlecht. Der erste britische Ravensbrück-Prozess 1946/47 in Hamburg*, Berlin: Metropol.

Lorber, Judith (2008), 'Constructing gender: the dancer and the dance', in James A. Holstein and Jaber F. Gubrium (eds), *Handbook of Constructionist Research*, New York: Guilford Press, pp. 531–44.

Luciak, Ilja A. and Cecilia Olmos (2005), 'Gender equality and the Guatemalan peace accords: critical reflections', in Dyan Mazurana, Angela Raven-Roberts and Jane Papart (eds), *Gender, Conflict, and Peacekeeping*, Lanham, MD: Rowman & Littlefield, pp. 202–19.

McCall, Leslie (2001), 'The complexity of intersectionality', *Signs. Journal of Women in Culture and Society*, **30**(3), 1771–99.

McKelvey, Tara (ed.) (2007), *One of the Guys*, Berkeley, CA: University of California Press.

Meintjes, Sheila, Anu Pillay and Meredeth Turshen (eds) (2001), *The Aftermath: Women in Post Conflict Transformation*, London: Zed Books.

Melander, Erik (2005), 'Gender equality and intrastate armed conflict', *International Studies Quarterly*, **49**(4), 695–714.

Meuser, Michael (1998), *Geschlecht und Männlichkeit: Soziologische Theorie und Kulturelle Deutungsmuster*, Opladen: Leske & Budrich.

Meuser, Michael (2007), 'Serious games: competition and the homosocial construction of masculinity', *Nordic Journal for Masculinity Studies*, **2**(1), 38–51.

Moser, Caroline O. and Fiona C. Clark (eds) (2001), *Victims, Perpetrators or Actors? Gender, Armed Conflict and Political Violence*, London: Zed Books.

Nanda, Serena (2000), *Gender Diversity. Crosscultural Variations*, Long Grove, IL: Waveland Press.

Nordstrom, Carolyn (2004), *Shadows of War: Violence, Power and International Profiteering in the Twenty-First Century*, Berkeley/Los Angeles, CA: University of California Press.

Pateman, Carole (1988), *The Sexual Contract*, Stanford, CA: Stanford University Press.

Peterson, Spike V. and Anne Runyan (1993), *Global Gender Issues*, Boulder, CO: Westview Press.

Reardon, Betty A. (1985), *Sexism and the War System*, Syracuse, NY: Syracuse University Press.

Rehn, Elisabeth and Ellen Johnson Sirleaf (2002), *Women, War and Peace. The Independent Experts' Assessment on the Impact of Armed Conflict on Women and Women's Role in Peacebuilding*, New York: United Nations Development Fund for Women.

Reimann, Cordula (2001), *Towards Gender Mainstreaming in Crisis Prevention and Conflict Management. Guidelines for the German Technical Co-Operation*, Eschborn: GTZ.

Reimann, Cordula (2004), 'Assessing the state-of-the-art in conflict transformation – Reflections from a theoretical perspective', in Alex Austin, Martina Fischer and Norbert Ropers (eds), *Transforming Ethnopolitical Conflict. The Berghof Handbook*, Wiesbaden: VS Verlag, pp. 41–66, available at: www.berghof-handbook. net/documents/publications/reimann_handbook.pdf.

Ruppert, Uta (1998), 'Theorien internationaler beziehungen aus feministischer perspektive', in Uta Ruppert (ed.), *Lokal bewegen – global verhandeln. Internationale Politik und Geschlecht*, Frankfurt a.M and New York: Campus Verlag, pp. 27–55.

Sahm, Astrid, Egbert Jahn and Sabine Fischer (eds) (2002), *Die Zukunft des Friedens weiterdenken – Perspektiven der Friedens – und Konfliktforschung*, Wiesbaden: VS Verlag für Sozialwissenschaften.

Sauer, Birgit (2009), 'Staatlichkeit und geschlechtergewalt', in Gundula Ludwig, Brigit Sauer and Stefanie Wöhl (eds), *Staat und Geschlecht*, Baden-Baden: Nomos, pp. 61–74.

Schäfer, Rita (2008), *Frauen und Kriege in Afrika. Ein Beitrag zur Gender-Forschung*, Frankfurt a.M.: Brandes & Aspelt.

Scheub, Ute (2010), *Heldendämmerung. Die Krise der Männer und warum sie auch für Frauen gefährlich ist*, München: Pantheon.

Schroer, Miriam (2010), *Gender und Konfliktbearbeitung*, Bonn: Bundeszentrale für politische Bildung.

Senghaas, Dieter (1995), 'Frieden als Zivilisationsprojekt', in: Dieter Senghaas (ed.), *Den Frieden denken. Si Vis Pacem, Para Pacem*, Frankfurt a.M.: Suhrkamp, pp. 196–223.

Streicher, Ruth (2010), 'The constructions of masculinities and violence: youth gangs in Dili, East Timor', Working Paper No. 2, Center for Middle Eastern and North African Politics, Berlin.

Tickner, J. Ann (1992), *Gender in International Relations: Feminist Perspectives on Achieving Global Security*, New York: Columbia University Press.

Tickner, J. Ann (2001), *Gendering World Politics*, New York: Columbia University Press.

Toch, Hans (1992), *Violent Men. An Inquiry into the Psychology of Violence*, Washington, DC: American Psychological Association.

Tuider, Elisabeth (2007), 'Diskursanalyse und Biographieforschung. Zum Wie und Warum von Subjektpositionierungen', *Forum Qualitative Sozialforschung*, **8**(2), Art. 6.

United Nations (UN) (2008), *The Role of Men and Boys in Achieving Gender Equality*, New York: UN Division for the Advancement of Women.

Wasmuht, Ulrike (2002), 'Warum bleiben Kriege gesellschaftsfähig? Zum weiblichen Gesicht des Krieges', in Cilja Harders and Bettina Roß (eds), *Geschlechterverhältnisse in Krieg und Frieden. Perspektiven der Feministischen Analyse Internationaler Beziehungen*, Opladen: Leske & Budrich, pp. 87–103.

World Economic Forum (2009), 'The Global Gender Gap Report', Geneva, available at: http://www.weforum. org/issues/global-gender-gap (accessed September 17, 2012).

Yuval-Davis, Nira (2003), *Gender and Nation*, London: Sage.

Zarkov, Dubravka (2005), 'Sexual violence and war in former Yugoslavia', CORDAID Debate Gender Crimes – A Future after Humiliation, available at: www.iccwomen.org/news/docs/CORDAID_Debate_Jan05_Zarkov.doc (accessed September 24, 2010).

Zdunnek, Gabriele (2002), 'Akteurinnen, Täterinnen und Opfer. Geschlechterverhältnisse in Bürgerkriegen und ethnisierten Konflikten', in Cilja Harders and Bettina Roß (eds), *Geschlechterverhältnisse in Krieg und Frieden. Perspektiven der Feministischen Analyse Internationaler Beziehungen*, Opladen: Leske & Budrich, pp. 143–61.

Zwingel, Susanne (2002), 'Was trennt Krieg und Frieden? Gewalt gegen frauen aus feministischer und völkerrechtlicher Perspektive', in Cilja Harders and Bettina Roß (eds), *Geschlechterverhältnisse in Krieg und Frieden. Perspektiven der Feministischen Analyse Internationaler Beziehungen*, Opladen: Leske & Budrich, pp. 175–88.

33. Trafficking and gender
Julie Ham*

I INTRODUCTION

When most people talk about gender and trafficking, they usually (but not always) are talking about trafficking of women. Most of the current evidence on trafficking focuses exclusively on women, and the intersection of men's gendered experiences and trafficking unfortunately remains a great gap in research. This chapter explores the impact of a gendered discourse on women. Policy and public conversations around trafficking reflect social ideas about women, specifically ideas about women's vulnerabilities. In addition, the chapter outlines the connections often made between trafficking and the gendered experiences of women, and identifies when these links help or hurt our ability to work for the rights of trafficked persons and other directly affected groups such as migrants. For example, trafficking prevention activities can be made more effective by incorporating an understanding of the way gender-based discrimination increases the risk of trafficking. But when gender is linked with trafficking incorrectly (such as when all prostitution or sex work is defined as trafficking), it has actively harmed certain groups of women, including migrant women and sex workers.

By gaining a better understanding of the intersections between gender and trafficking, readers will be empowered to think critically about messages they receive about trafficking; to provide assistance to trafficked persons in a more empowering and respectful manner; and to press governments to fix harmful anti-trafficking policies (those that criminalize certain groups of women) and implement helpful policies that stop trafficking while protecting the human rights of trafficked persons, addressing the root causes of trafficking and ensuring access to justice for trafficked persons.

Following a discussion of what trafficking is and who is trafficked (Section II), I explore the relationship between trafficking, migration, labor, and violence against women (Sections III and IV), before delving into the limitations of contemporary anti-trafficking campaigns and the gendered aspect of anti-trafficking services themselves (Section V). I also examine the linkage between trafficking and sex work (Section VI). Ultimately, understanding the links between trafficking and the gendered experiences of women can improve anti-trafficking work. Although this is a challenging endeavor, it is a crucial one as we continue to press for the end of modern day slavery and the ability for girls and women to exercise agency and voice in their everyday lives. Section VII concludes.

II WHAT IS TRAFFICKING? WHO IS TRAFFICKED?

The Human Trafficking Protocol in the 2000 UN Convention on Transnational Organized Crime includes the definition of trafficking that is now widely used as an international standard (United Nations Office on Drugs and Crime, 2010). The trafficking definition has three parts: actions (the recruitment, transportation, or receipt of persons); means (threat or use of force, coercion, or deception); and purpose (exploitation, such as sexual exploitation, forced labor, slavery, or removal of organs).

The 2000 Human Trafficking Protocol was an improvement from the 1949 UN Convention on Trafficking, which equated prostitution with trafficking. Discussions leading up to the 2000 Protocol hinged around ideas of women's ability to consent and the element of coercion in trafficking (see Wijers and Lap-Chew, 1997; GAATW, 2001; Doezema, 2002; Lansink, 2008). Some anti-prostitution advocates called for a protocol that would define all prostitution as trafficking and make the issue of consent irrelevant (that is, women were thought to be incapable of providing consent in sex work). Other groups, including the Global Alliance Against Traffic in Women (GAATW), formed a Human Rights Caucus and called for a protocol that would recognize the distinction between sex work and trafficking, and recognize coercion as an element of the trafficking definition. This meant that the trafficking of men could also be recognized as a human rights violation.

When we look at the question of who is trafficked from a gender perspective, we see that the current evidence is biased toward seeing trafficked persons as predominantly female. As this chapter will show, it is problematic to depict women as 'vulnerable' because so doing entrenches vulnerability as an identity for women, and masks both women's agency and root causes such as discrimination.

Accurate information about who is being trafficked and why, how, where, and when is needed to ensure that anti-trafficking policies address the needs of trafficked persons and vulnerable groups. In actuality, there still is not a sufficient body of research that accurately measures how many people are trafficked globally and how many of these are women, men, transgendered individuals, and/or children (United Nations, 2009). One significant limitation has been researchers' selective focus on a particular type of trafficking, specifically trafficking of women for forced prostitution. For example, a scan of the academic literature found 661 articles for 'trafficking and women', almost none of which addressed trafficking for purposes other than forced prostitution. Using the keywords 'trafficking and men' turned up only one article that acknowledged men's experiences as trafficking victims. The absence of research interest in trafficked men or women in other forms of trafficking does not mean that it does not exist or that it is only a minor concern. Rather, it raises questions about why women are at the center of research and discussions about trafficking.

While policy and public assumptions about trafficking have often linked trafficking with women, this link has not always been based on evidence or been made critically. Policy and public conversations around trafficking reflect social ideas about women. On the one hand, the focus on women is understandable given the various forms of discrimination against women in many parts of the world. Discrimination against women has been identified as one of the root causes of trafficking as discrimination can affect where and when a woman can work, travel, migrate, and make her own decisions. It ultimately affects whether and how her human rights are respected.

Yet an isolated focus on women's vulnerability can further entrench a woman's vulnerability by assuming that she cannot act on her own behalf. If our work starts with the idea that women are vulnerable, then it can be hard to see anything else – women's strength, decision-making, responsibilities, or power. We have found that women show a great deal of resourcefulness and strength in whatever circumstances they find themselves. Anti-trafficking efforts need to understand this in order to be successful. For instance, in a 2010 feminist participatory action research project by SEPOM (Self-Empowerment Program for Migrant Women, an organization led by returnee migrant women in Thailand), women talked about the strategies they used once they were trafficked, which included writing letters to embassies, learning the language of the destination country, talking to clients and planning their escape with clients, learning the street names and orientation of the city they were in, arguing and fighting back, planning escape with other women trafficked into the same workplace, and working collectively with other sex workers (SEPOM, 2010).

The focus on women as being victims of, and vulnerable to, trafficking also masks women's other roles in trafficking processes – as traffickers, recruitment agents, or as those who benefit from other women's exploitation (for example, employers of exploited domestic workers). Furthermore, focusing on women's vulnerability rather than women's rights can lead to anti-trafficking measures that harm more than help. Anti-trafficking measures can result in further restrictions on women's mobility if it is assumed that a woman's vulnerability is something that is an inherent part of being a woman rather than the result of a discriminatory context. For instance, research at the San Paulo airport found that Brazilian women were being refused entry to European Union countries and repatriated from European airports because they were suspected of being in the sex industry (Piscitelli, 2006). It may be more accurate to speak of how women are 'vulnerabilized' by certain practices rather than how they are 'vulnerable'.

Since research and policy has typically focused on the trafficking of women, this means that there is still a lack of comprehensive quantitative and qualitative data about the scope and nature of traffic in men (Surtees, 2008). The absence of public data on trafficked men also makes it unclear where men are trafficked to and whether human rights violations differ between trafficked men and trafficked women. Why is it difficult to imagine that certain men might be at risk of being trafficked? A woman's gender identity (or the fact of her being a woman) is assumed to be an important factor in identifying her as a trafficked person, her vulnerability to being trafficked and the type of assistance she is assumed to need. Given the lack of information on trafficked men (GAATW, 2007), it is hard to gauge what identities (if any) are considered important in identifying and assisting men. Does men's gender 'disappear' once they become a 'trafficked person'?

It is not known whether the exclusion of men from the anti-trafficking sector or the lack of identifying trafficked men is harming or helping men who have been trafficked. While 'women were often perceived to be more likely to be victimised by crime than men and, as such, victimisation is often perceived as a feminine and feminising experience' (Surtees, 2007, p. 26), vulnerability is not part of social ideas of masculinity. It may be that a trafficked man is more often identified, assisted or talked about based on another vulnerable identity, for example, as a racialized man or as a migrant. It may be that men who are trafficked are accessing assistance through other means such as labor court cases. Trafficking is considered a grievous harm to individuals – the fact that we know little about trafficked men indicates an important need in research, policy, and service provision.

Another important issue is whether anti-trafficking initiatives should or should not group women and children together. Doing so may risk treating women as children and it ignores the distinct human rights protection needs of children. Internationally, there are distinct conceptual and international frameworks for women's rights (the Convention on the Elimination of All Forms of Discrimination Against Women: CEDAW) and children's rights (the Convention on the Rights of the Child: CRC). In practice, the connections made between women and children can emerge in interesting ways. For example, in some contexts racialized or lower-class girl children or female youth may be sexualized or treated as sexually available adult women. In the northern region of the British Columbia province in Canada, the violence toward and murder of migrating Aboriginal female youth has been mistakenly described as trafficking of women (Hunt, 2010). At GAATW's 2009 Asia Regional Consultation, Asian member organizations discussed the challenges of providing appropriate assistance to older youth in sex work who express a wish to stay in a risky environment and how to handle cases of older youth in sex work when youth are granted sexual freedom in their teens (such as in the US) or when youth are married at an early age (as in Nepal).

Working for the rights of trafficked and migrant women requires a nuanced understanding of the blurred lines between womanhood, female youth, and girl children. For instance, an action research project with migrant women who had returned to their rural community enabled LRC–KJHAM (a community-based legal resource center in Indonesia) to find that travel documents were falsified for youth so that they could travel and work abroad as domestic workers; 16-year-old youths were being listed as 20-year-old migrants (LRC-KJHAM, 2010).

III   TRAFFICKING, MIGRATION, AND LABOR

The root causes of trafficking can include micro factors such as violence within the home or community or macro factors such as gender-based discrimination and economic policies that result in a lack of livelihood options in countries of origin. A lack of livelihood opportunities in a person's place of origin may stem from discrimination (barriers in education and the workforce that differentially impact groups), unequal economic policies (structural reform policies impacting local economies), conflict, displacement (loss of land tenure or violation of land rights), changing environmental conditions, or other economic, social or political changes in local contexts (for example, if local food production is no longer permitted or feasible).

Other factors contributing to trafficking include poverty and unemployment, globalization, trade policies, feminization of poverty and migration, development strategies, restrictive migration laws and policies, anti-sex work laws and policies, particular cultural or religious practices, and corruption of authorities and involvement of organized crime (see Wijers and Lap-Chew, 1997; GAATW, 2010). These factors affect the lives of most people across the globe and on occasion can result in trafficking. However, these root causes of trafficking are likely exacerbated for women due to gender-based discrimination.

Many women are trafficked as they attempt to migrate. Migration becomes necessary if there is a lack of socially meaningful and/or economically sufficient livelihood opportunities in a person's place of origin. But people migrate for professional, economic, social, cultural, and personal opportunity as well. While women's migration may often be tied to women's roles as family caregivers or economic providers, migration can also provide opportunities for independence, autonomy and self-creation, particularly for women who may not fit social or gender norms in their home village, town, or city (Constable, 1999).

Today, nearly half of all migrants are women, and in developing countries female migrants outnumber male migrants. The term 'feminization of migration' has been used to describe the increasing number of working-class women migrating autonomously for often precarious (temporary, insecure, and strenuous) work (Piper, 2003; Lipszyc, 2004; Jolly, 2005; Arriola and Kinney, 2009). This is the result of various factors including the lack of livelihood opportunities for women in countries of origin and increasingly globalized economies reliant on cheap labor sources. Within this context, migrant women workers are seen as a desirable labor source because they are perceived to be cheaper, harder working, more manageable, and less union savvy than their male counterparts, particularly in the garment industry, small-scale manufacturing, and horticulture.

Labor issues overlap with the first (recruitment practices) and third (exploitation) components of the 2000 UN Human Trafficking Protocol. Migrant women workers contribute greatly to the economies and development of their families, their communities, their countries of origin, and their countries of destination. Yet often governments do not adequately regulate migrant worker issues and pay minimal attention to migrant workers who have experienced problems such as nonpayment and abuse. This is particularly problematic in the informal sector. For example, a 2009–10 action research project with migrant women working in Nairobi (by FIDA-Kenya) found that women working as informal sector vendors and small-scale entrepreneurs faced higher risks of longer hours, unreliable income, theft, harassment, and gender-based discrimination (for example, suppliers preferring to deal with men vendors) (FIDA-Kenya, 2010).

While most of the literature on trafficked women has focused on the informal sector (in contrast to the documented instances of trafficked men, which have been in the formal sector), this is not necessarily a reflection of global trafficking trends. Women's participation in formal labor (such as in the manufacturing sector) is largely unrecognized in the academic literature on trafficking. Although an Indian study of the Jharkland mining industry found that sexual violence against women trafficked into the mining industry was more likely to get media coverage, the study found inadequate and incomplete media coverage among local and regional newspapers on the trafficking of women in this industry (Bose, 2009). This illustrates another knowledge gap that we need to fill.

Of course, even where trafficking is not involved the challenges of migration are not limited to destination countries. Migration shifts gender roles in workers' villages or towns of origin, and in some cases migration was a way women simultaneously contradicted and fulfilled traditional gender roles. In addition to being responsible for their families' well-being, women also became economic providers (traditionally masculine roles). This caused tensions in some families. But although migration was still perceived as outside the norm for women, migrating for work did become a way of fulfilling one's duties as a mother, sister, and family caretaker. In many of the feminist participatory action research projects coordinated by GAATW in 2009–10, women stressed their familial roles as the most important factor determining their migration and labor experiences. These roles both served as the motivation for leaving and enabled women to endure exploitation,[1] for example, thinking of one's children to help one endure an exploitative work environment. At the same time, women were emphatic about the emotional and social costs of family separation and the impact their migration/migration status had on their ability to parent.

After working abroad, women face social and economic consequences when returning to their home villages or towns. Women have to manage their families' and communities' expectations about the money they earned. They also have to be careful how they speak about their migration experiences in order to avoid negative social consequences within their home community such as ridicule (for returning home without adequate savings) or stigma. As migrant women workers in the informal sector in Nairobi, Kenya noted, 'Our husbands do not want us to work. They accuse us of being prostitutes when we go out to trade or say that we will desert them when we start making money' (FIDA-Kenya, 2010, p. 33). Women who had been trafficked and returned to their hometown were especially concerned how stigma would affect them as the trafficking identity sometimes carries strong stigma associated with sex work.

It is also important to realize that illegal and unsafe migration channels exacerbate trafficking. As the United Nations High Commissioner for Refugees has noted, 'European nations are playing into the hands of human traffickers by tightening immigration policies at a time when their economies increasingly depend on migrant labor and when new factors like climate change are swelling the ranks of those eager to come' (Bennhold and Brothers, 2009). Without access to legal or safe travel channels, women and men from economically disadvantaged countries have to resort to traffickers to access routes barred by governments. In Mongolia, for example, many recruitment agents do not accept women as clients and this is further compounded by a migration policy that allows only men to obtain travel permits. Women seeking to move abroad, then, are obliged to seek illegal channels of migration (GAATW, 2006).

Women can also encounter harassment or exploitation from border officials and other migration gatekeepers, particularly where a migration decision is seen as, for instance, the rejection of social norms to stay at home and take care of children. Although women can be vulnerabilized during migration due to gender-based discrimination, women's (and men's) migration experiences are also influenced by their class and racialized identities. For example, countries' economies require working-class workers but immigration policies favor professional workers; that said, a professional woman from the US is likely to have a much more favorable migration experience than a professional woman from a poorer country. Men from particular religious, national, racial and class backgrounds are also particularly vulnerable to discrimination during migration in the post-9/11 era.

Although domestic work is a great need in many countries (evidenced by the number of domestic workers employed globally), this sector of work is still largely unrecognized in countries' immigration policies or labor policies. Even in instances where legal channels may exist for women to take up domestic work in other countries, government policies often still structure domestic work as temporary or circular employment (where migrants travel to another country to work but return back to their country after a certain period), meaning that migrant women may not enjoy a sense of belonging and establishment. Further, even for women working as domestic workers in their own country, domestic work is largely unrecognized as work in global labor laws.

In addition, a purely vulnerability-based focus can impact women negatively if

women's travel and migration is restricted as a protective or anti-trafficking prevention measure. At a 2010 consultation between the Special Rapporteur on Trafficking in
Persons and Thai organizations, Women's Fight for Life (a returnee migrant women's
group in Thailand working with Foundation for Women) reported that passports were
being denied to women who had been trafficked in the past as a measure to 'protect'
women from being trafficked again.[2]

The intersections between anti-trafficking and gendered ideas about women's vulnerability provide an interesting contrast to intersections between anti-trafficking and
migrant identities. Women migrants may more readily be seen as vulnerable whereas
men migrants are often conceptualized as a social threat (IMISCOE, 2008). While public
messages around trafficking and women often highlight the victimization aspects of
a woman's story, the migrant identity is publicly seen as a more assertive but easily
criminalized identity.

These two constructions of trafficked persons have very different social uses and risks,
particularly when it comes to developing public awareness campaigns. Anti-trafficking
practitioners have remarked on how useful the gender/victim identity is in generating
public interest and attracting funds, sometimes to the detriment of other issues deserving attention and resources (for example, violence against women). In comparison, use
of the migrant/criminalized identity can result in xenophobic or racist backlash and less
public, media, and donor interest.[3]

One of the unique challenges anti-trafficking practitioners face is accessing justice for
women and men who can be defined both as a victim (of trafficking) and a criminal (of
not possessing proper identification documents, for example) within a legal framework.
It is unknown which identity legal processes have recognized more (a victimized gender
identity or a criminalized migrant identity) but anecdotally, member organizations
have expressed the challenges they encounter when trying to access justice for trafficked persons with irregular migration status. This sharp victim/criminal dichotomy
also appears in social ideas of women in sex work; they are either trafficking victims or
criminals.

There is a lack of interventions and government policies that recognize this complexity. Some trafficking survivors have experienced the possibility of punishment or
deportation if they cannot be classified as victims according to certain requirements.
Anti-trafficking advocates can help counter the 'passive victim' stereotype within anti-
trafficking work by learning from migrant rights organizations. Migrant rights organizations have been successful in identifying human rights violations in a way that does not
discount migrants' resourcefulness and strength. For example, Transient Workers Count
Too (TWC2), a migrant rights organization in Singapore, uses messages and imagery
that call for attitudinal change while recognizing migrant contributions.[4]

IV   TRAFFICKING AND VIOLENCE AGAINST WOMEN

Another issue to consider is the connection between trafficking and violence against
women (VAW). VAW can refer to an act or acts of violence against women because
they are women, but it can also be used to refer to a wider social movement, a conceptual framework of power over women, and/or a human rights violation. As an act,

violence against women can refer to physical abuse, sexual abuse, psychological and emotional abuse, social abuse (such as isolation or stigma), or financial abuse (having no control over one's income). Violence against women can occur within a woman's family (domestic violence), in one's community (as a result of discrimination, hatred, stigma), in one's workplace (for example, abuse of domestic workers), in situations of conflict, and as a result of systemic or structural policies (such as colonialism), to name a few examples.

Women who have been trafficked may have experienced violence in various forms. Women fleeing abuse or violence may turn to brokers, recruiters, and traffickers. Women who have been trafficked may encounter abuse and violence from their employers and/or from their agents or brokers (for example, using violence to prevent a woman's escape). Unfortunately, a woman may also experience violence if she has escaped her trafficker. She may encounter violence by authorities in detention centers or law enforcement, or by service providers who control women's movements as a method of 'saving' them. Violence can also be a risk when a woman returns to her community, either from traffickers or from her community as a result of the stigma around trafficked women.

Starting from the 1970s, the VAW movement sought to identify violence against women as a grave human rights violation and to understand violence against women as the result of patriarchy or unequal power relations between men and women. Trafficking emerged as a women's rights issue in the 1990s from the VAW movement, but public awareness and efforts addressing VAW differ globally. In some countries or local contexts, women's rights advocates are still struggling to convince people and/or governments that violence against women is a grave human rights violation stemming from social, political, and economic inequities. In other countries and/or contexts, the VAW issue has become a politically strong movement and publicly visible issue, and is associated with a well-funded nonprofit sector.

Regional contexts also differ with respect to what forms of violence are recognized and what forms are not. In North America, the VAW movement has opened up private spaces to public accountability (or politicized the personal), particularly on violence within interpersonal relationships and families. However, there has been less focus on gender-based violence as a result of government policies (for example, violence against Aboriginal women as a result of colonial policies), violence experienced in workplaces (for example, employer's abuse of domestic workers or migrant workers) and violence against transgendered women (Piper, 2003). Countries also differ in their recognition of violence against women in other nonrelationship contexts, such as violence against women due to their sexual orientation, police brutality against sex workers (Rao and Sluggett, 2009), and violence against women human rights defenders, to name a few examples.

As trafficking is about the control and exploitation of human bodies, the VAW movement has contributed to an understanding of who has the power to control women's movements and women's bodies. Within the UN, CEDAW's General Recommendation No. 19 on Violence against Women, the Vienna Declaration and Programme of Action, and the Beijing Declaration and Platform for Action all refer to trafficking within the context of violence against women. The VAW movement can also provide some valuable lessons to anti-trafficking practitioners. For instance, women's shelters have developed safety protocols on client confidentiality and the assessment of counseling needs for domestic violence survivors, which can provide a useful knowledge base in creating shelters for trafficking survivors.

In other instances, linking violence against women with trafficking can mask, or present a limited view of, other important issues related to trafficking. Trafficking is also about exploitation and profit. Violence against women is commonly viewed as violence perpetrated by a man against a woman. However, trafficking can also be understood as violence against women that is perpetrated by nongendered individuals (for example, brokers, employers) and by the state (in the form of border policies, immigration policies, or labor protection measures).

Some have challenged the VAW framework's emphasis on abuses rather than women's agency and women's rights, such as the right to dignity, the right to livelihood, and the right to self-determination. Some have also questioned the VAW framework for emphasizing the oppression of women by men rather than an allowing for an intersectional and structural analysis based on factors such as race and class. The VAW movement's focus on patriarchal oppression has led some women's organizations to exclude transgendered women from their organizations or from accessing assistance if they experience violence[5], despite the fact that transgendered women are at increased risk of violence (Noushin and Fereshteh, 2010).

V   THE GENDER DIMENSION OF ANTI-TRAFFICKING CAMPAIGNS AND SERVICES

Certainly, anti-trafficking public awareness campaigns and media depictions of trafficking have exacerbated particular social perceptions about victims of trafficking. Most public awareness campaigns have a strong focus on women, children, or both (and extremely little recognition of trafficked men). The messages are often based on ideas about women's vulnerability rather than a gender-based analysis of the issue. The traditional 'helpless/hopeless victim' storyline that is communicated in these campaigns very often leaves out other storylines, such as how a trafficked person decided to migrate, how she resisted exploitation, or how she survived, escaped, and recovered.

A strategic reliance on stories of victimhood generates a great deal of media and fundraising interest, but leaves the status quo intact by focusing on violence by one person as perpetrated against another person and by excluding discussion about broader contexts that contribute to trafficking (such as a lack of legal migration opportunities for working-class women). The use of racialized women in western anti-trafficking public awareness campaigns also provides a socially acceptable way to sustain ideas about women's vulnerability by defining a certain type of women in need of assistance from women in wealthier countries, for example, female victims from the 'third world' needing rescue.

Interestingly, while media or campaigns may explicitly detail the abuses a trafficked person has suffered, these abuses are not often publicly identified in campaign materials as human rights violations. A human rights-based approach can be more empowering for trafficked persons and includes a more holistic approach to human needs, focusing on the right to livelihood and right to health, so it is puzzling why a human rights-based approach is not more embraced in public awareness campaigns. Trafficked persons may be more able to exercise their power and their agency in a human rights-based framework. A human rights-based approach can also maintain the focus on redressing the wrongs done to a person rather than a protective approach's focus on what makes certain persons weaker or more vulnerable. A protectionist approach can perpetuate the pattern of doing something 'to' a person whereas a human rights-based framework allows more space for people to assert what they are entitled to.

Irresponsible anti-trafficking public awareness campaigns can also replicate traffickers' methods or attitudes. For instance, trafficking has been described as one way of commodifying people yet this tactic has also been used in public awareness campaigns by depicting women in boxes or as frozen grocery meat.[6] Some anti-trafficking campaigns implicitly suggest that it is best to act for women who are assumed not to know what is best for themselves. But anti-trafficking advocates must ensure that interventions based on an awareness of exploitation do not inadvertently perpetuate discrimination against women.

Measures that seek to protect or rehabilitate women despite women's refusals perpetuate discrimination against women by violating women's rights to choose. Anti-trafficking advocates may unwittingly replicate the behavior of traffickers if they forcibly control women's movements by locking women inside shelters during the day, forcibly removing them from their workplaces (such as in 'raid and rescue' missions), or violating women's rights in 'rehabilitation centers' (for example, harassment by guards, unsanitary conditions, lack of access to healthcare, or inadequate food and shelter) (see Soderlund, 2005; Women's Network for Unity, 2008; Ditmore, 2009; FIRST, 2009a). Other organizations may prioritize women's particular roles when providing assistance, such as by choosing to assist women who are mothers because they are mothers rather than assessing women as autonomous individuals.

The implementation of assistance programs for trafficked persons also depends on donors' ideas of who is most in need (Surtees, 2008), yet donors' ideas may not necessarily reflect the people or cases service providers actually encounter. This is particularly true if we consider how trafficked men might be assisted. If we consider that many service providers assisting women work within feminist or VAW frameworks, it is interesting to think about how assistance might be shaped for men who have been trafficked. For instance, how does assistance to a woman trafficked into factory work differ from assistance to a man trafficked into the construction sector? How can feminist principles be used to develop assistance options for trafficked men? Is it more empowering to seek assistance as a trafficked person or as an exploited migrant laborer?

Part of the support given to trafficked persons is meant to restore what has been lost. Therefore, would assistance to trafficked men be based on aims to restore feelings of independence, pride, and strength – all social ideas about masculinity? Action research by the nongovernmental organization La Strada Moldova (2010) found that men who had returned to Moldova after migrating abroad rarely spoke about their negative migration experiences due to stereotypes of men as 'strong, undefeatable' persons. Who decides what a trafficking victim has lost and what should be restored? Are these ideas based on a person's gender?

A related issue is that anti-trafficking assistance and identification processes are largely influenced by legal and criminal justice processes, since trafficked persons are essentially victims of a crime. Yet legal and criminal justice processes traditionally have not been gender sensitive or helpful for all women. Women can be re-victimized or re-traumatized when seeking help within patriarchal medical and legal frameworks (Campbell et al., 2001). For example, women may have their claims dismissed or belittled, or their morality can be inappropriately questioned when their private histories are assessed and judged by legal and medical professionals (see Campbell, 1998; Campbell et al., 2001; Waugh, 2006).

In addition, legal frameworks are typically focused on prosecution rather than bringing justice to victims (Anderson and Andrijasevic, 2008). Trafficked persons may have different views on what constitutes justice for them. At a workshop held for Burmese women who had experienced numerous human rights violations, participants ultimately defined justice as 'having one's life back'.[7] If justice is formulated this way, then access to justice could also entail reintegrating women into the workforce and reducing stigma against trafficked persons in addition to seeking compensation from traffickers through the legal system.

Finally, trafficked persons may have a variety of reasons for refusing assistance (Brunovskis and Surtees, 2007). Seeking assistance may pose serious risks because trafficked persons have identities that are both victimized (as trafficked person) and criminalized (as a person without proper documentation or a person in illegal sex work). Seeking assistance can be a gamble which some individuals will take. Others will not and will, for example, refuse to call the police or go to the hospital because of fears of deportation.

VI   TRAFFICKING AND SEX WORK

The link between gender and trafficking has perhaps been most public in feminist arguments over trafficking, prostitution, and sex work and how they are connected. Some groups (including GAATW) have advocated strongly for sex workers' rights and have argued that confusing trafficking and prostitution does little to combat trafficking while actively hurting women in sex work. Many others in the feminist movement continue to see a strong link between prostitution and trafficking, and maintain that trafficking cannot be addressed without abolishing prostitution. Most of the global discussions around trafficking have only focused on women in sex work with almost no mention of male sex workers or transgender sex workers.

Notwithstanding the diversity of opinions on sex work, most agree that sex workers have the right to organize themselves and assert their rights, that violence against women in sex work is a grave human rights violation, that trafficking is a distinct phenomenon from sex work, and that anti-trafficking policies must also factor in sex workers' concerns and knowledge (for example, concerns about the impact of raids on business/ clients). While women can be trafficked for forced prostitution, not all or even the majority of sex workers are trafficked. Sexual exploitation is a risk in any situation (not just sex work) where a woman experiences human rights violations. While sex workers can be sexually exploited (for example, if a client refuses to pay for a received service, or if a brothel owner demands sexual favors from an employee), commercial sex work (between two consenting adults who have agreed on a price for a service) is not inherently exploitative.

Policies created or actions performed in the name of anti-trafficking have at times resulted in gross human rights violations against sex workers, including economic exploitation and physical and sexual violence by law enforcement. For example, sex workers' rights groups in Cambodia are working to change the country's anti-trafficking law which they argue punishes sex workers (by forbidding them to work publicly) and creates a mechanism where law enforcement officers can extort sex workers for money or sex in return for non-arrest (Overs, 2009). In addition, when prostitution is mistakenly equated with trafficking, trafficked persons can also be stigmatized and receive threats of violence when they return home or when they seek assistance as a 'trafficked person' (Asia Pacific Forum on Women, Law and Development, 2010).

Some nongovernmental organizations have made a deliberate choice not to use the term 'sex trafficking' based on concerns that all human rights violations against trafficked persons across all occupational sectors should be addressed, not just the sexual aspects of trafficked persons' experiences. There is also a worry that the term 'sex trafficking' encourages voyeurism by directing public attention to the sensationalistic aspects of what women were forced to do rather than the full range of human rights violations women experienced and the human rights protections they are entitled to. A sole focus on trafficking for the purposes of prostitution can also divert attention and urgently needed resources from human rights violations in other sectors, such as labor exploitation or the 'trafficking-like' effects of particular government overseas labor programs.

Sex workers and advocates for sex workers' rights have asserted their voices in global discussions around trafficking. Various sex workers' rights organizations and projects have organized fora and produced informational resources about trafficking and sex work (FIRST, 2009b; Urban Justice, n.d.), advocated and lobbied for changes in anti-trafficking legislation and policy (ECP, n.d.; Chan, 2009), demanded changes to exploitative and misleading anti-trafficking campaigns (ABC News, 2009; Pivot Legal Society, 2009), and worked to increase sex workers' control over their work environments (Chez Stella, n.d.; UK Network of Sex Work Projects, n.d.; Zi Teng, 2002). Some sex workers have wanted to assist law enforcement (for example, by sharing information about trafficking activities) but fear that they will be criminalized if they come forward with information (Redfern, 2009).

The Women's Network for Unity (WNU), a sex worker-led organization in Phnom Penh, Cambodia, and the Asia-Pacific Network of Sex Workers (APNSW) connected sex workers' rights and globalizing economic agendas in a counter-campaign to the MTV EXIT anti-trafficking campaign. The counter-campaign was called MTV No EXIT. Cambodian sex workers argued that irresponsible, anti-trafficking campaigns and misguided anti-trafficking policies that focus only on sex workers can justify or rationalize mass round-ups and arrests of sex workers (as was happening in Cambodia). Such campaigns also justify the detention of sex workers in 'rehabilitation centers' where sex workers experienced further abuses, or placement into forced or coerced training programs geared toward preparing women to work in factories and export processing zones for the interest of wealthier nations.[8]

The above example shows that fighting 'sex trafficking' engenders a socially acceptable positioning of poorer countries as 'villains' and wealthier countries as 'rescuers'. A campaign against 'sex trafficking' may also be directly implicated in priming women for work in lower-paid (but socially more acceptable) jobs such as factory work.

VII   CONCLUSION

While gender is one factor that influences trafficking and anti-trafficking activities, in reality it is hard to separate a trafficked person's identity as a woman from her multiple identities as a racialized person, a migrant, a mother, an autonomous worker, an urban or rural resident, and so forth. At the same time, the intersection between trafficking and women's gendered experiences are often specifically linked to ideas about women's sexuality. One example is migration labor opportunities that tie women's employment to their reproductive status (for example, deporting workers who become pregnant). Another example is anti-trafficking campaigns that rely on sexualized images of violence against women.

A trafficked woman's gender identity and her other identities (for example, race, class) influence her opportunities (or lack thereof) in her place of origin, how she is treated during the migration process, what opportunities are available to her in her place of destination and what assistance is available to her. The gendered aspects of women's experiences have also proved relevant to researchers, border officials, governments, and policy-makers. What is less known is the relevance of a trafficked person's gender identity to herself in relation to her experience of being trafficked. For example, does a woman who has been trafficked feel wronged as a woman (young or old), as a migrant, as a citizen from a relatively poor country, as a youth, or as part of another group? What aspects of her identity does she identify as being salient to her migration, labor, and recovery experiences and do they include her status as a victim of trafficking?[9]

The anti-trafficking framework is ultimately a criminal justice framework and therefore the trafficked person identity is ultimately that of victim. While this entitles persons to compensation and redress, practitioners should take care that a legal designation as a 'victim of trafficking' does not become victimizing. It is good to have 'gender-based rights that advocates can positively fight *for* (rather than only negatively pointing to violations) [which] include the right to gender equality, to bodily integrity, to equality before the law, to freedom of movement, to freedom from discrimination, to freely choose a spouse and more' (GAATW, 2008, p. 36, original italics).

When we examine trafficking issues with a holistic and critical understanding of women's gendered experiences, it can help address discrimination against women and otherwise promote women's rights. But when the gendered aspects of women's experiences are linked with trafficking as a result of unawareness or misinformation, the outcome may be gross human rights violations against marginalized groups of women such as sex workers, or the creation or further entrenchment of women's vulnerability. Anti-trafficking activities that reinforce gender stereotypes may thus harm rather than help trafficked persons, particularly women. Many awareness campaigns wrongly draw on exploitative imagery and victimizing depictions of women who have been trafficked into forced prostitution. Service providers must take care that anti-trafficking assistance services do not end up perpetuating discrimination against women by making important decisions on behalf of trafficked persons without their knowledge or consent.

At this point governments need to take several steps. First, governments must analyze and understand gendered labor migration trends (why, how, and where women are migrating for work) in order to respect, protect, and uphold the human rights of all migrants. Second, governments need to ensure that citizens and migrants working in the

informal sector have access to full labor rights, and that safe and legal migration channels for working-class migrants are established. For instance, women in Indonesia have
recommended that Indonesian women be allowed to seek labor migration opportunities
without the interference of a recruitment agent (Indonesians are required by law to seek
work abroad through agents, who often charge prohibitive fees) (LRC-KJHAM, 2010).

Governments need not (and should not) work alone. A range of civil society actors can
help to ensure that anti-trafficking legislation, policy, and programs are rights enhancing
and empowering, reducing discrimination against women. It is important to minimize the
negative impact of legal and medical procedures on a trafficked person's recovery. But
top-down approaches should be avoided; consultation and collaboration with migrant
workers and informal sector workers, particularly sex workers, is crucial to accurately
identify measures to prevent abuses. Furthermore, public awareness campaigns should
include empowering imagery and messages, such as emphasizing people's right to a
livelihood and the resourcefulness women show in restrictive situations. Finally, it is
important to demonstrate flexibility when specifying the beneficiaries of anti-trafficking
programs. Due to the changing nature of trafficking, donors' ideas of assistance may not
match service providers' experience at the community level. In other instances, women
may feel safer if they can access anti-trafficking services without publicly having to identify as having been trafficked (SEPOM, 2010).

Above all, it will be difficult to move forward if we do not improve the public's understanding of the multifaceted links between trafficking and gender. Although this is a
challenging endeavor, it is a crucial one as we continue to press for social change and
policies which recognize women as political subjects and which create a rights-enhancing
environment.

NOTES

*   This chapter is a revised version of 'Beyond borders: exploring links between trafficking and gender', a
    working paper published in 2010 by the Global Alliance Against Traffic in Women (GAATW).
1. References to various FPAR projects are incorporated throughout this chapter.
2. January 18, 2010, Royal Princess Hotel, Bangkok, Thailand.
3. For example, the annual US Trafficking in Persons report ranks countries according to their effectiveness
    in addressing trafficking. Countries that receive aid from the US or have trade relations with the US must
    be perceived by the US to be addressing trafficking (countries must be at least at Tier 2 to avoid being
    penalized). At times, the US's stance on trafficking has been criticized for confusing prostitution with traf-
    ficking and for a lack of transparency regarding ranking assessments. This has resulted in many countries
    feeling that their anti-trafficking policies are governed by US anti-prostitution agendas rather than sound
    evidence based on the scope and nature of trafficking within a particular country. Sex workers' groups
    have argued that this has led to arbitrary crackdowns on the sex industry (regardless of the actual need or
    risk) so that their governments can demonstrate their allegiance to the US's anti-prostitution stance.
4. For more information, visit their website at www.twc2.org.sg.
5. For example, Vancouver Rape Relief and Lu's Pharmacy (both in Vancouver, Canada) have excluded
    transgendered women. Vancouver Rape Relief excluded a transgendered woman from volunteering on
    their shelter's crisis line; for more information, see http://dawn.thot.net/nixon_v_vrr.html (Kimberly
    Nixon vs. Rape Relief). Lu's Pharmacy excluded transgendered women from services provided to women
    in Vancouver's low-income urban area, the Downtown Eastside; for more information, see http://www.
    straight.com/article-239961/transgender-ban-vancouver-womens-pharmacy-could-violate-professions-
    code-ethics (Lu's Pharmacy).
6. Image used in anti-trafficking campaign by the Union of Finnish Feminists, Finland.
7. Personal communication, March 2007, Justice in Transit Workshop, Chiang Mai, Thailand.

8.   More information about the MTV No EXIT campaign can be found at: http://swannet.org/node/1520; http://www.youtube.com/watch?v=PsFBRFQYwJg;   http://www.facebook.com/group.php?gid=39176319005; http://www.youtube.com/user/apnsw.
9.   For more information on the different social impacts of a woman's multiple identities, see the Association for Women's Rights in Development (AWID, 2004).

REFERENCES

ABC News (2009), 'Salvos apologise to sex workers over ads', May 22, available at: http://www.abc.net.au/news/stories/2009/05/22/2577913.htm?section=australia (accessed December 17, 2009).

Anderson, Bridget and Rutvica Andrijasevic (2008), 'Sex, slaves and citizens: the politics of anti-trafficking', *Soundings*, (40), 135–45.

Arriola, Elvia and Ashley B. Kinney (2009), 'The feminization of migration: an interdisciplinary bibliography', available at: http://www.womenontheborder.org/globaleconomics.html (accessed April 27 2010).

Asia Pacific Forum on Women, Law and Development (2010), *My Body, My Life, My Rights: Addressing Violations of Women's Sexual and Reproductive Rights*, Changmai, Thailand: Asia Pacific Forum on Women, Law and Development.

Association for Women's Rights in Development (AWID) (2004), 'Intersectionality: a tool for gender and economic justice', *Women's Rights and Economic Change*, 9, available at: http://www.hhh.umn.edu/centers/wpp/flf/pdf/AWID_intersectionality.pdf (accessed December 20 2009).

Bennhold, Katrin and Caroline Brothers (2009), 'E.U. urged to open doors to migrants', *New York Times*, December 14, available at: http://www.nytimes.com/2009/12/15/world/europe/15iht-migrants.html?_r=3 (accessed December 20 2009).

Bose, Tarun Kanti (2009), 'Do media have a space? For women trafficked in mining in Jharkhand', Friedrich Ebert: New Delhi, India Stiftung, available at: http://www.scribd.com/doc/13768489/Trafficked-Women-Media (accessed 9 February 9, 2009).

Brunovskis, Anette and Rebecca Surtees (2007), 'Leaving the Past Behind? When Victims of Trafficking Decline Assistance', Fafo Report No. 40, Fafo: Oslo.

Campbell, Rebecca (1998), 'The community response to rape: victims' experiences with the legal, medical, and mental health systems', *American Journal of Community Psychology*, **26**(3), 355–79.

Campbell, Rebecca, Sharon M. Wasco, Courtney E. Ahrens, Tracy Sefl and Holly E. Barnes (2001), 'Preventing the "second rape": rape survivors' experiences with community service providers', *Journal of Interpersonal Violence*, **16**(12), 123–59.

Chan, Dyna (2009), 'Law on suppression of human trafficking and sexual exploitation', presentation at GAATW's Asia Regional Consultation, Kathmandu, Nepal, September.

Chez Stella (n.d.), 'Tools by and for sex workers', available at: http://www.chezstella.org/stella/?q=en/tools (accessed December 20, 2009).

Constable, Nicole (1999), 'At home but not at home: Filipina narratives of ambivalent returns', *Cultural Anthropology*, **14**(2), 203–28.

Ditmore, Melissa (2009), *Kicking Down the Door: The Use of Raids to Fight Trafficking in Persons*, New York: Sex Workers Project at the Urban Justice Center.

Doezema, Jo (2002), 'Who gets to choose? Coercion, consent, and the UN trafficking protocol', *Gender and Development*, **10**(1), 20–27.

English Collective of Prostitutes (ECP) (n.d.), 'Areas of work', available at: http://www.prostitutescollective.net/IPCpage.htm (accessed December 20, 2009).

FIDA-Kenya (2010), 'The realities and agency of informal sector workers: the account of migrant women workers in Nairobi', GAATW Feminist Participatory Action Research Series, GAATW, Bangkok..

FIRST (2009a), 'Rights, not rescue', FIRST, Vancouver, September 24, available at: http://www.firstadvocates.org/rights-not-rescue-open-letter-salvation-army (accessed September 24 2009).

FIRST (2009b), 'Trafficking facts and fictions', Working TV, Vancouver, June 16, available at: http://www.workingtv.com/first-16june09.html (accessed December 20, 2009).

GAATW (2001), *Human Rights and Trafficking in Persons: A Handbook*, Bangkok: GAATW.

GAATW (2006), *Prevention of Trafficking: Report of the Global Consultation*, Consultation proceedings of the Global Consultation, Bangkok: GAATW.

GAATW (2007), *Collateral Damage: The Impact of Anti-Trafficking Measures on Human Rights Around the World*, Bangkok: GAATW.

GAATW (2008), *Gender–Migration–Labor–Trafficking Roundtable: Exploring Conceptual Linkages and Moving Forward*, GAATW Bangkok, August 6–9.

GAATW (2010), 'Beyond borders: exploring links between trafficking, globalization, and security', GAATW Working Paper Series, Bangkok.

Hunt, Sarah (2010), 'Colonial roots, contemporary risk factors: a cautionary exploration of the domestic trafficking of Aboriginal women and girls in British Columbia, Canada', *Alliance News*, **33**, 27–31.

International Migration, Integration and Social Cohesion in Europe (IMISCOE) (2008), 'Illegal migration: how gender makes a difference', Policy Brief, No. 10.

Jolly, Susie (2005),'Gender and migration', BRIDGE Brighton, UK, available at: http://www.bridge.ids.ac.uk/reports/CEP-Mig-OR.pdf (accessed April 27, 2010).

La Strada Moldova (2010), 'A look at the linkages: how does gender, migration, labour and trafficking intersect in women's lives? A qualitative research based on migration and labour experiences of women from Ursoaia Village', GAATW Feminist Participatory Action Research Series, GAATW, Bangkok.

Lansink, Annette (2008), 'Human rights focus on trafficked women: an international law and feminist perspective', *Agenda*, 78, 45–56.

Legal Resources Center for Gender Justice and Human Rights or Legal Resource Center untuk Keadilan Jender dan HAM (LRC–KJHAM) and the Rowobertanten Women Migrant Workers Group (Kelompok Perempuan Mantan Buruh Migrant Rowoberanten) (2010), 'The linkages between migration, labor, gender and trafficking among women migrant workers: feminist participatory action research (FPAR) in Rowoberanten Village, Ringinarum Sub District, Kendal Districk, Central Java, Indonesia', *GAATW Feminist Participatory Action Research Series*, GAATW, Bangkok.

Lipszyc, Cecilia (2004), 'The feminization of migration: dreams and realities of migrant women in four Latin American countries', Urbal red12mujerciudad, Barcelona, available at: http://www.diba.es/urbal12/PDFS/CeciliaLipszyc_en.pdf (accessed April 27, 2010).

Noushin, K. and Fereshteh (2010), 'Understanding needs, recognising rights: the stories, perspectives, and priorities of immigrant Iranian women in Vancouver, Canada', GAATW Feminist Participatory Action Research Series, GAATW, Bangkok.

Overs, Cheryl (2009), *Caught Between the Tiger and the Crocodile: The Campaign to Suppress Human Trafficking and Sexual Exploitation in Cambodia*, Phnom Penh, Cambodia: Asia-Pacific Network of Sex Workers, Oslo: Fafo and Nexus Institute.

Piper, Nicola (2003), 'Feminization of labor migration as violence against women: international, regional, and local nongovernmental organization responses in Asia', *Violence Against Women*, **9**(6), 723–45.

Piscitelli, Adriana (2006), as cited in Frans Nederstigt and Luciana C.R. Almeida (2007), 'Brazil', in GAATW (ed.), *Collateral Damage: The Impact of Anti-Trafficking Measures on Human Rights Around the World*, Bangkok: GAATW, p. 99.

PIVOT Legal Society (2009), 'Advocacy groups denounce Salvation Army's human trafficking campaign', available at: http://www.pivotlegal.org/News/09-09-24--Salvation_Army_campaign.html (accessed December 17, 2009).

Rao, Sandhya and Cath Sluggett, (2009), *Who Stole the Tarts? Sex Work and Human Rights*, Maharashtra, India: Center for Advocacy on Stigma and Marginalisation.

Redfern, Katrin (2009), 'Sex workers seek policy partners', *The Phnom Penh Post*, July 28.

Self-Empowerment Program for Migrant Women (SEPOM) (2010), '"Trafficked" identities as a barrier to community reintegration: five stories of women rebuilding lives and resisting categorisation', GAATW *Feminist Participatory Action Research Series*, GAATW, Bangkok.

Soderlund, Gretchen (2005), 'Running from the rescuers: new U.S. crusades against sex trafficking and the rhetoric of abolition', *National Women's Studies Association (NWSA) Journal*, **17**(3), 64–87.

Surtees, Rebecca (2007), 'Trafficked men as unwilling victims', *St Antony's International Review*, **4**(1), 16–36.

Surtees, Rebecca (2008), *Trafficking of Men – A Trend Less Considered: The Case of Belarus and Ukraine (IOM Global Database Thematic Research Series)*, Geneva: International Organization for Migration (IOM).

United Nations (2009), Special rapporteur on trafficking in persons, especially women and children, 'Promotion and Protection of All Human Rights, Civil, Political, Economic, Social and Cultural Rights, Including the Right to Development', February 20, (submitted to the 10th HRC, Agenda item 3, No. A/HRC/10/16), United Nations,Geneva.

United Nations Office on Drugs and Crime (2010), 'What is human trafficking?', available at http://www.unodc.org/unodc/en/human-trafficking/what-is-human-trafficking.html (accessed April 23, 2010).

UK Network of Sex Work Projects (n.d.), 'Resources: documentation', available at: http://www.uknswp.org/resources.asp (accessed December 20, 2009).

Urban Justice (n.d.), 'Projects: sex workers', available at: http://www.urbanjustice.org/ujc/projects/sex.html (accessed December 20, 2009).

Waugh, Louisa (2006), 'Why trafficked women must be "perfect"', *New Statesman*, September 4, available at: http://www.newstatesman.com/node/154154 (accessed January 18, 2010).

Wijers, Marjan and Lap-Chew Lin (1997), *Trafficking in Women, Forced Labor and Slavery-Like Practices in Marriage, Domestic Labor and Prostitution*, Utrecht and Bangkok: Foundation Against Trafficking in Women (STV) and Global Alliance Against Trafficking in Women (GAATW).

Womyn's Network for Unity (2008), 'Impact of law enforcement and raids campaign on sex workers', Womyn's Network for Unity, Phnom Penh, Cambodia.

Zi Teng (2002), 'Things to know before you go', Zi Teng, Hong Kong, available at: http://ziteng.org.hk/pub/dl_e.html (accessed December 20, 2009).

Index

Acker, Joan 188–9
Afghanistan 152, 403–4
  maternal mortality ratio of 438
African Development Bank (AfDB) 136
  projects financed by 140
agency 527
  focus in 'doing gender' 527
  influences upon 55
  role in empowerment of women 151
Agricultural Development Projects (ADPs)
  World Bank support for 473
agriculture 121, 135, 136, 138, 504
  credit provision for 472–3
  decline in funding for 470
  modernization of 115
  presence of women in developing world
    sector 121, 162, 468–70, 472–3,
    480
  self-employment in 359, 362
  small-scale 340
  subsistence 140, 330
Albelda Randy 23
Algeria 152, 537
  self-employed population of 362
Allied Social Science Association
  annual meetings of 21
American Economic Association
  annual meetings of 21
  members of 19
Arab Spring 47
Argentina 125, 406
  education system of 158
Arrow, Kenneth
  model of 'statistical discrimination' 237
Asia-Pacific Network of Sex Workers
  (APNSW) 553
Asian Development Bank (ADB) 119, 136
  use of gender action plans 144–5
Asian Financial Crisis (1997–8) 378
Association for Social Economics
  members of 12
Australia 123, 311, 314
  self-employed population of 365
Austria 104–5, 205, 239–40, 246, 249, 277,
    293–4
  economy of 98
  poverty risk for single-parent families in
    95

rate of part-time employment of women in
    295
  Vienna 242
Azerbaijan
  self-employed population of 362

Baker, Anne 78
Bangladesh 14, 121, 138, 145, 152, 372, 403,
    456, 463–4
  energy infrastructure of 135
  Female Secondary School Stipend Project
    428–9
  Grameen Bank 360, 370–71
  land rights of women in 471
Bangladesh Rural Advancement Committee
    (BRAC) 366
  impact on women's contraception use 370–71
Bangladesh Rural Development Board
    (BRDB) 370–71
  impact on women's contraception use 370–71
  RD-12 program 366
Bank of Japan 347
Barriteau, Eudine 117
Becker, Gary 237–8
  Treatise of the Family (1991) 238
Bedford, Kate 125
Belarus
  maternal mortality ratio of 438
Belgium 277, 293, 407
  Flanders 247
  gender wage gap in 401
  human development loss due to gender
    inequality in 403
  poverty risk for single-parent families in 95
  rate of part-time employment of women in
    295
  trade union activity in 283
Beneria, Lourdes 25
Benin 406
Bergeron, Suzanne 39
Bergmann, Barbara
  concept of occupational crowding 211
Berlusconi, Silvio
  feminist opposition to 107
Binder-Oaxaca decompositions 231
  concept of 230
Bolivia 426
  education system of 425